EMPIRE OF ASHES

ALSO BY JAMES M. SCOTT

Black Snow:
Curtis LeMay, the Firebombing of Tokyo, and the Road to the Atomic Bomb

Rampage:
MacArthur, Yamashita, and the Battle of Manila

Target Tokyo:
Jimmy Doolittle and the Raid That Avenged Pearl Harbor

The War Below:
The Story of Three Submarines That Battled Japan

The Attack on the Liberty:
The Untold Story of Israel's Deadly 1967 Assault on a U.S. Spy Ship

WITH JACK CARR

Targeted: Beirut
The 1983 Marine Barracks Bombing and the Untold Origin Story of the War on Terror

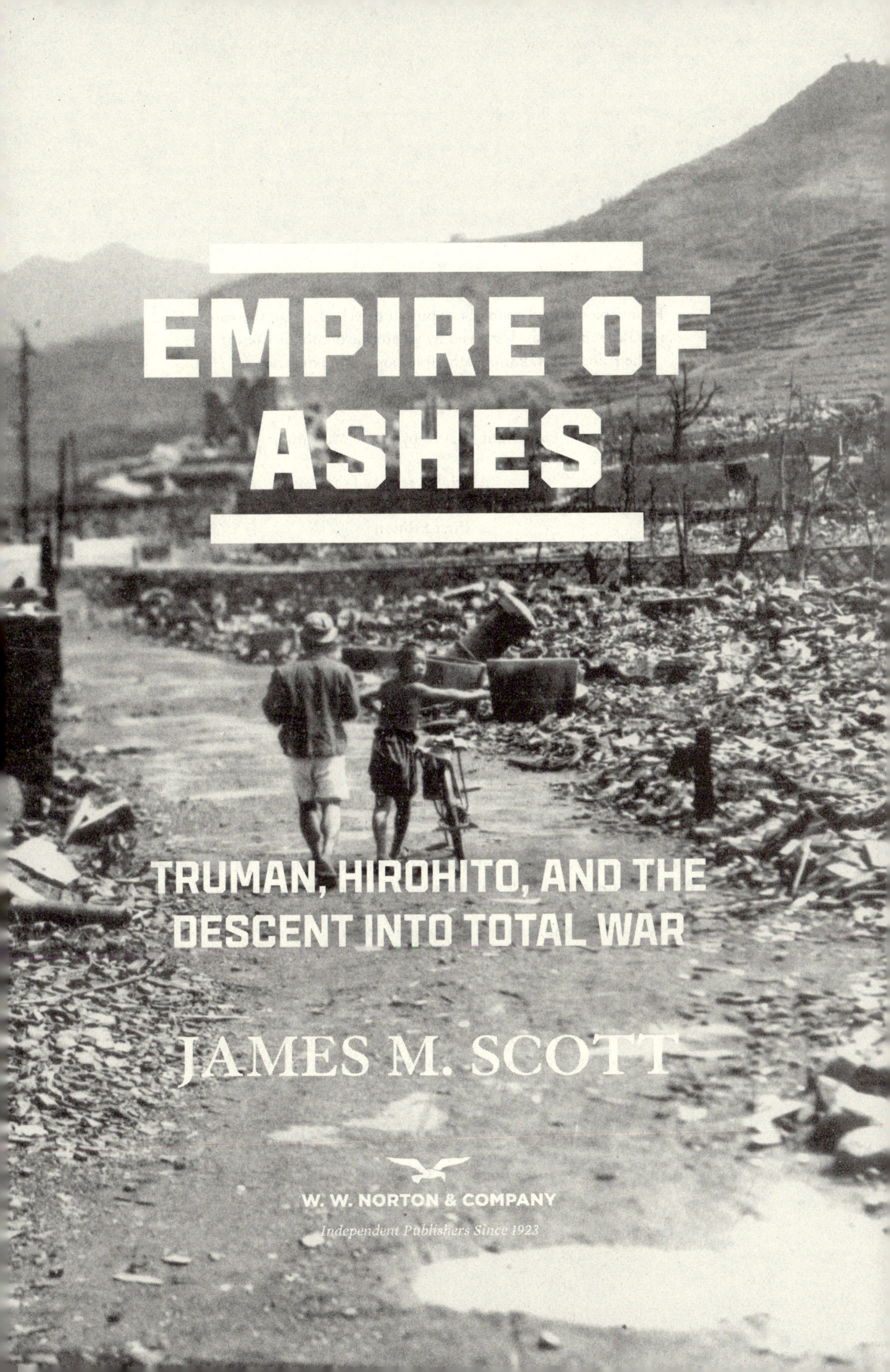

EMPIRE OF ASHES

TRUMAN, HIROHITO, AND THE DESCENT INTO TOTAL WAR

JAMES M. SCOTT

W. W. NORTON & COMPANY
Independent Publishers Since 1923

Frontispiece: Two young boys push a bicycle through the ruins of Nagasaki, which was destroyed by an atomic bomb on August 9, 1945. The ruins of Urakami Cathedral loom in the distance. *(NARA)*

Printed in the United States of America
First Edition

Manufacturing by Lakeside Book Company
Book design by Dana Sloan
Production manager: Anna Oler

ISBN 978-1-324-06548-7

W. W. Norton & Company, Inc., 500 Fifth Avenue, New York, NY 10110
www.wwnorton.com

W. W. Norton & Company Ltd., 15 Carlisle Street, London W1D 3BS

Authorized EU representative: EAS, Mustamäe tee 50, 10621 Tallinn, Estonia

10 9 8 7 6 5 4 3 2 1

For my mother, Sue Scott,
who inspired my love of stories.

"One must reap the harvest of the seeds one has sown."

—JAPANESE PROVERB

CONTENTS

EMPIRE OF ASHES

INTRODUCTION

For more than a decade, I have studied and written about America's air war against the Empire of Japan. It has been a journey that has taken me to archives, museums, and battlefields around the world. Along the way, I have interviewed bomber pilots, gunners, and navigators as well as survivors of the devastating fire raids and atomic attacks that decimated dozens of Japan's cites. My first book on the subject, *Target Tokyo: Jimmy Doolittle and the Raid That Avenged Pearl Harbor*, chronicled the dark early days of the war following Japan's surprise attack on Hawaii. From that despair emerged the audacious plan for sixteen army bombers to take off from an aircraft carrier and attack Tokyo on April 18, 1942, a virtual suicide mission that marked America's first strike back against the enemy's homeland. I followed that with *Black Snow: Curtis LeMay, the Firebombing of Tokyo, and the Road to the Atomic Bomb*, which examined America's abandonment of high-altitude bombing for low-level fire raids. That work spotlighted the mission of March 9, 1945, that not only incinerated sixteen square miles of Tokyo but began a 159-day air campaign virtually unrivaled in its destruction.

Empire of Ashes: Truman, Hirohito, and the Descent into Total War builds on those earlier works, serving in many ways as the end of an unofficial trilogy. This final volume, which covers the last four months of the war with a focus on the atomic attacks, is as much a scientific and political story as it is an operational one. The narrative explores the creation of the bomb, the roiling debate over its possible use, and of course, the missions that destroyed Hiroshima and Nagasaki. But it also delves into the political maneuvering in Washington and Tokyo. As the book demonstrates, there is a difference between defeat and surrender. The former is a state of a nation's military and economy; the latter is a political decision. As such, I have framed this story around two disparate and seemingly unlikely leaders, who managed to defy expectations in their respective countries and navigate the challenges of war termination as the conflict devolved into a level of violence never before seen.

Harry S. Truman, who had served only eighty-two days as the nation's vice president, was a figure few people in America knew until that April evening in 1945 when he placed his hand on the Bible and assumed the role of the nation's thirty-third president. Washington officialdom scoffed at this plainspoken former artilleryman and Missouri farmer with no college education. Largely ignored by his predecessor, Truman had to navigate relations with British prime minister Winston Churchill and Soviet premier Joseph Stalin. Closer to home, he had to contend with rebellious scientists who had unlocked the awesome power at the heart of an atom but feared the weapon would ignite a global arms race. He likewise faced a State Department divided over whether America should soften its demands in order to entice an early Japanese surrender. And then there was the restless American public, anxious for the war to end.

Against this backdrop, Truman faced the most consequential decision of his presidency. To hurry up and end the war—and save hundreds of thousands of American lives from an otherwise bloody invasion—should he order the atomic annihilation of the enemy's cities?

Truman's counterpart on the opposite side of the Pacific was Emperor Hirohito. Though the Japanese monarch stood at the center of his nation's political, cultural, and spiritual life, Hirohito was little more than a figurehead, albeit one with stooped shoulders and a nervous twitch. Though revered by millions, the emperor, like so many others, lived in the shadow of the nation's militarists and under the threat of assassination. He had proved too weak to prevent the outbreak of the war, left to watch from his palace in the heart of Tokyo as American bombers incinerated his cities each night in the lead-up to the atomic attacks. Only in the end, with his empire reduced to ashes and faced with the threat of atomic obliteration, did he find the strength to push his nation toward the painful decision to surrender. Even then he faced a reluctant military, willing, if necessary, to sacrifice everything to avoid such a fate.

Truman and Hirohito: a former farmer and a socially awkward monarch. Upon the shoulders of this unlikely pair rested the fate of two nations and millions of lives.

PROLOGUE

"I never believed he'd die, until he did."

—MICHAEL REILLY
CHIEF OF THE WHITE HOUSE
SECRET SERVICE DETAIL

President Roosevelt was dying.

Those closest to him could see the telltale signs.

The sixty-three-year-old commander in chief, whose battle with polio had left him tethered to a wheelchair for nearly a quarter of a century, now struggled with the little things. He could no longer button his own shirt, shave, or lift himself atop the toilet. Never a robust figure, Roosevelt was unusually gaunt. His skin hung off his cheeks while his pale blue eyes appeared recessed in their dark sockets. His weakness, his aides noted, even reflected in his signature. Gone was his bold, ink-rich stroke. Much like the president, his handwriting now faded on the page. "He is slipping away from us," his secretary Bill Hassett confided to the president's doctor, "and no earthly power can keep him here."

To the tiny hilltop town of Warm Springs, Georgia, where he had convalesced after he was stricken with polio in 1921, the exhausted president had once again returned in search of rest, arriving by train on March 30, 1945. In the thirteen days since, he had settled into a routine of sleeping late, followed by a little work in his white clapboard cottage, before stretching out for a nap or a drive through the countryside, where the dogwoods and azaleas bloomed. Only the day before, Roosevelt had taken just such a trip with his cousin Margaret "Daisy" Suckley, longtime mistress Lucy Mercer, and, of course, his Scottish terrier, Fala.

Much to the relief of his aides, the president's color had recently improved. So too had his appetite, prompting him to gain a much-needed eight pounds. To celebrate, his aides had chipped in to host a barbecue for him on the night of April 12, complete with a fiddler.

The stress of his job no doubt contributed to his failing health.

Roosevelt had served as president for a staggering 4,422 days, time in which he had helped reshape America and the world. He had taken the nation's helm in March 1933 at the height of the Great Depression and the Dust Bowl. More than four thousand banks had collapsed in the first few months of that year, while unemployment soared to 25 percent. The American army had then ranked nineteenth in the world, sandwiched between those of Portugal and Bulgaria.

In the years since—and as war enveloped the globe—Roosevelt had helped resurrect America's economy and had transformed the once-isolationist nation into the world's greatest military power, a fact underscored by workers at a single Ford Motor Company plant who cranked out a new B-24 Liberator every sixty-three minutes.

Germany, by contrast, which had steamrolled across Europe in 1939 at the start of World War II, had suffered an incredible reversal of fortune. The Third Reich, destined to last a thousand years, at least according to Adolf Hitler, would in the end survive only twelve. The German ruler who had boldly declared war on America three years earlier now lived in a bunker deep under the smoldering ruins of Berlin while hungry residents picked through the debris or crowded inside suffocating shelters as the dreaded Russian army closed in from the east.

The Japanese had fared little better in the Pacific.

The bespectacled Emperor Hirohito, who had once dominated a quarter of the globe, watched his own cities burn under the nightly rain of incendiary bombs delivered by America's awesome new B-29 Superfortress. Less than two weeks earlier, American soldiers and marines had sloshed ashore on Okinawa, the final stepping stone in the long march toward the enemy's homeland, a dire reality that had triggered the collapse of the Japanese cabinet. In the remote mountains of northern New Mexico, scientists hustled to create a top-secret new weapon, one that promised to annihilate cities and at last bring an end to the war.

All this had occurred on Roosevelt's watch.

But the president was not yet finished—too much was at stake. The specter of Woodrow Wilson, who had helped win World War I only to see his hopes for a permanent peace fade after the guns fell silent, haunted Roosevelt. As such, in the fall of 1944, he had run again and won an unprecedented fourth term. In a recent speech to a joint session of Congress—the first time in which he had to forgo his usual leg braces and sit—Roosevelt reiterated the imperative of winning the war and building an international framework to guarantee a lasting peace. "The structure of world peace cannot be the work of one man, or one party, or one Nation," the president warned. "It must be a peace which rests on the cooperative effort of the whole world."

Such concerns weighed on him as he opened his eyes shortly before 9:20 a.m. on April 12. Naval physician Commander Howard Bruenn, who had accompanied him to Warm Springs, checked on the president soon after he rose. "He had slept well," the doctor noted in his report, "but complained of a slight headache and some stiffness of the neck. He ascribed this to a soreness of the muscles, and relief was experienced with slight massage."

The White House mail pouch, which was flown in daily, arrived late that Thursday morning. Fog had blanketed the capital the night before, forcing aides to send the mail by train. Secretary Hassett collected the pouch and headed over to the president's cottage shortly before noon, where he was surprised to find Roosevelt already up and dressed in a double-breasted gray suit with a crimson necktie, all in preparation to have his portrait painted. Roosevelt relaxed in a leather chair at the card table by the fireplace, his back facing the windows that framed the pine trees in the distance. Daisy perched on the sofa crocheting while fellow cousin Laura "Polly" Delano pinballed around the wood-paneled room watering the plants.

Hassett placed documents before the president to sign, which ranged from postmaster appointments to Legion of Merit citations for distinguished foreigners. The secretary then scattered the records around the room to allow the president's signature to dry. "A typical State Department letter," Roosevelt joked at one point. "It says nothing at all."

As if on an assembly line, the president cycled through the papers, including a bill passed by Congress to increase the borrowing power of the Commodity Credit Corporation.

"Here's where I make the law," he announced.

The president then scrawled his approval along with his signature and the date.

Moments later Lucy arrived with artist Elizabeth Shoumatoff, who clutched an easel, paint box, and palette in her arms. The watercolor artist, who had painted the president two years earlier, had been in and out of the cottage all week as she prepared to compose a new portrait. "Oh, come right ahead," Roosevelt told her. "Bill is waiting for his laundry to dry."

Shoumatoff set up her easel by the door to the porch and began mixing paint. She could not help but notice his improved color. "Mr. President," she declared, "you look so much better than yesterday. I am glad I did not start working before today."

At 12:40 p.m., an attendant brought a silver tray with a cup of oatmeal and a small pitcher of cream. Daisy got up, poured the cream into his cup, and mixed it for him while he worked. Hassett departed, leaving a folder for Roosevelt to review while he ate lunch.

"We have fifteen minutes more to work," the president announced.

Daisy returned to the sofa. At 1:15 p.m., the president's face suddenly fell forward. He raised his left hand to his temple and then ran it along his forehead, a gesture that caught Daisy's attention. She put aside her crocheting and approached.

"Have you dropped your cigarette?" she asked.

"I have," the president whispered, "a terrific pain in the back of my head."

She instructed him to lean his head back in his chair. Polly came in and with the help of Lucy tilted his chair back. Daisy grabbed the phone. "Please get in touch with Dr. Bruenn," she urged the operator, "and ask him to come at once to the President's cottage."

Shoumatoff summoned the president's valet, Arthur Prettyman, and his Filipino steward, Irineo Esperancilla. The two men tried unsuccessfully to lift Roosevelt. Daisy and Polly joined the effort, grabbing his legs while the gentlemen lifted his upper body. The foursome carried the president to his bed in the adjacent room, where Daisy opened his collar and loosened his tie. She then clutched his right hand while Polly fanned him. Lucy returned with camphor and held it under his nostrils. "Two or three times, he rolled his head from side to side, opened his eyes," Daisy recalled. "I could see no signs of real recognition in those eyes."

At one-thirty p.m., Bruenn arrived, joined by medical aide George Fox. The doctor asked everyone to step outside. The men undressed the president, swapping his suit for pajamas. He was unconscious, cold, and sweating profusely. "Pupils of the eyes were at first equal," Bruenn observed, "but in a few minutes the right pupil became wildly dilated."

In addition to hot water bottles and blankets, Bruenn injected him with papaverine—a drug designed to help blood flow—along with amyl nitrite to relax his labored breathing. The president, Bruenn concluded, had suffered a massive cerebral hemorrhage. He phoned Dr. Ross McIntire in Washington, the president's primary physician. McIntire, in turn, summoned Dr. James Paullin, an Atlanta heart specialist about eighty miles away.

Michael Reilly, who headed the White House Secret Service detail and had long served as the president's personal guard, rushed into the cottage.

"Mike," Bruenn leveled with him, "this is very serious."

Reilly phoned Hassett and Grace Tully, the president's personal secretary. Hassett arrived to find Polly and Daisy sitting in silence. Tully walked in moments later, took a seat, and began whispering a prayer. Roosevelt's labored breathing hung over them all. In the neighboring bedroom, the doctors, whose muffled voices could be heard outside, continued to tend to the president. At 2:12 p.m., Hassett stepped inside the bedroom. "His eyes were closed—mouth open—the awful breathing," he wrote in his diary. "No one spoke."

The president appeared to stabilize—his color improved and his heart rate was good—only to deteriorate again at 3:31 p.m. His breathing stopped, replaced by occasional gasps. Dr. Paullin arrived from Atlanta. "The President," he wrote in his report, "was *in extremis* when I reached him. He was in a cold sweat, ashy gray, and breathing with difficulty."

Bruenn administered caffeine sodium benzoate and began artificial respiration. "On examination his pulse was barely perceptible," Paullin noted. "His heart sounds could be heard, but about three and a half minutes after my arrival, they disappeared completely."

Paulin injected adrenaline into the president's heart. "Within five minutes after my entrance into the room," Paullin added, "all evidence of life had passed away."

The time was 3:35 p.m.

Bruenn emerged from the bedroom. Gone was the soundtrack of the president's tortured breathing, as a sudden silence now settled over the cottage. All eyes stared up at the doctor. "He said nothing," Reilly recalled. "Just lowered his head and shook it."

The president was gone.

PART I

"It is still a long, tough road to Tokyo."

—PRESIDENT FRANKLIN ROOSEVELT

MARCH 1, 1945

A Marine with the 1st Marine Division aims at a Japanese sniper during the battle of Okinawa, which would prove to be one of the bloodiest fights of World War II. *(NARA)*

CHAPTER 1

"The untimely death of Franklin Roosevelt is truly a loss to mankind."

—*VICKSBURG EVENING POST*
APRIL 14, 1945, EDITORIAL

Vice President Harry S. Truman wrapped up work on Capitol Hill shortly before five p.m. on a rainy Thursday. The bespectacled Missouri native had spent the afternoon presiding over a dull debate in the Senate regarding a water treaty with Mexico. Truman had distracted himself amid the stodgy speeches by penning a three-page letter to his mother and sister. Upon adjournment, the vice president stopped by his office before he hustled over to see House Speaker Sam Rayburn. A Texas Democrat, the balding Rayburn enjoyed an afternoon bourbon and branch water with colleagues in a hidden office tucked away on the ground floor, one that featured a fireplace, overstuffed leather chairs, a sofa, and a frayed rug. Lawmakers who fraternized there dubbed the afternoon bull sessions the "Board of Education."

Truman navigated the Capitol's marble halls in a double-breasted gray suit complete with a blue-and-white-polka-dot bowtie and matching pocket square, a dapper outfit that reflected a love of fashion developed during his brief ownership of a Kansas City haberdashery a quarter-century earlier. The sixty-year-old, who had served as the nation's vice president for only eighty-two days, arrived at 5:05 p.m. to find Rayburn gathered with House parliamentarian Lewis Deschler and White House congressional liaison James Barnes.

"Harry," Rayburn announced, "Steve Early wants you to call him right away."

A former journalist, Early had long served as Roosevelt's trusted press secretary.

"Want me to get him for you?" Rayburn added.

"No," Truman replied. "I'll get it."

Truman poured a bourbon, picked up the phone, and rang the White House switchboard. "This is the V.P.," he said. "I understand Mr. Early wants to talk to me."

Early clicked on the line, his voice anxious. "Please come right over," the press secretary said, "and come in through the main Pennsylvania Avenue entrance."

Deschler watched the color drain from the vice president's face.

"Jesus Christ and General Jackson!" Truman declared when he replaced the receiver.

Everyone looked up at him.

"Steve Early wants me at the White House immediately," Truman announced. "Boys, this is in the room. Something must have happened."

Truman sprinted across the Capitol to his office, shedding his Secret Service detail along the way. He paused only long enough to grab his hat and inform his staff that he had been called to the White House. Truman climbed into the back of chauffeur Tom Harty's limousine for the two-mile trip to 1600 Pennsylvania Avenue. Alone in the back seat, Truman speculated on his sudden summons. Roosevelt's possible death was a perennial concern, prompting the Democratic Party to swap out the eccentric and liberal Vice President Henry Wallace for the more moderate Truman in the recent election. But Truman's first thought was that Roosevelt had returned for the funeral of his friend Bishop Julius Atwood. He suspected the president might have a congressional task for him before he headed back to Warm Springs.

Truman arrived at 5:25 p.m. White House ushers took his hat and escorted him to the oak-paneled elevator. A moment later Truman emerged on the second floor and was ushered into Eleanor Roosevelt's study, where he found the first lady along with her daughter Anna, son-in-law Col. John Boettiger, and Early. Truman sensed the gravity of the situation. That was confirmed when Eleanor approached and placed her arm on his shoulder.

"Harry," she said, "the President is dead."

Truman froze. "It was the only time in my life," he wrote in a letter that week to his mother and sister, "that I ever felt like I'd had a real shock. I had hurried to the White House to see the President and when I arrived, I found I was the President."

"Is there anything I can do for you?" he finally stammered.

"Is there anything *we* can do for *you*?" she replied. "For you are the one in trouble now."

A knock on the door interrupted them. Secretary of State Edward Stettinius entered with tears in his eyes. Stettinius and Early suggested Truman call an immediate cabinet meeting, to which he agreed. Truman asked Eleanor again if there was anything she needed. Would it be all right, she asked, for a government plane to fly her down to Warm Springs? "I assured her that the use of such a plane was right and proper," Truman recalled, "and I made certain that one would be placed at her disposal, knowing that a grateful nation would insist on it."

Truman left the study and headed for the Cabinet Room. Attorney General Francis Biddle began to summon members of the cabinet while Truman phoned Supreme Court Chief Justice Harlan Fiske Stone, asking him to come to the White House to swear him in as president.

He then phoned his family. His twenty-year-old daughter Margaret answered.

"Let me speak to your mother," Truman said.

"Are you coming home to dinner?" Margaret asked. "*I'm* going out!"

"Let me speak to your mother," he repeated.

"I only asked you a civil question," his daughter countered.

"Margaret," he pleaded, "will you let me speak to your mother?"

She handed the phone off in a huff and retreated to her bedroom.

"Bess," Truman began. "I'm at the White House. President Roosevelt died about two hours ago in Warm Springs. I'm sending a car for you and Margaret. I want you here when I'm sworn in."

The nation's soon-to-be first lady put the phone down in shock. With tears in her eyes, she made her way down the hall to her daughter's room, where Margaret was prepping for her date. "Mother," Margaret said, "what's the matter? What is it?"

"President Roosevelt is dead," Bess announced.

"Dead?" Margaret repeated.

Bess sized up her daughter, who wore a party dress, dancing slippers, and white gloves.

"You'd better change your clothes," she said. "Pick out something dark."

Inside the Cabinet Room, Truman collected himself. A series of French doors with arched transoms faced out onto the Rose Garden, where the last of the day's light faded. A fireplace anchored the room's northern end beneath a mantel adorned with a clock. Over it hung a portrait of Woodrow Wilson. An elongated wooden table stood at the center of the room surrounded by high-backed leather chairs where Truman sat. "He looked," recalled press officer Jonathan Daniels, "like a little man as he sat waiting in a huge leather chair."

Members of the cabinet filed in one after the other along with other senior governmental leaders, including Speaker Rayburn, House Majority Leader John McCormack, and House Minority Leader Joseph Martin. The only two in uniform were Adm. William Leahy, Roosevelt's chief of staff, and Maj. Gen. Philip Fleming, administrator of the Federal Works Agency. Emotions were raw. Secretary of Labor Frances Perkins wept. "It was a very somber group that had gathered," War Secretary Henry Stimson noted in his diary. "I think every one of us felt very keenly the loss of a real personal friend. I know I did."

Steve Early and Jonathan Daniels hunted around for a Bible as three wire service reporters were ushered in to witness Truman's swearing-in ceremony. The last to arrive were Truman's wife Bess and daughter Margaret. "If ever I have felt the awesome dimensions of history," Margaret recalled, "it was in that room, that night."

Truman stood at the head of the table beneath the portrait of Wilson with Bess and Margaret to his left. Others crowded around with mournful faces. Truman picked up a Bible bound with black covers and pages edged in red. He raised his right hand. Truman, who had never attended college and had once plowed the fields of Missouri as a farmer, stood on the precipice of history, about to be sworn in as the nation's thirty-third president.

At 7:08 p.m., Chief Justice Stone began to read from the oath, which Truman repeated. "I, Harry S. Truman," he began, as cameras flashed, "do solemnly swear that I will faithfully execute the office of the President of the United States, and will to the best of my ability, preserve, protect and defend the Constitution of the United States."

Bess dabbed her eyes while Margaret said a silent prayer. "Give him the strength," she asked. "Let everything be all right. Let him be equal to it. Let him live through it."

"So help you God," Stone said, ad-libbing.

"So help *me* God," Truman concluded.

At 7:09 p.m.—three hours and thirty-nine minutes after Roosevelt died in his bed in Warm Springs—Truman officially became president. "After repeating the oath," one reporter observed, "he bowed his head, lifted the Bible to his lips and kissed it."

Truman kissed Bess and Margaret, letting them know he would be home soon. The new president met with his cabinet with the exception of Postmaster General Frank Walker, who was ill. Early interrupted. Reporters wanted to know if the United Nations Conference on International Organization would still be held in San Francisco starting on April 25. Truman confirmed it would.

The new president then said he would be pleased if the current cabinet members remained in their posts. "It was my intention," he recalled, "to continue both the foreign and the domestic policies of the Roosevelt Administration." Truman made clear he would be his own president and assume responsibility for his own decisions, but he welcomed their advice and encouraged them to speak freely. All policy decisions in the end would be his. "I added that once such decisions had been made, I expected them to support me."

When the meeting ended, Stimson lingered, informing the new president that he needed to meet with him soon about "a most urgent matter." "Stimson told me," Truman recalled, "that he wanted me to know about an immense project that was under way—a project looking to the development of a new explosive of almost unbelievable destructive power."

At 7:40 p.m., Truman left the White House for his $120-a-month rental home at 4701 Connecticut Avenue, a modest second-floor apartment that featured five rooms and a single bathroom. French doors led onto a small porch that offered views of the courtyard below where reporters and onlookers gathered under the watchful eye of added police and the Secret Service. The media clamored for an interview with the new president, but Truman demurred. At his request, Early put out a statement. "For the time being I prefer not to hold a press conference," it quoted the president. "It will be my effort to carry on as I believe the President would have done, and to that end I have asked the Cabinet to stay on with me."

Truman had not eaten since noon. The most powerful leader in the world dined that night on a turkey sandwich, courtesy of his next-door neighbor. Before going to bed, he phoned his ninety-two-year-old mother Martha Ellen in the tiny Missouri town of Grandview.

"Be good, Harry," she advised him. "But be game, too."

CHAPTER 2

"The presidency falls upon a minor figure, chosen from among minor figures for political considerations."

—*AUSTIN AMERICAN*
APRIL 13, 1945, EDITORIAL

At 5:45 p.m. on April 12—at about the time Truman headed to the Cabinet Room to await his swearing-in ceremony—Steve Early prepared to alert the world of Roosevelt's death. The fifty-five-year-old Virginian, who began his career three decades earlier as a reporter with United Press, had served as the White House press secretary since 1933. During those twelve years, the veteran reporter had helped transform how the administration interacted with the media to better inform the public. He created regular press conferences open to all journalists and helped Roosevelt develop his famous fireside chats. In this role, Early had helped guide America on matters ranging from the Great Depression and the New Deal to World War II. Early, in fact, was the one who broke the news of the Japanese attack on Pearl Harbor.

This story would no doubt rival that one.

The White House switchboard arranged a conference call with the nation's three leading wire services: the Associated Press, International News Services, and United Press. "This is the White House," the operator announced as reporters joined the call. "Hang on."

Another voice ran through a quick roll call.

"Here," each reporter replied.

"Just a moment please," came the response.

The phone clicked again—and a new, albeit familiar voice joined the call. "This is Steve Early," the press secretary announced. "I have a flash for you."

The reporters started scribbling.

"The President died suddenly this afternoon," Early began.

"Do you mean President *Roosevelt*?" someone on the call interrupted.

"Christ!" a frustrated Early exclaimed, exhibiting his notorious temper. "There's only one president. *Of course* I mean President Roosevelt."

Inside the International News Service bureau, reporter Arthur Herman didn't wait for clarification before he jumped to his feet. "Flash!" he hollered. "F.D.R. Dead!"

The night wire operator Charles Sparkenbaugh punched out the first alert and hit transmit at 5:47 p.m. The Associated Press and United Press followed seconds later.

In newsrooms across the nation, bells clamored as the wire services spat out the first reports of the president's passing. Editors pored over the brief bulletins and barked orders to prepare extra editions while radio broadcasters interrupted evening programs. In New York, stunned commuters emerged from subways and buses, begging police officers for confirmation. Shopkeepers turned speakers toward the street, trumpeting the news.

"The president's dead" was a common phrase in Times Square.

At the Stage Door Canteen in the basement of Broadway's Forty-Fourth Street Theater—a venue that catered to service members—the evening show had just begun when the director signaled the orchestra to stop. As silence settled over the theater, the director addressed the troops in the audience. "I have a terrible announcement to make," he began, "but out of respect to the memory of the president of the United States this show cannot go on."

But few had heard the news.

"The president," the director added, "has just died."

Audience members began to weep.

People flooded out of movie houses and department stores in tears. Others swarmed newsstands and crowded around parked cars to listen to reports over the radio. Church bells tolled in the president's native Hyde

Park in New York. Many wrestled with disbelief, including one woman in Spokane, Washington, who questioned the veracity of such reports. "Lady," the exasperated news hawker replied, "I dunno any more about it than you do. It came off the press that way, and it wouldn't be in the paper if it wasn't true."

The lowering of the White House flag to half-staff brought pedestrians to a halt. As the afternoon sun vanished, hundreds of mourners crowded adjacent Lafayette Square, watching as an army of reporters filed inside and limousines dropped off cabinet members. By mid-evening, the number of silent mourners had soared into the thousands.

The *Washington Evening Star*, which had not printed an extra edition since Pearl Harbor, published four that night, totaling more than 39,000 copies. But even that was not enough to satisfy the public's insatiable appetite as readers stampeded the paper's lobby.

A similar story unfolded in towns and cities nationwide.

Residents jammed newspaper and radio phone lines. Tired of the busy signal, others rang the police and even the Red Cross. The call volume proved so high in St. Louis that it shut down the city's phone service for half an hour, prompting local radio stations to broadcast pleas for people to stay off the lines. The same occurred in the nation's capital, where residents found it briefly impossible to get a dial tone. The four major networks canceled commercial programs, dedicating the airtime instead to news and tributes to the late president.

Across the nation, many theaters, concert halls, and nightclubs closed while saloon jukeboxes sat silent. The Yankees and Dodgers exhibition game at Ebbets Field in Brooklyn was canceled; so too was the scheduled Cubs-versus–White Sox game in Chicago. The New York Philharmonic-Symphony Society called off its Carnegie Hall concert for only the second time in history, the first being the assassination of President Abraham Lincoln. Those few revelers who ventured out on to Miami's famed South Beach found only a ghost town.

News of the president's death likewise brought life in the suburbs to a standstill, where families gathered in kitchens and living rooms to listen to news reports. Many schools announced special assemblies for the following morning or canceled classes. "Ordinary street noises of children and vehicle traffic became strangely hushed," observed a reporter with the

Evening Herald in the small town of Shenandoah, Pennsylvania. "Some passed along the word to neighbors, who were assembled on porches or about some daily chores in gardens. All of them quietly went into their homes, too surprised and grieved to offer any comment."

Armed with notepads and pencils, reporters captured the mood of a sorrowful nation, where many young people had never known life without Roosevelt as the leader. Interviewees equated the president's death to losing a father or a dear friend. "He was the greatest man we ever had or will ever have," declared Samuel Gross of Philadelphia.

"I am completely overcome," added Lt. William Murphy.

World leaders ranging from British prime minister Winston Churchill to Soviet premier Joseph Stalin cabled condolences, while senior Washington politicos praised him in the press. "I am too shocked to talk," stammered Senate Majority Leader Alben Barkley of Kentucky. "It is one of the worst tragedies that ever happened to this nation or the world." Chinese Nationalist leader Gen. Chiang Kai-shek, in contrast, proved more composed. "His name and his ideals," he wrote, "will be a beacon of light to humanity for centuries to come."

As telegrams flooded the White House by the thousands, newspapers big and small rushed to publish editorials lauding the president, many printed on the front page of extra editions. Some compared his death, on the eve of victory over Germany and Japan, to the assassination of Abraham Lincoln, who was killed five days after the guns of the Civil War fell silent. Wisconsin's *Chippewa Telegram-Herald* went so far as to parrot the famous statement made by War Secretary Edwin Stanton upon Lincoln's passing. "The greatest American of his generation," the paper wrote of Roosevelt, "now belongs to the ages."

Others observed that Roosevelt's leadership stretched far beyond the borders of the United States, a loss that would reverberate around the globe. "Something incalculably great," wrote Alabama's *Birmingham Age-Herald*, "has gone out of the life of the Nation, out of the life of all the world." *The Atlanta Constitution* echoed that theme. "His death comes as a blow, not to the people of this nation alone," the paper lamented, "but to all mankind."

Such anguished reactions only underscored the extraordinary challenge Truman faced. Compared to Roosevelt, who many thought of as a family member, Truman was virtually unknown, having served as vice president for less than twelve weeks. The nation's spotlight—as Eleanor Roosevelt had warned him it would—now shifted to the man from Missouri.

To Truman fell the job of defeating America's enemies and securing the lasting peace Roosevelt had so desperately sought. Mixed in with the calls for national unity and the need to support the nation's new president were some of the same questions that had dogged Truman upon his selection as vice president. Could this plainspoken former farmer with no college education be a worthy successor to Franklin Roosevelt? Was Truman, who only a decade earlier had served as a county official, ready to take the helm as the nation's commander in chief? "Today a great weight falls upon the shoulder of Harry Truman," wrote California's *Chico Enterprise*. "Whether or not Mr. Truman can bear up under that weight remains to be seen."

CHAPTER 3

"A dazed and questioning world today watched Harry S. Truman pick up the banners of war and peace that slipped yesterday from the lifeless fingers of Franklin Delano Roosevelt."

—JACK BELL, ASSOCIATED PRESS
POLITICAL NEWS EDITOR
APRIL 13, 1945

Truman was everything Roosevelt was not.

The latter had been born into a world of wealth and privilege, a member of America's aristocracy. Unlike Truman, Roosevelt had enjoyed a luxurious childhood on a 110-acre estate north of New York City that featured stables, orchards, and a majestic view of the Hudson River. He traveled to Europe in the summers and vacationed at the family's waterfront home on Campobello Island in Canada's Bay of Fundy. The private tutors and governesses of his adolescence were followed by his tenure at the elite Groton School and later Harvard, where he served as editor of the *Crimson*. He studied law at Columbia University and spent several years with a prestigious Manhattan firm before he traded a career as a litigator for politics. Though Roosevelt had certainly faced adversities, he had never nursed the callused hands of a farm laborer, felt the fear of a thundering battlefield, or gone financially bust.

Truman, by contrast, had experienced all those things.

And more.

The five-foot-nine Missourian, who wore glasses, loved bow ties, and spoke in a twangy midwestern accent, was a product of rural America, a world comprising dirt roads and farms and governed by rainfall, frost, and the seasons. He was born in the tiny town of Lamar in the southwestern corner of the state, a farming community that was home to just seven hundred residents and where legendary gunslinger Wyatt Earp began his career as a lawman. The future president spent much of his early youth on his family's farm, where he feasted on homemade apple butter and pickled pigs' feet and learned to read from his mother using the Bible.

In 1890, when Truman was six, the family moved to Independence. Though larger than Lamar, the town of six thousand was a community where roosters announced each new day, goats grazed in people's backyards, and horse-drawn buggies rumbled through the town square. The Civil War still cast a shadow over American life. One of Truman's teachers regaled students with stories of her father, who was shot three times during Pickett's charge at the Battle of Gettysburg, while many of the town's older Black residents had been born in bondage.

Truman's need for glasses prompted him to shun sports, but he proved to be a talented piano player who enjoyed school, developing strong relationships with many of his teachers. "To tell the truth," he often joked, "I was kind of a sissy." The youth instead gravitated toward books, alternating histories of ancient Greece and Rome with biographies of famous leaders, from Andrew Jackson and Robert E. Lee to Julius Caesar and Genghis Khan. "My debt to history is one which cannot be calculated," he said. "I know of no other motivation which so accounts for my awakening interest as a young lad in the principles of leadership."

At age fourteen, Truman landed his first job at Clinton's Drugstore, where he opened the shop at six-thirty a.m., swept the sidewalk, and mopped the floors, all before school. "There must have been a thousand bottles to dust and yards and yards of patent-medicine cases and shelves to clean," he said. "I never finished the bottles and shelves by schooltime and had to start the next morning where I'd left off the day before. By the time I got around them all, it was time to start over." Beyond work, Truman's job introduced him to the hypocrisy of some of the town's citizenry. Though Independence had bars, many church leaders and members of the Anti-Saloon League would visit the store early in the morning to drink whiskey from a secret closet for ten cents an ounce. "This procedure," Truman said, "gave a fourteen-year-old boy quite a viewpoint on the public front of leading citizens and 'amen-corner-praying' churchmen."

After graduation from high school in 1901, Truman hoped to attend either West Point or Annapolis, but his poor eyesight robbed him of any such opportunity. His father, speculating on grain futures, lost the 160-acre farm his wife had inherited along with $40,000 in cash, leaving the senior Truman no choice but to earn a living as a night watchman.

Any hope Truman had of going to college vanished.

Over the next few years, Truman cycled through several jobs, including one as a construction timekeeper for the Santa Fe Railroad, a task that paid thirty dollars a month. He lived with the laborers in tents, monitored each worker's time, and then paid them every two weeks in a saloon that doubled as his office. "I learned," he said, "what it meant to work ten hours a day for $1.50." More than just hard work, the job was an initiation to those on the rougher edges of society. When the job ended after six months, the foreman publicly congratulated him. "Truman's all right," he announced, "from his asshole out in every direction."

Truman went to work in the mail room at *The Kansas City Star* before landing a job in 1903 as a clerk in the vault at the National Bank of Commerce, eventually earning forty dollars a month, a salary that surpassed his father's wages. Two years later he jumped to Union National Bank where he earned seventy-five dollars a month. His hard work soon warranted a raise to one hundred, a terrific salary in Kansas City. On Saturday afternoons, he ushered at the vaudeville shows at the Orpheum. "All I got out of it," he said, "was to see a show, which was for nothing."

On June 14, 1905, at the age of twenty-one, Truman enlisted in the Missouri National Guard. "Every citizen," he once wrote, "should know something about military, finance, or banking and agriculture." He proudly dressed in his new guard uniform and showed it off to his maternal grandmother, Harriet Young, a Confederate sympathizer.

"Harry," she admonished him. "This is the first time since 1863 that a blue uniform has been in this house. Don't bring it here again."

Truman's father, sick of laboring as a night watchman, rented an eighty-acre farm and returned to work the land. After a spring flood washed out his corn crop, he moved in with his mother-in-law to run her six-hundred-acre farm in Grandview. The work proved too much for him, so in 1906 he asked his son to leave the bank and join him, a temporary situation that would stretch on for more than a decade. Life on the farm was austere and primitive, a throwback to the pioneering days. The seven-room, white-frame home, which the young Truman lived in with his parents, two siblings, grandmother, and hired hands, had no electricity or running water. The toilet consisted of an outhouse while a telephone served as the family's only connection to modernity. Truman's father would wake him each morning long before sunrise, which instilled in him a discipline and work ethic he would carry for the rest of his life. He would then milk the cows, feed the livestock, and help his mother and sister prepare breakfast.

As one year bled into the next, Truman watched the sun rise and set each day over this one-square-mile patch of Missouri earth he called home. The seasons changed; so too did the crops, corn, clover, and oats in the spring followed by wheat in the fall. Along with crops, the family raised Black Angus cattle, Hampshire hogs, and chickens. The work was arduous, even dangerous, like when a three-hundred-pound calf fell on him and broke his leg. Beyond the fields, Truman built fences, nailed down shingles, and castrated hogs. He lost his voice hollering at plow horses while the sun baked his neck and the wind dried his cheeks. In the winter, he would walk alongside the plow to keep warm, dressed in a sweater, two coats, and an overcoat.

Truman applied his zeal for learning to farming, studying the latest technologies. He bought a manure spreader and solicited animal waste from his neighbors, which he used to fertilize the fields. He likewise learned to rotate the crops, a move that, he proudly noted, prompted his wheat output to jump from thirteen to nineteen bushels per acre while his corn doubled to seventy bushels an acre. Truman learned to enjoy the solace of plowing fields—he could cover five acres in as few as ten hours—followed by quiet nights spent around the piano with his family or reading his favorite author, Mark Twain. "Riding one of these plows all day, day after day, gives one time to think," he later said. "I've settled all the ills of mankind in one way and another while riding along seeing that each animal pulled his part of the load."

Truman's connection to the world beyond the farm came through

Elizabeth "Bess" Wallace, whom he had first met as a six-year-old when he moved to Independence and attended Sunday school at First Presbyterian Church. "I thought," he recalled, "she was the most beautiful and sweetest person on earth." The two had attended school together—she sat behind him in sixth and seventh grades as well as high school—but drifted apart after graduation. A social chasm existed between them. The Trumans were farmers while the Wallaces were city people, part of the town's high society who frowned upon people with callused hands.

But Harry Truman refused to acknowledge any such social obstacle. He saw an opportunity to rekindle his affections when he visited his cousins in 1910, who lived across the street from the Wallaces. Madge Wallace had recently sent over a cake. The empty plate needed to be returned, a task for which Truman eagerly volunteered.

When he knocked, Bess opened the door.

"Come in," she said.

That afternoon launched Truman's courtship, much of which was conducted via letters. The hundreds of pages he wrote capture the daily rhythm of his life on the farm, from baling hay to putting rings in the noses of hogs, all of which would later stand in stark contrast to his life as the most powerful leader in the world. "My very best friends," he wrote in one such letter, "would refuse to recognize me if they ever saw me in town in my farm rags."

"A two-hundred-pound hog," he explained in another, "can almost jerk the ribs loose from your backbone when you get him by the hind leg."

Even as he recounted such experiences, Truman recognized the mundanity of his life. "I do hope you won't find this letter as dull as it sounds to me."

When he could get away, Truman visited Bess in town, which despite only being fifteen miles away required a cumbersome trip via foot, buggy, train, or streetcar that took several hours. In a letter on June 22, 1911, he summoned the courage to ask her to marry him. "Would you wear a solitaire on your left hand should I get it?" Truman proposed. "You know, were I an Italian or a poet I would commence and use all the luscious language of two continents. I am not either but only a kind of good-for-nothing American farmer."

Bess, however, refused, but she did so graciously, which Truman appreciated. "I never was fool enough to think that a girl like you could ever care for a fellow like me," he confessed, "but I couldn't help telling you how I felt." Her refusal, however, only motivated him more. "I've always said I'd have you or no one and that's what I mean to do."

In 1914, Truman's father developed a severe hernia straining to lift a boulder, which an October X-ray revealed had caused internal blockage. The doctor advised that he could either have surgery or expect to die. He elected for surgery, but afterward his condition worsened, leaving him largely bedridden. Truman juggled the work on the farm with his concern for his father. "I am half worried to death," he wrote, "for fear he'll not get all right."

The younger Truman's worry proved wise.

As his health failed—and friends and family came to say goodbye—the senior Truman confided in a neighbor he felt his life had been a failure. He slipped away on the morning of November 2, 1914. "I was with him," Truman recalled. "I had been sitting with him and watching a long time. I nodded off. When I woke up he was dead."

Truman's anguish over his father's passing was reflected in his letters. "I've been in the habit of running the farm for some time, but Papa always made it go," he wrote to Bess. "There are things that I don't suppose I'll ever learn that were entirely natural to him."

Truman continued to work the land, but his interests widened. If he planned to marry Bess, he knew he could not remain a farmer and share his father's fate. Along with his neighbor Thomas Hughes and attorney and promoter Jerry Culbertson, Truman bought a zinc and lead mine 150 miles south near Commerce, Oklahoma. He turned the family farm over to hired hands and relocated. Just as he had done with the farm, he worked tirelessly, buying a cot that allowed him to live at the mine. His letters to Bess showed his eternal optimism. "In six months," he bragged, "we expect to be on velvet and an income of about $400 a week apiece."

"We are going to have a real mine," he added in another, "even better than expected."

But his optimism was not enough.

By May 1916, Truman realized the mine had largely run dry. Faced with financial ruin, the normally positive Truman fell into despair. "I shall join the class who can't sign checks of their own I suppose," he wrote to

Bess. "There was never one of our name who had sense enough to make money. I am no exception." A generous local banker provided additional capital, which allowed him to hang on until September, but all that did was prolong the inevitable. "I have been holding a postmortem over the mine; closed it down yesterday after paying out the last cent I've got," he wrote. "There's nothing like going entirely busted."

Truman sought to bounce back by going to work in the oil business, which was sweeping across the Midwest. He joined forces again with Culbertson and a new partner, David Morgan, an attorney with experience in the industry. Truman would serve as the company's treasurer and a one-third partner with an investment of $5,000 in notes backed by his mother. The group secured fifteen hundred acres for drilling. Morgan scouted additional lands while Truman sold shares in the new business. The outbreak of World War I, however, created a labor shortage, forcing the company to dispose of its leases. Only later would Truman learn that subsequent owners struck what became known as the Teeter Oil Pool, one of the largest deposits ever discovered in Kansas. Truman just missed his chance at millions. "I seem to have a grand and admirable ability," he wrote to Bess, "for calling tails when heads comes up."

On April 2, 1917, as European armies battled amid mud-filled trenches, President Woodrow Wilson declared war on Germany. The thirty-three-year-old Truman answered the nation's call. "I believe that the great majority of the country was stirred by the same flame that stirred me in those great days," he later wrote. "I felt that I was a Galahad after the Grail." To Bess, Truman admitted that he hoped to test himself. "Maybe a little war experience will tone me down and make a man of me," he confessed. "I hope it will anyway."

Over the years, the couple's relationship had strengthened. Though Bess had refused his marriage proposal six years earlier, the two now planned on a life together, but Truman wanted to wait until after he returned safely from the war. "Bess," he wrote, "I'm dead crazy to ask you to marry me before I leave but I'm not going to because I don't think it would be right for me to ask you to tie yourself to a prospective cripple—or a sentiment."

On September 26, 1917, First Lieutenant Truman reported to Camp Doniphan in Oklahoma as a member of the 129th Field Artillery

Regiment. There on the Great Plains, Truman marched, dug trenches, and fired artillery while alternately battling dust storms and blizzards. In addition, he served as the regimental canteen officer aided by Sgt. Edward "Eddie" Jacobsen, whom he had met years earlier working in the bank. To supply the canteen, the duo collected two dollars from the eleven hundred men in the regiment as startup capital. The men stocked the canteen with everything from cigarettes and candy to soda and shoelaces. The business proved so successful that Truman and Jacobson added a barber and a tailor. The duo soon paid everyone back and within six months distributed more than $10,000 in dividends. "The canteen is a whiz," Truman wrote to Bess. "I did four hundred dollars worth of business today."

The Camp Doniphan experience came to an end on March 19, 1918, when Truman boarded a train east. Ten days later he steamed for France aboard the USS *George Washington*, a German passenger liner seized by the United States. "There we were," he recalled, "watching New York's skyline diminish and wondering if we'd be heroes or corpses." As America receded in the ship's frothy wake, Truman's thoughts drifted back to Missouri. "The sunsets on the sea," he wrote, "aren't half as good to see as those on our prairies at home."

Two weeks later, on April 13, Truman landed at Brest. Much to his frustration, he spent his first couple of months in artillery school learning to shoot the French 75mm guns. "We'll all be nuttier than an Arkansas squirrel if we study this hard much longer," he complained in a letter to Bess. Beyond his work, a theme in much of his correspondence was his admiration for the beauty of the French landscape with its tree-lined country roads and picturesque towns. If he could no longer be a Missourian, he confessed, he would want to be French. "It's a shame," Truman added, "that our business is to tear up all the pretty places and villages."

Truman returned to his regiment in June as a newly promoted captain and a battalion adjutant. Col. Karl Klemm, who commanded the 129th Field Artillery, summoned Truman the following month. "Harry," he asked, "how would you like to command a battery?"

"Well, sir," Truman replied. "I hope to be able to do that some day."

"All right, you'll take command of D Battery in the morning."

Battery D had the worst reputation, filled with rowdy Irish and German Catholics. Truman would be the unit's fourth leader, a job in which he would have 194 men under his command as well as four guns. "I've been very badly frighted several times in my life and the morning of July 11, 1918, when I took over that battery was one of those times," he recalled. "I was rather doubtful of my ability to handle that obstreperous battery."

That morning he rallied his troops. Unlike the farm or the mine, where he had often toiled alone, Truman now had to serve as a leader, which was particularly unnerving. "If I can only make good at it," he confided in Bess, "I can hold my head up anyway the rest of my days."

As he surveyed the troops, Truman froze in fear. He could not speak, but he could feel the eyes of the nearly two hundred men on him, each one sizing him up.

"Dismissed," he finally uttered.

To his horror, the troops gave him the so-called Bronx cheer, a flatulence-like noise made when a person blows air through pursed lips. Later that day some of the men purposefully unleashed the unit's horses to create a stampede. That was followed by a drunken barracks fight that night that landed four soldiers in the infirmary. Truman had to crack down.

The next morning troops woke to find a notice tacked on the bulletin board. Truman had busted the culprits down in rank. He summoned the noncommissioned officers. "I didn't come over here to get along with you," he warned. "You've got to get along with me. And if there are any of you who can't, speak up right now and I'll bust you right back now."

Truman's firm approach set a new tone. His men understood he was in charge. While he would not tolerate such shenanigans, he soon developed a reputation for being fair.

"You soldier for me," he often told them, "and I'll soldier for you."

Truman ran his men through daily exercises and gunnery drills, which improved the battery's efficiency. Despite the unit's reputation for mischief, Truman discovered his troops were quite capable. His letters during this time reveal a newfound confidence and pride in his success. "You have no idea the experience I am getting," he wrote to Bess.

"I have had a university education and then some in the last year," he added in another.

Truman and his battery gained some initial combat experience in late August 1918 near the Vosges Mountains, which would further bolster's his men's confidence in him.

"We have a captain," one declared, "who cannot be beaten."

The following month Truman and his men were ordered to march from the Vosges Mountains to the Argonne Forest, where Allied forces were preparing for what would later be known as the Meuse-Argonne Offensive. The fight, which planners hoped would at last break Germany and bring an end to the war, required fifteen American divisions. Some 600,000 troops had to converge on the front along with 90,000 horses and 3,000 artillery pieces. To hide the massive movement from the enemy, troops marched from dusk until dawn along a handful of rural and congested roads, sleeping during the day in nearby woods and bushes. The grueling two-week slog robbed Truman of forty pounds as his weight plummeted to 135. The horses, which had to pull the guns, caissons, and wagons of food, suffered the worst. "Every night," one of Truman's men recalled, "it seemed we would lose one or two horses."

As the nights passed and the distances added up—troops marched a total of 125 miles—Truman felt the pressure weighing upon him. "You've got no idea," he wrote Bess, "what an immense responsibility it is to take 194 men to the front." As motivation, he kept a picture of her in the front left pocket of his uniform, closest to his heart. "Dear Harry," Bess scrawled on the back. "May this photograph bring you safely home again from France."

The men moved into position near Neuvilly early in the morning on September 23, 1918. "This was a heartbreaking job," Truman wrote in his report. "The fields were muddy and full of shell holes. The carriages would hang up, the horses go down, and men would slip into shell holes half filled with water." Three days later the 129th Field Artillery went into action, firing 18,000 rounds. Of those, Truman's battery fired 2,018. Hour after hour, the guns thundered. To keep the barrels from overheating, men periodically swabbed them with sal soda and water and covered them with wet gunny sacks. "It was one continual deafening roar. Men who serviced the guns became stone deaf for weeks after," Truman noted. "The sky was red from north to south as far as the eye could reach. It was like a continual play of lightning."

Truman then pulled out and moved to a new spot that forced his battery to cross no man's land. "The distance traveled was only about a mile and a half, but it was nothing but a bog," he recalled. "Mud, mud, mud."

Dead Germans, discarded grenades, and machine guns littered the landscape. At one point, the men discovered dozens of dead Americans piled up near a fork in the road, victims of a hidden German machine-gun nest. "One or two had their heads completely severed," Truman said, "and one was simply sawed in two at the waist."

On September 28 near Montblainville, an American reconnaissance plane dropped a flare near Truman's position. The captain seized on the illumination to scan the landscape around him with field glasses, spotting a six-gun German artillery battery moving into position along the front line and close enough to endanger the Allied infantry. Truman waited for the Germans to unhitch the horses and escort them to the rear, which would prevent them from quickly moving the guns once he opened fire. The captain felt anxious. The afternoon light was fading, and he would soon not be able to see to adjust fire. Unable to wait any longer, he ordered his men into action. The guns barked, hurling forty-nine rounds that obliterated the German battery.

Colonel Klemm, the regiment's martinet-like leader who had promoted Truman to a battery commander, threatened to court-martial him for firing into another division's territory. "Go ahead!" Truman challenged him. "I'll never pass up a chance like that."

But Klemm let it go.

The days soon turned to weeks as the guns continued to thunder. By the first of November, the novelty of combat faded. Buried French and German troops populated the landscape around Truman's battery. Every time a shell hit, he noted, it scattered the remains of the dead. Surrounded by disinterred rotting corpses, Truman thought back to the green pastures of Missouri. "If I ever get home from this war whole," he wrote, "I am going to be perfectly happy to follow a mule down a corn row the balance of my days."

At daybreak on November 11, 1918, just hours before the eleven a.m. armistice between Germany and the allies was set to begin, Truman's battery fired 68 rounds. A final barrage of 164 rounds followed later that morning, with the last shell fired at 10:45 a.m. The war, which had killed or wounded 40 million people in the span of just four years, ended fifteen minutes later. "The silence that followed almost made one's head ache,"

Truman observed. "We stayed at our positions all day and then crawled into our pup tents that evening."

Truman had accomplished his goal. He had led his troops in combat, firing more than ten thousand rounds without losing a single soldier to the enemy. His men rewarded him with the gift of a silver striking cup, which reflected the mutual respect and affection that had developed between Truman and his troops. "Captain Harry S. Truman," the engraving read. "Presented by the members of Battery D in appreciation of his justice, ability and leadership."

The demobilization would take months, allowing Truman time to explore Paris, where he visited Notre Dame and Napoleon's tomb and saw *Manon* and *Carmen* at the opera. He picked out an engagement ring for Bess and gained back much of the weight he had lost on the march. In addition to Paris, he traveled to Nice, Marseilles, and Monte Carlo. "The view from my window is simply magnificent," he professed in a letter. "There isn't a painting in existence that could do it justice. There is no blue like the Mediterranean blue."

The captain tried to keep his men busy through marches, drills, and inspections, but the inevitable boredom led some into mischief, forcing a reluctant Truman to discipline them. "You've got no idea how I hate to call a man down," he wrote. "I'd almost rather take a beating than tell a man how good for nothing he is when he's done something he shouldn't." The flu pandemic of 1918, which would kill an estimated 50 million people worldwide including 675,000 Americans, distracted his troops, who anxiously awaited news from home. "Every day nearly someone of my outfit will hear that his mother, sister, or sweetheart is dead," he wrote. "It is heartbreaking almost to think that we are so safe and so well over here and that the ones we'd like to protect more than all the world have been more exposed to death than we."

On April 9, 1919, Truman and his men boarded the German steamer *Zeppelin* for home, landing eleven days later on Easter Sunday. "I've never seen anything," he wrote, "that looked so good as the Liberty Lady in New York Harbor." Now with the war at last behind him, Truman could marry Bess. "Please get ready to march down the aisle with me just as soon as you decently can when I get back," he wrote to her. "I haven't any place to go but home and I'm busted financially but I love you as madly as a man can."

The couple wed on June 28, 1919—eight years after he first asked her to marry him—in Trinity Episcopal Church in Independence, the same day Germany and the Allied powers signed the Treaty of Versailles that formally ended the war. Truman, who had no money or even a place of his own, moved into Bess's family's residence at 219 North Delaware Street, which he would call home for the next sixteen years until he moved to Washington.

Truman looked at last to put life on the farm behind him. He teamed up with Eddie Jacobsen—the sergeant with whom he had so successfully run the canteen at Camp Doniphan—and opened a haberdasher in downtown Kansas City in November 1919. To pay for it, he sold his share of the family farm, earning $15,000. Truman served as the bookkeeper, and Jacobson the buyer, while a clerk managed the till. The store, which offered men's shirts, ties, and underwear, initially boomed, selling more than $70,000 of merchandise the first year.

But the recession in 1921–22 proved calamitous. As the economy spiraled down, the duo was left with $35,000 in inventory that could barely fetch $10,000. "We were," as Truman confessed, "hopelessly in debt."

Jacobson declared bankruptcy in 1925, but Truman held out, struggling to repay his creditors. That debt would trail him for another decade until he finally resolved it in 1935, albeit for pennies on the dollar. "This was," he admitted, "a hard experience for me."

The Pendergast family—the local political muscle in Missouri—stepped in to rescue Truman at this perilous point, tapping him to run for county judge in 1922. The job, which paid $3,465 a year, offered Truman a financial lifeline. Despite the title, a county judge functioned less like a jurist than like a traditional county commissioner. At thirty-eight—having worked as banker, farmer, miner, oilman, soldier, and haberdasher—Truman prepared to launch a new career in politics, one that would ultimately come to define him.

His campaign centered on improved roads and better fiscal stewardship of taxpayer money. But Truman was not a natural campaigner. He proved to be a terrible public speaker. At one event, he went up in a biplane, only to get airsick as the pilot circled the audience. Upon landing, he vomited in front of everyone. What he lacked in political polish, however, he more than made up for in hustle. Perched behind the wheel of an old Dodge roadster—weighted down by two bags of cement—he visited every precinct in the district. "I want men for road overseers who know roads and who want work," he declared, "men who will do a day's work for a day's pay, who will work for the county as they would for themselves."

Elected on November 7, 1922, Truman immersed himself in the job. "I became completely familiar with every road and bridge in the county," he wrote. "I visited every state institution in which the county had patients." Though he lost reelection two years later, his political good fortune returned in 1927 when voters chose him as presiding judge of Jackson County, a job he would hold for two terms. As the county's top administrator, he oversaw a $7 million budget and seven hundred employees. During his eight years at the helm, he reduced the number of employees, lowered the county's borrowing costs, installed a budget system, and launched a road and public building program. "I was taught that the expenditure of public money is a public trust and I have never changed my opinion on that subject," he said. "No one ever received any public money for which I was responsible unless he gave honest service for it."

In a letter to Bess on May 7, 1933—on the eve of his forty-ninth birthday—Truman paused to reflect on his nearly half century of life. His priorities in public service mirrored his personal values. His time on the farm had made him industrious and fiscally responsible. Even years later in the White House, where he had a staff to look after him, Truman would go around at night and make sure the windows were secure. He was, in many ways, old-fashioned. Truman never smoked, though he enjoyed a glass of bourbon. He frowned on women drinking or smoking, and believed men should refrain from imbibing in front of them. He never learned to dance and viewed jazz as "modern noise." He likewise avoided technological conveniences, including the telephone and typewriter. When not reading Mark Twain or Charles Dickens, he chuckled over his favorite comic strip, *Andy Gump*. An avid reader and letter writer, Truman was a notoriously bad speller; the name of his own street, Delaware, often flummoxed him. "He had been more at home," biographer David McCullough kindly observed, "in the older era."

Family remained Truman's top priority. He doted on his mother and sister along with Bess and the couple's daughter Margaret, who was born in 1924. Throughout all his many experiences—both the wins and the hardships—Truman remained an idealist. "Tomorrow I'll be forty-nine and for all the good I've done the forty might as well be left off," he wrote. "Take it all together though the experience has been worthwhile; I'd like to do it again."

As Truman's time as presiding judge wound down, he looked toward his next goal. He wanted to run for either governor or the House of Representatives, but the Pendergast political machine had tapped other people to support for those races. Truman appeared headed toward the political sidelines when the Pendergast family approached him about the Senate. Truman had not been the first choice; three other candidates had passed. In Kansas political circles, many questioned whether a county official could handle the job. "I don't think he's heavy enough for the Senate," one politico said of Truman at the time. "I can't imagine him there."

But Truman could.

He announced his candidacy on May 14, 1934. As he had previously done, he hit the road, visiting sixty of the state's 114 counties. A tireless campaigner, he made anywhere from six to sixteen campaign appearances a day. In a state hit hard by the Great Depression, where more than eighteen thousand farms had folded, Truman's rural roots proved to be a political winner. "I went from town to town and from county to county and from daylight until midnight made speeches and shook hands with about a hundred thousand people."

Truman swore the oath of office as a United States senator on January 3, 1935. "I was as timid," he later admitted, "as a country boy arriving on the campus of a great university for his first year." Despite his eagerness, the junior senator from Missouri found Washington a cold and inhospitable place. Many viewed Truman as a product of the Pendergast political machine, which gave him the taint of corruption even though he had done nothing wrong. Truman furthermore realized he was far poorer than many of his colleagues, most of whom chose to ignore him. His desk sat in the last row of the chamber, while his suite in the Senate Office Building consisted of just three rooms and a view of the inner courtyard. His request for a meeting with President Roosevelt took five months to materialize. "The appointment was for fifteen minutes," one biographer noted, "and the senator came out after seven."

"Harry, don't start out with an inferiority complex," the Illinois senator and whip Ham Lewis graciously advised him. "For the first six months you'll wonder how the hell you got here, and after that you'll wonder how the hell the rest of us got here."

Truman took that advice to heart.

Just as he had done on the farm, Truman rose early, arriving in the office at seven a.m., where he labored until seven p.m. Bess did not love life in Washington, often leaving him alone in the capital while she managed the couple's affairs in Independence. This freed him up to carry papers home at night to review in his rented apartment. On national affairs, Truman proved socially progressive, including supporting legislation to stop lynching and abolish poll taxes. He pressed for a robust national defense to counter the rise of Nazi Germany, going so far as to plaster the walls of his office with his old army maps so he could track the advance of Hitler's armies. Over time his colleagues began to take him more seriously.

Nonetheless Roosevelt largely ignored the senator, even though Truman consistently backed the administration's positions, including the president's controversial 1937 effort to enlarge the Supreme Court. In March 1939, after the administration asked Truman to rush back to Washington during a nighttime snowstorm to cast a tie-breaking vote, Truman hit his breaking point. He phoned the White House in a huff, only to reach Steve Early. "I'm here at your request," Truman began, "and I damn near got killed getting here."

"Well, Senator," Early said, "what is it you want?"

"I don't want a thing," Truman replied. "My vote is not for sale."

Early listened.

"I vote my convictions, just as I always have, but I think the President ought to have the decency and respect to treat me like the Senator from Missouri and not like an office boy, and you can tell him what I said. If he wants me to, I'll come down and tell him myself."

"All right, Senator," Early replied. "I'll tell the President."

In September 1939, Missouri governor Lloyd Stark announced he was going to primary Truman. The senator had introduced Stark to Roosevelt.

While Truman struggled to get the White House to return his calls, Stark enjoyed invitations to play poker on the president's yacht. Roosevelt publicly stayed out of the campaign, offering Truman no endorsement, much less encouragement. Behind the scenes, however, Roosevelt advocated for his poker buddy. Early phoned Truman in January 1940, offering him a lifetime appointment to the Interstate Commerce Commission, a job that paid more than a senator.

"Tell them to go to hell," Truman sneered.

The senator could sense he was facing stiff headwinds.

He organized a meeting in St. Louis of his friends, who unanimously advised him to bow out graciously. Tom Pendergast, whose political muscle Truman had long enjoyed, had since gone to prison, brought down by a gambling addiction that had led to graft and fraud. Missouri's major newspapers, many owned by Republicans, likewise despised Truman for his support of the president's New Deal policies. "In addition to all this," Truman said, "I lacked an organization and I had no money to put into an expensive state-wide campaign."

Rather than quit, the plucky senator vowed to fight for his political life. He came out swinging, announcing that he was opposed to Roosevelt seeking a third term, even though he supported many of his policies. "There is no indispensable man in politics," he wrote. "When a republic comes to a point where a man is indispensable, then we have a Caesar. I do not believe that the fate of the nation should depend upon the life or death of any one man."

Truman's friends and political allies stepped up, providing him vital campaign cash, though he still had to borrow $3,000 against his life insurance policy. "I went into seventy-five counties during the hot months of July and August," Truman said, "speaking day and night and meeting hundreds of thousands of voters in the cities, towns, and villages."

As the campaign progressed, voters rallied around him. Farmers liked his humble roots as well as his support of the New Deal. So did organized labor. His wartime service helped with veterans while his progressive ideas brought him minority support. "I always made it my business to speak plainly and directly to the people without indulging in high-powered oratory," he said. "The truth, I felt, is what voters need more than anything else."

Of the 665,000 votes cast, Truman beat Stark by just 7,976. The November 1940 general election against Republican Manville Davis in a largely Democratic state, produced a far easier victory. "I was still," he noted, "the United States senator from Missouri."

Truman began his second term on January 3, 1941.

War consumed Europe. Since 1939, German forces had seized Poland, Denmark, Norway, Belgium, Luxembourg, and France, while Yugoslavia and Greece would fall in a matter of months. The senator felt it was only a matter of time before America joined the fight. He went to see Gen. George Marshall, informing the army chief of staff that he would like to quit the Senate and climb back into uniform as a field artillery colonel or instructor.

"Senator," Marshall asked. "How old are you?"

"Well, I'm fifty-six years old."

"You're too damned old. You'd better stay home and work in the Senate."

"He was right, of course," Truman later acknowledged, "but it hurt my feelings and I decided to do something for the war effort on a constructive basis."

Truman started to hear complaints from his Missouri constituents about potential financial irregularities in the construction of Fort Leonard Wood, a basic training camp. Alarmed by the news—and fearful it might be endemic as the nation ramped up for war—the senator set out to investigate. He jumped in his car, driving a three-thousand-mile loop around the eastern half of the country. Along the way, he visited new military camps and defense plants that had mushroomed across the landscape. Much of the construction, Truman discovered, was being done on a cost-plus basis, which had no checks or balances over the work. Upon his return, Truman discussed his findings with William Helm, a reporter with the *Kansas City Journal-Post*.

"Why don't you call for a committee to investigate this rotten situation?" Helm said. "That would be doing something besides just making a speech, wouldn't it?"

"It surely would," Truman replied.

"You, of course, would head that committee; you'd be its chairman," Helm added. "You'd have the power of the United States behind you."

"You're right, Bill!" Truman declared. "You're absolutely right. I *will* do something about it. I'm going to do just what you've suggested."

On February 10, 1941, Truman rose before his Senate colleagues and called for a special committee to examine defense expenditures. Aware of the political land mines surrounding such a request, Truman was careful not to appear unpatriotic or on a witch hunt. "I consider public funds to be sacred funds," he told fellow lawmakers, "and I think they ought to have every safeguard possible to prevent their being misused and mishandled."

Truman asked for $25,000, but the Senate Committee on Audit and Control authorized only $15,000. Still, Truman had his start. "We were interested in doing a surgeon's job to cure," he said, "not in performing an autopsy to find out why the patient died."

The Special Committee to Investigate the National Defense Program, as Truman's group became known, avoided social issues, focusing exclusively on war costs ranging from base construction to the army's motion picture division. Truman worked hard, guided by the simple motto "There is no substitute for a fact." The committee held hearings not only in Washington but in hotel rooms in dozens of cities around the country. At the end of the first year, the committee had conducted seventy hearings and interviewed 252 witnesses. "We were not seeking headlines. We did not want publicity," Truman said. "We wanted only results."

The committee's budget soon jumped from $15,000 to $50,000, allowing Truman to increase the staff to fifteen investigators while broadening inquiries to include aluminum shortages, gasoline rationing, and the German U-boat threat. The fear of investigation was often enough to keep organizations honest. Truman's committee ultimately held more than four hundred hearings, interviewed 1,798 witnesses, and produced thirty-two reports. The success landed him on the cover of *Time* magazine on March 8, 1943. "In all," he wrote, "the committee had made recommendations resulting in the estimated saving of fifteen billion dollars to the American taxpayer. This had been accomplished at a cost of approximately four hundred thousand dollars, the amount of total appropriations granted for the committee's work."

During this time, Truman stumbled across the top-secret development of the atomic bomb. Investigators had begun questioning expenditures related to a plant in rural Washington near Hanford, where scientists worked to create plutonium. This prodding prompted a call from War Secretary Stimson on June 17, 1943. The transcript shows the conversation was short yet cryptic. "Now that's a matter which I know all about personally," Stimson said, "and I am one of the group of two or three men in the whole world who know about it."

"I see," Truman replied.

"It's part of a very important secret development."

"I herewith see the situation, Mr. Secretary," Truman said. "You assure that this is for a specific purpose and you think it's all right. That's all I need to know."

"Not only for a specific purpose," Stimson added, "but a unique purpose."

As the war progressed—and Roosevelt's third term neared the end—it became clear that the president's health was in decline. Not only had decades of paralysis worn him out, but on March 27, 1944, his doctor diagnosed him with heart disease. Dr. Howard Bruenn, one of the president's physicians, summed up his condition with two words: "God-awful."

But that did not stop Roosevelt from seeking an unprecedented fourth term with the hopes of guiding America through the end of World War II. His Republican rival was Thomas Dewey, a former mob prosecutor and current governor of New York. Few believed Roosevelt would survive another four years in office, which elevated the importance of his vice president. Over the course of three terms, Roosevelt had had two vice presidents, John Garner followed by Henry Wallace. An Iowa farmer, intellectual, and pioneer in the field of crop genetics, Wallace was viewed by many as brilliant but eccentric and even odd, a characteristic underscored by his unusual skill throwing a boomerang and his fascination with Russian mystics.

Democratic Party leaders, who deemed Wallace too liberal and likely to damage the ticket in the conservative South, set out to find a replacement. Truman was no one's first choice, but as party leaders moved down the list of possible candidates, the Missouri farmer's homespun appeal only increased. Word reached Truman of his consideration, but he was adamant that he did not want the job. After years of hard work, he had finally achieved seniority in the Senate. In addition to his own investigatory committee, he served on several other important bodies, including

Appropriations, Military Affairs, and Interstate Commerce. "Every effort was made by me to shut it off," Truman later said. "I liked my job as a senator, and I wanted to stay with it. It takes a long time for a man to establish himself in the senate."

But party leaders faced greater challenges than just Truman.

Wallace had no intention of stepping aside. At the same time, the presidential aide and confidante Jimmy Byrnes felt the job should be his. The South Carolinian sported an impressive résumé, including service in the House of Representatives and the Senate and time on the bench as a Supreme Court justice. He currently served as director of the Office of War Mobilization, a position in which he worked so closely with Roosevelt that he earned the nickname "assistant president." But like Wallace, Byrnes carried political baggage. Not only did organized labor dislike him, but Byrnes was a segregationist whose efforts as a lawmaker to kill a federal anti-lynching bill made him unpopular with minority voters. In the contest for vice president, neither Wallace nor Byrnes would step aside unless Roosevelt personally told them to do so. For a president who shunned personal conflict, such an ask proved impossible. If anything, Roosevelt only encouraged the hopes of both, setting up a fight at the convention.

Democrats poured into Chicago for the convention, which kicked off on July 19, 1944. Even as party leaders coalesced around him, Truman maintained his reluctance. "Hell," he confided in a news reporter, "I don't want to be president."

When Byrnes asked if he would make a speech nominating him for vice president, the Missouri senator agreed. But events soon superseded Truman's desires. Party officials released a letter from Roosevelt. "I have been associated with Henry Wallace during his past four years as Vice President," he wrote. "I like him and I respect him and he is my personal friend. For these reasons I personally would vote for his nomination if I were a delegate to the convention." This yawn of an endorsement, described in one account as the "coolest and cruelest brushoff in all the long Roosevelt career," would soon be known as the "kiss-of-death" letter.

Byrnes proved a bigger challenge, as he had locked up 400 of the 589 votes needed to secure the nomination. Party leaders jumped onto a call with Roosevelt, who was headed to San Diego. Byrnes's surging momentum, many feared, had to be halted, or else Roosevelt might lose the election. The president needed to put this weight on the scales.

"Go all out for Truman," Roosevelt instructed them.

Truman could feel the pressure. He phoned Tom Evans, a Kansas City businessman and longtime supporter who owned a chain of drugstores. "Are you my friend?" the senator asked.

"I hope so," Evans replied. "Why?"

"If you are," Truman continued, "I need you up here to help keep me from being vice president. How soon can you get up here?"

"I can come right away."

"Well, come on," Truman said. "I need you."

When Evans arrived, Truman protested that he did not want to be vice president. He wanted Evans to spread the word.

"Why, that's ridiculous," his friend told him.

"I don't want to drag out a lot of skeletons out of the closet." Truman had put his wife and daughter on his Senate payroll, which was common at the time, but he knew critics would use it against him. He also didn't want anyone to report that his father-in-law had died by suicide in 1903, which would devastate Bess.

Evans assured him his fears were unfounded. "Lord," he said. "That isn't anything terrible."

On the opening day of the convention, party leaders summoned Truman to a suite at the Blackstone Hotel. The senator perched on one of the twin beds.

Opposite him sat Democratic National Committee chairman Robert Hannegan, who phoned Roosevelt.

"Bob," the president began, "have you got that fellow lined up yet?"

"No, he is the contrariest Missouri mule I've ever delt with."

"Well," Roosevelt replied before slamming the phone down, "you tell him if he wants to break up the Democratic Party in the middle of a war that's his responsibility."

"To say I was stunned," Truman admitted, "is to put it mildly."

Truman rose and paced the room, all eyes on him.

"Well, if that is the situation," he finally announced, "I'll have to say yes, but why the hell didn't he tell me in the first place."

Byrnes dropped out of the race and left the convention, bitter at what he felt was Roosevelt's betrayal. Immediately following Roosevelt's nomination on the evening of July 20, 1944, Wallace's supporters stampeded Chicago Stadium to try to force the vote.

"We want Wallace!" his supporters chanted. "We want Wallace!"

Hannegan rushed to shut the convention down for the night before any vote. Truman's supporters used the time to convince as many delegates as possible to support favorite-son nominations, a strategy designed to water down Wallace's support. The tactic worked the following afternoon, as Wallace garnered 429 votes to Truman's 319, not enough to secure victory. Party officials meanwhile continued to rustle up votes for Truman.

Rather than recess for dinner, Hannegan pushed for an immediate second vote, a move that would limit the infusion of evening ticket holders who might support Wallace. As delegates voted, the tally appeared close until Alabama senator John Bankhead switched his support to Truman. "That really was the spark," one reporter wrote, "which ignited the tinder."

South Carolina followed.

Then Illinois, Indiana, Wyoming, New York, and Ohio.

"The stampede," added another journalist, "was on."

Delegates jumped to their feet as the chorus of voices rose to a crescendo.

At 8:14 p.m., the final tally revealed 1,031 votes for Truman to Wallace's 105. The junior senator from Missouri, who only days earlier had fought to avoid this fate, was now Roosevelt's vice-presidential running mate.

Before a crowd of thousands, this former farmer, soldier, and haberdasher gave one of the shortest acceptance speeches in convention history. "You don't know how very much I appreciate the very great honor which has come to the state of Missouri. It is also a great responsibility which I am perfectly willing to assume," he began. "Nine years and five months ago I came to the Senate. I expect to continue the efforts I have made there to help shorten the war and win the peace under the great leader, Franklin D. Roosevelt."

Truman's elderly mother beamed. "I knew that boy would amount to something from the time when he was nine years old," she said. "He could plow the straightest row of corn in the county. He could sow wheat so there wasn't a bare spot in the whole field."

But not all of the country was so sure, including some senior White House aides who had never even met him. "Who the hell is Harry Truman?" Adm. William Leahy, Roosevelt's chief of staff, famously asked upon hearing the news of his selection.

His lack of familiarity, however, was only one concern.

The press highlighted the fact that Truman's ascension—dubbed the "Missouri Compromise"—was the product of a backroom deal by party bosses, drawing comparisons to his earlier and controversial support from the Pendergast political machine. Others questioned whether the junior senator was the best person to stand in Roosevelt's shadow. "Truman is a first-rate second-rate man, rather than a topflight potential successor in the White House—and being an honest and modest person, he knows it," argued the *Columbus Dispatch*. The *Pittsburgh Post-Gazette* agreed. "Truman emerges," the paper declared, "from the hottest race ever conducted for the office as one of the weakest candidates ever to be nominated."

Despite the criticism, some saw the wisdom. "However much Truman's origin in national life may be held against him, there is no doubt that in the last few years he has become one of the most valuable men in Washington," the *St. Lous Post-Dispatch* declared. "Truman's committee has been a scourge to wrongdoers and a public benefit of inestimable importance."

Others pragmatically noted that the "colorless" Truman, as he was occasionally characterized in the media, failed to alienate any key constituencies. "The assumption is that Senator Truman, if not actually strengthening the ticket, will at least not cost it any votes," conceded the *Washington Evening Star*. "But there may be some doubt about this."

Truman, as he always did, simply soldiered on.

A month later, on August 18, 1944, Truman joined Roosevelt for lunch on the south lawn of the White House. It was a sultry summer day, and despite the shade of a magnolia tree, the two men shed their jackets. Though only three years apart, Roosevelt looked much older. Truman, by contrast, appeared trim and vigorous as the two men ate sardines and toast.

Roosevelt confided in his running mate that he would have to do most of the campaigning. He also forbade him to fly on a plane. "Harry, I'm not a well man," he said. "We cannot be sure of my future."

Truman, of course, had already made that deduction, noticing how the president's hands shook as he poured from the creamer. He struggled at times just to talk. "It doesn't seem to be any mental lapse of any kind," Truman observed, "but physically he's just going to pieces."

Though Truman admired Roosevelt's accomplishments, there was no real fondness between the men, who rarely saw each other. Truman no doubt recalled how Roosevelt had worked against him in his previous Senate election. Despite that, he labored hard on the campaign trail that fall, making fifty-four speeches in which he highlighted Roosevelt's successes along with the need to win the war. In keeping with his frugal ways, Truman often washed his socks in his hotel room and hung them up at night to dry.

The November 7, 1944, election was an electoral landslide. Roosevelt won thirty-six of forty-eight states, claiming 432 electoral votes to Dewey's 99. The popular vote was closer, but Roosevelt still bested his mustachioed rival by 3.5 million votes. For Roosevelt, it was the narrowest win of his four presidential campaigns. On January 20, 1945, the duo was sworn in on the rear portico of the White House as snow blanketed the capital.

Fears over the president's health haunted Truman that winter, who—outside cabinet meetings—saw Roosevelt only twice after the election, both times in March 1945. Despite his ill health, Roosevelt made no effort to educate Truman. As he always did, Roosevelt kept the war and his plans close, leaving Truman to busy himself in the Senate.

Over Truman hung the reality of Roosevelt's declining health, a point hammered home to him as he escorted his army friend Eddie McKim out of a White House reception. "Turn around and take a look," McKim said. "You're going to be living in that house before long."

"I'm afraid I am," Truman said. "And it scares the hell out of me."

CHAPTER 4

"We all turn now to our new leader, to Harry S. Truman, in complete dedication."

—*BIRMINGHAM AGE-HERALD*

APRIL 13, 1945, EDITORIAL

Truman rose at six-thirty a.m. on his first full day as president.

He ate breakfast, went for a walk, and then prepared to head to work. Joined by the Secret Service, the president emerged from his Connecticut Avenue apartment, where he spotted Associated Press reporter Tony Vaccaro waiting by the curb. Truman had grown fond of the Memphis native who followed him during his days on the campaign trail.

"Come on in, Tony," he said, waving him over to the car. "Let's get started."

On the five-mile ride to the White House, Truman confided to the journalist his feeling of inadequacy. "There have been few men in all history the equal of the man into whose shoes I am stepping," he told him. "I pray God I can measure up to the task."

Vaccaro scribbled down his comments.

As vice president, Truman added, his door had always been open, allowing everyone from congressional colleagues to old army buddies to drop in on him. He doubted that would be possible now that he was president. "I'm going to miss all that," he lamented.

At the White House, Truman hustled to the Oval Office. The staff had cleared the desk of Roosevelt's collection of toys and bric-a-brac, but the rest of the first-floor office still reflected the former president, whose death had occurred barely eighteen hours earlier. Ship models perched on tables and Hudson River prints adorned the walls, representing Roosevelt's lifelong love of sailing. Press officer Jonathan Daniels watched Truman approach the desk, the same one his predecessor had sat behind for twelve years. Atop the desk, crafted from American wood with a Michigan maple veneer, Roosevelt had signed the nation's most important legislation, from the declarations of war against Japan and Germany to the GI Bill.

The new president pulled back the leather chair and sat, his back to the three windows. He swiveled the chair, as though to test it. "It seemed still Roosevelt's desk and Roosevelt's room," Daniels recalled. "It seemed to me, indeed, almost Roosevelt's sun which came in the wide south windows and touched Truman's thick glasses."

Roosevelt's possessive hold over the presidency had left his successor woefully handicapped as he now assumed the office of the most powerful leader in the world. The former president had purposefully isolated his understudy. In January, when he had left to attend the Yalta Conference with Churchill and Stalin, Roosevelt instructed Truman to message him only if it was "absolutely urgent" and to keep his cables "as brief as possible." When he returned and the two met in March, Roosevelt did not brief him on the decisions made or dwell on any policy or plans. Nor had any of the president's senior lieutenants, like Secretary of State Stettinius or War Secretary Stimson, ever bothered to tutor Roosevelt's political heir. The first time, in fact, that Truman met Stettinius had been in Eleanor Roosevelt's study just the night before.

Those oversights came into sharp focus as Truman settled in behind his new desk, a leader armed only with a high school diploma and who had not been abroad since he returned from France at the end of World War I. Fear and uncertainty spread like a wildfire through the political system. "We in the State Department shared the concern of all Americans whether the 'little man from Missouri' could rise to the occasion," noted Charles Bohlen, the agency's Russia expert. Leahy agreed. "One cannot yet see," he wrote in his diary, "how the complicated critical business of the war and the peace can be carried forward by a new President who is completely inexperienced in international affairs." Truman, of course, shared their doubts, as evidenced by his comments to a Senate colleague: "I'm not big enough for this job."

At 10:15 a.m., Stettinius arrived in the Oval Office for what marked the beginning of Truman's presidential education. The forty-five-year-old Chicago native, who had worked as an executive with General Motors and the United States Steel Corporation, jumped into public service in 1939 as chairman of the War Resources Board. Stettinius later helped provide military aid to the Allies and served as a special assistant to the president before Roosevelt appointed him undersecretary of state in 1943. The following year, on December 1, 1944, he took over as the nation's top diplomat, replacing the ailing Secretary of State Cordell Hull.

On this Friday morning, Stettinius asked Truman for a few moments of his time.

"Take as long as you want," the president replied.

Stettinius updated him on the inaugural meeting of the United Nations. Roosevelt, who had served as assistant secretary of the navy during World War I, had supported President Woodrow Wilson's creation of the League of Nations, an organization designed to prevent another global conflict. Much to Roosevelt's frustration, the Senate had refused to ratify the treaty, and America never joined. The toothless organization subsequently foundered—and war erupted again two decades later. The United Nations was Roosevelt's answer to that earlier failure. His desire to avoid the same fate, according to his close aide Harry Hopkins, was one of his main motivations in selecting Truman to be his vice president, knowing the Missouri lawmaker was popular in the Senate. "The President," Hopkins added, "wanted somebody that would help him when he went up there and asked them to ratify the peace."

The inaugural meeting was set to begin in days in California, where representatives from fifty nations would gather to draft a charter. "I have decided," Truman announced, "that I shall not go to San Francisco—the President has appointed a delegation, the plans are made—you will go to San Francisco and conduct the meetings with great success."

The secretary of state listened.

"If you wish me to deliver a message," Truman added, "I shall be glad to do so."

Stettinius concurred. The secretary of state noted that under Roosevelt, communications between the White House and the State Department had been poor, a relationship he hoped would change with Truman. Relations with Russia likewise had deteriorated since Yalta, to which Truman said it was important for America to be firm. "He gave me the impression," Stettinius wrote in his diary, "that he thought we had been too easy with them."

The secretary of state encouraged Truman to seek out Roosevelt's friend and confidant, Harry Hopkins, who had enjoyed good relations with both Churchill and Stalin. Stettinius also urged the new president to meet soon with Churchill, to which he agreed.

"Do you wish me to take steps to push that along?" Stettinius asked.

"Any steps you take to encourage an early visit by Winston Churchill to this country will be a great service," Truman concluded.

The president met next with the nation's senior defense leaders, including Stimson, Marshall, Leahy, Chief of Naval Operations Adm. Ernest King, Navy Secretary James Forrestal, and Lt. Gen. Barney Giles, commander of the Army Air Forces in the Pacific. "I knew and respected all these men," Truman said, "and it was comforting to know that I would be advised by leaders of such ability and distinction."

Conservative estimates predicted the fall of Germany within six months, though most believed it would occur much sooner. Just that week American troops had liberated some twenty-one thousand starving prisoners from the Nazi concentration camp at Buchenwald. The famed journalist Edward Murrow visited the camp, describing piles of emaciated bodies stacked like cordwood. "God alone," Murrow declared, "knows how many men and boys have died there."

Unlike Germany, the defeat of Japan, military leaders informed Truman, could take up to eighteen months. Only thirteen days earlier, American troops had sloshed ashore on the island of Okinawa in what already was shaping up to be a hellacious fight. Headlines that morning revealed that Japanese kamikazes had sunk the destroyer USS *Mannert L. Abele* and damaged several others. *Baltimore Evening Sun* reporter Philip Heisler, who was aboard one of the wounded ships, captured the terror in a first-person story, describing smoke-filled passageways and sailors suffering from flash burns and missing limbs. "I saw men fight fire till they fell down from exhaustion," he wrote, "then get up and fight fire until they fell again."

Truman's meeting was brief, just forty-five minutes. Unlike Roosevelt, who often joked and spun stories, the new president was practical and direct. The diaries of Stimson and Leahy revealed a cautious optimism about the commander in chief, who was not afraid to seek help. "He was confident that we understood the terrific burden that had been unloaded on him and asked us to help him all we could," Leahy observed. "We were directed to adhere to the same lines of procedure we had followed with his predecessor." The war secretary agreed. "He made the impression on me of a man who is willing and anxious to learn and to do his best."

Despite the kind words, many still harbored doubts. That was evident in General Marshall's private comment to Stimson on the car ride back to the Pentagon. "We shall not know what he is really like," he said, "until the pressure begins to be felt."

After the meeting Truman asked Leahy to stay behind. The sixty-nine-year-old Iowa native and graduate of the Naval Academy had enjoyed a storied career. The chain-smoking admiral had fought in every major conflict, ranging from the Spanish-American War and the Philippine Insurrection to the Boxer Rebellion and World War I. He later served as chief of naval operations—the nation's top sailor—as well as governor of Puerto Rico and ambassador to Vichy France. Roosevelt, who first met Leahy decades earlier when he served as assistant secretary of the navy, tapped the admiral in 1942 to serve as White House chief of staff and the de facto chairman of the Joint Chiefs. The slender and bespectacled Leahy, whom a reporter once noted looked more like a chaplain than a fleet commander, had a reputation for being blunt and crusty, a fitting personality for a man who answered to the nickname "Sandpaper."

Truman asked Leahy to remain at the helm.

"Are you sure you want me?" he replied. "I always say what's on my mind."

"I want the truth, and I want the facts at all times," Truman assured the admiral. "I want you to stay with me and always to tell me what's on your mind. You may not always agree with my decisions, but I know you will carry them out faithfully."

"You have my pledge," Leahy said. "You can count on me."

Truman visited Capitol Hill at noon for lunch accompanied by an army of police and Secret Service agents, who encircled him as he walked the marble floors, the same ones he had dashed across alone only the afternoon before. Though protocol dictated that lawmakers visit the White House, Truman felt otherwise. "It was his instinct," observed United Press reporter Allen Drury, "to come home for reassurance in his terrifying hour."

The stakes for Truman and the nation could not have been higher as he prepared to face his former colleagues for the first time as their president.

And everyone knew it.

"There is a governmental crisis so deep and disturbing and tremendous that even the most political minded or the most irresponsible now feels that this is no time for anything less than unreserved support and cooperation," *Time* reporter Frank McNaughton wrote in a memo to his editor. "The honeymoon will not last forever, that is certain." In the short term, however, Republican lawmakers, who had long battled Roosevelt, even during times of war, rallied around Truman, sending him a resolution of support. "In this critical and sorrowing hour when you are called to the supreme responsibility of the republic," it stated, "we send you this expression of our faith and trust in you and the assurance of our sustaining prayers."

"This was probably the most sincere resolution the caucus has passed in a year or more," McNaughton observed. "It sprang from a personal liking of Harry Truman, a sympathy for his tremendous load and the humanity and humility with which he shouldered it."

"He's one of us," proved a common refrain.

In Secretary of the Senate Les Biffle's office, Truman dined with senior lawmakers, a roster that counted thirteen senators and four House members. Over a meal of salmon, potatoes, peas, and cornbread, Truman asked permission to address a joint session of Congress after Roosevelt's funeral, which was scheduled for the weekend. He wanted to use the speech to assure the nation he planned to continue his predecessor's policies.

"Harry," one senator said, "you were planning to come whether we liked it or not."

"You know I would have," the president answered, "but I would rather do it with your full and understanding support and welcome."

The president turned serious, reminding his colleagues that he had been thrust into a "terrible" position, one in which he would need their help and cooperation. "There will be times when we may disagree, when it will be impossible for me to go along with you," he said. "I value your opinions, I expect to consult you, and I want to cooperate with you."

Despite the doubts that swirled in the minds of many, those who had worked closely with the former Missouri farmer felt reassured. "Truman will not make a great, flashy president like Roosevelt. But by God, he'll make a good president, a sound president," House Speaker Sam Rayburn confided in a reporter off the record. "He's got stuff in him." Republican Senator Homer Ferguson of Michigan agreed. "Truman is a good, solid man. He knows the terrific responsibilities of the job," he said. "The people should have faith in him."

As he departed the lunch, Truman ran into a gaggle of congressional pages who wanted to meet him. News reporters joined the fray as Truman took time to shake hands.

"Well, isn't this nice," he said. "This is really nice."

The journalists crowded around.

"Boys," he said, "if you ever pray, pray for me now."

"Good luck, Mr. President," one of the reporters said.

"I wish you didn't have to call me that," he replied.

CHAPTER 5

"All this very strange; worked with F.D.R. in the hilltop cottage at Warm Springs last Thursday. Today—Monday—he sleeps in the rose garden at Hyde Park."

—BILL HASSETT

APRIL 16, 1945, DIARY ENTRY

The funeral train carrying Roosevelt's remains rolled into Washington's Union Station at 9:50 a.m. on April 14, 1945, ending the twenty-three-hour journey from Warm Springs. Throngs of men, women, and children—some of whom waved flags, saluted, or placed their hats over their hearts—had watched the train rumble northward across the hills and piedmont of Georgia, the Carolinas, and Virginia. The president's flag-draped coffin, which occupied the final coach under the care of a military honor guard, was illuminated at night, allowing mourners at rural crossroads and in tiny towns a glimpse of Roosevelt. At each stop along the 750-mile route, thousands crowded along the tracks and platforms, some standing in silence or singing hymns. "Everywhere," Bill Hassett wrote in his diary, "grief and reverence."

Truman stood on the platform that Saturday morning joined by Jimmy Byrnes and Henry Wallace, his former rivals for the vice presidency whom he had asked to accompany him so as to send a message of unity to the nation. A military-led procession departed Union Station soon after, taking a route that would pass the U.S. Capitol and then turn onto Fifteenth Street and lastly Pennsylvania Avenue before entering the northwest gate of the White House. The military deployed 2,300 soldiers to line the streets. That figure was soon dwarfed by the estimated half-million mourners, many crowded five deep along the two-mile route, hoping for a glimpse of Roosevelt's casket carried atop a black caisson and pulled by a team of six white horses. Others peered from rooftops at the procession, which at times was so quiet that those gathered could hear the footfalls of the marching service members who escorted the president's remains, reminding one news reporter of the rumble of a faraway surf.

The Roosevelt family followed the caisson in two black limousines while a third carried Truman. The new president studied the faces of those in the crowd. The anguish he witnessed not only reflected his predecessor's popularity but served as a reminder of the challenge he faced in reassuring a sorrowful nation as he tried to step out from Roosevelt's shadow. "I shall never forget the sight of so many grief-stricken people. Some wept without restraint. Some shed their tears in silence. Others were grim and stoic, but all were genuine in their mourning," Truman recalled. "It was impossible now to tell who had been for him and who had not."

The procession reached the White House at 11:14 a.m., where a Marine band played "The Star Spangled Banner." Eight service members escorted Roosevelt's casket inside and down the red-carpeted hall to the East Room where, almost eighty years earlier to the day, Abraham Lincoln had lain in state. Body bearers placed the president before an altar, which anchored the center of the windowed east wall. Behind it loomed a towering row of calla lilies, red roses, orchids, carnations, and daffodils. "On one side," observed reporter Tom Reedy, "stood a vacant wheelchair, a mute symbol of the malady which struck the President down in his prime but couldn't keep him down." Portraits of George and Martha Washington—rescued by Dolley Madison when the British torched the White House during the War of 1812—looked down on the casket, where Roosevelt, visible through a glass enclosure, wore a gray-blue suit, matching necktie, and white shirt. "He looked younger in death," one reporter observed, "than when last seen here by friends in Washington where his office weighed so heavily."

That afternoon Eleanor Roosevelt stopped by the White House usher's office. "Can you dispense with the Honor Guard for a few moments," she asked, "and have the casket opened? I would like to have a few moments alone with my husband."

She waited in the office while the undertaker opened the casket and the Honor Guard—composed of two soldiers, one sailor, and one marine—marched out the door.

"Please don't let anybody come in," she added.

Assistant chief usher James West watched as the former first lady looked down upon the face of her husband of four decades and the father of the couple's six children. Eleanor then slipped a gold ring from her finger and placed it on her husband's hand. "She straightened, eyes dry, and she left the room," West recalled. "The coffin was never opened again."

As staff hustled to complete final preparations for the funeral, Truman met briefly at 2:15 p.m. with Jimmy Byrnes. The veteran politico offered some wise advice to Truman following his comment to reporters the day before at the Capitol, lamenting the fact that the press now had to call him president. The nation's long-serving and beloved former leader had died. The country was in crisis. It was no time for Truman to be self-deprecating. "Every man, woman and child of America in every hamlet, village and city want to look up to their President," Byrnes advised. "Harry, you must put yourself up on a pedestal and stay there."

Truman agreed.

At four p.m., two hundred mourners crowded inside the East Room, so many that some overflowed into the Blue and Green rooms. Included among the invited guests were sixty diplomats and thirty congressmen, fifteen from each house. Mourners ranged from cabinet members and Supreme Court justices to military leaders and foreign dignitaries. His former rival Governor Thomas Dewey was on hand; so too was Mrs. Woodrow Wilson, widow of the twenty-eighth president, and Crown Princess Martha of Norway, the wife of the future King Olaf V. Throughout the White House, directives called for all work to cease. Members of the household staff gathered in the basement, where speakers were set up to broadcast the funeral.

Episcopal bishop Angus Dun led the twenty-three-minute service, reminding attendees of one of Roosevelt's most famous lines from his first inaugural address on March 4, 1933, a time when he sought to rally a nation gripped by economic calamity and despair.

"The only thing we have to fear," Dun said, "is fear itself."

The mourners listened.

"As that was his first word to us," the bishop concluded, "I am sure he would want it to be his last."

A crowd congregated across the street that evening to watch as body bearers loaded the president's casket into a hearse for the trip back to Union Station. Truman joined the Roosevelt family on the overnight train to Hyde Park. In death, the former president had chosen to return home to his family's estate, overlooking the Hudson River, where as a boy he had ridden horses and romped in the woods before polio later robbed him of the use of his legs.

At ten a.m. on a cool yet clear Sunday in April, family, friends, aides, and dignitaries gathered in the rectangular rose garden encircled by a towering hedge of hemlock. Included among them were Canadian prime minister Mackenzie King, Gen. George Marshall, and Adm. Ernest King, not to mention his beloved Scottish terrier, Fala. Rifle fire from West Point cadets announced the arrival of the president's horse-drawn caisson. "One by one, evenly spaced, came the staccato shots of the President's salute," Bill Hassett noted in his diary. "They echoed and re-echoed across the Hudson Valley and faded into silence."

The Reverend George Anthony led the procession into the garden. Nine pallbearers trailed him followed by the Roosevelt family. The minister read from the Book of Common Prayer before the former president's bronze casket was lowered. "We commit his body to the ground," Anthony concluded. "Earth to earth, ashes to ashes, dust to dust."

The mournful notes of taps floated over the garden.

Roosevelt's burial brought an end to the formalities of death and mourning that had consumed the nation since the first news bulletin rattled off the teletype barely seventy-two hours earlier. With Roosevelt now forever at rest just steps away from the bedroom in which he was born, the spotlight shifted to Truman, an unlikely leader whom the nation depended on to win the war and secure the peace.

No one felt the pressure more than Truman. "Back in Washington that evening, I felt that an epoch had come to an end," he recalled. "A great President, whose deeds and words had profoundly affected our times, was gone. Chance had chosen me to carry on his work, and in the three days I had already experienced some of the weight of its unbelievable burden. As I went to bed that night I prayed I would be equal to the task."

CHAPTER 6

"Tragic fate has thrust upon us grave responsibilities. We must carry on."

—PRESIDENT HARRY TRUMAN

APRIL 16, 1945

Truman hustled to educate himself.

The Oval Office resembled a revolving door as a parade of senators and House members along with ambassadors and world leaders cycled through, ranging from Philippine president Sergio Osmena to Chinese foreign minister Tse Vung Soong. Truman even met with three of the six marines in the famous Joe Rosenthal photograph of the flag-raising atop Iwo Jima's Mount Suribachi on February 23, 1945. "Everyone, including Truman himself," Leahy observed, "knew that in the field of international relations he had much to learn."

Outside work, the president swapped his apartment on Connecticut Avenue for Blair House, realizing that it was unfair to his neighbors to burden them with his army of Secret Service agents. Blair House furthermore was right across Pennsylvania Avenue, allowing him to stroll home each night, though he occasionally had to patiently wait at the stoplight, his arms loaded with briefing books to study. Truman planned to remain at Blair House as long as needed, giving Eleanor Roosevelt time to pack her family's possessions.

Beyond his briefing books, Truman sought out Roosevelt's former aides for advice. "I haven't been elected president," he confided in one staffer. "I'm going to try to follow Roosevelt's policy as much as possible." One of the first people he reached out to was Harry Hopkins, the former president's trusted confidant. Hopkins had lost two-thirds of his stomach in a 1937 battle with cancer, leaving him frail, anemic, and malnourished. His pale and spindly stature, coupled with his reputation as a midwestern Machiavelli, led one senior leader to characterize him as a "strange gnome-like creature," while Truman thought he looked downright "cadaverous." Despite Hopkins's ailments, Roosevelt so valued his counsel that he invited him to move into the White House, where he had resided for several years in Abraham Lincoln's study, helping to manage the administration's alliance with the Soviet Union.

"How do you feel, Harry?" the president began.

"Terrible," he predictably replied.

"I hope you don't mind my calling you in at this time," Truman continued. "But I need to know everything you can tell me about our relations with Russia—all that you know about Stalin and Churchill and the conferences at Cairo, Casablanca, Teheran, Yalta."

"Stalin is a forthright, rough, tough Russian," Hopkins said. "He is a Russian partisan through and through, thinking always first of Russia."

The president nodded.

"But he can be talked to frankly," Hopkins concluded.

Truman decided to replace Stettinius with Jimmy Byrnes, though he would wait until after the inaugural conference of the United Nations, so as not to undermine his secretary of state while he negotiated the creation of the world peace organization. The president's reasons for the swap were plentiful. Despite Stettinius's impressive career, Truman didn't think he had the intellectual horsepower needed for the job, an observation shared by others. "Stettinius," Truman once said in a moment of brutal candor, "was as dumb as they come."

In the case of Byrnes, Truman hoped an appointment to such an illustrious post would serve as a balm to soothe any residual burn he might feel over the ugly fight for the vice presidency. Roosevelt had done the same for Wallace, naming him secretary of commerce shortly before his death. But soothing a bruised ego wasn't Truman's only motivation. Under the law at the time, should tragedy befall him, power would pass to Stettinius, a businessman who had never been elected to public office. "It was my feeling that any man who stepped into the presidency should have held at least some office to which he had been elected by a vote of the people," Truman said. "I regarded Byrnes as the man best qualified."

The sixty-two-year-old Byrnes was certainly far more capable than Stettinius—he had served in the legislative, executive, and judicial branches—and the inexperienced Truman knew he needed the help of a veteran political hand. Byrnes was best characterized by a Washington reporter as "an expert wire puller," but he had his own issues. The bald and slender southerner, who stood just five foot seven, was a strong political fixer, but he was also notoriously ambitious. Byrnes understood better than anyone how politics had robbed him of the nation's top job, a fact that his aide Walter Brown recorded in his notes the day Roosevelt died. "In the back of both our minds was the one fact that neither of us mentioned—by all rules of the game he should now be president and not Truman," Brown wrote. "We both knew Truman was a weak man." Truman recognized these flaws in Byrnes, characterizing him in his diary as "able and conniving." "All country politicians," he added, "are alike." Byrnes even drew the ire of Stalin at Yalta, who described him as "the most honest-looking horse thief."

Beyond Byrnes, Truman made other staff changes, but none as high profile. Many longtime aides feared that Roosevelt's death would end their employment, a fact exacerbated by the sudden appearance of new faces in hallways of the West Wing.

"Confusion and uncertainty prevail all around the White House," Assistant Press Secretary Eben Ayers noted in his diary.

"There seem to be all sorts of strange people coming and going," he added in another entry. "Missourians are most in evidence."

Truman tried to calm the tensions, asking many veteran staffers to remain in his administration, including Secretary Bill Hassett, a former journalist who had served Roosevelt since 1935. Hassett said he considered it his duty to Roosevelt to assist Truman any way, but he added that he understood if the new president wanted his own people.

"No, I need you," Truman assured him. "I want you to stay."

To the Roosevelt loyalists, the arrival of Truman's entourage—dubbed the Missouri gang—sparked elitist whispers. "He had been a good senator," observed Jonathan Daniels. "But he seemed to be a tragically inadequate substitute for Franklin Roosevelt."

Much of the snobbish criticism echoed what Truman had faced throughout this life, including from his wife's family, who had looked down upon him as a simple farmer. "Roosevelt's White House was a place of power, where the winds of destiny blew through the corridors and one heard the voice of the future," wrote the journalists Joseph and Stewart Alsop. "The White House of Harry S. Truman, for all his modesty, patriotism and goodwill, is more like the lounge of the Lion's Club of Independence, Mo., where one is conscious chiefly of the odor of 10¢ cigars and the easy laughter evoked by the new smoking-room story."

On April 16, 1945—the day after Roosevelt's burial—Truman returned to Capitol Hill to address a joint session of Congress. He worked on the eighteen-hundred-word speech Sunday afternoon on the train back to Washington, wrapping up a draft later that night in Blair House, though he continued to pencil in changes Monday morning. Dressed in a black suit with a blue pocket square—and an American Legion button pinned on his left lapel—Truman entered the chamber at 1:02 p.m. to thunderous applause. In a break from protocol, he used the rear center door, the one preferred by lawmakers, cabinet members, and the court. "It was a neat touch," *Time*'s Frank McNaughton observed. "He's President, but he uses the same door he always used."

In his speech, which lasted just eighteen minutes, Truman received seventeen additional ovations, described by McNaughton as "generous and prolonged." The United States, he vowed, would settle for nothing less than total victory. "So that there can be no possible misunderstanding, both Germany and Japan can be certain, beyond any shadow of a doubt, that America will continue the fight for freedom until no vestige of resistance remains!" Truman declared. "Our demand has been and remains—unconditional surrender."

Lawmakers and the nation loved it.

"Here was real sincerity," said Republican Representative Dewey Short of Missouri. "No braggadocio in that speech, but genuine modesty and humility."

"I liked what he said," added a Washington taxi driver. "All he wants to do is serve his God and his people. You can't ask any more than that."

"There's a real man," declared a Capitol police officer.

Carrying on the tradition of his predecessor, who gave 998 press conferences during his time as president, Truman hosted reporters for his first news briefing at ten-thirty a.m. the following morning. Roosevelt had held two briefings a week, but Truman opted to scale them back to one a week, giving him more time to focus on work. A record 348 journalists crowded inside the Oval Office that Tuesday morning, so many, in fact, that some spilled out onto the adjacent terrace. With reporters packed elbow to elbow, temperatures inside soared.

"All in," an aide hollered.

The president reviewed the briefing rules and then read aloud a letter of appreciation from Eleanor Roosevelt to the nation for the generous outpouring of support.

Truman then opened the floor for questions.

"Mr. President," a reporter asked, "is there any possibility that you will go to the United Nations Conference at San Francisco?"

"There is not," he replied.

"Will you send a message?"

"I shall probably welcome the delegates by an opening statement when they arrive."

"Could you tell us," a reporter pressed, "some of the considerations that led to your decision not to go to San Francisco?"

"I have a competent delegation going," Truman said. "I shall back them up from this desk," he added, pausing to rap on the wood, "where I belong."

Over the course of eleven minutes, reporters lobbed a wide range of questions. Did the president plan to meet with Soviet foreign minister Vyacheslav Molotov?

Would Bess Truman hold press conferences?

Any chance he might lift the ban on horse racing?

"Some of these I refused to discuss," Truman later said. "Some I answered. Some I merely put off to a more appropriate time."

Reviews of his first press conference proved positive. "One gathered instantly that he was in command of the situation, and would command any other situation presented to him," observed the columnist Mark Sullivan in *The Washington Post*. "He was a man with a mind habitually affirmative, poised and ready." White House aides agreed. "The new president made an excellent impression," Assistant Press Secretary Ayers observed in his diary. "He answered their questions directly and avoided none of the queries put to him."

Truman followed his morning briefing with a ten p.m. broadcast to the armed services, assuring them, as he had done with Congress and the American public, that the United States remained committed to victory. "As a veteran of the First World War, I have seen death on the battlefield," Truman declared. "I know the strain, the mud, the misery, the utter weariness of the soldier in the field. And I know, too, his courage, his stamina, and his faith in his comrades, his country, and himself. We are depending on each and every one of you."

At noon on April 20, 1945, Truman met with Averell Harriman, the ambassador to the Soviet Union. The son of a railroad baron, Harriman had inherited one of the largest fortunes in America soon after his graduation from Yale. In the years since, he had grown his family's wealth through investments in banks, shipping companies, and railroads before transitioning into public service. He had worked with the National Recovery Administration—an organization designed to jump-start businesses after the Great Depression—and later the Office of Production Management and the Lend-Lease Administration, where he coordinated American wartime aid for England and Russia. Outside business, the eccentric ambassador's personal pursuits reflected his affluence. Harriman enjoyed polo, trained champion Labrador retrievers, and collected art by Pablo Picasso, Henri Matisse, and Vincent Van Gogh.

Harriman wanted to brief Truman before the president's meeting with Foreign Minister Molotov, who was passing through en route to San Francisco. In a half-hour session attended by Stettinius, Undersecretary of State Joseph Grew, and the department's Russia expert Charles Bohlen, Harriman outlined concerns over Stalin's efforts to turn neighboring eastern European nations into an orbit of pro-Soviet satellite states. This new "barbarian invasion of Europe," as Harriman characterized it, not only threatened to undermine democracies but could lead to the creation of secret police forces as well as the eradication of critical liberties, like free speech. That said, Harriman believed Russia needed America's help too much in postwar reconstruction to risk a break in ties. "For this reason," he explained, "America could afford to stand firm on important issues without serious risk."

"The Russians," Truman concluded, "need us more than we need them."

The flashpoint was Poland.

England and the United States wanted to see the creation of a unity government representative of the Polish people. Along those lines, the two nations had supported an anti-Communist government formed in exile in London. The Soviets, by contrast, backed the Polish Committee of National Liberation—often dubbed the Lublin government because of the city where it was headquartered—which was effectively a Russian puppet regime.

To solve the crisis, the three allies had struck a compromise during the Yalta Conference in February, which Roosevelt had attended along with Churchill and Stalin. Under that plan, the Polish Committee of National Liberation would be expanded to include pro-democracy leaders in both Poland and from abroad. This new government would then commit to holding free elections as soon as possible to allow the people to choose their own leaders.

Since the conference, however, Russia had stonewalled.

Harriman suspected Stalin knew that the Polish people, if given a choice, would oust any Russian-backed regime. But the issue was delicate. "The question of the future status of Poland and its government," as one briefing paper outlined for Truman, "remains one of our most complex and urgent problems both in the international and the domestic field."

The United States wanted Russia to help win the war in Europe and the Pacific. Truman likewise knew Stalin had been tepid about joining the United Nations, which was America's proposed framework for building a lasting peace. Stalin had initially balked at sending Molotov to the conference, opting for a lesser-level diplomat. The Soviet leader had relented only after Roosevelt's death. Though Harriman felt his acquiescence was little more than a gesture, Stalin likely wanted Molotov to size up America's new leader. If the Soviet ruler pulled out of the United Nations, the president knew, it would mortally wound the infant agency. "Without Russia," Truman acknowledged, "there would not be a world organization."

The president likewise understood that if Russia succeeded in Poland, then the Senate would never vote to join the United Nations. That would doom the fledgling organization, just as lawmakers had done to Woodrow Wilson's League of Nations in the wake of World War I. Truman's best option was to make Russia adhere to its commitments.

"I intend to be firm in my dealings with the Soviet government," he declared.

After the meeting, Harriman pulled Truman aside. "Frankly," he began, "one of the reasons that made me rush back to Washington was the fear that you did not understand, as I had seen Roosevelt understand, that Stalin is breaking his agreements."

Truman listened.

"My fear," the ambassador continued, "was inspired by the fact that you could not have had time to catch up with all the recent cables. But I must say that I am greatly relieved to discover that you have read them all and that we see eye to eye on the situation."

"I am glad that you are going to be available to our delegation in San Francisco," the president concluded. "And keep on sending me long messages."

At eight-thirty p.m. on April 22, 1945, Truman hosted Molotov for an informal evening at Blair House, joined by Stettinius, Harriman, and Bohlen. The fifty-five-year-old Soviet diplomat, whom Churchill noted had a head shaped like a "cannonball," was one of Stalin's most loyal lieutenants. As a young man, Molotov helped plot the 1917 Russian Revolution that overthrew Czar Nicholas II, later serving as a pallbearer in Vladimir Lenin's funeral. He had since held powerful posts in the Soviet leadership, including eleven years spent as premier. In his current role, Molotov had negotiated the August 1939 German-Soviet Nonaggression Pact, which had carved up eastern Europe between the two nations until Hitler reneged. He likewise brokered the April 1941 Soviet-Japanese Neutrality Pact. But the foreign minister's greatest notoriety no doubt rested on his namesake weapon—the Molotov cocktail. The crude bomb fashioned from a gasoline-filled bottle with a cloth wick was christened by Finnish fighters who hurled them at Soviet invaders in the 1939–40 Russo-Finnish War.

The bespectacled Molotov, who wore his thinning black hair slicked back, sported a small moustache, and fancied dark pinstriped suits, suffered from a healthy dose of paranoia that had prompted him, on a previous trip to the White House, to pack his own food and sleep with a revolver. But he was good at his job—exceedingly so. Over the years, his ability to endure hours of negotiation without any compromise in his position had earned him the nickname "Iron Pants." American diplomats who tangled with him understood that better than anyone. "Molotov is a hard trader and blunt but effective tactician," one senior Pentagon leader noted in his diary. "At the same time, he is exasperating, rude, and deeply suspicious." The Russian's "verbal adroitness and imperturbable demeanor" infuriated even Churchill. "I have never seen a human being who more perfectly represented the modern conception of a robot."

Truman began by assuring the Soviet foreign minister of his admiration for Stalin and his wartime accomplishments, adding that he hoped to maintain the same relations with the Soviet Union that Roosevelt had enjoyed. The president stressed that the United States stood firm behind all its previous agreements, including Poland, which had become a symbolic barometer for the public about whether the United States could work with Russia.

Poland was an even bigger concern to the Soviet Union, Molotov replied, since the two nations bordered each other. But the Yalta decision, he added, was a suitable basis for a solution. The president concluded with his desire to meet Stalin, which Molotov said his boss would welcome. "Truman then offered a toast to the good health of Marshall Stalin," Harriman recalled. "Molotov amended it to include Churchill and the President as well."

But Molotov's reputation for obstinacy emerged the next day in meetings at the State Department, where Iron Pants balked at expanding the Polish government as the allies had agreed to at Yalta. Stettinius went so far as to warn Molotov that the San Francisco conference and even the future of the United Nations was at risk, but the Soviet foreign minister refused to budge. "Molotov clung doggedly to his fixed position," Harriman lamented. "It became clear that the Moscow deadlock had simply been transferred to Washington."

At two p.m. on April 23, Truman sat down with Stettinius, War Secretary Stimson, Navy Secretary Forrestal, General Marshall, admirals Leahy and King, Harriman, and Bohlen. "Overnight the atmosphere had changed," Stettinius reported. "In fact, a complete deadlock had been reached on the subject of carrying out the Yalta agreement on Poland."

The president, who was scheduled to meet that afternoon with Molotov, was irritated. The Yalta agreements had so far, he said, been a one-way street. That could not continue. The conference of the United Nations would happen with or without Russia's participation, but the time to get tough had arrived. "It was," Truman declared, "now or never."

The president then surveyed the opinions of his advisers. On one side stood Stimson and Marshall, both of whom urged caution. The war secretary noted that the political battle over Poland was news to him, but he felt it was important to determine Stalin's objective, reminding everyone that before World War I, Russia had controlled much of Poland. On the battlefield, Russia had not only met its military obligations, Stimson added, but had often exceeded them. American forces had come to depend on them. Without understanding Stalin's intent, the war secretary feared, America could stumble into dangerous waters.

Marshall likewise had been unaware of the controversy. The general said that with the war in Europe nearing an end, the United States hoped the Soviets would join the battle against Japan. Such tensions might trigger the Russians to delay entry into the conflict until America had done most of the fighting. A break with Russia, he concluded, would be serious.

On the opposite side were Harriman and Forrestal. In response to Stimson, Harriman said Russia's motivation was simple. The puppet government stood on shaky ground. Any change in in its makeup would likely doom Russia's hopes to dominate its neighbor. The navy secretary added that if America relented, Poland would be the first domino to fall in Russia's efforts to expand its influence. Stalin had mistakenly concluded that America would not object to a Soviet takeover of eastern Europe. It was time, Forrestal said, to push back.

Leahy, in contrast, occupied the middle ground. The admiral said he left Yalta convinced that Stalin would never allow a free government in Poland. Leahy believed a break with Russia would be serious but that Truman should demand Poland be free.

The president thanked his advisers, stating he had no intention of delivering an ultimatum. His goal was to make clear the position of the United States.

Russia needed to live up to its agreements.

At five-thirty p.m. that Monday, Truman welcomed Molotov to the Oval Office. The foreign minister was joined by Russian ambassador Andrei Gromyko and interpreter Vladimir Pavlov. Other attendees included Leahy, Stettinius, Harriman, and Bohlen.

Truman was blunt, stating he was sorry to learn that no progress had been made on Poland. "The United States Government," he added, "could not agree to be a party to the formation of a Polish government which was not representative of all Polish democratic elements."

America and other member countries planned to hold the United Nations conference despite any problems that might arise. Failure of the three allied nations to agree on Poland, however, would cast doubt on their ability to collaborate after the war. Truman reminded Molotov that on April 1—twelve days before his death—Roosevelt had warned Stalin that no policy would succeed in the United States without public support. That would apply to postwar economic aid, which the Russians would be wise to appreciate.

Molotov replied that it was important for the three governments to work together as equals without two nations forcing their will on the third.

All Russia needed to do, Truman interjected, was follow the agreement.

Aides watched as the tensions rose, marked by the president's terse delivery, which Leahy noted consisted of "language that was not at all diplomatic."

Truman's sharpened tone was not lost on Molotov. "*What kind of president is he?*" the foreign minister thought.

But Truman was not finished.

The United States, he continued, planned to faithfully follow all the agreements reached at Yalta, and he expected the same from Russia. America welcomed Russia's friendship, he added, "but I wanted it clearly understood that this could be only on a basis of the mutual observation of agreements and not on the basis of a one-way street."

The president at last fell silent.

"I have never been talked to like that in my life," Molotov protested.

"Carry out your agreements," Truman fired back, "and you won't get talked to like that."

CHAPTER 7

> *"My chief purpose was to end the war in victory with the least possible cost in the lives of men in the armies which I had helped to raise."*
>
> —WAR SECRETARY HENRY STIMSON

On April 24, 1945—the day after he met with Molotov—Truman received a cryptic note from Stimson. "I think it is very important that I should have a talk with you as soon as possible on a highly secret matter," he advised. "I mentioned it to you shortly after you took office but have not urged it since on account of the pressure you have been under. It, however, has such a bearing on our present foreign relations and has such an important effect upon all my thinking in this field that I think you ought to know about it without much further delay."

The president penciled a seven-word response across the bottom of the page, requesting his appointment secretary to schedule the meeting for the following day.

The seventy-seven-year-old Stimson arrived at noon that Wednesday. Much like Franklin Roosevelt, Stimson was a member of America's aristocracy. The son of a New York surgeon, he had attended the nation's top schools—Phillips Academy, Yale, and Harvard Law School—and spent his summers exploring Europe, mountain climbing, or hunting grizzlies, moose, and elk. Stimson began his career as a Wall Street lawyer under the tutelage of Elihu Root, who served as secretary of war under William McKinley and secretary of state for Teddy Roosevelt. He followed his mentor into public service when Roosevelt appointed him U.S. attorney for the Southern District of New York, launching a career that would parallel America's transformation from isolationist nation to global powerhouse. "The profession of law," he admitted, "was never thoroughly satisfactory to me, simply because the life of the ordinary New York lawyer is primarily and essentially devoted to the making of money."

Stimson's one venture into electoral politics—a 1910 run for New York governor—ended in defeat, after which he realized his reserved personality was better suited in more advisory roles. "He was a man of great integrity, large experience, courage and capacity," observed John McCloy, Stimson's deputy. "He was thoughtful, bold, and elegant." A World War I veteran, Stimson served as defense secretary under President William Howard Taft and later secretary of state during President Herbert Hoover's administration. Roosevelt had tapped him to serve once again as war secretary in 1940, a job in which he had helped grow America's armed forces as well as manage the development of the top-secret atomic bomb. With a head full of gray hair, a matching moustache, and a hawk-like nose, Stimson presented himself as a wise grandfatherly figure. That no doubt helped assuage a wounded nation in the days after the attack on Pearl Harbor. "It's the last shots," he reminded Americans, "that count."

Stimson stood in the Oval Office for just that reason.

The war secretary handed the president a three-page memo, outlining details on the atomic bomb. Truman, of course, was not totally unaware. The day after he took office, Jimmy Byrnes had shared with him some of the weapon's details, none of which, however, rivaled the in-depth briefing he was about to receive. Stimson asked Truman to review the memo. "Within four months," it began, "we shall in all probability have completed the most terrible weapon ever known in human history, one bomb of which could destroy a whole city."

The nine-point memo explained that the United States had shared the weapon's development with England, but America controlled all the resources needed to build it. "No other nation," the document added, "could reach this position for some years."

Despite that assurance, other countries would eventually catch up. The scientific community beyond America's borders was aware of the burgeoning field of nuclear physics, while the high cost of such technology would decrease. Those factors foreshadowed the terrifying possibility that one day a rogue nation or even group could build such a weapon in secret and use it against a more powerful adversary. In such a scenario, a small nation could topple a rival in a matter of days. "The world in its present state of moral advancement compared with its technical development would be eventually at the mercy of such a weapon," the memo warned. "In other words, modern civilization might be completely destroyed."

Future control of this new technology would be a critical postwar challenge. Since the weapon had yet to be completed or even tested, it was too early to approach any world peace organization, like the new United Nations. Furthermore, the war secretary believed American leaders first needed an actual appreciation of the power of such a weapon.

The question of sharing this technology with other nations and under what terms, Stimson added, would become the primary question of American foreign relations after the war. "Our leadership in the war and in the development of this weapon has placed a certain moral responsibility upon us which we cannot shirk without very serious responsibility of any disaster to civilization which it would further," he wrote. "On the other hand, if the problem of the proper use of this weapon can be solved, we would have the opportunity to bring the world into a pattern in which the peace of the world and our civilization can be saved."

Stimson concluded with a request that Truman create a committee to guide the executive and legislative branches on how to handle the weapon once the veil of secrecy was lifted. Such a committee would also suggest actions for the War Department. "All recommendations," he concluded, "would of course first be submitted to the President."

"I listened," Truman said, "with absorbed interest."

Maj. Gen. Leslie Groves then joined the meeting. Stimson started to introduce him, but Truman cut him off. "Oh, I know General Groves very well," the president said. "I have known him for many years."

To maintain secrecy with so many reporters huddled in the president's anteroom, Groves had purposely arrived after Stimson and entered the White House and the Oval Office via little-used doors. For the same reason, General Marshall chose not to attend the session.

The forty-eight-year-old Groves headed the Manhattan Engineer District, which was the organization tasked to develop the atomic bomb. The mustachioed general, who grew up the son of a Presbyterian Army chaplain, could be an intimidating figure, both physically and mentally. He stood five feet eleven inches tall and weighed close to 250 pounds, the by-product of the chocolate he loved to munch, even as he avoided the cigarettes and coffee so common among his peers. To hide his bulging physique, he wore large, heavily starched uniforms and hiked his pants up over his belly. Despite his girth, he was a tireless worker, hustling up to fourteen hours a day, six days a week. Throughout the war, he took no vacation or sick days. The efficiency reports that filled his personnel file often highlighted his diligence. "A very alert, painstaking, capable officer of high initiative," one report declared. "His work," added another, "has been of such nature as to clearly stamp him as of superior caliber."

"One of the most efficient & finest officers I have ever known," exclaimed a third.

But Groves had a reputation for being difficult. Having graduated fourth in his class at West Point, where he had wrestled and played football, he demanded the same level of dedication from those who worked for him. As such, he could be notoriously irascible, terse, intolerant, and even arrogant, leaving a long trail of bruised and battered egos. "Groves not only behaves like he can walk on water," one colleague complained, "he acts like he invented it." People either loved him or hated him. "General Groves was a man of extraordinary ability and capacity to get things done," observed John Lansdale, who served as his special assistant for security. "He was in fact the only person I have known who was every bit as good as he thought he was." The general's harshness at times carried over to his family. "Even if you have no regard for your own honor," he wrote once to his son, a cadet at West Point, "for the honor of your old man, please buck up." Groves signed the letter: "Disgustedly yours."

That relentless drive had propelled Groves up the ranks of the Army Corps of Engineers. His most recent assignment prior to the Manhattan Project was to supervise the construction of the Pentagon, perched on the banks of the Potomac River in Arlington, Virginia. The five-story behemoth featured more than six million square feet of floor space and seventeen miles of corridors, not to mention eight cafeterias, two medical clinics, a bank, a post office, a barbershop, and even a museum. The sprawling structure, which rested atop 42,000 concrete pilings, proved triple the size of the Empire State Building. To accomplish the job, Groves depended on an army of twelve thousand laborers, who toiled daily in three shifts, including at night illuminated by floodlights. In the end, a building that should have taken four years to construct was finished in just sixteen months. "It is doubtful," one defense department official noted, "that any building of comparable size and utility has been constructed before or since or so expeditiously."

Stimson and Groves could not have been more different, but the two men who stood before Truman in the Oval Office had come together to spearhead one of the greatest and most complex endeavors of the war. "With regard to building the bomb," as one historian observed, "Stimson acted as chairman of the board with Groves as chief executive."

The general handed the president a twenty-four-page memo that served as a primer on the development of the weapon. No doubt conscious of his full schedule, Truman objected to the lengthy document. "Why," he protested, "I don't like to read papers."

"We can't tell you this in any more concise language," Stimson countered.

Truman listened.

"This is a big project," the war secretary added.

Stimson, in fact, had reviewed the memo only the day before as he crafted his own. The document described the science behind the bomb along with the development of its two primary fuels—uranium and plutonium. At three top-secret sites, tucked away in the backcountry of Tennessee, Washington State, and New Mexico, teams of scientists, engineers, and technicians now raced to enrich the fuel and build the weapon.

Truman reminded Stimson of when his investigators tried to gain access to the plant in Washington. "Now I understand," he added, "why you didn't want me to investigate."

Seven senior lawmakers, the memo continued, were briefed on the project because of the need for congressional appropriations, which closed in on $2 billion, a staggering sum that included securing massive uranium deposits from the Belgian Congo. England had assisted the United States, prompting the two nations to sign the secret Quebec Agreement in August 1943, which banned the use of atomic weapons against one another or a third party without mutual consent. The same consent was required before the technology could be shared.

Intelligence confirmed that German scientists were working on a bomb, but at this late stage in the war, such efforts appeared futile. "As far as is known," the memo added, "there is no prospect that Japan could develop an atomic bomb for use in the present war."

America had the tactical advantage.

Each bomb would deliver an equivalent payload between 5,000 and 20,000 tons of TNT, a figure that could eventually equal as much as 100,000 tons. The first test was expected in July, while the first bomb would be ready by August 1. A composite group with the Twentieth Air Force was preparing to deploy to the Pacific. "If our scientific progress continues as expected we should be prepared to drop one of these bombs every ten days starting in the latter part of August," the memo declared. "The target is and was always expected to be Japan."

This could be, as Groves said, a decisive weapon.

The memo closed by echoing Stimson's request for the creation of a select committee to help guide the use of this dangerous new technology. "Atomic energy, if controlled by the major peace loving nations, should insure the peace of the world for decades to come," Groves concluded. "If misused it can lead our civilization to annihilation."

Truman finished the report and returned it, feeling it unwise to hang on to it. "The president did not show any concern over the amount of funds being spent," Groves noted, "but made it very definite that he was in entire agreement with the necessity for the project."

The meeting ended after forty-five minutes.

"Mr. President," Groves asked. "How on earth do I get out of here?"

The report of America's awesome new weapon—and the tremendous responsibility that came with it—weighed on Truman. He had been president only thirteen days—and now he faced the prospect that to end the war and save American lives, he might have to obliterate Japan's cities. Such a weapon would kill tens of thousands of men, women, and children.

These thoughts consumed him when he bumped into Leonard Reinsch, his aide for press and radio affairs. "Leonard," Truman began, "I have just gotten some important information. I am going to have to make a decision which no man in history has ever had to make."

Reinsch listened.

"I'll make the decision, but it is terrifying to think about what I will have to decide."

PART II

"We were reaching into the unknown and we did not know what might come of it."

—BRIG. GEN. THOMAS FARRELL

JULY 16, 1945

At Oak Ridge, Tennessee, workers with the top-secret Manhattan Project operate the master control room of the gas diffusion plant, which enriches uranium to be used in atomic bombs. *(NARA)*

CHAPTER 8

"All during this time the most of us have been working toward a goal about as concrete as a fairy story."

—EDGAR RILEY, OAK RIDGE EMPLOYEE
AUGUST 14, 1945, LETTER

The road to the atomic bomb began with an agitated Hungarian immigrant.

At first glance, forty-one-year-old Leo Szilard did not appear to be a harbinger of doom, the man whose prophetic vision would launch one of the largest and most expensive endeavors in American history and end in the annihilation of two Japanese cities.

If anything, he resembled an absent-minded professor.

Szilard stood just five feet six inches tall and sported glasses. He was pudgy and unathletic, as evidenced by the fact that he never learned how to swim or even ride a bike. Physical violence made him ill, which was ironic given the role he would ultimately play in history. If anything, he was lazy. Only seldom, for example, did he publish academic papers. His favorite pastime was languishing in the bathtub, where he did most of his thinking. Emptying his dirty bathwater, like flushing the toilet, was beneath him.

That was, he said, a maid's job.

But Szilard understood humanity and had a finely tuned political radar—one that had kept the Jewish scientist one step ahead of the storm that swept over Europe.

The rise of antisemitism in Hungary in the wake of World War I had led Szilard in 1919 to flee to Germany, where he had earned his doctorate. Hitler's ascendancy, a little more than decade later, prompted him to pack his bags again, first for England and later for the United States. Before he departed, he visited his family in Budapest. "Hitler and the Nazis are going to take over Europe," he warned. "Get out now. Leave Europe—before it's too late!"

Hitler's rise coincided with rapid advances in the field of physics. For decades, scientists had probed at the atom, the basic building block of all matter. In 1911 the New Zealand physicist Ernest Rutherford was the first to theorize that every atom had a positively charged core filled with energy called a nucleus. But how to unlock that potential power remained a mystery until 1932, when physicist James Chadwick discovered the neutron, a particle with no electrical charge that could penetrate an atom's nucleus. Chadwick's discovery led to a stampede of atomic research across Europe. The tipping point came in December 1938 when the German scientists Otto Hahn and Fritz Strassmann split a uranium atom in what physicists later called nuclear fission. Scientists realized that if splitting atoms could be perpetuated, this chain reaction could provide a new source of energy or heat—not to mention a bomb. "The news of fission," as one historian observed, "swept the world of physics like a firestorm."

And that terrified Szilard.

With the world on the precipice of war, Szilard feared Germany might rush to develop just such a weapon. It was doubtful that German leaders were unaware of the scientific advances. Not only had the first atom ever split occurred in Germany, but scientists in 1939 published nearly a hundred articles on nuclear fission. Hitler's annexation of Czechoslovakia meant he controlled one of the world's larger uranium deposits. Adding to Szilard's fear, Germany suddenly banned the export of uranium. The Nazis appeared headed for a bomb.

Szilard's focus shifted to the Belgians, who were mining uranium in the Congo. Someone needed to alert them. Szilard knew just the person: his former mentor and friend, Albert Einstein. Despite a nearly two-decade age difference, the duo had worked together in 1930 to develop a refrigerator that used a liquid metal coolant. Though it worked, the fridge proved a noisy and commercial failure. "It howled," Szilard later said, "like a banshee."

Szilard knew that Einstein was friends with the royal family of Belgium, so on July 12, 1939, he set out with fellow physicist Eugene Wigner to track down the sixty-year-old genius, who was vacationing in a summer cottage in the Long Island hamlet of Peconic.

The two physicists, who had no address, drove around aimlessly for an hour.

"Let's give it up and go home," Szilard finally said. "Perhaps fate intended it."

"But it's our duty to take this step," Wigner protested.

"How would it be if we simply asked where around here Einstein lives," Szilard suggested. "After all, every child knows him."

The scientists spotted a boy on a nearby street corner. Szilard leaned out the window. "Say," he asked, "do you by any chance know where Professor Einstein lives?"

"Of course I do," the youth replied, pointing them down the road.

The famous physicist, who resided in a two-story white cottage on Old Grove Road, was dressed that summer day in an undershirt and rolled-up long pants. On a screened porch and over glasses of iced tea, Szilard explained his concern that a nuclear chain reaction could lead to the development of an atomic bomb.

"I haven't thought of that at all," Einstein admitted.

Belgium was a natural focus, given that nation's uranium deposits in the Congo. But Wigner suggested it might be wise to also inform the American State Department. The legendary scientist agreed to help sound the alarm. "The one thing most scientists are really afraid of is to make a fool of themselves," Szilard recalled. "Einstein was free from such a fear and this above all is what made his position unique on this occasion."

But Einstein was only part of the solution.

Szilard still needed to determine how to alert the government. "We didn't know our way around America," he admitted. "We did not know how to do business, and we certainly did not know how to deal with the government." An associate suggested he reach out to the economist Alexander Sachs, who knew President Roosevelt and served as a vice-president of Lehman Corporation, a Wall Street investment firm. Sachs, in turn, recommended the scientists forget Belgium and focus on Roosevelt. Szilard and Einstein went to work on a letter. "We did not know just how many words one could put in a letter which a president is supposed to read," Szilard remembered. "How many pages does the fission of uranium rate?"

Szilard did most of the work, sending drafts to Einstein. The duo eventually settled on a two-page letter that totaled fewer than five hundred words. That short missive, dated August 2, 1939—signed solely by Einstein—explained that uranium could be used to create a nuclear chain reaction. Such an event might release vast amounts of power that could be used for weapons. The United States lacked access to uranium, which could be mined in Czechoslovakia, but the largest deposits were in the Belgian Congo. The scientists suggested Roosevelt create a permanent liaison between the administration and physicists working in the field. This person could work with government departments, help secure money to speed up research, and secure support from industrial laboratories. The physicists closed with a warning that Germany had banned the sale of uranium from Czechoslovakia, a sign the Nazis were headed down this path. "A single bomb of this type," the letter warned, "carried by boat and exploded in a port, might very well destroy the whole port together with some of the surrounding territory."

The outbreak of World War II hampered Sachs's ability to arrange a meeting with Roosevelt. He finally visited the White House on October 11, 1939, a time when tensions were running high across the globe. Only five days earlier, Poland had fallen.

"Alex," the president declared, "what are you up to?"

Sachs gave Roosevelt a briefing, distilling the threat America faced.

"What you are after," the president said, "is to see that the Nazis don't blow us up."

"Precisely," the economist replied.

The president summoned his military adviser, Gen. Edwin "Pa" Watson.

"This," he declared, "requires action!"

The White House created the Advisory Committee on Uranium, which would be chaired by Dr. Lyman Briggs, director of the National Bureau of Standards. Col. Keith Adamson of the Army Ordnance Department and Cmdr. Gilbert Hoover of the Navy Bureau of Ordnance served as the committee's other two members. The new body met for the first time in Washington ten days later on October 21, 1939. Joining the three committee members where two Washington physicists, Fred Mohler of the Bureau of Standards and Richard Roberts with the Carnegie Institution. The Hungarian scientists Szilard, Eugene Wigner, and Edward Teller rounded out the meeting. The group had invited Einstein, but he demurred.

Szilard explained that it was possible to split uranium atoms and create a nuclear chain reaction, one that could be controlled using graphite. A single kilogram of fission uranium could produce a destructive force comparable to twenty thousand tons of TNT.

"In Aberdeen," Adamson interrupted, "we have a goat tethered to a stick with a ten-foot rope, and we have promised a big prize to anyone who can kill the goat with a death ray. Nobody has claimed the prize yet. I don't believe any of this nonsense you scientists are talking."

But others on the committee fortunately did.

"How much money do you need?" Hoover asked.

"For the first year of this research," Teller interrupted, "we need six thousand dollars."

"All right, all right," the colonel huffed. "You'll get your money."

That $6,000 would prove to be a tiny down payment on a $2 billion weapon of nightmarish proportions. The committee's November 1, 1939, report to the president urged further research into creating a nuclear chain reaction. "If the reaction turned out to be explosive in character," the report concluded, "it would provide a possible source of bombs with a destructiveness vastly greater than anything now known."

Work limped along until June 27, 1940, when Roosevelt created the National Defense Research Committee (NDRC), the brainchild of Dr. Vannevar Bush, the former vice-president of the Massachusetts Institute of Technology and president of the Carnegie Institution. The tall and slender Bush, who was equal parts inventor, engineer, and businessman, had grown alarmed at the rise of Nazi Germany and its powerful military. The United States, by contrast, still recovering from the decade-long Great Depression, had fallen behind in the development of new battlefield technologies. The NDRC, which included the Uranium Committee, was designed to mobilize the nation's scientific community for help with military research.

But the NDRC was like a toothless tiger, lacking the power to move past research and develop new weapons for the battlefield. That prompted the president a year later to create the superseding Office of Scientific Research and Development, again under Bush's leadership. The bureaucratic reshuffling, accomplished via executive order on June 28, 1941, not only opened up the nation's wallet but meant that Bush now reported directly to Roosevelt. "I knew," he later said, "that you couldn't get anything done in that damn town unless you organized under the wing of the president." Over the course of the war, scientists would help with the development of everything from sonar and radar to bazookas and incendiary bombs.

And of course, the atomic bomb.

Across the Atlantic, British scientists likewise focused on atomic energy. The biggest challenge centered on the fuel for a possible bomb. Uranium is a heavy metal commonly found in the earth's crust. While the uranium-235 isotope could be split, scientists discovered, its counterpart uranium-238 could not. The challenge, of course, was that the isotope needed for a bomb was rare, comprising just 0.7 percent of all uranium. That meant scientists would have to separate the uranium, which could prove laborious and expensive.

In July 1941, British scientists concluded that just twenty-five pounds of uranium-235 was enough to produce an enormous explosion. Such a weapon likewise could be made small enough to fit into a plane. Despite the challenge of separating uranium, scientists predicted a weapon could be ready in as little as two years. "The committee considers that the scheme for a uranium bomb is practicable and likely to lead to decisive results in the war," scientists concluded. "It recommends that this work be continued on the highest priority and on the increasing scale necessary to obtain the weapon in the shortest possible time."

Bush shared the British report with Roosevelt on the morning of October 9, 1941. Joining him was Vice President Wallace. During the ten-minute conference, Bush walked the president through the report's conclusions, explaining the possible cost and time needed to build a bomb. He emphasized that there was no guarantee of success, but he did want to consult with the army about construction. "I had no illusion as to the gravity of the decision," Bush recalled. "I knew that the effort would be expensive, that it might interfere seriously with other war work. But the overriding consideration was this: I had great respect for German science. If a bomb were possible, if it turned out to have enormous power, the result in the hands of Hitler might indeed enable him to enslave the world. It was essential to get there first."

Roosevelt agreed, instructing Bush to expedite the work but not to advance past research and planning.

Bush had one more request, given the price tag. "I would feel more comfortable if I shared responsibility," he said, "if I had something like a board of directors."

"Fine," Roosevelt said. "We will set it up."

The president created the Top Policy Committee made up of Wallace, Stimson, Marshall, and James Conant, the president of Harvard. Bush meanwhile reached out to Dr. Arthur Compton, a 1927 Nobel laureate and chairman of the physics department at the University of Chicago. Compton served on the National Academy of Sciences Committee on Uranium, a panel Bush had previously convened to advise the government on atomic energy. Bush asked Compton to evaluate the British conclusions. To help, Compton consulted some of the nation's top scientific minds, including Wigner, Glenn Seaborg, Robert Oppenheimer, Enrico Fermi, Ernest Lawrence, and Harold Urey, the latter three all Nobel laureates.

Compton's seven-page report, dated November 6, 1941, was less optimistic than the British. He estimated that it would require between two and one hundred kilograms of uranium-235 to produce an atomic weapon, a process that could take up to four years and cost taxpayers more than $100 million. But like the British, Compton determined that it was a job that needed to be done. Atomic weapons would determine military superiority. "Adequate care for our national defense," he warned, "seems to demand urgent development of this program."

The following month Japan attacked Pearl Harbor.

Five days later Germany declared war on America.

The clock was ticking.

By June 1942, the project prepared to move from theory to construction. The challenge was how best to separate the uranium. Rather than spend precious time experimenting, plans called for work to proceed simultaneously using three different means, including high-speed centrifuges, gas diffusion, and electromagnetic separation. To do this, scientists first had to convert uranium into a gas. Spinning centrifuges then worked like a cream separator, dividing the lighter uranium-235 from its heavier counterpart. Gas diffusion, by contrast, depended on a porous barrier through which only lighter molecules could pass. Lastly, scientists determined that sending charged particles through a magnetic field would separate them.

But there was a new twist.

Scientists discovered a way to convert uranium-238 into a new element, plutonium. Named after the planet Pluto—uranium was similarly named after Uranus—plutonium is found only in trace amounts in nature, but it can be manufactured. More important, like uranium-235, plutonium can be split. This opened a second path to a bomb.

To create plutonium, scientists had to make a nuclear reactor, which involved stacking large quantities of uranium metal to create a chain reaction. Uranium-235 produced neutrons, which were captured by the uranium-238. That resulted in the creation of plutonium. To control the chain reaction, scientists proposed using either graphite or heavy water, which is made with deuterium, an isotope of hydrogen but with twice the mass.

The Office of Scientific Research and Development had no experience in engineering or construction. To remedy that deficiency, Bush wanted to bring in the Army Corps of Engineers, which offered the added benefit of hiding the project's ballooning costs in the War Department's budget. On August 13, 1942, the Army Corps of Engineers created the Manhattan Engineer District—its temporary headquarters in New York City—under the command of Col. James Marshall. That same month Roosevelt and Churchill formalized a secret plan where America would take the lead on the development of atomic weapons. Marshall's lack of urgency, however, frustrated Bush, who advocated for a change in leadership.

After more than two years in Washington, during which time he oversaw the construction of the Pentagon, Col. Leslie Groves was ready for a change—and he wanted to go overseas. Domestic construction of bases, depots, and ordnance and manufacturing plants had peaked in July 1942, as the war prepared to shift to Europe and the Pacific. That's where the action would be, building airstrips, bridges, and hospitals. On the morning of September 17, 1942, after testifying before a congressional committee on a military housing bill, Groves met outside the hearing room with Lt. Gen. Brehon Somervell, the commander of Army Services of Supply. Groves needed to secure permission for an overseas assignment.

But Somervell had other plans for him. "The Secretary of War has selected you for a very important assignment," the general informed him, "and the President has approved the selection."

"Where?" Groves asked.

"Washington."

"I don't want to stay in Washington," Groves protested.

"If you do the job right," Somervell told him, "it will win the war."

Groves's heart sank. Though the atomic bomb project was secret, Colonel Marshall had consulted with Groves, who understood that a bomb was at best a long shot. In addition, it was a step down. The project's budget at the time was about $100 million, a pittance considering that the Army Corps of Engineers oversaw $600 million worth of work each month.

"Oh, that thing," Groves said.

"You can do it," Somervell said. "If it can be done."

Groves paid a visit later that morning to Maj. Gen. Wilhelm Styer, who served as the chief of staff of Army Services of Supply. Styer confirmed that his new assignment was to head the Army's atomic bomb project. The only plus was that the job came with a promotion to brigadier general. "The basic research and development are done," Styer explained to Groves. "You just have to take the rough designs, put them into final shape, build some plants and organize an operating force and your job will be finished and the war will be over."

As Groves would soon learn, Steyer's view was wildly optimistic.

Groves wasn't the only one unhappy with his appointment. That afternoon he met with Vannevar Bush who, despite having pushed for a change of leadership, did not yet know the abrasive Groves was the pick. Groves fired off questions, which Bush dodged. "In short," Groves recalled, "the meeting was far from satisfactory for both of us." Bush met with Styer afterward, who confirmed Groves was the project's new leader. Though the two would later become friends, Bush initially feared that

Groves would clash with the scientists. "I doubted whether he had sufficient tact for the job. He agreed the man is blunt, etc., but thought his other qualities would overbalance," Bush wrote that day. "I fear we are in the soup."

That first week, as Groves hustled to educate himself, he realized just how much work had to be done. "I was not happy with the information I received; in fact, I was horrified," he recalled. "It seemed as if the whole endeavor was found on possibilities rather than probabilities. Of theory there was a great deal, of proven knowledge not much. Even if the theories were correct, the engineering difficulties would be unprecedented."

Converting those theories into reality would require the project to have top priority. That, of course, was a challenge, given the massive number of projects America had undertaken for the war. Everyone needed something—and fast. To Groves, however, it was simple. If the atomic bomb was in fact the most important project in the pipeline, then it should receive the highest priority. On September 19, 1942, Groves visited Donald Nelson, head of the War Production Board, but Nelson pushed back. That's fine, Groves replied, adding that he would just have to tell the president his pet project would have to be abandoned.

Nelson caved.

Groves strove to emulate Civil War General William Tecumseh Sherman, who on his legendary march to the sea managed to consolidate his entire headquarters in a single escort wagon. Along those lines, Groves set up his own headquarters in just two rooms on the fifth floor of the War Department Building, perched on the corner of Twenty-First and Virginia Avenue just a short walk from the Lincoln Memorial. Over the course of the war—and as the Manhattan Project, as it was called, grew—his headquarters necessarily expanded to include adjacent rooms, but overall, he remained proud that his proved to be one of the smaller operations in Washington, particularly considering the size and scope of the mission. From the beginning, he emphasized the need for secrecy. "Compartmentalization of knowledge, to me, was the very heart of security," Groves said. "My rule was simple and not capable of misinterpretation—each man should know everything he needed to know to do his job and nothing else."

One of the general's first moves was to lock down supplies of uranium ore. One of the largest known sources came from the Shinkolobwe Mine in the Belgian Congo, which was controlled by the Union Minière du Haut Katanga. Edgar Sengier, who served as the company's managing director, understood the importance of uranium. In late 1940, he ordered his representatives in Africa to ship 1,250 tons of uranium ore to a warehouse on Staten Island, where it sat in some two thousand steel drums. He had since tried unsuccessfully to entice the State Department to buy it, but officials were unaware of the element's importance.

"As I told you previously during our conversation," Sengier continued to prod, "these ores containing radium and uranium are very valuable."

But the State Department still balked.

Groves dispatched Col. Kenneth Nichols, who had taken over for Marshall as the Manhattan Project's district engineer, to seal the deal. "Colonel," an exasperated Sengier began, "will you tell me first if you have come here merely to talk, or to do business."

"Business," Nichols confirmed.

With the fuel source secure, Groves turned to the development of the industrial plants needed to separate uranium and create plutonium. Before Groves took over, Colonel Marshall had set his eyes on a spot in rural Tennessee. Within days of assuming command, Groves hopped a train to inspect the property. The 59,000-acre site was about twenty miles west of Knoxville, an area comprising farmland, woods, and hills. The parcel, which measured seventeen miles long by seven wide, had access to highways and railroads as well as water and electrical services.

Groves liked what he saw, greenlighting the property's purchase for $3.5 million and forcing the relocation of about a thousand families, many of whom lived on farms without running water or electricity. Not everyone, however, wanted to go. "The only difference," one resident complained, "is when the Yankees came before we could shoot at them."

Crews broke ground on February 1, 1943, on what was initially called the Clinton Engineer Works, a title derived from a tiny nearby hamlet. At the suggestion of employees, the name would later be changed to Oak Ridge. Over the next few years, an army of 110,000 construction workers—chosen from 400,000 security-screened applicants—hustled to build everything from war plants and utilities to homes, schools, and stores.

Oak Ridge ultimately would serve as the Manhattan Project's hub for the separation of uranium. Early plans called for using high-speed centrifuges, but scientists soon abandoned that route, choosing instead to focus solely on the gas diffusion and electromagnetic methods. Engineers situated the two main plants in separate valleys and away from the proposed residential area, a move that not only allowed for easier security but also would spare unnecessary deaths in the event of an accidental explosion. The distances likewise increased the odds that if one plant were destroyed, the other could still operate, guaranteeing that the project could still move forward. "Always we were driven by the need to make haste," Groves recalled. "Consequently, research, development, construction and operation all had to be started and carried on simultaneously and without appreciable prior knowledge."

The first project that the workers tackled was the electromagnetic plant known as Y-12, which was designed to send atoms through a magnetic field in circular arcs dubbed "the racetrack." The lighter and heavier atoms would then separate onto different paths, allowing scientists to collect the more valuable uranium-235. "The construction," as the Manhattan Project's official history noted, "was one of the most complex and difficult problems ever undertaken by a construction contractor." Proof could be found in the 12 million square feet of blueprints that were required just to build the facility.

Plans were not the only item needed in such bulk. Workers used 37,562,000 feet of lumber, enough to build more than 7,600 homes. A shortage of copper forced the army to borrow nearly fifteen tons of silver—valued at more than $300 million—from the treasury to make electrical conductors, though with the promise that it would be returned at the war's end. The completed plant, which numbered 170 buildings spread over 500 acres, cost taxpayers $427 million and employed 22,000 men and women. "There's equipment like nothing you've ever seen," one employee remarked. "Right out of Rube Goldberg."

The gas diffusion plant, commonly referred to as K-25, followed on September 10, 1943. This method involved pumping uranium hexafluoride—the gas form of the element—through porous barriers containing billions of holes infinitely smaller than the tip of a pin. The lighter uranium more easily passed through the barrier, allowing scientists to collect it. The larger of Oak Ridge's processing facilities, the gas diffusion plant added another $512 million to the taxpayers' tab, much of it needed to cover the sixty thousand railroad cars of bricks, steel, and equipment required to construct it. The completed building, which depended on its own steam-generating plant, included a half-million valves and more than one hundred miles of piping, plus another 130,000 specially engineered instruments. The U-shaped structure sprawled over forty-four acres—the perimeter stretched nearly a mile—and employed twelve thousand people. The plant was so large that supervisors used bicycles to shuttle about inside.

But industrial plants were only one part of Oak Ridge.

Workers had to build a community just to house the employees. The top-secret town, like the uranium plants, was encircled by barbed wire with access via seven gates. The initial plan called for 13,000 residents. That was revised upward to 42,000 and then 66,000. Even then the population topped out in the spring of 1945 with 75,000 men, women, and children, making Oak Ridge the fifth-largest city in Tennessee, bested only by Memphis, Nashville, Knoxville, and Chattanooga. "To accommodate this population, we had to construct from scratch and then operate a whole city's infrastructure, a sewage system, water supply, and roads, and create fire and police departments as well as provide theaters, churches, stores, libraries, schools, offices, cafeteria, hotel, laundry service, etc.," Nichols said. "We even built a jail, but then had to face the jurisdictional question of whether we had the authority to lock the door."

Construction proved perpetual, starting with more than three hundred miles of paved roads, including a four-lane artery that wound through the valley and linked the town and the plants. The cacophony of bulldozers, screeching saws, and pounding hammers rattled residents. "I knew something was wrong when I first came, but I couldn't figure it out right away. Then, I realized," one woman remarked. "There were no birds. The noise had driven them away."

"There was no night," added another resident. "Bright streetlights and spotlights illuminated the area as people worked shifts around the clock."

The constant churning of the earth filled the summer air with clouds of dust, which led to a hacking cough that doctors dubbed the "Oak Ridge croup." The damp and cooler months turned the dirt to mud. "Oak Ridge might be dedicated to manufacturing bombs," one local recalled, "but dust and mud were the physical elements that went into its making."

As the town mushroomed in size, leaders battled a continual shortage of beds, forcing new arrivals to sleep in cars, tents, and barns. Workers would ultimately build a range of homes, including 10,000 family units, 13,000 dormitory spaces, 5,000 trailers, and more than 16,000 hutments and barracks spaces. "Oak Ridge," as Nichols observed, "was a city without a past, and it was not designed to have much of a future. We tried to design only for the duration of the war, in order to conserve money, materials, and labor." The primitive and often prefabricated housing coupled with the wooden boardwalks contributed to the town's frontier feeling. "There was a touch of the Klondike," one historian observed, "the fervor of a boom."

Despite the town's temporary nature, residents still needed services, including transportation. A fleet of 840 buses made 5,500 trips per day, logging enough miles to circle the globe every twenty-hour hours. Health care was another priority, prompting the army to build a 337-bed hospital. Doctors delivered the first of 2,810 babies on November 11, 1943. Education proved another must. The army constructed seven schools to supplement the three existing county ones while administrators recruited more than three hundred teachers from forty states. The first academic year in Oak Ridge began on October 4, 1943, with just 830 students, a number that would grow to 8,223 by the war's end. "The school system posed a special problem," Nichols said. "The school population increased every day. Additional teachers and school buildings had to be made available as needed for children arriving at Oak Ridge from all parts of the United States and all having different backgrounds and educational needs."

As residents flooded Oak Ridge, the demand for commercial enterprises skyrocketed. The nine businesses available in 1943 would climb to 165 in two years, ranging from thirteen grocery stores and nine pharmacies to seven theaters. The town had seventeen major eating establishments, including nine cafeterias, five restaurants, and three lunchrooms that served a total of forty thousand meals a day. Beyond the basics, residents could shop for roses at the florist, pick out a model train at the hobby shop, or have a portrait painted. Other services ranged from tailors and cobblers to typewriter and sewing machine repair shops. For Connie

Green, a youth at Oak Ridge, the best was the public library, home to more than nine thousand books. "On my first visit I stood at the doorway in awe," she recalled. "How would I ever look through so many books?"

Residents formed twenty-nine churches, so many that groups took over schools, recreation halls, and theaters for worship. Recreational activities blossomed. The army built ballparks, tennis courts, and swimming pools. Locals could thumb through the *Oak Ridge Journal*, a weekly paper that would grow from four mimeographed pages to twelve and had a circulation of 26,000 readers. Others organized more than a hundred civic groups, ranging from Alcoholics Anonymous and the Municipal Band to the Rabbit Breeders Association and the Cat Fancier's Club. Such groups, which leaders encouraged to help create a social fabric, gave like-minded people a chance to meet one another. "In the beginning," one resident recalled, "if you wanted music, any kind of music, you had to go out and make it yourself."

But life on the atomic frontier was not easy, particularly for the fifteen hundred African Americans who called Oak Ridge home. The same discrimination that plagued American cities existed at Oak Ridge, as blacks were forced to sit in the back of the bus, drink from separate water fountains, and use different bathrooms and cafeterias. "Segregation was total," the historian Valeria Steele wrote. "Blacks lived day in and out under oppressive conditions."

Life was hard in other ways, too, especially in the early days. "There was always a line," Edgar Riley recalled of that period, "so that the simple process there of getting mail and groceries took two to three hours and a great deal of energy." Work went on seven days a week, twenty-four hours a day, with shifts beginning at seven a.m., three p.m., and eleven p.m. A culture of secrecy pervaded Oak Ridge. "There was," wrote the head psychiatrist Erik Kent Clark, "an amazing lack of curiosity as to what your neighbors worked at or where." Riley agreed. "Eventually all of Oak Ridge got the habit of silence, and it created an unreal sort of atmosphere," he wrote. "People talked of sports and shortages and the weather, but never about their work."

A similar story unfolded some two thousand miles to the northwest in the remote desert of Washington State. There the army built a second secret atomic city, this one to process plutonium. Army officials had originally considered Oak Ridge, but the uranium plants taxed the power grid. Groves sent Col. Franklin Matthias to scout six sites in California, Oregon, and Washington, but it was the expansive swath of land near the tiny town of Hanford that captured his attention. The nearby Grand Coulee and Bonneville dams promised hydroelectric power, while the Columbia River offered abundant water to cool the reactors. The rock and gravel landscape likewise could be used to make the concrete foundations.

"This is it," Matthias thought. "There's nothing like it in the country."

He relayed his impressions to Groves. "I don't see any point of going down to Southern California," he added, "because there are too many strikes against it."

But Groves urged his engineer to be thorough and inspect all sites. "It will only take a few more days," the general added.

Matthias did as ordered, scouring southern California over to the Arizona border. But nothing compared to Hanford, so he returned to Los Angeles and phoned Groves.

"All right," the general relented, "come on back."

Groves inspected the site on January 16, 1943. Just as Matthias predicted, he liked what he found. Similar to Oak Ridge, Hanford was a rural area with a population average of just 2.2 residents per square mile. "Most of the farms in the area," Groves noted, "conveyed the distinct impression that the owners were having a pretty hard time making them pay." The absence of people appealed to him, given the inherent risks. "While I felt that the possibility of serious danger was small, we could not be absolutely sure," the general said. "No one knew what might happen, if anything, when a chain reaction was attempted in a larger reactor."

The army, via purchase, lease, and the transfer of already owned federal land, secured 428,000 acres for the sum of $5,148,462, making Hanford Engineer Works the largest single acquisition of its kind in the country. As at Oak Ridge, the seizure of farms caused distress. "It was a pretty hard thing," remembered Kathleen Hitchcock. "My mother never really adjusted to it. The fact that the government could come in and take your home away."

The plan called for building three water-cooled nuclear reactors—dubbed B, D, and F—along the banks of the winding Columbia River, each a windowless monolith that would eventually rise to the height of a twelve-story building. To guard against any hazard, the reactors would be spaced six miles apart. In addition, workers would construct four chemical separation plants, where scientists would extract the plutonium. These would be built in pairs eight miles south of the reactors. "The insensible but deadly powers of radiation," the project's official history noted, "influenced every feature of this strange man-made world."

The heart of each reactor was the so-called pile, comprising more than 75,000 meticulously stacked graphite blocks, each weighing up to sixty pounds. These blocks played a critical role, helping to moderate the nuclear chain reaction. Each cubelike structure measured 41 feet tall by 46 feet wide and 37 feet deep, sat atop a 23-foot-thick concrete foundation, and was encased in a thermal shield of cast-iron block. More than two thousand holes ran through each two-story pile, allowing engineers to insert uranium slugs as well as water to cool the reactor, a necessity since each pile would produce 250,000 kilowatts of heat. Once completed, workers pumped thirty thousand gallons of water per minute through each reactor. The three together guzzled enough aqua to quench the thirst of a city of nearly one million inhabitants. "This Swiss cheese pile," as one reporter noted, "is all there is to an atomic oven."

But nuclear reactors were only one part of the plutonium puzzle.

Workers had to construct four eighty-foot-tall separation centers, where irradiated uranium would be transported by rail in shielded casks filled with water. At these centers, uranium would undergo a series of chemical processes to separate out the plutonium. The creation of one pound of plutonium required four thousand pounds of uranium. Scientists monitored the process behind concrete shields, using televisions and periscopes. Each narrow structure was 65 feet wide by 800 feet long, more than double the length of a football field. "The building," as the official history noted, "looked like a huge aircraft carrier floating on a sagebrush sea."

Workers staked out the first reactor building on October 9, 1943. Much like Oak Ridge, Hanford represented a construction bonanza. Officials pulled laborers from 745 cities across forty-seven states, the District of Columbia, Alaska, and even Canada. The only state excluded was Tennessee, since its labor pool was needed for Oak Ridge. "We had recruiters all over the country. It was kind of scraping the bottom of the barrel," recalled Robley Johnson, Hanford's chief photographer. "The war was on and a lot of people were gobbled up by the Army." Security was a priority. Over the course of the project, officials interviewed 262,040 applicants, of whom 94,307 were hired. The force hit its peak on June 21, 1944, with 45,096 laborers, who ranged from carpenters and electricians to concrete and steel workers. The need for a large force was evident by the requirements to build a single reactor—390 tons of structural steel and 17,400 cubic yards of concrete, plus another 121,000 concrete blocks and bricks.

To house the legions of construction workers, the army erected 1,175 temporary barracks and hutments. These were joined by 4,300 trailers, all of which combined to give Hanford the primitive feel of a logging or mining camp, even though its population made the community the fifth largest in the state. The army built eight mess halls that ran the length of a football field, each capable of serving 2,700 people breakfast, lunch, and dinner. The rugged character of the camp underscored the fact that life was hard on the empty desert plateau, triggering constant turnover and a need for more workers. "It was a depressing sort of a place," recalled Robert Bubenzer, who helped supervise the 1,395 patrolmen who worked at Hanford. "It was almost like being in prison." Others agreed. "It was so damned bleak," one new arrival from Denver recalled. "If I'd had the price of a ticket, I wouldn't have stayed."

Many did not. "Well, Rob," Johnson remembers his boss announcing one afternoon, "we got two people on the rolls today. We hired 650 and 648 quit."

Temperatures swung from a frigid negative eighteen in the winter to a sweltering 110 in the summer while dust storms battered the area, a problem that was exacerbated once workers stripped the sagebrush to begin construction. "Your face would get black in the storms," remembered one worker, "and you felt grit in the food, on your hands and clothes, and everywhere." To make life bearable, the army built theaters, recreation halls, and arranged visits by traveling entertainers. "There was a beer parlor with 1,000 stools," one reporter observed, "and barmaids blind to any patron who left less than a 50-cent tip."

Many others got into trouble, from prostitution and bootlegging to gambling and brawling. From March 15, 1943, through August 28, 1944,

Hanford's patrolmen investigated 3,156 cases of intoxication, 1,124 burglaries, and 522 assaults, among other crimes. "We had murders, we had rapes," Johnson recalled. "It was a microcosm of society."

"When you have construction workers," added Francis McHale, "you have fights."

The Wild West nature of the Hanford camp contrasted sharply with the master-planned community of Richland Village, a 2,500-acre town designed to house the scientists and plant operators. The community, which would top out with 17,500 residents, comprised 4,300 one-, two-, and three-bedroom homes as well as twenty-five dormitories and a 114-room hotel. Planners designed the village with a downtown commercial district, schools, and abundant recreation, including a riverfront park with a swim area. "Those of us going into operation knew that Richland Village was a nice little place, unique of its kind," recalled one resident, "but it was going to seem pretty colorless after the roaring construction camp." But others welcomed the improved digs, including Nell MacGregor. "We felt," she said, "unspeakably elegant in rooms with plastered walls, painted woodwork and splinterless floors."

The last of the Manhattan Project's three secret atomic sites was located in the remote high desert of New Mexico, where scientists raced to design and build the bomb. To head the weapons laboratory, Groves tapped Robert Oppenheimer, who would become one of the project's most famous figures. Just thirty-eight years old when appointed in October 1942, the New York native dabbled in mysticism, wrote poetry, and devoured the classics. Despite a stellar intellect, Oppenheimer was a physical wreck who failed the military's fitness exam. The curly-haired physicist with blue eyes stood five feet ten inches tall but weighed less than 130 pounds. He preferred cigarettes to food, chain-smoking five packs of Chesterfields a day, which no doubt contributed to his chronic cough and the bad teeth that he used to gnaw on his fingernails.

Beyond his poor health, the Harvard-educated scientist had other strikes against him, including his earlier interest in Communism, which ultimately held up his security clearance. "Adding to my cause for doubt," Groves added, "no one with whom I talked showed any great enthusiasm about Oppenheimer as a possible director of the project."

"He couldn't run a hamburger stand," one colleague quipped.

But Oppenheimer's biggest disadvantage was his lack of a Nobel Prize, an award held by many on the Manhattan Project. The lack of such an honor, Groves feared, would cost him prestige among his fellow scientists, on whom he depended for success. Despite those deficiencies, Groves picked him. "I thought he could do the job," he said. "In all my inquiries, I was unable to find anyone else who was available who I felt would do as well."

The first task was to find a place to build a weapons laboratory, which was known as Project Y. Like Oak Ridge and Hanford, the lab would need strong rail and air transportation. Groves likewise sought access to water as well as a temperate climate that would allow year-round work, including outdoors. "As before, we sought an isolated area so that near-by communities would not be adversely affected by any unforeseen results from our activities," he said. "Yet this installation would be different, because here we were faced with the necessity of importing a group of highly talented specialists, some of whom would be prima donnas, and of keeping them satisfied with their working and living conditions."

Groves and Oppenheimer focused on New Mexico, an area the latter was familiar with since he leased a 154-acre ranch in the Sangre de Cristo Range and often spent summers exploring the area on horseback. "My two great loves are physics and New Mexico," Oppenheimer once wrote a friend. "It is a pity they can't be combined."

Or could they?

On November 16, 1942, Groves, Oppenheimer, and several others made a scouting trip to Jemez Springs near Albuquerque. The proposed site offered access to water, but the surrounding canyons prevented any expansion and blocked the magnificent views.

"This will never do," Groves declared.

"If you go on up the canyon you come out on top of the mesa and there's a boys' school there which might be a usable site," Oppenheimer suggested.

The Los Alamos Ranch School, which opened its doors in 1917, sat perched atop a mesa 7,300 feet above sea level. The property counted a total of fifty-four buildings, including twenty-seven houses, dorms, and living quarters. The other half ranged from stables and barns to an icehouse, carpentry shop, and sawmill. The school's notable alums included the novelist Gore Vidal and the infamous William Burroughs. Groves, Oppenheimer, and the others drove up to the school that brisk November day. "It was late afternoon," recalled the physicist Edwin McMillan. "There was a slight snow falling; it was just a tiny, drizzly type of snow. It was cold and there were the boys and their masters out on the playing field in shorts."

The men surveyed the scene.

"This," Groves declared, "is the place."

The army arranged to buy the 470-acre campus, which the scientists would later dub "the Hill," allowing the school to hand out its final diplomas to graduates in January 1943. But the school was only a minuscule part of the army's 49,383-acre acquisition. Since the federal government already owned 45,737 surrounding acres, the total cost to taxpayers for the remainder was just $414,971. "One of the deciding factors in the selection of Los Alamos was the existence of buildings which could be immediately utilized as housing," the project's official history noted. "This was the nucleus around which the project developed."

Similar to Oak Ridge and Hanford, planners hustled to create a community. Workers built a power plant along with sixty-seven miles of dirt, gravel, and paved roads. Septic tanks served as the sewer system while engineers piped in water from local reservoirs and wells near the Rio Grande River. The 3,500 men and women who arrived in Los Alamos in 1943 jumped the following year to 5,675 before topping out at 8,200 by the war's end. The ballooning population meant that housing was a constant challenge, even as workers rushed to remodel school buildings and construct 617 apartments, duplexes, and houses. These would be joined by thirty-six dormitories and fifty-five barracks plus hundreds of primitive hutments and trailers, many heated with furnaces that belched black smoke. "To control the temperature in our rooms," remembered the physicist Luis Alvarez, "we opened and closed the windows."

Laborers added other necessities, ranging from mess halls, a post office, and a commissary to a barbershop, dry cleaner, and shoe repair. A military police force of nearly five hundred manned forty-four full-time posts and patrolled the community, while the camp's nearly one hundred firefighters responded to dozens of calls each month, from brush and chimney fires to structure and vehicle blazes. Residents could attend

Catholic mass as well as Protestant and Jewish services. A school system that began in 1943 with 140 children would eventually grow to more than 350 students. Los Alamos likewise featured a nursery school for children ages two to five plus a hospital. "Medical service," Groves bragged, "was entirely free."

Scientists could hit tennis balls, enjoy a game of bowling, or play a few rounds of golf on the makeshift course. In the winter, others skied on the primitive slopes, which were built using explosives to knock down trees, while the lift consisted of a tow rope operated by the army's enlisted men. Other pursuits ranged from the chess and pistol clubs to a touch football league and a pottery group. Los Alamos even featured a six-member town council—elected to six-month terms—and a school board. "All civilian residents of Los Alamos over 18 years of age," the project's history noted, "could vote for the desired candidate or candidates."

The task of recruiting the scientists fell to Oppenheimer, who landed in Los Alamos on March 15, 1943. The job, as he discovered, was not an easy sell. The weapons lab required recruits to move to a remote area at a time when scientists were in high demand for wartime jobs, many of which were located in major cities that had great cultural amenities. The government likewise could not offer high pay or even financial bonuses. Despite those obstacles, most of the scientists Oppenheimer asked agreed to come to Los Alamos. "Almost everyone realized that this was a great undertaking. Almost everyone knew that if it were completed successfully and rapidly enough, it might determine the outcome of the war," he said. "Almost everyone knew that this job, if it were achieved, would be part of history."

Los Alamos, as most discovered, was a unique place, reminiscent of a college campus filled with brilliant young individuals. "There were practically no old people. Those of us in our early forties were the senior citizens," recalled Bernice Brode, a so-called human computer who ran calculations for the project's theoreticians. "We had no invalids, no in-laws, no unemployed, no idle rich, no poor, and no jails." Residents fed off one another's energy, observed Elsie McMillan, wife of the physicist Edwin McMillan. "I don't think," she wrote, "I shall ever live in a community that had such deep roots of cooperation and friendship."

"Los Alamos," added Alvarez, "was stimulating."

But life on the mesa came with challenges.

Scientists often bristled at the military restrictions, including the need for passes, badges, and inspections as well as censored mail and monitored phone calls. "The fence had a real effect on the psychology of the people behind it," remembered Ruth Marshak, who taught third grade at Los Alamos. "It was a tangible barrier, a symbol of our isolated lives." Laura Fermi, wife of the physicist Enrico Fermi, echoed her. "We were too many of one kind, all packed together," she said. "None of us had lived in such conditions, conditions so similar to those of a concentration camp that some European-born scientists could not stand them and quit."

Adding to the stress was the job's tremendous pressure, over which hung the moral question of designing a bomb powerful enough to wipe out cities. "I've never drunk so much as there at the few parties, because you had to let off steam," recalled Elsie McMillan, "you had to let off this feeling eating your soul, oh God are we doing right?"

The spectacular scenery often served as a tonic to remedy the frustrations that were part of life on the Hill. "Whenever things went wrong at Los Alamos, and there was never a day when they didn't, we had this one consolation—we had a view," Marshak said. "Los Alamos was a world unto itself, an island in the sky." Brode agreed. "We could gaze beyond the town, fenced in by steel wire, and watch the seasons come and go," she said. "The aspens turning gold in the fall, the dark green evergreens, blizzards piling up snow in the winter, the pale green of spring buds, and the dry desert wind whistling through the pines in the summer."

The endurance required of the men and women at Los Alamos was not lost on President Roosevelt, who understood the monumental task he had placed upon them, as evidenced by the letter he wrote to Oppenheimer on June 29, 1943. "I wish you would express to the scientists assembled with you my deep appreciation for their willingness to undertake the tasks which lie before them in spite of the danger and the personal sacrifices," Oppenheimer read aloud. "I am sure we can count on their continued wholehearted and unselfish labors. Whatever the enemy may be planning, American science will be equal to the challenge."

The three top-secret atomic cities were interdependent. Engineers at Oak Ridge and Hanford churned out the uranium and plutonium while the scientists at Los Alamos were tasked to turn this fuel into a bomb which, despite the investment of billions of dollars, existed only as a theory. "Even after the establishment of Los Alamos," the project's official history noted, "there was still no absolute experimental confirmation of the feasibility of the bomb in terms of its basic nuclear processes."

To help turn that theory into reality, Oppenheimer created various departments, ranging from chemistry and physics to electronics and ordnance. This coincided with the construction of multiple laboratories stocked with everything from massive meteorological balloons to the minuscule tools used by jewelers. A research library offered more than 3,000 titles plus monthly subscriptions to 160 academic journals along with another 1,500 microfilm copies of specific articles and portions of books that the scientists needed. "In the beginning, Los Alamos was purely a research organization," Groves wrote. "The work there was so scientific and so highly theoretical that, in its early stages, almost all the responsibility was carried by the scientists rather than by the engineers. As time went on, however, the balance shifted."

The scientists had to determine the shape of a bomb, figure out how to arm, fuse, and detonate it, and of course, calculate the size of its blast. Such a weapon likewise needed to be small enough to fit into a bomber. "It was impossible to wait until everything was ready, for it never would have been," Groves added. "Days counted, and they could not be wasted."

One of the biggest challenges centered on how to detonate the bomb.

Scientists and engineers developed the so-called gun method, which required shooting one mass of uranium-235 into another. The collision of these two created a critical mass, which kicked off a chain reaction that ended with a nuclear explosion.

But analysts discovered a major problem: The gun method would not work with plutonium. The bullet and the target could not be brought together fast enough before the plutonium started a premature chain reaction and fizzled. This challenge threatened to render obsolete the tremendous work—and millions of taxpayer dollars—that had gone into creating the Hanford nuclear reactors.

The brilliant minds at Los Alamos scrambled for a solution, ultimately devising what became known as the implosion method. This involved wrapping plutonium in conventional explosives that would compress the core. "The force of this blast," Groves explained, "literally squeezed the material together until it reached a critical mass and detonated."

The two methods dictated the different shapes for each bomb. The 9,700-pound uranium bomb would be long and cylindrical, stretching ten feet in length by two feet in diameter. The 10,800-pound plutonium bomb, in contrast, would be more bulbous, measuring eleven feet by five. The distinct shapes contributed to each weapon's unique nickname. Scientists dubbed the uranium bomb Little Boy while the plutonium bomb earned the moniker Fat Man.

Other questions remained, including what would serve as the bomb's fuse?

Teams investigated a wide range of possibilities, from barometric switches and proximity fuses to simple timers, the latter of which was the least preferable since it introduced the possibility of human error into the equation. A barometric switch seemed the best solution, but tests in 1944 revealed it was not fail-safe. Given the extraordinary taxpayer investment in the bomb, success had to be guaranteed. "Triggering devices," as the official history noted, "that fail only one percent of the time, on the average, were hardly acceptable."

Scientists learned that the air force was developing a tail warning device that used radar to signal the rear approach of other aircraft. This offered a promising alternative. Engineers worked to modify the APS-13—known simply as the Archie—to convert it into a radar altimeter. This would prove to be the critical component of a three-step fusing system.

At a predetermined altitude above the target, the Archie would close a relay. Four such units would go into each bomb. When any two relays closed, it would send a firing signal to the next stage. The second stage consisted of a bank of clock-operated switches. These were activated as soon as the bomb dropped from the plane by pulling arming wires from the clocks. As a fail-safe, the clock switches would not close for fifteen seconds, allowing the bomb to fall about 3,600 feet. This was designed to guard against a possible radar bounce from the plane that might trigger the Archies and prompt an early detonation. The third stage and final arming device was a barometric pressure switch, which would not close until the bomb reached seven thousand feet. Once all relays were closed, the firing signal in the uranium bomb would go to the gun primer. In the plutonium bomb, it closed a high-voltage circuit and triggered the implosion.

How to deliver the bomb was another question, prompting Groves to reach out to Gen. Henry "Hap" Arnold, commander of the Army Air Forces in the spring of 1944. The fifty-eight-year-old Arnold was an air-power pioneer who had learned to fly from Orville and Wilbur Wright in an Ohio cow pasture, under the watchful eye of a local undertaker. The only reason early aviators wore those classic goggles, in fact, was because a bug hit Arnold in the eye one time while landing. In the span of his career, Arnold had watched aviation advance from primitive wood and fabric biplanes to muscular four-engine bombers, capable of bridging oceans and turning entire nations into battlefields. In 1938 the general, with a head full of grandfatherly white hair, had taken command of an air service composed of twenty thousand aviators and a few hundred planes, converting it in just seven years into a global strike force that counted nearly 2.4 million airmen and eighty thousand fighters, bombers, and transports.

Along the way Arnold had made one of the biggest gambles of the war when he ordered the development of the B-29 Superfortress. The massive four-engine bomber—the largest in America's arsenal—had cost taxpayers an astounding $3.7 billion, making Boeing's aeronautical monster the single most expensive weapons system of the war, with a price tag nearly double that of the atomic bomb. An engineering marvel, the revolutionary bomber was constructed out of 55,000 parts along with 600,000 rivets. With a tail that rose as high as a three-story building, the B-29 flaunted the largest propellers ever fitted onto an airplane, along with a gigantic 141-foot wingspan—twenty feet longer than the Wright brothers' first flight. The first of the new bombers departed the factory for combat in the spring of 1944, just in time for the air war against Japan. "It was just so big," one pilot recalled, "I just couldn't imagine that it would fly."

But Groves could—and he had the perfect mission in mind.

He met with Arnold, informing him that the bomber would likely need some modifications to carry its unique payload. If for any reason it would not work, Groves added, he thought he might use a British Lancaster, which the prime minister would no doubt make available for the mission. "This brought from him the characteristic reply that I had hoped and expected to hear: that he wanted an American plane to deliver our bomb, and that the Air Force would make every effort to ensure that we had a B-29 capable of doing the job."

The two generals worked out a plan in which the air force would have three responsibilities. It would provide modified bombers capable of carrying the atomic weapons to the heart of Japan. The air force would organize, equip, and train a combat unit to deliver the weapon. Lastly, the bomb had to be dropped without fail on the target.

The original plan had called for three B-29s to be modified under a program codenamed Silverplate. That initial order was later increased to fifteen, then twenty-four, forty-eight, and finally fifty-four bombers, though only forty-six would be completed before war's end. Workers hustled to begin the extensive modifications, which required that all planes be capable of carrying either the tubular uranium bomb or the bulb-shaped plutonium one. Workers added high-strength internal supports along with a massive shackle, capable of holding a five-ton weapon by a single lug. Others installed bracing to keep the bomb in place amid rough air. A pneumatic system allowed the quick opening and closing of the doors while new fuel-injection engines would increase range. Reversible-pitch propellers would not only allow the plane to back up but would also help stop the massive bomber in shorter distances. To lighten the B-29, laborers removed upper- and lower gun turrets as well as armor plating. All told, each bomber required six thousand hours of work all done by hand to complete the modifications.

With the alterations underway, the air force began assembling a special combat unit under the command of Col. Paul Tibbets, Jr. The 509th Composite Group, based at Wendover Air Force Base in Utah, was officially activated on December 17, 1944. The 509th consisted of a bombardment and troop carrier squadron, an air service group, a headquarters and base services squadron, engineering, air matériel, and ordnance units, plus a military police company to provide security. All told, the 509th consisted of 225 officers and 1,542 enlisted men. "The Group," as the unit's official history observed, "was designed to stand alone."

By the spring of 1945, the Manhattan Project was rushing toward its climax. Over the course of two and a half years, Groves had spent a staggering $2 billion of taxpayer money. Of that, $1,188,352,000 had gone to the development of Oak Ridge, another $390,124,000 to Hanford, and

$74,055,000 to Los Alamos. That money had employed more than two hundred major contractors, who in turn hired thousands of subcontractors. A revolving door of 600,000 people had worked on the project. Along the way, Groves had transformed forests and deserts into bustling cites, constructed sprawling industrial complexes that appeared ripped from the pages of science fiction novels, and harnessed the greatest minds of the nation—all in the single pursuit of victory. But one critical question remained.

Would the bomb actually work?

CHAPTER 9

"The precedents of history were surely all against us."

—MAJ. GEN. LESLIE GROVES

On April 27, 1945—two days after Truman sat down with Stimson and Groves—the first Target Committee meeting kicked off at 8:40 a.m. The group's mission was ominous.

Determine which Japanese cities Truman should obliterate.

The eleven men who had assembled that Friday morning in the Pentagon were the direct result of an earlier conversation between Groves and General Marshall. With the bomb expected to be completed soon, the time had arrived to discuss how precisely to use it.

Groves had asked Marshall to designate an officer in the Operations Planning Division of the General Staff who could spearhead such an operation, but the nation's top soldier had resisted. "I don't like to bring too many people into this matter," Marshall confided in Groves. "Is there any reason why you can't take this over and do it yourself?"

"No, sir," the general replied. "I will."

Groves had then met with Gen. Hap Arnold to discuss the challenges of such a mission. "Our most pressing job," Groves said, "was to select the bomb targets. This would be my job." The main factor, Groves believed, was to pick targets that would destroy the will of the Japanese people. For Groves, that meant Kyoto, which was the historic and cultural heart of Japan with its nearly two thousand temples. In addition, he wanted military targets, like headquarters, troop centers, and factories. "To enable us to assess accurately the effects of the bomb," he added, "the targets should not have been previously damaged by air raids."

To help nail down a list of target cities, Groves had assembled the morning's committee. The general was normally no fan of decisions made by consensus, though he had one exception, based on the advice he had gleaned early in his career from a wise former chief of engineers. "I have no objection to committees," he said, "as long as I appoint them."

At the top of his handpicked list of members this morning was Brig. Gen. Thomas Farrell, whom Groves had recently chosen as his deputy. As the Manhattan Project ballooned, Stimson had grown alarmed that an unforeseen tragedy might befall Groves. No one else knew as much as he did. That had prompted Stimson to bar the general from flying to London to brief Churchill in December. Groves protested, even though he had similarly barred Oppenheimer from flying or even driving a car for more than a few miles.

"You can't be replaced," Stimson had leveled with Groves.

"You do it, and General Marshall does it," he had countered. "Why shouldn't I?"

"As I said before," Stimson replied, "you can't be replaced, and we can."

That exchange had prompted a larger discussion. The fate of a project as large and important as the atomic bomb could not hinge upon a single person. "I want you to get a Number Two man immediately who can take over your position," the war secretary continued. "You can have any officer in the Army, no matter who he is, or what duty he is on."

Groves had drafted a list of six individuals. He then ran it by Col. Kenneth Nichols, who as the Manhattan Project's district engineer, oversaw the uranium and plutonium development. Given Nichols's central role in the project—and the fact that he would have to work with any replacement—Groves felt it was vital for him to approve.

Nichols crossed out several names, including a close friend of Groves. He eyed the general to see if he objected.

"Well," Groves said, "he's out."

Do you have any preference among the remainder? the general asked.

"You name him," Nichols said, "and I'll tell you."

At the top of the list, Groves said, was Brig. Gen. Thomas Farrell.

"He would be my first choice, too," Nichols confirmed.

Like Groves, the fifty-three-year-old Farrell was a tireless worker, going so far as to give up golf for the duration of the war. A New York native, he had fought heroically during World War I, earning the Distinguished Service Cross, three Silver Stars, and a Purple Heart. Most recently he had served as chief engineer in the China-Burma-India Theater, overseeing the development of bomber bases as well as the Ledo Road, one of the largest construction projects of the war, a 478-mile highway that cut through jungles and bridged ravines to connect British India and China. For Farrell, the war had become very personal. His son and namesake had been killed in action on the Anzio beachhead in Italy on February 24, 1944.

In addition to Farrell, four other committee members seated around the table worked on the Manhattan Project, including Maj. Jack Derry and doctors John Von Neumann, Robert Wilson, and William Penney. The remaining four came from the Army Air Forces. Seated at the table was Arnold's chief of staff, Brig. Gen. Lauris Norstad, who was joined by Col. William Fisher and doctors Joyce Stearns and David Dennison.

Groves began the morning's meeting by explaining the importance of the mission and the need for absolute secrecy. The general believed that the group ultimately should select four of the enemy's cities as possible targets. "I emphasized General Marshall's opinion," he added, "that the ports on the west coast of Japan should not be ignored as possible targets, since they were vital to the Japanese communications with the Asiatic mainland." Groves then turned the session over to Norstad, who explained that the resources of the Twentieth Air Force would be made available to help in any way needed. Colonel Fisher and Dr. Sterns, Norstad added, could provide the group with maps, operational analyses, and target data.

Groves and Norstad then departed, leaving Farrell to run the session.

Throughout the morning and afternoon, the group hammered out the fundamental criteria for the first proposed atomic mission. That included determining the maximum range of a loaded B-29, which was fifteen hundred miles at an altitude of thirty thousand feet. The group likewise agreed that the mission demanded visual bombing, which was far more accurate than radar.

Other factors included predicting the weather over the possible targets, particularly in the months of July, August, and September, the earliest the bomb might be ready. Aircrews in the Pacific had already learned the difficulties of attacking Japan, given the island nation's notoriously foul weather. "Absolutely essential that we get a good day for the initial mission," the minutes show Farrell stated. "Exhaustive study should be made so as to enable prediction within a 3 day period of the day of the mission from 3 possible target areas."

Armed with eleven years of data, a weather expert warned the group to expect only seven good days in July. That would decrease to five in August, while September would be worse. Aircrews might have to wait two weeks between clear days. Japan's weather was so unpredictable that meteorologists could forecast an operational day only twenty-four hours in advance. One solution would be to send planes ahead of the bomber to scout the weather over target cities. The crew would then be given a primary target and two alternates. "Only once in 5 years," minutes stated, "have there ever been 2 successive good visual bombing days of Tokyo."

Another challenge was a dwindling list of cities.

The group wanted populated urban areas of at least three miles in diameter between Tokyo in the north and Nagasaki in the south. "The target and/or aiming point," the group agreed, "should have a high strategic value." Aircrews under the leadership of Maj. Gen. Curtis LeMay, head of the Twenty-First Bomber Command, had begun incendiary strikes on Japan's major industrial cities. LeMay's first raid on Tokyo on March 9 had burned sixteen square miles of the capital. Subsequent attacks had gutted portions of Nagoya, Osaka, and Kobe. "Tokyo is a possibility," the group conceded, "but it is now practically all bombed and burned out and is practically rubble with only the palace grounds left standing."

Each week brought more ruin, as the thirty-eight-year-old LeMay, who chewed on cigars to hide the residual effects of his battle with Bell's palsy, worked his way down a list of thirty-three priority targets with the aim of eventually dropping 100,000 tons a month. "It should be remembered that in our selection of any target, the 20th Air Force is operating primarily to laying waste all the main Japanese cities, and that they do not propose to save some important primary target for us if it interferes with the operation of the war from their point of view."

But there was one possibility.

"Hiroshima is the largest untouched target not on the 21st Bomber Command priority list," the group discovered. "Consideration should be given to this city."

In addition, the group settled on sixteen other possible targets, including the area around Tokyo Bay, Kawasaki, Yokohama, Nagoya, Osaka, Kobe, Kyoto, Kure, Yawata, Kokura, Shimosenka, Yamaguchi, Kumamoto, Fukuoka, Nagasaki, and Sasebo. For each city, the group requested data on possible targets, the type of buildings, and the nature of industry.

Farrell assigned various members to follow up on critical topics, including the projected size of the bomb blast, the amount of damage expected, and the expected kill radius. Others would dig into the meteorological data and hunt down details on proposed targets. The group concluded at four p.m. with a plan to meet again in two weeks at Los Alamos.

The target was slowly coming into focus.

CHAPTER 10

"I can't bear to have an empty stomach day after day."

—TSUNEJIRÔ TAMURA
MARCH 5, 1945, DIARY ENTRY

Emperor Hirohito brooded.

The forty-four-year-old ruler could only watch from his palace in the heart of Tokyo as his once-mighty empire burned. With a slight frame, stooped shoulders, and an oddly high-pitched voice, the bespectacled Hirohito appeared a far cry from history's great warriors, conquerors like Alexander the Great, Julius Caesar, or Napoleon Bonaparte.

At first glance, Hirohito appeared better suited for a library than a battlefield. He stood just five feet six inches tall and weighed a little more than 120 pounds. The emperor was clumsy and unathletic—even though he had grown up swimming and sumo wrestling—and had what one historian characterized as a "twitchy nervousness." Socially awkward and lonely, Hirohito had spent his life walled off from any real friends as well as the population at large, having lived, as even he later acknowledged, much like a "bird in a cage."

The emperor in whose name millions had fought and died enjoyed solitary pursuits. He wrote poetry and relished natural history and marine biology, collecting slugs, starfish, and hydrozoa. The West fascinated him based on his one trip abroad in 1922, so much so that he kept busts of Abraham Lincoln, Charles Darwin, and Napoleon in his study. Despite residing on a 531-acre compound in the heart of Tokyo—the largest open space in the capital, complete with a nine-hole golf course—Hirohito lived modestly. He rose at seven a.m., after which he thumbed through the newspapers and prayed before beginning his work. He ended each day with a stroll through the palace gardens. His meals likewise were simple. Breakfast consisted of oatmeal and black bread, while he ate cooked vegetables and dumpling soup for lunch. He neither smoked nor drank alcohol, though he did have the habit of talking to himself when anxious.

He no doubt had much to say these days.

Japan had suffered an extraordinary reversal of fortune since the heady early days of the war when Hirohito had ridden his white horse through Tokyo to shouts of banzai from the adoring citizenry. At its peak in the spring of 1942, after steamrolling across the Pacific, Hirohito had presided over an empire that stretched across 20 million square miles and seven time zones. The press and senior leaders bragged at the time that it would be easy for the nation's soldiers to invade and seize California or host a naval review in New York Harbor.

"Japan," as the *Asahi* newspaper trumpeted, "leads the world."

But Hirohito's sprawling empire, much like Hitler's vaunted Third Reich, had proved ephemeral, a short-blooming flower that withered under the string of defeats from Midway and Guadalcanal to the Philippines and Marianas. The weight of that hung on Hirohito, the 124th emperor in a dynasty that purportedly stretched back 2,600 years.

All that was now at risk.

Upon the death of his father, twenty-five-year-old Hirohito had ascended to the throne on Christmas Day 1926, during a tumultuous period in political life, one that would test the inexperienced new monarch. Following the 1868 Meiji Restoration, which ended shogunate rule and restored the monarchy at the head of Japan, the military played an increasingly powerful role in the government, one where the emperor served both as head of state and as supreme military commander. Military leaders usurped authority, withheld classified information from civilian rivals, and boasted the power to topple cabinets. "The military used its independent authority as broadly as possible to impose its priorities on the nation," noted the Japanese historian Saburô Ienaga. "If legal methods and the skillful use of institutional advantages were inadequate, they used their monopoly of force to terrorize and destroy opponents."

The 1930s proved a turbulent decade marred by overseas conquests and political violence. Driven by a need for resources—and acting against the wishes of the nation's civilian political leaders and Hirohito—the army seized Manchuria in 1931, a move that provided Japan with coal, steel, and nonferrous metals. At home, economic depression fueled the rise of nationalism and a turn against the West, highlighted by Japan's withdrawal from the League of Nations in 1933. That was followed four years later by the 1937 invasion of northern China, which kicked off an undeclared war that would drag on for eight years, cost millions of lives, and draw condemnation from world powers. China, in short, had become a tarpit. "A withdrawal," one postwar analysis concluded, "was politically impossible. The political standing of the army was predicated upon the maintenance of the Chinese stronghold."

Those trends coincided with a rise in political violence against anyone who threatened the military. On May 15, 1932, navy cadets assassinated Prime Minister Tsuyoshi Inukai in broad daylight in his office. Six years later on February 26, 1936, twenty-two junior army officers and fourteen hundred enlisted men launched a coup d'état, seizing the Army Ministry and Metropolitan Police Headquarters. The unsuccessful four-day siege concluded with the murder of Lord Keeper of the Privy Seal Makoto Saitô, Finance Minister Korekiyo Takahashi, and Inspector General of Military Education Jôtarô Watanabe, all political moderates whom Hirohito trusted most. Despite his role as the military's supreme commander, the emperor was reluctant to speak out or go against the brass. Over him hung the threat of assassination. "Domestic conflicts," argued Hirohito's biographer, Herbert Bix, "were more dangerous than the escalation of war."

The military's tightening grip on national political life dovetailed with the creation of societal guardrails to control everything from education and the media to public assembly, speech, and opinion. Schools played a central role as authorities revised textbooks to indoctrinate youth on the importance of citizenship, nationalism, and the divinity of the emperor. "War and patriotism," observed Ienaga, "were to be stressed in every subject." English vanished from the curriculum; youth were even urged to stop using the popular words *mama* and *papa*. The government assigned a military officer to every school. Daily calisthenics were incorporated into the curriculum, while Western sports, like baseball, were swapped for judo and kendo. "During recess," recalled the reporter Joseph Newman, "I frequently saw boys, who could not have been more than twelve years old, being taught by army officers how most effectively to bayonet straw dummies set upon the playground of a primary school."

Those efforts, however, stretched beyond schools. As far back as 1925, Japan had passed the first of a series of sweeping laws designed to curb speech and later even public assembly. A force of so-called thought police monitored unions, political parties, and educational organizations, while agents interviewed the friends, neighbors, and family members of potential suspects. The wealth of political spies and informants—coupled with the arrest of some 76,000 people—had a chilling effect on society, as the populace proved reluctant to speak out. Others were afraid even of confiding in private diaries. "Some prisoners were tortured and physically mistreated; others were held indefinitely, placed in a psychological limbo," Ienaga reported. "There were people who died from the effects of long years in prison."

The press proved another target. Under the guise of a newsprint shortage, the government forced the mergers of many major newspapers, slashing the number of outlets from 848 to just 54. Reluctant owners faced suspension or even closure, often on trumped-up offenses. That was the case with the *Japan Advertiser*, accused of offending the imperial family with a blurred photo of the eight-year-old crown prince. "At that point," the editor Wilfred Fleisher recalled, "I felt the situation was almost hopeless." Such aggressive moves succeeded. "By the time the war began, the newspapers had become no more than official bulletins," wrote Masuo Kato, a journalist with Domei, the government's wire service. "Any newspaper that wished to remain in business had to be an enthusiastic supporter of government policy."

The army and navy vetted all military articles, while the Foreign and Greater East Asia ministries approved all stories dealing with international news. The Censorship Department of the Home Ministry's Police Bureau reviewed everything from books, magazines, and films to records and even toys. Similar to newspapers, authorities overhauled the magazine and book industries, replacing top editors with government-friendly ones and blacklisting writers, including authors of romance novels and comic books. The number of periodicals were slashed in half, from 1,970 before the war to 965 a few years later. Book publishers likewise plummeted from 3,664 to 204. This coincided with a drastic reduction in titles, which fell from 28,138 in 1941 to just 875 by the war's end. "Controls on intellectual and political activity," Ienaga said, "were tightened again and again until civil rights virtually ceased to exist."

With schools, civic organizations, and the media under control, the government turned to the population at large. In towns and cities nationwide, authorities assembled every ten to twenty households into a *tonarigumi*, a neighborhood organization whose roots reached back to feudal times. Such associations not only helped with the distribution of rationed food and official announcements but also provided a means for authorities to surveil potential saboteurs and spies. This coincided with a repudiation of Western culture and luxury, an ideology best captured by the popular slogan "Extravagance is the enemy." The government banned cosmetics and limited women's hair permanents to just three curls. Men were pressed to drop Western-style business suits. Women wore *monpe*, a form of baggy work pants. English words were struck from baseball terminology while authorities prohibited the works of American and British composers; only German and Italian music was allowed. Ukeleles, steel guitars, and banjos were barred. "Jazz was condemned," Kato noted, "as a sign of decadence."

The restructuring of Japanese society, however, could do little to improve the nation's economic challenges. Outside of a few industries, like silk, fish oil, and sulfur, Japan had almost no material self-sufficiency, forced to import its most important food source, rice. Ships arrived in port loaded with bauxite to build fighters, cotton to sew uniforms, and rubber to manufacture tires. But Japan's greatest weakness—and the one most critical for war—was the oil it needed to power its battleships, bombers, and tanks. At the outbreak of the war, Japan could produce just two million barrels a year, a figure that equated to just 0.1 percent of the world's oil output. The United States in comparison—the world's largest producer—delivered seven hundred times that amount. "If our reserves were dribbled away, Japan would grow weaker and weaker like a tuberculosis patient gasping along till he dropped dead on the road," observed Ayakota Okazaki, who oversaw resource mobilization for the navy. "A grim and humiliating end."

Japan's hunger for raw materials to feed its military machine drove its dream of conquest, beginning with its first moves into Manchuria and later northern China. "Without crude oil, bauxite, rubber, tin, nickel and copper," the economist Jerome Cohen observed, "the pomp and power of empire were pretense and sham." Japan looked to Formosa to provide sugar and rice. Korea could offer electric power and light metals. Manchuria was rich in coal, iron ore, and soybeans. The Dutch East Indies had oil and bauxite, while Malaysia could provide tin and rubber. "With these materials in her grasp," Cohen added, "Japan would be self-sufficient and unchallengeable." But war promised more than just resources needed for Japan's empire. "There would be colonial posts for her young men, commands for her militarists, markets for her manufactured goods, and raw material for her industries."

But Japan opted to launch a war against the United States without a plan for victory—and amid much doubt by senior military leaders that such a fight could be won. That crystallized in a November 1, 1941, meeting of the Cabinet Liaison Conference at the Imperial Headquarters. "We can fight effectively for about two years, but no prediction can be made for after that," declared Adm. Osami Nagano, chief of the navy's general staff.

"In war a reasonable prospect of victory is enough," interjected the bespectacled Hideki Tojo, who served Japan as both war and prime minister. "Even if there is apprehension that we may be defeated, the nation should trust the military and move ahead."

Despite such assurances, Hirohito remained skeptical. His brother Prince Takamatsu visited him on November 30, 1941, arguing that senior navy leaders still doubted Japan could win. The emperor shared his concerns with Lord Keeper of the Privy Seal Marquis Koichi Kido. "Once you grant the imperial sanction," Kido warned, "there can be no going back."

Hirohito summoned admirals Nagano and Shigetaro Shimada. "Once an arrow is fired, it will become a long-drawn out war," he said. "Are you ready?"

Nagano confirmed.

"As navy minister," Hirohito added, turning to Shimada, "are you prepared?"

"Both men and supplies are fully ready," the admiral replied. "We are waiting for an imperial mandate."

Just as he had done throughout the war in China, the emperor, faced with extraordinary pressure from the militarists, caved.

Japan would go to war.

The military's plan was to knock out the American Navy in a surprise attack on Pearl Harbor, which would buy time to seize the resource-rich nations it desired and build defensive rings around the home islands. One of America's greatest flaws, the Japanese believed, was democracy. Strategists gambled that the American public would never allow the military to fight an expensive and bloody war on the opposite side of the Pacific against Japan's superior soldiers. The United States would have no choice but to make peace and allow Japan to hold on to its territorial gains. "Japan's militarists stoutly affirmed that morally and spiritually no American could begin to compare with a Japanese. This was axiomatic," noted historian Robert Butow. "Japan's strength lay in her spirit; America's weakness in her lack of it."

And that assumption would eventually prove fatal.

The war immediately taxed Japan's labor force, which was already at full capacity when bombers swarmed the skies over Pearl Harbor that Sunday morning of December 7, 1941. "This was a politician's dream," noted the historian Thomas Havens, "but a mobilizer's nightmare." To increase productivity, the government eliminated the twelve-hour workday limit and repealed protective laws that barred women and children from dangerous jobs, a move that allowed females to dig coal in Hokkaido's mines. Authorities prodded half of the nation's 50,000 convicts into factories, who were later joined by more than 30,000 prisoners of war. The government likewise barred men between the ages of fourteen and forty-five from working in more than a dozen fields, from barbers and cooks to salesmen and streetcar conductors. Okayama went further, adding gardeners, tree surgeons, and tombstone cutters to the list. As the war progressed, the government tapped 3 million students ages ten and older to toil on farms and in factories, a figure that equaled one-tenth of the civilian labor force.

To free up additional workers, officials shuttered nonessential businesses, from book and toy stores to dressmaking, typing, and art schools. Tokyo alone saw the closure of eleven thousand small shops. Restaurants, nightclubs, and kabuki theaters likewise went dark, robbing the public of the few diversions. "There was nowhere to go. The beerhalls, cafes, and bars, so many that once there had been one at every corner, were locked up," the Philippine diplomat León María Guerrero complained in his diary. "Life was no fun anymore." Authorities even bolted the doors on more than 3,000 teahouses, a move that put 10,000 geishas out of work, some of whom landed as secretaries and typists in government ministries or businesses. "A geisha out of her element is like a bird fallen from its nest," observed the French reporter Robert Guillain. "Many even let themselves be drafted into the labor service where hands trained to pour sake and arrange flowers learned to sew white-silk parachutes and fashion aluminum parts."

The loss of amusements coincided with the military's appetite for raw materials, particularly metals. Authorities demanded residents surrender everything from teapots and hibachis to watches, glasses, and dishware. Even gold teeth and diamonds proved fair game, the latter of which could be used for radio production. Buddhist priests relinquished gongs, statues, and bells from temples. Workers yanked the armrests off park benches, wrenched handrails from bridges, and tore down the iron fences that encircled cemeteries. Others toppled lampposts, pried up boilers, and plucked heating pipes and radiators out of walls, all of which scarred sidewalks and marred buildings. "Tokyo had never been a beautiful city, but it was now dirty as well as homely," Guillain added. "Every morning the capital awoke a little more sordid, as though stained by the sinister night into which it had just been plunged."

The citizenry, constantly urged to give more, saw little come to it in return. Vital necessities dwindled and then vanished, ranging from sugar and soap to matches, thread, and medicine, forcing the Japanese to scavenge for substitutes. Residents sipped sake distilled from acorns and sweet potatoes and smoked cigarettes made from eggplant and persimmon leaves as well as knotweed and cornsilk. "The most edifying solution," as one historian noted, "was to roll shredded black-market tobacco in pages torn from pocket dictionaries."

Bamboo replaced steel needles on phonograph machines while engineers in Hokkaido experimented by swapping wood for iron train rails. To conserve leather and rubber, the government implored residents to wear wooden clogs. Shark, whale, and salmon skin—dubbed sea leather—replaced cowhide. Cotton rationing coupled with the mixing of bark and wood pulp fibers decreased the quality of fabrics, much to the frustration of residents whose socks and shirts disintegrated after one or two wears. "Our clothes are in tatters," one Tokyo resident complained in her diary. "It's almost as though we have been defeated in battle."

But it wasn't only the living who suffered.

"One borrows coffins for the dead but cannot buy them," author Kiyoshi Kiyosawa observed in his diary. "They are used any number of times."

Such shortages only exacerbated hardships on the home front, where even before the war the typical Japanese person lived a far more meager lifestyle than the average American. Meat, milk, and butter were rare in a diet composed largely of rice, bean paste, and fish. Japanese homes were simple, constructed of wood and paper. Cars, radios, flush toilets, and washing machines—all staples in an American household—were an extravagance. Consumer expenditures before the war totaled just one-fifth of the United States and a quarter even of Germany. "Living from hand to mouth," Cohen wrote, "the Japanese civilian economy had no cushion, no 'fat' upon which it could fall back in case of a prolonged conflict."

As early as 1942, a family of five in Tokyo had to wait in line 4.5 hours a day to obtain enough food to survive. The following year a lack of fuel slashed the national fish catch in half. "Everything was rationed," recalled Ayako Koshino, a kimono maker. "Even a tiny mackerel had to be divided among ten families." To survive, residents bartered on the black market, which by 1944 provided half of all food purchased—and often at ten times the official price. "Those who could not pay," one postwar report noted, "simply did not eat." That disparity fell heaviest on the poor, who grew resentful of the wealthy, a theme captured in the diary of Tsunejirô Tamura. "It's the age," the elderly Kyoto resident wrote, "of the strong eating the weak."

City dwellers pilgrimaged by the thousands to the countryside in search of vegetables, prompting a crackdown by authorities. But crafty women swaddled rice sacks to disguise them as infants. "The trains were packed full of grim housewives loaded down with knapsacks knobby with potatoes or redolent of radish," Guerrero wrote. "Fish blood dripped from baggage racks." Others foraged in cemeteries and vacant lots. Ishii Tominosuke, a librarian in Odawara, plucked dandelions from his stone wall to make soup. The diary of Tsunejirô Tamura often noted his hunger. "Our stomachs," he wrote, "are getting emptier and emptier."

By late 1944, Tamura's diary grew even more desperate. "There's no end," the seventy-five-year-old wrote on November 11, "to our feelings of hopelessness." He returned to his agony nine days later. "We simply are waiting," he wrote, "to starve to death."

Even Hirohito learned to live more frugally, scaling his daily diet back to rice mixed with barley once a day coupled with a bowl of soup. His protein consisted of a piece of fish and an egg. The empress, in turn, wandered the palace grounds picking edible wild grasses.

The shortage of food sparked a rise in theft. People swiped children's lunch boxes from trains and railroad stations. Twelve-year-old Katsumoto Saotome, who labored at Kubota Iron Works, learned to keep his lunch tied to his waist. An Osaka University professor, arrested for stealing tomatoes from a vegetable field, was sentenced to five years in prison. Thieves stripped trains of hanging straps and cut out the leather upholstery. Slippers and soap vanished from bathhouses along with keys and even doorknobs from inns. Overcoats and shoes disappeared from the entry hall of private residences. "There is not a house," Kiyosawa wrote in his diary, "that has not had things stolen." Some perpetrator even nabbed the author's hat from a restaurant chair along the Ginza. "Japan," he complained, "has become a nation of thieves."

The military was equally starved for resources. The loss of oil imports forced engineers to scrounge for substitutes. Workers built almost forty thousand small distilleries, including some on the golf courses of tony Tokyo clubs, to harvest oil from pine roots. "Traveling through the country," Kato observed, "one could see evidence of the failure of the program in the many piles of pine roots abandoned and rotting by the roadside." The government likewise experimented with a gasoline made from shale and sardines. But few of these measures helped. Essential vehicles puttered around burning charcoal while the nation's once-muscular battleships sat in port, relegated to antiaircraft duty. The loss of fuel even sparked the creation of the nation's kamikaze corps, which made its first combat appearance on October 25, 1944, during the Battle of Leyte Gulf in the Philippines. "Suicide attack," recalled Lt. Col. Naomichi Jin, an air army operations staff officer, "was the only sure and reliable attack by airmen whose training had been limited because of the shortage of fuel."

The winter of 1944–45 proved particularly brutal on the home front as temperatures plummeted, freezing the water inside homes. Coal and charcoal, which were hard to find even at the start of the war, were luxury items. At night, people chopped down trees in parks to use as firewood. Others stripped wood from bridges. Wealthier individuals burned home libraries and furniture. A lack of fuel forced many bathhouses to close. Those few that remained open were often packed with long lines. "Our neighbor," Guerrero wrote in his diary, "says he once stuck his leg into a crowded pool and could neither take it out again nor get in after it."

"Don't push," people barked at one another. "Don't push."

Many residents could do little more than shiver in drafty homes beneath tattered blankets. "With no firewood, no split wood, and only a little charcoal," Tamura wrote, "it's a life-or-death situation." Others agreed. "I feel lucky to have survived for another day," Tokyo secretary Hisako Yoshizawa noted in her diary, "but I have absolutely no hope."

As American bombers began to target Japan, the government evacuated 1,303,200 children in grades three through six from cities, resettling them in rural temples, inns, and schools in what amounted to another blow to domestic life. Homesick youth often ran away, only to be found later wandering the train tracks that most seemed to think would deliver them home. Others wet their beds and grew despondent. Schoolteachers, who evacuated and cared for students, monitored their letters home, afraid that mentioning hardships might upset parents. "Mother, as soon as this letter arrives, please come to see me that very day. Please, Mother," one sixth grader wrote. "Mitsuko might die if you don't come to see me."

Just like their families at home, the evacuated children battled hunger. Students bullied one another while desperate teachers stole food from the youths. Children resorted to eating grasshoppers, snakes, and stream crabs as well as tooth-cleaning powder, paint, and crayons. Others foraged for chestnuts and grasses. "Malnutrition," one historian noted, "even drove many children to lick the sores on their own bodies." Only the lice grew fat. "On sunny days we stripped the children naked and boiled their clothes to kill the lice," recalled Mitsuko Ôoka, a teacher. "The water would turn red from all the blood the lice had sucked."

The situation grew dire in 1945. The rice crop, which amounted to one-quarter of the previous year's harvest, was the smallest in thirty-six years. America's submarine blockade slashed imports, which were one-tenth of normal. In April 1945 the government nixed the importation of raw materials for food, recognizing that starvation loomed on the horizon. "Human efficiency," noted reporter Masuo Kato, "was declining everywhere."

Worker absenteeism soared while sexual appetites plummeted. The stray dogs that once skulked about cities vanished, either starved or eaten. The 2,007 calories the average person consumed daily at the outbreak of the war plummeted to just 1,680. Malnutrition led to diarrhea and fatigue. The infant mortality rate climbed to a rate three times higher than either England or Germany. New mothers often proved too malnourished to produce milk, forcing hospitals to bottle-feed newborns radish and turnip juices, both rich in vitamin C. Older children suffered from rickets, a disease sparked by a prolonged vitamin D deficiency that causes soft and deformed bones. Cases of tuberculosis meanwhile soared. "One had only to open one's eyes and ears," Guillain noted, "to detect the contagion in the surrounding crowds."

An outbreak of lice in Japan's major cities only added to the misery as people increasingly grew hostile toward one another. "Riding trains and streetcars was a mad commotion," recalled a housewife in Ogaki. "People became irritable due to lack of food. They are always hungry and dissatisfied and naturally they try to blame their suffering on someone." Others upbraided military leaders, triggering the arrest in the war's last full year of some six thousand people accused of harboring antiwar sentiments or disseminating rumors. "Oftentimes, when we ladies got together, we used to talk about Tojo and his cohorts, wondering what kind of clothes they wore and what kind of food they ate," recalled the wife of a Nagano farmer. "We were darn sure it wasn't the kind of food that we ate." Others agreed. "The leaders," a Kyoto fireman added, "were getting more than their share of food and what we got was leftovers."

The public's frustration manifested in other ways, including when an official messenger tried to inform a mother of the loss of her son in the war. "Did you say the emperor?" she bitterly interrupted. "I don't want to hear any more of that crap."

The government struggled to prop up the nation's morale with bogus victories in the press. "Journalism," Ienaga wrote, "did a complete about-face from balanced dissent to inflammatory cheerleading." The military, meanwhile, disguised defeats with colorful euphemisms, so that a retreat became a "transfer of forces" or a "strategic withdrawal." Others fell back on empty slogans that did little to buoy morale. "Japan may be weak in resources, but she is strong in spirit," proclaimed one. "This will lead the nation to victory!"

"We ask for nothing but to win the war," declared another.

The military, much to the frustration of the populace, continued to hound the public to donate more to the war effort, posting placards around major cities. "Give cotton!" demanded one such notice. "It can be made into gunpowder that will sink enemy ships!"

"Turn in your silver—the army needs it!" added another.

The public tired of the government's lies. How could Japan be victorious if American bombers buzzed the capital's skies? "I couldn't help but feel contempt for the authorities who treat us as though we were stupid," Tokyo resident Aiko Takahashi wrote in her diary. The novelist and poet Jun Takami agreed. "We are clearly being pushed back by the enemy," he wrote. "We are losing. Why can't they write this plainly? It's the same old story." Despite the private grumblings, few dared to speak out, much less revolt. "The whole population," Ienaga wrote, "suffered brain damage from incessant propaganda shock value."

The public's mounting frustration and exhaustion were not lost on senior leaders, who increasingly feared that such simmering hostility might threaten the throne. "The people are disgusted with the military and with the government," Reserve Gen. Kanji Ishiwara confided in his diary. "They do not care anymore about the outcome of the war."

Even Hirohito, who unlike the public knew the true state of the war, understood this reality. The emperor's initial reluctance to fight had faded after Japan's early victories, only to return in force as America rebounded, prompting him to gripe in meetings with senior leaders. "Are the army and navy seriously trying to work together?" he barked.

"Is there any way we can defeat American forces in a frontal attack somewhere?"

"Somehow," he decried, "we have to defeat the United States."

Hirohito's frustration magnified in June 1944 as America closed in on Saipan, an island just fifteen hundred miles south of Tokyo. "If we ever lose Saipan, repeated air attacks on Tokyo will follow," he warned Tojo. "No matter what it takes, we have to hold there."

But the emperor's demands were not enough.

The fall of Saipan had for many senior leaders crystallized the inevitability of the nation's downfall. "Japan has lost the war," retired navy Adm. Mitsumasa Yonai confided to a colleague. "We have been defeated beyond doubt." Hirohito consoled himself by watching fireflies in the palace garden. "Under the circumstances," the emperor's cousin wrote in his diary, "there is nothing better for him than to divert himself and to recuperate."

"Hasn't Tojo committed hara-kiri yet?" anonymous callers hounded his wife.

No, but Saipan's loss did bring an end to the bespectacled leader's 876 days as prime minister. Tojo was replaced by Kuniaki Koiso, a sixty-four-year-old general. Saipan was soon followed by the fall of Tinian and Guam. The capture of those three islands had for the first time placed Japan's major cities in range of American bombers, an alarming reality best captured in the four words Admiral Nagano uttered to the emperor: "Hell is on us."

And hell it soon would be.

Japanese leaders understood that the bombing of the nation's cities was a prelude to an invasion of the homeland. To prepare, Hirohito approved the outline for Ketsu-Go on January 20, 1945, an ambitious army-and-navy operation to counter the anticipated American assault. The strategy called for fortifying perimeter strong points, like Iwo Jima and Okinawa, while ground forces prepared to battle the enemy on the southern island of Kyushu and the main island of Honshu. In anticipation, Japan planned to reserve its air strength to use as kamikazes hell-bent on crashing into warships. Rather than battle on the beaches, military strategists envisioned a defense in the cities, towns, and villages. The backbone of this plan would fall to civilians, who were being trained in schools and businesses to fight with bamboo spears. "The final decisive battle of the war," the plan's opening sentence declared, "will be waged in Japan proper."

At the same time, Hirohito took the unorthodox step of consulting with former senior statesmen known as the *jûshin*, a move that had to be done in secret so as not to draw attention from the militarists who might object—or worse. Despite interruptions from air raids, Hirohito met individually between February 7 and 26 with six former prime ministers, including Kiichiro Hiranumu, Koki Hirota, Fumimaro Konoe, Reijiro Wakatsuki, Keisuke Okada, and Tojo, as well as the former keeper of the privy seal, Nobuaki Makino. All pushed for the war's continuance except Prince Konoe. "When I think of the madmen leading the present situation," he once said, "I can't help but feel weary of life." In his February 14 meeting, Konoe urged Hirohito to make peace. Loss of the war would threaten the *kokutai*, the traditional imperial political system. "Regrettably," Konoe said, "I think that defeat is inevitable."

Hirohito pushed back, arguing that Japan needed one more victory to secure a better bargaining position and avoid America's demand for unconditional surrender.

"Is that possible?" Konoe pressed.

"If we hold out long enough in this war, we may be able to win," the emperor said that day, "but what worries me is whether the nation will be able to endure until then."

Those fears came into much sharper focus seven minutes past midnight on March 10, 1945, when LeMay sent 279 B-29s on a low-altitude fire raid against the capital. Armed with napalm-filled incendiaries, the bombers rained fire across Tokyo, turning night into day. The initial blazes merged to create a firestorm, which rolled like a tidal wave across the capital, devouring homes, shops, and businesses. As the heat soared, people's eyelashes melted. Clothes and hair burst into flames. Temperatures reached as high as 2,800 degrees, hot enough to liquefy asphalt, fuse metal coins, and vaporize thousands. The sun rose the following morning to reveal an apocalyptic wasteland. "There was still a light wind blowing," the journalist Kato observed, "and some of the bodies, reduced to ashes, were simply scattering like sand."

That one raid destroyed 15.8 square miles of Tokyo, incinerating 267,171 homes, stores, and businesses. Literally one out of every four buildings had vanished. The attack killed 105,000 men, women, and children, wounded another 40,918, and left one million homeless. Rescuers fished the dead from clogged canals, where many had boiled in superheated waters. Others had to pry apart charcoaled corpses. Distinguishing men from women was at times impossible. The dead would go on to fill sixty-seven temporary cemeteries dug into the grounds of schools, parks, and temples. The ruin stunned Hirohito, who left the palace for the first time in months to tour the capital. "Tokyo," he said, "has been reduced to ashes."

The firebombing represented a radical shift in American strategy. Gone were the earlier high-altitude attacks on Japan's industry. America had escalated to total war.

And Tokyo was only the start.

American bombers went on to hit Nagoya, Osaka, Kobe, and Nagoya again. In five missions flown over a span of barely ten days, LeMay's bombers scorched a staggering thirty-two square miles of four of Japan's largest cities. Word spread of the devastation. "Tokyo has become a burned-out field," Tamura wrote in his diary. "Nagoya is weeping over a similar fate; and corpses are piled up in the burned-out fields that is now Osaka."

"For the first time," Aiko Takahashi added, "I began to be afraid."

But Japan's challenges soon magnified.

Iwo Jima fell on March 26, 1945. American troops sloshed ashore at Okinawa on April 1. Four days later, the Soviet Union announced it would not renew its Neutrality Pact with Japan, which for four years had helped maintain peace between the neighboring nations. What Japanese leaders did not know was that during the February 1945 conference in Yalta, Stalin had agreed with Roosevelt and Churchill to enter the Pacific war within three months of the fall of Germany. The empire's prospects faded. Japan's cities burned, Russia was preparing to come off the war's sideline, and America was readying a city-killing weapon.

Tojo's fall in the summer of 1944 had given hope to those who favored peace, an aspiration that his replacement, Prime Minister Koiso, had failed to deliver. The invasion of Okinawa brought an end to Koiso's brief eight-month tenure. To replace him, the *jûshin* turned to Kantaro Suzuki, a seventy-seven-year-old former admiral who protested the job. A veteran officer of nearly four decades, Suzuki had fought valiantly in the First Sino-Japanese War in 1894 and in the Russo-Japanese War ten years later, becoming the nation's most respected living war hero. Over the years, he had served as commander of the Combined Fleet and chief of the navy's general staff before retiring in favor of politics. "He was the consummate samurai," as one historian observed, "a proud, noble, clean-living warrior respected by almost everyone from the lowliest peasant to the Emperor as a sterling example of Japanese manhood."

Beyond the battlefield, Suzuki had served as the grand chamberlain to the emperor, developing such a rapport with Hirohito that the monarch often referred to him as *oyaji* or uncle. "To Suzuki," Hirohito said, "I could pour out my heart." With a wrinkled brow and a thick moustache, Suzuki appeared less a warrior than a grandfatherly figure, a practicing Taoist who enjoyed reading Laotse, the famed Chinese philosopher whose classic *Tao Te Ching* was one of many works that filled his extensive twenty-thousand-volume personal library.

Though the public adored the former hero, Suzuki's moderate views had made him a target in the 1936 coup in which he had miraculously survived being shot four times in the head, chest, shoulder, and groin—a surgeon had to pluck a bullet from one of his testicles. His brush with death had scarred Suzuki both physically and emotionally. When his son offered to serve as his private secretary, he refused. "Don't accompany me to death," he warned him. "I have come a long way but you still have far to go."

On April 5, 1945, Marquis Koichi Kido, a close confidant of the emperor and the lord keeper of the privy seal, pulled Suzuki aside during a dinner with the *jûshin*. The next prime minister would have to assemble a cabinet that could at last put the nation on the road to peace. "Japan's situation has become so critical," Kido said, "that I, as Lord Keeper of the Privy Seal, must implore you to make a firm decision to save the nation."

The waffling Suzuki met at ten p.m. with Hirohito, where he again protested the assignment, citing his advanced age, poor hearing, and weak grasp of the politics.

"Your unfamiliarity with politics is of no concern, nor does it matter that you are hard of hearing," Hirohito assured him. "Therefore, accept this command."

Suzuki, at last, did as ordered.

CHAPTER 11

"When the last Japanese division has surrendered unconditionally, then only will our fighting job be done."

—PRESIDENT HARRY TRUMAN

MAY 8, 1945

On May 7, 1945, Truman at last moved into the White House.

It had taken Eleanor Roosevelt and the White House staff six days to pack up twelve years of her family's life. Ushers had gone room by room, pulling down paintings from the walls, carefully wrapping ship models and photographs, and boxing books by the crate. Over Roosevelt's four terms in office, the family had accumulated so much that movers required a convoy of twenty army trucks. Eleanor stopped by Blair House as she departed on April 18 to thank the Trumans—and to warn them their new home was in shambles.

And she was right.

The next day Bess and Margaret Truman visited with assistant chief usher James West. "The White House upstairs is a mess," Margaret complained in her diary. "I was so depressed when I saw it." Much of the furniture was worn, while dust coated the walls, which had faded to reveal the outline of picture frames. Sagging drapes often failed to match the furniture. "What little was left," West recalled, "gave it the appearance of an abandoned hotel."

"How much redecorating can we do?" Bess asked.

"Actually," West replied, "you'll be able to do quite a lot."

Over the next few weeks, Bess worked with West and a Kansas City decorator, who arrived each morning armed with fabric swatches and paint samples. The Trumans shipped much of their Connecticut Avenue furniture back to Missouri, opting instead to use the provided tables, chairs, and mirrors. The exception was Margaret's baby grand piano, which had to be hoisted through a second-floor window. Movers likewise swapped Roosevelt's hospital gurney for an antique four-poster bed. Staffers dusted and reupholstered furniture as others painted and hung new drapes. When it was finished, Truman inspected. "When you think of all the great men who've lived in this house," he said, "you can't help but feel a sense of awe."

The president woke up on May 8—his sixty-first birthday—for the first time in the White House. But he had more to celebrate than just his birthday. Only eight days earlier Hitler had retreated to his private study in his underground bunker, pressed the barrel of his Walther PPK to his right temple, and squeezed the trigger. The last of the enemy's resistance crumbled. The Allies planned to broadcast news of Germany's surrender to the world at nine a.m. Before doing so, however, Truman took a moment to pen a letter to his mother. "This will be a historical day," he wrote. "Hostilities will cease on all fronts at midnight tonight. Isn't that some birthday present?"

Truman headed to his office at eight-thirty a.m., joined by Bess and Margaret. Others gathered for the historic occasion ranged from Chief of Staff Leahy, General Marshall, and Admiral King to members of the cabinet and congressional leaders, including Speaker of the House Sam Rayburn and Kenneth McKeller, the president pro tempore of the Senate.

"You're forty years old!" McKeller announced.

"Yes," Truman replied, "forty years old—plus!"

"Happy birthday, Mr. President," McKeller added.

"All right," Truman said. "We are ready."

Aides opened the doors at 8:35 a.m., allowing in a stampede of 123 reporters. "Good morning," Truman said. "I sure made you all get up this morning, didn't I?"

The reporters laughed.

"All in," one of the president's aides announced.

Truman proceeded to brief the press pool, alerting them that the news was embargoed until nine a.m. He then read aloud his remarks, which he would momentarily broadcast to the nation. As soon as he finished, the reporters dashed for the door, anxious to phone in the news. In the mad scramble, the United Press reporter Merriam Smith tripped and broke his arm.

"Did you ever see such a rush," McKeller declared.

"Each one's afraid the other is going to beat him to the punch," Truman replied.

The president then proceeded to the Diplomatic Reception Room, where his predecessor had delivered his fireside chats. Promptly at nine a.m., Truman began his historic broadcast, informing the public via a roughly seven-hundred-word address that the war against Germany was at long last over. Most already knew, as the Associated Press had leaked the news the day before, which had sent thousands into the streets to celebrate. But Truman's word served as the official confirmation. "This is a solemn but a glorious hour. I only wish Franklin D. Roosevelt had lived to witness this day," the president began. "The flags of freedom fly all over Europe."

But the fight, as Truman warned, was far from over.

"Our victory is but half-won. The west is free, but the east is still in bondage to the treacherous tyranny of the Japanese," the president continued. "The job ahead is no less important, no less urgent, no less difficult than the task which now happily is done. I call upon every American to stick to his post until the last battle is won."

Truman then read a second statement, which totaled less than two hundred words. This one served as a warning to the miliary leaders of Japan, who would now suffer the full force of American might. "The Japanese people have felt the weight of our land, air and naval attacks," he began. "So long as their leaders and the armed forces continue the war, the striking power and intensity of our blows will steadily increase and will bring utter destruction to Japan's industrial war production, to its shipping, and to everything that supports its military activity.

"The longer the war lasts," he continued, "the greater will be the suffering and hardships which the people of Japan will undergo—all in vain. Our blows will not cease until the Japanese military and naval forces lay down their arms in unconditional surrender."

What does unconditional surrender mean? Truman asked.

"It means the end of the war," he continued.

"It means the termination of the influence of the military leaders who have brought Japan to the present brink of disaster," the president declared. "It means not prolonging the present agony and suffering of the Japanese in the vain hope of victory. Unconditional surrender does not mean the extermination or enslavement of the Japanese people."

In big cities and small towns, Americans tuned in as the president's twangy midwestern accent crackled over the nation's airwaves. In war plants and factories, administrators piped the speech over the public address systems for workers while students congregated in cavernous school auditoriums to hear the news. Elsewhere people paused on the street as radios trumpeted the news from corner drugstores and in restaurants and hotel lobbies. Ailing Gen. John "Blackjack" Pershing, the American commander during World War I, tuned in at Walter Reed Hospital. So did the president's mother from her home in Missouri. According to the Columbia Broadcasting System, Truman scored an audience rating of 64.1, a record-breaking figure that totaled more than 36 million people. That bested the previous high of 59.6, which was Roosevelt's famous speech to Congress 1,247 days earlier, after the attack on Pearl Harbor.

Official word of Germany's defeat sparked a renewed celebration among many. Half a million people surged into New York's Times Square, including scores who knelt in prayer as confetti rained down. Across the nation, stores closed while churches opened their doors for worshipers. Trolley bells clanged and ship horns blared. The brownout ended, prompting the Statute of Liberty to once again shine over New York Harbor.

But the euphoria was tempered by the fact that the fight still raged in the Pacific, a fact Stimson highlighted in his diary. "It was not a day of exuberance or hysterical demonstrations," he wrote, "but rather of sober satisfaction and of pulling in the belt for further effort." Half a world away American soldiers and Marines battled the Japanese on the island of Okinawa while B-29 bombers in the skies overhead continued to burn the enemy's cities. "The war is not over," as one sign reminded shoppers in Syracuse. "Remember Pearl Harbor."

The Marines on Okinawa understood that better than anyone. "Nazi Germany," as one said, "might as well have been on the moon." The war correspondent Gordon Cobbledick, who reported from the frontlines, contrasted the celebration of victory over Germany with the scene that unfolded before him that day on Okinawa, where he witnessed a frightened and shell-shocked Marine break down. "Oh, Jesus, I can't stand it anymore," the youth howled. "I can't stand it."

Flame tanks torched Japanese pillboxes, Cobbledick reported, while ambulances filled with bloodied Americans bounced over coral roads. "Some stared into space through eyes that were dull with the look of men to whom nothing mattered greatly. Some screamed with pain that the morphine couldn't still. And some lay very quiet under ponchos that covered their faces," he concluded. "It was V-E Day, but on Okinawa the forests of white crosses grew and boys who had hardly begun to live died miserably with the red clay of this hostile land."

CHAPTER 12

"Can Japan see that she, like ancient Carthage and modern Germany, is doomed?"

—*HONOLULU ADVERTISER*
MAY 11, 1945, EDITORIAL

The Target Committee reconvened at nine a.m. on May 10, 1945—two days after Truman's radio address to the nation—in Oppenheimer's office at Los Alamos. Several of the project's senior scientists joined the meeting, including Dr. Hans Bethe, who ran the Theoretical Division, and Dr. Robert Brode, whose team developed the bomb's fuse. The thirteen items on the agenda that Thursday morning ranged from the psychological factors behind target selection to the coordination of air operations and the ultimate delivery of the bomb.

The seven-page meeting minutes summarize the discussions, which began with the determination of what altitude each bomb should be set to explode. This was a critical issue. If the bomb detonated too low, the ground would absorb much of the energy and restrict the potential blast radius. On the flip side, if the weapon exploded too high, much of the energy would disperse into the air. "All we would produce," Groves explained, "would be a spectacular pyrotechnical display which would do virtually no damage at all."

The challenge was that no one yet knew how big an explosion either bomb would produce. Scientists conservatively estimated that Little Boy might produce a comparable explosion in the range of 5,000 to 15,000 tons of TNT. "For this weapon." Groves said, "the corresponding desirable height of detonation would vary then from 1,550 feet to 2,400 feet." Fat Man, by contrast, was expected to produce a smaller blast, ranging from 700 to 5,000 tons of TNT. "This would require," the general added, "detonating heights between 700 feet and 1,500 feet." Given the uncertainty, the committee decided that fuses should have four different altitude settings: 1,000, 1,400, 2,000, and 2,400 feet. "With present information," the panel agreed, "the 1,400 feet fuse would be most likely to be used for both the Fat Man and the Little Boy."

The group next turned to the challenge of the weather: "For this we should be prepared to wait until there is a good weather forecast in one or more of three alternative targets." Estimates showed that there was only a 2 percent chance that this would require a wait longer than two weeks. "When the mission does take place," the committee agreed, "there should be spotter aircraft over each of the three alternative targets in order that an alternative target may be selected in the last hour of flight if the weather is unpromising over the highest priority target."

Despite such precautions, the possibility existed that the aircrew might find the primary and alternative targets obscured. In that case, the group decided, the bomber should plan to return to base and make a normal landing under the watchful eye of fire and rescue personnel. Such an operation posed a risk, but the committee believed the chance of a crash detonating the weapon was small. If the plane proved unable to land for any reason, Fat Man could be jettisoned from a low altitude in shallow water. "Extreme care would have to be exercised," Groves said. "Under no circumstances should it be jettisoned near American-held territory." Little Boy, however, was a challenge, as water leakage would trigger a nuclear reaction. "The best emergency procedure that has so far been proposed," the committee concluded, "is considered to be the removal of the gun powder from the gun and the execution of a crash landing."

The committee next looked at targets.

The previously established criteria mandated that the target be a large urban area of more than three miles in diameter, capable of being damaged by the blast, and unlikely to have been destroyed by August. Based on those prerequisites, the group zeroed in on five of the original seventeen target cities. At the top of the list was Kyoto, the ancient capital of

Japan, which had a population of one million. The burning of so many other cities had prompted Japan to start moving industries into the area. "From the psychological point of view," the committee agreed, "there is the advantage that Kyoto is an intellectual center for Japan and the people there are more apt to appreciate the significance of such a weapon."

Hiroshima stood second on the list. The city in southwestern Honshu served as an important army depot and port of embarkation for troops, all in the middle of a sizable urban industrial area. The city's many waterways had made it a poor choice for an incendiary attack, which meant that it had so far been spared the damage of other cities. Hiroshima's adjacent hills likewise would produce a focusing effect, which would amplify the blast.

The third potential target was Yokohama, which like Hiroshima had so far been spared, despite the fact that the city played a critical role in Japan's production of planes, machine tools, electrical equipment, and oil. The destruction of its neighbor Tokyo meant that many of those industries had relocated to Yokohama, which only increased its value as a military target. Yokohama's drawback, however, was the concentration of antiaircraft guns.

Kokura was the fourth potential target. Home to one of the largest arsenals in Japan, the city housed light ordnance, antiaircraft shells, and beach defense materials. The fifth and final possible target was Niigata, a port city on the northwest coast that had grown increasingly valuable as bombers destroyed other waterfront areas. In addition to the port, Niigata was home to machine tool industries and oil refineries. "The possibility of bombing the Emperor's palace was discussed," the minutes state. "It was agreed that we should not recommend it but that any action for this bombing should come from authorities on military policy."

Of the five targets, the committee ultimately scratched Niigata, ranking the remaining four in order of importance as Kyoto, Hiroshima, Yokohama, and Kokura. The committee decided to request reservations on the targets, meaning the air force would be prohibited from bombing them. Members also sought additional target data, including photo reconnaissance, related to specific industries and exact locations. Other requests centered on the nature of the construction, the area, and the heights, contents, and roof coverage of buildings.

Atomic weapons offered American leaders a great psychological tool—the ability to shock Japan's leaders. That was made evident following the March destruction of Tokyo, a fire raid that had caused tremendous loss of life and property damage but failed to bring about any change in the war. The initial use of an atomic bomb therefore needed to be "sufficiently spectacular." "In this respect," the group agreed, "Kyoto has the advantage of the people being more highly intelligent and hence better able to appreciate the significance of the weapon. Hiroshima has the advantage of being such a size and with possible focusing from nearby mountains that a large fraction of the city may be destroyed. The Emperor's palace in Tokyo has a greater fame than any other target but is of least strategic value."

Oppenheimer presented a memo stating that to avoid radioactivity, no aircraft should be within two and a half miles of the point of detonation. "To provide against blast effects," Groves added, "a distance of five miles was advisable." Though an incendiary mission right afterward would benefit from the destruction of fire and rescue services, the group decided it should be avoided until more was known about radioactive clouds. In the meantime, members of the 509th Composite Group would begin training that summer in the Pacific using mock atomic weapons, referred to as pumpkins. "It was agreed by all," the minutes concluded, "that very complete rehearsals of the entire operation are essential to its success."

The Target Committee reconvened two weeks later at nine a.m. on May 28, 1945, at the Pentagon. General Farrell announced that generals Groves and Arnold had concluded that control of the atomic weapon would remain with Washington and not the commander in the Pacific. Too few people, Groves felt, appreciated the gravity of the bomb. "This was too complicated and all-important a matter," he said, "to be treated so casually."

Col. Paul Tibbets, Jr., commander of the 509th Composite Group, joined the Monday meeting to review the rehearsal program and give an update on the training of the aircrews. After four months, he said, the initial twenty-one crews had been reduced to fifteen. Each bombardier, he added, had made at least fifty practice bomb releases at altitude with most having made between eighty and one hundred. Crews likewise had practiced radar bombing. To simulate the mission, crews had taken off with a gross weight of 135,000 pounds, flown 4,300 miles with a 10,000-pound bomb load, and then dropped it at 32,000 feet and returned to base.

At this third and final meeting, the committee adjusted the potential targets one last time, albeit only slightly. Yokohama came off the list, replaced by Niigata.

The four final targets were Kyoto, Hiroshima, Kokura, and Niigata.

Given the accelerated pace of America's bombing campaign, it was imperative to block those cities from attack. Orders went out to Hap Arnold, Navy Pacific Fleet Cmdr. Admiral Chester Nimitz, and Gen. Douglas MacArthur, supreme commander of Allied forces in the Southwest Pacific. "Kyoto, Hiroshima, Kokura, and Niigata will not—repeat—not be attacked by any forces under your command unless further directions are issued by the Joint Chiefs of Staff," the top-secret directive mandated. "Knowledge of the above instructions will be limited to the minimum number of persons essential to carry out the instructions."

With the targets decided, Groves sat down to prepare a proposed operational plan for General Marshall's approval. On a visit to the Pentagon on May 30, 1945, Stimson asked if he had completed his plan for the first-ever atomic attack. Groves confirmed but added he had not yet had a chance to proof it. "I want to be sure," he said, "I've got it just right."

"I would like to see it," the war secretary insisted.

Groves was reluctant to step outside the chain of command, afraid General Marshall might object. He stalled, noting that the plan was in his office across the river.

"I have all day," Stimson replied, pointing to the phone on his desk.

The general blinked.

"Call your office," Stimson said, "and have them bring that report over."

Groves made one last objection, arguing that since the plan involved a military operational matter, Marshall as chief of staff should review it first.

"This is one time I'm going to be the final deciding authority," Stimson declared. "Nobody's going to tell me what to do on this. On this matter, I am the kingpin."

Groves did as ordered. As the general stewed waiting on the report's arrival, Stimson asked what cities the committee had selected. Groves rattled off the list.

"I don't want Kyoto bombed," Stimson protested.

The war secretary, who had visited Kyoto when he served in the Philippines, explained that it was too important a cultural and religious site to be destroyed, one that might engender decades of resentment and handicap postwar efforts to remake Japan.

Groves pushed back, pointing out that it had a population of one million people. Armed with his report, which just arrived, he added that the city had 26,446,000 square feet of known factory floor area with another 19,496,499 square feet of suspected war industry. "The city's peacetime industries had all been converted to war purposes and were producing, among other items, machine tools, precision ordnance and aircraft parts, radio fire control and gun direction equipment," Groves recounted. "The industrial district occupied an area of one by three miles in the total built-up area of two and one-half by four miles."

But Stimson still balked, opening the door that separated his office from General Marshall's. "If you're not busy," he asked, "I wish you'd come in."

The chief of staff appeared.

"Marshall," Stimson began, "Groves has just brought me this report on the proposed targets. I don't like it. I don't like the use of Kyoto."

General Marshall read the target description for each of the four cities. "He did not express too positive an opinion, though he did not disagree with Mr. Stimson," Groves said. "It was my impression that he believed it did not make too much difference either way."

Groves left in a huff.

"I particularly wanted Kyoto as a target because, as I have said, it was large enough in area for us to gain complete knowledge of the effects of an atomic bomb," he said. "Hiroshima was not nearly so satisfactory in this respect. I also felt quite strongly, as had all the members of the Target Committee, that Kyoto was one of the most important military targets in Japan."

CHAPTER 13

"It is clear that the president still finds it difficult to realize he is president."

—EBEN AYERS
MAY 26, 1945, DIARY ENTRY

The situation with Russia continued to deteriorate.

After his confrontation with Molotov, Truman had initially been proud of himself as he recounted the story for Joseph Davies, the former ambassador to the Soviet Union. "I gave it to him straight. I let him have it," he bragged. "It was the straight one-two to the jaw."

But beneath the bluster the inexperienced president doubted himself. "Did I do it right?" he sheepishly asked.

Davies hedged, which was enough for Truman to know he had erred.

"What should be done?" the president asked. "What can I do?"

"Your conference with Molotov commanded their respect," Davies replied. "You must now command their confidence in our good will and fairness."

Poland remained the central challenge—and Truman's tirade did nothing to sway Stalin. The Soviet leader stood firm in his belief that for its own security, Russia should be able to influence the future government of its neighbor. "I am ready to fulfill your request and do everything possible to reach a harmonious solution, but you demand too much of me," Stalin cabled Truman after his meeting with Molotov. "In other words, you demand that I renounce the interests of security of the Soviet Union, but I cannot turn against my country."

Stalin's stonewalling dimmed any hope of an easy solution. "We were making very little headway," the president acknowledged, "over the explosive Polish question."

A breakdown in relations between the three Allies on the eve of victory could prove calamitous, a fear Truman and Churchill both shared.

But Churchill's worries ran deeper. The British prime minister saw Poland as a symbol of Russia's efforts to dominate Europe in the wake of the war. The collapse of the Third Reich, which had steamrolled across much of the continent, meant that other previously conquered countries would face similar challenges over future governance, particularly as American troops prepared to fall back to previously agreed-upon occupational lines. That would leave vast swaths of Europe under Stalin's control. Much to Churchill's alarm, the Russians had already set up a provisional government in Austria. Other countries risked being swept up in a "tide of Russian domination," including Germany, Czechoslovakia, Bulgaria, Romania, Yugoslavia, and the Baltic provinces. Many of Europe's great capitals—Berlin, Vienna, Budapest, Belgrade, and Bucharest—would fall under Russian control. "This would be an event," Churchill cabled Truman, "which, if it occurred, would be one of the most melancholy in history."

This threat made it imperative to set the right precedent over Poland.

Churchill's fears only magnified when he learned that America had begun to transfer troops out of Europe to join the fight against Japan. "Anyone can see that in a very short space of time our armed power on the Continent will have vanished except for moderate forces to hold down Germany. Meanwhile what is to happen to Russia?" he pleaded with Truman. "An iron curtain is drawn down upon their front. We do not know what is going on behind."

Unlike Churchill, Truman had his own concerns over Russia.

Stalin had previously agreed to join the fight in the Pacific three months after Germany's defeat, a time frame that would allow him to move an additional thirty divisions to the Far East, to make a total of sixty divisions. He would likewise need to build up a three-month reserve of supplies, given the limited capacity of the Trans-Siberian Railroad. Truman now counted on those Russian forces to tie down the 713,000 Japanese troops in Manchuria and prevent them from reinforcing the homeland when American troops hit the beaches of Kyushu later that year. "As our forces in the Pacific were pushing ahead, paying a heavy toll in lives, the urgency of getting Russia into the war became more compelling," the president wrote. "Russia's entry into the war would mean the saving of hundreds of thousands of American casualties."

In expectation of that help, America had launched Project Milepost, a top-secret supply mission to send everything from food and fuel to locomotives and ships to Russia to prepare for the invasion. Stalin had provided the United States a shopping list calculated to maintain a force of 1.5 million troops equipped with 5,000 planes and 75,000 motor vehicles, including 3,000 tanks. Over the course of many months, no less than 171 ships steamed the Pacific, ultimately carrying 1,252,385 tons of clothing and medicine, barbed wire, and explosives. The secret supply mission dovetailed with Project Hula, a plan to train Russian sailors in how to operate American ships in Cold Bay, Alaska. Some 12,000 Russian officers and men would pass through the secret base before taking command of 149 minesweepers, subchasers, frigates, and landing craft. Despite America's generosity, many still feared Russia might wait and let America battle Japan, only to come in at the end of the war to reap the rewards.

Given the stakes, it was important Truman deftly manage relations.

So far, he wasn't. But the brouhaha with Molotov was only one setback.

On May 8—just as the first Milepost supply ships departed for Russia—Foreign Economic Administrator Leo Crowley and Under Secretary of State Joseph Grew came to see Truman with a proposed order for him to sign. The duo explained that with Germany defeated, America should cut back on wartime supplies provided to Allies, a program known as Lend-Lease. "What they told me made good sense to me; with Germany out of the war, Lend-Lease should be redecided," Truman recalled. "They asked me to sign it. I reached for my pen and, without reading the document, I signed it. The storm broke almost at once."

Germany was out of the war, but Russia was not.

And Stalin had been counting on those supplies.

Crowley immediately placed an embargo on all shipments to Russia and other European nations, a move that led some ships already at sea to be rerouted back to port. The order hurt the British the worst, but the ever-suspicious Stalin assumed it was aimed at him, particularly given the impasse over Poland. The president rescinded the order, but the damage had been done. "The Russians complained about our unfriendly attitude," Truman said. "We had unwittingly given Stalin a point of contention which he would bring up every chance he had."

Given the deadlock and all the tensions, Churchill suggested the three Allied leaders meet in person, possibly in an unburned city in Germany. Truman agreed, recognizing that he needed to practice face-to-face diplomacy rather than continue to manage relations by cable, but he preferred not to meet until after America's June 30 fiscal year ended.

In the meantime, the president prepared to send envoys ahead to sit down with the two world leaders. "It was imperative for me to know whether the death of Roosevelt had brought any important changes in the attitudes of Stalin and Churchill," Truman said. "I wanted personal, on-the-spot reports from men with judgment and experience."

To meet with Churchill, he tapped Davies, the former Soviet ambassador. "Davies was not well. In fact, when I saw how drawn he looked, I was hesitant to make such great demands upon him," Truman said. "But he waived any consideration of his health and agreed to go." For Russia, he turned to Harry Hopkins, whom he had had in mind for such a task since the two talked on the train ride back from Roosevelt's funeral. "Why don't you send Harriman back on a special mission," Hopkins had suggested, "since he is already our ambassador there?"

But Truman disagreed; so did Harriman, who felt Hopkins was a better choice given his relationship with Stalin as well as his symbolic link to Roosevelt. Hopkins's health, as always, was bad, but he agreed to go. Truman cabled the news to Stalin. "I am sure you are as aware as I am of the difficulty of dealing by exchange of messages with the complicated and important questions with which we are faced," he wrote. "Pending the possibility of our meeting I am therefore sending Mr. Harry Hopkins with Ambassador Harriman to Moscow in order that they may have an opportunity of discussing personally with you these matters."

Hopkins stopped by the White House for instructions before he departed. Truman's message was the same as he had told Molotov—Stalin needed to follow through on his commitments. "I made it plain to Hopkins," he said, "that in talking to Stalin he was free to use diplomatic language or a baseball bat if he thought that was the proper approach."

Davies met with Churchill for a total of eight hours between May 26 and May 29 at the prime minister's country house Chequers as well at 10 Downing Street. Given the portly prime minister's notoriously nocturnal schedule, one meeting ran from eleven p.m. until four-thirty a.m. Another took place while the seventy-year-old Churchill languished in bed. Churchill's greatest fear was the withdrawal of American troops from Europe—and he was nothing if not dramatic. "He would be equally great in a courtroom, on the stage, or in any intellectual or fighting field," Davies reported to Truman. "He was at his oratorical and powerful best."

Churchill, who Davies added appeared "tired, nervous, and obviously under great stress," played the victim, framing England as abandoned amid a swarm of Russian forces. "England, he proclaimed, would stand her ground alone, if she had to," Davies wrote. "England was not a negligible factor in world affairs. England could still protect herself."

Truman's envoy dismissed Churchill's fears. "The Prime Minister is one of the greatest men of our time, and the greatest Englishman of this or any other time, in my opinion. But he is first and foremost an Englishman," he reported. "I could not escape the impression that he was basically more concerned over preserving England's position in Europe than in preserving peace."

Davies told Churchill that no American president could justify leaving massive amounts of troops in Europe after the war's end and hope to keep his job. He furthermore warned Churchill that his hostility toward Russia carried real risks. "His attitude," Davies cautioned, "placed not only the future, but possibly the immediate peace in real danger."

Hopkins was equally as blunt in his six meetings with Stalin, which took place at the Kremlin between May 26 and June 6. Despite standing just five feet, four inches tall, the sixty-six-year-old Russian premier, who sported a bushy moustache, exuded strength. "Stalin is impressive—he speaks with force, a good voice and a strong body," one senior Pentagon official observed in his diary. "He is intelligent and tactful. He is aware of his own power and position." To this bear of a leader, the small and cadaverous Hopkins delivered a deathly warning: The American public's

The flag-draped remains of President Franklin Roosevelt are transferred from a funeral train to a caisson at Washington's Union Station on the morning of April 14, 1945. *(NARA)*

Inside the White House Cabinet Room, Harry Truman recites the oath of office to become the nation's thirty-third president at 7:09 p.m. on April 12, 1945. *(NARA)*

A young Harry Truman rides on the back of a cultivator on his family farm in 1910. *(Truman Library)*

Captain Harry Truman, who served as an artillery officer, writes at his desk during World War I in France. *(Truman Library)*

After World War I, Harry Truman briefly owned a men's haberdashery in Kansas City with an army friend before the economy soured, forcing them out of business. *(Truman Library)*

On October 4, 1934, Harry Truman, perched in the back of a truck, delivers a campaign speech in Sikeston, Missouri, in his run for the U.S. Senate. *(Truman Library)*

On August 18, 1944, Harry Truman enjoys lunch with President Franklin Roosevelt under the shade of a magnolia tree on the White House lawn shortly after he was chosen to join the ticket as the vice presidential candidate. *(NARA)*

Japanese Emperor Hirohito, pictured here on horseback in 1932, served as the center of Japanese political, cultural, and spiritual life. *(NARA)*

Major General Leslie Groves was a driving force behind the top-secret Manhattan Project, which developed the first-ever atomic bombs. *(NARA)*

Dr. Robert Oppenheimer was tasked to oversee the Manhattan Project's top-secret weapons lab in Los Alamos, New Mexico, where scientists worked to design and build the atomic bomb. *(NARA)*

Dr. Leo Szilard, a Hungarian physicist who helped spur America to develop the atomic bomb, later became a fierce opponent of the weapon's use. *(NARA)*

Oak Ridge, Tennessee, was the largest of America's three top-secret atomic cities, and accounted for half of the bomb's $2 billion price tag. *(NARA)*

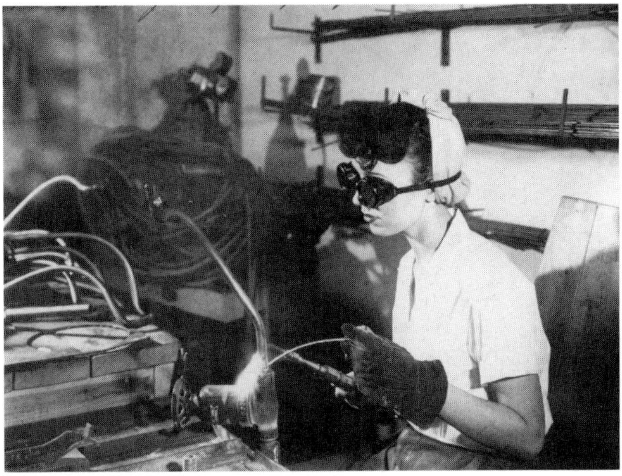

At its peak, Oak Ridge, Tennessee, was home to 75,000 men, women, and children, like this welder, who worked on the Manhattan Project. *(NARA)*

Residents of the atomic cities enjoyed diversions, like this game of baseball, played at Hanford, Washington, where workers created plutonium. *(NARA)*

Harry Truman and Secretary of State Jimmy Byrnes enjoy some fresh air on the deck of the U.S.S. *Augusta* en route to Europe for the Allied conference at Potsdam, Germany, in July 1945. *(NARA)*

President Truman took time while onboard the *Augusta* to eat lunch with the ship's crew. *(NARA)*

Harry Truman met British Prime Minister Winston Churchill for the first time at Potsdam. *(NARA)*

War Secretary Henry Stimson, pictured here outside the White House, was an instrumental force behind the Manhattan Project. *(NARA)*

President Truman, Secretary of State Jimmy Byrnes, and Admiral William Leahy tour the wreckage of Berlin in July 1945. *(NARA)*

Winston Churchill, Harry Truman, and Joseph Stalin met at Potsdam to discuss how best to end World War II and plan for the postwar era. *(NARA)*

Truman talks with Soviet Foreign Minister Vyacheslav Molotov, whose tough negotiating tactics earned him the nickname "Iron Pants." *(NARA)*

For the first-ever test of an atomic weapon, codenamed Trinity, workers built a small base camp in the remote desert of New Mexico that resembled a frontier town. *(NARA)*

The first atomic bomb, which was hoisted atop this one hundred-foot-tall tower in the New Mexico desert, was successfully tested on the morning of July 16, 1945. *(NARA)*

At 5:29 a.m. on July 16, 1945, scientists detonated the first-ever atomic bomb in the remote desert of New Mexico. *(NARA)*

opinion of Russia had plummeted in the last six weeks over the issue of Poland. The struggle had become symbolic of whether the nations, which had worked together well throughout the war, could continue to do so in a time of peace.

Stalin reiterated his security concerns, noting that Germany had twice invaded via Poland, a horrific experience neither England nor America had endured. "These German invasions were not warfare but were like the incursions of the Huns," he said. "In these circumstances either Poland had been too weak to oppose Germany or had let the Germans come through. Thus Poland had served as a corridor for the German attacks on Russia."

In regard to the Pacific, Stalin said Russia would be ready to enter the war against Japan on August 8, precisely three months after the defeat of Germany, which was news Truman wanted to hear. Hopkins asked if Stalin favored forcing Japan to accept unconditional surrender. The Russian ruler confirmed, adding that he felt Japan needed to be occupied and the position of emperor eliminated. A war of this magnitude, he added, could happen only once in a hundred years. "It was better to take advantage of it," he said, "and utterly defeat Japan."

Unconditional surrender meant that Japan would have to be destroyed militarily, which could be costly. The only way to avoid that, he suggested, would be to accept a conditional surrender and then use a harsh occupation to weed out the anti-Western sentiment that plagued the military. "In other words," Stalin said, "unconditional surrender by stages."

Stalin agreed to meet Truman and Churchill in the German city of Potsdam, a suburb of Berlin. Truman suggested July 15 for a meeting; the others agreed. In his report afterward, Ambassador Harriman praised Hopkins for his finesse with the Russian premier. "He is a realist in all of his actions, and it is hard for him to appreciate our faith in abstract principles," Harriman wrote. "It is difficult for him to understand why we should want to interfere with Soviet policy in a country like Poland which he considers so important to Russia's security unless we have some ulterior motive. He does, however, appreciate that he must deal with the position we have taken."

CHAPTER 14

"Japan is on the verge of terrible punishment."

—DEWITT MACKENZIE,
ASSOCIATED PRESS WAR ANALYST
MAY 10, 1945

The first meeting of the Interim Committee kicked off at nine-thirty a.m. on May 9, 1945, in Henry Stimson's fifth-floor office at the Pentagon. The president had approved of the committee's creation during his April 24 Oval Office meeting with Stimson and Groves, the day he first learned of the Manhattan Project. Unlike the Target Committee, which focused on which cities to destroy, Stimson's group would handle policy, ranging from drafting postwar legislation to preparing White House news releases to inform the public about the bomb. But the committee, as Groves explained, had a larger purpose: to send a message to the American public and to world leaders that the decision to use atomic weapons had been made not solely by the War Department but by individuals far removed from the influence of men in uniform.

The unique task assigned to each committee dictated its membership. The Target Committee was made up of military leaders and Manhattan Project scientists, while the Interim Committee consisted of eight civilians. Stimson served as chairman, joined by George Harrison, president of New York Life Insurance Company, who would be his deputy and moderate in his absence. Jimmy Byrnes, who would take over as secretary of state in July, would likewise assist, shuttling back and forth between his native South Carolina and Washington, where he resided at the Shoreham Hotel and had briefings at night from State Department chiefs. Stimson made a point of alerting the others that Truman had designated Byrnes as his personal representative. "The membership," as historian Richard Rhodes noted, "was thus put on notice that Byrnes enjoyed special status and that his words carried extra weight."

Other members included Dr. Vannevar Bush, Under Secretary of the Navy Ralph Bard, Assistant Secretary of State William Clayton, MIT president Dr. Karl Compton, who also served with the Office of Scientific Research and Development, and Dr. James Conant, president of Harvard and chairman of the National Defense Research Committee. Neither General Marshall nor General Groves was a member, but minutes show both were invited at times to sit in on the sessions. Groves, in fact, attended them all and at times contributed to the discussion, though he understood his role. "There was never any question in my mind or the minds of any members of the committee," he said, "that they were the jury and I was a witness."

The inaugural meeting that Wednesday would be the first of eight sessions—totaling a little more than twenty-eight hours—that would take place over the next sixty-one days. The purpose of the committee, as outlined in the invitation to members, was to study and report on war controls and publicity and later make recommendations on postwar research, development and controls, and legislation to effectuate them. The letter made no mention that the committee likewise would debate and recommend whether America should use atomic bombs against Japan, though that ultimately would become its defining purpose. "All subjects were open and there were no holds barred," recalled the committee's secretary, Second Lt. Gordon Arneson. "Everyone was free to speak on whatever he wanted to talk about."

The three-page minutes show that Stimson began by outlining both the Manhattan Project and the role of the committee. "It was termed an 'Interim Committee,'" the war secretary said, according to the minutes, "in view of the fact that, at the proper time, Congress would probably establish by law a permanent body to supervise, regulate, and control the entire field."

Stimson read aloud the twenty-three-page memo Groves had initially used to brief Truman, followed by the Quebec Agreement signed by Roosevelt and Churchill. "The Committee strongly expressed the view," the minutes state, "that all possible steps should be taken as promptly as possible to build up our supplies of uranium and thorium."

The group reconvened five days later on May 14, 1945, during which time members agreed to create a scientific panel made up of Robert Oppenheimer, Ernest Lawrence, Enrico Fermi, and Arthur Compton, the latter three all Nobel laureates. Lawrence ran the Radiation Laboratory at the University of California at Berkeley, which focused on electromagnetic separation, while the University of Chicago's Fermi was the first to build a nuclear reactor that served as the basis for Hanford. The foursome would no doubt help guide the committee on scientific matters, but the panel was also designed as a response to the rising frustration of some scientists, who wanted a voice in the decision over whether the bomb should be used. This group would serve as a conduit for those individuals.

Karl Compton, whose brother had agreed to serve on the Scientific Panel, was acutely aware of the political need to allow the project's experts to be heard. "The scientists," Compton said, "feel a very strong sense of responsibility for having brought this thing into being and that their future cooperation on the one hand or their criticism on the other hand will be affected by the decisions which are reached and particularly by the opportunity which they may be given to express their points of view." Others on the committee agreed. "The Scientific Panel," the minutes state, "should be free not only to discuss technical matters but also to present to the Committee their views concerning political aspects of the problem."

To craft press releases for the Manhattan Project, the committee tapped William Laurence, the Pulitzer Prize–winning science reporter for *The New York Times* who was under contract to prepare a history of the project. On Laurence's immediate horizon was the first test of an atomic weapon, which was planned for July at Alamogordo Bombing Range in New Mexico, some two hundred miles south of Los Alamos. If the first test yielded poor results, Laurence would write a short release announcing that a munitions dump had exploded. But if the bomb proved a success—as the scientists predicted—a more robust news release would eventually be necessary. "Such a statement," the minutes concluded, "should be made by the President and should indicate the general nature of the weapon, trace the history of its development and of the controls, both national and international, that are contemplated."

The Scientific Panel joined the committee's ten a.m. meeting on May 31, which was also attended by Marshall and Groves. For the benefit of the new guests, Stimson began that Thursday morning session in the Pentagon by again outlining the committee's history and purpose. The war secretary emphasized that it was important for everyone to understand that this was more than just a new bomb in the nation's arsenal. Though developed for the war, the implications and responsibilities of the new technology would carry long past the enemy's eventual defeat. "This project should not be considered simply in terms of military weapons, but as a new relationship of man to the universe. This discovery might be compared to the discoveries of the Copernican theory and of the laws of gravity, but far more important than these in its effect on the lives of men," the war secretary said. "It must be controlled if possible to make it an assurance of future peace rather than a menace to civilization."

The group discussed the future of atomic weapons, noting that over time the bombs would only grow stronger. The weapons were currently expected to create an explosion comparable to between 2,000 and 20,000 tons of TNT, Oppenheimer said, but scientists could eventually produce one that rivaled 100 million tons. "As I heard these scientists," Byrnes confessed, "I was thoroughly frightened. I had sufficient imagination to visualize the danger to our country when some other country possessed such a weapon." It was important, members agreed, to build stockpiles of nuclear materials, keep the industrial plants intact, and open the door for industrial development. Oppenheimer noted that atomic research was already well known around the world. The United States might be wise to offer the free interchange of information with an emphasis on the development of peacetime uses. "The basic goal of all endeavors in the field should be the enlargement of human welfare," he said. "If we were to offer to exchange information before the bomb was actually used, our moral position would be greatly strengthened."

The United States needed a better understanding, Stimson replied, of the nonmilitary potentials of nuclear fission before it could consider such an exchange. An international body would likely be needed, one with the power to perform inspections.

But what kind of inspections would be effective, the war secretary continued, and how would democratic governments handle totalitarian regimes? "Everyone recognized," recalled Arneson, "that there would be a very serious problem of adequate inspections."

The critical concern, of course, was the Soviet Union.

Russia had been friendly to science, Oppenheimer noted, so it might be worth a general approach without revealing any details. "We might say that a great national effort had been put into this project and express a hope for cooperation with them in this field," the physicist suggested. "We should not prejudge the Russian attitude in this matter."

Marshall spoke up, covering the military's wartime experience of working with the Russians, which at times consisted of charges and countercharges, most of which turned out to be bogus. He favored building a coalition of like-minded nations, which would put pressure on Russia to fall in line. Marshall even suggested inviting a couple of prominent Russian scientists to attend the July atomic test. "The seemingly uncooperative attitude of Russia in military matters," the general added, "stemmed from the necessity of maintaining security."

Byrnes, by contrast, pushed back. As the incoming secretary of state and confidant of Truman, he knew the administration's concerns over Russia and its efforts to dominate Poland and other neighbors, including Hungary and Romania. Furthermore, the veteran congressman and senator understood the bare-knuckle reality of domestic politics to know many lawmakers would not be happy to learn America gave away $2 billion in atomic secrets to a questionable ally. Given the Quebec Agreement, which Byrnes also did not like, he feared Russia would demand a similar status as the British. "If information were given to the Russians, even in general terms," he warned, "Stalin would ask to be brought into the partnership."

Not even the British, Bush noted, had access to the blueprints for the uranium and plutonium plants. Byrnes's interjection appeared to end any talk of atomic cooperation with the Soviets. "The most desirable program," the committee concluded, "would be to push ahead as fast as possible in production and research to make certain we stay ahead and at the same time make every effort to better our political relations with Russia."

The group adjourned for lunch at 1:15 p.m. In the Pentagon dining room, where members sat at adjoining tables, the debate continued. "Throughout the morning's discission," Compton recalled, "it seemed to be a foregone conclusion that the bomb would be used."

That prompted the mustachioed Compton, seated to Stimson's left, to ask whether it might be possible for America to conduct a demonstration of the bomb, so as to impress on the Japanese the need to surrender without killing thousands of civilians.

Stimson tossed the question out to the group, which sparked a spirted discussion. Oppenheimer doubted any demonstration might be spectacular enough to convince the Japanese to surrender. Other concerns likewise arose. What if the Japanese shot down the B-29 or brought American prisoners of war to the proposed bomb site? "If we were to warn the Japanese of the new highly destructive weapon in the hope of impressing them," Byrnes argued, "and if the bomb then failed to explode, certainly we would have given aid and comfort to the Japanese militarists." Stimson agreed. "Nothing would have been more damaging to our effort to obtain surrender," the war secretary wrote, "than a warning or a demonstration followed by a dud—and this was a real possibility. Furthermore, we had no bombs to waste."

At a minimum, Groves believed, a demonstration would eliminate the element of surprise that America had worked so hard to preserve and that would be needed to shock the Japanese into surrender. "A nation fighting for its very existence," he noted, "doesn't give up that easily." He pointed to Confederate General Robert E. Lee, who fought for two years after his defeat at Gettysburg. The Germans likewise battled on after Stalingrad. Such a move, Groves felt, would only lead the Japanese to doubt America's determination to force them into submission. "Our failure to use the bomb," he said, would be seen "as a sign of weakness."

"Various possibilities were brought forward," concluded Compton, who had initiated the debate. "One after the other it seemed necessary they should be discarded."

When members reconvened an hour later—and went back on the

record—the focus remained on Japan, specifically the enemy nation's will to fight.

How would, someone asked, a nuclear attack differ from a fire raid?

Oppenheimer jumped on the question, describing for the group what it would look like at the exact moment an atomic weapon detonated in the heavens over Japan. "The visual effect of an atomic bombing would be tremendous," he replied. "It would be accompanied by a brilliant luminescence which would rise to a height of 10,000 to 20,000 feet. The neutron effect of the explosion would be dangerous to life for a radius of at least two-thirds of a mile."

The committee reviewed various types of targets, discussed the expected effects, and debated whether America should warn Japan before it unleashed an atomic inferno on its homeland. "After much discussion," the minutes state, "the secretary expressed the conclusion, on which there was general agreement, that we could not give the Japanese any warning; that we could not concentrate on a civilian area; but that we should seek to make a profound psychological impression on as many of the inhabitants as possible."

Conant suggested a desirable target would be a vital war plant surrounded by worker housing. Would it be wise, someone else asked, to execute multiple simultaneous atomic strikes? a question that Groves addressed. Multiple bombs, the general said, risked making the mission appear to the Japanese more like a regular air force raid than a unique operation. In addition, assembling multiple bombs would require a rush job on the part of technicians, which could lead to errors. "We would lose the advantage," the general concluded, "of gaining additional knowledge concerning the weapon at each successive bombing."

The meeting concluded with a discussion about the frustration of some of the project's scientists. The hub of discontent was the Metallurgical Laboratory at the University of Chicago, where scientists had worked to develop the first nuclear reactor. With Hanford in operation—and work winding down in Chicago—scientists had time to consider the consequences of atomic weapons. That had led to a range of concerns from whether the bomb should be used to the possibility that America might trigger an arms race. The questions raised by some had, in fact, been one of the factors that had led to the creation of the Interim Committee, even though it infuriated Groves. "The program," he complained, "has been plagued since its inception by the presence of certain scientists of doubtful discretion and uncertain loyalty."

But what could the committee do at this point?

Nothing, the members concluded, at least until after the bomb had either been used against Japan or tested in the New Mexico desert. "After some publicity concerning the weapon was out," the committee agreed, "steps should be taken to sever these scientists from the program and to proceed with a general weeding out of personnel no longer needed."

The political motivation behind the creation of the panel—to provide upset scientists a voice—was evident in the minutes during the closing discussion about what the four physicists should tell fellow colleagues. "The scientists should be permitted to explain that they had met with this Committee and had been given complete freedom to present their views on any phase of the subject," the minutes state. "The impression should definitely be left with their people that the Government was taking a most active interest in this project."

The committee met again on June 1, 1945, with generals Marshall and Groves once again in attendance. Similar to the Scientific Panel, the committee invited four business leaders whose companies had served as critical contractors. Attendees included Westinghouse president George Bucher, DuPont president Walter Carpenter, Union Carbide vice president James Rafferty, and James White, president of Tennessee Eastman. These men addressed another key concern for Byrnes: how long it might take for Russia to develop atomic weapons. The industrialists estimated that Russia, suffering from a lack of recourses as well as skilled and educated labor, would take years to catch up. "I concluded," Byrnes said, "that any other government would need from seven to ten years, at least, to produce a bomb."

Only two days earlier, the Target Committee had held its final meeting, identifying four Japanese cities worthy of attack. The question remained: What would the Interim Committee recommend? Driving the debate was Byrnes, who knew of the planned invasion of the Japanese homeland. He understood that the heavy casualties that troops had suffered on Okinawa would worsen once troops hit the beaches of Kyushu. "Under these circumstances," he said, "it was certainly essential to end the war as soon as possible and avoid the invasion."

That sentiment motivated the incoming secretary of state. "Byrnes felt," as Secretary Arneson recalled, "that it was important there be a final decision on the question of the use of the bomb." Even though there was no written mandate for the committee to make such a decision, Byrnes understood that an order to wipe out an enemy's cities with atomic weapons would be scrutinized, just as some of the project's scientists where already doing. For a new and untested president, a decision from a committee of civilians to drop the bomb would no doubt give important political cover and send a message to the public and the world.

The question before the committee was first: Would America use the atomic bomb?

And if so, when and how?

The minutes of the afternoon session do not record any debate, only that Byrnes made the recommendation. The other seven committee members, who had gathered in executive session in Harrison's office, all agreed. "The present view of the Committee," the minutes state, "was that the bomb should be used against Japan as soon as possible; that it be used on a war plant surrounded by workers' homes; and that it be used without prior warning."

Byrnes met with the president that afternoon to share the news. "Mr. Truman told me," Byrnes recalled, "he had been giving serious thought to the subject for many days, having been informed as to the investigation of the committee and the consideration of alternative plans, and that with reluctance he had to agree that he could think of no alternative and found himself in accord with what I told him the Committee was going to recommend."

Stimson followed five days later, sitting down with Truman on the one-year anniversary of the D-Day invasion. The war secretary announced he was trying to rein in the air force's firebombing campaign, which night after night incinerated Japan's cities. "I was anxious about this feature of the war for two reasons," he said, "First, because I did not want to have the United States get the reputation of outdoing Hitler in atrocities; and second, I was a little fearful that before we could get ready the Air Force might have Japan so thoroughly bombed out that the new weapon would not have a fair background to show its strength."

Stimson walked the president through the Interim Committee's recommendations, noting the desire to hold off on sharing any information with Russia until the bomb had first been used against Japan. This might, Stimson feared, cause some complication when Truman met next with Churchill and Stalin at the upcoming Allied conference planned for Potsdam. For that reason, Truman replied, he had pushed the start of the conference back to July 15. If the Russians for any reason brought up the atomic program and wanted to be included as partners, Stimson encouraged the president to take the same approach Stalin aways did. "Namely to make the simple statement," he said, "that as yet we were not quite ready to do it."

Despite his apprehension over fire raids, Stimson agreed with Byrnes that the atomic bombs were necessary. "The committee's function was, of course, advisory," he recalled after the war. "The ultimate responsibility for the recommendation to the President rested upon me, and I have no desire to veil it. The conclusions of the committee were similar to my own, although I reached mine independently. I felt that to extract a genuine surrender from the Emperor and his military advisers, they must be administered a tremendous shock which would carry convincing proof of our power to destroy the Empire. Such an effective shock would save many times the number of lives, both American and Japanese, that it would cost."

Japan was now in the bull's-eye.

CHAPTER 15

"I personally thought that using the bomb against the cities of Japan would be a great mistake."

—DR. LEO SZILARD

MAY 22, 1956

Leo Szilard was once again agitated.

Exceedingly so.

With a little help from Albert Einstein, the pudgy Hungarian physicist had launched America down the nearly six-year, $2 billion road to the atomic bomb. And now, like Dr. Victor Frankenstein, he feared the monster he had helped create.

Szilard had become the de facto leader of the project's concerned scientists who had caught the attention of the Interim Committee. The physicist was no doubt the one who Groves had in mind when he referenced individuals of "doubtful discretion and uncertain loyalty."

The burly general had long despised the outspoken Szilard, who had bristled from the start over what he viewed as the military's authoritarianism and rigid security protocols. Groves, who initially saw Szilard as a disruptive force who could sidetrack the important work of his colleagues, had increasingly begun to question the scientist's loyalty, a suspicion that was likely reinforced by his Hungarian accent. "He was a parasite," Groves once said of Szilard, "living off the brains of others." The general went so far in October 1942 as to draft a letter to the attorney general. "It is considered essential for the prosecution of the war," he wrote, "that Mr. Szilard, who is an enemy alien, be detained for the duration of the war."

Stimson, however, had balked at signing the unconstitutional order. "This was the answer I expected," Groves admitted, "but I thought that there was no harm in trying." The tenacious general, however, instead marginalized his foe, ordering Szilard tailed by investigators and his mail read. "Few enemies," Groves griped, "were causing us as much trouble."

The physicist who had first predicted the potential of atomic bombs had once again peered into the future and feared what those weapons might mean for America.

Szilard outlined his concerns on September 21, 1942, in an eleven-page paper he distributed to his colleagues at the University of Chicago's Metallurgical Laboratory.

"What Is Wrong with Us?" he had boldly titled it.

Szilard's fear centered on postwar controls of atomic weapons. "One has to visualize a world in which a lone airplane could appear over a big city like Chicago, drop his bomb, and thereby destroy the city in a single flash," he wrote. "Not one house may be left standing and the radioactive substances scattered by the bomb may make the area uninhabitable for some time to come." The physicist's solution was for his colleagues to take a more active role in shaping the policy of atomic weapons. "Perhaps," he concluded, "it would be well if we devoted more thought to the ultimate political necessities which will rise out of our present work."

Szilard's concerns had only magnified as the months turned to years and the bomb's reality appeared a certainty. Unlike many of his colleagues, who ultimately relocated to Los Alamos, Groves ordered Szilard left behind in Chicago. "Nobody could think straight in a place like that," he huffed. "Everybody who goes there will go crazy."

On January 14, 1944, Szilard wrote to Vannevar Bush, arguing that work on the bomb should speed up. The American public needed to see the destructive force of such a bomb in order to be prepared to make the necessary sacrifices to guarantee a lasting peace, which could include seizing the world's uranium deposits by force. "This weapon will be so powerful," he warned, "that there can be no peace if it is simultaneously in the possession of any two powers unless these two powers are bound by an indissoluble political union."

With Germany's defeat inevitable, Szilard's views began to change. "What is the purpose of continuing the development of the bomb," he wondered, "and how would the bomb be used if the war with Japan has not ended by the time we have the first bomb?"

Like other émigré scientists from Europe, Szilard had focused solely on the horror of Hitler. "He had been willing to approve and even to urge the use of the bomb against the Germans, for in this case it would be an evil less than that of the human destruction he felt sure would result if the Nazis should gain the victory," observed Arthur Compton. "He could not persuade himself that the case was the same with regard to the Japanese."

In short, destroying Germany with atomic weapons was justified.

But destroying Japan was not.

By early 1945, Szilard decided that the only person who could help was President Roosevelt, to whom he had first reached out in 1939. He set his concerns down on paper, crafting a three-page letter in which he outlined his fear of an arms race between the United States and Russia. The costs of the weapons would decrease while the power of the bombs would increase. This, he feared, would boomerang on the United States, which was uniquely vulnerable given the density of many cities. "Most of our major cities," he wrote on March 25, 1945, "might be completely destroyed in one single sudden attack and their populations might perish."

Szilard's answer was to refrain from using the bomb until a system of controls was developed. Scientists likewise should have a seat at the policy table. "This situation," he demanded, "can be evaluated only by men who have first-hand knowledge of the facts involved, that is, by the small group of scientists who are actively engaged in this work."

The physicist once again turned to his friend Albert Einstein, who, with the aid of Eleanor Roosevelt, helped him secure a meeting with the president on May 8, 1945. With his appointment in hand, Szilard went to see Compton, the director of the Metallurgical Laboratory. Szilard shared his memo with his boss, expecting that he would be scolded.

"I hope," Compton replied to his surprise, "that you will get the President to read this."

Szilard returned to his office when a knock on the door brought news that Roosevelt had died. "There I was now with my memorandum, and no way to get it anywhere."

The physicist enlisted the aid of a Kansas City associate to help secure an appointment with Truman. He then traveled to Washington accompanied by his friend Dr. Walter Bartkey, the associate director of the Metallurgical Laboratory. The two physicists arrived at the White House on May 25, 1945. Szilard handed Einstein's cover letter and the memo he had prepared to Truman's appointment secretary, Matt Connelly, who reviewed the materials.

"I see now this is a serious matter," Connelly said. "At first I was a little suspicious, because this appointment came through Kansas City. The President thought that your concern would be about this matter, and he has asked me to make an appointment with you with James Byrnes, if you are willing to go down to see him in Spartanburg, South Carolina."

Szilard replied that he was happy to travel. Connelly picked up the phone to make the appointment. Would it be all right, Szilard asked, if he also brought Dr. Harold Urey, a Nobel laureate chemist working on the Manhattan Project at Columbia University?

He could bring whomever, Connelly replied.

The following day the three scientists boarded a Southern Railway train at Union Station for an overnight trip to South Carolina, unknowingly trailed by one of Groves's investigators. Szilard, who did not know Byrnes would soon take over as secretary of state or that he served on the Interim Committee, was left to wonder why Truman had sent him south to see a former politician living as a private citizen in South Carolina. As the train lumbered south across Virginia, the three physicists discussed a plan. "We were concerned about two things: we were concerned first about the role which the bomb would play in the world after the war, and how America's position would be affected if the bomb were actually used in the war," Szilard recalled. "We were also concerned about the future of atomic energy, and about the lack of planning as to how this research might be continued after the war."

The scientists stepped off the train on May 28, 1945, just four days before the Interim Committee would unanimously decide that Japan should be bombed as soon as possible and with no warning. Szilard and his colleagues walked the mile and a half from the station to Byrnes's home on Otis Boulevard, a quiet tree-lined street in the upscale Converse Heights neighborhood. The men climbed the front steps of a two-story brick home, where the former congressman, senator, and Supreme Court justice welcomed them into his living room.

Byrnes was not unaware of Szilard's concerns, having been briefed in advance by Truman. Szilard handed Byrnes Einstein's letter and his memo, which he read. The physicist then said he feared that if America used the bomb against Japan, it would only encourage Russia to seek to become an atomic power and kick-start an arms race.

"General Groves tells me there is no uranium in Russia," Byrnes interjected.

Szilard corrected him, stating that there was a limited amount of rich uranium ore in Czechoslovakia, which Russia could access. He added that a nation the size of Russia was also likely to have low-grade uranium. As a result, it would be a mistake for America to use the bomb before adequate protocols had been established. "Once the bomb has been tested and shown to go off," he cautioned, "it would not be possible to keep it a secret."

If America did not test the weapon, Byrnes countered, people would conclude it had failed. It was imperative, after spending $2 billion of taxpayer money, to prove the value of that investment. "How would you get Congress to appropriate money for atomic energy research," he continued, "if you do not show results for the money which has been spent already?"

Szilard conceded that point.

According to Szilard's account, Byrnes then highlighted his concern over Russia's postwar behavior, pointing out that Stalin's troops were in Hungary and Romania. "Russia," he said, "might be more manageable if impressed by American military might."

The comment floored Szilard.

"Well, you come from Hungary," Byrnes added, according to the physicist, "you would not want Russia to stay in Hungary indefinitely."

"I certainly didn't want Russia to stay in Hungary indefinitely, but what Byrnes said offended my sense of proportion," Szilard later wrote. "I was concerned at this point that by demonstrating the bomb and using it in the war against Japan, we might start an atomic arms race between America and Russia which might end with the destruction of both countries. I was *not* disposed at this point to worry about what would happen to Hungary."

Byrnes, by contrast, made no mention of Russia in his recollection of the meeting. "Szilard," he wrote, "complained that he and some of his associates did not know enough about the policy of the government with regard to the use of the bomb. He felt that scientists, including himself, should discuss the matter with the Cabinet, which I did not feel desirable."

It is not hard to understand why Szilard's demand might have been poorly received by Byrnes. The physicist, whose pushy arrogance had a way of offending people, had in short told the nation's incoming secretary of state that neither he nor other senior American leaders were bright enough to grasp the reality of the bomb and therefore needed the help of scientists. Byrnes may not have held a doctorate in physics, but he had served at the highest levels of the legislature and judiciary and had even come within a whisper of being Roosevelt's heir.

Szilard had overstepped his bounds. He and other scientists had been tasked to build a weapon. If, when, how it was used would fall to senior military commanders and civilian leaders, namely the president and commander in chief. "His general demeanor," Byrnes said, "and his desire to participate in policy making made an unfavorable impression on me."

Byrnes showed the scientists out. "I was rarely as depressed as when we left Byrnes's house and walked toward the station," he said. "I thought to myself how much better off the world might be had I been born in America and become influential in American politics, and had Byrnes been born in Hungary and studied physics. In all probability there would have been no atomic bomb, and no danger of an arms race between America and Russia."

Despite his frustration, Szilard had, in fact, achieved his goal. He had wanted to bring his concerns to the attention of America's top leaders—and he had done so in the living room of Truman's confidant and the future secretary of state. Furthermore, the arguments he presented—and those of his colleagues at the Metallurgical Laboratory—had, in fact, made it onto the agenda of the Interim Committee, where the civilian members with the help of senior project scientists had debated the issues. Szilard's irritation, however, stemmed from the fact that senior officials did not agree with him. He failed to understand that while he may not have wanted to see the bomb used in combat, others including Stimson, Byrnes, and Truman did.

Szilard stopped off in Washington to see Oppenheimer, who had arrived to attend the Interim Committee. During a meeting on May 30, 1945, Szilard said it would be a mistake to use an atomic bomb against Japan, a view Oppenheimer did not share.

"The atomic bomb is shit," Oppenheimer added, according to Szilard's recollection.

"What do you mean by that?" the Hungarian asked.

"This is a weapon which has no military significance," Oppenheimer continued. "It will make a big bang—a very big bang—but it is not a weapon which is useful in war."

That said, Oppenheimer added it was important to inform the Russians that America had developed the bomb and planned to use it rather than surprise them with it.

But Szilard did not think that went far enough.

"Well," Oppenheimer concluded, "don't you think that if we tell the Russians what we intend to do and then use the bomb in Japan, the Russians will understand?"

"They'll understand it only too well," he replied.

CHAPTER 16

"We believe that these considerations make the use of nuclear bombs for an early, unannounced attack against Japan inadvisable."

—FRANCK REPORT
JUNE 12, 1945

Szilard, of course, was not the only concerned scientist.

Arthur Compton returned to the Metallurgical Laboratory after the June 1 Interim Committee meeting and sat down the following day with the scientists. The committee, he said, was open to additional input. Any concerns should be put in a report. Compton said he was leaving on June 14 and would like any suggestions to be turned into him by then so he could submit them. Inside the lab, Dr. James Franck chaired a committee on the social and political implications of atomic energy. The sixty-two-year-old German physicist and Nobel laureate, who had served on Oppenheimer's doctoral exam committee, had fled Nazi Germany in 1933. Others on Franck's committee included doctors Donald Hughes, Jame Nickson, Eugene Rabinowitch, Glenn Seaborg, Joyce Stearns, and of course, Leo Szilard.

Franck and his team jumped at the opportunity. "By an accident of history, we were among a very few who were aware of a new, world-threatening peril," Seaborg recalled. "We felt obligated to express our views." Members spent the next nine days hammering away on a report. Franck, who spent many sleepless nights walking the Midway, began drafting the report but struggled with the language, prompting him to eventually turn his notes over to Rabinowitch to complete it. "While the authorship of the whole report was mine," he said, "the fundamental orientation was due above all to Leo Szilard and James Franck."

The committee turned in its final report on June 11, 1945. Unlike Szilard's earlier memo to the president, which totaled just three pages, the committee's nearly five-thousand-word report spanned sixteen. Szilard's fingerprints were all over it. The brief echoed the same fears he had shared in his earlier memo, citing the vulnerability of American cities. "All of us," the group wrote, "live with the vision before our eyes of sudden destruction visited on our own country, of a Pearl Harbor disaster, repeated in thousandfold magnification, in every one of our major cities." Such a threat, the scientists argued, would require a radical redesign of American cities so as to scatter the population and industry. "If no efficient international agreement is achieved," the report added, "the race of nuclear armaments will be on in earnest not later than the morning after our first demonstration of the existence of nuclear weapons."

The best way to prevent an arms race was to refrain from dropping the bomb in combat, which the scientists derided as too weak to make a difference in the outcome of the war. "It is doubtful," the report stated, "whether the first available bombs, of comparatively low efficiency and small size, will be sufficient to break the will or ability of Japan to resist, especially given the fact that the major cities like Tokyo, Nagoya, Osaka and Kobe already will largely be reduced to ashes by the slower process of ordinary serial bombing."

The group instead advocated that America perform a demonstration of the bomb for representatives of the United Nations in either the desert or on a barren island.

"You see what weapon we had but did not use," America would be able to state, according to the report. "We are ready to renounce its use in the future and to join other nations in working out adequate supervision of the use of this nuclear weapon."

The military could afterward—with the approval of the United Nations and the American public—use the weapon against Japan. In an effort to counter Byrnes's earlier statement on the need to validate the expenditure of so much taxpayer money, the scientists argued that the public would understand that it is sometimes desirable to develop a weapon and keep it in readiness for use only in extreme emergency. The reputational harm to the nation, the panel added, outweighed the potential lives saved. "The military advantages and the saving of American lives achieved by the sudden use of atomic bombs against Japan," the report concluded, "may be outweighed by the ensuing loss of confidence and by a wave of horror and repulsion, sweeping over the rest of the world and perhaps, dividing even public opinion at home."

On June 12, 1945, Arthur Compton wrote a two-page letter to Stimson to accompany the report, outlining the concerns of the scientists in Chicago. The report had not yet been reviewed by other members of the Scientific Panel, he noted, but that would occur in a few days. The panel would write a report in response. "In the meantime," Compton said, "because time is short for making the necessary decisions, I have personally taken the liberty of transmitting this memorandum to you for the consideration of your committee."

Compton highlighted the main point of the report. "The proposal is to make a technical, but not a military demonstration, preparing the way for a recommendation by the United States that the military use of atomic explosives be outlawed by firm international agreement," Compton wrote. "It is contended that its military use by us now will prejudice the world against accepting any future recommendation by us that its use be not permitted."

The director singled out two important considerations that the scientists omitted. The first was that failure to use the bomb could make the war last longer and prove more costly in human lives. Second, absent the bomb, America would likely squander the opportunity to "impress the world with the need for national sacrifices in order to gain lasting security."

The scientists wanted Franck to deliver his report in person. Compton agreed to accompany him. In Washington, the men met with Interim Committee secretary Gordon Arneson on June 12, 1945. According to Compton, Arneson told them Stimson was out of town, though he would not actually leave for vacation for several more days. Three days later Arneson discussed the report with Stimson's deputy George Harrison, the same day the war secretary left for a holiday at Highhold, his hundred-acre estate on Long Island.

"This report," Harrison said, "really ought to be examined and commented upon by the Scientific Panel before the Interim Committee is asked to express its views."

Oppenheimer invited Compton, Lawrence, and Fermi to spend that weekend at Los Alamos to discuss the report. Should America attempt a technical demonstration of the bomb or use the weapon in combat? That was the exact question that Interim Committee members had, in fact, already discussed and ruled out, but the panel agreed to reexamine the issue. The four physicists felt pressure from all sides. In addition, over them hung the reality that without the bomb, American troops faced what promised to be a bloody invasion. "We were determined to find, if we could, some effective way of demonstrating the power of an atomic bomb without loss of life that would impress Japan's warlords," Compton said. "If only this could be done!"

One by one, each member gave up such hope.

Lawrence held out the longest, but in the end he too caved. "Experience with the determination of Japan's fighting men," Compton conceded, "made it evident that the war would not be stopped unless these men themselves were convinced of its futility."

The bomb, the four agreed, offered that potential.

The physicists drafted a one-page response. The Scientific Panel recommended that before the use of the bomb, America should alert Britan, Russia, France, and China and ask for future cooperation in making the development of atomic energy contribute to improved international relations. "The opinions of our scientific colleagues on the initial use of these weapons are not unanimous; they range from the proposal of a purely technical demonstration to that of the military application best designed to induce surrender," the panel wrote. "We find ourselves closer to these latter views; we can propose no technical demonstration likely to bring an end to the war; we see no acceptable alternative to direct military use."

The Interim Committee reconvened on June 21, 1945, to review the report. "The committee," the minutes state, "reaffirmed the position taken at the 31 May and 1 June meetings that the weapon be used against Japan at the earliest opportunity, that it be used without warning, and that it be used on a dual target, namely, a military installation or war plant surrounded by or adjacent to homes or other buildings most susceptible to damage."

CHAPTER 17

"The progress of the war in Okinawa, to my regret, makes me believe that it is destined inevitably to result in a miserable fiasco."

—LORD KEEPER OF THE PRIVY SEAL MARQUIS KOICHI KIDO

JUNE 8, 1945, DIARY ENTRY

Armed with a recommendation from the Interim Committee—and with the first test of the bomb planned for July—Truman set out to decide the best option for how to win the war. Should he order Japan's cities destroyed with atomic weapons?

What about an invasion of the enemy's homeland?

Should America blockade Japan and continue firebombing cities?

Or would Japan's defeat come from a combination of some or all of these options?

The president directed Leahy to gather the Joint Chiefs for an Oval Office meeting on the afternoon of June 18, 1945. The sole topic on the agenda: the war against Japan.

Leahy fired off a memo to senior military leaders. The president required a breakdown of the soldiers and ships needed for an invasion as well as the time required and an estimate of American casualties. For comparison, Truman wanted similar figures if he chose to blockade Japan and pummel it with sea and air forces. What role would Russia play? How about other Allies? "It is his intention to make his decisions on the campaign with the purposes of economizing to the maximum extent possible in the loss of American life," Leahy concluded. "Economy in the use of time and in money cost is comparatively unimportant."

In short, saving American lives—not money—was Truman's goal.

Since the summer of 1944, American strategists had begun developing plans for the invasion of the Japanese homeland. Code-named Operation Downfall, the plan was twofold. The first part, known as Olympic, called for landing in November 1945 on the southern island of Kyushu. Unlike Okinawa, Kyushu was a sprawling island—Japan's third largest—covering more than fourteen thousand square miles, making it thirty times larger than Okinawa. A mountain range split the island, walling off the southern half, which was the objective of the United States. To take Kyushu, the United States planned an armada of three thousand ships, including twenty-seven heavy and light aircraft carriers, twenty-two battleships, and more than five hundred cruisers and destroyers, along with thousands of troop transports, minesweepers, and service ships. These forces would be backed up by 1,850 land-based fighters and bombers plus another two thousand carrier planes. Under the protection of this sea- and airpower, the United States planned to land fourteen divisions—eleven army and three marine—a force double the size of the Normandy invasion.

Olympic would be followed in the spring of 1946 by an invasion of the Kanto Plain called Coronet. The six-thousand-square-mile lowland on the main island of Honshu was home not only to 18 million people but to half of Japan's major war industries, much of them centered in cities of Tokyo, Kawasaki, and Yokohama. The invasion would dwarf Kyushu, requiring twenty-five divisions in what would prove the largest amphibious operation of the war.

The question that hung over any proposed invasion—and that was forefront in Truman's mind—was just how costly such a fight would be for America.

If history demonstrated anything, it would be bloody.

Over the course of the war, American forces had grown accustomed to the battlefield ferocity of the Japanese, a characteristic solidified during the November 1943 capture of Tarawa in the Gilbert Islands. On that tiny atoll eight thousand miles from Tokyo—a coral speck smaller than New York City's Central Park—Japan's nearly five thousand defenders fought to the death, suffering a 99.7 percent fatality rate. The seventy-six-hour battle cost America 3,407 dead and wounded, creating such a pervasive stench of rot that mortuary teams were forced to wear gas masks. "You could not dig a grave for a body," one recalled, "without exposing another body." So horrific was the fight that *Time* magazine labeled the island "one square mile of hell."

But Tarawa had proved only the beginning.

As American forces closed in on the Japanese mainland—and the ability to bypass islands vanished—the bloodletting had only escalated. Beginning in June 1944, a month that saw American forces storm the beaches of both France and Saipan, the United States experienced what the army later characterized as a "casualty surge." The surge consisted of a year of violence in which the army suffered an average of 65,000 killed or wounded each month, a figure that did not include losses from sickness or disease, which were considerable given the prevalence of dysentery, malaria, and dengue in the Pacific. Those numbers likewise did not include the heavy losses suffered by the navy or the marines. The army's casualties had peaked in December 1944, when the nation recorded a staggering 88,000 dead and wounded.

The calamitous casualties reflected the gruesome battles that had defined the last year of the war, combat accentuated by fanatical banzai charges, mass civilian suicides, and of course, terrifying kamikaze attacks, monsoons of metal and flesh that rained down on American warships. That began with the June 1944 invasion of Saipan in the Mariana Islands. The bloody twenty-four-day battle included the largest Japanese banzai charge of the war, in which soldiers fought hand to hand, killing 4,300 enemy troops in a span of hours. That was followed by the mass suicides of hundreds of Japanese civilians, many of whom jumped from cliffs into the ocean. "It's just the damnedest feeling deep in your stomach when you see somebody die like that," remembered one American sailor, "especially women and young kids, babies even." The brutality even stunned Lt. Gen. Holland Smith, the marine commander of the ground forces. "It was war such as nobody had fought before," he wrote, "a campaign in which men climbed, crawled, clubbed, shot, burned and bayonetted each other to death."

But Saipan paled compared to the fight that awaited the marines in

February 1945 on Iwo Jima, an eight-square-mile volcanic rock devoid of fresh water and that stank of sulfur. Islands like Tarawa and Saipan had taught the Japanese valuable lessons that would shape the war's remaining battles. The goal was no longer victory but attrition. As such, troops swapped wasteful suicide charges and beach defenses for fortified caves, digging eleven miles of tunnels through the lunar landscape. The thirty-six-day fight, which cost America 27,000 dead and wounded, was the only battle where the United States suffered more casualties than the Japanese. The reporter Robert Sherrod, who stumbled over a string of intestines, recounted the grisly scene. "Along the beach," he wrote, "lay many dead. About them, whether American or Jap, there was one thing in common. They died with the greatest possible violence. Nowhere in the Pacific war have I seen such badly mangled bodies. Many were cut squarely in half."

The Japanese demonstrated similar defensive skill during the Battle of Manila, which occurred alongside Iwo Jima. The urban fight proved particularly instructive as it gave war planners the best approximation of what a battle inside Tokyo, Osaka, or Nagoya might involve. Some seventeen thousand enemy troops had fortified the Philippine capital, using land mines, overturned trucks, and railroad axles sunk upright into the pavement to block more than fifty intersections. The Japanese converted modern concrete-and-steel-reinforced buildings into fortresses, barricading passageways and forcing American soldiers to fight room by room through university halls, hotels, and even the Rizal Memorial Stadium. The twenty-nine-day battle not only flattened 613 blocks of the former Pearl of the Orient but left an estimated one hundred thousand civilians dead, many of them massacred by the Japanese. "If anything should happen to Tokyo," one American general wrote afterward to his wife, "the Japanese have asked for it."

These battles set the stage for the climactic showdown on Okinawa, which had begun on April 1, 1945, twelve days before Truman ascended to the presidency. For the Japanese, it was a pivotal fight. Barely four hundred miles south of the mainland, Okinawa served as the final stepping stone before American troops reached Japan's shores. Kamikazes, which had first appeared in the Philippines during the Battle of Leyte Gulf in late 1944, swarmed like hornets. The Japanese executed 1,900 kamikaze attacks that destroyed thirty-six ships and damaged another 368. Thirteen carriers, ten battleships, and five cruisers were among those hit. The Japanese even targeted the hospital ship *Comfort*. All told, the navy suffered 9,731 casualties, including 4,900 killed, the majority in kamikaze attacks. That figure amounted to one-seventh of the navy's entire losses for the war. "They would come in at you in such numbers and so low that you could see the expressions on the faces of the pilots," recalled one sailor. "It was awful to see the guys who got burnt in the fires these planes set off. They looked like charcoal logs."

The battle on shore proved equally as horrendous, as evidenced by the twenty-four Medals of Honor that would eventually be awarded. "We were surrounded by maggots and decay," recalled Eugene Sledge, a marine. "Men struggled and fought and bled in an environment so degrading I believed we had been flung into hell's own cesspool." The eighty-two-day fight proved to be the bloodiest single battle of the Pacific war, second only to the Battle of the Bulge. Nearly a quarter-million people died, including 107,539 Japanese troops. Of the nearly 50,000 American casualties, 12,274 were killed. The United States suffered another 26,000 nonbattle injures, the majority due to combat fatigue, the largest for any single battle in the war. Civilians paid a tremendous price with nearly 150,000 killed, a figure that amounted to nearly one out of every three of the island's inhabitants. "Every single person," recalled Maj. Art Shaw, "who survived the battle for Okinawa knew they were lucky to still be alive."

The American public was stunned at such violence.

"Please for God's sake, stop sending our finest youth to be murdered," one distraught mother wrote to the Navy Department in the wake of Iwo Jima. "Why can't objectives be accomplished some other way? It is most inhuman and awful—stop, stop!"

Many others questioned what it meant for the invasion of the enemy's homeland. "If it took almost three months to conquer Okinawa," asked *The New York Times*, "how much life, treasure and time must we expend to conquer Kyushu and Honshu?"

That was the question uppermost in Truman's mind.

Each service had its own solution for how best to end the war. General Marshall and the army supported an invasion, a position reinforced by the fact that airpower alone had proved unable to bring an end to the war in Europe, forcing troops to charge ashore on the beaches of France. Admiral King and the navy, in contrast, advocated a strategy of continued blockade coupled with bombardment, which would strangle Japan. B-29s had recently joined the submarine service in that fight as part of Operation Starvation, the navy's efforts to mine the empire's waters. Over 1,529 sorties, Superfortresses would plant 12,053 mines into the waters of Japan, China, and Korea and ultimately sink or disable 431 ships.

General Arnold and his senior air commanders believed that the city-burning campaign would eventually bring Japan to its knees. LeMay, in fact, expected to run out of cities to burn by October 1, 1945, one month before the proposed invasion of Kyushu. And of course, there was always the atomic bomb—though it was still a yet-to-be-proven solution. That was the option favored by Stimson and Groves, the latter of whom was anxious to justify the extraordinary taxpayer expense of the Manhattan Project. Stimson, in contrast, believed the bomb had the greatest chance to shock Japanese leaders into surrender. "The atomic bomb was more than a weapon of terrible destruction," he noted, "It was a psychological weapon."

These were the competing viewpoints Truman had to wade through to make a decision. The president's diary shows that he recognized the task before him. "I have to decide Japanese strategy—shall we invade Japan proper or shall we bomb and blockade?" he wrote. "That is my hardest decision to date. But I'll make it when I have all the facts."

At three-thirty p.m. on June 18, 1945, members of the Joint Chiefs marched into the Oval Office. Around the room that Monday afternoon sat Marshall, King, Stimson, Assistant Secretary of War John McCloy, Navy Secretary James Forrestal, and Lt. Gen. Ira Eaker, who represented General Arnold, currently in the Marianas for a conference with LeMay. Brig. Gen. Andrew McFarland took notes. Truman stated that he wanted to be informed about the campaign against Japan, as was spelled out in Leahy's memo.

The president first asked Marshall his opinion. The situation, the general said, was practically identical with the one that preceded the invasion of Normandy. To best capture his views, Marshall referred to a nineteen-page memo he had brought with him, drafted by the Joint Staff planners, titled "Details of the Campaign Against Japan." American air and sea power, he explained, had slashed Japanese shipping south of Korea and would within the next few months reduce it to a trickle, if not choke it off completely. That rendered pointless any need to seize positions south of Korea. Both Gen. Douglas MacArthur and Adm. Chester Nimitz, who had spearheaded the planning for Operation Downfall, had agreed with the Joint Chiefs on a November 1 target date for the invasion of Kyushu. By then, American bombers would have destroyed every industrial target in Japan as well as most cities. "The Japanese Navy, if any still exists, will be completely powerless," Marshall said. "Our sea action and air power will have cut Jap reinforcement capabilities from the mainland to negligible proportions."

Important considerations bearing on the November 1 date, Marshall continued, were weather and the need to give the enemy as little time as possible to prepare a defense. After November, he warned, deteriorating weather could delay an invasion by as much as six months. "The Kyushu operation is essential to a strategy of strangulation and appears to be the least costly worthwhile operation following Okinawa," he added. "The basic point is that a lodgment in Kyushu is essential, both to tightening our strangle hold of blockade and bombardment on Japan, and to forcing capitulation by invasion of the Tokyo Plain."

The others around the table listened.

Short of a total defeat, the general continued, the Japanese would capitulate only when faced with the hopeless prospect of a total blockade and bombardment coupled with an invasion and possibly the threat of or entry by the Soviet Union into the war. "We are bringing to bear against the Japanese every weapon and all the force we can employ."

Projected casualties, he admitted, were tricky. "Our experience in the Pacific war is so diverse," Marshall said, "that it is considered wrong to give any estimate in numbers."

The general ran through a breakdown of battles in the last year. America suffered 17,000 killed, wounded, or missing on Leyte compared to 78,000 Japanese. That equated to one American casualty for every 4.6 of the enemy. The battle for Luzon was similar, with 31,000 Americans killed or wounded to Japan's 156,000 for a ratio of one to five. The ferocity of fighting on Iwo Jima and Okinawa had tightened that ratio with one American casualty for every 1.25 of the enemy on the former and one to two on the latter.

The wide range of casualties made it hard to discern precisely what American forces might face on Kyushu. For the first thirty days, Marshall estimated casualties would be more comparable to the fight for Luzon than for Iwo Jima or Okinawa. "It is a grim fact," he added, "that there is not an easy, bloodless way to victory in war and it is the thankless task of the leaders to maintain their firm outward front which holds the resolution of their subordinates."

Russia's entrance into the war, the general noted, could be decisive in forcing the Japanese to capitulate. The Soviets also would help tie down Japanese troops in Manchuria, who might otherwise be shipped to Kyushu to defend the homeland.

Marshall said he asked MacArthur for his opinion, which he had received and shared with the Joint Chiefs. "I believe the operation presents less hazards of excessive loss than any other that has been suggested and that its decisive effect will eventually save lives by eliminating wasteful operations of non-decisive character," Marshall read aloud from the telegram. "I regard the operation as the most economical one in effort and lives that is possible. In this respect it must be remembered that the several preceding months will involve practically no losses in ground troops and that sooner or later a decisive ground attack must be made."

The general concluded MacArthur's cable.

"The operation against Kyushu," Marshall urged, "was the only course to pursue."

Airpower alone would not be enough to end the war. It had failed to do so against the Germans. Japan, if anything, would be a much greater challenge. Generals Eaker and Eisenhower, Marshall noted, agreed. "Against the Japanese, scattered through mountainous country, the problem would be much more difficult than it had been in Germany," he said. "This plan offered the only way the Japanese could be forced into a feeling of utter helplessness."

Admiral King agreed. The more he studied the operation, the more convinced he became of the island's strategic advantage. "Kyushu followed logically after Okinawa," King declared. "It was a natural setup." After the capture of Kyushu, he continued, there would be time to judge the impact on the war of any possible operations by the Russians and the Chinese. In the meantime, however, plans should continue for the seizure of the Tokyo Plain. "Once started," the admiral concluded, "they can always be stopped if desired."

Marshall concurred.

Truman asked if a later decision over Tokyo would depend on what the Russians agreed to do, which the others agreed would have considerable influence.

The president asked Leahy for his views.

The admiral returned to the early concern over casualties. He pointed to Okinawa, which he, unlike Marhsall, felt served as a better estimate for what America would experience on Kyushu. He asked for the total number of troops planned for the invasion.

Unlike Okinawa, King interjected, where troops had faced a frontal attack under heavy fire, Kyushu offered many diverse landing beaches, which would reduce casualties. He estimated casualties would fall between what America experienced on Luzon and Okinawa.

Total assault troops for Kyushu, Marshall replied, were planned as 766,700. As for enemy opposition, he expected eight Japanese divisions or about 350,000 troops. The general noted that enemy divisions were still being raised, and it was possible Japan could bring in reinforcements from other areas, but it was becoming harder to move them.

Truman pressed him on Japan's ability to move troops south from other islands.

America, the general replied, planned to destroy all communications from Kyushu. King added that Japan would have to rely on shipping for any reinforcement. Kyushu, Leahy noted, had a mountain range, which would be difficult for enemy troops to cross.

Okinawa had proved to be a hellacious fight, not just for American troops but for the public who had followed the battle at home in the press. Kyushu was far larger and carried greater symbolic importance for the Japanese since it was one of the nation's four principal islands, ultimately ensuring a rough fight. An invasion of Kyushu, Truman said, risked creating another Okinawa, a word that had become synonymous in his eyes for bloodletting.

The Joint Chiefs all agreed.

The president turned to Eaker for his opinion.

The airman supported Marshall. The capture of the Tokyo Plain would require Kyushu, which could accommodate forty groups of heavy bombers. "Those who advocated the use against Japan of air power alone," he explained, "overlooked the very impressive fact that air casualties are always much heavier when the air faced the enemy alone."

Truman asked if the Joints Chiefs, after weighting all possibilities, were still of the unanimous opinion that the Kyushu operation was the best solution.

"The Chiefs of Staff," the minutes state, "agreed that this was so."

Truman next asked Stimson for his views.

The war secretary said there was no other choice. Stimson said he believed there was a large percentage of the Japanese populace who did not support the war. It was important, if at all possible, that this group's influence be felt before any invasion. "This submerged class," he said, "would fight and fight tenaciously if attacked on their own ground."

Would an invasion by Westerners, Truman asked, unite the Japanese?

There was every prospect of this, the war secretary replied.

The president lastly consulted Forrestal.

Even if America besieged Japan for a year or even a year and a half, the navy secretary said, troops would still eventually have to storm ashore and take Kyushu. "The sound decision," Forrestal advocated, "is to proceed with the operation against Kyushu. There will still be time thereafter to consider the main decision in the light of subsequent events."

Truman said one of his goals in the upcoming conference with Allied leaders in Potsdam was to secure Russia's help with the defeat of Japan. What did he need to do in advance to guarantee he was in the strongest possible position when he faced Stalin?

Leahy interjected that he disagreed with those who felt that anything less than Japan's unconditional surrender equaled a loss for America. Japan was beaten and posed no threat in the foreseeable future. "Our insistence on unconditional surrender," he added, "would result only in making the Japanese desperate and thereby increase our casualty lists."

It was with that thought in mind, Truman replied, that he had left the door open for Congress to take whatever action appropriate on that policy. With that said, the president did not feel that he alone could take any action to change public opinion. Truman then told the assembled military leaders that he approved of the seizure of Kyushu and would decide later on the invasion of the Tokyo Plain. He reiterated his concern over casualties, hoping "there was a possibility of preventing an Okinawa from one end of Japan to the other."

Absent from the printed minutes was any discussion about the possible use of atomic bombs, the first test of which was scheduled in less than a month. If successful, what role might such weapons play in ending the war? Would an invasion even be necessary? The last line of the minutes provide only a cryptic hint of this unanswered question. "The President and the Chiefs of Staff," the minutes conclude, "then discussed certain other matters."

CHAPTER 18

"The devastation was so bad that I wondered whether I was really in the center of Tokyo."

—AIKO TAKAHASHI
JULY 25, 1945, DIARY ENTRY

As spring rolled into summer, life in Japan unraveled.

After the March 10 raid on Tokyo, American bombers returned to the capital five more times in the lead-up to the final assault on May 25. Those six fire raids—spread over a span of seventy-six days—incinerated a staggering 56.3 square miles of homes, shops, and businesses, reducing an area nearly three times the size of Manhattan to rubble and ash. "Tokyo," as one postwar American report gloated, "got the super deluxe treatment."

Even the palace was not spared America's fury. Despite protection from ten thousand soldiers and firefighters, flames from the final May assault hurdled the moat and burned twenty-seven of the complex's buildings, including the principal hall. The emperor was safe, since he and his family had moved into the protected Obunko, a concrete building complete with an underground bunker. But upon hearing news of the loss, he turned pale and fell silent.

"So," Hirohito finally said, "the Palace has burnt down."

The capital's destruction stunned residents, including Aiko Takahashi, who watched rescuers stack the wounded like cordwood in the back of a truck. "I had never seen such pathetic figures, not even in medieval hell screens," she penned in her diary. "Humans had done this to other humans." Beyond the dead and wounded, residents now struggled just to orient themselves in a wasteland devoid of familiar landmarks. "The limitless acres of ruin seemed to spread everywhere, like a desert, in a drab and monotonous panorama of hopelessness," recalled reporter Masuo Kato. "The fires had swept away trees and flowers, schools and monuments and parks, along with munitions works and factories, so there was little to relieve the drabness. Unsightly, reddish-orange rust had painted lavishly the tangled metal that lay here and there—automobile bodies, printing presses, metal lathes, iron safes, plumbing, roofing and the other scattered bits of metal left over from a city that had been mostly wood."

But the devastation spread far beyond Tokyo.

Night after night Boeing's monstrous Superfortresses systemically scorched Japan's cities, like fire-breathing dragons. The thirty-two square miles that America destroyed in March more than tripled by June as bombers burned 102.67 square miles of Tokyo, Osaka, Nagoya, Yokohama, Kobe, and Kawasaki. With Japan's six major industrial cities largely in ruins, American forces turned to the nation's secondary and even tertiary cities. The tempo of attacks likewise increased, as more bombers and crews arrived each month in the Marianas. As a result, one out of every three Japanese people would personally experience raids while one out of five would suffer the loss of property. "Air raids," as one postwar report concluded, "brought the war home, psychologically as well as physically, to the Japanese people."

The struggles that dominated daily life before the raids only worsened under the added threat of air attack. "Merely to subsist," Kato noted, "had become the goal of each Japanese." Along with homes and business, the fires wrecked bus, trolley, and train systems, knocked out water and electric utilities, and destroyed schools and hospitals, disrupting all aspects of life. Residents were left to hunker down in the dark under severe blackout restrictions, wondering each night if it would be their last. Hunger coupled with the fear of fire exhausted many, a theme common in a survey of survivor diaries. "Living each day amid this destruction has become unbearable," Hisako Yoshizawa wrote in hers. "Is this natural selection?"

"How long," she added in another entry, "can this life continue?"

The only people who seemed to welcome the raids were locksmiths, who prowled the smoldering ruins offering to open up the fireproof safes that dotted the landscape. "We open safes!" was a common sales pitch. "Twenty yen each! Just ten minutes!"

The nation's military, which had once conquered a quarter of the globe, proved powerless to stop the Americans, who controlled the skies and seas. The relentless raids laid bare the government's failure to prepare the populace for the inevitability of attacks on the homeland. Few public shelters existed, leaving residents to dig primitive foxholes in home gardens, where many either suffocated or roasted to death. Concrete buildings, like schools and train stations, often functioned as ovens, reducing the bodies inside to ashes and bone.

The nation's fire departments were woefully inadequate, plagued by decades-old trucks and pumpers, a lack of training, and mediocre personnel, a fact that only worsened as the war progressed and able-bodied men were drafted. "Fire-fighting equipment in common use," one report noted, "would, in a large part, have been shunned by small-town volunteer departments in the United States." Equally appalling was the dependence on neighborhood associations to fight fires, where residents wielded brooms, buckets of water, and sand to combat napalm incendiaries. "It was officially drilled into them," recalled reporter Robert Guillain, "that with speed and order their equipment was adequate to put out even the most violent fires."

Fighter planes that could be used for air defense were hoarded to counter America's expected invasion, while antiaircraft guns guarded only military targets. Seventy-six percent of the population, according to one survey, felt air raid safeguards were deficient. "We were unprotected," a Kokura resident testified. "It was the same all over Japan."

Post-attack welfare likewise was nonexistent. Residents were fortunate to collect a blanket, some hardtack, and a train ticket. "I did not receive any help from the government or anyone else," a Yokohama resident said. "We just had to look after ourselves; nothing was given to us. I felt bitter toward the government and wished we had never started the war."

Many could do little more than wallow in fear. "The raids almost seemed continuous in Tokyo," one survivor recalled. "I could stand everything else but I couldn't help worrying about the air raids." Others developed a sense of resignation. "There was no reason to become more frightened," another Tokyo resident said. "Everything would be destroyed anyway. Fate would decide who would be next." Unlike the daily struggle for food on the black market, where the wealthy won out over the less fortunate, air raids did not discriminate. "Everyone suffered equally," one report concluded. "The rich and poor alike lost their homes."

In the absence of hope, many turned to superstition. Wearing Western-style clothes, for example, was alleged to protect a person; so was rubbing an onion on one's head or placing a pickled onion atop a bowl of rice and beans. Others speculated that certain cities had been spared because friends of Truman or MacArthur lived there. Another rumor falsely asserted that Kyoto was off limits because MacArthur's mother was buried there.

Japan's most visible response to the attacks was to hack firebreaks through the nation's dense wooden cities. The program, which began in 1944, accelerated once the fire raids began, as workers slashed lanes up to 120 feet wide through residential and business districts. All told, workers tore down 614,698 homes, businesses, and shops, including 214,203 in Tokyo, 82,508 in Osaka, and another 41,607 in Kobe and Kyoto. "Grids were traced in straight lines running through flat, densely overpopulated neighborhoods where thousands of houses were marked for demolition," recalled Guillain. "The people living in them were given a week at most—sometimes only two to three days—to get out with their meager possessions, their bedding, their rags. Then the troops arrived and, often aided by schoolboys and older students, embarked on a kind of brutal, rapid sack of the city. Lined up for miles, khaki-clad soldiers smashed buildings, chopped at them with axes, pounded them with battering rams, pulled them down with ropes; in less than three hours, the old wooden houses crumbled into dust."

The Philippine diplomat León María Guerrero witnessed one such demolition in Tokyo, noting that authorities marked houses with chalk. On the street outside, residents hawked their belongings, the most coveted of which were bottles needed for soy sauce, beer, and sake rations. "Tokyo was a vast flea-market," Guillain added, "in which all the articles unobtainable for months, even on the black market, suddenly reappeared: sets of porcelain, chest of drawers, European furniture, new and used sandals, charcoal, straw mats, and the thousand knickknacks that adorned prosperous homes: silk paintings, luxurious cushions, cases, lacquered boxes, Japanese books, incense burners. And all of it went for a pittance."

These yard sales coincided with the mass exodus from Japan's major cities. Trains were so packed that passengers climbed through the windows and crowded inside bathrooms, leaving children to defecate on the floors. Since March, 886,904 people had escaped Osaka, Japan's second-largest city, where the prewar population had totaled 3,254,380. Nagoya experienced a similar flight as more than 487,000 residents departed. Tokyo saw the greatest evacuation, with more than 4,729,000 abandoning the capital, the majority in the last year of the war. That figure amounted to three out of every four residents. Across Japan, more than 8.5 million people fled to the countryside, roughly one-fourth of the entire urban population. "Most people," as the historian Thomas Havens observed, "in the timeless pattern of war refugees everywhere, wordlessly left town riding bicycles, sitting atop oxcarts, or trudging on foot."

The flood of people into the country's rural areas created added hardships as well as frictions. "The food problems were the chief cause of this," one schoolmaster noted. "There simply wasn't enough for everyone, and the people felt that additional mouths complicated the situation, while the evacuees felt that they had as much right as anyone to eat."

Those who chose to remain in the cities often suffered post-traumatic stress as the attacks continued. Many were sensitive to flashes of light and sounds, including train whistles and planes. An estimated 227,000 people settled in the scorched ruins of Tokyo, hoping that American bombers would not target those hard-hit areas again. In neighboring Yokohama, another 100,000 squatted amid the rubble, with 90,000 more in Osaka. Life in the ruins was hard as men, women, and children bedded down in shanties made from salvaged wood and metal, without electricity or water. Garbage and waste littered the area over which hung the smell of human excrement. "Every day I burn scraps of wood taken from destroyed houses to cook my meals," the writer and playwright Kafu Nagai wrote in his diary. "Life in a defeated country—no water, no fire. One can fairly say that we have reached the extreme of misery."

Twelve-year-old Katsumoto Saotome spent his days scavenging for food amid the ruins. "I was like a stray dog," the youth said, "picking whatever looked valuable on the ground." Others attempted to grow vegetables amid the vast wasteland. "When you dig in the burned-out areas, you find all sorts of things," Yoshizawa wrote in her diary. "I found a bottle opener, a curling iron, charcoal, a pair of tongs, a camera, and much else. Everything we dug up showed signs of being used, and I wondered about the owners of these objects."

Morale plummeted as the scope of the military's lies came into sharper focus. America's raids had at last punctured the propaganda. "Thousands and thousands of houses have been burned, set afire, destroyed. And men, women, children with them. The sky turns red in the night, pitch black in the day," Tokyo professor Kazuo Watanabe wrote in his diary. "This is the time when all Japanese must become truly aware of what war is, what militarism is, and what politics are when led by fanaticism." Kato agreed. "To each family that watched its home and belongings go skyward in a rush of smoke and flame, the news from Okinawa, true or false, meant little," he wrote. "For them, their personal war was already lost."

Most grasped the inevitability of defeat. "Everywhere one goes, the topic of conversation turns toward the point of asking when the war will probably end," author Kiyoshi Kiyosawa wrote in his diary. "One can infer from this that everyone has had enough war."

"Everyone now realizes," Yoshizawa added, "there will be no victory."

Even as the misery spread, the military prepared for a final decisive battle against the Americans, who would soon appear on the nation's doorstep. The army hustled to transfer troops from Manchuria to Kyushu. Others, meanwhile, dug fortifications. Kato visited Chiba peninsula to inspect the work, which he noted appeared far more primitive than the concrete bunkers the Germans had erected along the beaches and cliffs of Europe. "Those that I inspected were hand-made and crude," he reported. "No materials existed for modern fortifications."

American troops battling on Leyte and Okinawa knew that rudimentary fortifications made from toppled trees and earth could prove formidable obstacles. But Kato was not convinced. "To an amateur, at least, there was a question whether the army intended making a serious defense of the homeland at all or would merely offer a face-saving token defense," the reporter wrote. "It seemed obvious that no successful resistance could be made. Perhaps Japan was fighting on only from habit and because she did not know how to stop."

The defense of the homeland likewise fell to evacuated students and teachers, the latter of whom were taught to fly gliders that could be used for kamikaze missions. Children performed calisthenics, took long hikes, and swam, all to get in shape for the battle. Physical training was mixed with education, including lessons on national heroes, watching propaganda films, and singing war songs. Veterans and service members visited the youth to encourage them. "The children's lives," as one historian noted, "were focused completely on the war."

As the threat of invasion drew nearer, children practiced hand-to-hand combat, throwing hand grenades, and fighting with wooden swords and spears.

"They're still there," instructors cried. "Spear them! Spear them!"

One youth chronicled the experience in her diary. "It was really fun," she noted. "I was tired, but I realized that even one person can kill a lot of the enemy."

That same practice occurred in larger cities, including Tokyo. "Everywhere there is training with bamboo spears," Kiyosawa noted in his diary. "Probably the Japanese spirit encourages the idea that when one sees B-29s, they can be dealt with bamboo spears and judo." That spirit was likewise reflected in the press. "If there are no rifles, bamboo spears will do fine," opined the *Asahi* newspaper. "If bamboo spears are broken karate will do fine."

CHAPTER 19

"How many people in Japan are still confident that we will win the war? Aside from the young suicide pilots and other simplehearted youths, I doubt that there is anyone."

—MUSEI TOKUGAWA
MAY 20, 1945, DIARY ENTRY

Japanese leaders courted catastrophe.

Absent any dramatic change or intervention, the nation's political inertia propelled it toward a climactic and bloody showdown against American forces on the beaches of Kyushu, a fact that the Japanese Army capitalized on that summer when it issued the "Basic Policy for the Future Conduct of the War." Under the proposed plan, the militarists anticipated that kamikazes would sink a quarter of American forces at sea. Another quarter would be destroyed on the beaches, while the remaining half would be wiped out in the subsequent battle. "It contemplated the possibility neither of surrender nor defeat," as one Japanese historian noted. "It was concerned only with a final, and ultimately successful, battle on Japanese soil."

The army planned to pitch its proposal to Japan's Supreme Council for the Direction of the War on June 6, 1945, the same day Stimson briefed Truman on the Interim Committee's recommendations. The military's next step was to seek approval from the Diet in a special session scheduled for the middle of June. Such an extraordinary move would not only cement the army's plans in stone but commit the nation to a brutal fight to the finish.

The Supreme War Council, which functioned as an inner war cabinet, was colloquially known as the Big Six. The council consisted of four cabinet members; the prime minister, foreign minister, war minister, and navy minister, as well as two military leaders, the chiefs of the army and navy general staffs. Originally designed to serve as a liaison between the military and the cabinet, the Big Six had evolved over time into Japan's most powerful political body, one tasked to examine the nation's highest policies from the economy to the direction of the war. The group not only set its own agenda but had direct access to the emperor, and while decisions made by the Big Six had to be ratified by the full cabinet, such approvals were routine. This small group of a half-dozen men served, as one historian noted, as "a jury of six deciding Japan's fate and affecting the lives of millions in distant areas around the world."

Suzuki had been tapped to serve as prime minister in April with the hope of bringing about an end to the war. The scars he carried from the 1936 failed coup served as a reminder that to push too hard against the nation's militarists could be deadly. This prompted the cautious septuagenarian to try to thread the political needle. With the military and the public, Suzuki advocated increased war effort and a determination to fight to the finish while he simultaneously looked for a diplomatic exit ramp that might save Japan. One of the prime minister's first moves was to commission an analysis of the nation's capability to continue the war. That study revealed that not only could Japan not replace aircraft and shipping losses, but it likewise faced a looming food crisis and rising antiwar sentiment. In short, Japan was doomed. "It has become increasingly difficult to meet the requirements of total war," the study concluded. "Moreover, it has become necessary to pay careful attention to the trends in public sentiment."

Another of Suzuki's moves was to recruit Shigenori Togo to serve as the nation's foreign minister, a dapper career diplomat who fancied striped shirts with French cuffs and pocket squares that matched his ties. The bespectacled sixty-two-year-old, who came from a long line of samurai, had studied German literature at Tokyo University before joining the foreign service. Soon after World War I, he was posted to Germany, an assignment that highlighted the struggles of life in a defeated country.

Over the years, Togo pinballed between various capitals, including those of Russia and the United States. Those experiences had convinced him that war against America would be a grave mistake, a fact he pressed unsuccessfully once appointed foreign minister in the lead-up to the attack on Pearl Harbor. After the outbreak of the war, differences of opinion with Hideki Tojo led Togo to resign in 1942. Even as a private citizen, he had followed the war, tracking Japan's defeats in the Solomon Islands, the Marianas, and the Philippines. "As the war progressed," Togo lamented, "the hope of victory for Japan receded."

Togo had initially refused to join Suzuki's cabinet, believing the prime minister failed to appreciate just how dire a situation Japan faced. Togo's concerns were justified. In the final months of the war, the aging prime minister seemed to sway between those who favored immediate peace and the militarists who wanted to continue the fight, a tendency that not only frustrated colleagues but created challenges. If anything, Suzuki's public comments parroted the militarists. "Should I die," he told the public at the swearing-in of his cabinet, "I hope that you will advance over my dead body to continue the fight against the enemy."

"I am resolved," he said another time, "to sacrifice everything to continue the war."

Historians have long speculated on Suzuki's waffling, particularly during the critical period between April and June 1945. Some have attributed his ambiguous and at times contradictory positions to everything from his age to his habitual loyalty to the military he long served. The threat of assassination no doubt weighed heavily on Suzuki along with the realization of the precarious role he played as the central political figure caught between opposing sides. In the case of Shigenori Togo, pressure from other peace advocates—along with an understanding from Suzuki that he would be free to pursue a diplomatic end to the war—convinced Togo at last to join the new prime minister's cabinet. "From the moment of the outbreak of the war," Togo later wrote, "I had had in mind the ending of it."

But Togo's goals collided with those of the military.

That was clear when the Big Six gathered at nine a.m. on June 6 for the army's presentation of its plan. In addition to the regular members of the Supreme War Council, several bureau chiefs and cabinet ministers joined. Togo felt sandbagged, given that the military had suddenly called the conference. "Upon attending the meeting," he complained, "I was astounded to find that its purpose was to determine the fundamental policy for carrying on the war."

Throughout the daylong session, a parade of military leaders extolled how the battle for the nation's homeland would be far different from the string of bloody defeats Japan had suffered on Saipan, Iwo Jima, and Okinawa. "When the enemy attempts to invade Japan proper," one officer declared, "he will be met at the point of landing by an overwhelming Japanese force, which will continue its attack until he is defeated and turned back."

Of the Big Six, only Togo raised any objections, pointing out that Japan's national strength had faded. That reality was compounded by the fire raids coupled with the loss of wartime production. Japan had neither command of the skies nor allies. "No external help," Togo warned, "could be anticipated now that the war had become so desperate."

In the end, only Togo opposed the army's plan.

Navy Minister Admiral Mitsumasa Yonai did not speak while the remaining four members agreed to support it, including Suzuki. The next day the prime minister went before the cabinet. "There is only one way to win, and that is by determination," he declared. "When the whole nation possesses this will, then we shall be able to achieve victory!"

The cabinet rubber-stamped it.

The army's final step was to secure Hirohito's approval in an Imperial Conference. At 10:05 a.m. on June 8, the Big Six and seven other senior officials appeared before the emperor. Suzuki requested that the proposed policy be read aloud. "I ask all those," Suzuki then said, "who have any opinions on the subject to express them now."

This time no one spoke.

"Japan's situation at the present moment is indeed critical," he said. "She has reached the point where she can, so to speak, pull continued life out of the jaws of death."

At the end, everyone rose, faced the emperor, and bowed. Throughout the nearly two-hour conference, Hirohito did not say a word. "His silence was customary," as one Japanese historian noted. "He was never expected to speak, only to lend by his presence the final imperial authority to the decision that had already been reached by his ministers."

Japan would fight to the finish.

Hirohito met at 1:50 p.m. that afternoon with Marquis Koichi Kido, the lord keeper of the privy seal, a job that required him to guard the emperor's signature stamps, which were used to ratify official state records and rescripts. But in all reality, the fifty-five-year-old with thinning hair, a bushy moustache, and glasses was one of the most powerful leaders in Japan. "He was the Emperor's eyes, ears, and voice," one historian noted, "as well as his chief adviser." A member of the Tokyo aristocracy, Kido had studied law at Kyoto Imperial University and later worked as a bureaucrat before migrating into politics. Over the years he had served as the nation's education minister and as the welfare and home minister before landing in the palace as Hirohito's principal political adviser in 1940.

During the afternoon meeting at the Obunko, the dejected emperor pushed the army's papers across the table. "This," Hirohito said, "is what has been decided."

Kido scanned the army's plan, recognizing immediately the nation's peril. Suzuki, who both men had hoped would steer the nation toward peace, was either playing the army's game or playing for time; either could lead to disaster. That afternoon Kido returned to his office and started work on a counterplan. "By the latter part of this year," he began, "we will be all but incapable of conducting the war on all fronts." The enemy, he realized, would continue its fire raids, which threatened to wipe out city after city, village after village. Along with the homes and businesses would go vital stores of food, clothing, and necessities. "The extreme shortage of provisions," he wrote, "that will sweep the country in the latter part of this year and thereafter—in light of the approaching chilly season—will cause serious unrest among the people at large. And, in consequence, the situation will be beyond salvation."

Based on enemy broadcasts, the Allied goal was to eliminate the militarists who had led Japan into the war. At the same time, Kido noted, it was imperative to safeguard Japan's national polity, particularly the throne. Time was imperative. If Japan waited too long, it might share the same fate as Germany, forced to accept an unconditional surrender.

There was, Kido realized, only one solution.

Hirohito had to intervene.

Kido recommended that Japan—via a personal message or envoy

from the emperor—appeal to the Soviet Union to serve as an intermediary. Japan would then be willing, Kido wrote, to end the war on "very generous terms." He suspected Japan would have to surrender its conquered territories and withdraw its military forces. "In regard to the reduction of armaments, we must be prepared for pretty strong demands being forced on us," the privy seal concluded. "There will be no choice for us but to be content with a minimum defense."

Overcome by anxiety, Hirohito took to bed for two days, leaving Kido to sell his plan. On June 13, the lord keeper of the privy seal met with Navy Minister Yonai, a sixty-five-year-old admiral who stood more than six feet tall and weighed close to 180 pounds. A liberal, Yonai had resisted the enlargement of the Axis pact, earning him the enmity of his army colleagues who had then undermined his six-month tenure as prime minister in early 1940. Yonai had subsequently sat out much of the war until the ouster of Hideki Tojo's government. Like the foreign minister, he felt Japan was doomed. "I think the turning point of the war was the start," he said. "I felt from the very beginning that there was no chance of success."

Yonai agreed to support Kido's plan; so did Suzuki and Togo. Kido next met with War Minister Gen. Korechika Anami on June 18, the same day Truman green-lit the invasion of Kyushu. Unlike Togo, the fifty-eight-year-old Anami was no intellectual; he had, in fact, failed the war college entrance exam four times before he finally passed. But he was a charismatic leader with a samurai's ability to focus, a skill he developed through kendo and archery, the latter of which he practiced each morning in his garden. Anami, who sported a trim moustache, receding hairline, and short cropped hair, had fought in China, where his son was killed in a battle he had planned. The loss had devastated the general, whose only comfort came when he learned his son had refused treatment to spare the overwhelmed medics. "Accept my son's death," he implored the gods, "as an offering."

Away from the battlefield, Anami had served as the aide-de-camp to Hirohito, of whom he had grown exceptionally fond. His greatest treasure was a white shirt the emperor had worn and later presented to him as a gift. Anami understood his nation was doomed, but he believed Japan should continue the fight. Only after America had been badly bloodied on the beaches of Kyushu could Japan hope to obtain a better position at the bargaining table.

"Our ability to continue the war is virtually nonexistent," Kido told him. "Now is the time, then, for us all to concentrate our efforts on ending it."

"As a soldier," Anami replied, "I believe that we must first defeat the enemy when he invades the homeland. Then, when we negotiate for peace."

"And do you," Kido countered, "believe the enemy will be inclined to agree to our peace terms after he has completed his landing on Japan? If he does not, then we shall have no choice but to continue fighting, and that can only mean the utter annihilation of the country."

Anami listened.

"The emperor himself," Kido added, "is of the opinion that it would be futile for us to go on with the war, and he is deeply concerned about our plight."

The mention of the emperor changed the dynamics—and placed Anami in a predicament. On the one hand, as the war minister, he was bound to prosecute the war to its end. At the same time, he was a subject of the emperor and beholden to his will.

Faced with this conundrum, Anami relented. Though he disagreed with Kido, he would not interfere with his efforts. At 1:50 p.m. on June 20, Kido met with Hirohito. The only way to overturn the military's plan was for the emperor to intervene. "There is no other way," Kido assured him, "to revoke a decision already reached in the imperial presence."

"Very well," Hirohito said. "Let it be done."

At three p.m. on June 22—the same day America declared Okinawa secured—Hirohito met with the Big Six. Though the imperial conference on June 8 had determined that Japan should continue the fight, the emperor wanted to explore other ways to end the hostilities. "We have heard enough of this determination of yours to fight to the last soldier," Hirohito declared. "Now we want action. We want you to consider methods of ending this war."

CHAPTER 20

"Japan has never lost a war in modern times. We therefore have no yardstick to measure the eventual impact on the Japanese mind of the cataclysm of destruction and defeat."

—JOSEPH GREW
DECEMBER 12, 1944,
CONGRESSIONAL TESTIMONY

Scientists were not the only ones pushing Truman.

As the war neared its climax, a small group of senior American leaders urged the president to abandon the demand for unconditional surrender. If the emperor were assured of his safety, officials argued, Japan would be more likely to capitulate.

But such a change, as the president knew, would be momentous. Unconditional surrender, after all, had become more than just a demand—it was a rallying cry.

The ultimatum dated back to the Casablanca Conference in January 1943, when Roosevelt had met with Churchill in the coastal Moroccan city. The president had learned a valuable lesson from World War I. The botched peace that had brought an end to the bloodshed had proved to be fertile soil that nurtured the seeds of the current conflict. Many Germans never felt the agony of defeat, since much of the war was fought elsewhere in Europe. That was followed by what many viewed as punitive reparations, which were exacerbated by the economic meltdown in the 1930s. Those factors fertilized the resentment and hostility that formed the heart of Nazism—and set Germany once again on the path toward war.

The only way to prevent another future conflict, Roosevelt believed, was to remake the warring societies. The victor, in short, would have total control over the vanquished. That would allow the Allies to rip out the roots of the Nazism that had overgrown Germany as well as the militarism that had done the same in Japan. "It is of the utmost importance that every person in Germany should realize that this time Germany is a defeated nation," Roosevelt explained to Stimson. "The fact that they are a defeated nation, collectively and individually, must be so impressed upon them that they will hesitate to start any new war."

At a press conference on January 24, 1943, Roosevelt mentioned Gen. Ulysses S. Grant. The Union commander had earned the nickname "Unconditional Surrender Grant," which was a play on his initials, for his insistence on those terms following the capture of Tennessee's Fort Donelson from the Confederates in February 1862. "The elimination of Germany, Japanese, and Italian war power means the unconditional surrender by Germany, Italy, and Japan," Roosevelt told reporters in Morrocco. "It does not mean the destruction of the population of Germany, Italy, or Japan, but it does mean the destruction of the philosophies in those countries which are based on conquest and the subjugation of other people."

The president had from the outset explained that the ultimatum meant the eradication only of the warmaking ideologies and not the lives of the men, women, and children.

But over time and through repetition, much of that nuance was stripped away as the demand was reduced to two simple words. "Unconditional surrender" had since become one of the most recognizable policies of the war, a slogan rivaled only by "Remember Pearl Harbor" or MacArthur's famous vow after his escape from the Philippines, "I shall return."

Over the years, Roosevelt continued to clarify his policy. On March 1, 1945, in his last speech before he died, he explained that for Germany, the policy meant the obliteration of Nazism and the Nazi Party, the destruction of its institutions, and the repeal of its racial laws. Included among those demands was national disarmament, the prosecution of war criminals, and the destruction of military hardware and armaments factories.

The same, of course, applied to Japan.

Truman had inherited this policy from his predecessor, and those in the State Department who opposed it hoped that since he was not its creator, he might be more likely to walk away from it. Since taking over, however, Truman had held firm.

But Germany's defeat had changed the calculus.

Americans were increasingly anxious for the conflict to end, particularly after the Battle of Okinawa illuminated the expected horror that awaited troops in the fight for the enemy's homeland. Years of war had exhausted many Americans, who were sick of sending their husbands and sons to battle on the beaches and in the malarial jungles of faraway islands and atolls. That weariness was exacerbated by the military's insatiable hunger for recruits—in the first six months of the year, it had conscripted 900,000 new soldiers and sailors. This came as troops in Europe began arriving stateside for a brief reprieve before joining the fight in the Pacific. "America is not their destination," New York opinion writer Max Lerner reminded readers. "Japan is their stopping point: America is only a waystation."

War bond posters in the nation's press urged people to remain strong in the face of fatigue. "The Japanese war is far bigger than most people think!" declared one such advert. "The home front must be protected from these temptations to compromise."

"You can't afford to get tired of war," added another, "no more than those boys facing our fanatical, crazed, barbarous enemies."

But such fatigue stretched far beyond those in the foxholes.

The war, which at its pinnacle consumed ninety-six cents of every federal dollar spent, had transformed all aspects of American life. Not only did it demand the service of 16 million men and women in uniform, but millions more labored on the home front. The conversion of civilian factories to war plants meant the severe reduction or elimination of scores of consumer industries, ranging from bicycles and baby carriages to musical instruments, jukeboxes, and lawn mowers. This, in turn, triggered a scarcity of basic items. Bobby pins vanished from store shelves; so did razor blades, mattresses, and even caskets.

America's ravenous war machine prompted the rationing of everything from paper, rubber, and cotton to sugar, butter, and meat, much of which was overseen by 5,600 local boards manned by an army of 127,000 paid staff and volunteers. "Rationing," as one government report noted, "reached into virtually every home and business in America." *The Washington Post* even ran a column called "Rationing Made Easy," offering tips for readers to help them cope. "About 50 million pairs of shoes are lying idle in closets," one such column advised. "The ration order should put these idle shoes to work." To encourage Americans, Roosevelt took to the airwaves in a fireside chat, reminding them that not all wartime sacrifices were on the front lines. "Never in the memory of man," the president extolled, "has there been a war in which the courage, the endurance, and the loyalty of civilians played so vital a part."

Over the course of the war, Americans had learned to survive with much less. Many navigated life with as little as two gallons of gasoline a week, which, coupled with a shortage of tires, sparked the creation of carpools. To conserve fabric, cuffs vanished from men's pants along with jacket pleats. The government likewise banned suit vests. Women's dresses and skirts grew shorter while two-piece swimsuits proved popular. To compensate for rationed food, Americans planted victory gardens and donated old golf clubs, radiators, and kitchen utensils for scrap. Many others celebrated Christmas without a tree, the result of labor and railway shortages, and scooped up the turkey grease at Thanksgiving, which was used to make gunpowder. "One to two billion pounds of waste fats are thrown away each year," one government official urged. "Every pound of it can be used in America's munitions factories."

Germany's defeat had led to the relaxation of some wartime restrictions on the American home front, including the revocation of the midnight curfew and the ban on horseracing, but much else remained in place. Magazine and newspaper advertisements teased future refrigerators and washing machines, radios, and vacuum cleaners. A gray two-door Ford sedan—the first civilian car produced since February 7, 1942—rolled off a Detroit assembly line that summer, one of 690,000 that workers would hammer out over the next nine months. A survey by the War Production Board revealed that Americans, who sat on $150 billion in savings ready to unleash on the consumer market, were anxious to buy more than 12 million alarm clocks, 6 million refrigerators, and 3.5 million sewing machines. "Following the end of the Japanese war," one senior government official predicted, "the demand of the American people, dammed up now for nearly four years, will exceed anything this country has ever known."

The defeat of Japan was all that stood in the way.

How to hurry the enemy's surrender had become the fixation of Joseph Grew, the State Department's second-in-command. The sixty-five-year-old Bostonian, who, like Roosevelt, was a product of Groton and Harvard, stood over six feet and sported thick bushy eyebrows and a moustache to match. Grew had spent his more-than-four-decade career in the foreign service, including posts as ambassador to Denmark, Switzerland, and Turkey. But it was his final assignment before the war—a decade as the ambassador of Japan—that cemented his status. Grew had landed in Tokyo in 1932, just five years after Hirohito assumed the throne. The ambassador had a front-row seat in the turbulent era that included assassinations, a failed coup, and Japan's war with China. His navigation of the tempest had landed him on the cover of *Time* in 1934, followed by a generous profile in *Life* in 1940 by journalist John Hersey, who characterized Grew as "unquestionably the most important U.S. ambassador."

When the war broke out, Grew was interned at the American embassy in Tokyo and eventually repatriated in the summer of 1942. Upon his return, he served as special assistant to Secretary of State Cordell Hull before his promotion in 1944 to undersecretary of state. Unlike Nazi Germany, a nation he had long felt would collapse, Grew doubted the same pressure would apply to Japan. "I know the Japanese intimately," he said. "The Japanese will not crack. They will not crack morally or psychologically or economically, even when the eventual defeat stares them in the face. They will pull in their belts another notch, reduce their rations from a bowl to a half bowl of rice, and fight to the bitter end. Only by utter physical destruction or utter exhaustion of their men and materials can they be defeated."

But Grew recently had become convinced there might just be another way. The April appointment of Prime Minister Suzuki, a presumed moderate who had survived an assassination attempt during the 1936 coup, foreshadowed a potential move toward peace.

The linchpin, he knew, would be Hirohito.

The emperor was largely a figurehead, but one adored by the Japanese public who viewed him as a deity. Years of conflict had done little to dim that view, a fact confirmed by interrogations of Japanese prisoners of war as well as interviews with civilian internees on Saipan. Unlike Germany, Japan had never been defeated in a modern war, which meant analysts had no precedent from which to gauge how the public or millions of enemy troops might react. That unknown variable was a cause for serious concern. The Japanese air force and navy had largely been destroyed, but the army still counted more than 5 million men under arms. In Grew's eyes, that uncertainty raised the importance of the emperor.

Hirohito was the one person who might unite his nation in defeat—and convince millions of zealous Japanese soldiers to lay down arms and surrender. That could save America from the horror of a bloody guerrilla war. But the only way Hirohito was likely to help, Grew reasoned, was if he had some assurance that he and his dynasty might survive.

Truman needed to offer Hirohito a lifeline.

But Grew's ideas, which he pitched to his colleagues at the State Department on May 28, 1945, divided the agency's senior leaders. Those who had served in Japan agreed with the undersecretary, who advocated that America issue a statement and set of terms, the most important one being that Japan could keep its dynasty, if the public so desired. Based on his experience, Grew believed that America could, in turn, harness the monarchy as a building block for peace in postwar Japan. "We must remember," Grew warned, "that the Japanese are a fanatical people and are capable, if not likely, of fighting to the last ditch and the last man. If they do this, the cost in American lives will be unpredictable."

But others inside the department disagreed, including fellow assistant secretary of state Dean Acheson, who went so far as to label Grew the "prince of appeasers." Acheson and others viewed the throne as archaic and Hirohito as either a weak or a willing tool of the militarists, who either way had used him to lead Japan down the path to war. "The institution of the Emperor," as one declared, "offered a basis for much of the beastly behavior of the Japanese."

Grew faced an even bigger challenge convincing the American public, who remained bitter after years of war. Fueling that animosity were news reports of Japanese atrocities in places like Nanking, Manila, and

Bataan, where troops had abused and starved captured American soldiers and slaughtered men, women, and children by the thousands. In the eyes of most, Japan deserved little sympathy. A Gallup poll showed one out of three respondents wanted Hirohito executed. The rest believed he either should be tried as a war criminal, locked up for life, or exiled. Only 4 percent felt America should do nothing. "The average American," the poll concluded, "thinks he should be treated like any other war criminal."

Grew was not the only one searching for options on how to end the war.

The military, in fact, had already begun grappling with similar challenges as the fight moved into its violent final act. The core issue boiled down to a single question: How would a nation like Japan, where capitulation was viewed as shameful, ever embrace unconditional surrender? Such a concept was completely foreign to the Japanese, where troops fought to the death and defeated commanders often committed seppuku. If Japan could not be convinced to surrender, commanders faced a hellacious fight to the finish, one that could prove incredibly costly for American troops. "Unless a definition of unconditional surrender can be given which is acceptable to the Japanese," one report concluded, "there is no alternative to annihilation and no prospect that the threat of absolute defeat will bring about capitulation."

Like Grew, Assistant War Secretary John McCloy had begun exploring whether there might be another way to entice Japan's surrender. The fifty-year-old McCloy, who had served as an artillery officer during World War I, had spent much of his career as a Wall Street lawyer before landing in the War Department in 1941. Short and stocky—as well as tremendously energetic—McCloy served as the chief troubleshooter for Stimson. To his boss, McCloy had begun to raise many of these issues. "What attitude do we intend to take toward Japan after the war?" he asked on May 28, 1945. "Is it a Carthaginian one? Is it one which will induce her to cooperate with us? Or do we administer a defeat and then just let her alone?"

McCloy sensed, much like Grew, that some Japanese leaders were looking for an exit. The insistence on the phrase *unconditional surrender* might serve as a roadblock. Could America, he asked, accomplish its goals without the use of *that* term? "It may hold them off," McCloy noted, "to the point where we go on digging them out of caves at considerable cost to ourselves when our important objectives can be won without this attrition." Stimson agreed, suggesting to George Marshall on May 30 that the war's objective be changed from "unconditional surrender" to the "complete defeat and permanent destruction of the war making power of Japan."

But changing those two simple words was no easy matter.

The nation and the world were now wedded to the slogan. Not only did any such change risk upsetting the populace, Marshall warned on June 9, but it could rattle America's allies, whose help was needed in order to secure victory over Japan. More important, the general feared what such a change would say to the Japanese, particularly in the wake of Okinawa, a fight that had proved so brutal that Marshall had considering using poisonous gas against the enemy. The general worried the Japanese would interpret it as a weakening of American resolve, which might stiffen the enemy's resistance and make a battle for the homeland more costly. "We should," Marshall advised, "diligently avoid giving any impression that we are growing soft."

But the voice that mattered most in this debate was Truman's.

And the president so far was not convinced that any change was needed, even as he listened to the opinions of his senior advisers. He went further, seeking out the views of former president Hebert Hoover and Secretary of State Hull, two leaders who had experience dealing with the Japanese. The seventy-year-old Hoover, who had been commander in chief when Japan invaded Manchuria in 1931, echoed Grew, arguing that America should issue a declaration along with other allied nations, laying out specific terms for Japan's surrender. An early peace, he predicted, could save up to one million American lives. "There could be no greater gift to the world than to give it peace," Hoover told Truman in a White House meeting, "and to have peace would be of enormous advantage to us and the world."

But Hull disagreed. A former judge, congressman, and senator, the seventy-three-year-old Tennessean had served as the nation's top diplomat for almost twelve years, the longest tenure of any secretary of state. In that time, he had seen the rise and fall of both Nazi Germany and militant Japan, all while he laid the foundation for the United Nations, a feat that would earn him the Noble Peace Prize in 1945. Few people better understood the former president's policies and views on war termination.

Given Hull's stature, his words mattered. Hoover's recommendation, he told Truman on June 12, was an "appeasement proposal."

Faced with split opinions, the president decided on June 18—the same day he green-lit the invasion of Kyushu—to punt the issue to Potsdam. That would allow him a chance to discuss the issue with Churchill and Stalin. Waiting also offered him several additional advantages. An ultimatum issued from the conference would send a message to Japan and the world that the Allies were united. More important, it created time to confirm if the Soviets planned to join the war as well as for America to test the atomic bomb. "If the test of the bomb was successful, I wanted to afford Japan a clear chance to end the fighting before we made use of this newly gained power," Truman said. "If the test should fail, then it would be even more important to us to bring about a surrender before we had to make a physical conquest of Japan."

But Stimson refused to let it go. "This is a matter about which I feel very strongly," he noted in his diary, "and feel that the country will not be satisfied unless every effort is made to shorten the war."

The war secretary began work on a memo to Truman that spelled out the need for an ultimatum to Japan, which he shared on June 26 with Grew and Navy Secretary James Forrestal, who together formed the Committee of the Three. McCloy, in turn, worked with staffers from the State, War, and Navy departments to draft a proposed warning.

At eleven a.m. on July 2, 1945—five days before the president would leave for Potsdam—Stimson sat down with Truman, handing him his four-page memo that explained why America needed to issue a warning to Japan. "There is reason to believe that the operation for the occupation of Japan following the landing may be a very long, costly, and arduous struggle on our part," he began. "The terrain, much of which I have visited several times, has left the impression on my memory of being one which could be susceptible to a last-ditch defense such as has been made on Iwo Jima and Okinawa and which of course is very much larger than either of those two areas." As soon as troops landed, the die would be cast for a battle that would likely exceed anything in Europe. "The Japanese are highly patriotic and certainly susceptible to calls for fanatical resistance to repel an invasion," he continued. "Once started in actual invasion, we shall in my opinion have to go through with an even more bitter finish fight than in Germany. We shall incur the losses incident to such a war and we shall have to leave the Japanese islands even more thoroughly destroyed than was the case with Germany."

To avoid such a fight, Stimson urged Truman to issue an ultimatum, which he believed enemy leaders might find favorable considering Japan no longer had any allies and was forced to carry the costly burden of battling alone. America likewise had obliterated its navy while its cities burned and Soviet forces swelled along the Manchurian border. The United States, by contrast, had inexhaustible resources plus the moral superiority that came with being a victim of enemy aggression at Pearl Harbor. "Japan is not," the war secretary concluded, "a nation composed wholly of mad fanatics of an entirely different mentality from ours."

Stimson next handed the president a copy of the proposed ultimatum, which consisted of thirteen points including the surrender of all captured territories, the disarmament of the military, and the prosecution of war criminals. The retention of the emperor would be permitted if the world could be assured Japan would remain peaceful. "The Japanese shall not be enslaved as a race or destroyed as a nation," the ultimatum declared. "Democratic tendencies among the Japanese people shall be supported and strengthened. Freedom of speech, of religion and of thought, as well as respect for the fundamental human rights shall be established."

According to Stimson, Truman appeared impressed by his memo, which he characterized as "a very powerful paper." The war secretary told Truman that the ultimatum was obviously a draft and could not be completed until America knew what it planned to do with the atomic bomb. Along those lines, Stimson shared the proposed statement, drafted by the Interim Committee, to be issued by Truman after the bomb's use. The war secretary noted that Truman appeared to agree to his suggestion for how to handle Japan. "The president so far has struck me as a man who is trying hard to keep his balance," Stimson noted that day in his diary. "He certainly has been very receptive to all my efforts in these directions."

PART III

"Our job was started on faith, carried through all its strenuous months on faith and won out in the end on faith—faith of our leaders in American capacity to do the impossible and to do it in time."

—MAJ. GEN. LESLIE GROVES
NOVEMBER 19, 1945

Workers hoist the first-ever atomic bomb atop a one hundred-foot tower in the desert of New Mexico in preparation for the top-secret test on July 16, 1945. *(NARA)*

CHAPTER 21

"I'm on the way to the high executioner. Maybe I'll save my head."

—PRESIDENT HARRY TRUMAN
JULY 6, 1945, LETTER TO BESS TRUMAN

At 6:01 a.m. on July 7, 1945, President Truman climbed the gangplank of the USS *Augusta*, a heavy cruiser moored along the south side of Pier 6 in Newport News, Virginia. At the president's request, his arrival aboard ship was a low-key affair with few honors rendered. Truman had come that Saturday morning via an overnight train from Washington's Union Station, which had departed at eleven p.m. and covered the 192 miles in seven hours. Truman's destination was Potsdam, a suburb of Berlin where he would meet with Winston Churchill and Joseph Stalin. Amid the ruins of a vanquished Third Reich, the three Allied leaders would negotiate the terms for the end of the war and the peace that would follow.

Only eighty-six days had passed since a stroke had felled Franklin Roosevelt and catapulted Truman into the nation's top office. To the new president, those three months no doubt had felt like an eternity, as he pored through briefing books, met with world leaders, and struggled to overcome his learning curve. In that brief time, he had seen the fall of Germany, learned of America's top-secret atomic program, and green-lit the invasion of Kyushu. The first test of an atomic bomb in the remote desert of New Mexico loomed on the horizon, offering a potential new solution to the war in the Pacific. "He had to accomplish," as one aide later marveled, "a greater learning in less time than almost any other man in history."

On a personal level, it had been a busy spring and summer before he departed for Europe. Soon after he moved into the White House, he sent the presidential plane nicknamed *Sacred Cow* to Missouri to pick up his elderly mother. Born a decade before the Civil War, she remained, as Truman colorfully noted, an "unreconstructed rebel."

"You tell Harry, if he puts me in the room with Lincoln's bed in it I'll sleep on the floor."

When she stepped onto the tarmac in Washington after her first-ever trip in an airplane, she was mobbed by reporters and photographers. "Oh, fiddlesticks!" she declared. "Why didn't you tell me there was going to be all this fuss, and I wouldn't have come."

On May 31, 1945, Bess and Margaret had left Washington to return home to Missouri. The president had accompanied them to Union Station and then ridden with them as far as Silver Spring before he said good-bye, disembarked, and returned alone to the White House. Their absence was immediately felt by the president, a devoted husband and father. The family spent so much time together that the White House staff referred to them as the three musketeers. "The Trumans were the closest family who lived in the White House during the twenty-eight years I worked there," assistant chief usher James West later observed. "They did everything together—read, listened to the radio, played the piano, and mostly talked to each other."

With his familial support group gone, Truman had felt adrift. "I'm always so lonesome when the family leaves," he confided in his diary. "I have no one to raise a fuss over my neckties and my haircuts, my shoes and my clothes generally." The president cheered himself up by phoning them often. "I can't help wanting to talk to my sweetheart and my baby every night," he wrote in another entry. "I'm a damn fool I guess because I could never get excited or worked up about gals or women. I only had one sweetheart from the time I was six."

On June 1, 1945, the Sunday after their departure, Truman sneaked out of the White House, crossed Lafayette Square, and slipped into the back pews of St. John's Church. "Don't think over six people recognized me," he bragged in his diary. Other times he entertained dinner guests, including Leahy and Joseph Davies. But most nights the president preferred to work alone in his upstairs oval study, cooled by the summer breeze that whipped through the open window. "I sit here in this old house and work on foreign affairs, read reports, and work on speeches—all the while listening to the ghosts walk up and down the hallway and even right here in the study," he wrote in a letter to Bess. "The floors pop and the drapes move back and forth—I can just imagine old Andy and Teddy having an argument over Franklin. Or James Buchanan and Franklin Pierce deciding which was the more useless to the country. And when Millard Fillmore and Chester Arthur join in for place and show the din is almost unbearable."

In recent weeks, Truman had begun to make changes within his administration, beginning with the Oval Office. He gifted the maple-veneer desk that his predecessor had used for twelve years to Eleanor Roosevelt, who planned to display it in a library dedicated to her husband up at his family home in Hyde Park. In its place, Truman had the staff return the 1903 mahogany pedestal desk used by Teddy Roosevelt and five subsequent presidents. With the exception of a tiny red rabbit, the desk was empty of everything but his office essentials. Truman likewise swapped out Roosevelt's beloved Currier & Ives lithographs for paintings of George Washington and Simón Bolívar. A globe stood on a table behind his desk along with photos of his wife and mother. "I suppose I am old fashioned," he told a news reporter on a visit to his office, "but much of the painting that now passes for art looks like scrambled eggs to me."

The president likewise had begun to clean out the cabinet he had inherited from Roosevelt, few of whom he felt any loyalty to or even respected as capable civil servants. "The weakness of any president," he often remarked, "is having too many ass-kissers around." Byrnes was sworn in as secretary of state on July 3 while outgoing chief diplomat Edward Stettinius would become America's first ambassador to the United Nations. Other changes included swapping Labor Secretary Frances Perkins with Lewis Schwellenbach. Attorney General Tom Clark took over for Francis Biddle, while Agriculture Secretary Claude Wickard was replaced by Clinton Anderson. Amid this transition, Interior Secretary Henry Morgenthau demanded to accompany Truman to Potsdam. The president, who viewed him as a "blockhead" and a "nut," saw no need.

"Morgenthau," he colorfully griped, "didn't know shit from apple butter." To another aide, he snarked that he would not even appoint him as dog catcher. When Truman refused his request to go to Potsdam, Morgenthau threatened to resign.

"If that is the way you feel," the president said, "I'll accept your resignation right now."

Other changes involved lower-level staffers, members of the so-called Missouri Gang, who had allowed access to power to get the best of them. "Some of my boys who came in with me are having trouble with their dignity and prerogatives," Truman wrote in his diary. "It's hell when a man gets in close association with the President. Something happens to him."

Truman's popularity meanwhile soared.

A Gallup poll published on the eve of his trip revealed that 87 percent of the country approved of the president's job performance. That trumped Roosevelt's highest-ever approval rating of 84 percent, which followed the attack on Pearl Harbor. *Newsweek* attributed Truman's popularity to his sensible nature, rapport with lawmakers, and appointment of seasoned leaders. "His folksy personality," the magazine added, "goes across well."

Many who had doubted and even scoffed at the plainspoken chief executive during his swearing-in ceremony only three months earlier had come to appreciate his hard work and drive. Truman rose early, ate breakfast, and reported to his office by eight-thirty a.m. Unlike Roosevelt, he maintained a rigid schedule. He slashed the length of cabinet meetings in half while visitors were allotted a strict fifteen minutes. After work, he swam laps in the White House pool and studied at night, so much so that he had to delay a new vision exam so that his eyes could recover. "His sincerity and his desire to do what is right is continually evident," Assistant Press Secretary Eben Ayers noted in his diary. "The opinion in political circles is practically unanimous that Mr. Truman has made a good start," added *New York Times* reporter Bertram Hulen. "The country has rallied behind him and he has seemingly won its confidence."

The president likewise had earned the respect of the Beltway press, who crowded the Oval Office each week for his news conference. Before each session, Truman made time to chat with the reporters, whom he jokingly labeled "vultures" and "wolves." To Merriam Smith, who broke his arm racing out of a press conference two months earlier, Truman penned a personal note. "I was going to come out to see you, but you moved home too quickly," the president joked with Smith upon his return to the press pool. "What I am particularly interested in is, are you going to sue the President for damages for falling out of that door?"

The other reporters all laughed.

"If I go too fast, you put on the brakes," Truman advised the journalists during another session. "You fellows always cause me to go fast, you ask so many questions."

Truman's aides admired his rapport. "He is making a decided hit with the correspondents," Ayers observed. "He stands during the conferences and replies decisively and directly to questions without attempting to evade any. If he cannot discuss a subject, he says so. He speaks rapidly, facing his questioner, and smiles frequently." Reporters agreed, appreciating how he never went off the record or dodged questions. "The quality of his own performance is rapidly dispelling the early doubts as to his ability," wrote Cabell Phillips of *The New York Times*. "He is creating a role of his own and playing it with ability and distinction."

Outside the Oval Office, Truman had busied himself with a trip to California to celebrate the signing by fifty countries of the United Nations Charter on June 26, 1945. The successful conclusion of the nine-week conference, which had at times been in doubt, was a major victory. Truman had accomplished Roosevelt's dream to forge an international body that would hopefully help prevent another world war. Unlike with the previous League of Nations, which America had refused to join, the Senate would ratify this charter in the weeks ahead by a vote of 89–2. While in San Francisco, Truman had enjoyed a parade seated in the back of an open sedan, waiving his hat to an estimated half-million cheering spectators who lined the streets. "You have created a great instrument for peace and security and human progress in the world," Truman applauded delegates. "The world must now use it!"

On his way back to Washington, the president stopped off in Missouri to enjoy some time with Bess and Margaret at the family's home at 219 North Delaware Street, where neighbors had been busy mowing lawns in expectation of his arrival. He had his hair cut by his trusted barber, Frank Spina, and popped in to see his old friend and former business partner Eddie Jacobson, who once again ran a menswear store. During a speech at Kansas City University, where he was awarded an honorary doctorate, Truman reminded attendees of his unlikely rise to the presidency following his predecessor's death. "It was necessary for me," he said, "to assume a burden greater, I think, than any man has assumed in the history of the world." As such, he implored the ten thousand attendees to support him in the difficult days ahead. "There are two things that I must accomplish as President of the United States. The first one is we must win the war with Japan—and we are winning it," Truman declared. "The next one is to win the peace."

The war in the Pacific, as evidenced by his remarks, dominated the president's thoughts as America prepared for the violent conclusion of the fight that had begun on a Sunday morning three years and seven months earlier in the cool waters of Pearl Harbor. The possible use of the atomic bomb, which no one yet knew for certain would work, had set off a firestorm among the scientists, some of whom questioned the weapon's morality. Other senior administration leaders argued over whether America should relinquish its insistence on unconditional surrender to entice Japan to abandon its hopeless fight. Beyond that were the fears over just how bloody a battle awaited troops when they charged ashore on the enemy's beaches amid a storm of kamikazes. All of this weighed on Truman as he headed to Potsdam. "My immediate purpose," he said, "was to get the Russians into the war against Japan as soon as possible."

A secret analysis of the enemy, distributed the day after Truman boarded the *Augusta*, provided a snapshot of Japan's deteriorating position. "The basic policy of the present government is to fight as long and as desperately as possible in the hope of avoiding complete defeat and of acquiring a better bargaining position in a negotiated peace," the report stated. "Japanese leaders are now playing for time." Japan's navy was largely destroyed while commanders rushed to convert the air force into suicide attackers. "The incendiary bombing," the report added, "has had a profound psychological and economic effect on the Japanese." The enemy's greatest strength, however, remained its army, which estimates placed at 110 infantry and four armored divisions for a total of 4.6 million troops. Planners not only expected that force to grow by thirty divisions but also highlighted Japan's National Volunteer Army, which depended on youth and grandparents to fight with bamboo spears. "Fanatical resistance," the report noted, "will be offered in the defense of any of the Home Islands."

The primary preoccupation of the Japanese high command was the defense of Kyushu and Honshu. Planners estimated Japan would have more than thirty-five active divisions plus fourteen depot divisions for a force of more than 2 million troops. All available aircraft and naval units would be deployed in suicide operations. "Japan will use," the report stated, "all political means for avoiding complete defeat or unconditional surrender." That included cementing the belief that any invasion would prove costly and bloody. At the same time, Japan could be expected to make territorial concessions to the Soviets to keep them out of the war while trying to pit the Russians against the Americans and British. Last, Japan might try to pull the Soviets in to serve as a mediator or put out intermittent peace feelers to either negotiate an end to the war or weaken Allied resolve. "The Japanese believe," the report concluded, "that unconditional surrender would be the equivalent of national extinction. There are as yet no indications that the Japanese are ready to accept such terms."

Despite his popularity, Truman was no doubt nervous. This would be his first face-to-face meeting with two veteran world leaders who had helped lead the Allies to victory over Germany. Truman was the president of the United States and a former senator, but he could not escape the fact that just ten years earlier he had been a county official in Missouri. If ever he felt inferior, this was the moment—and his anxiety showed in his letters and diary. "Wish I didn't have to go," he complained in one missive to his mother, "but I do and it can't be stopped."

"I wish this trip was over. I hate it," he added in another.

"How I hate this trip!" he griped in his diary.

To compensate for his anxiety, Truman did what he always did.

He worked hard.

In between packing his tuxedo, tails, and top hat, he had studied the minutes of the Yalta Conference and interviewed the participants, including Stettinius, Hopkins, Byrnes, and Leahy. The State Department and the Joint Chiefs of Staff had prepared exhaustive background materials for him on all subjects, which he had pored over during a quiet July 4 holiday review session aboard the USS *Potomac*, the presidential yacht.

To assist on his first trip abroad as president, Truman had brought a fifty-three-person entourage, ranging from mess attendants and Secret Service agents to senior leaders like Byrnes and Leahy. Included among them were four print reporters, two photographers, and one newsreel reporter as well as five military photographers. "The White House," Truman said, "in a sense, had to be moved to Potsdam for the duration of the conference."

Aboard the *Augusta* that Saturday morning, Truman met the skipper, Capt. James Foskett, his executive officer, Cmdr. Charles Freeman, and several department heads. Attendants then escorted the president to his quarters. For the journey to Europe, Truman would reside in the admiral's spacious cabin. Byrnes meanwhile took over the captain's stateroom while Leahy settled into the chief of staff's quarters. Other senior aides took nearby staterooms in what was dubbed "Flag Country." A map room and communications center were set up in the ship's first lieutenant's office to keep Truman apprised of the war.

The 9,100-ton warship, named for the city in Georgia, stretched 600 feet long, nearly the length of two football fields. Crewed by sixty-four officers and 760 enlisted men, the *Augusta* boasted a barbershop, a tailor, and a soda fountain, where thirsty sailors could buy soft drinks and ice cream. A small library offered a diverse selection of books, from Fyodor Dostoevsky's *Crime and Punishment* to Stephen Crane's *The Red Badge of Courage*. Those searching for a little lighter fare might check out a Sherlock Holmes mystery by Sir Arthur Conan Doyle. The library even had a copy of Hitler's controversial tome *Mein Kampf*.

At seven a.m., the *Augusta* departed, passing the Fort Wool Light house at 7:47 a.m. Twenty-eight minutes later, the *Augusta* joined the light cruiser USS *Philadelphia*, trailing by a thousand yards. The two ships formed Task Force 68 under the command of Rear Adm. Allan McCann. With the war in Europe over—and no threat from German U-boats—security was relaxed. No destroyer or air escort was required, nor were blackout conditions.

The journey across the Atlantic would take eight days, during which time the president, as he always did, awoke each morning at 6:15 a.m. Truman often enjoyed a stroll on deck before he sat down to breakfast an hour later. His staff, unaccustomed to living in such close quarters with the commander in chief, felt the pressure to be seen and keep pace, prompting one of them to complain that the president always had to wake up at the crack of dawn.

"He's the man," replied another, "who cracks the dawn."

Truman's days included a mix of activities, including long hours spent reviewing materials with Byrnes, Leahy, and other senior aides. "He took advantage of the conferences aboard the *Augusta* to absorb information and ask pertinent questions," recalled Charles Bohlen, the State Department's Russia expert. "He rarely philosophized about the future of the world; he preferred to address himself to the practicalities of questions. During our conferences, Truman spent little time on small talk and jokes. He stuck to business."

The president did make time to explore. The Secret Service, long accustomed to his wheelchair-bound predecessor, struggled to keep up. "He toured the ship, from the crow's nest to the machinery spaces," recalled naval aide William Rigdon. "He took part in every lifeboat drill. He shook hands with every ship's officer. He talked with scores of bluejackets."

As a former artillery officer during World War I, Truman particularly enjoyed the gunnery exercise in which the *Augusta* fired upon the *Philadelphia*, an event that Truman and his entourage watched through binoculars from the navigating bridge. The practice was a so-called offset exercise, meaning the *Augusta*'s deflection sight scales were four degrees to the right of the line of target. "Thus while the fire," the trip's log noted, "was actually directed at the target ship, the shots landed some 500 yards or more astern of the *Philadelphia*."

On Sunday he attended Protestant church services with the crew in the mess hall. He returned a few days later to lunch with the men, going through the chow line with his aluminum tray. Over lunch with two sailors from Missouri, he feasted on boiled ham and mashed potatoes, along with tomato soup, buttered carrots, and string beans. Coffee and apple cobbler served as dessert. Dinners proved far more formal, including music offered by the ship's orchestra, which played pieces ranging from Mozart's *Magic Flute* Overture to Johann Strauss II's "Blue Danube Waltz." Afterward Truman and his aides often retired to Byrnes's stateroom to watch movies ranging from the Bob Hope film *The Princess and the Pirate* to Humphrey Bogart in *To Have and Have Not*, based on the novel by Ernest Hemingway.

Never much of a movie fan, Truman at times skipped, recruiting aides and reporters to play poker in his stateroom, including Robert Nixon with International News Service. "He was an expert at cards," Nixon recalled, "because he had played cards so long."

Truman's poker playing eventually drew the ire of the secretary of state. "Mr. Nixon," Byrnes scolded the reporter, "will you boys please leave the President alone?"

"Mr. Secretary," he replied, "what are you talking about?"

"I mean leave him alone in the evening," Byrnes continued. "Stop occupying all of his hours. I've got to tell him what's supposed to go on at this conference."

"Well, Mr. Byrnes, I will have to apologize, but I have no control over this," Nixon said. "Why don't you go to the President and ask him to leave *us* alone."

The *Augusta* reached the Belgian coast early on the morning of July 15, entering the Scheldt Estuary en route to the port of Antwerp. Truman was up early, pacing the cruiser's deck. At one point, the ship passed a few hundred yards from a prisoner of war camp, where thousands of Germans stared back from behind barbed wire. "As we passed one little town after another on our way up the estuary," the trip's log reported, "the President was cheered by hundreds of wildly enthusiastic Belgians and Hollanders lining the south bank."

The *Augusta* moored at 10:04 a.m. in Antwerp, ending the 3,837-mile journey. Waiting for the president on the pier were Gen. Dwight Eisenhower, the Supreme Allied Commander, and Adm. Harold Stark, commander of America's naval forces in Europe, along with various other Allied officials. Truman disembarked at 11:10 a.m., where he was greeted by Belgian diplomat Jean van den Bosh, who thanked him for America's help in the war.

"I have always been a great admirer of your country," he replied.

The president climbed into a sedan, which was part of a forty-car caravan, for the thirty-five-mile drive to Brussels. At the airport, he boarded the *Sacred Cow* for the 460-mile flight to Berlin. Two other planes carried the rest of his entourage. Upon landing, Truman was greeted by Stimson,

Assistant War Secretary John McCloy, and assistant secretaries of state William Clayton and James Dunn, among others. From the airport, the president traveled the ten miles to Babelsberg, a small suburb located between Berlin and Potsdam.

Truman settled into No. 2 Kaiserstrasse, a three-story yellow stucco residence on Lake Griebnitz, which was soon known as the Little White House. The thirty-room property, surrounded on three sides by trees, had been stripped during the war. In advance of the conference, the Russians refurnished the home, but little of it matched. The windows likewise lacked screens, allowing swarms of mosquitoes inside to attack. Truman took over a suite on the north side of the second floor, which consisted of a bedroom, sitting room, office, and breakfast room. A small sun porch that overlooked the lake was the suite's highlight. Byrnes moved into a first-floor suite while Leahy and other members settled in nearby rooms.

Technicians installed a map room and communication center with direct lines to Frankfurt and Washington. This was complemented by a telephone exchange and switchboard set up in the basement of the residence. That first evening Truman called Bess in Missouri, the first call from Berlin to the United States since 1942.

Food and bottled water came from Washington aboard the *Augusta*. The army provided additional supplies. The State Department and Joint Chiefs of Staff took over lodging nearby for the conference. Churchill settled into a property at 23 Ringstrasse, about two blocks away, while Stalin would reside in another property about one mile away.

After the long trip, the president and his aides dined at six p.m. and then retired to bed. He would start early the next day, beginning what would prove to be a long and stressful conference for America's new leader. "Truman's personal goals at Potsdam were quite simple. He wanted to prove to Stalin that he was his own man, a real leader, in firm command of the United States government," recalled Bohlen. "And above all, he wanted to make sure that the Kremlin would honor the agreement to enter the war against Japan."

CHAPTER 22

"If the project proves a failure, it will then be subjected to relentless investigation and criticism."

—JIMMY BYRNES

MARCH 3, 1945, LETTER TO FRANKIN ROOSEVELT

Half a world away, tensions soared.

In the remote desert of New Mexico, Groves, Oppenheimer, and an army of scientists prepared for the first-ever test of an atomic bomb on the morning of July 16, 1945.

Five years, eight months, and twenty-five days had passed since financier Alexander Sachs had presented Einstein's two-page letter to Roosevelt, hypothesizing about a revolutionary new weapon. In the years since, American taxpayers had spent $2 billion, hired hundreds of thousands of workers, and built three top-secret cities with the hope of unleashing a potential war-ending fury hidden in the heart of a microscopic atom.

All that now came down to this one test.

To this one morning.

And that was why the lanky Robert Oppenheimer could not sleep.

The test was scheduled for four a.m. in the desert near Alamogordo, just one day after Truman arrived in the suburbs of Berlin. The president had, in fact, purposefully delayed the Potsdam Conference, so as to give scientists extra time to test the bomb.

Like so much else with the Manhattan Project, the Monday morning test represented the culmination of tremendous effort, which began in March 1944, months before American troops stormed the beaches of France. Eight sites were initially considered as scientists scoured California, Colorado, Texas, and New Mexico in search of a flat landscape that would minimize any extraneous effects on the blast. The location needed to be remote, far from homes and towns to guarantee safety and security as well as offer consistently clear weather with limited haze, dust, and only light winds. Scientists had surveyed the various locales by air and auto before selecting a 432-square-mile site in the northwestern corner of the Alamogordo Air Base. Some two hundred miles southwest of Los Alamos, the test site was wedged between two mountain ranges in a valley named by conquistadors as Jornado del Muerto or Dead Man's Walk.

Kenneth Bainbridge, the physicist tasked to oversee the test, phoned Oppenheimer with news of the selection and a question: What code name would he suggest for the site?

Oppenheimer, who at that moment was grasping a book by English poet John Donne, glanced down at the opening lines of the sonnet he had just read.

Batter my heart, three-person'd God; for, you
As you but knock, breathe, shine, and seek to mend.

"Trinity," the physicist said. "We'll call it Trinity."

To develop the site, workers had constructed more than forty miles of new blacktop roads along with barracks, officers' quarters, a mess hall, laboratories, warehouses, an explosives magazine, and a hospital. Others dug wells, installed generators and lights, and ran more than two hundred miles of phone lines, setting up a communications and public address system. Workers accomplished this while battling tarantulas, rattlesnakes, and the scorching summer heat. The completed base camp resembled a primitive frontier town during the Wild West.

Ten miles to the north of base camp rose a hundred-foot steel tower capped with a sheet-metal shed with a removable center section to allow workers to hoist up the bomb. Three large bunkers situated ten thousand yards away encircled the tower on the north, south, and west sides. Of the three, the southern bunker—or S-10, as it was called—served as the control center. Made of wood with walls reinforced by concrete, each bunker was buried under a layer of earth and sand, providing observers protections from the projected shock wave. Five hundred miles of wiring were required to connect the test weapon to the blast-proof shelters.

To date, Oak Ridge laboratories had enriched only enough uranium for a single weapon. Scientists furthermore felt confident that the gun method would work. The combination of these two factors ruled out a test of a uranium bomb. But doubts still surrounded the implosion method needed to detonate a plutonium weapon, especially since most of the bombs projected to come online in the months ahead were of the same design. A test was imperative.

Four days earlier, on July 12, the bomb's thirteen-pound plutonium core—divided into several subcritical pieces so as to prevent any accidental chain reaction—had arrived at the test area in the backseat of an army sedan. One minute past midnight the following morning, the preassembled bomb casing left Los Alamos for the trip to Trinity. As the convoy rumbled across the New Mexican desert, a team of eight scientists, huddled inside an old adobe ranch house that had been converted into a makeshift laboratory, began reassembling the weapon's core.

At noon on July 13, the explosives truck backed up to the base of the tower. Inside a tent, scientists inserted the bomb's plutonium core, which was surrounded by 5,300 pounds of conventional explosives. At eight a.m. on July 14, a motor-driven hoist lifted the five-ton weapon to the top of the tower at a rate of one foot per minute. "The bomb," as one journalist later observed, "swayed on its cable like the blunt sword of Damocles."

The following day, with the bomb assembled and atop the tower, scientists could at last relax or, as one leader urged his staff, go "look for rabbits' feet and four-leaf clovers." Distinguished visitors had arrived that day, including Groves, Farrell, Vannevar Bush, and James Conant. The *New York Times* reporter William Laurence, who had been hired to write press releases for the Manhattan Project, was also on hand. The fifty-seven-year-old reporter, who had spent the last three months touring the atomic cities, fired off a letter to his boss at the paper on the eve of the test. "This story is much bigger than I could imagine, fantastic, bizarre, fascinating and terrifying," he wrote. "When it breaks it will be an Eighth Day wonder, a sort of Second Coming of Christ yarn. It will be one of the biggest stories of our generation."

Project leaders evacuated all other unnecessary personnel while additional doctors arrived in case of an emergency. All air traffic between Albuquerque and El Paso was halted.

But there was one critical element no one could control.

The weather.

About four p.m. on July 15—twelve hours before the scheduled test—thunderstorms rolled across the desert. By that evening, lightning illuminated the heavens accompanied by rain and winds. Groves worried the moisture might cause problems with the electrical connections need to fire the bomb. The wind, however, was his bigger fear. The general did not want the radioactive cloud to drift over any populated areas that might require evacuation.

Many of the scientists urged Oppenheimer to delay the test, but Groves disagreed. Truman and his advisers at Potsdam were anxious for news of the bomb's success. Other fears hung over him, from a possible saboteur to the strain on the scientists. "I knew," he added, "that every day's delay in the test might well mean the delay of a day in ending the war."

Oppenheimer was a physical wreck. The project's stress coupled with a recent case of chickenpox had whittled his weight down to 115 pounds, an astonishingly low figure for an individual who stood five feet ten inches tall. His constant cough, the product of his five-pack-a-day Chesterfield habit, left the emaciated physicist constantly hacking. "He seemed," as one historian noted, "to be literally disappearing little by little, day after day."

"He resembled a scarecrow," added another.

The general pulled Oppenheimer aside that night. "Get some sleep," he urged.

But the physicist refused, passing the time smoking.

At midnight, the duo reviewed the situation again, deciding to leave base camp and head for the control dugout. Groves reluctantly pushed the test back an hour to five a.m.

"If we postpone," Oppenheimer warned, "I'll never get my people up to pitch again."

But the weather failed to improve.

Groves delayed the test again, this time to five-thirty a.m.

Every few minutes the duo stepped outside. "I was devoting myself during this period to shielding Oppenheimer from the excitement swirling about us," Groves recalled, "so that he could consider the situation as calmy as possible, for the decisions to be taken had to be governed largely by his appraisal of the technical factors involved." The general, in contrast, appeared at ease. "Groves," Farrell noted, "was about the calmest of the lot."

At 3:45 a.m., the base camp mess hall served a breakfast of powdered eggs, French toast, and coffee. Fifteen minutes later conditions started to clear, a fact confirmed by the 4:45 a.m. weather report. High altitude winds had lessened. Cloud cover was expected to soon dissipate, after which there would be a two-hour window of low wind and clear skies. Test director Bainbridge jumped on a conference call with Oppenheimer, Groves, and meteorologist Jack Hubbard. The test had been delayed twice already. Dawn fast approached.

Should the test be scrubbed?

The decision was unanimous.

"Prepare to fire at five-thirty," Bainbridge ordered the control center.

Scientists initiated the arming procedure while the five guards stationed at the foot of the test tower climbed into jeeps and departed. At 5:10 a.m., the final countdown began.

"It is now zero minus twenty minutes," the control center broadcast.

Throughout the test area, scientists, technicians, and observers buzzed. The rain, which earlier had threatened the test and sapped the spirits of all involved, suddenly vanished, replaced by an excitement as the dawn of the nuclear age approached. For safety reasons, Oppenheimer and Groves planned to monitor the test separately. The physicist would remain in the control dugout while the general hopped a ride back to base camp. "Our preparations here were simple," Groves recalled. "Everyone was told to lie face down on the ground, with his feet toward the blast, to close his eyes, and to cover his eyes with his hands as the countdown approached zero. As soon as they became aware of the flash they could turn over and sit or stand up, covering their eyes with the smoked glass with which each had been supplied."

A green rocket shot skyward, signaling five minutes to detonation.

More than 500 witnesses comprising over 300 scientists and 250 military personnel hunkered down in a half-dozen spots. Those included the three earthen bunkers, base camp, an observation point on Compania Hill twenty miles northwest of the tower, and another post situated on a flat plain about twenty-seven miles from the test site. "With the darkness and the waiting in the chill of the desert," wrote Laurence, the *Times* man, "the tension became almost unendurable." One of the scientists with him on Compania Hill passed around sunscreen. "It was an eerie sight," he added, "to see a number of our highest-ranking scientists seriously rubbing sunburn lotion on their faces and hands in the pitch-blackness of the night."

Inside the control dugout, tensions soared.

Four minutes ticked down to three and then two.

"Lord," Oppenheimer muttered, "these affairs are hard on the heart."

The physicist clutched a post and stared ahead. Twenty people crowded inside the bunker, but Farrell kept his focus on Oppenheimer, who appeared not to breathe as the seconds slipped past. "That scene inside the shelter was one of the highlights of my life," Farrell recalled. "There was nothing to compare with the tension and the drama of sitting there."

"Zero minus ten seconds!" the announcer cried.

Another green flare briefly illuminated the heavens.

Five seconds before the expected detonation, thirty high-speed cameras mounted behind bulletproof glass in the northern and western bunkers began to whirl.

"Zero minus three seconds!"

"From the east," Laurence observed, "came the first faint signs of dawn."

"Now!" the announcer shouted.

The two and a half tons of conventional explosives detonated, compressing the bomb's plutonium core, as one journalist later described, "from about the size of an orange to that of a lime." The bomb exploded, unleashing a spectacular nine-thousand-degree fireball. "There rose from the bowels of the earth a light not of this world, the light of many suns in one," Laurence wrote. "It was as though the earth had opened and the skies had split. One felt as though one were present at the moment of creation when God said, 'Let there be light.'"

From the control center, Farrell echoed him, describing a searing light brighter than the midday sun that suddenly illuminated the desert. "It was golden, purple, violet, gray and blue," he wrote in his report. "It lighted every peak, crevasse and ridge of the nearby mountain range with a clarity and beauty that cannot be described but must be seen to be imagined."

"The sun can't hold a candle to it!" someone exclaimed.

"My God," declared another, "the long-hairs have lost control!"

Residents as far away as Amarillo, Texas—some 450 miles to the east—reported seeing the bomb's flash while windows shattered in homes 235 miles away. The bright flare even stunned Georgia Green, a blind University of New Mexico student who was accompanying her brother-in-law in a car ride to Albuquerque. "What's that!" she declared.

The explosion not only vaporized the steel tower but sucked sand up into the heavens, which rained down like a bright green glass that resembled jade. Eviscerated wild jackrabbits meanwhile littered the ground as far as eight hundred yards from ground zero. Scientists would later measure the crater twelve hundred feet across and twenty-five feet deep in the center.

All eyes watched as the brilliant fireball ascended into the heavens, which turned into a mushroom cloud that would rise 41,000 feet. The explosion was followed by the roar of the blast, which reached some observers as much as two minutes later. "The thunder reverberated all through the desert, bounced back and forth from the Sierra Oscuro, echo upon echo," Laurence wrote. "The ground trembled under our feet as in an earthquake."

Oppenheimer, who watched the birth of his creation, was reminded of a verse of Hindu scripture from the Bhagavad Gita. "I am become death, the destroyer of worlds."

Worlds, no—but cities, yes.

"Buddy," a soldier said, "you just saw the end of the war."

That thought percolated in the minds of many, including Farrell. "As to the present war," he wrote in his report, "there was a feeling that no matter what else might happen, we now had the means to insure its speedy conclusion and save thousands of American lives."

At base camp, Groves watched the cloud rise above the desert. Conant reached over and shook his hand; so did Bush. As cheers erupted around him, the weight of the historic moment hit Groves. He thought of the days, weeks, and years that had passed since Lt. Gen. Brehon Somervell had informed him of his appointment to lead the Manhattan Project, a task which many believed at the time was impossible, an assignment Groves had tried to refuse. "You can do it," Somervell had assured him that morning. "If it can be done."

And Groves did it.

"I personally thought of Blondin crossing Niagara Falls on his tight rope," the general wrote in his report, "only to me this tight rope had lasted for almost three years."

Despite the early hour, someone passed around a bottle of bourbon and paper cups to aid in the celebrations. "We share a feeling," the physicist Ernest Lawrence wrote hours later in his report, "that we have this day crossed a great milestone in human progress."

Amid the relief and euphoria, however, others harbored a sense of foreboding. "I am sure," one scientist commented, "that at the end of the world—in the last millisecond of the earth's existence—the last man will see what we have just seen!"

Such an image was on Bainbridge's mind when he turned and shook hands with Oppenheimer. "Now," the test director said, "we're all sons-of-bitches."

Oppenheimer and Farrell arrived at base camp by jeep.

"I'm proud of all of you," Groves told the physicist.

"Thank you," he replied.

"The war is over," Farrell interjected.

"Yes," Groves replied. "After we drop two bombs on Japan."

CHAPTER 23

"It was a great new force to be used for good or for evil."

—BRIG. GEN. THOMAS FARRELL

JULY 16, 1945

On July 16, 1945, the same day scientists detonated the first-ever atomic bomb, Truman awoke unusually late by his standards, beginning his first full day at Potsdam at eight a.m. Anxious for news of the test in New Mexico, the president spent the morning reviewing mail and meeting with Byrnes and Leahy. At eleven a.m., Winston Churchill arrived at the Little White House, joined by his daughter Mary, Foreign Minister Anthony Eden, and naval aide Cmdr. Charles Thompson. The early morning appointment no doubt pained the notoriously nocturnal prime minister, whose daughter noted that he had not been up so early in ten years. "He came to call on me, but I did not feel that I was meeting a stranger," Truman recalled. "I had an instant liking for this man who had done so much for his own country and for the Allied cause. There was something very open and genuine about the way he greeted me."

The feeling proved mutual, as evidenced by Mary's letter to her mother. The prime minster, who spent two hours with Truman, liked America's new president immensely and was certain he could work him. "I nearly wept for joy and thankfulness, it seemed like divine providence," she wrote. "I can see Papa is relieved and confident."

Truman, who had created an agenda for the meeting, asked if Churchill had one.

"No," the prime minister replied. "I don't need one."

A minor heart attack delayed Stalin's arrival, which forced the postponement of the afternoon session. Truman seized the opportunity to tour Berlin, sandwiched between Byrnes and Leahy in the back seat of a sedan. The president's motorcade rolled out at 3:40 p.m.

On the outskirts of the capital, Truman found the Second Armored Division deployed along the right side of the highway for his inspection. The motorcade stopped, and honors were rendered. Truman hopped into an open half-track reconnaissance car, which proceeded to escort the president along the two-mile line of troops plus eleven hundred vehicles. "Men and tanks were arrayed down the highway in front of me as far as the eye could see," Truman said. "The line was so long it took twenty-two minutes to ride from the beginning to the end of it."

The force's size stunned even the veteran sailor Leahy, who was accompanied on the inspection by the division's commanding officer, Brig. Gen. John Collier.

"This is the most powerful land force I have ever seen," the admiral said. "I do not see how anybody could stop them if they really wanted to go somewhere."

"Nobody has stopped them yet!" Collier replied.

As an old artillery officer, Truman could not help but feel a pang of envy. "I am only sorry," he said, "that I didn't get a chance to participate in some phase of this war myself."

The motorcade resumed its trip into the center of Berlin, turning down Wilhelmstrasse toward the ruins of the Reich Chancellery, where Hitler used to deliver his fiery speeches from the now-broken balcony. "This one-time great and beautiful metropolis," Leahy noted, "capital of a proud nation which many times I had desired to visit, was wrecked beyond repair."

The motorcade slowed to a stop outside of the battle-scarred Chancellery, where Truman, dressed in a blue suit and gray hat, spoke to news reporters.

"It is a terrible thing," he said, shaking his head, "but they brought it on themselves. It just demonstrates what man can do when he overreaches himself."

Reporters jotted down his comments.

"I never saw such destruction," the president concluded.

Churchill followed on his own tour, stopping about ten minutes after Truman departed. Unlike the president, who chose not to enter so as not to appear to gloat, Churchill demanded a tour. American soldiers had recently swarmed the Chancellery hunting souvenirs, including several who hammered off pieces of Hitler's marble desktop. Among them was Pvt. Larry Hirschbach, who swiped the führer's personal ink blotter and stationery, which he used to write a letter. "It is just about worth your life to walk around the place—holes everywhere, chunks of plaster and concrete as big as a house hanging on the reinforcing bars that strengthened them, walls with no visible means of support ready to topple at any moment, chandeliers hanging seemingly on cobwebs, and columns of beautiful polished marble scored, cracked and pitted with small arms and shrapnel marks," Hirschbach wrote. "Serves them right."

With a cigar in hand and escorted by Russian guides, the prime minister marveled at the Chancellery's shattered galleries, visited Hitler's now-looted office, and climbed down into the stench-filled bunker where the führer had shot himself. "The course Hitler had taken," Churchill said, "was much more convenient for us than the one I had feared."

Others who visited over the course of the conference likewise explored the bunker, including Assistant War Secretary John McCloy, who reflected on the devastation as he picked through the ruins, ultimately snagging an ornate chair from the underground bedroom of Eva Braun, Hitler's companion. "The whole world conflict finally welled up around this man's very feet," McCloy wrote of the führer in his diary. "The forces he set in motion only ended in his very hideout just in front of his office. If he were here now, he could look out from his office onto as complete a scene of destruction and frustration as one could wish to see. I never can understand how the Germans allowed him to get so far and bring them so low."

Up ahead in the president's car, Leahy surveyed the vast sea of rubble and ruin. "It was not hard to distinguish," he noted, "between the effects of artillery and of aerial bombing." Artillery often left a telltale hole in a masonry wall while the property behind it was obliterated. Other buildings that Leahy observed appeared to have been destroyed from the top down, with many left flattened into rubble. "That," the admiral added, "would be from bombing."

The president's motorcade passed the Tiergarten, the wrecked Reichstag, the Sports Palace, and the German Foreign Office, all in ruin. "After looking at the buildings," one Truman aide observed, "you wondered where anyone in Berlin could live."

A far more depressing sight was the endless procession of old men, women, and children, many filthy and carrying what was left of their lives. The fortunate ones had a cart or wagon, often piled high with furniture, bedding, and other salvaged belongings. "There were no young men among them," Leahy observed. "Any men we saw were old beyond military age or crippled and lame." The scene reminded Truman of similar moments in history, including the sack of Carthage, Jerusalem, and Rome. A parade of conquerors likewise ran through his mind from Genghis Khan and Alexander the Great to Civil War General William Sherman. "In that two-hour drive I saw evidence of a great world tragedy," Truman said. "I was thankful that the United States had been spared the unbelievable devastation of this war."

McCloy was horrified to watch starving men, women, and children tear apart a dead horse in the street. "How the people of this city," he wrote in his diary, "can live and not damn Hitler and his gang of ruffians every minute of the day, I do not understand."

The scene upset Stimson, who on his tour the following day could not help but feel a pang of personal guilt over America's role in Germany's destruction. "I felt," he lamented, "as though I had done a distasteful duty."

At seven-thirty p.m., a courier arrived at Stimson's quarters to deliver a cable from George Harrison with the first news of the successful atomic test that morning in New Mexico. The war secretary, who was visibly pleased, handed the notice to McCloy. "Operated on this morning," the top-secret message declared. "Diagnosis not yet complete but results seem satisfactory and already exceed expectations. Local press release necessary as interest extends great distance. Dr. Groves pleased. He returns tomorrow. I will keep you posted."

The size of the blast, which scientists would later determine was comparable to 21,000 tons of TNT, had generated queries far beyond the barbed-wire fences that encircled the Alamogordo Air Base, forcing the release of a planned cover story. "A remotely located ammunition magazine containing a considerable amount of high explosives and pyrotechnics exploded," the release stated. "There was no loss of life or injury to anyone, and the property damage outside of the explosives magazine itself was negligible."

Cable in hand, the war secretary rushed to see Truman at the Little White House, leaving McCloy to reflect on the significance. "I hope it does not augur the commencement of the destruction of modern civilization," he wrote in his diary. "In this atmosphere of destruction and callousness of men and their leaders, the whole things seems ominous."

The president sat down to an eight p.m. dinner with Leahy, Averell Harriman, Joseph Davies, and ambassador Edwin Pauley. Against the backdrop of music provided by the Second Armed Division band, the group discussed the breadlines, refugees, and poverty that marked the afternoon's tour. "There was no mood of vindictiveness or revenge," Leahy noted of the conversation, "but rather a realization brought home to those of us who fought the war from Washington of the horrible destructiveness of modern combat."

Upon Stimson's arrival fifteen minutes later, the president summoned his secretary of state for a meeting in the home's library. Behind closed doors, Stimson shared the news. "Both he and Byrnes," Stimson jotted in his notes, "were delighted." Though information consisted of just seven sentences, the mere fact that the bomb worked represented a potential war-ending solution. "As I read the message from Stimson, I realized that the test not only met the most optimistic expectation of the scientists but that the United States had in its possession an explosive force of unparalleled power," Truman said. "We were now in possession of a weapon that would not only revolutionize war but could alter the course of history and civilization."

Shortly before noon the next day, the Russian premier called on Truman. "I looked up from the desk and there stood Stalin in the doorway," the stunned president wrote in his diary. "I got to my feet and advanced to meet him. He put out his hand and smiled." Stalin was joined by Foreign Minister Molotov and interpreter Vladimir Pavlov. Truman welcomed the Russian leader along with Byrnes, Leahy, and Bohlen. "Stalin looked tired and older than he had a few months before," Bohlen observed. "He seemed to be most cautious."

Given the hour, Truman asked him to stay for lunch.

But Stalin refused.

"You could if you wanted to," the president persisted.

Stalin relented, and the two dined, discovering that the Russian leader proved fond of the California wine. "I told Stalin that I am no diplomat," Truman wrote in his diary, "but usually said yes & no to questions after hearing all the argument. It pleased him." The conversation turned to the war in the Pacific, which was at the forefront of Truman's mind. Stalin assured the president that he would keep his agreement and join the fight. Truman was ecstatic. "Most of the big points are settled. He'll be in the Jap War on August 15th. Fini Japs when that comes about," he wrote. "I can deal with Stalin. He is honest—but smart as hell."

A second message arrived at eight-thirty a.m. on morning of July 18 after Groves landed back in Washington. "Doctor has just returned most enthusiastic and confident that the little boy is as husky as his big brother," the top-secret message stated. "The light in his eyes discernable from here to Highhold and I could have heard his screams from here to my farm."

The coded message, which referred to Stimson's Long Island estate, made sense to the war secretary. Light visible from Washington to Highhold alerted him that the bomb's flash could be seen some 250 miles away. The war secretary likewise knew that Harrison's farm was in Upperville, Virginia, meaning the thunder of the explosion could be heard at a range of fifty miles. The message confirmed that the test was a stunning success, far greater, in fact, than anyone had initially hoped. The news prompted a relieved Stimson to turn to his aides. "Well," he declared, "I have been responsible for spending two billion of dollars on this atomic venture. Now that it is successful I shall not be sent to prison in Fort Leavenworth."

At 10:10 a.m., the war secretary hustled to see Truman, meeting for fifteen minutes in his office at the Little White House. The president, as Stimson jotted in his notes, was "tremendously pleased." Truman summoned Byrnes, Leahy, Marshall, King, and Hap Arnold to join them. "We reviewed our military strategy in the light of this revolutionary development," Truman wrote. "We were not ready to make use of this weapon against the Japanese, although we did not know as yet what effect the new weapon might have, physically or psychologically, when used against the enemy. For that reason the military advised that we go ahead with the existing military plans for the invasion of the Japanese home islands."

It was not until 11:35 a.m. on July 21, 1945—five days after the test—that a full report on Trinity arrived via special courier. Groves had written the first paragraph to set the tone and then handed it over to Farrell along with an outline to complete. The two leaders then revised the thirteen-page report, which included four attachments. "For the first time in history there was a nuclear explosion," Groves began. "And what an explosion!"

The general outlined in detail the scene of the test in the desert, from the early morning weather delay to the size of the crater and the height of the ensuing mushroom cloud. Groves quoted from Farrell's report, who was in the control center with Oppenheimer, and added his own personal observations. "We are all fully conscious that our real goal is still before us," he concluded. "The battle test is what counts in the war with Japan."

Page after page, line by line, Stimson pored through the report. "It was an immensely powerful document, clearly and well written and with supporting documents of the highest importance," the war secretary noted in his diary. "It gave a pretty full and eloquent report of the tremendous success of the test and revealed far greater destructive power than we expected."

The account likewise wowed McCloy. "I should have liked to have been there—the description of it leaves little doubt that we are on the edge of a new world—that of atomic force," he wrote in his diary. "God give us the intelligence and character to use it for good purpose!"

Stimson made an appointment to see Truman at three-thirty p.m., requesting that he summon Byrnes. The war secretary read aloud the report. The detailed account made clear that there might be an alternative to a bloody fight to the finish on Kyushu, a fact that relieved Truman. The end of the war was in sight. "The President was tremendously pepped up by it," Stimson recalled. "He said it gave him an entirely new feeling of confidence."

That confidence was evident to Churchill later that afternoon when he met with Stalin and Truman, the latter of whom was far more forceful in his dealings with the Soviets. At a 10:40 a.m. conference the next morning, during which time Stimson shared the top-secret report, Churchill suddenly realized the reason for the president's newfound toughness. "Now I know what happened to Truman yesterday. I couldn't understand it," he exclaimed. "When he got to the meeting after having read this report, he was a changed man."

The prime minster finished reading the report, which stunned him, as it had everyone. The ramifications of atomic energy dwarfed all else. "What was gunpowder?" Churchill declared. "Trivial. What was electricity? Meaningless."

Stimson listened.

"This atomic bomb," Churchill concluded, "is the Second Coming of Wrath."

CHAPTER 24

"It is impossible to accept unconditional surrender under any circumstances."

—FOREIGN MINISTER SHIGENORI TOGO
JULY 25, 1945, TELEGRAM

Hirohito likewise was anxious to end the war.

On July 7—the same day Truman climbed the gangplank of the *Augusta*—the emperor met with Prime Minister Kantaro Suzuki. During his June 22 meeting with the Big Six, Hirohito had demanded that senior leaders find a diplomatic way to end the fight. But efforts to do so via Russia's ambassador to Japan so far had produced no results, much to the emperor's frustration. Time was running out, particularly as the Allies prepared to gather at Potsdam.

Hirohito recommended that Japan bypass Russia's ambassador and send a special envoy to Moscow to seek help to mediate an end to the conflict. Time was of the essence. That same day Foreign Minister Shigenori Togo traveled to the mountain resort town of Karuizawa to recruit Prince Fumimaro Konoe. Of the members of the *jûshin* Hirohito had consulted in February, Konoe was the only one who had urged the emperor to make peace.

At three p.m. on July 12, Hirohito met privately with Konoe. During the fifteen-minute session, Hirohito asked for his views on the war. Konoe was alarmed by the great disparity between the army's and navy's estimates on the state of the war. Public morale, he added, had plummeted, so much so that some spoke ill of the emperor. The only hope many clung to was that somehow the throne could navigate a way out of the debacle.

Hirohito listened.

"The war," Konoe concluded, "should be terminated without delay."

At 8:50 p.m. that evening, Togo cabled Naotake Sato, Japan's ambassador to the Soviet Union, requesting permission from Molotov for a visit by Konoe. "As long as America and England insist on unconditional surrender, our country has no alternative but to see it through in an all-out effort for the sake of survival and the honor of the homeland," Togo directed Sato to explain. "The resulting enormous bloodshed of the citizens of the belligerent powers would indeed be contrary to His Majesty's desires, and so it is His Majesty's earnest hope that peace may be restored as speedily as possible for the welfare of mankind."

For Japan, it was too little, too late.

And Sato knew it.

"I believe it no exaggeration to say," he replied, "that the possibility of getting the Soviet Union to join our side and go along with our reasoning is next to nothing." The Soviets were realists, who would not respond to vague or empty peace offers. Such efforts, he predicted, would go nowhere. "If indeed our country is pressed by the necessity of terminating the war, we ourselves must first of all firmly resolve to terminate the war," he said. "Without this resolution, an attempt to sound out the intentions of the Soviet Union will result in no benefit."

What was to be gained, given the accelerated pace of American air raids, by prolonging the war and sacrificing hundreds of thousands of conscripts plus millions of innocent civilian lives in incinerated towns and cities? Japanese leaders needed to understand that even if the Soviets intervened, the nation at best faced an outcome that would closely resemble unconditional surrender. "I have expressed my extremely unreserved opinion in the foregoing and I beg your pardon for such frank statements at this time," Sato concluded. "In international relations there is no mercy, and facing reality is unavoidable."

On July 13, 1945, Sato had attempted to see Molotov, who was unavailable. The ambassador requested a conference with Vice Foreign Minister Alexander Lozovsky. During the five p.m. meeting, Sato provided a rundown of Hirohito's request and asked him to share it with

Molotov, handing him a Russian translation of the message. The special envoy, Sato stressed, was being sent at the emperor's request. A fast reply, he concluded, was desired.

Sato warned Togo that if Konoe's mission was approved, the envoy needed to come ready to deal. Japan could not, he stressed, simply rehash vague previous propositions. To do so risked creating trouble for the throne. "As long as the dispatch of an important special mission from afar has been determined," the ambassador wrote, "I believe that its purpose should be nothing other than a proposal for peace and termination of hostilities."

At midnight, Lozovsky phoned Sato to inform him that a Soviet answer would take a few days. In a message to Tokyo, Sato speculated on reasons for the delay. Maybe, he ventured, Russia did not want to rankle relations with America and England at a delicate time. Or perhaps Stalin wanted to sound out Truman and Churchill before he replied. "In the final analysis," Sato concluded on July 15, "if our country truly desires to terminate the war, we have no alternative but to accept unconditional surrender or something very close to it."

But Togo pushed back.

Securing Soviet help in mediating an end to the war, he acknowledged, would be difficult. Japan, in fact, faced a challenge just to keep Russia from joining the fight alongside America and England. But the Allied demands were impossible. "If the enemy insists on unconditional surrender to the very end," he wrote, "then our country and His Majesty would unanimously resolve to fight a war of resistance to the bitter end."

The exchange of cables revealed the depth of the Japanese government's obstinacy. Though Hirohito claimed to want peace, his government proved unable to make the necessary concessions, even as Japan's cities burned and millions fled to the countryside. American forces prepared to invade Kyushu while Russian troops crowded the Manchurian border.

In this dire moment, Sato emerged as the lone voice of reason.

And time was running out.

The ambassador's earlier speculation on the Russian delay proved prophetic. At three p.m. on July 18—the same day Truman received the second update on the success of the Trinity test—the president, Byrnes, and Bohlen called on Stalin at his villa. The Russian leader informed

Truman that the Soviets had received a message from Hirohito, requesting to send a special envoy to Moscow. He handed a copy of the cable to the president.

But Truman was not surprised.

Intelligence had forewarned of just such a possibility only the day after the president left Washington for Europe. But American awareness of Japanese moves ran much deeper. The United States had long since cracked the enemy's diplomatic code, allowing analysts to decipher and read the encrypted messages between Japan and its many embassies. Since the early days of the war, that intelligence windfall had been assembled daily into top-secret reports that ranged from six to thirty-two pages—dubbed the "Magic Diplomatic Summary"—that were distributed to the White House and other senior officials.

Included among the latest reports were the messages between Togo and Sato, which leaders had known of for days but did not want to share with the Russians for fear of alerting them of American intelligence capabilities. "Things are moving," McCloy had observed earlier that week in his diary. "What a long way we have come since that Sunday morning we heard the news of Pearl Harbor!" Sato's pragmatic evaluation had even made an impression on Forrestal. "The gist of his final message," the navy secretary wrote in his diary, "was that it was clear that Japan was thoroughly and completely defeated."

Was it worthwhile for him to respond? Stalin asked Truman.

"The President replied," according to a memo of the conversation, "that he had no respect for the good faith of the Japanese."

Russia was not at war with Japan, Stalin countered. "It might be desirable," he added, "to lull the Japanese to sleep." The premier suggested he could give a general and nonspecific response, noting that the exact nature of the mission was too vague. Or he could ignore the message and not answer or simply refuse the emperor's request. "The President," the memo noted, "said that he thought the first course of action would be satisfactory."

It would be completely factual, Molotov interjected, since it was not clear what the Konoe mission would have to offer. Byrnes speculated that fear of what the Soviets intended to do motivated the Japanese, but Molotov countered that he thought the Japanese could guess Russia's plans. Stalin agreed with his foreign minister, noting that the Japanese had no doubt seen the Soviet buildup of troops and tanks in Manchuria.

War with Russia was obviously coming.

That night in Moscow, Lozovsky sent a confidential note to Sato. Per Stalin's suggestion, which Truman approved, he explained that the imperial views were "general in form" and contained "no concrete proposal." The Konoe mission likewise was not clear. "The Government of the USSR, accordingly, is unable to give any definite reply either as to the message of the Emperor of Japan or to the dispatch of Prince Konoe as special envoy."

Sato saw the message for precisely what it was, a Russian rejection of Japan's overture. The following day the ambassador reiterated his earlier recommendation: Tokyo needed a concrete proposal for how to end the war. Sato reached out again on July 20, highlighting the continued American fire raids. With the nation's large urban areas all destroyed, he noted, bombers now incinerated midsize cities and even small towns. The American Navy, meanwhile, prowled the waters off Honshu. Japan had lost command of the seas and the skies. "Our Empire," the ambassador wrote, "can do nothing to combat the above circumstances; we are at the mercy of the enemy and committed to whatever the enemy should will."

The Japanese people, despite the dire circumstances, would fight to the last man, if the emperor so ordered. But was that worth it? "Do you think," the ambassador wrote, "the Emperor's safety can be secured by the sacrifice of seventy million citizens?"

The time for peace, he urged, was now.

The Japanese would have to endure harsh conditions, but further bloodletting had to stop. The honor of the military and the pride of the people could no longer take precedence over the state. "Our country is literally standing at the crossroads of destiny," he wrote. "We should protect the survival of our country even by enduring every kind of sacrifice." The prospects of the present war were desperate. The hope of wearing down the Americans after an invasion of the mainland was a fallacy. "The resulting imbalance of the opposing forces," he wrote, "cannot be rectified no matter how heroically our soldiers and people fight."

If the emperor chose to fight, America would destroy the country and Japan would still lose. It was imperative to end the war and stop the sacrifice of hundreds of thousands of lives. "I realize that it is a great crime to dare to make such statements, knowing that they are contrary to the views of the government," Sato concluded. "The reason for doing so, however, is that I believe that the only policy for national salvation must coincide with these ideas."

On July 21, Togo instructed Sato to explain to Moscow that Konoe's mission would be to seek Soviet help in terminating the war. In a follow-up message that same day, Togo brushed aside Sato's impassioned pleas. Though the emperor wanted Russia's help mediating peace, Japan was willing to go only so far. America and England needed to understand. "We cannot," he wrote, "accept unconditional surrender in any situation. Although it is apparent that there will be more casualties on both sides in case the war is prolonged, we will stand united as one nation against the enemy if the enemy forcibly demands our unconditional surrender."

American code breakers continued to intercept the messages between Togo and Sato, monitoring in real time the dialogue between the capitals. The message traffic showcased Japan's obstinacy even as its cities burned. American policymakers likewise understood this was not some low-level diplomat but Japan's foreign minister, transmitting the wishes of the emperor. Togo's words mattered—and he was blunt. "Tokyo," as the July 17 American intelligence summary noted, "says no unconditional surrender."

"Tokyo *again* says no unconditional surrender," added the July 22 report.

Sato's realistic portrait of his nation's future coupled with his impassioned plea for Japan to surrender once again drew special notice from Forrestal, who commented on it in his diary on July 24. Togo's reply, as the navy secretary noted, was unambiguous. "The response," he wrote, "was that the war must be fought with all the vigor and bitterness of which the nation was capable so long as the only alternative was unconditional surrender."

Like Forrestal, other senior American leaders, who now contemplated how best to end the war, read these messages literally. Despite the successful test of Trinity, Truman and his senior military advisers had decided days earlier to hold off on using atomic bombs and to continue with plans for the invasion. But it was clear now that Japan had no intention to meet

Allied demands for unconditional surrender, which Stimson and Grew had long suspected. This was coupled with intelligence that revealed the rapid buildup of enemy forces on Kyushu, which threatened to turn America's invasion into a bloodbath. "If she should persist in her fight to the end," Stimson concluded, "she had still a great military force."

CHAPTER 25

"That the war against Japan has now become plain murder has become entirely Japan's fault."

—*WASHINGTON POST*

AUGUST 1, 1945, EDITORIAL

Leo Szilard refused to give up.

Despite his repeated failed efforts to influence American policymakers, the Hungarian physicist proved relentless in his quest to stop the use of atomic weapons.

The Franck Report, he believed, argued against the bomb's use on the grounds of expediency. The scientists, he felt, now needed to make a moral case—and this time, rather than appeal to the secretary of war, Szilard set his sights on the commander in chief.

In the first few days of July, as the president prepared to leave for Potsdam, Szilard drafted a two-page petition, arguing that the use of such weapons against Japan could not be justified. "Atomic bombs," Szilard wrote, "are primarily a means for the ruthless annihilation of cities." The air force had already upped the moral stakes by incinerating dozens of Japan's cities and towns, a trend America had protested only a few years earlier when Germany did the same to England. "Our use of atomic bombs in this war would carry the world a long way further on this path of ruthlessness," he added. "A nation which sets the precedent of using these newly liberated forces of nature for purposes of destruction may have to bear the responsibility of opening the door to an era of devastation on an unimaginable scale."

America should publicly announce terms for Japan and offer its leaders a chance to surrender. Only if Japan's leaders refused to surrender should America then reexamine its position. "In view of the foregoing," Szilard concluded, "we, the undersigned, respectfully petition that you exercise your power as Commander-in-Chief to rule that the United States shall not, in the present phase of the war, resort to the use of atomic bombs."

Szilard circulated the July 3, 1945, petition among his colleagues at the Metallurgical Laboratory in Chicago. "The fact that the people of the United States are unaware of the choice which faces us," the physicist wrote in his cover letter, "increases our responsibility in this matter since those who have worked on 'atomic power' represent a sample of the population and they alone are in a position to form an opinion and declare their stand."

Fifty-three physicists and biologists signed it, but to Szilard's surprise, not everyone agreed with him. Some, in fact, welcomed the use of the atomic bomb, while others wanted a petition with milder language. "His colleagues," recalled former lab director Arthur Compton, "saw that other factors also needed consideration, among them that thousands of men were daily being killed on both sides, and that we would be guilty of permitting this slaughter to continue if we did not use what power we had to bring the war to a close."

Szilard went back to work.

On July 17, 1945, one day after the Trinity test, he circulated a second petition. Szilard nixed references to burning Japan's cities along with some of the more incendiary language. He likewise softened his blunt demand that Truman not use atomic weapons, advocating instead that the weapons be used only if "the terms which will be imposed after the war on Japan were made public in detail and Japan were given an opportunity to surrender."

This time seventy scientists signed.

Szilard's advocacy, which he had hoped would stop the bomb, instead sparked a robust debate, not just in Chicago but throughout the atomic cities. Those who opposed him or who had different ideas circulated additional petitions. Others fired off letters to Compton.

Eighteen scientists at Oak Ridge, who largely agreed with Szilard, signed another petition that called for responsibility to be shared by all allies. Sixty-seven others in Tennessee backed a competing proposal, which argued that a demonstration of the weapon should be made first, after which Japan should be given a chance to surrender before the bomb was dropped. "We feel that this course of action," the petition stated, "will heighten the effectiveness of the weapon in this war and will be of tremendous effect in the prevention of future wars."

A counterprotest led by George Parker at Oak Ridge—and which drew only one supporter—advocated the immediate use of the weapons. The chemist challenged Szilard's view that the scientists should have a greater say in the decision-making process than other Americans, including the parents of the troops in the trenches and on warships. "Are not the men of the fighting forces a part of the nation? Are not they, who are risking their lives for the nation, entitled to the weapons which have been designed?" the petition asked. "In short, are we to go on shedding American blood when we have available a means to a speedy victory? No! If we can save even a handful of American lives, then let us use this weapon—now!"

Others questioned why the atomic bomb was worse than America's conventional attacks. "It is hard to imagine anything more conclusive than the devastation of all the eastern coastal cities of Japan by fire bombs; a more fiendish hell than the inferno of blazing Tokyo is beyond the pale of conception," argued chemist Evan Young. "Then why do we attempt to draw the line of morality here, when it is a question of degree, not a question of kind?"

Compton had one distressed young physicist barge into his office. "I have buddies who have fought through the battle of Iwo Jima," the young man said. "Some of them have been killed, others wounded. We've got to give these men the best weapons we can produce. If one of these men should be killed because we didn't let them use the bombs, I would have failed them. I just could not make myself feel that I had done my part."

The flood of feedback revealed a lack of consensus. "It was difficult from such petitions," Compton noted, "to get a balanced view of how our men were thinking."

Military intelligence tipped Groves off of the furor. The general did not object so long as the petitions remained classified. To better discern opinion, Groves suggested Compton conduct a poll. Farrington Daniels, who succeeded him that month as director of the Metallurgical Lab, took charge.

Daniels's questionnaire offered scientists five choices. The first was to use the bomb in a manner most effective to bring an end to the war with minimal cost to American lives. The second was to conduct a demonstration in Japan followed by a renewed call for surrender before the full use of the weapons. The third involved a demonstration in this country for representatives of Japan. The fourth was to withhold military use but do a public demonstration. The fifth option was to keep the weapons secret and never use them.

The scientists, who ranged from physicists and chemists to biologists and metallurgists, placed a number in an envelope. Only three scientists—or just 2 percent—voted against any use of the weapon. Another sixteen people voted to withhold all military use but to make a public demonstration. The remaining 131 scientists—totaling 87 percent—voted to use the bomb in some fashion. Of those, 108 preferred a demonstration either in America or in Japan, followed by an invitation to surrender. Twenty-three scientists equaling 15 percent voted for the bomb's immediate use. "My experience with this questionnaire," Compton said, "confirmed my faith in the reliability of democratic processes in judging matters of human concern."

On July 23, Col. Kenneth Nichols visited Compton. "Washington wants at once the results of the opinion polls on the use of the bomb," the district engineer said.

Compton, who had assembled the many petitions, letters, and surveys, summarized the findings as best he could, only for Nichols to return an hour later.

"Washington wants to know what *you* think," he said.

If he said he were opposed to the bomb, Compton felt he might prevent an atomic attack on Japan. "I knew all too well the destruction and human agony the bombs would cause. I knew the danger they held in the hands of some future tyrant. These facts I had been living with for four years," he said. "But I wanted the war to end. I wanted life to become normal again. I saw a chance for an enduring peace that would be demanded by the very destructiveness of these weapons. I hoped that by the use of the bombs many fine young men I knew might be released at once from the demands of war and thus be given a chance to live and not to die."

"My vote is with the majority," he said. "It seems to me that as the war stands the bomb should be used, but no more drastically than needed to bring surrender."

The following day Compton forwarded a complete packet to Nichols along with a one-page memo, highlighting the fact that the majority of the scientists polled favored the use of the bomb following a military demonstration in Japan, coupled with a renewed opportunity to surrender before the full use of the weapon was employed. "This coincides," Compton concluded, "with my own preference and is, as nearly I can judge, the procedure that has found most favor in all informed groups where the subject has been discussed."

Nichols, in turn, drafted a two-page cover letter to Groves to which he attached nine documents. Those records included Szilard's original and revised petitions, the latter of which the physicist sealed inside an envelope with instructions that it should be opened only by the president's representative. Other records included Farrington's poll, the various additional and counterpetitions, and letters submitted to Compton. "Contrary to the hopes of Mr. Leo Szilard, who started the original petition," Nichols wrote on July 25, "it is believed that that these collective papers generally support the present plans for the use of the weapon."

Seven days later, on August 1, 1945, Groves forwarded the materials to George Harrison, Stimson's deputy on the Interim Committee. Truman was, of course, in Potsdam. Unlike the special report on Trinity, no effort was made to send these files by courier. Groves, who thumbed through the petitions, felt the records were little more than a rehash of already expressed concerns. "The petitions," he added, "contained nothing new."

A top-secret memorandum for the record, drafted by Interim Committee secretary Gordon Arneson after the war, revealed that Truman never saw the files. By then, the memo stated, the question over the use of the bomb had already been fully considered and settled. In short, Szilard's final try to stop the bomb had failed. "As far as the scientists employed on the project were concerned, they had been given adequate opportunity to express their views on this or any other question relating to the project to the Interim Committee through the Scientific Panel," Arneson concluded. "In view of the foregoing, it was decided that no useful purpose would be served by transmitting either the petition or any of the other attached documents to the White House, particularly since the President was not then in the country."

CHAPTER 26

"Japan's military position has deteriorated to the point where the choice facing her is literally one of surrender or suicide."

—BARNET NOVER

WASHINGTON POST, JULY 12, 1945

The first successful test of an atomic bomb—coupled with Japan's refusal to accept unconditional surrender—elevated the importance of issuing an ultimatum to the enemy before the use of the new weapon. Since arriving in Europe, Stimson had continued to press the issue. The first full day at Potsdam, the war secretary wrote a top-secret memo to the president, laying out his argument and forwarding a copy to Byrnes. "The Japanese soldier has proved himself capable of a suicidal, last ditch defense; and will no doubt continue to display such a defense on his homeland," Stimson wrote on July 16, 1945. "Yet we have enormous factors in our favor and any step which can be taken to translate those advantages into a prompt and successful conclusion of the war should be taken." Japan's recent overtures to Russia, he added, meant such a time had arrived. He urged Truman to complete the warning based on the draft prepared by the State, War, and Navy departments. "It seems to me," the war secretary concluded, "that we are at the psychological moment to commence our warnings to Japan."

But Byrnes balked.

The new secretary of state, who had taken over a fiercely divided department, had followed Truman's lead and sought out Cordell Hull. Hull had previously warned that softening the administration's position would be appeasement. He instead advised Byrnes to hold off until the climax of America's bombing campaign and Russia's entry into the war.

Much to Stimson's frustration, Byrnes had agreed.

Word of the acrimonious debate had since leaked. Not only did the press report that Truman carried a draft ultimatum to Potsdam, but reporters zeroed in on the central battle—the fate of the emperor. "So hot has it become," one journalist observed, "that some who believe in retention are afraid to speak up lest they be called 'reactionaries' or even 'Fascists.'"

Back in Washington, lawmakers jumped into the fray, reflecting the division that had dogged the State Department for weeks. Republican Senator Wallace White of Maine took to the floor, demanding Truman clarify unconditional surrender. "Much might be gained by such a statement," the minority leader cautioned. "Nothing could be lost."

Senator Homer Capehart agreed, arguing that America suffered eight thousand casualties a week at a cost of $1 billion every four days. "It isn't a matter of whether you hate the Japs or not. I certainly hate them," the Indiana Republican howled. "But what's to be gained by continuing a war when it can be settled now on the same terms as two years from now?"

But others stood in opposition, including Senate Majority Leader Alben Barkley, who questioned why a victorious America would even engage in such a debate that served only to stiffen the enemy's resistance. "Defeat of Japan must be a complete defeat," the Kentucky Democrat declared. "It must be a defeat which she recognizes as a defeat."

Opinion page editors and columnists likewise sounded off.

The famed journalist Walter Lippmann argued that since Hitler had usurped all authority from the German state, he had to be destroyed. But as history had shown, the Japanese emperor was less a ruler and more of a figurehead. "It is quite conceivable then that he might continue to reign," Lippmann wrote, "but that the country would be ruled by men who had surrendered the conquests and military power of Japan and had given guarantees."

The New York Times disagreed, stating that America had been clear all along on its demands for Japan. A lack of clarity was not what prolonged the war, but rather Japanese obstinacy. "We could shorten the war, of course, if we softened our demand," the paper opined. "But to do so would be as shortsighted as it would be faint-hearted."

The debate trickled down to the citizenry who, like opinion page writers, lawmakers, and State Department diplomats, had fierce opinions. "There is no short-cut to victory in the Pacific," Ramon Lavalle of San Francisco wrote in a letter to the editor. "It is either unconditional surrender or destruction, no matter how long it may take and how costly it may turn out to be. Unconditional surrender cannot contain a single compromise."

But Trinity had proved a game changer.

And as the flurry of message traffic revealed, events were now moving at a rapid pace, forcing leaders to make consequential decisions. "Operation may be possible any time from August 1 depending on state of preparation of patient and condition of atmosphere," Harrison cabled on July 23. "From point of view of patient only, some chance August 1 to 3, good chance August 4 to 5 and barring unexpected relapse almost certain before August 10."

That reality brought into sharper focus the need for an urgent warning to Japan, if America, in fact, planned to unleash atomic fury on the enemy's homeland. Though the Interim Committee had initially recommended that the bomb be dropped with no warning, senior leaders increasingly feared world opinion would turn against the United States if it obliterated a city—and killed tens of thousands of men, women, and children—without first offering Japan a chance to surrender. "Every effort," as General Marshall advised, "should be made to keep our record of warning clear." Armed with the proposed dates for the bomb's possible use, Truman at last approved the ultimatum that Stimson, McCloy, and Grew had worked on for weeks.

The president shared the warning with Churchill and Chiang Kai-shek. Since Russia was not in the war, Stalin would not be asked to sign, though Truman privately informed him of the ultimatum. Much to Stimson's frustration, Byrnes had convinced the president to strike out any mention of the emperor's fate. During a 9:20 a.m. meeting on July 24, Stimson urged Truman, if dynastic continuity became an obstacle to peace, to reassure the Japanese verbally through diplomatic channels. "He said that he had that in mind," Stimson noted, "and that he would take care of it." Despite his concern over some of the edits, the war secretary was pleased overall with the ultimatum, which he noted offered the enemy two paths. "It was designed to promise destruction if Japan resisted," Stimson said, "and hope, if she surrendered."

With the ultimatum complete, a bigger question remained.

Would Truman approve the weapon's use?

For such a monumental decision—to destroy a city with an atomic bomb—there is little in the way of a documentary record for precisely when the green light was given. No single meeting—or set of meeting minutes—records any such conversation, much less decision. Even an internal review by Truman's staff after the war failed to nail down an exact date, concluding that it likely occurred between July 22 and July 24. During those days, the president met often with all the key players, from his senior lieutenants to British prime minister Winston Churchill. In all likelihood, as some historians have surmised, Truman's decision resulted not so much from a single meeting as from several that shaped his views.

The largest factor that weighed on the president—and the one he had made clear when he met with the Joint Chiefs of Staff in June—was just how bloody an invasion would be. The latest intelligence intercepts sparked alarm. The strategic situation on Kyushu had changed dramatically since the president's approval of the invasion barely five weeks earlier. The Japanese, who had correctly concluded that Kyushu was America's next target, had begun to rush troops to the island to build a defensive force. By the third week of July, code breakers had detected ten combat divisions on Kyushu with another en route plus two depot divisions. The Japanese reinforcement efforts, which showed no signs of slowing down, were on track to create a total force of 916,218 troops by the time American forces stormed the beaches in November. That was nearly three times the number of troops General Marshall had told the president planners expected. To complement ground troops, Japan hustled to build an air force of 10,440 kamikazes made up 3,230 fighters and 1,810 bombers, plus another 5,400 trainers.

Much as at Iwo Jima and Okinawa, the goal was not victory but attrition. Japanese leaders highlighted that at Okinawa dogged troops had held off a force five times larger for nearly three months. America was facing a bloodletting. "This threatening development," as one intelligence report warned, "if not checked, may grow to a point where we attack on a ratio of one to one, which is not a recipe for victory."

Soaring estimates of potential casualties complemented reports of Japan's buildup on Kyushu. A War Department study prepared by future Nobel laureate William Shockley painted a brutal image of an invasion's cost. "We shall probably have to kill at least 5 to 10 million Japanese," Shockley concluded in his July 21 report. "This might cost us between 1.7 and 4 million casualties including 400,000 and 800,000 killed."

During a conference with his top aides, Truman asked Marshall what an invasion of Kyushu and Honshu would cost. Though his numbers were lower than some Pentagon estimates, the math was still painful. "It was his opinion," Truman recalled, "that such an invasion would cost at a minimum one quarter of a million casualties, and might cost as much as a million, on the American side alone, with an equal number for the enemy."

The others present agreed.

But those casualties were only one part of the bloody equation. Each month the conflict continued, more people across Asia died, victims not only of fire raids and fighting, but famine and disease, the latter the tragic by-products of a conflict that now claimed the lives of an estimated 500,000 men, women, and children each month.

The war, in short, had to end.

Truman turned to Stimson, asking what cities might be targeted. The secretary rattled off the list, which included Hiroshima, Kokura, Nagasaki, and Niigata.

"It is my suggestion," Truman added, "that we pick out a place to drop the bomb as near a war plant as possible so as not injure any more people than necessary."

In the years since, some have questioned Truman's role in approving the bomb. Was the weapon's use a foregone conclusion, or did the former Missouri farmer really have a say? "Truman made no decision because there was no decision to be made," recalled aide George Elsey. "He could no more have stopped it than a train moving down a track." Groves likewise noted that the project had built up an incredible momentum. "As time went on, and as we poured more and more money and effort into the project, the government became increasingly committed to the ultimate use of the bomb," he said. "As far as I was concerned, his decision was one of noninterference—basically, a decision not to upset the existing plans."

The fact remains that as commander in chief, Truman certainly could have stopped the bomb. The bigger question is, why would he have wanted to do so?

None of his senior lieutenants urged him to stop.

Stimson supported the weapon's use; so did Byrnes and Marshall. The Interim Committee, which had examined the issue, had urged Truman to use the bomb as soon as it was ready. "No man," Stimson said, "in our position and subject to our responsibilities, holding in his hands a weapon of such possibilities for accomplishing this purpose and saving those lives, could have failed to use it and afterwards looked his countrymen in the face." Churchill agreed. "The decision whether or not to use the atomic bomb to compel the surrender of Japan was never even an issue," he added. "There was unanimous, automatic, unquestioned agreement around our table; nor did I ever hear the slightest suggestion that we should do otherwise."

After the war, Truman took full responsibility for what would prove to be one of the most consequential decisions ever made by an American president and one that would forever define his legacy. His goal, he proclaimed, was to save lives. "The final decision of where and when to use the atomic bomb was up to me," he declared. "Let there be no mistake about it. I regarded the bomb as a military weapon and never had any doubt that it should be used."

On July 25, the same day the Pentagon issued orders for the atomic strike, Truman recorded his decision in his diary. "We have discovered the most terrible bomb in the history of the world. It may be the fire destruction prophesied in the Euphrates Valley Era, after Noah and his fabulous Ark," he wrote. "This weapon is to be used against Japan between now and August 10." Truman wrote that he instructed Stimson to target military objectives and avoid killing women and children which, though a noble intention, was an impossibility. As Trinity had demonstrated, the bomb was not a scalpel but a sledgehammer. "Even if the Japs are savages, ruthless, merciless and fanatic, we as the leader of the world for the common welfare cannot drop this terrible bomb on the old capital or the new,"

Truman wrote. "The target will be a purely military one and we will issue a warning statement asking the Japs to surrender and save lives. I'm sure they will not do that, but we will have given them the chance."

Despite Japan's recent peace feelers to Moscow, few believed their sincerity—and with good reason. After all, only four years earlier, Japanese diplomats had negotiated peace right up until the attack on Pearl Harbor. Furthermore, as intercepted cables made clear, Japan still refused to accept unconditional surrender. "We faced a terrible decision," Byrnes wrote. "We could not rely on Japan's inquiries to the Soviet Union about a negotiated peace as proof that Japan would surrender unconditionally without the use of the bomb."

Truman's decision raised another important question.

With the bomb, did the United States still need Russia in the war?

Marshall reiterated that the original goal was for Soviet forces to tie down the Japanese in Manchuria and prevent the reinforcement of forces on Kyushu. The buildup of Russian troops along the border had prompted the Japanese to respond in kind, which had helped accomplish that goal. Despite that, he added, there was little else America could do. "Even if we went ahead in the war without the Russians, and compelled the Japanese to surrender to our terms, that would not prevent the Russians from marching into Manchuria anyhow and striking, thus permitting them to get virtually what they wanted in the surrender terms."

The last item on Truman's checklist was to inform Stalin of the bomb.

The president and his aides had gone back and forth in recent months over whether to alert the Russian leader before or after the bomb's use. In the end, Truman decided it would be best to let Stalin know in advance but not to reveal any more details than necessary.

The president's talk with Stalin on July 24, 1945, which has been described by some historians as one of the most memorable moments of the conference, is surprising for how unmemorable it actually was. The conversation, which lasted at most thirty seconds, occurred at the end of the afternoon's session at Cecilienhof Palace. As attendees rose to leave, Truman walked around the wooden table to greet Stalin. The only witnesses were the two translators. The president spoke in hushed tones and was likewise cryptic, never actually using the word *atomic*. "I casually mentioned to Stalin that we had a new weapon of unusual destructive force," Truman recalled. "The Russian Premier showed no special interest. All he said was that he was glad to hear it and hoped we would make 'good use of it against the Japanese.'" Churchill watched the interaction. "I knew what the President was going to do. What was vital to measure was its effect on Stalin," the prime minister wrote. "He seemed to be delighted."

"How did it go?" Churchill asked Truman afterward.

"He never asked a question," the president replied.

Stalin's seeming lack of interest stemmed from the fact that he already knew. The Soviet ruler had a mole buried inside the project, the German-born physicist and naturalized British citizen, Klaus Fuchs, who worked at Los Alamos and had witnessed the Trinity test.

With the decision made and Stalin informed, Truman needed only to warn Japan. At 9:20 p.m. on July 26, 1945, the president issued the thirteen-point ultimatum that would forever be known as the Potsdam Declaration. The 658-word warning, signed by Truman, Churchill, and Chiang Kai-shek, served as Japan's last chance to end the war before America unleashed atomic Armageddon on its cities. Diplomats handed the message to representatives of the neutral nations of Switzerland and Sweden for delivery to the Japanese. Shortwave radios in San Francisco and New York meanwhile broadcast the warning in two dozen languages while newspapers worldwide published the ultimatum in full. "The prodigious land, sea and air forces of the United States, the British Empire, and of China, many times reinforced by their armies and air fleets from the west, are poised to strike the final blows upon Japan," the declaration began. "This military power is sustained and inspired by the determination of all the Allied Nations to prosecute the war against Japan until she ceases to resist."

The ruins of Germany served as an example of what Japan would face if it continued its futile resistance. "The full application of our military power," the message continued, "backed by our resolve, will mean the inevitable and complete destruction of the Japanese armed forces and just as inevitably the utter devastation of the Japanese homeland."

The time had arrived for Japan to decide its fate: Would it continue to follow the militarist leaders down the path of annihilation, or would it choose reason and peace?

"Following are our terms," the declaration stated. "We will not deviate from them. There are no alternatives. We shall brook no delay." The Allies demanded an end to control by the nation's militarists coupled with the forfeiture of conquered territories. Japan's military, once disarmed, would be returned home. "We do not intend that the Japanese shall be enslaved as a race or destroyed as a nation," the message continued, "but stern justice shall be meted out to all war criminals, including those who have visited cruelties upon our prisoners."

Democratic principles would be strengthened, including freedoms of thought, speech, and religion, while respect for human rights would be established. Japan would be allowed to maintain industries needed to sustain its economy, but none that might permit it to rearm for war. No mention of the emperor was made, but the declaration stated that the government would be chosen through the freely expressed will of the Japanese people. Likewise absent from the ultimatum was any reference to the newest weapon in America's arsenal. Once Japan fulfilled these obligations, occupying forces would leave. "We call upon the Government of Japan to proclaim now the unconditional surrender of all the Japanese armed forces," the declaration concluded. "The alternative for Japan is prompt and utter destruction."

Headlines around the country and world trumpeted the demands. "Allies Order Japan to Quit or Be Destroyed," declared *The New York Times*.

"Last Call to Japan: Surrender Now," added *The Philadelphia Inquirer*.

"U.S. Warns Nips That Nation Is Doomed," touted the *Tallahassee Daily Democrat*.

Editorial pages in big cities and small towns likewise weighed in, with most agreeing that it would be not just perilous but foolhardy for the Japanese to continue the fight. "The fate of Japan is up to her leaders," declared the *Indianapolis News*. "The question for them to decide is whether they will attempt to lead the empire into national suicide."

"Quit now or be destroyed, that is the sole choice," added the *Ventura County Star Free-Press*.

"Japan is finished," opined the *Duluth News-Tribune*. "But how soon will she admit it?"

That was the question to which the world now waited for an answer.

If Japan accepted the Allied ultimatum, Truman informed Stimson he would rescind his order. But time and American patience were running out, a fact McCloy noted in his diary. "Maybe the Secretary's big bomb may not be dropped—the Japs had better hurry if they are to avoid it." In the meantime, however, America's military machinery moved quickly to prepare to execute the president's orders. Despite Stimson's earlier insistence that Kyoto be spared, Groves once again advocated that America destroy Japan's ancient capital, which he believed would deliver the necessary seismic shock to propel the enemy to surrender. "All your local military advisors," Harrison cabled the war secretary, "definitely favor your pet city."

But Stimson continued to balk. "Aware of no factors to change my decision," he curtly replied within hours. "On the contrary new factors tend to confirm it."

The war secretary went so far as to raise his concern with Truman, seeking validation of his decision to spare Kyoto from the commander in chief. "As to the matter of the special target which I had refused to permit," Stimson wrote in his diary, "he strongly confirmed my view and said he felt the same way." The war secretary likewise shared Harrison's cables with Gen. Hap Arnold, whose airmen would deliver the bomb. "He told me," Stimson added, "that he agreed with me about the target which I had struck off the program."

Kyoto was once again safe.

Directives went out to senior army, navy, and air force commanders in the Pacific, lifting the previous embargo against attacking the designated target cities, but with a key caveat. "The targets," the orders said, "are released to the Commanding General, U.S. Army Strategic Air Forces for attack only by the 509 Composite Group, 20th Air Force."

At the same time, directions landed in Hap Arnold's inbox, outlining the top-secret plan for the world's first atomic attack, codenamed Centerboard. The uranium bomb Little Boy would be ready to deploy between August 1 and August 10. "Plans are to drop it," the memo stated, "the first day of good weather following readiness." The four designated target cities were listed in order as Hiroshima, Kokura, Niigata, and Nagasaki. "All four cities are believed to contain large numbers of key Japanese industrialists and political figures who have sought refuge from major destroyed cities," the memo continued. "The attack is planned to be visual to insure accuracy and will await favorable weather. The four targets give a very high probability of one being open if the weather varies from that forecast, as they are considerably separated."

The job of overseeing the bomb's delivery would fall to Gen. Carl Spaatz, whom Arnold had tapped to command the newly formed U.S. Army Strategic Air Force in the Pacific, making him the senior airman in the theater. A veteran of the European war, the fifty-four-year-old Spaatz had opposed firebombing, so much so his family later said that he had been reluctant to take the job in the Pacific for fear it would be worse than Germany. "When the atomic bomb was first discussed with me," he confided in his diary, "I was not in favor of it just as I have never favored the destruction of cities as such with all inhabitants being killed. It was pointed out to me however that the use of the atomic bomb would certainly mean that an invasion would be unnecessary and that thousands of American lives would be saved."

Aware of the bomb's awesome power—as well as the controversy that would no doubt surround it—Spaatz demanded his orders in writing. "If I'm going to kill 100,000 people, I'm not going to do it on verbal orders," he said. "I want a piece of paper." Groves drafted the directive, which was then circulated among senior leaders in the air force and Interim Committee before it was sent to Marshall and Stimson for final approval. Orders in hand, Spaatz would fly to the Pacific to brief MacArthur and Nimitz. "The 509th Composite Group, 20th Air Force will deliver its first special bomb as soon as weather will permit visual bombing after about 3 August 1945," orders stated. "The foregoing directive is issued to you by direction and with the approval of the Secretary of War and of the Chief of Staff, USA."

A study on Guam of the target cities raised a concern. "Hiroshima according to prisoner of war reports is the only one of four target cities for Centerboard that does not have Allied prisoners of war camps," Spaatz's headquarters cabled Washington. "Advise."

For senior leaders, there was little that could be done. "Targets previously assigned for Centerboard remain unchanged," the reply stated. "However if you consider your information reliable Hiroshima should be given first priority among them. Information available here indicates that there are prison camps in practically every major Japanese city."

Continued studies of the Trinity test illuminated what could be expected when the bomb detonated over Japan. Scientists concluded that to obtain maximum damage, the fuse should be set to explode at 1,800 feet. At that height, the blast would be lethal to anyone on the ground at a range of 1,000 feet while the heat and flames would likely extend the kill zone out to 2,000 feet. Serious injury could be expected as far away as 3,500 feet. "Practically all structures in an area of one or two square miles should be completely demolished," one report predicted, "and a total area of six to seven square miles should be so devastated that the bulk of the buildings would have to have major repairs to make them habitable." Scientists likewise described what the bomb would look like to witnesses on the ground. "At 10 miles for a few thousandths of a second the light will be as bright as a thousand suns; at the end of a second, as bright as one or possibly two suns," the memo concluded. "The effect on anyone about a half mile away who looks directly at the explosion would probably be permanent sight impairment; at one mile, temporary blindness; and up to and even beyond ten miles, temporary sight impairment."

Japan's response did not take long.

At six a.m. on July 27, 1945, Tokyo radio receivers picked up the broadcast from San Francisco. Vice Minister of Foreign Affairs Shunichi Matsumoto, who spent the morning poring over the ultimatum, advised Togo that Japan should accept. At a minimum, Matsumoto advocated, the full ultimatum should be shared with the Japanese public.

"Wait," the foreign minister instructed, "it's not going to be as easy as that."

Matsumoto listened.

"The army," Togo added, "will never accept the proclamation as it stands."

The foreign minister noted that the Allies had dropped the demand for the "unconditional surrender of Japan" and replaced it with the "unconditional surrender of all the Japanese forces." That important softening of demands, he concluded, signaled a possible willingness to negotiate. Despite Moscow's clear reluctance to help mediate, Togo held out hope that Stalin might intervene on Japan's behalf. He sent a cable to Sato to urge him to try again.

At ten-thirty a.m., the Supreme War Council met to review the ultimatum. Togo highlighted the lessening of Allied demands, urging his colleagues that it would be "extremely impolitic" to reject the ultimatum. Despite pushback from his hawkish counterparts, the foreign minister convinced the majority to hold off on any reply to see if the Soviets might still help.

The question of how best to inform the public dominated the Japanese Cabinet meeting that afternoon. Togo again led the debate, arguing that the government should say nothing until leaders determined how to answer to the ultimatum. Some of his colleagues questioned whether Japan could do that, given that the American radios blared the news while bombers blanketed the nation with leaflets that carried a translation of the declaration. If the news was released, War Minister General Korechika Anami insisted that Japan should state its rejection of the demands, an opinion seconded by the army and navy chiefs of staff. Despite the kaleidoscope of opinions, the cabinet reached a compromise in which Japan would release the news but downplay it and make no official statement. Prime Minister Suzuki said he would *mokusatsu* the proclamation, a tricky and in this case dangerous word that could be translated in several ways. The softer interpretation, which Suzuki no doubt intended, was to "remain in a wise and masterly inactivity" or essentially to "wait and see." A harsher translation—and the one the Japanese press used—meant to "kill it with silence" or to "treat with silent contempt."

At a four p.m. press conference the next day, the seventy-seven-year-old Suzuki hoped to clarify the delicate situation, only to veer further off script. "The government does not regard it as a thing of any great value; the government will just ignore it," the prime minister said. "We will press forward resolutely to carry the war to a successful conclusion."

And that was the message the world heard.

In a large font and with bold print, newspaper headline writers heralded the enemy's reply. "Japs Refuse to Surrender," announced the *Indianapolis News*.

"Cabinet Decides to Fight On," added the *Los Angeles Times*.

"Demand to Be Ignored," declared the *Fort Worth Star-Telegram*.

With the bomb now a certainty, one of the last items to tackle was Truman's proposed press statement—the brainchild of the Interim Committee—to be issued by the White House after the weapon's first use. The task of drafting it had fallen to reporter William Laurence of *The New York Times*. Stimson now needed Truman to sign off on the final statement, which he had edited in response to the Trinity test and the recent Potsdam Declaration. "The time schedule on Groves' project is progressing so rapidly that it is now essential that statement for release by you be available not later than Wednesday, 1 August," the war secretary wrote on July 30, 1945. "Sorry circumstances seem to require this emergency action."

Anxious to wrap up in Potsdam, Truman planned to depart on August 2 for the return voyage home. He wanted to be gone when the new weapon was unleashed on Japan, which would spare him any uncomfortable questions from Stalin. Truman read over Stimson's note and then flipped over the pink cable and reached for a pencil. The eleven words he scribbled on the back would prove to be his only written instructions greenlighting the bomb's use. In them, he made clear the first date on which the bomb could be dropped. "Suggestions approved," the president wrote. "Release when ready but not sooner than August 2."

Japan's fate was sealed.

PART IV

"Atomic energy knows neither friend nor foe. It is primeval force. It is a new beginning, a new world; or it is the end."

—MARQUIS CHILDS, SYNDICATED COLUMNIST
AUGUST 8, 1945

Battered religious relics stand watch on a hill overlooking the ruins of Nagasaki, which was destroyed by an atomic bomb on Aug. 9, 1945. *(NARA)*

CHAPTER 27

"The atomic bomb is unendurable."

—MAJ. GEN. LESLIE GROVES
SEPTEMBER 21, 1945

Tens of thousands of Japanese lives now rested in the hands of Col. Paul Tibbets, Jr. Japan's rejection of the Potsdam Declaration coupled with Truman's approval of the atomic bomb shifted the action from the battered ruins of Berlin to the tiny Pacific island of Tinian, home to the 509th Composite Group. Throughout the summer, atomic warfare had been debated around conference room tables in the Pentagon and State Department and in labs from Chicago to Los Alamos. In these bureaucratic settings, commanders armed with agendas argued over what cities to target, the morality of the weapon, and whether America needed to warn Japan. But those issues were now resolved. The time for action had arrived.

And that role fell to Tibbets.

"My job," he said, "was to wage atomic warfare."

At first glance, Tibbets appeared an unlikely leader to be trusted with the delivery of the first-ever combat atomic weapon, one that represented the culmination of a $2 billion investment as well as the herculean work of the nation's leading scientists and industrialists. Handsome, trim, and of medium build, Tibbets had had only recently turned thirty. On his shoulders he still wore the eagles of a colonel, not the stars of a general.

But Tibbets's youth disguised his drive and talent.

Born in the Prairie State, he had spent his childhood pinballing between Illinois, Iowa, and Florida, where his father sought refuge from the harsh midwestern winters. At the age of twelve, he took his first flight in a Waco 9 biplane with fabric wings and a wooden propeller. In the heavens over Miami, Tibbets caught what he later described as a delightfully incurable disease. "I could see the unfortunate earth-bound mortals crawling around like ants on the ground below," he said. "The flight was an important event in my life—more important than I realized at the time—because it was then that I subconsciously opted for a career in the sky."

After graduating high school from Western Military Academy in Illinois in 1933, Tibbets enrolled at the University of Florida in Gainesville. His father's desire for him to become a doctor prompted Tibbets to transfer after his sophomore year to the University of Cincinnati, where he planned to later attend medical school. He spent summers working in a urology clinic, administering shots to combat gonorrhea and syphilis. Tibbets's fascination with aviation soon superseded his interest in medicine, a fact his mentor Dr. Alfred Crum noticed.

"I'm not so sure you want to be a doctor," Crum said.

Tibbets agreed, informing him he had thought about dropping out of school.

"Why don't you do it?"

"I'm afraid of what my old man will say," he replied.

"If you want to go fly," Crum advised him, "go ahead."

Over Christmas break, Tibbets confided the same in his mother, who could sense his unhappiness. To his surprise, she, too, encouraged him. "If you want to fly," she said, placing her hand on his shoulder, "go right ahead and do it, because I know you will be all right."

Even his father, whose scorn he had so feared, proved far more receptive, though he questioned his son's judgment. "The die," Tibbets later said, "had been cast."

On February 25, 1937, Tibbets joined the Army Air Corps. Over the next few years, he earned his wings and began to climb the ranks and distinguish himself. When the war broke out, he deployed to England, where he commanded the 340th Bombardment Squadron of the 97th Bombardment Group. In that role, he led America's first bombing raid against occupied Europe on August 17, 1942. That mission, which targeted the French marshaling yards at Rouen, was the first of twenty-five Tibbets flew in Europe and later North Africa. Such missions could be brutal as pilots navigated through black clouds of bursting flak while dodging fighters. Tibbets discovered that firsthand when a 20-millimeter cannon shell tore into the cockpit, destroying a section of the instrument panel and wounding his copilot, though he would later recover. "A portion of his left hand had been torn off by the exploding shell," Tibbets recalled. "Blood was spraying over what instruments were left in the shattered cabin."

Tibbets's skills in the air led to prestigious assignments, including secretly flying Maj. Gen. Mark Clark to Gibraltar on October 19, 1942, so he could rendezvous with the French in advance of the North Africa invasion. A few weeks later Tibbets was tapped again, this time to airlift Gen. Dwight Eisenhower and his staff to the Rock on the eve of the landings. On November 5, the morning of the general's scheduled departure, rain and mist blanketed the southern coast of England. The fog proved so dense, Tibbets observed, that even birds refused to fly. "A successful takeoff," he added, "seemed out of the question."

But Eisenhower was anxious.

"If it was just the crew and me, I'd go," Tibbets told the four-star general. "But I've got to think about you and your staff."

"Well, son," Eisenhower replied, "I've got a war about to begin down there and that's where I have to be."

"Okay, sir," Tibbets said. "Let's go."

Tibbets lifted off into the fog, leveling off at two hundred feet to avoid any German fighters. Given the tight space on a B-17, the general wedged himself between Tibbets and his copilot on a makeshift seat fashioned from a two-by-four. "Eisenhower could see how nearly impossible the weather conditions were," Tibbets said, "but he never said a word or expressed a doubt about our decision." Eight hours later and some twelve hundred miles to the south, Tibbets touched down at Gibraltar. "All of us are well," Eisenhower cabled his headquarters, "although I must say that the trip by bomber is not something to be taken on your honeymoon."

Tibbets's strong self-confidence, which made him a daring pilot, at times prompted him to clash with his superiors. That was the case soon after he landed in Algiers as the assistant operations officer in January 1943 with the Twelfth Air Force. Col. Lauris Norstad, who was his boss, ordered a raid on the coastal Tunisian city of Bizerte at just 6,000 feet.

"If we send them in at 6,000 feet," Tibbets protested, "they'll be wiped out."

Tibbets's outburst in front of other staff officers undermined and infuriated Norstad, whose face reddened. Though Tibbets later admitted he should have been more tactful, any such self-reflection escaped him as the confrontation escalated. Rather than embrace Tibbets's knowledge, which he had earned on two dozen missions, Norstad turned that experience against him in an effort to humiliate him. "It appears Colonel Tibbets has been flying too much," Norstad proclaimed. "He may be suffering from combat fatigue."

The insinuation that he was a coward enraged Tibbets, particularly since Norstad had never flown a combat mission. "Something snapped in me at that moment," Tibbets later wrote. "Whatever I had learned of discipline and self-control left me."

"I'll tell you what I'm prepared to do," Tibbets barked at Norstad. "I'll lead that raid myself at 6,000 feet if you will come along as my co-pilot."

Norstad retreated, but not for long.

Lt. Gen. Jimmy Doolittle, commander of the Twelfth Air Force, summoned Tibbets. Norstad, who was politically connected, wanted Tibbets court-martialed. But Doolittle liked Tibbets, whom he considered "an excellent officer and bomber pilot." Rather than see his career wrecked, Doolittle offered a solution. "I've just received a message from Hap Arnold," he said. "He wants an experienced bombardment officer to come back to the States and help with the development of a big new bomber. I've recommended you for the job."

The bomber was, of course, the B-29, which at the time was in development by Boeing. Doolittle's staff car idled outside to take him to his apartment and then the airport. Seven days later Tibbets landed in the States, his eight months of overseas duty complete. "I didn't realize until I arrived home how tightly my nerves had been wound by the war," he said. "Every time I heard a siren on the street, I would jump. In the middle of the night I would wake up, listening for airplanes. I was home, but part of my subconscious was still at war."

In July 1943, Tibbets started work on the B-29 program, which at the time faced a crisis. On a test flight that February, one of the model bombers crashed into a Seattle meat processing plant, killing all eleven airmen plus twenty-one others. "It was," as Curtis LeMay later remarked, "a test program disaster of unparalleled proportions."

Tibbets served as a test pilot, which included flying the bomber at night and in inclement weather, like snow and ice. Other challenges centered on the engines, which often caught fire. "You could hardly get one in the air and bring it back," he said, "without an engine fire." On one such flight, an engine fire burned with such intensity that it fell off the plane. "We got the airplane back," Tibbets recalled. "The Good Lord smiled on me."

Despite those early challenges, which engineers later remedied, Tibbets came to love the B-29. "I had," he said, "the utmost faith in that airplane." His in-depth experience with the bomber, which would soon enter the war, led to his March 1944 assignment to Grand Island, Nebraska, where he was tasked to start a school to train B-29 flight instructors. The time home had given his nerves a break, but he was bored and restless. "After the excitement of combat over Europe and North Africa, my assignment to the States had been an emotional letdown," he recalled. "The war, which had been a day-to-day reality, now seemed remote."

But that all changed when he received a call from Gen. Uzal Ent, commander of the Second Air Force, requesting him to fly to Colorado Springs. Shortly before ten a.m. on September 1, 1944, Tibbets arrived at the general's office. In the outer area stood Lt. Col. John Lansdale, who served as Groves's special assistant for security.

"I'd like to ask you a few questions," he began.

A few questions, Tibbets learned, was a euphemism for interrogation. "The penetrating nature of Lansdale's questions baffled me," Tibbets recalled, "but, however embarrassing, I knew that tough questions called for honest answers."

Tibbets gave straightforward replies until finally Lansdale rose to his feet.

"Now," he said, "let's go see General Ent."

Inside the office, Tibbets greeted General Ent, who introduced him to navy Capt. William "Deak" Parsons and physicist Dr. Norman Ramsey.

Parsons was chief of the Ordnance Division at Los Alamos, while Ramsey served as his scientific and technical deputy.

"I'm well satisfied by Colonel Tibbets," Lansdale announced.

"That's good," the general replied. "I felt sure you would be."

Ent explained that Tibbets had been charged with leading an important and highly sensitive mission. The need for secrecy was utmost, including from family and even colleagues. Tibbets's job would be to organize and train a combat force to deliver a new weapon.

"Have you heard about atomic energy?" Ramsey interjected.

Tibbets said he was generally aware.

"Now, if I told you that we were in the process of making an atomic bomb that would be infinitely more destructive than any present bomb," he said, "what would you think?"

Ramsey proceeded to brief a stunned Tibbets on the developments in atomic science. The United States, he continued, had embarked on a crash program to build a bomb, which included creating three top-secret cities scattered around the country. General Ent added that the project was far enough along that it was imperative to now focus on how to deliver such a weapon safely. "Ours was not a nation with a kamikaze mentality," he explained. "When our bombers took off, the odds had to favor their safe return by at least ten to one."

Tibbets would have fifteen bombers and a force of eighteen hundred men in the newly created 509th Composite Group, a name that reflected the organization's unique composition. "The organization," Tibbets observed, "was to be completely self-contained with its own engineering, maintenance, and technical units, ordnance squadron, troops transport aircraft, military police, and a medical unit with specialists in the field of radiology." Tibbets, in short, had his own air force. "There had been nothing like it in this or any other war."

The general then reiterated the need for secrecy. "You can't tell your family, your friends, or anybody what you're doing, where you're going, or anything about it," he demanded. "You will put nothing in writing—you will have to remember everything." Ent then closed with a warning. "Paul," he concluded, "if this thing is a success, you're going to be a big hero. If it's a failure, you may wind up in prison because they'll crucify you."

On September 8, 1944, Tibbets established his headquarters at Wendover Airfield in the northwestern corner of Utah near the Nevada border, an isolated area surrounded only by miles of empty salt flats that guaranteed few prying eyes. The colonel next picked his key people, beginning with his former aircrew in Europe. He summoned bombardier Maj. Thomas Ferebee, navigator Capt. Theodore "Dutch" Van Kirk, tail gunner Staff Sgt. George Caron, and flight engineer Staff Sgt. Wyatt Duzenbury. He also drafted Capt. Robert Lewis, who had worked with him more recently on the B-29 program. These men would not only fly with Tibbets but would help train new recruits in those critical areas.

As with the other atomic cities, security was a major priority. "We read mail and monitored phone calls through the base switchboard and from pay phones on the base," Tibbets said. "If a sergeant's wife told him on the phone that she was pregnant, I'd make a point of having someone congratulate him. He didn't know how the other soldier knew of his wife's condition, but he and everyone else in the outfit became aware that they were being watched."

Questions over the operation and the demand for such secrecy confounded the airmen, prompting Tibbets to summon the entire outfit to a meeting. He could not share details of the mission, but he could give them a hint. "You have been brought here to work on a very special mission," the colonel began. "Those of you who stay will be going overseas."

The airmen perked up.

"You are going to take part in an effort that could end the war."

Scientists meanwhile had warned Tibbets that it would be unsafe to drop the bomb from less than 30,000 feet. Given the weapon's weight and the fuel requirements, such an altitude would strain the notoriously bad engines. The solution, Tibbets proposed, was to strip all guns except the one in the tail. Such a move would lighten the bomber by more than 7,000 pounds and therefore lessen the engine stress. The flip side, of course, was that the plane would be largely defenseless on a mission deep inside the enemy's homeland. Tibbets reasoned that at 30,000 feet, the bomber would cruise above the effective range of Japanese flak. Enemy fighters meanwhile would struggle to reach the plane at such an altitude, and if any were able, the lighter plane could more easily maneuver into position to use its tail guns.

Another challenge, scientists cautioned, was that the bomber needed to be at least eight miles away from the blast if the crew hoped to survive. Tibbets calculated that it would take two minutes to fly that distance. The problem, however, was that the bomb would detonate after just forty-three seconds. The explosion's shock wave would travel the speed of sound, which was about eleven hundred feet per second. That meant that it would take forty seconds to travel eight miles. That still was not enough. "It was obviously impossible," he realized, "to reach a point over the earth eight miles from the explosion in one minute and 23 seconds."

Tibbets solved the problem via trigonometry. From his bombing altitude of six miles, he realized, he needed to cover only five ground miles. The diagonal line from the explosion to his bomber would equal eight miles. The fact that he could cover six miles in the time before the shock wave hit gave Tibbets added wiggle room. "Calculations convinced me that the most effective maneuver would be a sharp turn at 155 degrees," he wrote. "This would put considerable strain on the airplane and would require a degree of precision flying unfamiliar to bomber pilots. Nevertheless, it seemed our best bet for survival."

With the escape plan determined, Tibbets began to train fellow pilots in the maneuver. Crews meanwhile practiced dropping a bomb from 30,000 feet onto a circular target that measured just 400 feet in diameter. To imitate the bomb's ballistics, airmen used bulbous dummy weapons the men dubbed pumpkins. "We would," Tibbets said, "accept a miss of no more than 200 feet from the aiming point." In addition to escape maneuvers and bombing, crews trained in navigation, including long overwater flights to Cuba. Tibbets flew to Washington to brief the members of the Target Committee and made frequent trips to Los Alamos to confer with the scientists, including Oppenheimer. Over time the inferiority he felt around the physicists lessened. "If their language in the area of nuclear physics was unintelligible to me," he said, "my own field of expertise was equally foreign to them."

As Tibbets readied his crews, preparations began for the move to the Mariana Islands, which served as the frontline of America's air war against the Empire of Japan. Groves had initially set his sights on Guam, but a February 1945 inspection had revealed Tinian to be a better option. The island was not only one hundred miles closer to Japan but far less congested than Guam, which was the headquarters of the Navy and Army Air Forces. Unlike neighboring Saipan, whose landscape was dominated by the 1,555-foot Mount Topochau, Tinian was relatively flat, which had made it conducive to sugarcane farming before the war.

Since its capture the previous summer, engineers armed with bulldozers and dynamite had rushed to convert the thirty-nine-square-mile island into the largest air base in the world with four 8,500-foot runways capable of handling the B-29s. Tinian's shape, which was reminiscent of Manhattan, had prompted the Seabees who designed the island's roads to mimic the Big Apple. Drivers rumbled down newly paved asphalt motorways that sported familiar names like Broadway, Park Avenue, and Forty-Second Street. "Tinian Island became known as Manhattan in the Pacific," Tibbets later recalled. "New York without subways."

The 509th Composite Group, whose members arrived by ship and plane in May and June, took over the northern tip of the island in an area commonly referred to as the Columbia University District. In preparation for the group's arrival, workers had constructed four air-conditioned buildings to house the bomb's fusing, detonator, pit, and observation teams. Three additional airconditioned structures were dedicated to the weapon's assembly. Other special requirements ranged from warehouses and magazines to two pits with hydraulic lifts that would hoist the bomb in the back of the B-29. Along with the airmen, fifty Manhattan Project scientists and technicians, under the command of Capt. Deak Parsons, deployed to Tinian as part of Project Alberta to help ready the bombs. Secrecy mandated that the scientists and airmen keep to themselves. "It was an island," as one observer recalled, "within an island." A team of 128 guards protected the barbed-wire compound, which sparked resentment from other airmen, who flew nightly missions to burn the enemy's cities while Tibbets's crews only practiced. At night, rival airmen liked to ride by and toss rocks atop metal roofs to rouse them. "To the other outfits on Tinian," Tibbets acknowledged, "we were a bunch of pampered dandies."

That practice came to an end at two a.m. on July 20, 1945, four days after the first successful test of an atomic bomb in the New Mexico desert. On that morning, ten crews of atomic airmen lifted off from Tinian for the first practice strike on Japan, dropping pumpkins filled with black powder or the explosive Torpex on the cities of Koriyama, Fukushima,

Nagaoka, and on Toyama Industries. LeMay's bombers had so wrecked Japan's urban areas that the airmen's objectives consisted of either industries of secondary importance or priority targets that had previously been damaged. "These targets," as one report noted, "varied all the way from converted textile mills to marshaling yards, and included almost every type of industry, including aircraft, oil, ordnance, chemical, steel, and shipbuilding, as well as airfields and harbors."

Crews would fly again four days later on July 24, targeting Sumitomo, Kobe, and Yokkaichi Industries. On July 26, bombers returned to Nagaoka and Toyama. Airmen flew a final practice mission over the empire on July 29, hitting Ube along with the prior targets of Koriyama and Yokkaichi Industries. All told, thirty-eight bombers flew a dozen missions against Japanese cities and industries, during which time only one plane was hit by flak. Tibbets's airmen learned what LeMay's crews had known for months: weather over the empire could be a challenge. "These flights," Tibbets added, "gave our pilots, navigators, and bombardiers the type of experience they would need when the time came to drop our nuclear weapons."

Even as Tibbets readied his airmen, LeMay refused to let up.

He kept punching.

And punching.

In mid-June, after torching 102 square miles of Japan's six major urban areas, LeMay shifted his focus to secondary- and even tertiary-size cities. With smaller targets, there was no need to send aerial armadas, which allowed him to divide up his force and pound multiple cities in a single night. In the latter half of June, LeMay's forces burned 15.24 square miles out of eleven cities. He more than tripled that figure in July, hammering thirty-seven cities for a total of 35.41 square miles destroyed. In Quonset huts on Guam, photo analysts struggled to keep up, poring over post-strike photos, so as to chart the destruction of Japan's cities down to the square mile, acre, and even foot. "We are certainly giving the Japs a going over," LeMay wrote to his wife. "If they don't give up soon, they are a lot dumber than I think they are."

And yet Japan refused to surrender.

LeMay's latest ploy was to blanket Japan with leaflets that listed eleven cities, four of which America planned to destroy in the days ahead. For the Japanese who picked up the flyers, the decision to stay was like a game of Russian Roulette.

Which of the eleven cities would be next?

"We hope to convince the Japanese people that they can do nothing about it," LeMay boasted to reporters, "that we can destroy any target we want to, city after city."

Against this backdrop, the cruiser *Indianapolis* eased into port on July 26, anchoring a half mile off Tinian's southern coast. Sailors unloaded a fifteen-foot wooden crate that held Little Boy's firing mechanism onto a tank landing ship. Two officers climbed into a motor launch with a heavy lead bucket, which contained the uranium projectile. The three uranium target rings needed to complete the gun assembly arrived two days later via airplane along with the plutonium required to assemble Fat Man, the second atomic bomb.

On July 29, Gen. Carl Spaatz landed on Guam to take command of the new U.S. Army Strategic Air Force in the Pacific, making him the senior airman in the theater. Spaatz tapped LeMay, who had led the Twenty-First Bomber Command, to be his chief of staff. Spaatz brought with him orders for the first atomic attack. No date had been set, but Truman had mandated that the weapon not be deployed before August 2. Tibbets met with Spaatz and LeMay. "I assured them that we were ready and that the bomb had been assembled, minus the two small slugs of uranium that were being kept under guard in the ordnance area."

With the crews trained, the weapon ready, and the orders in Spaatz's hands, final preparations for the attack began. Weather over Japan remained the biggest challenge. "Radar was to be used as an aid, but the actual bombing was to be accomplished visually," Groves insisted. "If this proved to be impossible, the bomb was to be brought back."

Hiroshima remained the favored target given Stimson's demand that Kyoto be scratched from the list. Perched at the head of Hiroshima Bay, the city traced its roots back to 1591, when it began as a fishing village. Over the centuries Hiroshima had grown to become Japan's seventh-largest city behind Tokyo, Osaka, Nagoya, Yokohama, Kyoto, and Kobe. The city's population peaked in June 1942 with 380,000 inhabitants, but five government-ordered evacuations—and a sixth currently underway—had slashed the number of full-time residents to 245,000. Those numbers were offset by an influx of troops and refugees from destroyed cities, which pushed the total to around 350,000 people. Despite the city's relatively small size, the population density remained high with 31,600 persons per square mile, an average greater than that of even New York City, a staggering statistic since most of Hiroshima's architecture consisted of one- and two-story buildings compared to the Big Apple's high-rises.

Unlike the majority of Japan's cities, Hiroshima had remained unburned, which was the result of its unique geography. Built on the delta of the Ota River, which emptied into the Inland Sea, the river's half-dozen tributaries had sliced the city into seven fingerlike islands, all connected by a network of eighty-one bridges. These waterways served as natural firebreaks, which had made Hiroshima a poor candidate for a fire raid. Other than a couple small air raids, the city had largely escaped the damage that had reduced scores of Japanese cities to rubble and ash. In addition, compared to other major cities, Hiroshima was less industrialized, a factor derived from its lack of hydroelectric power, coal, or iron, which had handicapped its growth. In August 1945, only three companies in the city employed more than five hundred workers, and most of those were devoted to the production of alcoholic beverages and tinned beef.

Much of the city's industry catered to military and government agencies. The headquarters for both the Second General Army and the Fifth Division, Hiroshima was home to 43,000 troops. Not only did the city feature scores of barracks, administration buildings, and ordnance depots, but the port served as the key point of embarkation for Japanese troops. "Probably more than a thousand times since the beginning of the war did the Hiroshima citizens see off with cries of 'Banzai' the troops leaving from the harbor," observed one Japanese report. Only 20 percent of port facilities, in fact, were dedicated to civilian use; the rest were controlled by the military. "Hiroshima," as one intelligence report noted, "is an army city." That was what made it such an appealing target. "It was a beehive of war industry," Groves added, "carried on in moderate-sized plants and in small shops as well as in almost every home."

The heart of the city centered on four square miles spread across the deltaic islands. Seventy-five percent of the population crowded in this area, which consisted largely of one- and two-story wooden homes with a density, as one postwar report noted, comparable to the "worst slum

Leslie Groves and Robert Oppenheimer (center) examine the remnants of the steel tower that once held the atomic bomb. *(NARA)*

Leslie Groves, pictured here after the first atomic test, beams with excitement, knowing that America now has a weapon that can potentially end the war. *(NARA)*

Col. Paul Tibbets, Jr., pictured second from left, commanded the 509th Composite Group, which was tasked with dropping the first atomic bomb on Japan. *(NARA)*

On the remote Pacific island of Tinian, workers hoist the uranium bomb, nicknamed Little Boy, in the back of the B-29 *Enola Gay* for the first atomic strike on Japan. *(NARA)*

On the morning of Aug. 6, 1945, Col. Paul Tibbets, Jr., smiles from the cockpit of the *Enola Gay*, a B-29 Superfortress which he named after his mother. *(NARA)*

American war planners selected Hiroshima, which served as the headquarters of Japan's Second General Army, as the first target for an atomic bomb. *(NARA)*

On the eve of the attack, the population of Hiroshima was approximately 350,000, including 43,000 troops. *(NARA)*

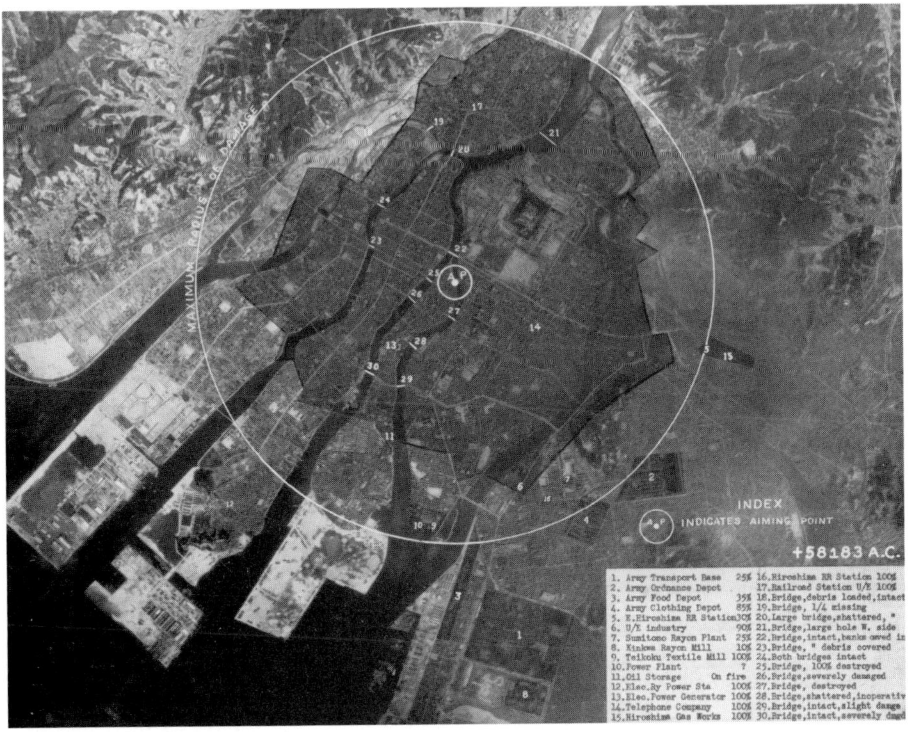

American war planners targeted the congested center of Hiroshima. *(NARA)*

At 8:14 a.m. on August 6, 1945, the first-ever combat atomic bomb detonated 1,968 feet over downtown Hiroshima. *(NARA)*

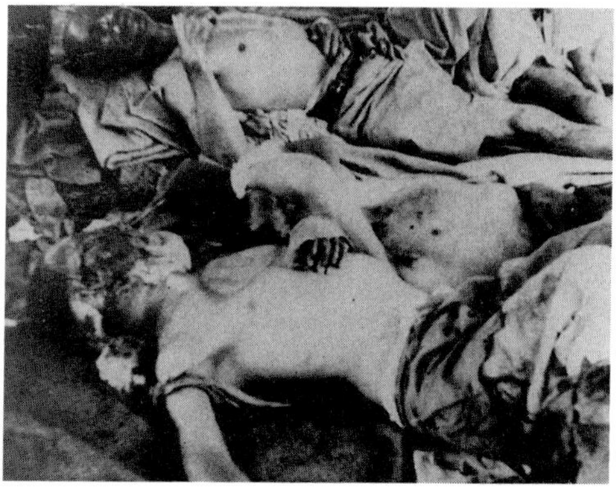

It would take thirty hours for outside rescuers to reach Hiroshima, leaving many of the atomic bomb survivors to crowd inside the few remaining structures, such as schools. *(NARA)*

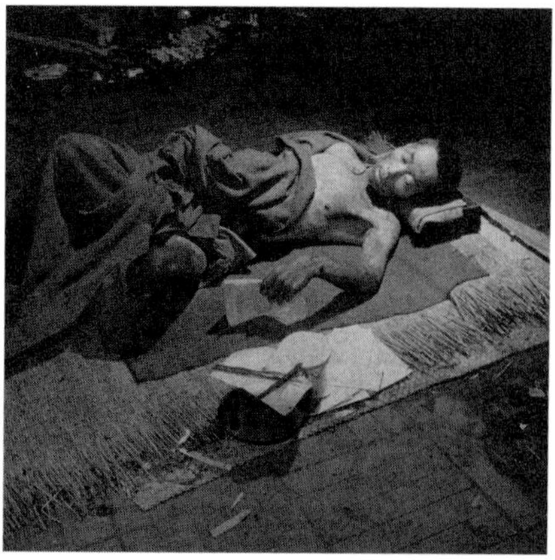

Survivors of the atomic bomb often struggled for weeks, like this man pictured in September 1945, who lies atop a tatami mat in a makeshift hospital inside a bank building. *(NARA)*

On the steps of the Hiroshima branch of the Sumitomo Bank near ground zero, rescuers discovered the shadow of one victim, who was seated at the time of the blast. *(NARA)*

The atomic blast and ensuing firestorm destroyed 4.4 square miles of Hiroshima. *(NARA)*

The ruins of the Hiroshima prefectural hall, which was located near ground zero, would become the iconic symbol of the attack. *(NARA)*

General Carl Spaatz awards Paul Tibbets, Jr., the Distinguished Service Cross upon his return from Hiroshima on August 6, 1945. *(NARA)*

Unlike Hiroshima, which was a flat deltaic city, Nagasaki was more mountainous, leading to many terraced areas and the need for steps. *(NARA)*

On Tinian, workers prepare to load the plutonium bomb, nicknamed Fat Man, into the back of the B-29 *Bockscar*. *(NARA)*

Tibbets shakes hands with Maj. Charles Sweeney, who would pilot *Bockscar*, before he prepares to take off for the second atomic strike on the morning of August 9, 1945. *(NARA)*

At 11:02 a.m. on August 9, 1945, a second atomic bomb detonates over Japan, this time in the city of Nagasaki. *(NARA)*

Nagasaki's mountainous geography corralled the force of the blast, but the attack still killed tens of thousands and left many more injured and homeless. *(NARA)*

The bomb ultimately destroyed more than two square miles of the Urakami River valley in Nagasaki, home to several large wartime factories. *(NARA)*

The ruins of the Urakami Cathedral tower over the city's remains, which, like the prefectural hall in Hiroshima, would become an iconic symbol of Nagasaki. *(NARA)*

A road that winds through the wreckage of Nagasaki is the only visible reminder of the city that once stood in this place. *(NARA)*

districts in large American cities." Compared to the rest of the city, the population density here soared to 46,000 people per square mile. Streets were narrow, sidewalks nonexistent, and open gutters carried wastewater and drainage. Scattered throughout were some masonry and concrete and rebar buildings, which averaged between two to four stories, with the tallest tapping out at seven, but overall the area reflected the traditional architecture that dominated much of Japan. Recognizing the threat of fire, which had devoured so many other cities, workers had begun tearing down homes to create 41,000 feet of additional firebreaks.

Beyond cutting firebreaks through the city, authorities had done very little to prepare for an attack. Public shelters were largely nonexistent, leaving residents to dig primitive foxholes in home gardens. The more than three dozen civilian hospitals and clinics had a combined total of about one thousand beds, but there were no designated first-aid stations and only ten ambulances to service the entire city. The fire department consisted of two main stations, each with seven pumpers, and eighteen substations with two pumpers assigned to each. Of the 411 firefighters, few were quality recruits. "The preparations," as one report noted, "which had been planned for emergency medical work were totally inadequate for any type of emergency."

And time was running out.

Armed with instructions from Groves, Tibbets sat down and drafted a proposed four-page field order, which detailed how the mission would proceed. The colonel then forwarded it to LeMay for approval. The authorized order came back on August 3, 1945, confirming Hiroshima as the mission's primary target. Kokura was designated as the secondary objective; Nagasaki the third. "No Tactical Mission Number is assigned to this mission," the order stated. "For record purposes, Special Bombing Mission Number 13 is assigned."

Seven bombers would fly the mission. Three would lift off in advance to scout the weather over each of the target cities. A strike force of three planes would follow. Tibbets would carry the weapon, while two additional bombers would transport scientific equipment and cameras to measure and record the explosion. The scientific equipment consisted of three slender aluminum cannisters, each equipped with parachutes and armed with special microphones that would gauge the blast's shock wave and radio the results back to the plane. In addition to traditional still and motion picture cameras, the second bomber would carry what was called a Fastax, a special high-speed instrument designed to photograph the explosion and growth of the fireball. A final B-29 would land at Iwo Jima to serve as a spare in case the main strike plane developed any sort of equipment trouble that necessitated a change. "No friendly aircraft, other than those listed herein, will be within a 50-mile area of any of the targets for this strike during a period of four hours prior to and six hours subsequent to strike time."

Tibbets and bombardier Ferebee pored over aerial photos of Hiroshima. Ferebee selected the initial point, which was where the plane would begin its bombing run. He next chose his aiming point, placing his finger on the Aioi Bridge, a T-shaped structure in the heart of the city. All the airmen needed now was a guaranteed day of clear skies over Japan.

At 2:45 p.m. on August 4, Parsons briefed the crews about what could be expected when the bomb detonated, explaining that the force of the explosion would be the equivalent of twenty thousand tons of TNT. He warned them to be sure and wear goggles. "I can say," Parsons assured them, "that this is the brightest and hottest thing on earth since creation."

The following day the clouds that had blanketed Japan began to clear. LeMay confirmed that the mission would likely run on August 6. In anticipation of the historic event, which would dominate global headlines, Tibbets decided to name his silver B-29 Superfortress, known until then simply as *No. 82*. As he contemplated a name, he was reminded of his red-haired mother, who in a moment of his personal anguish had encouraged him to abandon medicine and follow his dreams. That decision had led him to battle in the heavens over Europe and delivered him here to a tiny island in the Pacific on a mission many hoped would at last end the war. "Her name, Enola Gay, was pleasing to the ear," he wrote. "It was also unique, for I had never heard of anyone else named Enola. It would be a fine name for my plane: *Enola Gay*."

The following morning, Parsons raised a new alarm when he met with the so-called Tinian Joint Chiefs, a group composed of Tibbets, Brigadier General Farrell and other senior military officers, and Manhattan Project scientists who had deployed to the Pacific. The weaponeer had eyed the scorched remains of several crashed B-29s that littered the airfield. "You know," Parsons said, "if we crack up at the end of the runway tomorrow morning and the plane gets on fire, there is the danger of an atomic explosion and we may lose this end of the island, if not the whole of Tinian with every blessed thing on it."

"We will just have to pray that it doesn't happen," Farrell said.

But Parsons had a better idea. He proposed finalizing the bomb's assembly after takeoff, specifically by inserting the explosive charge and detonator.

"Are you sure you can do it?" Farrell asked.

"No," he replied, "but I've got all day to learn."

"Go ahead and try," Farrell advised.

Reporter William Laurance with *The New York Times* landed that afternoon on Tinian after being delayed for three days. He had originally hoped to fly the first atomic mission, but Farrell informed him he was too late, though he could go on the next one.

"There may not be any need for another mission," Laurence countered.

"I hope you are right," Farrell replied.

At two p.m. that afternoon, workers, many without shirts in the heat, used chains and pullies to hoist the 9,700-pound Little Boy onto a wheeled trailer, where it was then shrouded with a tarp. A truck towed it from the assembly building to the loading pit. Once lowered, Tibbets watched as a tractor guided the *Enola Gay* into position so that the bomb bay loomed above the pit. Workers removed the tarp before a hydraulic lift helped raise the weapon into the bay. "With its coat of dull gunmetal paint," Tibbets said, "it was an ugly monster."

A few airmen scribbled messages on the bomb, including one addressed to Hirohito that read "From the Boys of the *Indianapolis*," a reference to the cruiser that a Japanese submarine had sunk after it delivered the atomic bomb materials to Tinian. The *Enola Gay* then taxied to its hardstand under the watchful eye of military guards. Parsons climbed into the bomb bay, where temperatures soared over one hundred degrees, to determine if he could in fact finish the weapon's assembly in flight. After two hours he finally emerged soaked in sweat with his fingers bloodied. "For God's sake," Farrell exclaimed, "let me loan you a pair of pigskin gloves."

"I wouldn't dare wear them," Parsons replied. "I've got to feel the touch."

"He was confident," Tibbets observed, "that the task could be done."

Capt. Bob Lewis, who would serve as Tibbets's copilot on the mission, visited the airfield that afternoon, stunned to see *Enola Gay* stenciled diagonally across the nose of the silver bomber. "What the Hell is *that* doing on *my* plane?" he howled.

Lewis had served as the aircraft commander of the plane until Tibbets bumped him to the role of copilot for the historic flight. As group commander, Tibbets had every right to do that, but it still chafed Lewis. Now Tibbets had gone further and named the plane.

The captain went straight to the group headquarters and confronted Tibbets. "Colonel," he said, "you authorized men to put a name on my airplane?"

"I didn't think you'd mind, Bob."

But Lewis did.

Despite his protest, Tibbets was adamant the name would remain. "It was a decision," as one historian noted, "which would lead to a lasting conflict between the two men."

That afternoon and evening the men busied themselves. The weight of the mission hung over them. Some thought of their families. Others played cards, thumbed through magazines, or stretched out for a nap, though sleep proved elusive. A few turned to faith, including radar operator Sgt. Joseph Stiborik, who visited the Catholic priest to absolve him of his sins. "If something happened to me," he recalled, "I wanted to be sure to go to Heaven."

At ten p.m., all seven crews filed into the assembly building, sitting atop wooden benches. On a platform in front, Tibbets watched as his men settled in for the briefing. "I soon found that the tension that had been building up within me was shared by almost everyone else in the room," Tibbets recalled. "This was no dry run. It was the real thing."

Tibbets had no prepared speech, but Laurence scribbled down his remarks.

"Tonight is the night we have all been waiting for," he began. "Our long months of training are to be put to the test. We will soon know if we have been successful or failed."

The airmen listened.

"Upon our efforts tonight it is possible that history will be made," he continued. "We are going on a mission to drop a bomb different from any you have ever seen or heard about. This bomb contains a destructive force equivalent to twenty thousand tons of TNT."

Tibbets saw a look of shock spread across the men's faces.

"Because this bomb is so powerful, we must use different tactics."

The colonel then walked the crews through the operational plans. The weather planes would take off at 1:45 a.m. followed one hour later by the strike force. Tibbets informed the men that the radio call sign had been changed from Victor to Dimples, a move designed to confuse any enemy eavesdroppers who might have been monitoring the group's earlier communications. He likewise told the men that the altitude for the first leg of the mission would remain below five thousand feet, so Parsons could complete the weapon's assembly. Other information covered ranged from expected weather conditions to air-sea rescue operations. "Do your jobs," he concluded. "Obey your orders. Don't cut corners or take chances."

The three weather crews met a final time at eleven p.m. followed one hour later by the three strike crews. Tibbets repeated much of the same information during the final briefing. "The men," Laurence observed, "still wore the amazed look of two hours before." At the end, officials passed out goggles, similar to the ones worn by welders but with adjustable Polaroid lenses. "All were warned," Tibbets said, "to have the goggles ready for use as soon as the bomb was released in order to protect their eyes from a flash far brighter than the sun.

Chaplain Capt. William Downey, who before the war served at Hope Lutheran Church in Minneapolis, closed the briefing with a prayer. "May the men who fly this night be kept safe in Thy care, and may they be returned safely to us," he said. "We shall go forward trusting in Thee, knowing we are in Thy care now and forever. Amen."

At twelve-thirty a.m., the airmen marched from the briefing to breakfast. Mess Sgt. Elliot Easterly dished up a preflight meal of eggs, sausage, and rolled oats accompanied by bread and apple butter. Airmen downed the meal with cups of milk and hot coffee.

As Tibbets wrapped up his breakfast, flight surgeon Don Young appeared at his table, handing him a pillbox with twelve cyanide capsules, one for each crew member.

"I hope you don't have to use these," he said.

"Don't worry," Tibbets said. "The odds are in our favor."

The airmen returned to their quarters a little past one a.m. to grab their flight gear before trucks drove them down to the flight line, where the men were stunned to find floodlights illuminating the *Enola Gay*. Motion picture cameras whirred while flashbulbs popped, giving the scene the feel of a Hollywood premiere. "I had known," Tibbets recalled, "that there would be some routine picture-taking before departure, but I was unprepared for this."

Cameramen photographed the entire crew as well as each individual airman, pictures which could then be distributed to hometown papers. The photographers insisted as well on capturing Tibbets waving from the cockpit window. "The picture taking would have continued all night," he said, "if I hadn't called a halt shortly before two o'clock."

Lewis gave a quick pep talk to the airmen. "You guys," he said, "this bomb cost more than an aircraft carrier. Don't screw it up. We've got it made; we're gonna win the war."

Tibbets ran through his external preflight checks before he and the eleven other crewmen climbed aboard. For this mission, the colonel had chosen many of his former crew members from Europe, including Ferebee, navigator Dutch Van Kirk, tail gunner George Caron, and flight engineer Wyatt Duzenbury. He likewise had tapped Lewis as his copilot while Parsons would serve as the weaponeer aided by Second Lt. Morris Jeppson. Other crew members who fanned out through the bomber included Lt. Jacob Beser, the radar countermeasures officer, Sgt. Joseph Stiborik, radar operator, Sgt. Robert Shumard, assistant flight engineer, and Pvt. First Class Richard Nelson, the radio operator.

Once in place, crew members ticked through extensive checklists. The flight engineer flipped on the cabin pressure, checked the oxygen and lights, and set the throttles to start. The radioman inspected the antennas and flare gun while the bombardier adjusted the altimeter and synchronized his clock. Up in the cockpit, where Tibbets settled into the lefthand seat with Lewis to his right, the pilots ran through more than two dozen items.

Emergency cabin pressure release in place?

Check.

Landing gear switch and fuse?

Check.

Flight controls?

Check.

Ground crews pulled through the props, two men per each sixteen-foot propeller, spinning them to remove any oil from the cylinder. Once completed, Tibbets signaled Duzenbury to start the number-three engine, as he shot a glance out the side window. "It caught immediately," he observed, "with the customary tongue of flame spitting into the darkness."

Duzenbury next started engine number four followed by one and two. Tibbets shot a glance at the oil and fuel pressure gauges. With the brakes set, he flashed both thumbs up to the ground crew, signaling them to pull the wheel chocks at two-thirty a.m. After a final wave to the more than one hundred spectators, Tibbets began to taxi to the runway.

Farrell, Laurence, and others hopped into jeeps for the ride to the tower to watch the takeoff as Tibbets maneuvered into place on the western end of Runway Able. Through the cockpit windshield, he stared down the mile-and-a-half-long runway of chipped coral that ended at the edge of the ocean. Tibbets could not escape the significance of the moment. He had flown America's first bombing raid of the war 1,085 days earlier over France. He now prepared to fly what many hoped would be one of the last—if not *the* last—mission of the war.

The roar of the bomber's four 2,200-horsepower Wright Cyclone engines caused the plane to vibrate. He could see the scorched skeletons of crashed bombers along the side of the runway, a reminder of the danger of trying to lift off in a 150,000-pound plane, 16,000 pounds over max gross weight. In addition to 7,000 gallons of flammable aviation fuel, Tibbets carried a 9,700-pound atomic weapon. The fire trucks stationed along the edge of the runway were of little comfort. He squeezed the controls with sweaty palms and tried to steady his nerves. "This is just another takeoff," he reminded himself. "You've done it many times before."

"Dimples Eight Two to North Tinian Tower," he radioed. "Ready for takeoff on Runway Able."

"Dimples Eight Two. Dimples Eight Two," the tower replied. "Cleared for takeoff."

Tibbets released the brakes, and the *Enola Gay* lumbered down the runway, picking up speed from 75 miles per hour to 100. Up in the tower,

Farrell, Laurence, and others anxiously watched as the bomber continued to hug the runway.

One thousand yards turned to two, three, and then four.

"Will he ever lift her up off the ground?" Laurence wondered.

The *Enola Gay*'s speed reached 125 miles per hour. At the controls next to Tibbets, Lewis likewise grew nervous. "Come on, Paul," he finally said. "Let's go."

The copilot reached for his own controls.

"No!" Tibbets declared. "Leave it!"

The colonel kept the bomber on the ground, building up speed until the *Enola Gay* reached 155 miles per hour. As the end of the runway fast approached, Tibbets at last eased back on the controls, and the massive bomber clawed its way into the air.

The mission was a go.

CHAPTER 28

"Our people have not forgotten that the Japanese struck us the first blow in this war without the slightest warning."

—SENATOR RICHARD RUSSELL
AUGUST 7, 1945, TELEGRAM TO PRESIDENT HARRY TRUMAN

Dutch Van Kirk penciled his first notation into the navigator's log, recording the moment of takeoff as 2:45 a.m. Lewis retracted the wheels while Tibbets kept the bomber's nose down for another minute to continue to build up speed, before banking left over the dark waters. He eased back on the controls, climbing to a cruising altitude of 4,700 feet. Ten minutes later the *Enola Gay* passed over the northern tip of Saipan. It was there, only thirteen months earlier in the waning days of battle, that American troops had watched in horror as hundreds of Japanese men, women, and children had jumped from the cliffs into the swirling sea below.

The *Enola Gay*'s engines roared, though the pressurized compartment helped muffle the noise as Tibbets set his flight speed at 220 miles per hour. The cockpit windshield framed the evening sky ahead. "It was a pleasant tropical night, warm with a light breeze," Tibbets observed. "Around us were cream-puff clouds, their edges outlined by the faint glow of a crescent moon that had just appeared above the horizon to the east."

"Colonel Tibbets," Parsons announced over the intercom.

"Yes, Captain," he replied.

"If it's all right with you, sir, I'll begin."

"Okay," Tibbets replied.

At three a.m., Parsons and his deputy Morris Jeppson climbed into the bomb bay to insert Little Boy's explosive charge and detonator. Parsons had written out the eleven steps necessary to tackle the job, which he had shared with Farrell before he departed.

"Check that green plugs are installed," he wrote. "Remove rear plate."

Jeppson held the flashlight while Parsons ticked off one step at a time. Up in the cockpit, Tibbets kept a running relay of the progress for Farrell via radio.

"How is Parsons doing?" the general asked at one point.

"He hasn't come up yet," Tibbets replied.

Down below, Parsons used a wrench to unscrew the breech plug and inserted the four sections of the explosive charge. He then reinserted and tightened the plug before connecting the firing line. The final steps involved replacing the armor and rear plate before securing his tools. Fifteen minutes later, much to the relief of the others, the duo climbed back out of the bomb bay. By then, the *Enola Gay* had slipped out of radio range with Tinian, leaving Farrell in the dark. "With the bomb armed," Tibbets recalled, "tensions eased among our crew as we settled down for the long flight so familiar to other B-29 men on Tinian, who every night had been carrying incendiaries and bombs from the Marianas to the Japanese home islands."

Bill Laurence did not want to miss out on such an historic scoop even though his late arrival on Tinian had robbed him of the chance to fly on the mission. The crafty reporter improvised, asking Lewis to jot down notes for him. The copilot agreed, turning the backs of some old War Department forms into a makeshift journal of the mission.

"Everything," he scribbled at 3:45 a.m., "is going along smoothly."

With the mission safely underway, Lt. Jacob Beser seized a few minutes of shut-eye. Others did the same. Up in the cockpit, Tibbets checked in via radio with the other two bombers in the strike force as well as the spare; all had taken off at two-minute intervals after the *Enola Gay*. "The other planes were a few miles behind," Tibbets said. "It was our plan to rendezvous over Iwo Jima and complete the final leg of the mission together."

Before taking his own rest, Tibbets checked on the crew, including climbing through the cramped tunnel over the bomb bay to reach Stiborik, Shumard, and Caron. Though the airmen knew the mission involved a special new weapon, only a few had been told that the bomb was atomic. "Have you figured out what we're doing?" Tibbets asked Caron.

"Hell, Colonel," he replied. "I'd probably get in trouble with the security around here."

"We're on our way now," Tibbets said. "You can guess anything you want."

"Is it a chemist's nightmare?" the gunner asked.

"Not exactly, but you're warm."

"Are we splitting atoms today, Colonel?"

"That's about it," Tibbets replied.

Tibbets made his way back to the cockpit, where, like the others, he decided to take a nap in his seat, using his parachute and life jacket to make himself more comfortable. The colonel, who had enjoyed little rest in the last forty-eight hours, wanted to be sharp when it mattered most. He turned the controls over to Lewis and closed his eyes. "The colonel better known as the 'Old Bull,'" Lewis scribbled in his diary, "shows signs of a tough day, with all he had to do to help get this mission off he is deserving of a few winks."

Halfway around the world, Leslie Groves stewed.

Even though it was Sunday in Washington, the general busied himself in his office, awaiting word that the *Enola Gay* had lifted off. "I finally gave up," he said. "I decided that all of us in my office would be better off if I went out to play tennis for an hour."

Groves took an officer with him to sit by the court's phone. Every fifteen minutes the aide called for an update, but still no word arrived. A sweaty Groves hustled back to the office, where he continued to fret. At five p.m., General Marshall phoned, having just returned from his weekend home in Leesburg, Virginia. The duty officer offered to connect him with Groves, but Marshall demurred. "I don't want you to bother General Groves," Marshall told him. "He has enough to think about without answering any unnecessary queries."

Groves met his wife and daughter at the Army-Navy Club for dinner. George Harrison, Stimson's deputy on the Interim Committee, joined them. At 6:45 p.m., Groves was summoned to the phone, where he at last learned that the *Enola Gay* was airborne. "This report was about six hours late," he complained, "but still it was a relief to have something."

The general had his wife drop him off at his office, where he planned to spend the night waiting on the mission's strike report. Groves busied himself as best he could by working on papers, but the tension soared. To ease the stress, he slipped off his tie and rolled up his sleeves, which he hoped would create a more informal atmosphere for the staff. "The hours went by more slowly than I ever imagined hours could go by, and still there was no news."

In the cockpit of the *Enola Gay*, Lewis spied the first signs of dawn around five a.m., which was a relief after spending the previous half-hour dodging large cumulus clouds. "I think everyone will feel relieved when we have left our bomb with the Japanese and get halfway home," he scribbled in his diary. "Or better still all the way home."

Tibbets began his climb to 9,300 feet at 5:34 a.m. Iwo Jima came into view through the cockpit windshield, the eight-square-mile island that had proved so costly for America to capture. Perched on the southern tip of the island, Mount Suribachi loomed above the volcanic killing field. At 5:55 a.m., Tibbets circled Suribachi, which allowed the two strike planes—*The Great Artiste* piloted by Maj. Chuck Sweeney and an unnamed B-29 known as *No. 92* flown by Capt. George Marquardt—to catch up. A third bomber, *Big Stink*, piloted by Capt. Charles McKnight, likewise trailed, though it would land to serve as the mission's spare.

At 6:07 a.m., the three strike planes pressed on toward Japan, as the bright red sun began its climb up the eastern sky amid a few scattered clouds. Up ahead, along what veteran airmen dubbed the Hirohito Highway, three additional bombers—*Straight Flush*, *Jabit III*, and *Full House*—pressed on toward Japan to scout the weather over each of the target cities. *Straight Flush*, piloted by Maj. Claude Eatherly, would buzz Hiroshima while Maj. John Wilson in *Jabit III* would investigate Kokura, leaving Maj. Ralph Taylor in *Full House* to scope out Nagasaki. "If the first priority target was found to be obscured by clouds," Tibbets said, "we would turn westward toward Kokura or Nagasaki on the coast of Kyushu."

A thin layer of clouds appeared below, prompting a rise in tension

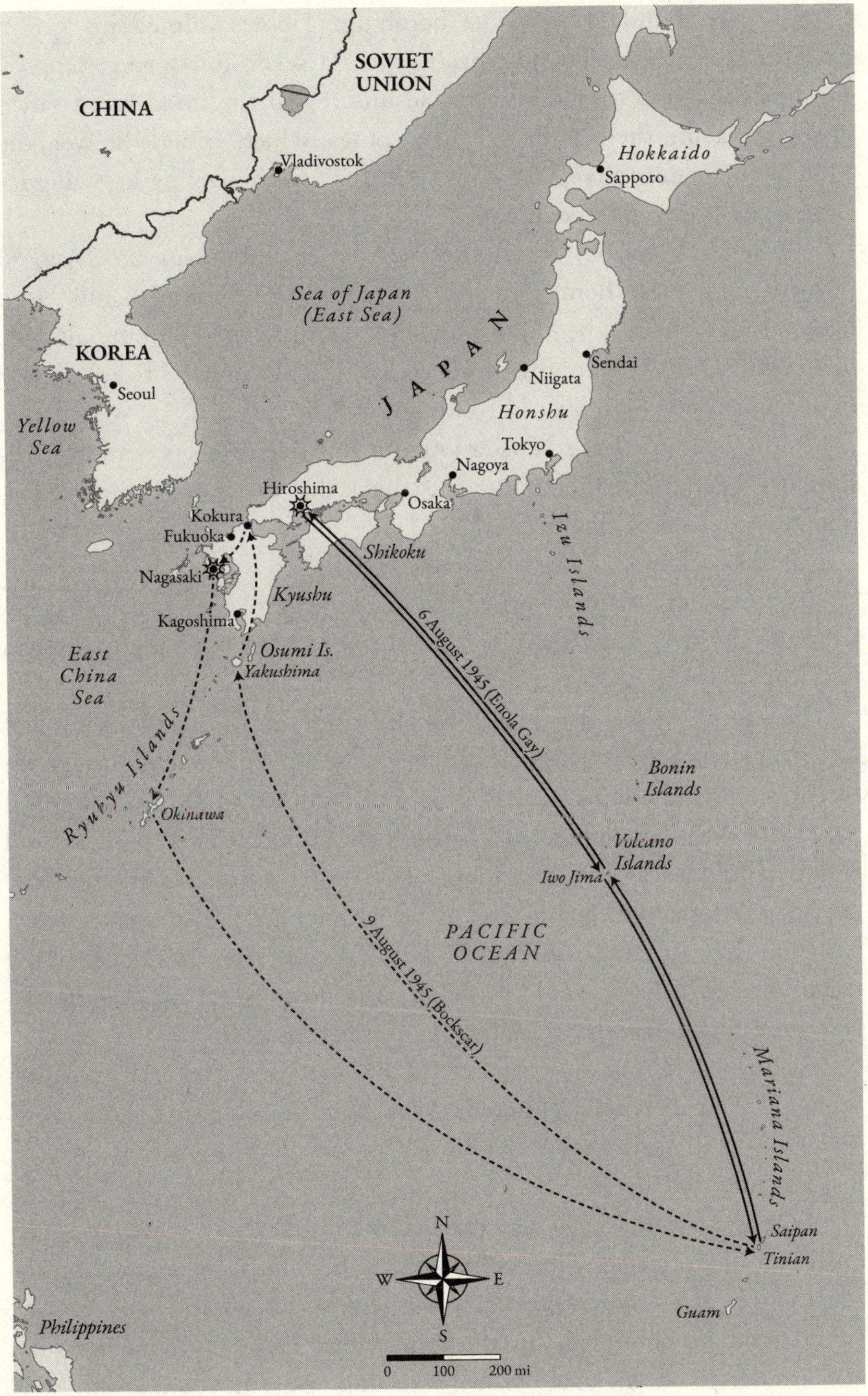
SOVIET UNION
CHINA
Vladivostok
Hokkaido
Sapporo
Sea of Japan (East Sea)
JAPAN
KOREA
Seoul
Niigata
Sendai
Yellow Sea
Honshu
Tokyo
Nagoya
Hiroshima
Osaka
Kokura
Fukuoka
Shikoku
Izu Islands
Nagasaki
Kyushu
Kagoshima
6 August 1945 (Enola Gay)
East China Sea
Osumi Is.
Yakushima
Ryukyu Islands
Okinawa
Bonin Islands
Volcano Islands
Iwo Jima
PACIFIC OCEAN
9 August 1945 (Bockscar)
Mariana Islands
Saipan
Tinian
Guam
Philippines
N
W
E
S
0
100
200 mi

since orders mandated a visual bombing. Tibbets calmed his nerves by puffing on his Kaywoodie briar pipe. At seven-thirty a.m., Jeppson climbed back into the bomb bay. He unscrewed the three green safety plugs, replacing them with red firing plugs, which armed the weapon. "The bomb is now alive," Lewis noted. "It's a funny feeling knowing it's right in back of you. Knock wood."

Tensions climbed as the minutes ticked past, and the *Enola Gay* closed in on the Japanese homeland. At 7:40 a.m., Tibbets once again eased back on the controls, beginning his slow climb to the bombing altitude of 30,700 feet. Fifty minutes later a coded message arrived from *Straight Flush*, which was high over Hiroshima: "Y-3, Q-3, B-2, C-1."

Radio operator Dick Nelson jotted it down as Tibbets read over his shoulder. "I translated the message to mean that the cloud cover was less than three-tenths at all altitudes."

"It's Hiroshima," Tibbets announced to the crew.

The crew members absorbed the news. "Right now we are 25 miles from the Empire," Lewis wrote, "and everyone has a big hopeful look on his face."

The small eastern island of Shikoku came into focus. To the relief of the crew, no enemy fighters or flak rose up to challenge them. In recent months, the Japanese had grown accustomed to the daily flight of American weather planes, which routinely buzzed the skies. Scattered clouds drifted below, but not enough, Tibbets determined, to threaten the mission. "We had studied maps and aerial photographs of the approach path and the city of Hiroshima," he said. "We knew every feature of the terrain over which we would be flying. And now the Japanese landscape was unfolding below us just as the pictures had promised."

Eight minutes out, and the city came into view. "The early morning sunlight," Tibbets noted, "glittered off the white buildings in the distance."

"Do you all agree that's Hiroshima?" he asked the crew.

The men concurred.

At 9:12 a.m., the *Enola Gay* reached the initial point, which was 15.5 miles east of the target. Tibbets banked the bomber sixty degrees left for a heading of 264 degrees. His flight was almost due west. That meant he would make his bomb run into the wind, which blew south that morning at ten miles per hour. The bomber's ground speed hovered around 330 miles per hour. As the *Enola Gay* closed in on the target, Tibbets reminded the crew to slip on their goggles, keeping them up on their forehead until the bomb was released.

"Okay, I've got the bridge," Ferebee announced ten miles out.

"No question about it," Van Kirk agreed, comparing it to a photo.

Ninety seconds out, Tibbets turned the bomber on autopilot over to Ferebee.

"It's all yours," he said.

The colonel released the controls and sat back. "My eyes were fixed on the center of the city," he said, "which shimmered in the early morning sunlight."

The pilot then scanned the sky for antiaircraft fire or enemy fighters.

None appeared.

"Goggles," Tibbets announced.

On the ground below, the time zone was one hour behind the *Enola Gay*. Local authorities had issued an air raid alert at 7:09 a.m. that morning, only to lift it twenty-two minutes later. With the alarm canceled, residents left for work, including 8,400 mobilized students tasked to clean up broken roof tiles, nails, and lumber from homes demolished under the city's firebreak program. The lack of any substantial attacks on the city in recent months had prompted residents to speculate why America had so far spared Hiroshima when dozens of other cities smoldered. Some erroneously hypothesized that Truman had family living in the area while others suggested it stemmed from many of the city's residents immigrating to America.

"Because Hiroshima is a strong Buddhist center," others theorized.

At 8:14 a.m., a searchlight battery on the outskirts of Hiroshima reported the roar of engines closing in on the city, a sound that soon reached the ears of army conscript Tadataka Sasaki, who marched past Hiroshima Castle. The twenty-five-year-old had recently come back from serving in Tokyo. "When I returned to Hiroshima, the city was beautiful, untouched, like nothing had ever happened in Japan," he later said. "It was a strange scene for me."

"There's a B-29!" a fellow soldier announced.

Sasaki looked skyward.

Elsewhere in the city, others paused for a glance up into the heavens, including thirty-three-year-old Futaba Kitayama, who worked that Monday to help clear fire lanes. "The plane looked very small," she recalled, "small enough to be held in my hands."

"That's beautiful!" she exclaimed. "Just like a picture."

"You must be a poet," her friend teased. "How else can you have that sort of idea at this time."

Six miles overhead bombardier Ferebee pressed his left eye against the viewfinder of the sight, watching the streets, bridges, and canals pass below.

"I've got the aiming point," he announced.

"That's the aiming point," Van Kirk again confirmed.

"We're on target," Ferebee declared.

One minute before the expected release, Ferebee hit a toggle switch, which activated a high-pitched radio tone that was audible to everyone in all three bombers. "There will be a short intermission," Lewis jotted in his diary, "while we bomb our target."

The tone stopped.

The pneumatic bomb bay doors sprang open, and Little Boy plummeted.

Tibbets shot a glance at his watch: 9:15 a.m. plus seventeen seconds.

"It's clear," Ferebee announced.

"Bomb away," Van Kirk scribbled in his log.

The loss of the 9,700-pound weapon caused the nose to jump upward. Tibbets wrestled control of the plane and banked 155 degrees into a diving right turn at full power. *The Great Artiste* released three aluminum canisters, each equipped with parachutes to measure the blast and radio the results, while the motion picture cameras onboard *No. 91* whirred.

"Now," Parsons said to himself, "it's in the lap of the Gods."

Ten seconds passed.

Then twenty.

And thirty.

Silence hung over the men as Tibbets struggled with the controls. Jeppson counted the seconds in his head. "Oh my God," he finally thought, "this thing is a dud." Others likewise agonized over the wait. "To some in the plane," Tibbets said, "it seemed an eternity."

"No one knew," added Lewis, "what to expect."

The bomb detonated after forty-three seconds, unleashing powerful radioactive forces that not only exposed X-ray films stored in the basement of a concrete hospital a mile from ground zero but made the fillings in Tibbets's teeth tingle. "The cockpit," Lewis recalled, "filled with a sickening purple light." Tibbets, who could not fly with the goggles, felt like flak hit him in his exposed face. "Everything," he said, "just turned white in front of me."

Tibbets continued his escape, trying to put as much distance between the *Enola Gay* and the blast as possible. Traveling at eleven hundred feet per second, the shock wave smashed into the bomber one minute later and nine miles out from the target. "Our B-29," Tibbets recalled, "trembled under the impact and I gripped the controls tightly to keep us in level flight."

"That's it—the shockwave," Parsons shouted. "We're in the clear now."

A second milder wave soon followed.

"Fellows," Tibbets announced, "you have just dropped the first atomic bomb in history."

The colonel banked the bomber and circled for a view of the devastation. A purple mushroom cloud roared up into the heavens, threatening to swallow the *Enola Gay*. On the ground below, amid the turbulent and boiling smoke, the crew could see multiple fires. "If Dante had been with us in the plane," Tibbets said, "he would have been terrified!"

"Holy moses," Caron declared. "What a mess!"

The others agreed. "There in front of our eyes," Lewis scribbled in his diary, "was without a doubt the greatest explosion man has ever witnessed."

The bright shimmering city, which Tibbets had seen so clearly only moments earlier, had vanished in a dark cloud that swirled up in the sky. The realization of the bomb's awful power hit them. "A feeling of shock and horror," Tibbets said, "swept over all of us."

"My God," Lewis wrote in his diary, "what have we done?"

CHAPTER 29

"When I looked in the direction of the city, there was no city. It looked like a winter field, bleak and desolate."

—YÔKO ÔTA, JAPANESE WRITER AND HIROSHIMA SURVIVOR

Little Boy detonated 1,968 feet above the Shima Hospital, a modern two-story brick clinic that sat just 550 feet east of the aiming point. Within one-millionth of a second, a single neutron sparked a supercritical chain reaction that sent temperatures soaring to several million degrees Fahrenheit, turning the bomb's casing into ionized gas. The ensuing fireball ballooned in less than a second to 900 feet in diameter. Temperatures on the ground below reached 7,200 degrees, hot enough to bubble clay roof tiles, fuse porcelain dishware, and melt coins, sewing needles, and even a bronze Buddha statute. Rescuers sifting through the city's debris would later find a skull with the victim's glasses melted inside the eye cavity.

The explosion carbonized people on the streets, leaving charred hands still wrapped around the hanging straps on trains. Organs evaporated, and birds vaporized in flight. Survivors inside the city center never even heard the explosion. "We saw blue-white lightning," recalled fourteen-year-old Ichiso Hori. "It was like the flash of a camera." That brilliant flash of infrared energy hurtling across the doomed city at the speed of light would leave haunting reminders of the split-second when the detonation occurred, including the shadow of a castor bean plant's leaves on a charred utility pole, the outline of a person seated on the steps of Sumitomo Bank, and the image of a man pulling a cart across the Bantai Bridge.

The sudden release of so much heat triggered a massive expansion of air, which unleashed a 984-mile-per-hour blast wave that smashed streetcars, snapped or uprooted trees, and flattened most of the city's homes, shops, and businesses. Windows shattered as far as seventeen miles away, while the force of the explosion drove shards of glass into masonry walls. Of the city's 76,327 buildings—85 percent of which were residences—the explosion and subsequent fires destroyed or damaged a staggering 70,147. Little Boy likewise crippled the city's public services. The blast toppled more than 4,000 utility poles, busted water mains, and wrecked power and gas plants. Sixty-five percent of Hiroshima's 123 trolley cars were ruined along with half of the city's eighty-five buses. "It is no exaggeration," as one postwar report observed, "to say that the whole city was ruined instantaneously."

Tadataka Sasaki, who had been walking seconds earlier with two soldiers, came to his senses, noticing immediately the sudden absence of cicadas. "I felt like I was dreaming," he said. "I was in the middle of the castle's outer moat, almost naked. My body was hideously burned, and I was wearing only tattered underwear and holding my bayonet."

"I'm injured," he heard a fellow soldier shout.

Tadataka pulled himself out of the moat and stumbled over to his colleague. "His back was deeply burned," he recalled. "I could see through to bone." He left his friend and climbed a nearby hill, reaching the top with the hope of surveying the damage. "There was nothing to block my view," he recalled. "The city of Hiroshima had disappeared."

Many others woke up under piles of debris from collapsed roofs, walls, and furniture. Dust from the shattered city, which would rise more than eight miles into the heavens in the form of a mushroom cloud, blotted out the summer sun, turning day into night. "I couldn't even see my wife's face as she lay right next to me," recalled newspaper photographer Yoshito Matsushige. "I squeezed her hand tightly." Survivors choked on air thick with pulverized concrete and timbers, hair and skin. The sudden trauma of the explosion disoriented many along with the drastically changed landscape. Gone were the city's businesses and neighborhoods, replaced by a sea of twisted lumber and warped sheet metal. "None of the buildings or trees that had stood there moments before could be seen," recalled thirteen-year-old Setsuko Iwamoto, who was less than a mile from the blast. "I was engulfed in an eerie silence and felt, for an instant, that I might be the only living thing on earth." Akihiro Takahashi, a middle school student, experienced the same. "For a moment I thought Hiroshima had vanished."

Survivors stumbled into this apocalypse, past victims whose white teeth stood out in marked contrast to their blackened bodies. "I saw a train stopped on the Aioi Bridge," recalled seventeen-year-old Hiroko Uchida. "The driver and the passengers, seated and standing both, were completely charred." The blast had left many naked or in shredded shirts and pants. Glass from blown-out windows coupled with wooden splinters riddled bodies, gouged out eyes, and sliced open bellies, exposing the intestines. Flash burns tattooed skin while blisters arose and ruptured on faces and torsos, exposing raw red flesh and leaving the skin to dangle, as one survivor later described, like apple peelings. "Some were wearing what I assumed to be tatters of clothing," remembered twenty-four-year-old Fumie Enseki, "but when I looked closer, I was shocked to find that the tatters were in fact hanging skin, burned and peeling off."

Naked children cried for parents while mothers and fathers hollered the names of their missing offspring. Victims crouched in the rubble, pleading for help. "Everywhere I looked," remembered Setsuko, "I saw the most horrible misery." Fifteen-year-old Michiko Yamaoka, who was walking to work at the Hiroshima Central Telephone Office, witnessed the carnage just a half mile from the hypocenter. "This wasn't the world I knew—it was a living hell."

"Water, give me water," victims begged. "I'm hot."

"Help me!" others pleaded. "Help me!"

Those who could fled toward the city's many waterways, propelled by an incredible thirst and a desperate desire to cool their burning flesh. Along the way, many dunked their faces in firefighting cisterns, gulping the inky-black water. "Wherever a puddle of water had collected from burst waterpipes, people gathered like ants around a honeypot," recalled Kosaku Okabe, noting that many perished at the water's edge. "Others clambered over the dead bodies to get at the water, only to die in the same way, their bodies piling one on top of another."

Fourteen-year-old Takahashi, who was in his schoolyard less than a mile from the blast, was in agony. Glass protruded from his body while the skin on the back of his head, torso, arms, and legs peeled, exposing the bright red flesh beneath. The youth plunged into the river. "The coolness of the water," he said, "was a priceless medicine to my burning body." Others guzzled the murky water. "Bodies were floating past on the current, so many that I had to push them aside with my hands to find space enough to take water into my cupped hands," one survivor recalled. "But no sooner had I pushed aside one corpse than another took its place."

The outgoing tide would carry scores of the dead out into the bay, so many in fact that human remains would continue to wash ashore for five months. The wounded crowded the banks, many with singed hair. Thermal burns prompted bodies and faces to swell so much that people's eyes appeared as slits. Even to loved ones, victims were often unrecognizable. "It was as if the skin had been broiled rather than burned," recalled survivor and writer Yôko Ôta, "ash-colored skin hung from their bodies, peeling off in strips, like the skins of roast potatoes." Massive doses of radiation sapped the energy of others and caused them to be sick. "Those with burns vomited continuously," Ota added. "The sound was nerve-wracking."

Other survivors stumbled toward Hijiyama Hill, a 230-foot-tall ridge a little more than a mile from the hypocenter. Taeko Teramae, who worked at the Hiroshima Central Telephone Office less than six hundred yards from the hypocenter, emerged from the ruins. In the darkness, she failed to realize that the blast had robbed her of her left eye. On her way to Hijiyama, she spotted a girl on the ground, her clothes ripped off. A boy stood over her, tugging her arm.

"You can't die!" he pleaded. "You can't die!"

But the horror had only begun.

The explosion had reduced Hiroshima to little more than a kindling pile of splintered lumber mixed with broken tables, chests of drawers, and shredded tatami mats. Three weeks with no rain had only exacerbated the combustibility. Radiant heat coupled with electrical shorts and toppled stoves immediately sparked fires, which feasted on the debris. In those few concrete buildings that still stood, dark cotton blackout curtains absorbed the heat and ignited; so did offices filled with papers. The blast had blown out windows and doors, allowing air to rush through while open staircases served as chimneys. Within ten minutes of the explosion, hundreds of fires erupted throughout Hiroshima. Twenty minutes later those blazes began to merge, creating a firestorm with winds up to forty miles per hour that would ravage the city's ruins. "The fires swelled up, became mountainous, burning everything in their path," Ota recalled. "The city was being destroyed a block at a time. The heat was unbearable."

Downed utility poles and debris blocked roads and fire hydrants, but that proved irrelevant since the bomb had destroyed the city's two main fire stations along with ten of the eighteen substations. Eighty percent of Hiroshima's on-duty firemen were killed or wounded. "The public fire department sustained an instantaneous paralyzing blow from which it could not recover," one postwar American report noted. "No public fire department as presently constituted could have prevented the conflagration from developing in this city, even if its equipment had not been destroyed or damaged and its personnel had not been killed or injured by blast and debris. The problem and task were overwhelming from the beginning."

Survivors struggling to recover from the shock of the bomb's blast now faced a rising inferno that would ultimately incinerate 4.4 square miles of the city center. "Hiroshima," recalled seventeen-year-old Haruto Seo, "became a sea of fire." Nineteen-year-old Tadashi Takahashi survived the blast in the basement of the Fukoku Seimei Building barely 350 yards from the hypocenter. He escaped from the battered building to witness the terrifying phenomena of fire tornadoes, stalking victims amid the wreckage. "It was like a pillar of fire," he remembered, "and it came with very hot wind, pieces of wood, stones, and many other things."

Shige Hiratsuka faced a horror that befell so many when the blast knocked down the family's home as her husband read the newspaper and she cleared the breakfast table. The couple wriggled out from under the ruins and began searching for their two children.

"Help, Mummy, help!" Shige heard her six-year-old daughter Kazuko cry.

She found her daughter pinned from the chest down under fallen plaster and timber. Shige shouted for her husband to help, but he was too injured to move. "It hurts, Mummy," Kazuko pleaded. "My legs hurt. I can't move. Hurry and get me out."

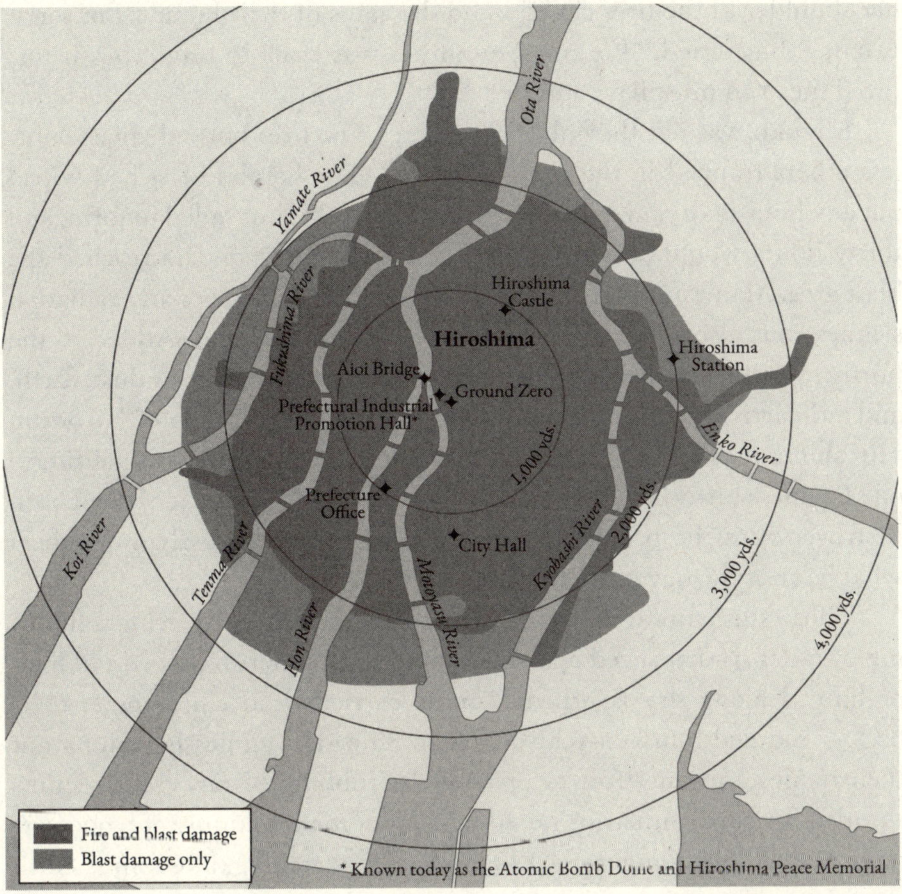

Shige struggled to pull her free, but Kazuko would not budge. "No matter how desperately I tried, I just could not free her," she recalled. "The fires were moving closer and closer. We would not be able to stay there much longer." The heat soared. "I realized," Shige said, "I was afraid to die. I could not let myself be burned to death."

With tears in her eyes, she pressed her hands together as if in prayer and begged her daughter's forgiveness. "Kazu," she pleaded, "I am a bad mother to you, but please forgive me. You don't want to die either, I know. Mummy isn't brave enough to stay here and die with you. I am afraid of the fire. Kazu, forgive me, forgive me."

She fled with her injured husband toward the river, looking over her shoulder as the fires closed in on the ruins of their home. "I'm sorry, Kazu," Shige cried. "Forgive Mummy. I was cruel to leave you. It tortured me. You must have suffered so."

Kazuko was not the only such victim. The fires burned alive countless others trapped in the city's wreckage. The bomb's blast had wiped out any hope of organized local rescue. First aid teams failed to form, and thirty hours would pass before the first outside responders reached the blast area. Many survivors not only struggled with injuries and radiation sickness but also shock that combined to paralyze them. Added to the horror was the mystifying phenomena of black rain, a mix of dust, earth, and radioactive material that fell across the city that afternoon. "No one in Hiroshima that day, or for many days afterward, had any sense of time," one Japanese historian observed. "Almost all watches and clocks had been destroyed. But the people seldom bothered to ask themselves or others what hour of the day it might be."

Those survivors who were able fled the burning city center, climbing over debris that sliced open hands and feet. Others followed rail lines or limped along dry riverbeds. "Some carried dead children on their backs," recalled fourteen-year-old Yoko Shineda, "aimlessly wailing out their names." In an effort to prevent the rubbing of raw flesh, victims shuffled forward with arms raised in front of them, reminiscent, one witness recalled, of a kangaroo. "I found myself watching, like some hellish marathon, a procession of ghastly, inhuman figures fleeing from the city. Their burned skin had peeled and was dangling in shreds," recalled Rikio Yamane. "It was impossible even to differentiate males from females."

Yoshito Matsushige, the thirty-two-year-old photographer for the *Chugoku Shimbun,* made his way to the Miyuki Bridge at eleven a.m., a mile and half from the hypocenter. Hundreds of evacuees had gathered, including housewives and schoolchildren in filthy uniforms who were caught outside in the blast. A lone police officer slathered burns with cooking oil.

"I'll get a quick picture of this," the photographer thought.

Yoshito lifted his camera. Through the viewfinder he saw the dark smoke and haze that hovered over the bridge, where a line of dazed and weary victims sat with heads down and legs drawn up to their chests. Many had singed hair coupled with burns and blisters on their faces, backs, and limbs. "The people around me," he said, "seemed barely alive." The photographer saw an infant clinging to the breast of a woman unable to move. Another hysterical mother cradled her baby. "Open your eyes!" she screamed. "Just open your eyes!" Yoshito froze. "I found it impossible to snap the shutter," the photographer said. "The scene before me was so gruesome that I merely stood there, paralyzed by the reality of this hell."

Twenty minutes passed before Yoshito summoned the courage to again raise his camera and click the shutter release. He snapped a wide-angle shot of the bridge before moving closer, taking a photograph of a police officer helping victims. Yoshito would shoot only three more images that day, including two of his home and one of a police officer issuing survivor certificates. Those five images, which he developed in the open at night with radioactive water, are the only pictures taken inside the city that day. "When I looked into the viewfinder," he said, "the figures I wanted to photograph were blurred and faint because of my tears."

The bomb gutted the city's healthcare system. Only three out of forty-five civilian hospitals still operated. The blast also wiped out two army clinics. Of the city's 298 doctors, 270 suffered casualties. Nurses fared similarly. Of the 1,770 in Hiroshima, a total of 1,650 nurses were killed or wounded. Another 132 dentists and 112 pharmacists were also casualties. Medical personnel suffered a 90 percent casualty rate. "For all practical purposes," one postwar report noted, "the well-prepared medical care system was rendered totally useless." Akihiro Takahashi agreed. "Just to find a doctor," Takahashi said, "was a matter for rejoicing."

Casualties swarmed the few surviving clinics, filling beds and crowding corridors. Triage was merciless. "Medicine was in such short supply," one report noted, "that those who were burned over more than a third of the body were considered hopeless and simply abandoned." Inside the Hiroshima Communications Hospital, located barely fifteen hundred yards from the hypocenter, patients sprawled out on tatami mats and pallets. The blast had left many naked, prompting some to improvise with clothes fashioned from hospital curtains or tablecloths. Patients wallowed in excrement and vomit while the foot traffic smeared the foul fluids throughout the clinic. "The people who were burned suffered most because as their skin peeled away, glistening raw wounds were exposed to the heat and filth," Dr. Michihiko Hachiya wrote in his diary. "This was the environment patients had to live in. It made one's hair stand on end."

With so few hospitals, the majority of the injured crowded inside schools that doubled as primitive rescue centers, often overflowing into classrooms. Within days, fifty-three such aid stations opened, ultimately admitting 105,861 men, women, and children and giving outpatient care to another 210,048 people. The scene inside such clinics appeared reminiscent of a horror movie. "I was scared," recalled eleven-year-old Akiyo Tagawa, "by the sounds of people wailing and screaming in pain." The youth along with other sixth graders at Hera Elementary School worked each day, hauling firewood and disposing of feces. "Some of the babies were dead," she said, "and yet the mothers would continue to hold them."

With so many injured—coupled with the loss of power and the sweltering summer heat—conditions throughout the city deteriorated. "The smell," recounted twelve-year-old Takeshi Tanaka, "of blood, burnt skin, and excreta mixed together was terrible."

Burns comprised most of the wounds. "There were few survivors with severe fractures, internal injuries and blood vessel injuries," observed a report by the Army Medical College and First Tokyo Army Hospital. "This no doubt was due to the fact that only those able to save themselves were brought into medical installations and those severely wounded were either instantaneously crushed to death or were left to die there." Medics applied the topical antiseptic Mercurochrome while orderlies passed out meager supplies of hardtack and rice gruel. Victims resorted to sliced cucumbers to cool burns. Others applied mashed potatoes or coated wounds with olive and tempura oil. "All we had," recalled Setsuko Iwamoto, "was folk medicine."

Swarms of flies crawled over open wounds, laying eggs in the rotten flesh. "Nurses would remove these maggots with tweezers," recalled Akiyo, "and then we helpers were supposed to take the maggots in newspaper and kill them by smashing them with our fingers." Tadataka Sasaki, the soldier blown into the moat of Hiroshima Castle, picked the worms from the wound on his neck. He looked on in horror after a man near him died. "When the nurses carried him out on a stretcher, his bed was covered in maggots," Tadataka remembered. "The nurses brushed the maggots off, clearing the space for the next patient."

Survivors arrived daily, prowling hospital hallways in search of missing loved ones. "Parents, half-crazy with grief, searched for their children," Haichya wrote in his diary. "Husbands looked for their wives, and children for their parents. One poor woman, insane with anxiety, walked aimlessly here and there through the hospital calling her child's name. It was dreadfully upsetting to parents, but no one had the heart to stop her."

Fourteen-year-old Yoko Shineda, who had left for work in a torpedo factory, rushed home to find the windows blown out and the roof peeled back. She ran to the elementary school, which was overwhelmed with victims, many of whom cried out in agony.

"Mother," Yoko hollered, "where are you? Put your hand up."

She searched the gymnasium as well as the first- and second-floor classrooms, passing row after row of victims. Yoko finally stopped, tears streaming down her cheeks. At that moment, someone seized her ankle. "I looked down at the person clutching me," she recalled. "I couldn't speak. Her face was swollen to twice or three times its normal size, and the skin on her hand fluttered back, exposing the red flesh beneath. It was a completely different face from the mother who had smiled and waved me off to work that morning."

"Let's go home," her mother whimpered.

Yoko located a handcart, and with the help of several people she lifted her mother. "When I tried to support her, her skin would stick to my hand," she remembered. "I can't imagine how much she must have been in pain." At home, she swept up the glass and placed her mother in the tatami room. "We put the egg white on my mother's skin and fed her the yolks," she said. "My mother was a brave person, but she struggled, groaned, suffered, and cried."

At daybreak on August 10, her mother died.

The summer heat and humidity swelled bodies, which erupted under the August sun. Workers hustled to collect the dead, including horses and dogs. Teiichi Teramura, a field officer with the 52nd Ship Construction Battalion, was assigned to recover corpses from the water. Protecting the dignity of the deceased eventually gave way to expediency as workers at times used gaffs to hook the dead. "We had to pull the charred bodies aboard with ropes and then take them ashore, where others were waiting to deal with them," he recalled. "There was no way of distinguishing the bodies by sex or age. Most had completely lost their clothes, and all were brown and swollen. Their skin had peeled off and hung dangling, like the peelings of a bruised, black loquat, and all their hair had fallen out."

Laborers dug burn pits throughout the city in schoolyards, empty lots, and along the riverbanks. Seventeen-year-old Tadaomi Furuishi was recruited for the job, searching the dead for nametags or personal items that might help with identification. With so many bodies to burn, workers eventually ran out of wood, forcing them to use light and heavy oil. "We carried the bodies on bamboo mats and wooden shutters to the trenches and ignited them with oil," he said. "The crackling of the burning bodies sounded like fish grilling."

The pyres burned day and night, often watched over by hungry dogs that rooted in the ashes. "Each evening," recalled Katsuyoshi Yoshimura, "we could hear the bugles blown by the soldiers and smell the indescribable odor of burning flesh." Families at times chose to cremate their own loved ones. That was the case for twenty-two-year-old Mitsuko Tsuchikawa. "It was a horrible thing," she recalled, "to have to burn your own mother."

CHAPTER 30

"Identification of the dead and the accurate count of casualties was impossible."

—UNITED STATES STRATEGIC BOMBING SURVEY

Up in the skies over Hiroshima, the crew of the *Enola Gay* continued to gaze down at the destruction on the ground below. From his right-side seat in the cockpit, Lewis focused on the mushroom cloud, which, already high above the bomber, continued its skyward climb. "I am certain the entire crew felt this experience was more than any one human had ever thought possible. It just seems impossible to comprehend. How many Japs did we kill? I honestly have the feeling of groping for words to explain this," he recorded in his makeshift diary. "If I live a hundred years I'll never quite get those few minutes out of my mind."

Tibbets at last banked the bomber to the south for the return flight to Tinian. He kept his airspeed above two hundred miles per hour as he slowly stepped down his altitude. "We were still groping for words to describe what we had witnessed," he recalled. "This spectacular consequence of a single bomb explosion was beyond our understanding."

"I think this is the end of the war," he said to Lewis.

Others felt the same.

Tibbets scrawled out a brief message, noting that he had visually attacked his primary target with positive results while encountering no fighter opposition or flak. He handed the message to radio operator Dick Nelson to transmit. Parsons likewise prepared a short report, though his contained more details. Back on Tinian, Farrell decrypted it. "Results clearcut, successful in all respects," it stated. "Visual effects greater than New Mexico test."

The mushroom cloud continued to grow as the minutes ticked past. The airmen could still see it at a distance of one hundred miles. Then two hundred.

And three hundred.

Not until an hour and a half later, when the bomber was nearly four hundred miles away, did the cloud at last vanish, obscured not by the curvature of the earth, but by the haze. "After a few last looks I honestly feel the Japs may give up before we land at Tinian. They certainly don't care to have us drop any more bombs of atomic energy like this," Lewis wrote. "Everyone on the ship is actually dumbstruck, even though we had expected something fierce."

The tension the men had felt that morning faded as the crew settled in for the long flight back to Tinian. Gone was the earlier silence, replaced by excited chatter about the end of the war and the hope to return home soon. "You would have thought you were at a family reunion," Tibbets recalled. As the adrenaline faded, however, drowsiness seized the airmen. "The rest of the ride back to base," he added, "was a bit like a slumber party."

A similar story unfolded onboard *The Great Artiste*, where Manhattan Project physicist Luis Alvarez used the downtime to pen a letter to his four-year-old son, Walt. "The story of our mission," he began, "will probably be known to everyone by the time you read this, but at the moment only the three crews of our three B-29s, and the unfortunate residents of the Hiroshima district in Japan are aware of what has happened to aerial warfare." The days of massive bombing raids were over, he continued, since a single plane could now destroy an entire city. "What regrets I have," he concluded, "about being a party to killing and maiming thousands of Japanese civilians this morning are tempered with the hope that this terrible weapon we have created may bring the countries of the world together and prevent further wars."

The *Enola Gay* reached Iwo Jima at 12:43 p.m. and banked southeast toward the Marianas. As the three bombers closed in on Tinian, the pilots of *The Great Artiste* and *No. 91* reduced speed and fell back to allow Tibbets to land first.

At 2:58 p.m., the *Enola Gay* touched down on the same runway it had taken off from some twelve hours earlier. More than two hundred officers and enlisted men awaited the crew as the bomber taxied to a halt. Tibbets climbed down first, his pipe in hand.

"Attention to orders," a voice shouted.

Everyone stiffened as a silence settled over the crowd. Gen. Carl Spaatz stepped forward—as Tibbets fumbled to hide his pipe—and shook hands. The general presented Tibbets with the Distinguished Service Cross, pinning the medal on his wrinkled flight suit. "It had been an easy mission," he would later write, "one of the most routine I had ever flown, except for the strain and anxiety occasioned by my knowledge of its overwhelming importance."

Back in Washington, Groves continued to stew.

He had received the report at dinner Sunday night that the *Enola Gay* had taken off, but since then nothing. He tried to distract himself with work as the hours crawled past.

At 11:15 p.m., Col. Frank McCarthy phoned. General Marshall had asked McCarthy, who served as secretary of the general staff, for any word of the mission.

"No," Groves admitted, "we have not received any."

Parsons's strike message rattled off the teletype fifteen minutes later followed by Tibbets's report. A relieved Groves phoned McCarthy. Marshall had since gone to bed, instructing the colonel not to bother him with any news, but wait until morning.

Should I wake the general? McCarthy asked Groves.

"I certainly would call General Marshall right away," he replied.

McCarthy followed his advice.

"Thank you very much for calling me," Marshall said.

Groves went back to work, preparing a rough draft of a report that he could present to Marshall in the morning. He planned to add more to it once he received a follow-up report after the crew landed on Tinian. With a draft complete, he crashed on a cot.

At 4:45 a.m., the duty officer woke Groves. A more detailed account had just arrived from Farrell. A reconnaissance plane had taken off to photograph Hiroshima but had not yet returned. The crew's account, however, was stunning. "Entire city except outermost ends of dock areas was covered with a dark grey dust layer which joined the cloud column," the report stated. "It was extremely turbulent with flashes of fire visible in the dust. Estimated diameter of this dust layer is at least three miles. One observer stated it looked as though whole town was being torn apart." Parsons and other observers who had witnessed Trinity felt the Hiroshima bomb was tremendous and awesome even in comparison with the New Mexico test. "Its effects," the report concluded, "may be attributed by the Japanese to a huge meteor."

Armed with this latest update, Groves revised his report. As his secretary typed it, he swapped unforms and then hustled to Marshall's office. He was waiting on him around seven a.m. when the general arrived. Groves handed him the three-page document. Gen. Hap Arnold and George Harrison soon joined. Marshall then phoned Stimson at 7:45 a.m., who had flown home from Potsdam and headed up to Highhold. Within hours, the White House would reveal to the world news of the atomic attack. Marshall warned that America should not appear to gloat, given the expected high number of casualties. "I was not thinking so much about those casualties," Groves replied, "as I was about the men who had made the Bataan Death March."

"I am glad you said that," Arnold told him afterward. "It's just the way I feel."

At Marshall's urging, Groves camped out that morning in Stimson's office while final considerations were given to the president's press release, which Laurence had drafted. Both Stimson and Truman had since approved the release, but Groves had concerns. Since the president's statement emphasized the bomb's strength, the general wanted to make sure America did not oversell the destruction. That had happened in the European theater, when the air force prematurely announced the complete destruction of Berlin, only to have to hit the capital again and again. Groves wanted to avoid a repeat of that embarrassment, but the challenge was that no one yet had visual evidence of Hiroshima's devastation; only the crew's testimony. "There were suggestions that we should delay our announcement. There were suggestions that we should soften it," Groves said. "There were innumerable suggestions."

And time was short.

At ten a.m., the frustrated general finally reached LeMay on Guam via teletype. "Important," he began, "that we make press announcement here immediately."

Groves pressed for any update on visual evidence of Hiroshima's destruction.

The only confirmation of the crew reports, LeMay replied, came from pictures shot from the *Enola Gay*'s tail camera. "Target area of approximately three miles in diameter is covered by a grey dust like smoke," LeMay said. "This smoke slopes to the center forming a mushroom of white smoke that rises to about 27,000 feet. The picture taken approximately three minutes after strike report the target completely covered with smoke and a column of dense white smoke rising to about 30,000 feet with a lesser concentration rising to 40,000 feet."

LeMay added that the reconnaissance plane that arrived four hours after the strike to photograph Hiroshima found the mushroom cloud still there and the city obscured by smoke. "Have oblique pictures," LeMay wrote, "but expect no detail from them."

Groves was running out of options.

Absent concrete proof, this would be a gut decision. And for that, Groves would depend on his trusted deputy. "Will you ask Farrell thru your relay setup if he sees any reason for not releasing information to the public in the United States without delay?"

"General Farrell," LeMay replied, "sees no reason why information on Hiroshima strike should not be released to American public at once and strongly recommends such release."

That was all Groves needed.

Within the hour, White House reporters, who had been alerted of an eleven a.m. announcement, shuffled in to see Eben Ayers, the assistant press secretary. Ayers held up the president's four-page statement, which would prove to be one of the most consequential press releases in history, detailing the world's first atomic attack and warning Japan of a new horror ahead. "I have got here," he began, "what I think is a darned good story."

CHAPTER 31

"As soon as I saw that explosion, I knew war had changed. We would never need 1,000 planes again. All we would need was one."

—PAUL TIBBETS, JR.

Groves was not the only one anxious for news.

Onboard the *Augusta*, which steamed across the Atlantic en route home to the United States, Truman eagerly awaited confirmation of the first atomic attack. It had been a long four days at sea for the president, who had departed Germany on August 2. Truman had spent eighteen tiring days at Potsdam, during which time he and his fellow Allied leaders had met in thirteen formal sessions. That did not include the various drop-ins, dinners, and preparatory conferences he had with his aides. In short, the president was whipped. "In a physical sense I found the conference to be exacting," Truman recalled. "Churchill and Stalin were given to late hours, while I was an early riser. This made my days extra long."

The conference had delivered mixed results. On the plus side, Truman had held his own alongside Allied leaders on the world's stage. He likewise secured Russia's commitment to enter the war against Japan, which had been his top priority when he left Washington. The president also welcomed Allied backing for the issuance of the Potsdam Declaration, an ultimatum that he hoped would entice Japan to surrender before a bloody invasion. On the flip side, the challenge of checking Soviet influence in Europe remained, particularly as it related to countries like Poland, Romania, and Bulgaria. Truman left Europe committed to preventing a repeat power struggle in the Pacific. "Force is the only thing the Russians understand," he realized. "While I was hopeful that Russia might someday be persuaded to work in co-operation for peace, I knew that the Russians should not be allowed to get into any control of Japan."

Wrapping up the conference, the president looked forward to returning home. As such, he had turned down offers to visit Denmark, Norway, and France, as well as an extended visit to England, though he did agree to stop over for a lunch of fish, mutton, and vegetables with King George VI. The *Augusta*, joined once again by the light cruiser *Philadelphia*, at last got underway from Plymouth at 3:49 p.m. on August 2. "It has been a delightful experience to visit you and your country," Truman later messaged the king. "I am sure that our two nations will cooperate in peace as they are now cooperating so effectively in war."

At eight-thirty a.m. on August 3, his first full day at sea, the president had summoned the traveling reporters to his stateroom. As Europe receded in the *Augusta*'s frothy wake, Truman's focus once again turned to the Pacific. When everyone was seated around the green-felt-covered table, the president opened a large loose-leaf notebook that contained the details of one of the war's greatest secrets. He then walked the reporters through the development of the atomic bomb, including the recent successful test in New Mexico. "Within a matter of twenty-four or forty-eight hours," Truman told them, "the bomb would be used for the first time."

The stunned journalists listened.

United Press reporter Merriam Smith, who had been in Warm Springs when Roosevelt died, noted that Truman appeared emotionally split. "He was happy and thankful we had a weapon in our hands which would speed the end of the war," Smith recalled. "But he was apprehensive over the development of such a monstrous weapon of destruction." Smith's focus, however, soon turned to his own dilemma. "Here was the greatest news story since the invention of gun powder. And what could we do with it?" he asked. "Nothing. Just sit and wait."

The president settled into shipboard life, much as he had done on the way to Europe. He rose as early as five a.m. each morning, after which he enjoyed strolls on the deck or chats with the reporters. Gone was the pressure he had felt to prepare for the conference. Truman instead reviewed reports, thumbed through the mail, and worked on a radio address he planned to deliver on his return. The reporters checked in daily with Truman, who, like them, was anxious for news of the atomic bomb. All the president could do, however, was shrug his shoulders.

"No word yet," he repeated.

By August 5, the tensions were palpable. "The secret was so big and terrifying," Smith recalled, "that we would not discuss it with each other."

The latest Japanese military intercepts only added to the pressure, revealing that the enemy's buildup on Kyushu had reached 600,000 troops with no sign of slowing down. The rapid reinforcement raised questions among American military leaders as to whether the invasion was feasible—or if the United States should abandon Kyushu and examine alternate sites. "We are," as one intelligence report noted, "in a race against time."

The president distracted himself by attending the ten a.m. Protestant church service in the crew's forward mess hall, joined by Byrnes and Rosenman as well as dozens of officers and enlisted men. Dressed in a light brown summer suit, Truman sang hymns, including one of his favorites, "The Old Rugged Cross," and joined in a reading of Psalm 107. "O give thanks unto the Lord for he is good," he recited, "for his mercy endureth forever."

On the morning of August 6, the fourth day at sea, the president woke to warmer weather as the ship entered the Gulf Stream, prompting the officers and crew to switch to khaki and white uniforms. Truman walked on deck, enjoying the sun and a concert by the ship's band before he retired to his stateroom to continue work on his proposed address to the nation.

A new poll that week by *Fortune* revealed that six out of ten Americans believed Japan would fight until the bitter end. This came as journalists and commentators continued to debate the enemy's astonishing refusal to accept the Potsdam Declaration, even as American bombers incinerated cities and threatened Japan with national extinction. "What is taking place over Japan now," observed *Atlanta Constitution* columnist Gladstone Williams, "is merely the prelude to the most horrible campaign of war devastation ever devised by man."

"How long," added the *St. Louis Post-Dispatch*, "can the Japs hold out?"

"Will the Japanese force the Allies to invade?" asked columnist David Lawrence.

At 11:45 a.m., Truman and Byrnes joined the crew in the after mess hall, sitting separately at tables filled with sailors. A few moments before noon, Capt. Frank Graham, the White House Map Room watch officer, handed Truman a message. "Hiroshima bombed visually with only one tenth cover at 052315Z. There was no fighter opposition and no flak. Parsons reports fifteen minutes after drop as follows: 'Results clear cut successful in all respects. Visible effects greater than in any test. Conditions normal in airplane following delivery.'"

This was the news Truman had waited to hear. "I could not keep back my expectations," he recalled, "that the Pacific war might now be brought to a speedy end."

The president sprang to his feet and shook Graham's hand. "Captain," he declared. "This is the greatest thing in history. Show it to the Secretary of State!"

Graham marched the message over to Byrnes.

"Fine! Fine!" the secretary exclaimed.

Ten minutes later a second message arrived, this one from Stimson. "Big bomb dropped on Hiroshima 5 August at 7:15 p.m. Washington Time," the cable stated. "First reports indicate complete success which was even more conspicuous than earlier test."

Truman again jumped to his feet.

"It's time for us to get on home!" he shouted to Byrnes.

Truman then addressed the crew. "Please keep your seats and listen for a moment," he began. "I have an announcement to make." The president waited as a hush settled over the room. "We have just dropped a new bomb on Japan which has more power than twenty thousand tons of TNT," he continued. "It has been an overwhelming success!"

The crew erupted in cheers.

"Mr. President," one sailor shouted, "I guess that means I'll get home sooner now!"

Against the backdrop of the crew's excitement, the president, with the message still clutched in his hand, darted to the wardroom to share the news with the officers. "There was a broad, proud smile on his face," Smith observed. "In the small dispatch which he waved at the men of the ship, he saw the quick end of the war written between the lines."

Inside the wardroom, the officers started to rise.

"Keep your seats, gentlemen," Truman began. "I have an announcement to make."

The officers sat down and listened as he repeated his message. Few in the wardroom could hear his final words, which were drowned out by the thunderous applause.

"Now we'll finish Japan off in a hurry," one officer declared.

A follow-up message from Stimson alerted the president that the White House had released his statement to the media at eleven a.m. The bomb was no longer a secret, though as a later bulletin noted, details of the damage remained a mystery. "Reconnaissance planes state that an impenetrable cloud of dust and smoke covered the target area," the release stated. "As soon as accurate details of the results of the bombing become available, they will be released by the Secretary of War." Truman called a press conference aboard ship with the embedded reporters, during which he praised Stimson. "If ever a man worked on a thing heroically, it was Secretary Stimson," the president declared. "He deserves great credit."

The ship's radio receivers began to carry news bulletins from Washington about the bomb, including Truman's approved release, which had earlier worried Groves. "Sixteen hours ago an American airplane dropped one bomb on Hiroshima," the statement began. "The force from which the sun draws its power has been loosed against those who brought war to the Far East." The eleven-hundred-word release, which was first conceived of by the Interim Committee and then drafted by Laurence, announced to the world the top-secret development of the atomic bomb, a battle fought not by soldiers and sailors but by industry and scientists. "We have spent two billion dollars on the greatest scientific game in history—and won," the release added. "What has been done is the greatest achievement of organized science in history."

The statement then zeroed in on Japan and the risk it faced if the war continued. "We are now prepared to obliterate more rapidly and completely every productive enterprise the Japanese have above ground in any city," the statement continued. "We shall destroy their docks, their factories, and their communications. Let there be no mistake; we shall completely destroy Japan's power to make war." Truman's message concluded with a reminder that the Potsdam Declaration, which Japan had rejected, was intended to spare the people from the utter destruction many now faced. "If they do not now accept our terms," the message stated, "they may expect a rain of ruin from the air, the like of which has never been seen on this earth."

Word of the destruction of Hiroshima swept the nation and the world. "Most terrible Engine of Ruin Ever Devised May End War Soon," trumpeted the *Pittsburgh Press*.

"Whole Jap City Believed Destroyed," added the *Atlantic City Press*.

"Quit or Be Atomized," declared the *Boston Evening Globe*.

For a secret that had been so carefully guarded, the Pentagon suddenly did an about-face, pumping out multiple press releases, including a statement from Stimson designed to calm any fears. "Every effort is being bent toward assuring that this weapon and the new field of science that stands behind it will be employed wisely in the interests of the security of peace-loving nations and the well-being of the world." Additional releases described Oak Ridge, Hanford, and Los Alamos while others highlighted Trinity and key figures like Groves. The media soaked it up. "Release at long last of the successful development of an atomic explosive," wrote syndicated columnist Marquis Childs, "is news that is literally earth-shaking."

Editorials sounded off on the bomb's use, with many speculating that the war seemed certain to conclude. "For the first time in history," declared the *Washington Evening Star*, "a great nation must surrender or accept the literal alternative of total destruction."

"Unless the Japanese people are utterly, hopelessly mad," added the *St. Louis Globe-Democrat*, "this secret weapon ought to bring the Pacific war to a sudden end."

Others marveled at the incredible scientific discovery at the heart of atom. "It is a different world from the world we woke up to twenty-four hours ago," observed the London *Express*. "The explosion that Hiroshima has seen destroyed a whole world of ideas." Many more touched on the responsibility and danger of such a weapon, echoing the argument long made by some of the Manhattan Project scientists. "Can mankind grow up quickly enough," asked *The New York Times*, "to win the race between civilization and disaster?"

CHAPTER 32

"That pillar of smoke above Hiroshima is a sign of warning to all the world."

—MARQUIS CHILDS, SYNDICATED COLUMNIST
AUGUST 8, 1945

Thirty-six-year-old Satoshi Nakamura, who served as the editor for the Hiroshima bureau of the Domei news agency, was eight miles outside the city, where he had spent the night in the home of a friend. Even at that distance, Little Boy's explosion blew out the windows and hurled him to the floor. The mushroom cloud ascending over Hiroshima ignited the dazed reporter's news instincts, prompting him to hop on a bicycle and pedal toward the devastated city. En route, he weathered a downpour of black rain that stained his fingers gripping the handlebars. Heavy winds soon prompted him to abandon the bike and continue on foot. Upon reaching Hiroshima's western edge, he found the bridge destroyed.

Nakamura diverted to the nearby village of Hara, where he encountered hordes of naked, burned, and bleeding survivors. Around 11:20 a.m. he reached the Japan Broadcasting Corporation's office. The local manager informed him that the broadcasting capabilities were fried, but a telephone line to Okayama still functioned, which Nakamura used.

"Please relay the message I will now give you," he announced into the receiver.

The reporter shared the few facts he had gathered. Hiroshima had been devastated early that morning in an attack by one or two planes, using what he surmised was a special bomb. "Casualties are estimated at one hundred and seventy thousand dead."

"Does that figure sound right to you?" he asked the station manager.

"No," the man cried. "It should be nearer two hundred thousand."

With his news flash filed, the exhausted Nakamura collapsed under an acacia tree outside. "So this," he scribbled in his reporter's notebook, "is the end of the war."

In a follow-up report describing the survivors he had seen, Nakamura encountered pushback from Susumu Uematsu, the head of the Okayama office. Uematsu instructed him to correct his earlier causality estimates, which must have been exaggerated.

"Why the army itself—" Uematsu added.

"You tell those bastards in the army," Nakamura interrupted, "that they are the world's biggest fools."

More than four hundred miles away in Tokyo, a picture of Hiroshima's devastation began to emerge as the afternoon faded, aided by government listening posts that had picked up the broadcasts of Truman's message. Lord Keeper of the Privy Seal Kido briefed Hirohito that afternoon, but neither the Big Six nor the cabinet convened. Not until dawn the following morning did the full scope of the horror emerge in the form of a report to Army Vice Chief of the General Staff Torashiro Kawabe. A single sentence framed the devastation. "The whole city of Hiroshima," it declared, "was destroyed by a single bomb."

CHAPTER 33

"If there is a semblance of sanity among the leaders of Japan, or among the hapless people they have led so far and so fast down the road toward national extinction, it must assert itself now."

—*PHILADELPHIA INQUIRER*
AUGUST 7, 1945, EDITORIAL

There was no letup on Tinian.

The next atomic attack was scheduled for August 11, 1945, but the scientific staff thought it might be possible to finish Fat Man's assembly and push it up by one day.

But even with that bump, another challenge soon arose over weather.

Meteorologists predicted clear skies over Japan on August 9, but after that, forecasters expected the weather to deteriorate and remain bad for five days.

Waiting, many feared, risked losing the initiative.

At an August 7 meeting between Spaatz, LeMay, Parsons, and Rear Adm. William Purnell, senior commanders decided to hustle to make it happen. Not only would a back-to-back strike shock Japan's leaders, but it would play a valuable role in psychological warfare, particularly since a third bomb would not be available until September. "The use of the second bomb the same week," Tibbets recalled, "was calculated to indicate that we had an endless supply of this superweapon for use against one Japanese city after another."

A press conference followed the morning meeting. At the U.S. Army Strategic Air Force headquarters on Guam, Spaatz and LeMay flanked Tibbets, who stood behind a table, the long sleeves of his uniform loosely rolled up. Reporters fired off a laundry list of questions. How did you feel, one asked, dropping the most fearsome weapon in history?

Do you think it will end the war? added another.

How was Hiroshima chosen as a target?

Tibbets ran through the questions, turning the press conference over at times to Parsons, who could handle the more technical aspects. The duo, as a *New York Times* reporter noted, "told this story, the greatest story of the war, with an air that was almost casual."

The atomic attack on Hiroshima had electrified the world.

And now Tibbets, as the pilot of the *Enola Gay* and commander of the secretive 509th Composite Group, would become the face of the mission. Reporters tracked down his parents in Florida, who were soon inundated with phone calls from neighbors and friends around the country. "We knew that he was on some secret mission, but what it was we couldn't guess," said his father, Paul Tibbets, Sr. "I am proud that my son, of all the millions of men in the armed forces, was picked to lead the mission that may bring this war to an end."

Journalists, of course, zeroed in on his red-haired mother, whose unusual name would forever be associated with the destruction of Hiroshima. Enola, she told them, is *alone* spelled backward. "That bomb," she declared, as she nervously played with a pencil, "it's a terrible thing, but if it brings Japan to time, it will save the lives of our own boys."

Reporters likewise found Tibbets's wife, Lucy, who was visiting her mother in Columbus, Georgia, where she had the couple's two toddler sons. "His father wanted him to be a doctor," Lucy Tibbets told the press. "And now look at what he's done."

"I think my daddy is a great guy," added four-year-old Paul Tibbets III.

Outside the glare of the press, analysts pored over photos of Hiroshima. The first reconnaissance flight, which had buzzed the city hours after the attack, found the city obscured by clouds. A follow-up flight on August 7, however, captured the destruction, bringing into sharp focus the horror of Oppenheimer's weapon. The attack had destroyed more than four square miles of Hiroshima or about 60 percent. A few concrete buildings still stood inside the blast zone even as additional damage spread far beyond the area. "No bomb crater," the report noted, "is visible." Analysts highlighted that the blast had flattened five military targets as well as critical industries, ranging from the Hiroshima Gas Works and Telephone Company to railway stations. Many of the city's bridges collapsed while debris clogged the waterways. "Very few moving vehicles and people are visible," the report concluded, "no moving streetcars." A follow-up message added a striking observation. "One peculiarity," the report noted, "is that no rubble is visible on hard surfaced streets. These seem as if swept clean by terrific wind."

The extent of the damage stunned even veteran combat commanders. "Early reports indicate that the destruction wrought this city is incalculable," LeMay's office diary noted. "Early estimates are that 50% of its population were killed by this single bomb."

With a new attack being readied, the air force wasted no time preparing warning leaflets. Orders called for dropping 16 million over the next nine days. The campaign would target forty-seven cities with a population greater than 100,000. Planes likewise would drop another half a million Japanese-language newspapers with stories on the attacks, while radio Saipan would broadcast details of the bombing every fifteen minutes.

To the Japanese People:

America asks that you take immediate heed of what we say on this leaflet.

We are in possession of the most destructive explosive ever devised by man. A single one of our newly developed atomic bombs is actually the equivalent in explosive power to what 2,000 of our giant B-29's can carry on a single mission. This awful fact is one for you to ponder and we solemnly assure you it is grimly accurate.

We have just begun to make use of this weapon against your homeland. If you still have any doubt, make inquiry as to what happened to Hiroshima when just one atomic bomb fell on that city.

Before using this bomb to destroy every resource of the military by which they are prolonging this useless war, we ask that you now petition the Emperor to end the war. Our President has outlined for you the thirteen consequences of an honorable surrender: We urge that you accept these consequences and begin the work of building a new, better, and peace-loving Japan.

You should take steps now to cease military resistance. Otherwise, we shall resolutely employ this bomb and all our other superior weapons to promptly and forcibly end the war.

EVACUATE YOUR CITIES

Orders for the second atomic mission were cut on August 8, 1945.

The main target was Kokura, the city and the arsenal. The secondary target was the Nagasaki urban area. No other alternate city was listed. "Niigata," as Groves explained, "was not made a third target because of its great distance from the other two cities."

Perched on the shores of northern Kyushu, Kokura was home to 168,000 residents. War planners put the bull's-eye on the city's sprawling arsenal, which covered more than two hundred acres, making it one of the largest in Japan. Workers there hammered out everything from automatic weapons and antiaircraft guns to combat vehicles and ordnance. Numerous part manufactures, machine shops, and electric power plants fed the arsenal.

Nagasaki, by contrast, had long served as one of Japan's principal maritime centers, dating back to the arrival of the Portuguese in 1571. Over the ensuing centuries, the city's prominence grew, aided by its possession of one of the best natural harbors on western Kyushu, which facilitated trade with mainland Asia. The area's mountainous geography had shaped its development. Though the metro area covered thirty-five square miles, the heart of the city centered around four square miles that ringed the harbor and stretched north into the valleys formed by the Urakami and Nakashima rivers. Population density in Nagasaki topped out at 65,000 residents per square mile, with many living in traditional one- and two-story Japanese homes constructed of wood and paper with clay roof tiles.

In more modern times, the city's rugged geography had handicapped its economic growth, making it difficult to cut roads and rail lines through the mountains. The city's naval base had since been superseded in importance by the one in Sasebo, while Nagasaki's waterfront had taken a back seat to the ports in Kobe and Yokohama. Despite those challenges,

Nagasaki, with a wartime population of 230,000, remained an important producer. Mitsubishi operated four major factories in the city, the largest being the shipyard that cranked out freighters, destroyers, and light carriers. Workers there, in fact, had built the *Musashi*, one of the two largest battleships in the world until American forces sank it off the Philippines on October 24, 1944. Other Mitsubishi operations included the Electrical Equipment Works, the Steel and Arms Plant, and the Ordnance Factory, the latter two located in the Urakami Valley. So dominant was Mitsubishi that nine out of every ten city laborers worked for the company.

Similar to the attack on Hiroshima, two bombers would take off first to scout the weather over the targets. These would be followed by a three-bomber strike force, one to carry the weapon and two others to transport instruments and observers. A spare B-29 would fly to Iwo Jima and remain in case of an emergency. All other aircraft would be forbidden from flying within fifty miles of the target for four hours prior to the strike. The first leg would be flown below 5,000 feet. After Iwo Jima, pilots would step it up to 10,000 feet until it came time to climb to bombing altitude. "No Tactical Mission Number is assigned to this mission," orders stated. "For record purposes, Special Bombing Mission Number 16 is assigned."

Tibbets planned to sit this mission out, turning it over to Maj. Chuck Sweeney, pilot of *The Great Artiste*, who would serve as the aircraft commander. The twenty-five-year-old Massachusetts native had grown up one of six children in an Irish Catholic family. After he graduated from North Quincy High School in 1937, Sweeney sold wholesale leather and studied at Boston University until, like Tibbets, he caught the flying bug, prompting him to enlist. On December 12, 1941—as rescuers still pulled the dead from the oily waters of Pearl Harbor—the six-foot-one Sweeney was commissioned as an officer in the Army Air Forces.

Sweeney had flown the Hiroshima mission days earlier, dropping the instruments designed to measure the blast. As such, the bomb bay was outfitted with special electronic equipment used to help measure radiation. Rather than transfer all the equipment from his plane, Sweeney opted instead to switch bombers. He would fly Capt. Fred Bock's Superfortress—nicknamed *Bockscar*—while Bock would, in turn, pilot *The Great Artiste*.

Throughout the compound, security was increased for fear of possible sabotage following the publicity surrounding the strike on Hiroshima. Guards were doubled while three machine guns were installed to protect the ordnance area. Laurence spent the morning there in the air-conditioned assembly building watching scientists complete the fabrication of Fat Man, an opportunity that afforded him a glimpse of the fourteen-pound plutonium core at the heart of the weapon. "It is a thing of beauty to behold," the *New York Times* reporter wrote. "In its design went millions of man-hours of what is without doubt the most concentrated intellectual effort in history. Never before had so much brainpower been focused on a single problem."

Laurence joined members of the crew and the brass, who gathered that afternoon to watch workers roll the bomb on a wheeled cart outside the assembly building. "It was painted a dull, mustard yellow and looked ominous as it sat on its cradle," recalled copilot Second Lt. Fred Olivi. "I was in awe of the fact that inside the ugly-looking bomb was something that would split atoms." Members of the crew were invited to sign the weapon, which in the end would carry a simple message stenciled in crayon: "Let's hope this is the last one."

Workers used a chain hoist to transfer the bomb onto a trailer, where it was covered with a tarp. A truck then pulled it to the loading pit, as Olivi and others walked alongside. At the pit, workers lowered Fat Man and then pulled off the tarp. Using reversible propellers, *Bockscar* backed over it. "Then, very slowly, the world's second atomic bomb was lifted up into the bomb bay," Olivi wrote. "You couldn't help but feel goosebumps."

At two p.m., Sweeney attended a briefing to study the maps and aerial photos of the targets. He was joined by pilot Lt. Don Albury and bombardier Capt. Kermit Beahan. "We knew these cities as well as we knew our own hometowns, perhaps better," Sweeney said. "Every inch of them—streets, buildings, bridges, factories, rivers, lakes—was committed to our memories. We walked through every sequence of the bomb runs at each city."

Intelligence officers reviewed the latest information on antiaircraft guns and fighters. The men were warned to expect significant flak over Kokura, which was ringed with antiaircraft batteries designed to protect the arsenal. "It sat smack in the heart of the city," Sweeney said of the target. "The Japanese war effort depended on keeping factories like this one operating." Nagasaki, by comparison, the airmen learned, was not as heavily defended as Kokura. "None of us had slept well over the past two days, and as the afternoon briefing dragged on, the tedium and tension grew," Sweeney recalled. "We finally finished up, and I returned to our hut to try to grab a little nap. The heat and anticipation made sleep impossible."

The crews assembled for the final briefing at twelve-thirty a.m. In addition to *Bockscar, The Great Artiste* would carry the instruments, and the *Big Stink*, piloted by Maj. James Hopkins, would serve as the camera plane. The *Enola Gay*, commanded this time by Capt. George Marquardt, would scout the weather over Kokura while Lt. Charles McKnight's *Laggin' Dragon* would buzz Nagasaki. Capt. Ralph Taylor in *Full House* would fly to Iwo Jima with the spare B-29. During the briefing, officers passed along the latest intel as well as updates on radio frequencies and air-sea rescue plans in case of an emergency. Laurence, who would join the mission as an observer on *The Great Artiste*, marveled at the meeting. "Each target was shown on detailed maps and in aerial photographs," he said. "Every detail of the course was rehearsed—navigation, altitude, weather, where to land in emergencies."

Thunderstorms en route ruled out Iwo Jima as a rendezvous for the three strike planes, forcing a change to Yakushima, a small island off the southern tip of Kyushu. Forecasters predicted clear skies over Kokura from eight a.m. until eleven a.m., giving them a tight window to reach and bomb the target. A calculation by navigator Capt. James Van Pelt revealed that *Bockscar* needed to be airborne by three a.m. Tibbets hammered two points: the crews were to wait no more than fifteen minutes at the rendezvous before flying to the target. As at Hiroshima, the bomb had to be dropped visually. "The orders," as Olivi recalled, "were very specific."

Chaplain Downey again closed the briefing in prayer.

"Above all else, our Father," he said, "bring peace to Thy world."

The airmen headed to breakfast and then climbed aboard trucks for the ride down to the hardstands. The scene that greeted them stood in sharp contrast from a few nights before, when the brass had crowded the tarmac and floodlights illuminated the *Enola Gay*. A few army cameramen were on hand along with a single newsreel photographer, but little else denoted the significance of the occasion. "That was the first atomic mission," Olivi recalled. "Ours was just number two. Now everyone knew what to expect. No reason to get excited."

Sweeney, Albury, and flight engineer Master Sgt. John Kuharek walked around the bomber. "The airplane looked in pristine condition," Sweeney said, "not a drop of fluid on the ground, tire pressures perfect, surfaces clean and clear, everything in tiptop condition."

Before climbing aboard, Sweeney gave the crew a quick talk, noting that the Hiroshima mission was flawless. "I want our mission to be exactly the same," he told the men. "We will execute this mission perfectly and get the bomb to the target."

Once on board, the airmen began preflight checks before starting the engines.

"Major," Kuharek announced to Sweeney, "we have a problem."

The bomber held 7,250 gallons of fuel, but during his checks Kuharek discovered that a transfer pump appeared to malfunction, preventing him from moving 640 gallons stored in two auxiliary tanks. That would reduce how much fuel Sweeney had for the mission. The question of whether the pump was broken or if the problem was a mechanical quirk that the substitute crew was unfamiliar with has long been a debate, but the reality is to the airmen at that time, it was a problem.

"How long to fix it?" Sweeney asked.

"With all the special precautions," Kuharek replied, "several hours."

Sweeney climbed down the nose ladder and relayed the news to Tibbets. "We have 600 gallons of fuel we can't use," he said. "It'll take too long to change pumps."

Each minute Sweeney loitered on the tarmac shortened his already limited window to reach and bomb the target. Time was of the essence. "I could tell by his expression," Tibbets wrote, "that he was looking to me for a solution to his problem."

"You don't need the damned fuel," Tibbets told him. "It is only in there to offset some of the bomb weight in the front." But he reminded Sweeney that as the aircraft commander, he could scrub the mission if he disagreed. "It's your call, Chuck."

"The hell with it," Sweeney replied. "I want to go. We're going."

"Before you go," Tibbets replied, "let me caution you to remember something." Given the late start, he said, it was vital that Sweeney not loiter at the rendezvous point and wait for the two other strike planes. Make one circle of the area, Tibbets instructed, then press on for the target. "You don't need those escorts to make a successful release."

CHAPTER 34

"It is the masses of the people who have so little to say about the starting or ending of wars who pay the additional cost."

—WINSTON CHURCHILL

Foreign Minister Shigenori Togo, on August 8, hustled to see Hirohito in the emperor's underground shelter dug into the 531-acre palace grounds. The purpose of Togo's meeting was to provide a report about American radio broadcasts, which trumpeted Truman's message on the atomic attack and the threat to destroy Japan. The situation was dire. The United States had burned dozens of Japanese cities even before the introduction of the atomic bomb. Now a single airplane could deliver a weapon that could wipe out an entire city.

"It was all the more imperative," Togo urged him, "that we end the war."

Togo's view presented a strong contrast to the nation's military. In the past forty-eight hours, army leaders had downplayed the attack, arguing that it was unlikely America had, in fact, used an atomic weapon. To confirm, Tokyo had dispatched Lt. Gen. Seizô Arisue, head of army intelligence, along with the nation's top nuclear physicist, Yoshio Nishina, to investigate. But even if it was an atomic bomb, such naysayers added, America likely did not possess abundant fissile material to build enough weapons to continue such strikes. World condemnation of the Americans likewise would prevent future attacks, a sentiment Japanese radio now stoked. "Hiroshima was subjected to the most inhumane and barbaric act yet to be reported in the annals of America," howled Radio Tokyo. "Men, women, and children, sick, crippled or helpless—the bomb has no mercy as to whom it kills."

But the militarists failed to sway Hirohito.

Only the day before, he had met with his senior political aide, Lord Keeper of the Privy Seal Marquis Koichi Kido. During the thirty-five-minute meeting in the palace library, Kido confirmed reports that the attack on Hiroshima had been catastrophic. Casualties topped 130,000 killed and wounded, a figure that stunned the emperor.

"The damage sustained by us," Kido warned, "is enormous."

"Under these circumstances," Hirohito replied, "we must bow to the inevitable."

America's new weapon, the emperor realized, had left Japan powerless to continue the fight. Not only could the United States easily wipe out Japan's remaining cities, but the bomb also rendered the army's plans for a water's edge defense moot. Hirohito requested Togo to inform the prime minister of his view. "Tell Suzuki," he instructed, "it is my wish that the war be ended as soon as possible."

But Japan's problems only worsened.

At five p.m. that afternoon in Moscow, Japanese ambassador Sato entered the Kremlin to meet with Molotov, who had recently arrived home from Potsdam. Speaking in Russian, the ambassador congratulated him on his safe return, but Molotov interrupted him, directing him to take a seat in his study. "I have here," he began, "in the name of the Soviet Union, a notification to the Japanese government which I desire to communicate to you."

Molotov read aloud a 225-word statement that announced the news that Japan had long feared. "The Soviet Government," Molotov said, "declares that from tomorrow, that is from August 9, the Soviet Union will consider herself in a state of war against Japan."

Two hours later the Red Army rolled into Manchuria.

CHAPTER 35

"Destiny chose Nagasaki as the ultimate target."

—WILLIAM LAURENCE
SEPTEMBER 9, 1945

Bockscar roared into the skies over Tinian at 3:47 a.m.

The turbulent weather prompted Sweeney to climb to 17,000 feet, where he planned to cruise for the next few hours until the time arrived to begin his ascent to 30,000 feet for the rendezvous over Yakushima. The increased altitude meant that the bomber burned more fuel, but it was a necessary trade-off, he reasoned, rather than risk rattling the weapon any more than necessary. Even at the higher altitude, however, the flight was rough. "Some of these damned cumulus and thunder clouds," Olivi noted in his diary, "are rough as hell!"

At four a.m., Navy Cmdr. Frederick Ashworth opened the small hatch and climbed down into the bomb bay. The mission's weaponeer then unscrewed the green safety plugs and replaced them with the red firing ones, which armed Fat Man. Ashworth relayed the news to Sweeney. Once *Bockscar* reached cruising altitude, Sweeney turned the controls over to Olivi. "Take it to Yakushima," he instructed. "I'm going to get some sack time."

The cockpit windshield framed the dark night as the bomber flew north, skirting the storm. "The lightning flashes illuminated the sky around us and were a pretty sight," Olivi recalled, "until we had to fly through one." About an hour into the flight, the storms finally broke.

Olivi passed the time marveling at the St. Elmo's Fire, atmospheric electricity that resembled blue lightning as it danced off the tips of the propellers and wings. "It was spectacular," he recalled, "and one of the best displays I had ever seen."

Others on the plane followed Sweeney's lead and snoozed. The early morning takeoff likewise caught up with Olivi, who struggled to stay awake at the controls. "God, I'm so tired I can barely keep my eyes open," he scribbled in his diary at five-thirty a.m. "Wish I could sleep too, but flying through these cumulus clouds sure wakes you up in a hurry."

One hour soon turned to two.

Then three.

Onboard *The Great Artiste*, Laurence likewise enjoyed the St. Elmo's Fire as he chatted with members of the crew, including Sgt. Ralph Curry, the radioman.

"Think this atomic bomb will end the war?" Curry asked.

"There is a very good chance," Laurence replied. "But if not, then the next one or two surely will. Its power is such no nation can stand up against it very long."

Bombardier Lt. Charles Levy invited Laurence to climb into the transparent nose, where he watched the morning brighten. "From that vantage point in space," he wrote, "one gets a view of hundreds of miles on all sides, horizontally and vertically. At that height, the vast ocean below and the sky above seem to merge into one great sphere." Laurence's thoughts turned to Japan and the mission ahead. In a few hours, he noted, one of the enemy's cities would vanish. "In one-tenth of a millionth of a second, a fraction of time immeasurable by any clock, a whirlwind from the skies will pulverize thousands of its buildings and tens of thousands of its inhabitants," he wrote. "Does one feel any pity or compassion for the poor devils about to die? Not when one thinks of Pearl Harbor and of the Death March on Bataan."

Back on board *Bockscar*, copilot Don Albury woke up. He split flying duties with Olivi until Sweeney rallied and took the controls. As the third pilot, Olivi perched behind them. Around seven a.m., the red light on the black box that held the bomb's fuse monitor began to flash, indicating that the weapon's firing circuits had suddenly closed. Tension on the plane soared. Assistant weaponeer Lt. Philip Barnes disassembled the box, inspecting the circuitry. "After a few moments he found the problem: someone on the ground had placed two rotary switches in the wrong positions, causing a malfunction in the monitor's circuits," a relieved Sweeney said. "The firing circuits had not closed. The fuses had not activated."

Sweeney eased back on the controls around eight a.m., beginning the climb to 30,000 feet. A little more than an hour later, *Bockscar* reached the rendezvous point. Within minutes, *The Great Artiste* appeared off the right wing, but the *Big Stink* failed to arrive. Crew members not actively working peered out the bomber's windows, scanning the horizon in search of the third plane. "We started circling," Laurence wrote. "We saw little towns on the coastline, heedless of our presence. We kept circling, waiting for the third ship in our formation."

The coded messages arrived from the *Enola Gay* and *Laggin' Dragon*, reporting that low morning haze hung over both targets, but the skies over Kokura were expected to clear while Nagasaki would see increased cloud coverage. "In non-meteorological terms, the conditions were fairly good at both cities," Sweeney said. "Good news for a change."

Five minutes passed.

Then ten.

And the *Big Stink* still failed to show.

Unbeknownst to Sweeney, the *Big Stink* had not been delayed or lost but was circling more than a mile and a half overhead. Mandatory radio silence prevented Sweeney from trying to raise Major Hopkins, leaving the airmen no option but to continue to search the heavens. "The harder we looked," Olivi said, "the more exasperated we became."

Tibbets had been clear: Wait no longer than fifteen minutes, and then head to the target with or without the two escort bombers. Despite those orders, Sweeney hesitated, erroneously concluding that the missing photographic plane was vital to the mission's success, even as his bomber burned through five hundred precious gallons of fuel each hour.

Fifteen minutes soon turned to twenty.

Then thirty.

And *Bockscar* still circled.

"Where the hell is he?" Sweeney said.

Navigator James Van Pelt used the time to consult the charts, confirming the direct route to Kokura. If needed, he charted the route from Kokura to Nagasaki.

Sweeney continued to scan the empty skies.

Forty minutes passed.

"That's it," he finally announced. "The hell with it. We can't wait any longer."

At 9:50 a.m., Sweeney wiggled his wings, signaling *The Great Artiste* that it was time to head for Kokura. Sweeney banked the bomber and aimed for the target, reaching the initial point at 10:44 a.m. Only the day before, LeMay's crews had firebombed the neighboring city of Yawata—known as the Pittsburgh of Japan because of its massive steel production—burning 1.22 square miles or about 21 percent of the urban area. Smoke from the fires wafted over Kokura, adding to the haze and mix of broken clouds. Despite that, Sweeney glimpsed the river, a few buildings, and even streets as he started his run. "Bomb must be dropped visually," Olivi noted in his diary, "but I don't think our chances are very good."

He was right.

"I can't see it!" bombardier Beahan yelled. "There's smoke obscuring the target."

Bockscar zoomed past the Kokura Arsenal.

"No drop," Sweeney announced over the intercom. "Repeat, no drop."

He banked the bomber, circling back to make a second run albeit on a different heading. The element of surprise had vanished. Antiaircraft fire thundered into the skies. "I was now doing something a bomber pilot rarely, if ever, does—making a second run on a target," Sweeney said. "Second runs gave antiaircraft guns second chances."

Sweeney climbed to 31,000 feet to throw off the antiaircraft gunners as he began his second approach. "I hoped," he recalled, "we could catch a break."

But hope was not enough.

"I can't see it!" Beahan again shouted.

"No drop," Sweeney announced. "Repeat, no drop."

Sweeney's problems worsened.

Radar countermeasures officer Lt. Jacob Beser picked up activity on Japan's fighter control frequencies. In addition to the antiaircraft fire that filled the sky with black clouds of bursting flak, *Bockscar* would soon have to face enemy fighters. This came as flight engineer John Kuharek warned that fuel was running low. Compounding challenges, like the faulty fuel transfer pump and cloudy weather, coupled with Sweeney's decision to spend some forty minutes over Yakushima, now placed the entire mission in jeopardy.

In the cockpit, Sweeney conferred with Kuharek and Navy Commander Ashworth before opting to make an unprecedented third pass over the target. If unsuccessful, *Bockscar* would have just enough fuel to execute a single run over Nagasaki, which was south of Kokura and along the general flight path out of Japan. But the question remained whether the bomber would have enough fuel to make it to an American airfield. Tinian was out of the question; so was Iwo Jima. The closest airfield was on Okinawa—and even that might be too far.

These challenges hung over the crew as Sweeney again banked the bomber. "As we came up for our third bomb run," Olivi said, "it was obvious to all of us in the cockpit that we wouldn't be dropping the Fat Man. The clouds and smoke were just too heavy."

Kokura was saved.

"Give me the heading for Nagasaki," Sweeney asked at eleven-thirty a.m.

"Roger," navigator Van Pelt replied before relaying the course.

"It's now or never!" Olivi scribbled in his diary. "Less than two hours of fuel left." Two minutes later, he put pen to paper again. "Reducing power to save gas—wonder if the Pacific will be cold? Our chances for ditching are—good!!! Bomb MUST be dropped for more reasons than one—Hope it goes off! It'll be a hell of a lot of sweat for nothing if it doesn't."

Tension gripped the crew. The original plan called for the bomber to circumnavigate the island to avoid enemy interception, but the fuel shortage forced Sweeney to fly south directly over Kyushu, which was crowded with Japanese fighter bases. Everyone on board knew the stakes. "Boys getting jittery," Olivi noted at 11:40 a.m. "Can't blame them."

At 11:50 a.m., the bomber closed in on the target.

Sweeney's heart sank.

Clouds flittered over Nagasaki, providing only the occasional peek at the coastline and harbor below. "If we didn't drop, we were out of options," Sweeney recalled. "We had about 300 gallons of fuel. If we stayed too long at Nagasaki by making a second bomb run, we might be forced to crash land on the ground in Japan or in the ocean. If we didn't get a visual on our first run and then depart, we'd have to dump the bomb in the ocean."

Others realized the same.

"This is going to be pretty tough," the bombardier told himself as he looked down on the city. "I don't know if we're going to be able to see the target visually or not."

Sweeney summoned Ashworth, who as weaponeer was responsible for the bomb. He explained that there was not enough fuel for more than one run. Though orders mandated a visual drop, it was clear that might not be possible. Radar was the only option. "I'll guarantee," Sweeney added, "we come within five hundred feet of the target."

"I don't know, Chuck," he replied.

Ashworth requested a moment to think while Sweeney prepared for a radar run over the target. "We had to get rid of the bomb," added Albury, "in order to reach Okinawa." Ashworth agreed, realizing there was no other choice, even if it meant disobeying orders. He returned to the flight deck. "This is going to be a radar approach," he instructed Beahan. "If you can get a sighting, good, but if you can't, then release by radar. I'll take responsibility."

Van Pelt and radar operator Staff Sgt. Edward Buckley—both glued to their scopes—worked to set up the bomb run. "No change in cloud coverage," Olivi noted at 11:56 a.m. "It's radar all the way so far—still hoping for visual sight of the target."

Bockscar began the run over the city. Beahan kept his eye glued to the sight when a hole suddenly opened in the clouds. "I've got it," he shouted. "I've got it!"

"You own it," Sweeney said.

Beahan took control of the plane, noting that the radarmen had made a solid approach. In the span of just twenty seconds, Beahan hustled to orient the bomber, kill the drift, and determine the drop angle. He chose an aiming point just north of the city center in the valley of the Urakami River, which was home to two large Mitsubishi armaments plants. "I picked out a racetrack below," Beahan said. "It stood out like a sore thumb from that altitude."

Everyone on board now waited.

"Bombs away," he shouted, then corrected himself. "That's bomb away."

Ashworth recorded the time in his log as 11:58 a.m.

Sweeney banked the bomber into a steep 155-degree dive to the left as he tried to put as much distance as possible between *Bockscar* and the blast. "Time seemed suspended," he said. "As the seconds ticked by, I began to wonder if we had dropped a dud."

Forty-five seconds later, bright light flooded the cockpit. "Even with my dark welders' goggles," Olivi said, "I winced and shut my eyes." Moments later the first of five diminishing shock waves rocked the bomber. Van Pelt climbed into the cockpit as Sweeney completed his escape maneuver. All eyes focused below. "The cloud was rising faster than at Hiroshima," Sweeney wrote. "It seemed more intense, more angry. It was a mesmerizing sight, at once breathtaking and ominous." Others agreed. "I could see tongues of flame shooting out of the mouth of the mushroom," Olivi added. "It resembled a huge, boiling cauldron. It was frightening." Beahan echoed him. "It looked like a picture of hell."

"By the time I got to the window," Beser added, "the city was gone."

At 12:01 p.m., Olivi made a note in his diary. "I have never seen anything like it!" he wrote. "Biggest explosion I've ever seen. Those poor Japs. But they asked for it."

Sweeney circled to allow Beahan to complete his strike report, which radio operator Cpl. Abe Spitzer transmitted: "Nagasaki bombed. Results good." Sweeney ordered Spitzer to call for air-sea rescue, but there was no reply. *Bockscar* was on its own with barely three hundred gallons of fuel. "Even if we slow down our rate of consumption," Kuharek advised, "the best we can do is get within seventy-five, maybe fifty, miles of Okinawa."

Van Pelt plotted the course and relayed the heading to Yontan Airfield. Sweeney aimed the bomber south, throttled back the engines, and began to step down his altitude, a technique designed to stretch his meager fuel reserves. "We're on our way to Okinawa," Olivi wrote in his diary at 12:06 p.m. "It'll be close but I think we're in. Sure hope so!"

To the anxious crew, minutes felt like hours. Would the bomber make Okinawa or go down in the Pacific? Olivi tightened his life preserver and mentally rehearsed ditching procedures. "The flight back," he said, "seemed as if it would last forever."

At one p.m., Olivi noted that Okinawa was visible in the distance. Sweeney tried to raise the tower to alert them of the emergency, but once again there was no reply.

"Yontan tower," he repeatedly radioed. "Mayday! Mayday! Over."

But only silence answered.

On the ground, air traffic controllers were busy landing dozens of B-24 Liberators and B-25 Mitchell bombers along with fighter escorts returning from a strike in Japan.

"Major," Kuharek said, "we're just about out. There's nothing left in the tanks!"

"Everyone," Olivi recalled, "started to sweat. This was a real emergency, and far more frightening than anything that had happened thus far on the mission."

Sweeney continued to try the tower with no success as he forced his way into the landing pattern. "Start firing the flares," he ordered Olivi. "We've got to get on the ground!"

Olivi did as instructed. He grabbed the gun and loaded it with a red flare, which meant that the bomber had wounded on board. He opened the small hatch, pushed the gun into the hole, and squeezed the trigger. Olivi reached down for another flare.

Then another.

And another.

Smoke wafted through the cockpit as Olivi ran through the flares. "It was stick the gun in the hole, fire, remove, reload—as fast as I could," he recalled. "Red—blue—pink—green—yellow—white—all the colors of the rainbow. One after the other."

Other planes banked away from the field, Sweeney observed, while on the ground fire trucks and ambulances now rolled. "I was now barreling in straight ahead, like a runaway freight train," he said. "In a few seconds we'd be on the ground, one way or the other."

The bomber roared over the concrete runway before touching down midway on the strip at 140 miles per hour. *Bockscar* bounced and then settled back down. "I was braced," Ashworth recalled, "fully expecting the B-29 to quickly gobble up the remaining short distance and go tearing through the boondocks." Sweeney hit the emergency brakes and flipped on the reversible propellers to slow the plane. As the bomber turned onto the taxi stop, the number-two engine died. "It wasn't pretty," Olivi said, "but we were on the ground in one piece!"

Bockscar rolled to a stop. Mentally and physically exhausted, Sweeney slumped in his seat. "For several moments no one said a word," Olivi added. "I think we were all caught up in our own thoughts about how close we had come to a fatal disaster."

Sirens wailed as firetrucks and ambulances roared up on the bomber. Sweeney opened the nose wheel door seconds before a head suddenly popped up through it.

"Where's the dead and wounded?" the rescuer asked.

"Back there," Sweeney said, pointing north in the direction of Nagasaki.

Before the men climbed down, Sweeney gave the crew an order.

"Let's not mention where we came from or anything about what we did," he instructed them. "We're just a B-29 looking for gas to get home after a mission."

On the ground, Ashworth conferred with the three pilots and Beahan, so he could pinpoint where the bomb had exploded. "As we compared notes, my fears were confirmed," Ashworth wrote. "Our best estimate showed we had missed the target."

Moments later a truck rolled up. Most of the crew climbed in and headed for the mess hall while Sweeney and Ashworth hopped into a jeep and ordered the driver to take them to the headquarters of Lt. Gen. Jimmy Doolittle, who had recently taken over as the commander of the Eighth Air Force based on Okinawa.

Ashworth went to the communications shack. "How long will it take to send a message to Guam?" he asked.

"Sorry," the duty captain replied. "We're busy."

"Where are General Doolittle's quarters?" he asked.

The officer directed the duo up the street, where a double-pyramidal tent served as the general's headquarters. "The irony struck me immediately. I was about to meet the man who had flown the first American air strike against Japan by bombing Tokyo in 1942," Sweeney recalled. "And I had just flown what might be the last mission of the war—a mission that had demonstrated to the Japanese people that they could be on the verge of annihilation in spite of what their military and civilian leaders were telling them."

Upon arrival, Ashworth introduced himself to the general's chief of staff. "We've just dropped the second atomic bomb over Nagasaki," he said. "We need to send a report back to Guam, but your communications people aren't cooperating."

The chief of staff ushered them in to see Doolittle.

"Well, son," the general said to Ashworth. "Sit down and tell me about it."

Ashworth related the mission.

"What do you think?" Doolittle asked. "Did you hit the target?"

"No, sir," Ashworth said. "I don't think we did."

The navy commander spread out a map out on Doolittle's desk. He pinpointed the original target as spelled out in the orders, followed by where the bomb detonated, which was approximately 1.5 miles outside the city center in the industrial river valley. "Son," Doolittle said, "I am sure that General Spaatz will be much happier that the bomb exploded where it did over the industrial area and not over the city. There will be far fewer casualties."

With Doolittle's assistance, Ashworth fired off a detailed report of the mission. He and Sweeney then found the crew in the mess hall. The airmen from *The Great Artiste* and *Big Stink* joined them, the latter of which had spent the morning orbiting between Kokura and Nagasaki after missing the earlier rendezvous. That crew learned of the mission's success when the mushroom cloud rose over Nagasaki, prompting Hopkins to buzz the city and photograph it. "Ate Spam as I expected," Olivi noted in his diary, "but it tasted good at that."

The airmen headed back to the flightline, where *Bockscar* was now refueled. At five-thirty p.m., the bomber roared back into the skies for the six-hour flight to Tinian. The long day caught up with the crew, who tuned in to Armed Forces radio as it belted out the music of Tommy Dorsey and Glenn Miller. "Not much was said on board the airplane," Beser noted. "There was none of the euphoria that was evident after the drop at Hiroshima. So far we had experienced fourteen long and trying hours, and although it was now all downhill, it wasn't over yet."

The sun sank in the western sky as *Bockscar* flew south. "I don't think any of us had any regrets," Olivi said. "We had done the job we were trained to do: fly an atomic bomb nicknamed Fat Man to a targeted city in the Japanese Empire, drop it, then return to our home base."

Bockscar touched down at ten-thirty p.m. on Runway Able, almost nineteen hours after the crew departed. Unlike Tibbets's return a few days earlier, there were no medals presented or bands of cheering airmen. Gone, too, were the floodlights and camera crews. A handful of senior leaders were there along with the ground crew and a single photographer. "We were home," Sweeney said. "We were alive. We had completed our mission." Olivi echoed him in his diary. "Tinian looks good," he wrote. "Real tired, but happy to be home safe."

The mission may have been over, but the criticism was only beginning. Tibbets fumed, believing that Sweeney had jeopardized the lives of his crew. "Come morning," he said, "I would be expected to peruse the various mission reports and decide what, if any action should be taken against the airplane commander, Charles Sweeney, for failure to command."

The following day after a press conference on Guam, LeMay met with Tibbets and Sweeney. "You fucked up, didn't you, Chuck?" LeMay began.

"The awkward silence that followed," Tibbets noted, "spoke volumes."

LeMay told Tibbets he didn't think an investigation would serve a useful purpose.

"You got any more of those things?" LeMay asked of the bombs.

"Yes, sir," Tibbets said. "We have another Fat Man bomb ready back at Wendover."

"Get it out here," he said. "If we need another mission, you are going to fly it."

CHAPTER 36

"This was the day of the apocalypse which Nagasaki will remember forever."

—DR. RAISUKE SHIRABE
AUGUST 9, 1945, DIARY ENTRY

It was a hot summer morning in Nagasaki.

Many of the residents were tired following a late evening of howling air raid alarms. The last had sounded at 1:10 a.m., but not until three a.m. did authorities issue the all-clear, allowing weary residents to finally climb out of shelters and back into bed. Sunrise that Thursday had brought little reprieve. A 7:50 a.m. siren sent many once again scurrying into bomb shelters dug in home gardens or carved into the surrounding hillsides. Officials canceled the warning at eight-thirty a.m., but the city remained on edge as residents began the day.

The morning mist that hugged the mountains and the harbor burned off as women lined up at rice stations or gathered in neighborhood groups to collect rations. Others hiked out into the terraced fields to pick eggplants and cucumbers. The pious popped by the Urakami Cathedral for morning prayers. The largest church in Asia, it catered to the estimated 20,000 Catholics in the city. At Nagasaki Medical College, more than 850 faculty and students resumed classes, creating a morning soundtrack of professorial lectures intermixed with the clinking of glass test tubes. Perched atop the college rooftop as well as a nearby hilltop, students manned a large bell and scanned the skies for the threat of any incoming bombers.

Doctors and nurses made rounds at the nearby Nagasaki University Hospital, which with its five hundred beds was the pride of the city and considered to be one of the finest institutions in Japan, rivaled only by the Imperial University Hospital in Tokyo. At the Mitsubishi Sports Field, which bombardier Kermit Beahan would site through his eyepiece, students armed with bamboo spears practiced drills. A similar scene unfolded at the morning assembly at the Mitsubishi Steel and Arms Plant, a sprawling complex along the Urakami River that cranked out ship-launched torpedoes, including the ones used in the attack on Pearl Harbor. An army officer atop a horse addressed the workers, including Yuriko Kitamura, one of 320 mobilized students from the Nagasaki Prefectural Girls High School.

"The war situation is becoming increasingly serious," the officer warned.

The students all listened.

"Even you young girls," he continued, "must prepare to fight against the enemy with bamboo spears in case they start landing in our country."

"Good heavens!" Kitamura asked herself. "What am I going to do?"

Like much of Japan, tensions ran high throughout Nagasaki. Night after night, American bombers incinerated Japanese cities. Nagasaki was not immune, though the damage suffered paled compared to what cities like Tokyo, Nagoya, and Osaka had endured. Nagasaki had suffered five small-scale raids in the previous twelve months that had destroyed or damaged 476 homes and another forty-five industrial buildings. The number killed or missing in those attacks totaled 390 residents with another 600 wounded. The most recent strike had occurred nine days earlier, when six bombs hit the operating room and laboratories at the University Hospital, killing three students and injuring as many as forty others.

The rise of such raids had prompted authorities to order precautions. Similar to other cities, workers had demolished 8,929 homes, shops, and businesses to serve as firebreaks. This was complemented by the evacuation of 51,761 men, women, and children. That number, which was less than other comparably sized communities, reflected the demand for laborers in the city's war factories. To protect those who remained, the city and neighborhood associations dug more than fifteen miles of tunnels in the hills to serve as bomb shelters.

The city's fire department, like so many others across Japan, was woefully inadequate to defend against modern flame weapons. The war's hunger for recruits had whittled the peacetime force of 249 firemen down to just 148. Equipment likewise was lacking. The department, which had one main fire station and five smaller ones, had a total of just seven trucks that could pump 350 gallons per minute. Voluntary police and fire groups complemented the department, adding 492 rescuers and twenty-one more vehicles. Medical efforts centered around the city's eighteen hospitals and clinics that offered a combined total of 1,240 beds. These were augmented by twenty-five first aid stations set up in public schools and doctor offices.

That Thursday morning, fears ran particularly high. Word of the destruction of Hiroshima three days earlier circulated around town. "Enemy Drops New-Type Bomb on Hiroshima," the *Asahi* newspaper heralded the day before. "Considerable Damage Done."

A handful of witnesses to Hiroshima's destruction had since returned home to share stories of the horror. Among them was fifty-five-year-old Takejiro Nishioka, the publisher of Nagasaki's leading daily newspaper, *Minyu*. Nishioka was on a train on the outskirts of Hiroshima when Little Boy detonated. Spared from the blast, he had disembarked and made his way on foot through the burning landscape of crushed buildings, toppled trees, and scorched vehicles. "The track was jammed with numberless victims of the blast, leaving the city on foot. The line seemed to be endless," Nishioka recalled. "It was a sight horrible beyond description. Many of the victims had the skin peeled from their faces and arms."

Upon returning home, Nishioka rushed to see Wakamatsu Nagano, the governor of Nagasaki Prefecture. Nishioka's descriptions proved so appalling that the governor asked if he had seen them personally or heard them from others, which drew a rebuke. "I told you," Nishioka barked, "that I was going to relate what I saw with my own eyes."

The governor summoned his police administrators and leaders to his office the night of August 8. At the end of the two-hour meeting, he suggested the group reconvene the next morning. "We concluded," Nagano said, "that Nagasaki might soon undergo a similar bombing attack, because it had not suffered terribly from air raids thus far."

The morning air raid alarm had delayed the meeting, which finally began in the governor's underground bunker. Nagano had spent the night debating what to do before deciding that he must order the city's evacuation. Such a move would be consequential, given Nagasaki's critical role in the war industry, but the governor saw no other solution. With senior police administrators at last all gathered, the governor prepared to pitch his plan.

"I want to suggest a drastic measure," he began.

At 10:53 a.m.—as the governor briefed police leaders, students jotted notes, and parishioners prayed—*Bockscar* closed in on the city. Despite the sirens that so often rattled the lives of residents, no alarm sounded as the minutes ticked past. Atop the Medical College roof, lookouts spotted the bomber and began to ring the bell. In classrooms down below, lecturers fell silent while students stopped writing. Inside the congested war plants that crowded the banks of the Urakami River, heavy machinery drowned out the roar of *Bockscar*'s four Wright Cyclone Engines. Elsewhere in the city, in homes or out in the fields, those who heard the bomber, more than five and a half miles overhead, paused to look up into the heavens.

"Isn't that a whir from an enemy plane?" one woman asked.

"It sounds like the buzzing of a B-29," her daughter replied.

Fat Man exploded at 11:02 a.m. local time 1,650 feet above a tennis court in the Urakami River valley. In Hiroshima the flat landscape had allowed the energy to disperse, but here the surrounding hills corralled and amplified the explosive force, flattening an oval-shaped area that ran two miles north to south and nearly a mile east to west. The soaring heat, which reached 7,200 degrees Fahrenheit at ground zero, carbonized people, horses, and cows. Clay roof tiles bubbled while porcelain, glassware, and coins melted. Rescuers would later find a helmet with pieces of a soldier's skull fused to the inside. The bomb's blast wave and winds obliterated neighborhoods, toppled granite gravestones, and bent the steel frames of factories, turning the city into shrapnel. Doctors would later pluck a stick from a survivor's skull and find glass and metal bits embedded in the stomachs, lungs, and even bones of victims.

Almost directly below the blast sat the Urakami Branch of the Nagasaki Prison, which was the closest building to ground zero. The explosion reduced the two-and-a-half-story penitentiary to rubble, killing 134 people, including the prison director, employees and their families, and eighty-one inmates. The bomb likewise demolished the Urakami Cathedral, leaving only a portion of the front brick edifice and a wall standing. Among the dead were two priests and ten parishioners. One of the hardest-hit areas surrounded the Nagasaki Medical College, a complex of multistory buildings that lay just five hundred meters east of the blast. Investigators would later tally the dead at 892 faculty and students, though a few survived, shielded by the concrete and rebar walls, which withstood the blast. "It was like a thunderbolt in a clear sky," recalled Dr. Takahasi Nagai, who was in the radiology laboratory. "I felt that the end had come."

Survivors stumbled outside the college to find a sea of bodies, all stripped naked from the violent winds. Gone were the homes, shops, and businesses that had populated the valley. Smashed roof tiles and timbers littered the landscape along with uprooted trees. "Not one leaf, not one

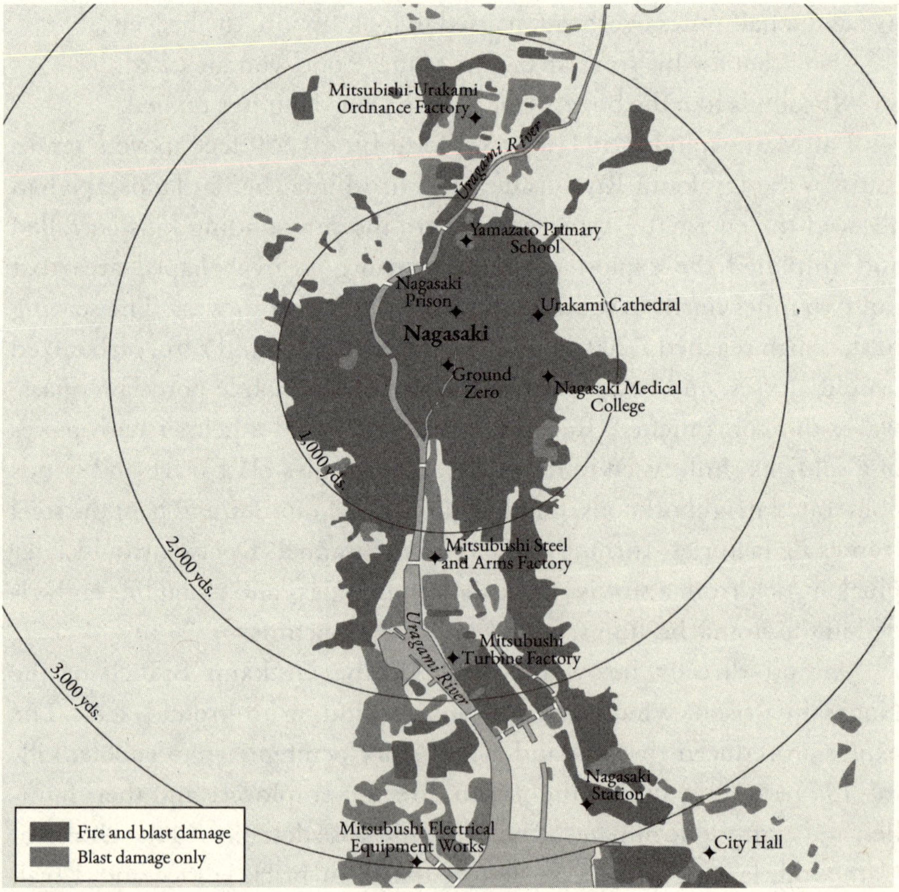

blade of grass remained," Nagai said. "The city had vanished and the mountains were bared right down to the rocks." Dust and smoke swirled into the sky, blocking out the midday sun as a silence settled over the area. "Everything got dark, almost as dark as night," recalled one survivor, "and cold, too, and pieces of burnt paper kept falling down out of the sky."

"Hell!" one nurse cried. "This is hell!"

And hell it was.

The bomb had destroyed or damaged 18,409 homes, or one out of every three houses in Nagasaki. The twenty neighborhoods within a half-mile radius of the hypocenter were obliterated by the heat and winds. About 80 percent of the twenty neighborhoods that surrounded those collapsed and burned. Public utilities likewise were devastated. The blast ruptured water lines, felled some fifteen hundred utility poles and steel transmission towers, and scorched electrical transformers and gas plants. The streetcar system, which on any given day shuttled 77,000 commuters around the city, saw thirty-nine of its fifty-six cars destroyed. Beyond the physical damage, the attack killed all but three of the 115 employees. The force of the bomb likewise wrecked ten bridges while the heat buckled rail lines.

The city's medical system bore the brunt of the attack, with as many as three out of every four doctors and nurses killed. The bomb slashed the number of functioning hospitals and clinics from eighteen to five. Aid stations went from twenty-five to ten. With 80 percent of the city's hospital beds located within 3,000 feet of ground zero, just 240 remained to handle one of the largest catastrophes of the war. The loss of Nagasaki Medical College, which the city had counted on as the centerpiece of its emergency plan, proved to be the biggest blow. Not only did the college provide many of the city's hospital beds, but authorities had stockpiled drugs and medical supplies in an onsite warehouse. "The explosion of the atomic bomb," Governor Nagano said, "obliterated the college and with it all of our preparations."

Absent immediate medical help, scorched survivors wriggled out of the wreckage and fled to the Urakami River, where many crowded the banks desperate for water. Others waded out into the water only to perish. So many, in fact, died in the water that the bodies impeded the flow of the river. "Hundreds and hundreds of corpses were sprawled over each other chaotically," recalled Chie Setoguchi, "forming a great dam of death in the river."

Others climbed the surrounding hills or trudged north and south out of the wasteland. "I met so many people coming from the direction of Urakami," said Keishi Yamaguchi, "crawling on their hands and knees like insects." Fujie Matsumoto recounted the same. On the outskirts of Urakami, she came upon a parade of wounded workers fleeing the destroyed Mitsubishi Ordnance Factory. All were naked, though some of the men still wore a leather belt around the waist while the women had *monpe* strings tied around their ankles. "They were stumbling along unsteadily," she recalled, "weeping crazily, forgetting even to be ashamed of their nakedness. Their faces, necks, and hands were blistered and on some of them I could see sheets of skin that had peeled right off and hung down flapping, all black with dust."

"For heaven's sake, what is it!" Matsumoto cried. "What's happened!"

"I don't know" was the common response. "All I saw was a sudden flash!"

Unlike Hiroshima, where organized rescue efforts had taken thirty hours to form, first aid teams assembled within two hours. Emergency vehicles could not penetrate the blast zone, where the roads were blocked with everything from corrugated metal and machinery to timbers, bricks, and stones. Rescuers had no option but to pick through the wreckage on foot, which proved perilous as fires gorged on destroyed homes and shops. Thirty-six-year-old firefighter Masayuki Yoshida was one of the first into the area, where smoke and whirling dust made it difficult to open his eyes. "Visibility ahead was almost zero," he said. "The streets nearby were scattered with scores of bodies, all of which were too miserably damaged to see."

In places the ground was so hot that shoes melted. Bodies dangled from overhead electrical wires. Others were decapitated or missing arms and legs. A child without hands begged for water. "I saw a mother with her abdomen ripped open," said Kyoko Araki, "and her baby hanging out by the umbilical cord." Jun Higashi found a crazed woman searching for her husband, son, and daughter. In her hands she clutched a bucket, which Higashi was horrified to discover contained her daughter's head.

"Burned corpses lay on the ground in a posture of grasping at the air, a last expression of their extreme distress in the sea of fire," he said. "The carnage of this day rendered utterly useless every word in my vocabulary."

Forty neighboring towns and villages organized emergency relief teams. Yasumasa Iyonaga, who served as the chief orderly at Omura Naval Hospital, twenty miles northeast of the city, accompanied one of the first such missions sent in that afternoon. "I do not know how many dead bodies we saw along the way," he said. "Most of them were charred black, almost carbonized." Like others, Iyonaga reported long lines of survivors dressed in rags. The heat had fried the hair off others, making it difficult to tell the men from the women, all of whom walked with arms outstretched, like ghosts. "Every one of them tottered by in total silence," he added. "There is no other way to describe them but as a procession of the living dead."

With the city's hospitals largely destroyed, authorities realized it was imperative to move survivors out of Nagasaki to neighboring communities. At the time of the blast, a southbound train had just pulled into Nagayo Station north of the city, providing a perfect vehicle. The train could approach as close as 0.8 miles from ground zero, where rescuers could load the injured who were carried out of the ruins on stretchers and even doors. The job, as rescuers discovered, was difficult, as the flesh of many of the wounded had melted. "When I lifted them up onto the stretcher the charred skin tore off and stuck to my fingers," Hisashi Aoki recalled. "I had to ignore it and keep going, because there were so many people to carry."

At 1:50 p.m.—less than three hours after the blast—the train made its first of four runs that day out of the shattered city, transporting 3,500 wounded men, women, and children to the nearby towns of Isahaya, Omura, Kawatana, and Haiki. Conditions onboard were horrendous. The wounded were crammed inside. Most were naked, covered in burns, and begging for water. Over them all hung the smell of burnt flesh. Each time the train passed through a tunnel, the locomotive's hot exhaust flooded the cars, drawing howls. "Everyone was groaning," said Fumiko Wakasugi. "If a person stopped groaning, it meant he was dead."

Miyo Kasahara, a nurse at Isahaya Naval Hospital, fifteen miles north of the city, helped unload the wounded from the first train that afternoon.

"A horde of injured people poured out," she recalled, "bloated and marred like rotten sweet potatoes." Dr. Masao Shiotsuki reported the same when he and his staff admitted the first of 758 survivors at eight p.m. that evening at Omura Naval Hospital. "When we shone our flashlights on them, we could see countless fragments of glass, wood, and metal still imbedded in their faces and backs and arms and legs," the doctor wrote. "It was hard to believe that these were human beings."

"The war is over," the twenty-five-year-old physician muttered to himself. "If butchery as horrible as this were to continue, people would choose to commit suicide."

Medics rushed to sort the patients, some of whom were dead upon arrival, including a baby found amid a pile of the injured. The scorched skin of others reminded Shiotsuki of the smell of roast cuttlefish, while the oozing flesh soon made his hands slippery. Victims suffering amputations, broken limbs, or penetrating fragments were rolled into surgery. The others were treated for burns, which were second and third degree. "The burns on all of my patients were so horrible," he wrote, "they surpassed the limits of medical knowledge."

"My god," Shiotsuki thought to himself. "What am I to do?"

The doctor injected those unlikely to survive—about one hundred patients died that first night—with a heavy dose of morphine. He instructed the nurses and orderlies to do the same. "As a result, I assisted in committing euthanasia. Or to put it another way, I was a mercy killer," he said. "Those people died peacefully, I believe, their pain and agony relieved."

Back inside Nagasaki, survivors could do little more than watch that first night as a large swath of the city burned. Those survivors who climbed the nearby hills had a ringside seat of the inferno, which would finally burn itself out the following day. "The fires below were raging more fiercely than ever," said Dr. Raisuke Shirabe. "The red glow became brighter and brighter as night fell, and the flames spread out like an ocean as far as the eye could see. The fearful roar of the blaze echoed everywhere. Sitting down on the hillside I gazed into the crimson inferno, and for some unknown reason my body trembled uncontrollably."

Emergency workers hustled to open rescue centers inside the city often aided by private practitioners, retired army physicians, and medical teams from neighboring communities. Eighty such centers—set up in schools, temples, and clinics—would help treat the wounded, who crowded inside larger facilities by the hundreds. "Patients," as one postwar report observed, "were treated wherever they could be laid out on a concrete floor." Iyonaga from Omura Naval Hospital helped work one such center at Inasa Primary School. "On the rubble-littered floor," the orderly said, "lay so many casualties you could scarcely move without stepping on them." Conditions inside such centers were hot, humid, and primitive, made all the worse by the cries of the wounded. "Call me the doctor immediately," the injured howled.

"Give me some medicine right now!" others cried.

"Kill me! It hurts! Kill me now, please!"

The most important of these centers was Shinkozen Primary School, a three-story concrete structure on the city's south side near the harbor that at maximum capacity housed 363 wounded. The blast had blown out the windows and opened cracks in the walls, but the building still stood. "The injured were lined up in four rows of 10 to 15 people with heads touching heads and feet touching feet," said Dr. Kenji Miake of the Sasebo Navy Hospital, who lost 168 patients his first day. "I remember vividly the sickening stench of burned flesh, like the smell of scorched chicken meat, that greeted us when we entered the classrooms."

The doctors converted a first-floor classroom into an operating suite with three tables. "Many had limbs missing or entrails hanging out," Miake said. "We performed amputations and stump formations and sewed up bellies." Faced with an absence of medical supplies, doctors turned to unorthodox solutions to soothe burns. "The method of treatment consisted simply of collecting seawater from Nagasaki Harbor in drum cans," the doctor added, "disinfecting this by boiling, then pouring it over the injured people with sprinkling cans."

As the days progressed, conditions worsened amid the summer heat. As in Hiroshima, maggots became a challenge, feasting on the rotten flesh of the wounded. "Making the rounds of the classrooms," he said, "was like walking through outhouses." Those who survived the blast often succumbed to radiation, which the doctors proved powerless to treat. "Often we went down a row of patients, performing whatever treatment we could, only to find when we came back along the adjacent row that a person who had been talking only minutes before was now dead," Miake said. "Without exception, the patients who developed fever, then infections and then nosebleeds died after one or two days. The corpses were carried away, still nameless and unidentifiable as men, women, children and senior citizens."

Workers used rakes and shovels to clear debris as rescuers searched for any wounded. Survivors picked through the rubble, hoping to find missing loved ones and friends. "In the gutted ruins of the classrooms I found the ashes of dead students in neat rows where their desks had been," recalled Dr. Nagai of his visit to the medical college. "In several places in the hospital I found the ashes of two people on top of each other, obviously the remains of students or nurses who were trying in vain to carry patients out of the conflagration."

Sixteen-year-old Akira Nagasaka was a mobilized student worker at a branch factory of Mitsubishi Steel when the bomb exploded. She returned to her family's home near the Urakami Cathedral to search for her mother, an area she found littered with the scattered bones and the ash outlines of the dead. "All I had to go by was the fact that she had had gold teeth," said Nagasaka, whose search would prove in vain. "I held skull after skull in my hands and peered into the jaw area. I wonder how many people's skulls I picked up during my search."

Tadao Nakazawa, who also lived near the cathedral, was at work 1.5 miles from ground zero. Days after the blast, he returned home to search for his wife's remains, armed with a garden hoe to help dig through the ash. "With the first stroke, out came a white skull like that of a cat," he said. "I picked it up—it was my wife's skull. She had been of very small stature, and from the size of the skull and the way the teeth were arranged I realized right away it was she. Instinctively I clutched it to me tightly. In just a few more minutes of digging I unearthed her whole skeleton; the bones were as white as if she'd been cremated."

Surrounded by so much death, some survivors soon became desensitized to it all, going so far as to make jokes about the black and bloated bodies that populated the ruins. "If only they were watermelons," people quipped, "you could eat them." But the disposal of the dead soon became a priority as swarms of flies attacked the remains. "The heavy odor of dead bodies," remembered Ryoko Okumura, "hung in the air day after day." At aid stations, orderlies hauled the remains outside each afternoon and burned them. "Day after day, the cremation smoke rose slowly to the murky early evening sky," observed Emiko Kinoshita. "Its unbearable odor permeated the whole area." Families, by contrast, often chose to cremate loved ones at home, gathering unburned timbers for fuel. "There were no coffins," recalled Fuie Matsumoto. "The bodies were put on piles of wood and burned. It was done like a fish fry at a picnic."

Garbage trucks rumbled through town to collect others, which were then burned in school yards and parks. Eighteen-year-old Hisae Aoki, whose younger sister succumbed to radiation, accompanied her remains out front of the hospital, where crews collected the dead.

"Please burn her carefully," she asked one of the workers.

The laborers picked up her sister. "It was an empty truck. The men threw her body in and it landed with a thud on the bottom," Aoki said. "As I stood there the truck was filled with corpses—a veritable mountain of death. The last body to be placed on the pile was a little one-year-old girl. Because the truck was filled to the brim, the tiny corpse slid off and fell on the ground. The worker immediately grabbed it by the hair and flipped it back up onto the pile. I knew it was a dead body but nevertheless it appalled me so much that I burst out crying. The body would probably fall again and again before the truck reached its destination."

CHAPTER 37

"The misery was boundless."

—MATSUE ATSUYUKI
AUGUST 11, 1945, DIARY ENTRY

Foreign Minister Togo showed up at Suzuki's home in northern Tokyo at eight a.m. on August 9. Togo was irate that the prime minister had postponed the meeting of the Big Six the day before, at a time when the nation's position worsened by the hour. "Valuable time had been lost," he complained. "The war must now be ended as soon as possible—or sooner."

The wasted twenty-four hours likewise upset the emperor. At 9:55 a.m., Hirohito met with Kido, instructing him to impress upon Suzuki the need to end the war. "I assured His Majesty," Kido wrote in his diary, "that I would discuss the matter with the premier at once." That opportunity arose fifteen minutes later, when Suzuki arrived at the palace. "I conveyed His Majesty's instructions to him," Kido wrote, "emphasizing the necessity of terminating the war by immediately taking advantage of the Potsdam Declaration."

At ten-thirty a.m., the Big Six at last convened. Joining Suzuki and Togo at the table that humid morning were Navy Minister Adm. Mitsumasa Yonai, War Minister Gen. Korechika Anami, Army Chief of Staff Gen. Yoshijiro Umezu, and Navy Chief of Staff Adm. Soemu Toyoda. These six men held the fate of the entire nation.

Suzuki began by arguing that the destruction of Hiroshima, coupled with Russia's invasion of Manchuria, made it impossible for Japan to continue. "I believe," he declared, "that we have no alternative but to accept the Potsdam Declaration."

The others listened.

"I would now like to hear your opinions," Suzuki then offered.

But no one moved.

"We can't get anywhere by keeping silent forever," Admiral Yonai finally said, breaking the awkward silence. "Do we accept the enemy ultimatum unconditionally? Do we propose conditions? If so, we had better discuss them here and now."

Others at last spoke up. The ensuing discussion revealed that the six leaders all agreed that Japan's imperial structure must be preserved. But opinions beyond that proved sharply divided. On one side stood Suzuki, Togo, and Yonai, all of whom favored accepting the Potsdam Declaration with the only condition being the retention of the monarchy.

On the opposite side stood War Minister Anami along with General Umezu and Admiral Toyoda, the respective chiefs of the army and navy general staffs. These officers, all imbued with the samurai ethos, wanted to add three additional conditions. Those included barring—or at least limiting—the occupation of the homeland, allowing officers to demobilize their own troops, and permitting Japan to oversee the trials of any suspected war criminals.

If Japan proposed a host of conditions, Togo warned, the Allies would likely refuse to negotiate at all, which could be dangerous given Japan's vulnerability.

The sixty-three-year-old Umezu, who had previously commanded the Kwantung Army, countered that Japan was not defeated. America had not even invaded. "If we are lucky, we will be able to repulse the invaders before they land," the war minister added. "At any rate, I can say with assurance that we will be able to destroy the major part of an invading army, that is, we will be able to inflict extremely heavy damage on the enemy."

Even if America's first assault failed, Togo shot back, it would only weaken Japan, which could not carry on indefinitely. "Japan must accept the Potsdam ultimatum *now*," he barked, "demanding no more than the preservation of the Imperial House."

An aide interrupted the meeting to bring news of the atomic attack on Nagasaki. In the span of just three days, America had destroyed two Japanese cities, raising doubt over the military's assertion that America might not have a stockpile of such weapons.

Despite the news, the council remained divided three to three.

At one p.m., Suzuki proposed the group take a break and reconvene later in the day after the cabinet met. During that time, the prime minister reported the morning's deadlock to Kido, who was alarmed. If Japan countered with multiple conditions, he realized, America would likely consider it a refusal to surrender, which could prove calamitous for Japan. At two-thirty p.m., the cabinet convened at the prime minister's residence. Around the table sat many of the same individuals from the morning session.

Togo began the session, giving a rundown of the events leading up to the Soviet declaration of war, including Japan's failed efforts to get them to mediate. The foreign minister concluded with a description of the attacks on Hiroshima and now Nagasaki.

Suzuki asked Admiral Yonai and General Anami to speak.

"We might win the first battle for Japan, but we won't win the second. The war is lost," Yonai said. "We must begin to consider at once how best to preserve our country."

The navy minister's comments drew a rebuke from Anami. "It is far too early to say that the war is lost," he countered, adding that Japan could still inflict severe losses on the enemy. "There is really no alternative for us but to continue the war."

But others disagreed, including the agriculture, commerce, transportation, and munitions ministers. Not only had America already converted Okinawa into a massive staging area for the invasion of Kyushu, but the nightly fire air raids continued to devastate the homeland. This had exhausted the already hungry population, who now faced a rice shortage. "Japan," these leaders argued, "had neither the strength nor the means to wage war any longer."

"Yes, yes!" Anami interjected. "Everyone understands the situation, but we must fight the war through to the end no matter how great the odds against us!"

Home Minister Genki Abe warned that surrender might spark violence, reminding everyone of the failed coup in February 1936 that resulted in the deaths of several senior leaders. Prime Minister Suzuki still carried a bullet lodged in his back from that time.

The cabinet recessed at five-thirty p.m. for an hour. When members returned, the debate resumed, but with no resolution. One hour soon turned to two.

And then three.

At ten p.m., Suzuki finally asked for a consensus. But the cabinet, the body that would ultimately approve any surrender, remained hopelessly split. Six members wanted to accept the Potsdam Declaration with the sole addition that the monarchy be preserved. Three others supported Anami's additional conditions. Five more fell in the middle, requesting more than one condition, but less than those recommended by the war minister.

The cabinet recessed for the night.

Suzuki and Togo rushed to the palace to see Hirohito. The situation was politically perilous. Any time either the cabinet or Big Six deadlocked, tradition called for the leaders to resign so that the emperor could form a new government. Such a move at this time would not only cost Japan valuable time but opened the nation up to additional atomic attacks. Togo reported on the outcome of the back-to-back meetings, making it clear that neither the Supreme War Council nor the cabinet could be expected to resolve the impasse. There was only one person, the two ministers knew, who could break the deadlock. The prime minister proposed that the Big Six reconvene that night, only this time with the emperor in attendance.

Hirohito agreed.

At 11:50 p.m., the six members of the Supreme War Council filed back inside in the palace's underground bunker. A few aides joined the meeting along with two Suzuki invitees, Chief Cabinet Secretary Hisatsune Sakomizu and Baron Kiichiro Hiranuma, the president of the Privy Council. The conference room, which measured thirty feet long by eighteen wide, was surrounded by dark wood-paneled walls beneath an overhead made of arched steel beams. The room was hot and poorly ventilated on this sultry August night.

Six men sat on one side with five on the other when Hirohito took his place in a straight-backed chair at the head of the table. Suzuki stood to his left. The prime minister asked the cabinet secretary to read aloud the Potsdam Declaration before he recounted the two meetings earlier that day. He apologized to the emperor, whose intervention he now sought.

Suzuki turned the floor over to Togo, who argued in favor of accepting the Potsdam Declaration with the sole addition that the monarchy be preserved.

"I agree," Admiral Yonai declared.

Anami sprang from his chair, advocating that Japan continue the fight. At a minimum, he added, if Japan did surrender, it must insist not only on the preservation of the throne but also on a limited occupation and the right to disarm itself and conduct its own war crimes trials.

General Umezu echoed him. "Japan was still more than a match for the enemy," he added. "Unconditional surrender now would only dishonor the heroic war dead."

Suzuki asked Baron Hiranuma to speak. A former prime minister, Hiranuma served as the president of the Privy Council, which, like the cabinet, would need to sign off on any surrender. Hiranuma, who was not as versed in the facts as the others, ran through a list of questions, ranging from the failed efforts to entice the Soviets to mediate to the various proposed conditions the group had debated, all of which Togo dutifully answered.

Hiranuma then addressed the military leaders, noting the increasingly dire circumstances Japan faced. Could the military, he asked, prevail? "We have been preserving our strength for future use," Toyoda replied. "But hereafter we expect to counterattack."

While it was imperative for the monarchy to continue, Hiranuma advised, Togo should not rule out trying to negotiate other concessions. Such a major decision, he concluded, should be approved by the throne. "In accordance with the legacy of Your Imperial Forefathers, Your Imperial Majesty is also responsible for preventing unrest in the nation," he said to Hirohito. "I should like to ask Your Majesty to make Your decision with this point in mind."

Admiral Toyoda spoke last, but all he did was reiterate the previous points made by his colleagues in uniform. "We cannot say that final victory is certain," he concluded, "but at the same time we do not believe that we will be positively defeated."

The minutes had turned to hours as August 9 rolled into August 10. It was close to 2:20 a.m. The group had debated for more than two hours yet deadlock prevailed, just as it had throughout the day. The prime minister at last turned to Hirohito. "Your Imperial Majesty's decision," he said, "is requested as to which proposal should be adopted."

Silence fell over the room as the emperor rose to his feet. Those around the table snapped to attention and bowed. "I have given serious thought to the situation prevailing at home and abroad and have concluded that continuing the war can only mean destruction for the nation and a prolongation of bloodshed and cruelty in the world," Hirohito began. "I cannot bear to see my innocent people suffer any longer. Ending the war is the only way to restore world peace and to relieve the nation from the terrible distress with which it is burdened."

Fortifications for an invasion, he continued, were still not yet completed. He likewise noted that experience had revealed a discrepancy between plans and performance, raising concerns over Japan's ability to repel the invaders. This uncertainty was coupled by his distress over the millions of lives lost on the frontlines as well as those who suffered in the bombing of the homeland. "It goes without saying," he said, "that it is unbearable for me to see the brave and loyal fighting men of Japan disarmed. It is equally unbearable that others who have rendered me devoted service should now be punished as instigators of war."

All eyes focused on him.

"Nevertheless," he concluded, "the time has come when we must bear the unbearable."

CHAPTER 38

"I urge Japanese civilians to leave industrial cities immediately, and save themselves from destruction."

—PRESIDENT HARRY TRUMAN
AUGUST 9, 1945

In the span of seventy-two hours, America had obliterated two Japanese cities with atomic weapons. Those were complemented by precision strikes on a refinery, aircraft factory, and arsenal as well as fire raids against Nishinomiya and Maebashi, which incinerated another 5.8 square miles of those two cities. America had reached the zenith of total war. "During those three days," Truman wrote, "we indicated that we meant business."

Despite the president's public bravado, the back-to-back atomic blows troubled Truman, who was pained by the devastation inflicted upon tens of thousands of Japanese civilians. That was evident in his exchange with Georgia senator Richard Russell, who urged him to resist pressure to give in to any Japanese demands. "Let us carry the war to them," he cabled, "until they beg us to accept the unconditional surrender." If America did not have enough atomic bombs, Russell urged the air force to continue with fire raids. "This was a total war as long as our enemies held all of the cards. Why should we change the rules now, after the blood, treasure and enterprise of the American people have given us the upper hand?" the senator asked. "The next plea for peace should come from an utterly destroyed Tokyo."

But Truman disagreed. "I know that Japan is a terribly cruel and uncivilized nation in warfare but I can't bring myself to believe that, because they are beasts, we should ourselves act in the same manner," he replied. "My object is to save as many American lives as possible but I also have a humane feeling for the women and children in Japan." He fired off another response to Samuel Cavert, general secretary of the Federal Council of the Churches of Christ in America, who cabled his concerns over the weapon's indiscriminate destruction while urging that Japan be given time to surrender. "Nobody is more disturbed over the use of atomic bombs than I am but I was greatly disturbed over the unwarranted attack by the Japanese on Pearl Harbor and their murder of our prisoners of war," Truman replied. "When you have to deal with a beast you have to treat him as a beast. It is most regrettable but nevertheless true."

That humane feeling prompted the president to order a halt on the future use of atomic bombs without his approval. That was made clear when Groves sent a message to Marshall, alerting him that a third atomic bomb could be ready by August 24. "It is not to be released over Japan," Marshall replied, "without express authority from the President."

But the president's reluctance did not stop the need for continued planning. The war was not yet over. Groves messaged Arnold, recommending Tokyo be added to the approved list of atomic targets. "You may wish to give consideration to easing the requirements for visual bombing of targets," he added, "so that the weather difficulties encountered in the last strike, which might well have resulted in failure, may be avoided on future strikes."

On August 9, hours after America leveled Nagasaki, Truman took a moment to dash off a two-sentence note to the men and women of the Manhattan Project. "If I live to be one hundred years old," the president would later say, "I'll never forget the day that I was first told about the atomic bomb." He felt not only a sense of awe but also appreciation for the army of scientists, engineers, and technicians who had toiled for years in secrecy to give America a war-ending weapon. "Atomic bombs have now been successfully employed against the enemy," Truman wrote. "A grateful nation, hopeful that this new weapon will result in the saving of thousands of American lives, feels a deep sense of appreciation for your accomplishment."

Later that evening, the president addressed the nation in a ten p.m. radio broadcast. Though he dedicated the majority of his half-hour speech to the Potsdam Conference, Truman seized the moment to send a warning to Japan. He struck a far steelier tone in public than he did in his private correspondence earlier that day with Senator Russell. "Having found the bomb we have used it," the president declared. "We have used it against those who attacked us without warning at Pearl Harbor, against those who have starved and beaten and executed American prisoners of war, against those who have abandoned all pretense of obeying international laws of warfare. We have used it in order to shorten the agony of war, in order to save the lives of thousands and thousands of young Americans. We shall continue to use it until we completely destroy Japan's power to make war. Only a Japanese surrender will stop us."

Truman did not need to wait long for an answer.

At 7:33 a.m. the next day, Radio Tokyo broadcast in plain language a message Japan had sent to the Swiss and Swedish governments for transmission to the United States, Great Brittain, Russia, and China. "The Japanese Government is ready to accept the terms enumerated in the joint declaration which was issued at Potsdam," the messaged stated, "with the understanding that the said declaration does not comprise any demand which prejudices the prerogatives of His Majesty as a sovereign ruler." One Truman adviser summed it up best: "What Japan was saying, in effect, was that she would capitulate if we did not hang the Emperor."

Truman summoned Leahy, Byrnes, Stimson, and Forrestal for a nine a.m. meeting.

The war secretary had just finished packing his car and was preparing to head to the airport for vacation when Col. Frank McCarthy reached him with news of the Japanese offer. "That busted our holiday for the present," he wrote in his diary.

Inside the Oval Office that Friday morning, the president went around the room, polling each of his senior lieutenants. "Were we to treat this message from Tokyo as an acceptance of the Potsdam Declaration?" Truman asked. "Could we continue the Emperor and yet expect to eliminate the warlike spirit in Japan? Could we even consider a message with so large a 'but' as the kind of unconditional surrender we had fought for?"

Opinions varied.

"I recommended accepting the Japanese proposal," Leahy recalled. "This did not mean that I favored the Emperor's retaining all his prerogatives. I had no feelings about little Hirohito, but was convinced that it would be necessary to use him in effecting surrender."

More important, the admiral added, the fate of the emperor was a "minor matter compared with delaying a victory in the war which was now in our hands."

Each day, as the men all knew, cost lives.

Stimson agreed. He had originally urged the Potsdam Declaration to include dynastic protection, but Byrnes and Truman had vetoed him. Now, just as he had feared, the emperor's fate had become an obstacle. The United States, he argued, would need Hirohito to convince millions of Japanese soldiers throughout Asia to surrender "in order to save us from a score of bloody Iwo Jimas and Okinawas all over China and the New Netherlands."

Byrnes, in contrast, pushed back. "I do not see why we should retreat from our demand for unconditional surrender," he argued. "That demand was presented to Japan before the use of the bomb and before the Soviet Union was a belligerent. If any conditions are to be accepted, I want the United States and not Japan to state the conditions."

Forrestal sought a compromise. "We might in our reply," the navy secretary suggested, "indicate willingness to accept, yet define the terms of surrender in such a manner that the intents and purposes of the Potsdam Declaration would be clearly accomplished."

Truman agreed, asking Byrnes to prepare just such a response.

The secretary of state hustled to draft a reply. Once completed, he shared it with Stimson. "I thought it was a pretty wise and careful statement," the war secretary confided in his diary, "and stood a better chance of being accepted than a more outspoken one."

Byrnes returned to the Oval Office before noon, armed with a hard copy of the Japanese offer, which had since arrived, and his proposed response. Over lunch the duo worked on an urgent message to Allied leaders, seeking concurrence with America's reply.

Truman summoned his cabinet for a two p.m. meeting. The president read aloud Japan's letter. Byrnes followed with his suggested response, which, as Forrestal had suggested, effectively punted on the question of the emperor. Hirohito's fate instead would be decided by the senior military commander, which would be Gen. Douglas MacArthur. "From the moment of surrender," the reply stated, "the authority of the Emperor and the Japanese Government to rule the state shall be subject to the Supreme Commander of the Allied powers who will take such steps as he deems proper to effectuate the surrender terms."

The emperor and military high command, the message continued, would have to sign the surrender terms and issue orders to all forces to cease hostilities and surrender arms. Japan likewise needed to transport all prisoners of war and civilian internees to places of safety. "The ultimate form of government of Japan shall, in accordance with the Potsdam Declaration, be established by the freely expressed will of the Japanese people."

During the meeting, Stimson noted that the Soviets would likely urge a delay, a move designed to give them more time to seize territory in Manchuria.

Truman added that he had given orders to stop additional atomic bombing. "He said the thought of wiping out another 100,000 people was too horrible," Henry Wallace noted in his diary. "He didn't like the idea of killing, as he said, 'all those kids.'"

Messages went out to the American ambassadors in Great Britain, Russia, and China along with a copy of Byrnes's proposed reply to the Japanese. Time was urgent. "Please deliver at once to the Secretary of State for Foreign Affairs the following message," the 3:45 p.m. telegram to London stated. "Please impress upon the Secretary of State for Foreign Affairs the urgency of a reply to this message and telegraph at once his reply."

Ambassador John Winant cabled that night. The British agreed but suggested removing the demand that Hirohito personally sign the surrender terms, allowing him instead to "authorize and ensure the signature" by the Japanese government and military. "The Prime Minister and the Foreign Secretary are standing by all night for your answer," Winant cabled. "Mr. Churchill telephoned me tonight. I feel you would be interested to know that this message is in line with his views. He believes that using the Mikado will save lives in outlying areas."

Chinese ruler Chiang Kai-shek likewise agreed, adding a personal note to Truman: "I congratulate you on the victory and wish you the best of health."

But Moscow, as always, proved problematic.

Ambassador Averell Harriman was meeting with Molotov about Japan's offer moments before Byrnes's message arrived. The Soviet view, the foreign minister explained, was "skeptical," since officials did not consider Japan's offer to be unconditional surrender. Soviet forces therefore planned to continue the advance into Manchuria. "He gave me the definite impression," Harriman cabled, "that he was quite willing to have the war continue."

Byrnes's message arrived and was translated for him, but Molotov was "noncommittal," suggesting he would provide an answer the next day. "I told him that this would not be satisfactory and that we wished it tonight," Harriman wrote. "He thereupon agreed to take it up with his Government and attempt to give me an answer tonight. If I do not hear from him in a reasonable time, I will telephone him and keep you informed of the developments."

Seventy minutes later, a follow-up from Harriman rattled off the State Department's teletype. Molotov had provided a four-sentence statement. The Soviets largely agreed with America's position but, as always, added a poison pill. "In case of an affirmative reply from the Japanese Government," Molotov wrote, "the Allied Powers should reach an agreement on the candidacy or candidacies for representation of the Allied High Command to which the Japanese Emperor and the Japanese Government are to be subordinated."

The Soviets, who had been in the war less than seventy-two hours, wanted to play an equal role in the postwar control of Japan, a position the administration opposed. America had won the war in the Pacific; America would be in charge. Beyond the question of equity, Soviet behavior in postwar Europe had proved alarming. "I was determined that the Japanese occupation should not follow in the footsteps of our German experience," Truman said. "I did not want divided control or separate zones. I did not want to give the Russians any opportunity to behave as they had in Germany and Austria. I wanted the country administered in such a manner that it could be restored to its place in the society of nations."

Harriman objected to Molotov's demand, arguing that it gave the

Soviets veto power over the selection of the supreme commander. The foreign minister suggested that there possibly could be two supreme commanders—one American and one Russian. "I stated that it was unthinkable that the Supreme Commander could be other than American," the ambassador wrote. "After a most heated discussion he insisted that I send his communication to my Government. I maintained, however, that in my opinion it would be unacceptable."

No sooner did Harriman reach his office than Molotov's secretary Vladimir Pavlov phoned, informing him that Molotov had talked to Stalin. There had been a misunderstanding. The Soviets did not want an agreement on the candidacy or candidacies of the supreme commander but only wanted America to consult with them over the selection. Harriman said that did not alleviate the Soviet demand that there be multiple commanders. "Within a few minutes he called back stating that Stalin had agreed to the deletion of these words."

With the issue resolved, Byrnes handed the Allied reply to the Swiss chargé d'affaires on the morning of August 11, 1945. "I was confident the Japanese would accept," Byrnes wrote, "but the feeling of responsibility for thousands of lives was inescapable."

CHAPTER 39

"It is certain this morning that the Great World War is about to come to an end."

—ADM. WILLIAM LEAHY
AUGUST 10, 1945, DIARY ENTRY

Tensions hung over Tokyo as August 11 rolled over to the twelfth.

Hirohito's intervention had broken the impasse, but it did not change the minds of the militarists who wanted to continue the fight. Those who advocated peace understood the ever-present threat of political violence and assassination. Such attacks often came at the hands not of senior commanders but of fanatical junior officers. That was the case in the failed February 1936 coup that left multiple politicians dead and wounded.

The emperor's intervention likewise was no guarantee that the Allies would accept Japan's demand that the monarchy be allowed to continue.

And why should they?

Armed with atomic bombs—and aided by the Soviet invasion of Manchuria—the Allies had no need to negotiate or even invade. Bombers could pound Japan night after night, reducing its cities to piles of radioactive ruin until leaders begged to accept unconditional surrender. A rumor already circulated that the next atomic bomb was aimed at Tokyo.

All anyone could do now was wait.

And hope no more cities vanished.

At 12:45 a.m. on August 12, the Foreign Office radio at last picked up America's broadcast of the Allied reply, eighteen hours before the official note would arrive via formal channels. Radiomen with the navy and the Domei news agency likewise copied down the reply, albeit a few hours later, meaning the Allied answer was soon widely circulated in political and military circles. Those who had hoped the Allies would simply agree to Japan's demand were disappointed by the stern note, but other challenges soon emerged.

The broadcast was made in Morse Code, which raised questions about the accuracy of its reception and transcription. Officials zeroed in on two additional concerns, the first being how to interpret the demand that the emperor would be "subject to" the supreme commander. After much deliberation, the Foreign Office viewed it to mean "controlled by" and not "obedient to," an interpretation that did not conflict with Hirohito's sovereignty. The second issue surrounded the Allied insistence that the Japanese people would decide the ultimate form of government. This, too, senior diplomats concluded, did not undermine Hirohito, who functioned outside the system of traditional governance. "The Allies had in general," Togo wrote, "confirmed the understanding which we had stated in our communication to them."

But the military disagreed.

At 8:20 a.m. that morning, army and navy chiefs of staff Genera Umezu and Admiral Toyoda marched to the palace to see Hirohito. Word of the negotiations had spread through the barracks, prompting many young officers to protest and raise the specter of violence. War Minister Anami experienced that firsthand that morning when his brother-in-law, Lt. Col. Masahiko Takeshita, and a dozen others confronted him. "The proposed surrender must not take place," Takeshita demanded. "If it does, the War Minister ought to commit suicide with his own sword." During their conference with Hirohito, Umezu and Toyoda likewise objected to the Allied demands. The emperor thanked the officers and assured them that no decision would be made until after the formal text had been received and studied.

Togo followed them at eleven a.m., informing Hirohito of the Allied reply and urging the emperor to accept. Hirohito agreed, instructing him to relay his desire to Suzuki. In response, the cabinet met at three p.m., at which time Suzuki read a translation of the reply.

Anami and Privy Council president Hiranuma objected to the demands, raising the same two concerns the Foreign Office had already considered and settled. To Togo's surprise, however, Suzuki, who had met that morning with Anami and Hiranuma, suddenly waffled, questioning whether Japan should clarify that the ultimatum guaranteed the retention of the emperor. If it did not, he added, Japan should continue the fight.

There was too much at stake, Togo feared, for the debate to spiral out of control. He needed to shut down the conversation and regroup. Suzuki's opinions, he suggested, demanded further study. "I therefore propose," he said, "that the meeting be adjourned and that the question be reopened after the official communication from the Allies has been received."

After the meeting, a furious Togo cornered the prime minister. "Unless we were resigned to rupture negotiations for peace," he argued, "there was no alternative to acceptance of their reply as it stood." Hirohito had insisted that Japan surrender—and his opinion mattered most. Togo threatened if needed to take his concerns to the emperor. "If you persist in this attitude," he concluded, "I may have to report independently to the Throne."

At six-thirty p.m., Togo met with Kido, informing the lord keeper of the privy seal that the needed support for surrender was crumbling. Kido understood the precarious moment. Rumors circulated of a potential military coup, including the possibility that the emperor might be captured and separated from the cabinet. Posters appeared around Tokyo, calling for the assassination of peace advocates, including Kido, who had moved into the palace for his safety. In response, the metropolitan police posted guards throughout the city and monitored suspected officers. If negotiations broke down, Kido knew, the war would resume with catastrophic consequences. "I feel," he wrote in his diary, "extremely anxious."

Kido met with Suzuki at nine-thirty p.m., stressing the importance of immediately ending the war. "If we do not accept the Allied position now," he said, "we will be sacrificing hundreds of thousands of innocent people to the continued ravages of war. If we do accept and internal upheaval ensues, we shall only have to lay down our own lives. Furthermore, it is *His Majesty's wish* that we advance on the basis of the views held by the Foreign Minister."

Suzuki at last fell back in line. "The premier," a relieved Kido noted in his diary, "answered that he concurred with my opinion. It was quite reassuring."

But convincing the military remained a challenge.

Anami showed up at the palace at 7:10 a.m. on August 13 to see Kido. He again argued that Japan should continue to fight. A decisive battle on the homeland would give the emperor better leverage at the surrender table. But Kido pushed back. Neither the emperor nor the Foreign Office agreed with the military's objections to the Allied demands. Japan needed to accept the ultimatum and end the war. "The course we must follow is clear," Kido said. "We must abide by the wishes of His Majesty. We must accept the Allied reply in its present form."

The Supreme War Council met at nine that morning. The battle lines broke down just as before. "The discussion," Togo griped, "dragged on for many hours." The council adjourned at noon and was followed by a four p.m. cabinet meeting, where the impasse continued as Togo and Anami continued to battle. "Often I felt wearied with fighting," Togo added, "but conditions were too tense to permit any personal feeling to deteriorate from the utmost sincerity in arguing the issues preoccupying us." This time twelve supported Togo, three Anami, and one was undecided. "Inasmuch as we have failed once again to agree," Suzuki said, "I propose to ask His Majesty for a second Imperial decision."

After the meeting adjourned at seven p.m., Anami approached Suzuki. The war minister was in a difficult situation, under pressure from Togo and Hirohito as well as junior officers, some of whom he knew were conspiring to overthrow the government. The easy solution would be to resign from the Cabinet, a move that would topple the government and wreck peace negotiations. But such a move, even though he opposed surrender, would be disloyal to the emperor. He instead did his best to prevent younger officers from rebelling. "Will you give me just two more days," he asked Suzuki, "before you go to the Emperor again?"

"I'm sorry," he replied. "Our opportunity is now—we must seize it at once."

A navy officer who overheard the exchange repeated the request.

"Impossible," Suzuki said. "If we don't act now, the Russians will penetrate not only Manchuria and Korea but northern Japan as well. If that happens, our country is finished. We must act now, while our chief adversary is still the United States."

"General Anami," the officer replied, "will kill himself."

"Yes," the prime minster said, "that will be very regrettable."

Millions of American leaflets rained down the next morning, featuring Japan's original surrender offer and the Allied reply. "One look caused me to be stricken with consternation," Kido said. "If the leaflets should fall into the hands of the troops and enrage them, a military coup d'état would become inevitable and make extremely difficult the execution of the planned policy. It would bring about the worst possible situation for our country."

At eight-thirty a.m. on August 14, Kido met with Hirohito followed ten minutes later by Suzuki. Kido asked if the prime minister had summoned the Big Six. The army, Suzuki replied, had urged him to wait until the afternoon, while the navy wanted to wait indefinitely.

"I am having a hard time," the prime minister confessed.

The two then met together with Hirohito. The only way to end this, Kido advocated, was for the emperor to call another imperial conference. Hirohito agreed, demanding a joint meeting that morning in his presence of the Supreme War Council and the cabinet.

The emperor gathered with the nation's senior military leaders at 10:20 a.m., including Field Marshall Shunroku Hata, commander of the Second General Army in Hiroshima. Hata, who had just returned from the devastated city, was the general tasked to repel the Kyushu invasion. Though Anami had hoped the esteemed leader would minimize the city's destruction and encourage Japan to continue the fight, Hata leveled with the emperor. Japan had no hope to win.

At 10:50 a.m., Hirohito assumed his seat behind a small table draped in a gold cloth. A gilded screen stood behind him while the senior statesmen filled the chairs in front of him. The heat and humidity once again soared, so much so that water droplets appeared on the walls. Suzuki opened the session, summarizing the opposing views before calling on the military leaders. Anami, Umezu, and Toyoda spoke, rehashing the by-now-very-familiar points.

Suzuki then climbed to his feet, apologizing again to the emperor for seeking his intervention. All eyes turned to Hirohito, who was dressed in his military uniform. For the second time in four days, Japan's fate hinged upon the words of the bespectacled forty-four-year-old monarch. "I have listened carefully," the emperor began, "to each of the arguments presented in opposition to the view that Japan should accept the Allied reply as it stands without further clarification or modification, but my own thoughts have not undergone any change. I have surveyed the conditions prevailing in Japan and in the world at large, and it is my belief that a continuation of the war promises nothing but additional destruction."

The men around the table all listened.

Hirohito explained that he understood that many distrusted Allied intentions, which was only natural. He also knew that it was difficult for men of arms to surrender and see the enemy occupy their homeland and their comrades tried as war criminals.

But to continue the fight would bring death to tens of thousands, if not hundreds of thousands. "The whole nation," he said, "would be reduced to ashes."

In closing, he instructed the cabinet to honor his wishes and accept the Allied reply. To alert the public, he asked his ministers to prepare a draft of an imperial rescript that he could broadcast to the nation. "Finally," he concluded, "I call upon each and every one of you to exert himself to the utmost so that we may meet the trying days which lie ahead."

CHAPTER 40

"In both Hiroshima and Nagasaki the tremendous scale of the disaster largely destroyed the cities as entities."

—"THE ATOMIC BOMBINGS OF HIROSHIMA AND NAGASAKI"
MANHATTAN ENGINEER DISTRICT, JUNE 29, 1946

Doubts still plagued Anami as he left the meeting.

He pulled Army Chief of the General Staff Umezu aside. "Do you believe that the war should be continued," he asked, "even at the risk of launching a coup d'état?"

"No, it is impossible, because the decision of His Majesty the Emperor has already been given," he said. "Launching a coup d'état in complete defiance of the Emperor's decision will, first of all, invite a split within military circles. Moreover, the nation will not follow us. There is nothing we can do now but to comply with the Emperor's decision."

In a nearby washroom, where he was joined by his adjutant Maj. Saburo Hayashi, Anami announced a rumor that an American landing force was near Tokyo Bay, a ripe target he wanted to strike. "Maybe," he declared, "we'll get the kind of peace terms we want."

"But the Emperor," his aide reminded him, "has already given us his decision."

Anami's excitement faded.

He next met with his brother-in-law, Lieutenant Colonel Takeshita, who along with a dozen others had confronted him a few days earlier.

Takeshita urged Anami to act and mobilize troops. "You have power," Takeshita said. "You could use it.

"No," Anami at last replied. "The Emperor has made his decision."

By the time he reached the War Ministry, where young officers swarmed him, Anami's doubts had vanished. Hirohito's decision spelled the end of the Japanese Army, which still numbered more than 5 million troops. American forces would soon land and occupy the homeland that Anami had fought so hard to protect. The war minister knew that history would record him as the last leader of the defeated Imperial Japanese Army, a shameful badge he would wear for eternity. But despite his own indignity, Anami realized it was vital to prevent the army from rebelling and leading the country into civil war. That was the message he needed to deliver to his men. "The emperor has spoken his decision," he said, "and we have no choice whatsoever but to obey it. Anyone who disagrees will have to do so over my dead body!"

But the war minister knew that to guarantee peace he needed to broadcast that message beyond just the men who crowded inside his office. That afternoon he called a meeting of all the officers scattered across the ministry's many sections. Once the men gathered, he stepped atop a small dais. The emperor, he informed them, had ordered Japan to accept the Allied demands. The army, like the rest of the nation, would obey. "No officer in the Imperial Army will disobey the Emperor's command," he said. "No officer in the army will presume to know, better than the Emperor and the government of the country, what is best for the country."

The job of preparing the emperor's rescript fell to Chief Cabinet Secretary Hisatsune Sakomizu and Michio Kihara, a former reporter with *Nippon Times* who was on temporary duty with the cabinet. That afternoon the two created a draft based on the emperor's comments in the two earlier meetings. Unlike everyday common language, Hirohito spoke using court Japanese, which was formal and archaic. To prepare the script, the duo had not only consulted multiple reference works but had sought advice from two Japanese experts on the classics, who could assist with the written characters that were derived from Chinese.

The aides presented the finished draft to the cabinet at four p.m. on August 14. The fifteen members seated around the table at the prime minister's residence spent the next three hours haggling over the language.

Most of the quibbles were minor, but Anami zeroed in on a phrase he viewed as problematic: "The war situation grows more unfavorable to us every day." If that sentence was not changed, Anami protested, he would refuse to sign. "We still have not lost the war," the war minister argued. "The situation has merely not turned in our favor."

"Japan is on the verge of destruction," Yonai shot back. "We have clearly been defeated."

Though the others did not immediately realize it, Anami's argument had nothing to do with semantics but was focused instead on the practical reality of trying to convince millions of zealous Japanese soldiers to surrender. An "unfavorable" war situation was no reason to give up, particularly for troops who had been trained to believe that surrender was dishonorable. Language mattered, and in this case, lives depended on it. Anami suggested the sentence be changed to read: "The war situation has not developed to Japan's advantage."

Yonai initially insisted on the original verbiage, until he realized Anami was not trying to be difficult but rather to spare more bloodshed. "On the question of the phrasing," the admiral said, "I would like to see it revised in accordance with the War Minister's desire."

The agreed-upon rescript went to the palace, where imperial scribes armed with brushes and ink made two copies on thick paper. One would become the signed official order, while the other would be used by the emperor for his broadcast. Hirohito proofed the rescript, ordering five minor changes. The edict consisted of 815 characters, too many for the scribes to redo, prompting them to cover the characters to be fixed with pieces of paper.

Hirohito signed the finished rescript at eight-thirty p.m. A sixteen-petaled gold chrysanthemum—the imperial seal of Japan—was then affixed to the edict. The cabinet met at nearly ten p.m., where Suzuki signed first, with a brush and ink, followed one after the other by the remaining members. When the task was done, Anami rose and approached Togo. He had seen a copy of the accompanying message the Foreign Office planned to send with the formal acceptance of the Allied demands. That message requested Japanese forces be allowed to disarm themselves, one of the concessions Anami had requested. The war minister bowed and thanked his former adversary. "I am most grateful to you," he said, "and feel I owe you an apology for some of the things I may have said in the heat of the argument."

"Everything," Togo replied, "has come out all right in the end."

Anami apologized next to Suzuki, telling him he was trying to represent the views of the army while protecting the monarchy. "I should have given you every assistance in this war," he said, "but I am afraid I have caused you a great deal of trouble instead."

"I fully appreciate your painful situation," Suzuki replied, warmly grasping the war minister's hand. "I have not yet lost hope for the future of Japan."

Anami presented the prime minister with a package of cigars before he saluted him and departed, escorted out by the chief cabinet secretary. When the secretary returned, Suzuki shared his fears. "I think the war minister," he said, "came to say goodbye."

Tokyo was a ghost town. American bombers had leveled more than fifty square miles of the capital, prompting millions to abandon the city. The remaining few huddled in the dark as required under the nation's strict blackout restrictions.

At the palace, a six-person team with the national broadcaster NHK set up a studio on the second floor of the Imperial Administrative Office, complete with a Matsuda A-type microphone, two K-type 14 recorders, and two amplifiers. Hirohito would then record his speech on a gramophone record that would be broadcast over the nation's airwaves the next day. Everyone bowed when the emperor entered at eleven-thirty p.m.

"How loudly should I speak?" Hirohito asked.

Normal tones, he was told, would be fine.

The emperor then proceeded to read his rescript.

"Was it all right?" he asked when he was finished.

A few words were not entirely clear, the engineer replied.

Hirohito then read the speech again, this time with tears in his eyes.

CHAPTER 41

"In this last great action of the Second World War we were given final proof that war is death."

—WAR SECRETARY HENRY STIMSON

The night was far from over.

For several days, a group of young officers had plotted a potential coup, a plan born in a bomb shelter under the War Ministry after news first spread of Hirohito's decision to surrender. The scheme called for the elimination of the peace advocates—Suzuki, Togo, Kido, and Yonai—coupled with the kidnapping of Hirohito, ostensibly for his own protection. The military would then seize control of the government under the command of the war minister.

But the plotters, who had shopped the idea around to senior officers, had failed to win the support of critical leaders. Eastern District Army commander Gen. Shizuichi Tanaka, whose force oversaw the defense of Tokyo and the Kanto region, shot them down. So did Lt. Gen. Takeshi Mori, head of the First Imperial Guards Division, whose job was to protect the emperor, his family, and the palace. "Unless the Emperor personally commands me," Mori told them, "I cannot and will not carry out any action contrary to the wishes of His Majesty even though said action is ordered by the War Minister himself."

The conspirators had likewise courted the nation's top soldier, General Anami, whose support was essential for any coup. Unlike Tanaka and Mori, who immediately shut down such talk, Anami did nothing to discourage the fanatics, even though he later confided to an aide that he doubted the plan would work.

The young officers first visited the war minister on August 12, during which time he listened to their complaints but refused to commit to join them. Anami strung them along again the following day, erroneously telling them that the emperor and other peace advocates were coming around to the army's position. Such a statement, whether intentional or not, no doubt helped stall any violence and buy time for the political process. Anami's flirtation with the conspirators—or at a minimum, his reluctance to outright order them to stop—may very well have tracked with his own seesawing emotions over what was best for Japan.

Any hope the plotters had of the general's help, however, ended when Anami returned to the War Ministry following the joint meeting of the Big Six and the Cabinet. By then, his own personal wavering was finished. He knew the path he had to take. "No officer in the Imperial Army," he warned his men, "will disobey the emperor's command."

Despite Anami's admonition, Maj. Kenji Hatanaka refused to relent. The junior officer, who worked in the ministry's military affairs section, conscripted a handful of others and hastily organized a new plan designed to stop the broadcast of Hirohito's rescript.

Time was running short.

Around eleven p.m., moments before the emperor recorded his speech, Hatanaka went to confront General Mori, hoping to convince the Imperial Guard commander to finally back them. He was joined on the mission by two fellow conspirators, Lt. Col. Masataka Ida and Capt. Shigetaro Uehara. Mori, who was meeting with others, kept the trio waiting until twelve-thirty a.m., much to Hatanaka's frustration, who paced the waiting room.

"There's no time," he repeated. "There's no time."

Tired of waiting, Hatanaka with Uehara in tow stepped out to call upon Lieutenant Colonel Takeshita, who had once supported the conspirators. Hátanaka told him a coup had begun and urged him to go see the general and convince him to join. Takeshita, after failing to dissuade Hanaka, agreed to at least try.

The duo's departure left Ida as the lone conspirator to meet with General Mori, who at last invited him inside his office. Mori was not alone, but was joined by his brother-in-law, Lt. Col. Michinori Shiraishi, who stood behind him. The general, who no doubt suspected what Ida wanted to discuss, killed time rambling about life.

"Hold on a minute," he would say each time Ida tried to interject.

After fifteen minutes, Mori finally fell silent and at last let Ida make his pitch. When Ida finished, the general once again reiterated his opposition to any coup. The emperor, as Mori explained, had made his decision. "As commander of the Imperial Guards, I must obey that decision," the general declared. "I must insist that my men obey it."

To soften the blow, Mori offered to go visit the Meiji Shrine to pray for guidance. He then summoned his chief of staff, Lt. Col. Kazuo Mizutani, requesting his opinion, but the officer demurred. Mizutani did not know enough about the plan, he said, to offer an opinion. As a result, Mori requested Ida go brief his chief of staff in his office.

Ida followed Mizutani down the hall, when Hatanaka and Uehara returned accompanied by several of the guard's staff officers. The duo walked into Mori's office as Ida sat down and began his briefing. Ida did not get far into his pitch before a gunshot crackled. Ida and Mizutani rushed down the corridor. Before the men reached the door, Hatanaka emerged from the general's office with a pistol in hand and his face pale. Ida peered inside. He was stunned to see Mori on the ground bleeding alongside Lieutenant Colonel Shiraishi, who was decapitated. Uehara stood over him, wiping the blood from his sword.

"Time was running out," Hatanaka said. "Please forgive me."

The plot had graduated from a coup to an assassination.

At 1:45 a.m., Ida and Mizutani, both in shock from the carnage, hopped into a staff car and drove to the Eastern District Army Headquarters, where Hatanaka hoped the duo could convince General Tanaka to join the coup. Hatanaka meanwhile fished Mori's personal seal from the general's desk and stamped his name on a fake directive—Imperial Guards Division Strategic Order No. 584—instructing the troops to "protect" the emperor and to occupy NHK and block all broadcasts. He sent the order by messenger to the Imperial Guard commanders. For his plan to work, however, Hatanaka knew he needed Tanaka and Anami to join him.

At the palace, Imperial Guards disarmed the police and sliced the phone lines. Others sealed the grounds, set up machine guns at the entrances, and captured some twenty hostages. That included the NHK team, who were apprehended heading back to the station. Through interrogation of the hostages, Hatanaka learned that Hirohito had made a recording of his rescript, which remained hidden somewhere on the grounds. What he did not know was that officials had locked the recording in an office safe that belonged to a member of the empress's staff. Hatanaka likewise discovered that Kido and Household Minister Sotaro Ishiwatari were also on site, prompting the conspirators to begin a hunt for the recording and the two senior officials.

Word quickly spread that the palace was under attack, prompting chamberlains to smuggle Ishiwatari into a secret underground room known as "the bank vault." Aides similarly found Kido at 3:20 a.m. The lord keeper of the privy seal quickly tore up and flushed important records down the toilet. Aides then hid Kido in the palace's doctor's office before smuggling him into the underground vault to join Ishiwatari. To protect Hirohito and his family, who resided in the Imperial Library, chamberlains barred the doors and windows.

Across the capital, several dozen additional army conspirators, armed with swords, handguns, and two light machine guns, attacked the official residences of Suzuki and Kido. Fanatics machine-gunned the front of the prime minister's home, who was not there at the time, and engaged in a firefight with guards at Kido's residence before being driven off. Others surrounded and then seized the NHK building, locking sixty employees in Studio 1.

Meanwhile another drama unfolded at the war minister's residence, where General Anami had returned after the evening's cabinet meeting to prepare to meet his end. Normally not a drinker, Anami downed cup after cup of rice wine. Between sips of sake, he used a brush and black India ink to write a one-sentence poem on a scroll, consisting of thirty-one syllables. "After tasting the profound benevolence of the Emperor, I have no words to speak." He signed it General Korechika and dated it the night of August 14, 1945. He then brushed a farewell note. "For my supreme crime, I beg forgiveness through the act of death." This time, he signed it with his full name and title, Korechicka Anami, Minister of War. Historians would later puzzle over his use of the word "crime." Was it a reference to the army's role in leading Japan into a disastrous war, or was it more personal, perhaps his dabbling with the coup plotters? After some time and a few more drinks, Anami picked up his brush and added a final line to the back of the scroll. "I believe," he wrote, "in Japan's sacred indestructability."

When Takeshita arrived at the war minister's home, Anami welcomed him and poured him a glass of sake. The general told his brother-in-law that he planned to commit *seppuku*. Under the circumstances, Takeshita said, he understood and would not interfere.

"I am glad you agree," the general said. "I was worried you might try to stop me."

Takeshita told him of the coup, but Anami said the Eastern District Army would never join. "If I don't succeed in killing myself," he asked, "will you give me the *coup de grâce*?"

Ida and Mizutani meanwhile reached the Eastern District Army Headquarters, where an excited caller had earlier alerted officers that the Imperial Guards were in revolt.

Would the Eastern District Army, the caller asked, join the rebellion?

Officers at the headquarters had been reluctant to believe the caller, given General Mori's insistence that he would follow the emperor's orders. The first words out of Mizutani's mouth, however, shattered any such illusion and proved another blow to the coup. "Mori's been murdered," Mizutani declared. "The Guards are occupying the palace."

Ida had already begun to lose faith in the coup, which was clearly unraveling with Mori's assassination, a fact he had initially hoped to hide from the officers at the Eastern District Army Headquarters. Ida now faced the challenge of trying to convince Tanaka that he and his forces should join the murderous rebellion, a cause he realized was likely hopeless.

And he was right.

A dispirited Ida left the headquarters by car and went to the palace to see Hatanaka, hoping to convince him to end his quixotic coup. Each passing hour only further highlighted the futility of Hatanaka's task. The maze of offices inside the Imperial Household Ministry had confounded the conspirators, who had no luck finding either Hirohito's recording or Kido and Ishiwatari. Time was now Hatanaka's enemy. "It's all over," Ida said. "If you occupy the Palace any longer, you'll find yourself fighting a battle against the entire Eastern Army."

"I'm not afraid of a battle," Hatanaka replied.

"Don't be a fool," Ida said. "Withdraw the soldiers before dawn."

Ida knew he next needed to report to Anami, who he found at his home preparing to commit suicide. Ida said he planned do the same, a comment that drew a sharp rebuke from Anami. It was imperative, the war minister explained, that Ida survive. "You must do your best to rebuild Japan," he ordered him. "That takes more courage than dying!"

General Tanaka was determined to stop the coup.

As the general rushed to the palace, his senior aides managed to get through by phone to the Imperial Guards command post, which was the one line the insurgents had failed to cut. Maj. Gen. Tatsuhiko Takashima, who served as Tanaka's chief of staff, spoke to Hatanaka, who begged the senior officer to understand his position. Just as Ida had done, the major general told Hatanaka that he was defeated and his situation hopeless. "The only thing you can do now," he said, "is to make sure there are no more unnecessary deaths."

At 5:10 a.m., General Tanaka reached the palace, where he discovered that Hatanaka had fled. Tanaka ordered the arrest of Maj. Sadakichi Ishihara, a staff officer of the Imperial Guards Division and one of Hatanaka's collaborators. Tanaka informed the guards that Division Order No. 584 was a forgery and that General Mori had been slain. "From this moment," Tanaka declared, "I am in command of the Imperial Guards Division."

Hatanaka refused to give up. He fled to NHK, where armed with a pistol, he demanded to be put on the air. He may have failed at the palace, but Hatanaka planned to plead his case to the nation, urging the citizenry to reject the government's surrender. Officials stalled, telling him that the station was prohibited from broadcasting when an air raid warning was in effect without permission from the Eastern District Army. As an added precaution, clever employees went so far as to unhook the cable that connected the studio and broadcasting tower.

But Hatanaka continued to bully the staff, waiving his handgun and threatening to kill everyone until a call came through from the Eastern District Army Headquarters. The terrified personnel at NHK listened as Hatanaka took the call and continued his now-familiar rant. He then fell quiet as he listened to the officer on the other end of the line.

"Very well," he finally said.

The staff watched as Hatanaka replaced the receiver. He then wiped tears from his eyes. "We've done everything we could," he announced to his conspirators. "Let's go."

Hatanaka and his cohorts departed without a single shot fired.

The leader of the failed coup had run out of options. Outside the palace later that morning, he raised his pistol to his forehead and squeezed the trigger.

The sun rose over the capital as the final drama played out in the war minister's home. Anami slipped on the white shirt the emperor had given him, one Hirohito had personally worn. He then prepared his dress uniform, pinning on his medals, before carefully folding it and setting it aside. On top he added a photo of his second son, who was killed in the war in China. "When I am dead," he asked Takeshita, "will you drape the uniform over me?"

The head of the secret police arrived at Anami's home to report on the failed coup. The general asked Takeshita to go speak to him, and he sent Ida to stand watch elsewhere, leaving him alone. The war minister then sat on his knees in typical Japanese fashion and faced the palace. He unsheathed his dagger and sliced open his abdomen.

When Takeshita returned, he saw the war minister, blade clutched in his left hand, searching for his carotid artery on the right side of his neck. Once found, Anami raised the blade and drew it across his neck. With each beat of his heart, the blood pulsed out, yet he remained upright on his knees.

"Shall I help you?" Takeshita asked.

"No," Anami said. "Leave me."

Takeshita did as instructed.

Anami remained upright, even as the blood continued to flow from his wounds and he slipped unconscious.

Takeshita picked up the blade and drove it into his neck.

The long saga was at last over.

CHAPTER 42

"If the Japs aren't quite ready to capitulate, they will quickly wish they had."

—*PITTSBURGH POST-GAZETTE*
AUGUST 13, 1945, EDITORIAL

Americans anxiously awaited news from Japan.

Throughout the Pacific, commanders urged troops to remain vigilant. "Take precautions against treachery even if local or general surrender should be suddenly announced," Pacific Fleet Commander Adm. Chester Nimitz ordered his forces. "Maintain all current reconnaissance and patrols. Offensive action shall be continued unless otherwise specifically directed."

Rumors of a possible peace deal swept through the press pool at the White House and the Pentagon, while newspaper switchboards from New York to San Francisco were jammed with calls. Others hovered over news tickers anxious for word. Such speculation did not last long, as the White House soon confirmed reports of Japan's offer. News of a possible peace deal electrified the world. People poured into the streets to celebrate. In Honolulu, where the war had begun on a cool December morning, cars and trucks filled with excited troops sped through downtown honking horns. "Londoners danced in the streets," one reporter observed. "Chinese celebrated in Chungking. Australians smashed windows and set fires in Sydney."

"Thank God, there will be no more invasions and no more bombing missions" was a comment heard often on the busy airbases throughout the Marianas.

In Manila, MacArthur addressed hundreds of cheering troops from his office balcony. "I hope from the bottom of my heart that this is the end of the war."

White House officials drafted a message to allies, informing them that MacArthur would serve as the supreme commander, while others prepared surrender documents. "With these steps completed," Truman said, "there remained nothing to do but to await that reply."

On Sunday, August 12, Truman arrived early in the Oval Office. Confident of a quick answer, officials urged reporters to show up at eight-thirty a.m. More than a hundred print, radio, and photo journalists swarmed the White House, pestering press aide Charles Ross. "Reporters went in and out of Secretary Ross's office looking for something significant in every casual move," one journalist observed. "Nothing was too trivial for inquiry."

A similar scene unfolded outside, where crowds gathered along Pennsylvania Avenue. Across the street in Lafayette Park, men, women, and children spread out on blankets to await the news. As the day passed, the number swelled to an estimated ten thousand people, many of whom passed the time playing cards and singing patriotic and service songs. Others huddled around radios at home, anxiously awaiting word on the war's end.

"Thank God," one soldier in the park said, "it's almost over."

The exuberance that marked the start of the day began to fade as the minutes turned to hours, and no word arrived from Japan. Ross's lack of news did not keep the reporters from hounding him, prompting the press aide to at last close his office door.

"I don't know," an exasperated Ross repeated.

The president busied himself while waiting by penning a letter to his sister, wishing her a happy birthday. "Since I landed last Tuesday there hasn't been a minute. The speech, the Russian entry into the war, the Jap surrender offer and the usual business of the President's office have kept me busy night and day," Truman wrote. "It seems that things are going all right. Nearly every crisis seems to be the worst one, but after it's over, it isn't so bad."

The afternoon turned to evening.

And still no word arrived.

At 9:34 p.m., radio broadcasters interrupted scheduled programs.

"Here it is!" one announcer crackled.

Across the capital, people mobbed radios.

"President Truman," the broadcast continued, "announces Japs accept surrender terms."

Celebratory gunfire erupted in some Washington neighborhoods. Others poured out of restaurants and drugstores as traffic slowed to a crawl. At National Airport, where the news was broadcast over the public address system, passengers cheered. In Lafayette Park, a woman screamed as others surged around a radio sound truck for news. Inside the White House press room, where scores of reporters had spent the day pacing, the phones began to ring at once. "On the other end of the wire," one reporter noted, "were city editors, news editors, managing editors—all demanding to know why they hadn't called in the news."

"Hold that flash," a broadcaster declared two minutes later. "We don't know what it is, but something is wrong. United Press has ordered a kill on that flash."

The erroneous report did little to dampen the enthusiasm of those gathered outside the White House. "We want Harry," people began to cheer. "We want Harry."

But the president, exhausted after a long day, had retired to his bedroom.

The vigil continued Monday. At 10:45 a.m., Ross addressed more than a hundred reporters. "It is safe to say," the press secretary declared, "the war is going on."

Journalists scribbled down his remarks.

"No word has been received from Japan," he continued.

"Might there be another atomic bomb?" someone asked.

"I do not know," he replied. "If I did, I wouldn't say."

The hours once again crawled past.

"No word from Japan," Ross told reporters at three p.m.

"Nothing new," he added at five-thirty p.m.

"The president has gone to bed," Ross concluded at ten-thirty p.m.

America needed to up the pressure on Japan.

After four days of no missions, General Marshall ordered America's bombers back into business: "The President directs that we go ahead with everything we've got."

Arnold jumped on the radio teletype to Spaatz. "It is desired that you start operations with your B-29s against Japan at once," he wrote. "What is the maximum that you can send out? One thousand looks good to me. Can you reach it? What can you do about this at once?"

Spaatz confirmed that he could send at least nine hundred planes.

"The maximum number possible must be sent over Tokyo so as to impress the Japanese officials that we mean business and are serious in getting them to accept our peace proposals without delay," Arnold replied. "What number can be used effectively over Tokyo?"

The Japanese capital was a flattened wasteland spread across fifty-six square miles. There were no other viable targets left for an incendiary attack. "Tokyo," Spaatz wrote, "is not a good target except for the atomic bomb." He instead listed six other targets, a mix of smaller cities along with various industries and arsenals. "Recommend utmost urgency," he added, "be given to placing third atomic bomb here to be dropped on Tokyo."

The air force launched 828 B-29s and 186 fighters, hitting the Nippon Oil Refinery, the Marifu railyard, and army and navy arsenals in Osaka and Tokuyama. Other Superfortresses lifted off to burn the cities of Isezaki and Kumagaya, home to a combined ninety thousand residents. For fourteen hours, American bombers mercilessly hammered targets across Honshu. It was a display of force, as *The New York Times* observed, "calculated to remind the Japanese of the certain fact that it was within our power to destroy them unless they quit immediately."

CHAPTER 43

"The desire and will to go on were submerged by the sorrow and sadness of defeat."

—DR. MICHIHIKO HACHIYA
AUGUST 16, 1945, DIARY ENTRY

At 7:21 a.m. on August 15, the radio announcer Morio Tateno's voice crackled over the nation's airwaves. "His Imperial Majesty the Emperor has issued a rescript. It will be broadcast at noon today. Let us all respectfully listen to the voice of the Emperor."

Tateno then paused.

"Let us all," he reiterated, "respectfully listen to the voice of the Emperor."

With the failed coup now over, palace officials unlocked Hirohito's recording and transported it to NHK for the midday announcement. The broadcast company planned to bump its power from the normal ten kilowatts to sixty, while utilities prepared to transmit power to districts normally blacked out during the day. Across Japan, workers set up radio receivers in railroad stations, post offices, and government buildings. Factories likewise planned to pipe the news over public address systems or via loudspeakers set up outdoors.

Rumors swirled over what the news might be. A few speculated about a possible run on the banks, but most suspected it centered on the fate of the war. "As I walked down the street," Tokyo secretary Hisako

Yoshizawa recorded in her diary, "I could hear whispered conversations, every one of them about what would happen if the war ended."

Down on the island of Kyushu, farmer Jingo Tanaka was irrigating his fields when he saw his friend Kyôchi Mazaki. "What sort of broadcast do you suppose it will be?" Mazaki asked. "I wonder if, by chance, it will say that we have surrendered."

"Maybe they surrendered," Tanaka replied.

At eleven a.m., a broadcaster reminded citizens to listen in an hour.

But no such notice was needed.

The announcement that the emperor would address the nation—a voice few had ever before heard—had electrified the population. Down in Hiroshima, Dr. Michihiko Hachiya and other physicians crowded into the hospital's communications bureau, where a radio had been set up. In a hotel in Odawara, where Philippine diplomat León María Guerrero had evacuated, local officials likewise gathered around an old receiver, standing elbow-to-elbow with German, Italian, and other foreign guests. As the broadcast time approached, hotel cooks, clerks, and maids stole a break from work and joined them. "There was complete silence as the clocks ticked toward noon," Guerrero wrote in his diary. "The waiting was oppressive."

At noon, radios nationwide buzzed to life. Many stood, removed hats, and bowed. "In an instant," Yoshizawa recalled, "the streets were dead quiet."

The broadcast began with the *Kimigayo*, Japan's national anthem, followed by the high-pitched voice of the emperor, known to many as the Voice of the Sacred Crane.

"To our good and loyal subjects," Hirohito began.

The emperor's speech, which totaled just 625 words when translated, lasted just four and a half minutes. Though he never mentioned the word *surrender*, his message was clear: Japan had been defeated. "The war situation," he explained, using the language Anami had insisted upon, "has developed not necessarily to Japan's advantage, while the general trends of the world have all turned against her." But the real blame, he said, was the atomic bomb, which in a span of less than seventy-five hours, had wiped out two cities and killed and wounded hundreds of thousands of people.

"The enemy has begun to employ a new and most cruel bomb, the power of which to do damage is, indeed, incalculable, taking the toll of many innocent lives," he said. "Should we continue to fight, not only would it result in an ultimate collapse and obliteration of the Japanese nation, but also it would lead to the total extinction of human civilization."

In rural areas, plagued by weak reception, people strained to hear the emperor's words amid the static. Others struggled to decipher his courtly phrases. But despite such difficulties, most observed that his tone was calm and deliberate, even if his voice betrayed a hint of weariness. As he listened, Guerrero shot glances at those around him. "All were expressionless as they stood, stiffly upright, their hands at their sides with the palms turned backward, head and shoulders bent low with reverence," he wrote. "Not a sound came from them." Tokyo resident Aiko Takahashi, in contrast, could not hold back her emotion. "As each word and phrase was etched on my heart, my eyes got quite warm and tears welled up," she wrote. "I had to wipe them with a handkerchief. Sadness and happiness. Happiness and sadness."

At the hospital in Hiroshima, Dr. Hachiya could barely hear the radio. "The broadcast was in the Emperor's own voice," the director finally announced, "and he has just said that we've lost the war. Until further notice, I want you to go about your duties."

"I had been prepared for the broadcast to tell us to dig in and fight to the end," Hachiya wrote in his diary, "but this unexpected message left me stunned."

Others agreed.

"Only a coward would back out now!" someone shouted.

Across Japan, many others felt the same. For years, Japanese residents had learned to live with less and less, all with the hope that it would ultimately bring victory.

But in the end that was not enough.

America, the nation once ridiculed by the Japanese press, had won. "The news on the radio was terrible," Ryôsaku Sutô wrote in her diary. "All of us sank into silence and didn't say a word. I felt in a daze, exasperated, and tears of resentment began to flow."

Jingo Tanaka, the Kyushu farmer, agreed. "We all felt the horror of being defeated," he wrote, "and the inexpressible horror of being the citizens of a defeated country."

Many others, by contrast, felt relief. There would be no more atomic bombs. No more fire raids. And hopefully soon, no more hunger. "It's ended at last," Taiko Hirabayashi wrote in her diary. "It's ended. The war, like everything else, has ended."

A more painful realization, however, crystallized for those whose loved ones had been killed in the war. That was the case for Matsuo Atsuyuki in Nagasaki, who lost three of his four children. The last to succumb was his wife of eighteen years, Chiyoko, who had died only the night before. On the morning of August 15, Atsuyuki carried her to the Irabayashi Primary School, where he built a pyre of salvaged wood near the sumo ring. He heard the *Kimigayo* waft from a nearby home. "We lifted Chiyoko up onto the bottom stack of lumber," he wrote in his diary, "piled another stack over her body, then set fire to the wood."

The static-filled broadcast mixed with the crackling flames made it impossible for him to hear Hirohito. A neighbor came over afterward and shared the news.

What? he asked in disbelief.

"Japan," the neighbor repeated, "has announced its surrender."

"I broke into tears," Atsuyuki wrote in his diary. "How can Japan surrender after all this? For what purpose did my wife and children die? Were their deaths for nothing?"

Atsuyuki's grief was shared by countless others, who were left to pick through the ashes of an empire while questioning why their husbands and wives, sons and daughters had to die. The emperor's speech may have ended the war, but for so many the work and the sorrow would only continue. That was evident in the devastated ruins of Hiroshima and Nagasaki. "I could see small fires here and there where people had gone back to cremating the dead," recalled Matsu Moriuchi, who, like Atsuyuki, incinerated her family that morning. "I watched the hundreds of columns of smoke climbing up, and I thought of the dead as sacrifices."

CHAPTER 44

"The bells are ringing, the wars are over. Nothing left but to thank God, the soldiers and sailors and the dead and begin the new job."

—ASSISTANT WAR SECRETARY JOHN McCLOY
AUGUST 14, 1945, DIARY ENTRY

At 1:50 a.m. on August 14, the Associated Press listening post in New York picked up a flash message broadcast by Tokyo radio. "It is learned," the announcer stated, "that an imperial message accepting the Potsdam proclamations will be forthcoming soon."

Forty minutes later Truman's naval aide Commodore James Vardaman, who had heard the broadcast, arrived at the White House to await any developments. Ross reported into the office at 7:02 a.m. to find reporters once again gathered in search of news.

"The president is up," he told the press, "and fully aware of all that's going on."

In the White House that Tuesday morning, after days of waiting, Tokyo's broadcast sparked a buzz. Truman was at his desk in his study at 7:15 a.m. before having breakfast at eight with Vardaman and then heading to the Oval Office to meet with Byrnes.

Did America expect a reply soon from Tokyo? a reporter asked as he departed.

"Yes, sir," the secretary of state exclaimed.

In his first press conference at 9:45 a.m., Ross echoed Byrnes, informing

150 reporters that the Swiss had received Japan's reply. The message would be decoded and then encoded for transmission to the United States, a process that would take several hours. Protocol mandated that the reply go first to Byrnes, who would then deliver it to the president. "It looks as if at last we are nearing the end of our long vigil," Ross concluded. "By that I mean some time today."

But Ross spoke too soon.

The press secretary summoned reporters to his office soon after for a second news conference. "I have here," he began, "a memorandum from the Legation of Switzerland in Washington through the State Department, which I shall read without comment."

The journalists listened anxiously.

"Very urgent," Ross read aloud. "Japanese Legation reports that coded cables it received this morning do not contain the answer awaited by the whole world."

"The confusion," as one reporter observed, "was reaching a peak."

Across the street from the White House, where crowds once again gathered, many began to ask questions. Were the Japanese stalling or trying to embarrass America?

How long would Truman wait?

What might America do to force the Japanese to decide?

No one knew.

At 12:01 p.m., Tokyo Radio broadcast another message. "The Japanese government's reply to the four powers is now on its way to the Japanese Minister at Bern."

Two and a half hours later, the Swiss chargé d'affairs, Max Grassli, informed Byrnes that the Japanese minister in Bern had received his government's reply. Tensions soared inside the State Department and White House. Would Japan accept America's demands, many wondered, or would leaders insist on further concessions? "A few minutes after 4 o'clock," Byrnes recalled, "I got the telephone call; it ended the longest wait I have ever experienced."

On the other end of the line was Leland Harrison, America's minister in Bern. In his hand he held the text of Japan's reply, which he read to Byrnes. After 1,346 days of war, Japan at last agreed to surrender. The war was finally over. "His Majesty the Emperor is prepared to authorize and ensure the signature by his Government and the Imperial General Headquarters of the necessary terms for carrying out the provisions of the Potsdam Declaration," Harrison read. "His Majesty is also prepared to issue his commands to all the military, naval, and air authorities of Japan and all the forces under their control wherever located to cease active operations, to surrender arms and to issue such other orders as may be required by the Supreme Commander of the Allied Forces for the execution of the above-mentioned terms."

Byrnes was euphoric. "It was," he said, "a complete acceptance of our terms." He rushed across West Executive Avenue to share the news with Truman before heading to the Pentagon. The War Department set up a radio circuit with London, Moscow, and Chungking. Byrnes suggested the Allied powers release the news simultaneously. To avoid the challenge of finding an agreeable time, he declared Truman would announce the news at seven p.m. and urged the others to follow his lead. "I did not believe," he said, "this happy news should be withheld from the people of the world because of an argument on the time of the release."

At 6:57 p.m., reporters filed into the Oval Office, standing shoulder to shoulder. Bess Truman was on hand; so were most of the cabinet members to whom the president apologized for the lack of advanced notice. Truman had even summoned ailing former secretary of state Cordell Hull. Dressed in a double-breasted blue suit, the president stood behind his desk, his typed remarks in hand. "I have received this afternoon a message from the Japanese government," he read aloud. "I deem this reply a full acceptance of the Potsdam Declaration which specifies the unconditional surrender of Japan. In the reply there is no qualification."

Reporters scribbled down his comments.

Arrangements, Truman continued, were being made for the formal signing of the surrender terms. MacArthur, who would serve as Supreme Allied Commander, would receive Japan's surrender joined by senior military leaders of Great Britain, Russia, and China. "Allied armed forces have been ordered to suspend offensive actions," he said. "The proclamation of V-J Day must wait upon the formal signing of the surrender terms by Japan."

Aides handed out several press releases, including one announcing that federal workers would receive two days off and another that ordered military inductions slashed from 80,000 recruits a month to 50,000. The president then read aloud Japan's reply.

"I congratulate you," a reporter shouted when he finished.

"That is all," Truman concluded.

Others scrambled outside to flash word of the news.

"It was simple and without dramatics, except for the drama of the news itself," one reporter observed. "The whole thing lasted only about two minutes."

A huge roar from the crowd shattered the calm night outside the White House. Car horns blared and traffic slowed to a crawl. Gunfire crackled against the backdrop of tolling church bells. Police estimated that as many as a half-million people poured into the streets with some climbing atop streetcars and blocking traffic. Ticker tape rained down from office windows, so much so that city collectors would sweep up thirty thousand pounds of paper. "I have never seen such a mess," the district refuse director said. "It looks like a snowstorm hit us."

"The city," as a *New York Times* reporter noted, "went mad with joy."

"It was the noisiest and most colorful night this Capital has ever known," added a journalist with the *Washington Times Herald*.

Outside the White House, an estimated fifty thousand men, women and children congregated. "We want Harry," people began to chant again. "We want Harry."

And Harry delivered.

Twenty minutes after the press conference, the president and first lady walked outside onto the North Lawn. Truman raised his hand and flashed the victory sign.

Participants erupted in cheers.

The president, who had taken the nation's helm only 124 days earlier, went back inside where, as he always did, he called his ninety-two-year-old mother to deliver the good news. "I'm proud of Harry," she told reporters. "I think everyone should be proud of Harry."

Like a balloon, the crowd outside 1600 Pennsylvania Avenue swelled. "The White House was the center of the celebration," a reporter noted. "Crowds moved toward it, sometimes, it seemed, not knowing just where they were going. But there they landed."

At eight p.m., Truman stepped back outside onto the North Portico, where a loudspeaker had been set up. "Ladies and gentlemen," the president began as people pressed closer. "This is a great day. This is the day we have all been looking for since December 7, 1941."

The crowd howled.

"This is the day for the democracies," he concluded.

"Harry, Harry," people shouted. "Harry, Harry."

But the president waved good night and walked back inside. He had one last task to perform before the day ended. At ten p.m., he phoned Eleanor Roosevelt in New York. The message he delivered to her was the same one he imparted on his staff earlier that evening. "I don't deserve the congratulations," he said at the time, pointing to Roosevelt's portrait on the wall. "There is the man who should be here. To him should go the congratulations."

EPILOGUE

> *"The explosion of the atomic bomb had an even greater impact on the world than it did on Hiroshima. It stands alone in the earth's history as a subject of world-wide discussion."*
>
> —LT. GEN. LESLIE GROVES
> JULY 31, 1948

President Harry Truman ordered the use of atomic bombs.

And he never regretted his decision.

In the aftermath of the war, the American public agreed. A Gallup poll in August 1945 revealed that 85 percent supported the bomb's use. The relief of a war-weary nation, which had faced a bloody invasion, was reflected in the comments at the time. "Two bombs cost two billion," one columnist quipped. "Well, it turned out to be the best bargain of the war."

The United States Strategic Bombing Survey, in an analysis compiled soon after the conflict's end, estimated that the attack on Hiroshima killed as many as 80,000 men, women, and children. Nagasaki, where the mountains corralled the blast, suffered another 40,000 fatalities. Japanese historians have since revised those numbers upward. The generally agreed-upon figures today are that 140,000 perished in Hiroshima with more than 73,000 others in Nagasaki.

The realization of the human cost of the attacks coupled with published accounts of the civilian suffering—most notably, John Hersey's

1946 book *Hiroshima*—have subsequently contributed to a softening of that support. In the war's aftermath, a number of senior military leaders questioned Truman's decision. Some, like Generals Hap Arnold and Curtis LeMay who argued that Japan was largely defeated, were no doubt motivated by professional rivalry, recognizing that the novel new weapon would steal the spotlight from the air force's hard-fought conventional campaign. Others were troubled by the morality of the bomb. "I disliked seeing the United States take the lead in introducing into war something as horrible and destructive as this new weapon was described to be," said Gen. Dwight Eisenhower. William Leahy echoed him, describing the bomb as "barbarous." "I was not taught to make war in that fashion," he wrote in his 1950 memoir. "Wars cannot be won by destroying women and children."

But Truman, who lived until 1972, never wavered.

"It was a question about saving hundreds of thousands of American lives," he declared. "I could not worry about what history would say about my personal morality. I made the only decision I ever knew how to make. I did what I thought was right."

Over the years, Truman received mail from both supporters and detractors. "The whole of humanity," one New York City resident wrote him, "will not forgive you for the massacre of noncombatant men, women, children and the unborn."

Thirteen years after the war, the former president even tangled with the chairman of the Hiroshima City Council, who sent him a resolution to protest televised comments he made about his lack of regret over his decision to drop the bomb. That prompted Truman to fire off a blistering two-page response, which he released to the public at a press conference. "As the executive who ordered the dropping of the bomb, I think the sacrifice of Hiroshima and Nagasaki was urgent and necessary for the prospective welfare of both Japan and the Allies," he concluded. "The need for such a fateful decision, of course, never would have arisen had we not been shot in the back by Japan at Pearl Harbor in December 1941."

Truman, of course, was not the only one to endure such enmity in the war's aftermath. *Enola Gay* bombardier Tom Ferebee's own grandmother chastised him.

"I hope the Lord will forgive you," she declared.

A rabbi went so far as to compare Paul Tibbets to Nazi leader Adolf Eichmann, who oversaw the deportation of millions to concentration camps. "Does service to one's country demand that a human being put aside all moral considerations?" David Arzt asked. "Maybe it would be healthy if your conscience would bother you just a bit."

"Can you," another person wrote him, "feel those people burning?"

More often than not, however, the reaction that Truman, Tibbets, and others received was positive. Much of it came from soldiers, sailors, and marines, all grateful for having been spared the need to invade. "With four battle stars and three beachhead operations to my credit, I don't think that my luck would have held much longer," Lloyd Whydotski wrote to Truman in 1970. "I feel that I have had these many years to enjoy because of you."

Over the last eight decades the pendulum likewise has swung back and forth among historians as to whether the atomic attacks were a necessary tool to end the war or were the unwarranted slaughter of tens of thousands of men, women, and children. Some have argued that Japan was on the verge of surrender. Others have claimed that Russia's entry into the war was what ended the conflict, or that America's use of the bombs was really calculated to send a warning to the Soviets in the postwar era. Researchers in any university library can find shelves packed with books and dissertations. Each new round of records declassification has contributed to the swelling literature, making it likely the most debated topic of the war.

America's submarine blockade coupled with the fire raids had devastated Japan's economy. It is true as well that the Imperial Navy was likewise destroyed. But the army remained a potent force, one that counted more than 5 million men under arms and had repeatedly demonstrated in places like Tarawa and Manila a willingness to fight to the last soul. On the southern island of Kyushu, more than 900,000 Japanese troops were preparing for a titanic battle, one that would have been aided by more than 10,000 kamikazes. Casualty estimates ranged widely, but it can be certain, based on the American experience on Iwo Jima and Okinawa, that such a fight would have proved horrific.

And Kyushu was only the start.

Americans next would have had to take the Tokyo Plain.

Japanese records reveal that senior military leaders remained committed to a fight to the very end. Two atomic bombs, in fact, had failed to convince hardline members of Hirohito's war council to surrender, forcing the unprecedented intervention of the emperor to break the three-to-three impasse. Even then fanatical officers on the eve of capitulation murdered senior leaders and seized the palace in a dangerous coup that nearly succeeded.

Russia's entry into the conflict certainly increased the pressure on Japanese leaders, but it was not the war's deciding factor. When the Soviets refused to renew the neutrality pact in the spring of 1945, Japanese leaders knew the clock was ticking on a Russian invasion. That was complemented by the buildup of troops and supplies in Manchuria as well as by Stalin's refusal to entertain the emperor's peace envoy in the war's waning days. Along similar lines, one of the more unfortunate claims is that Truman used the bomb, not to end the war, but to bully the Soviets in the postwar era. This allegation accuses Truman and his senior lieutenants of the murder of more than 200,000 civilians simply to flex political muscle over Stalin. A serious review of the historical record does not support such a spurious claim, but it does show the president's repeated position that he hoped to speed an end to the war and save lives.

In the decades since the atomic bombs, historians have pulled back the lens to examine the suffering, not just in Hiroshima and Nagasaki, but across Japan and Asia. This adds important context to the frantic final days of the fight. America's blockade of Japan had choked off the vital import of food, which coupled with a disastrous rice harvest that year raised the real threat of a future famine. This coincided with the drumbeat of fire raids that had incinerated more than 170 square miles of sixty-four Japan's cities, forcing more than 8.5 million people to abandon urban areas. All of this occurred before the atomic attacks.

But the suffering spread far beyond Japan. Across Asia, the war, which had already claimed millions of lives in China, the Philippines, the Dutch East Indies, and Indochina, had sparked famine and disease that in the final months of the conflict claimed an estimated 500,000 lives each month. Every day the fight continued, more people died.

After the war—and in response to the growing criticism—Henry Stimson explained the administration's decision-making in an article in *Harper's Magazine*, arguing that of all America's options, the bomb was the "least abhorrent choice." "The destruction of Hiroshima and Nagasaki put an end to the Japanese war," he wrote in 1947. "It stopped the fire raids, and the strangling blockade. It ended the ghastly specter of a clash of great land armies." Even at the highest levels of the Japanese government, there was a realization that Stimson was right. The bomb, coupled with Russia's invasion, offered Japan a way out of the fight, a fact best articulated by Navy Minister Adm. Mitsumasa Yonai. "The atomic bombs and the Soviet entry into the war," he said at the time, "are, in a sense, gifts from the gods."

For the people in Hiroshima and Nagasaki, the atomic attacks were anything but a gift. The horror that befell those cities was unimaginable. Equally so was the devastating impact the attacks had on hundreds of thousands of lives, not only those killed but the survivors who battled everything from radiation sickness and painful keloids to the loss of loved ones and homes. Both cities have since been rebuilt, but scattered throughout are monuments as well as a few scarred buildings that remind people of the tragedy that came from the sky more than eight decades ago. Making sure the world remembers has been a goal for many who survived. "I saw misery that day that I cannot believe was of this world," recalled Setsuko Iwamoto, who was thirteen at the time. "The voices of those war victims will never be heard. As a survivor, it is my mission to speak on their behalf and tell their story to the next generation."

ACKNOWLEDGMENTS

Any work of history is invariably a team effort, involving many archivists and librarians as well as fellow researchers and historians. This book is no exception. I remain indebted to myriad individuals and institutions who aided me over the years of research and writing, from the National Archives and the Library of Congress to Yale and Clemson Universities. A few deserve special mention, including the Harry S. Truman Institute, which graciously awarded me a grant that helped fund my research. Along similar lines, I would like to thank archivists David Clark, Randy Sowell, and Laurie Austin at the Truman Library, who were a great help guiding me through the many collections. I likewise want to thank my good friend George Cully, who aided me, as he has done many times before, in sorting through the voluminous records at the Air Force Historical Research Agency at Maxwell Air Force Base.

In Japan, I am grateful to my dear friend Yukako Ibuki, who has helped me tremendously over the years in tracking down information and connecting me with historians and survivors. Through Yuka, I had the privilege to meet and interview the late Katsumoto Saotome, Japan's leading historian on the March 1945 fire raid. Thanks to her I was also able to spend a couple of days with Shigeaki Mori, who survived the atomic attack on August 6, 1945. Mr. Mori generously invited me into his home, shared with me his powerful story, and escorted me on a personal tour of the Hiroshima Peace Memorial Museum. He likewise showed me the memorial he helped construct, honoring the twelve American prisoners of war killed in the atomic attack. Over in England, I want to thank Doctors Charlie Laderman, Jonathan Fennell, and Alessio Patalano at

King's College London, where I worked on this book as part of my ongoing doctoral research in war studies.

Closer to home, I owe much to my good friends and Citadel colleagues Doctors Brian Jones, Kyle Sinisi, David Preston, and Brian Laslie. In addition to all his duties as the dean of the School of Humanities and Social Sciences, Brian Jones found time to graciously read and comment on this manuscript. A special thanks is in order for the awesome staff at the Citadel's Daniel Library, who are always so helpful and never gripe at the scores of interlibrary loan requests I put in each year. Pacific War historians are a small but tight bunch, and I owe so much to my amazing friends and colleagues Rich Frank, Jon Parshall, and Dennis Giangreco. All three gave of their valuable time to read this book in advance and provide excellent feedback. Thank you, gentlemen. In addition, I have the privilege each spring of leading tours of the Marianas with Jon Parshall, who aside from being a tremendous historian makes the best mai tai I have ever tasted.

I am always grateful to my terrific friends at the National World War II Museum in New Orleans, who have generously brought me on board over the years as a travel historian. Through the museum, I have visited many of the places featured in this book, from the Philippines and the Marianas to Peleliu and Japan. The brilliant historians and staff at the museum always make the trips such fun. Thanks go to Sarah Kirksey, Darsey Walker, Ellie Fetzer, James Williams, John Curatola, Jeremey Collins, and Stephen Watson. I owe a similar thanks in England to my great friend Alan Rooney of the Cultural Experience, a topnotch company that, like the World War II Museum, specializes in battlefield tours. When I am not on the road with the World War II Museum, I am traveling with Alan, often to Japan and the Philippines. I want to say a special thanks as well to my dear friend and *Targeted* series coauthor Jack Carr. Jack has been a champion of this book since I first mentioned it to him several years ago.

I owe a very special thanks to my superb editor John Glusman at W. W. Norton, whom I have had the privilege of working with now on four books of World War II history. During the editing of my previous book *Black Snow*, John first brought up the idea of this book. Since then he has worked at every step to elevate the quality of the manuscript.

Thank you as well to his ever-patient associate Wick Hallos, who has helped keep me to my deadlines. Copyeditor Janet Biehl, whom I have worked with now on many books, is hands down the best in the business. As always, much is owed to Norton's terrific art and marketing departments, particularly my good friend Kyle Radler. Thank you as well to my agent, Wendy Strothman, whom I have now worked with for two decades. A special thanks as well to her associate Lauren MacLeod. Last but certainly not least, thank you to my amazing and patient wife, Carmen, and our wonderful children, Isa and Grigs, who have put up with my travel and countless weekends of work, not to mention the war stories intermixed with a few bad dad jokes.

A NOTE ON SOURCES

I always say that crafting a true story begins with a scavenger hunt through archives, libraries, and museums around the world to assemble the pieces of the narrative puzzle. Along those lines, the Truman Presidential Library and Museum in Independence, Missouri, is a must-stop for anyone interested in the nation's thirty-third president. The library is home to a wealth of information, from Truman's personal letters and wartime records to voluminous memos, reports, and cables. The museum likewise features among its collection the green safety plug that was removed from Fat Man while in flight from Tinian to Nagasaki.

In addition to archival work, I am indebted to several previous Truman biographers who plowed the rich ground of this former farmer-turned-statesman's life. David McCullough's magisterial book, *Truman*, is a wonderfully rich and enjoyable read for both the scholar and the general reader. Equally important are the many works by acclaimed historian Robert H. Ferrell. Though Ferrell's emphasis was less on storytelling, he did yeoman's work, parsing through Truman's papers to write and edit multiple books. Along similar lines, D. M. Giangreco has done exceptional work, producing several books on Truman's time in uniform, his decision to use the atomic bomb, and another on the bloody final year of the war.

The voluminous files of the Manhattan Project can be found amid several important collections at the National Archives and on microfilm. A vital set of records include "Manhattan Project: Official History and Documents," a twelve-roll microfilm series that details everything from the land acquisition for the three atomic cities to the construction of the reactors and the communities needed to house the army of workers.

Two other important collections are the five-reel "Correspondence ("Top Secret") of the Manhattan Engineer District, 1942–1946" and the nine-roll collection "Harrison-Bundy Files Relating to the Development of the Atomic Bomb, 1942–1946." Both sets include invaluable cables, meeting minutes, memos, reports, and correspondence of the project and War Department's senior leaders. The National Archives likewise is home to the personal papers of Leslie Groves, the dogged general who oversaw the development of the Manhattan Project. The personal papers of his deputy, Thomas Farrell, can be found at the U.S. Army Heritage and Education Center in Carlisle, Pennsylvania.

Other important archives include the Air Force Historical Research Center in Montgomery, Alabama, which holds the voluminous papers of the Twentieth Air Force, the 21st Bomber Command, and of course, the 509th Composite Group. These three collections tell the story of America's devastating air war against Japan, from the unsuccessful high-altitude raids through the shift to firebombing and lastly the escalation to atomic weapons. The archive likewise houses the personal papers of Paul Tibbets, Jr., which include mission files as well as his personal correspondence and a trove of newspaper and magazine articles that the *Enola Gay* commander collected over the years. The Library of Congress has the papers of other leaders, including Curtis LeMay, Carl Spaatz, Hap Arnold, Robert Oppenheimer, William Parsons, and William Leahy. Other important collections include the personal papers of War Secretary Henry Stimson and his deputy John McCloy, both of whom were terrific diarists. Stimson's papers can be found at Yale University while McCloy's are at Amherst College. Jimmy Byrnes's papers and those of his aide, William Brown, are at Clemson University.

I married my archival research with trips to numerous places featured in this book, from Oak Ridge, Tennessee, to many of the remote islands in the Pacific. To better understand the violence of the war, which shaped Truman's decision in the summer of 1945, I hiked up Mount Suribachi on the southern tip of Iwo Jima, climbed through many caves and tunnels on Okinawa, and peered down from atop the cliffs of Saipan, where hundreds of men, women, and children committed suicide. On multiple visits to Tinian, I explored the remnants of the University District, home of the 509th Composite Group, perched amid the tangled overgrowth on the island's northern end. Beyond the potholed roads that still carry the names given to them by the Seabees more than eight decades ago, much of the military's historic presence is gone or in ruins, but with a few notable exceptions. I explored the foundation of the atomic bomb's Assembly Building and stared down into the bomb pits—now protected under glass—where Little Boy and Fat Man were hoisted into the backs of the *Enola Gay* and *Bockscar*. The highlight for me was to walk along the crumbling coral and asphalt of Runway Able, the airstrip that launched the two atomic missions and that is now, after nearly a century, slowly being brought back into service by the United States Air Force as part of America's pivot toward Asia.

In Japan, where I spent a year in my twenties as a public school English teacher, I visited Tokyo, Hiroshima, and Nagasaki to better understand America's escalating air war. All three cities, of course, have long since been rebuilt, but hints of the past remain. The Center of the Tokyo Raid and War Damages, which is dedicated to the March 9, 1945, fire raid, is a necessary visit for anyone interested in the air war; so is the Great Kanto Earthquake Museum, which has a floor dedicated to the firebombing. The NHK Museum of Broadcasting in Tokyo is also worth a stop just to see the gramophone record on which Hirohito recorded his speech that brought an end to the war. Hiroshima and Nagasaki both have powerful museums dedicated to the atomic attacks, filled with painful artifacts, from bubbled roof tiles and stopped watches to charred lunch boxes and tattered clothes. In addition, I found it powerful to walk each city, visiting the few surviving buildings, and the markers denoting ground zero.

I have provided extensive notes and a bibliography of the many collections, archives, museums and libraries consulted as well as secondary sources. All quotations and dialogue in this book come from reports, memos, cables, letters, diaries, survivor statements, author interviews, oral histories, news stories, and memoirs of participants.

NOTES

ABBREVIATIONS

AFHRA	Air Force Historical Research Agency, Montgomery, Ala.
CMED	Correspondence ("Top Secret") of the Manhattan Engineer District, 1942–1946, National Archives Microfilm Publications, Microfilm Publication M1109, Washington, D.C.
CLP	Curtis E. LeMay Papers, Library of Congress, Washington, D.C.
FRUS	U.S. Department of State, *Foreign Relations of the United States: Diplomatic Papers, 1945*, vols. 1–2, *The Conference of Berlin (The Potsdam Conference).* Washington, D.C.: U.S. Government Printing Office, 1960.
GCMP	George C. Marshall Papers, George C. Marshall Library, Lexington, Va.
HBF	Harrison-Bundy Files Relating to the Development of the Atomic Bomb, 1942–1946, National Archives Microfilm Publications, Microfilm Publication M1108, Washington, D.C.
HLSP	Henry L. Stimson Papers, Yale University, New Haven, Conn.
HSTL	Harry S. Truman Library, Independence, Mo.
JJMP	John J. McCloy Papers, Amherst College Archives and Special Collections, Amherst, Mass.
LOC	Library of Congress, Washington, D.C.
LSP	Leo Szilard Papers, Special Collections & Archives, UC San Diego Library, La Jolla, Calif.
MDH	Manhattan District History
NARA	National Archives and Records Administration, College Park, Md.
USAHEC	United States Army Heritage and Education Center, Carlisle, Penn.
USSBS	United States Strategic Bombing Survey
WJBP	Walter J. Brown Papers, Clemson University Special Collections and Archives, Clemson, S.C.

Prologue

1 **"I never believed":** Michael F. Reilly, as told to William J. Slocum, *Reilly of the White House* (New York: Simon & Schuster, 1947), p. 226.

1 **He could no longer:** Jim Bishop, *FDR's Last Year: April 1944–April 1945* (New York: William Morrow, 1974), pp. 535–36.

1 **His weakness:** William Hassett, diary entry for March 30, 1945, in William D. Hassett, *Off the Record with F.D.R., 1942–1945* (New Brunswick, NJ: Rutgers University Press, 1958), p. 328.

1 **"He is slipping":** Ibid., p. 327.

1 **In the thirteen:** Grace Tully, *F.D.R.: My Boss* (New York: Charles Scribner's Sons, 1949), p. 359.

1 **Only the day:** Margaret (Daisy) Suckley, diary entry for April 12, 1945, in Geoffrey C. Ward, ed. *Closest Companion: The Unknown Story of the Intimate Friendship Between Franklin Roosevelt and Margaret Suckley* (Boston: Houghton Mifflin, 1995), p. 415.

2 **Much to the relief:** Ross T. McIntire with George Creel, *White House Physician* (New York: G.P. Putnam's Sons, 1946), pp. 239–40; Howard G. Bruenn, "Clinical Notes on the Illness and Death of President Franklin D. Roosevelt," *Annals of Internal Medicine* 72 (1970): 590.

2 **To celebrate:** Reilly, *Reilly of the White House*, p. 229; Merriam A. Smith, *Thank You, Mr. President: A White House Notebook* (New York: Harper & Brothers, 1946), pp. 175–88.

2 **More than four thousand:** Andrew J. Felton, "Regulation of the Banking Industry," in Steven Payson, ed., *Public Economies in the United States: How the Federal Government Analyzes and Influences the Economy*, vol. 2, *Economic Analysis of Legislation, Regulation, and Taxation* (Santa Barbara, California: Praeger, 2014), p. 372.

2 **The American army:** Barbara W. Tuchman, *Stilwell and the American Experience in China, 1911–1945* (New York: Macmillan, 1970), p. 203.

2 **In the years since:** Nigel Hamilton, *The Mantle of Command: FDR at War, 1941–1942* (Boston: Houghton Mifflin Harcourt, 2014), p. 387.

3 **"The structure":** Franklin Roosevelt, "Address to Congress Reporting on the Yalta Conference," March 1, 1945, in Samuel I. Rosenman, ed., *The Public Papers and Addresses of Franklin D. Roosevelt* (New York: Harper & Brothers, 1950), p. 13:579.

3 **"He had slept well":** Bruenn, "Clinical Notes on the Illness and Death of President Franklin D. Roosevelt," p. 590.

3 **The White House:** William Hassett Diary, entry for April 12, 1945, in Hassett, *Off the Record with F.D.R.*, p. 333.

4 **"A typical":** Bernard Asbell, *When F.D.R. Died* (New York: Holt, Rinehart & Winston, 1961), p. 33.

4 **"Here's where":** William Hassett Diary, entry for April 12, 1945, in Hassett, *Off the Record with F.D.R.*, p. 334; "Roosevelt Is Dead!" *Chicago Tribune*, April 13, 1945, p. 1.

4 **"Oh, come":** Asbell, *When F.D.R. Died*, p. 34.

4 **Shoumatoff set up:** Elizabeth Shoumatoff, *FDR's Unfinished Portrait: A Memoir* (Pittsburgh: University of Pittsburgh Press, 1990), pp. 115–16. See also Eileen Callahan, "The Last Portrait of Franklin D. Roosevelt," *Daily News*, May 27, 1945, pp. 42–43; "Roosevelt Jovial Before Collapse," *New York Times*, April 16, 1945, p. 1.

4 **"Mr. President, she declared:** Margaret (Daisy) Suckley Diary, entry for April 12, 1945, in Ward, *Closest Companion*, p. 417.

4 **"We have fifteen":** Shoumatoff, *FDR's Unfinished Portrait*, p. 117.

4 **"Have you dropped":** Margaret (Daisy) Suckley, diary entry for April 12, 1945, in Ward, *Closest Companion*, p. 418.

4 **"Please get":** Ibid.

5 **"Two or three":** Ibid., pp. 418–19.

5 **"Pupils of the eyes":** Bruenn, "Clinical Notes on the Illness and Death of President Franklin D. Roosevelt," p. 590.

5 **"Mike," Bruenn leveled:** Reilly, *Reilly of the White House*, p. 232.

5 **"His eyes":** William Hassett, diary entry for April 12, 1945, in Hassett, *Off the Record with F.D.R.*, p. 355.

5 **"The President":** James Paullin report, in McIntire, *White House Physician*, p. 242.

5 **"On examination":** Ibid.

6 **"Within five":** Ibid., pp. 242–43.
6 **"He said nothing":** Reilly, *Reilly of the White House*, p. 233.

PART I

7 **"It is still":** Roosevelt, "Address to Congress Reporting on the Yalta Conference," March 1, 1945, in Rosenman, *Public Papers and Addresses of Franklin D. Roosevelt*, p. 13:584.

Chapter 1

9 **"The untimely":** "Nation Mourns Death of President Roosevelt," editorial, *Vicksburg Evening Post*, April 14, 1945, p. 1.
9 **vice President:** Harry S. Truman, *The Memoirs of Harry S. Truman*, vol. 1, *Year of Decisions* (Garden City, New York: Doubleday, 1955), p. 4.
9 **Truman had distracted:** Harry Truman to Martha Ellen Truman and Mary Jane Truman, April 12, 1945, Box 19, Papers of Harry S. Truman Pertaining to Family, Business, and Personal Affairs, HSTL.
9 **A Texas Democrat:** Alfred Steinberger, *Sam Rayburn: A Biography* (New York: Hawthorn, 1975), p. 195.
10 **"Harry":** Robert J. Donovan, *Conflict and Crisis: The Presidency of Harry S. Truman, 1945–1948* (New York: W. W. Norton, 1977), p. 4.
10 **"This is the V.P.":** David McCullough, *Truman* (New York: Simon & Schuster, 1992), p. 341.
10 **"Please come":** Truman, *Year of Decisions,* p. 4.
10 **"Jesus Christ":** Donovan, *Conflict and Crisis*, p. 4.
10 **"Steve Early wants":** Ibid.
10 **Truman sprinted:** Truman, *Year of Decisions,* p. 4; Harry Truman, diary entry for April 12, 1945, in Robert H. Ferrell, ed., *Off the Record: The Private Papers of Harry S. Truman* (New York: Harper & Row, 1980), p. 15.
10 **Truman arrived:** McCullough, *Truman*, p. 342.
11 **"Harry," she said:** Truman, *Year of Decisions,* p. 5.
11 **"It was the only":** Harry Truman to Martha Ellen Truman and Mary Jane Truman, April 16, 1945, Box 19, Papers of Harry S. Truman Pertaining to Family, Business, and Personal Affairs, HSTL.
11 **"Is there anything":** Truman, *Year of Decisions,* p. 5.
11 **A knock on the door:** Ibid., p. 6; Donovan, *Conflict and Crisis*, p. 8.
11 **"I assured her":** Truman, *Year of Decisions*, p. 6.
11 **"Let me speak":** Margaret Truman with Margaret Cousins, *Souvenir: Margaret Truman's Own Story* (New York: McGraw-Hill, 1956), p. 83.
11 **"Bess":** Margaret Truman, *Bess W. Truman* (New York: Macmillan, 1986), p. 249.
12 **"Mother":** Truman, *Souvenir*, p. 84.
12 **"You'd better change":** Truman, *Bess Truman*, p. 250.
12 **"He looked":** Jonathan Daniels, "What I Learned About Washington," *Saturday Evening Post*, March 30, 1946, p. 9.
12 **"It was a very somber":** Henry Stimson, diary entry for April 12, 1945, HLSP.
12 **"If ever I have felt":** Truman, *Bess Truman*, p. 251.
13 **"I, Harry S. Truman":** McCullough, *Truman*, p. 347.
13 **"Give him":** Truman, *Souvenir*, p. 86.
13 **"So help":** Robert E. Ferrell, *Harry S. Truman: A Life* (Columbia: University of Missouri Press, 1994), p. 178.
13 **"After repeating":** C. P. Trussell, "Truman Is Sworn in the White House," *New York Times*, April 13, 1945, p. 1.

13 **"It was my":** Truman, *Year of Decisions*, p. 9.

13 **"I added":** Ibid., p. 10.

13 **"a most urgent":** Ibid.

13 **"Stimson told":** Ibid.

13 **At 7:40 p.m.:** White House Log, entry for April 12, 1945, Box 1, White House Chief Usher Files, HSTL; Truman, *Bess Truman*, p. 197.

14 **"For the time":** Trussell, "Truman Is Sworn in," p. 1; "Truman Goes Home and Bars Visitors After Taking Oath," *Washington Evening Star*, April 13, 1945, p. A6.

14 **Truman had not:** Truman, *Year of Decisions*, p. 13.

14 **"Be good":** Truman, *Bess Truman*, p. 253.

Chapter 2

15 **"The presidency":** "Roosevelt: Great Leader of This Century," editorial, *Austin American*, April 13, 1945, p. 4.

15 **The fifty-five-year-old:** Linda Lotridge Levin, *The Making of FDR: The Story of Stephen T. Early, America's First Modern Press Secretary* (Amherst, N.Y.: Prometheus, 2008), pp. 9–16.

15 **"This is the White House":** Asbell, *When F.D.R. Died*, pp. 76–80.

16 **In New York:** Meyer Berger, "City Is Stunned by News of Death," *New York Times*, April 13, 1945, p. 10.

16 **"The president's dead":** Ibid.

16 **"I have a terrible":** Ibid.

16 **People flooded:** John R. Bell, "Stunned Silence First Reaction of St. Louisans," *St. Louis Post-Dispatch*, April 13, 1945, p. 1.

16 **Church bells:** "Hyde Park's Church Bells Give the News," *New York Times*, April 13, 1945, p. 3.

17 **"Lady":** "City Staggered by Death News," *Spokesman-Review*, April 13, 1945, p. 1.

17 **The lowering:** Edwin A. Lahey, "News on Every Tongue Stuns Nation's Capital," *Detroit Free Press*, April 13, 1945, p. 10.

17 **As the afternoon sun:** "Death of President Leaves D.C. Residents Grave and Quiet," *Washington Evening Star*, April 13, 1945, p. A9.

17 **By mid-evening:** Dewey L. Fleming, "Roosevelt Dies at Warm Springs; Truman Takes Oath as President," *Sun*, April 13, 1945, p. 1.

17 **The *Washington Evening Star*:** "Star Staff Rushes Four Extras to Throng of Late Shoppers," *Washington Evening Star*, April 13, 1945, p. 8.

17 **Residents jammed:** "News Stuns City," *Kansas City Times*, April 13, 1945, p. 1.

17 **The call volume:** "Phone Lines Here Tied Up Half Hour by Flood of Calls," *St. Louis Post-Dispatch*, April 13, 1945, p. 3A.

17 **The same occurred:** "Death of President Leaves D.C. Residents Grave and Quiet," *Washington Evening Star*, April 13, 1945, p. A9.

17 **The four major:** "Radio Networks Cancel Commercial Programs," *New York Times*, April 13, 1945, p. 10.

17 **The Yankees:** "Yankee-Dodger Game Off," *New York Times*, April 13, 1945, p. 20.

17 **The New York:** "Philharmonic Cancels 2d Concert in History," *New York Times*, April 13, 1945, p. 8.

17 **Those few revelers:** "Grief-Stricken Miami Halts All Merriment," *Miami Herald*, April 13, 1945, p. 1.

17 **"Ordinary street":** "President's Death Stuns Shenandoah," *Evening Herald*, April 12, 1945, p. 1.

18 **Interviewees equated:** Bob Mahon, "Local Citizens Express Shock Over Sudden Death of Roosevelt," *Jackson Sun*, April 13, 1945, p. 1; "Citizens of Greenwood Mourn for President They Call 'Like a Friend," *Index-Journal*, April 13, 1945, p. 5.

18 **"He was the greatest":** "People Stunned by News, Find It 'Hard to Take,'" *Philadelphia Inquirer*, April 13, 1945, p. 8.

18 **"I am completely":** Ibid.

18 **World leaders:** "Leaders of All Nations Shocked by Sudden Death of Roosevelt," *Knoxville News-Sentinel*, April 13, 1945, p. 11.

18 **"I am too shocked":** Frederick R. Barkley, "Shock, Disbelief Echo in Congress," *New York Times*, April 13, 1945, p. 4.

18 **"His name":** "Chiang, the Pope and De Gaulle Join in Messages from Abroad," *St. Louis Post-Dispatch*, April 13, 1945, p. 1.

18 **As telegrams flooded:** "Thousands of Wires of Sympathy Pour into White House from Persons in All Walks of Life," *St. Louis Post-Dispatch*, April 13, 1945, p. 1.

18 **"The greatest American":** "Franklin Delano Roosevelt," editorial, *Chippewa Herald-Telegram*, April 13, 1945, p. 1.

18 **"Something incalculably great":** "Digest of Press Comment," *Washington Evening Star*, April 13, 1945, p. A10.

18 **"His death comes":** "A Voice the World Needed Is Stilled," editorial, *Atlanta Constitution*, April 13, 1945, p. 10.

19 **"Today a great weight":** "Roosevelt Dies," editorial, *Chico Enterprise*, April 13, 1945, p 8.

Chapter 3

20 **"A dazed":** Jack Bell, "Truman Faces Crisis Unprepared," *Jersey Journal*, April 13, 1945, p. 1.

21 **He was born:** Ferrell, *Harry S. Truman*, pp. 1–21; McCullough, *Truman*, pp. 37–65.

21 **"To tell the truth":** McCullough, *Truman*, p. 45.

21 **"My debt":** Truman, *Year of Decisions*, p. 119.

21 **"There must":** Ibid., p. 121.

22 **"This procedure":** Ibid., p. 122.

22 **After graduation:** Ibid.

22 **His father:** McCullough, *Truman*, p. 66.

22 **Over the next:** Ibid., pp. 67–73; Ferrell, *Harry S. Truman*, pp. 25–36.

22 **"I learned:** Truman, *Year of Decisions*, p. 123.

22 **"Truman's all right":** Harry Truman, interview by Jonathan Daniels, July 28, 1948, in Research Notes Used in Connection with Writing *The Man of Independence*, Part I, Notes on Interviews, Box 1, Jonathan Daniels Papers, HSTL.

22 **"All I got":** "The President's News Conference of Sept. 8, 1949," in *Public Papers of the Presidents of the United States: Harry S. Truman, Containing the public Messages, Speeches, and Statements of the President, January 1 to December 31, 1949* (Washington, D.C.: U.S Government Printing Office, 1964), p. 472.

22 **"Every citizen":** Robert H. Ferrell, *The Autobiography of Harry S. Truman* (Columbia: University of Missouri Press, 1980), p. 27.

22 **"Harry," she admonished:** Ferrell, *Harry S. Truman*, p. 35.

22 **Truman's father:** Ferrell, *Harry S. Truman*, pp. 33–52; McCullough, *Truman*, pp. 73–96.

23 **As one year:** Ferrell, *Autobiography of Truman*, pp. 27–37; Many of the details here are drawn from Harry Truman's extensive letters to Bess Wallace during the years he lived on the farm.

23 **"Riding one":** Ferrell, *Autobiography of Truman*, p. 30.

24 **"I thought":** Truman, *Bess Truman*, p. 10.
24 **"Come in":** Ferrell, *Harry S. Truman*, p. 50.
24 **"My very best":** Harry Truman to Bess Wallace, April 1, 1911, Box 1, Papers of Harry S. Truman Pertaining to Family, Business, and Personal Affairs, HSTL.
24 **"A two-hundred-pound":** Harry Truman to Bess Wallace, September 10, 1912, Box 2, ibid.
24 **"I do hope":** Harry Truman to Bess Wallace, November 28, 1911, Box 1, ibid.
24 **"Would you":** Harry Truman to Bess Wallace, June 22, 1911, ibid.
25 **"I never":** Harry Truman to Bess Wallace, July 12, 1911, ibid.
25 **"I've always said":** Harry Truman to Bess Wallace, November 4, 1913, Box 3, ibid.
25 **"I am half worried":** Harry Truman to Bess Wallace, September 8, 1944, Box 2, ibid.
25 **"I was with him":** Jonathan Daniels, *The Man of Independence* (New York: J.B. Lippincott, 1950), p. 74.
25 **"I've been":** Harry Truman to Bess Wallace, ca. November (no day listed) 1914, Box 3, Papers of Harry S. Truman Pertaining to Family, Business, and Personal Affairs, HSTL.
25 **Along with:** Ferrell, *Harry S. Truman*, pp. 52–55; McCullough, *Truman*, pp. 96–101.
25 **"In six months":** Harry Truman to Bess Wallace, March 5, 1916, Box 4, Papers of Harry S. Truman Pertaining to Family, Business, and Personal Affairs, HSTL.
25 **"We are going":** Harry Truman to Bess Wallace, April 16, 1916, ibid.
25 **"I shall join":** Harry Truman to Bess Wallace, May 19, 1916, ibid.
26 **"I have been":** Harry Truman to Bess Wallace, September 7, 1916, ibid.
26 **"I seem":** Harry Truman to Bess Wallace, May 28, 1917, ibid.
26 **"I believe that the great":** Ferrell, *Autobiography of Truman*, p. 41.
26 **"Maybe a little":** Harry Truman to Bess Wallace, July 14, 1917, Box 4, Papers of Harry S. Truman Pertaining to Family, Business, and Personal Affairs, HSTL.
26 **"Bess":** Ibid.
26 **On September 26, 1917:** Ferrell, *Harry S. Truman*, pp. 56–71; McCullough, *Truman*, pp. 102–40.
27 **"The canteen":** Harry Truman to Bess Wallace, October 14, 1917, Box 4, Papers of Harry S. Truman Pertaining to Family, Business, and Personal Affairs, HSTL.
27 **"There we were":** Ferrell, *Autobiography of Truman*, p. 45.
27 **"The sunsets":** Harry Truman to Bess Wallace, April 13, 1918, Box 4, Papers of Harry S. Truman Pertaining to Family, Business, and Personal Affairs, HSTL.
27 **"We'll all be":** Harry Truman to Bess Wallace, May 19, 1918, ibid.
27 **"It's a shame":** Harry Truman to Bess Wallace, April 23, 1918, ibid.
27 **"Harry," he asked:** Ferrell, *Autobiography of Truman*, p. 46.
28 **"I've been very":** Ibid.
28 **"If I can only":** Harry Truman to Bess Wallace, July 14, 1918, Box 5, Papers of Harry S. Truman Pertaining to Family, Business, and Personal Affairs, HSTL.
28 **"Dismissed":** G. M. Giangreco, *The Soldier from Independence: A Military Biography of Harry Truman* (Minneapolis: Zenith Press, 2009), p. 95.
28 **To his horror:** Ibid., pp. 95–96.
28 **"I didn't come":** Daniels, *Man of Independence*, p. 95.
28 **"You soldier":** McCullough, *Truman*, p. 118.
28 **"You have no":** Harry Truman to Bess Wallace, July 14, 1918, Box 5, Papers of Harry S. Truman Pertaining to Family, Business, and Personal Affairs, HSTL.
28 **"I have had":** Harry Truman to Bess Wallace, October 6, 1918, ibid.
28 **"You've got":** Harry Truman to Bess Wallace, August 13, 1918, Box 5, Papers of Harry S. Truman Pertaining to Family, Business, and Personal Affairs, HSTL.
29 **"We have a captain":** Giangreco, *Soldier from Independence*, p. 142.

29 **"Every night":** Floyd T. Rickets, oral history interview by James R. Fuchs, March 24, 1970, HSTL.

29 **"Dear Harry":** McCullough, *Truman*, p. 116.

29 **"This was a heartbreaking":** "Handwritten Account of Activities of Battery D, 129th Field Artillery," undated, Box 33, Papers of Harry S. Truman Pertaining to Family, Business, and Personal Affairs, HSTL.

29 **Three days later:** Ibid.; Giangreco, *Soldier from Independence*, p. 167.

29 **"It was one":** "Handwritten Account of Activities of Battery D," undated.

29 **"The distance":** Giangreco, *Soldier from Independence*, p. 179.

29 **"One or two":** Ibid., p. 181.

30 **"Go ahead!":** Ferrell, *Harry S. Truman*, p. 67.

30 **"If I ever":** Harry Truman to Bess Wallace, November 1, 1918, Box 5, Papers of Harry S. Truman Pertaining to Family, Business, and Personal Affairs, HSTL.

30 **"The silence":** Truman, *Year of Decisions*, p. 131.

31 **"Captain Harry":** Giangreco, *Soldier from Independence*, p. 257.

31 **"The view":** Harry Truman to Bess Wallace, November 29, 1918, Box 5, Papers of Harry S. Truman Pertaining to Family, Business, and Personal Affairs, HSTL.

31 **"You've got no idea":** Harry Truman to Bess Wallace, January 11, 1919, Box 6, ibid.

31 **"Every day":** Harry Truman to Bess Wallace, January 12, 1919, ibid.

31 **"I've never seen":** Harry Truman to Bess Wallace, April 24, 1919, ibid.

31 **"Please get ready":** Harry Truman to Bess Wallace, February 18, 1919, Ibid.

32 **He teamed up:** Ferrell, *Harry S. Truman*, pp. 72–90; McCullough, *Truman*, pp. 141–51.

32 **"We were":** Truman, *Year of Decisions*, p. 134.

32 **"This was":** Ibid., p. 136.

32 **The Pendergast:** Ferrell, *Harry S. Truman*, pp. 91–176; McCullough, *Truman*, pp. 151–342.

33 **"I want men":** Daniels, *Man of Independence*, p. 142.

33 **"I became":** Truman, *Year of Decisions*, p. 138.

33 **"I was taught":** Wes Cook, "From Farm to the Presidency, Truman Was Called Firm, Fair," *Winston-Salem Journal*, May 9, 1980, p. 8.

33 **He was, in many ways:** Ferrell, *Harry S. Truman*, pp. 178–83; McCullough, *Truman*, pp. 141–42.

33 **"He had been":** McCullough, *Truman*, p. 141.

34 **"Tomorrow, I'll be":** Harry Truman to Bess Truman, May 7, 1933, Box 7, Papers of Harry S. Truman Pertaining to Family, Business, and Personal Affairs, HSTL.

34 **"I don't think":** McCullough, *Truman*, p. 204.

34 **"I went from town":** Ferrell, *Harry S. Truman*, pp. 128–29.

34 **"I was as timid":** Truman, *Year of Decisions*, p. 142.

35 **"The appointment":** Ferrell, *Harry S. Truman*, p. 133.

35 **"Harry, don't start":** Truman, *Year of Decisions*, p. 144.

35 **"I'm here":** Ferrell, *Harry S. Truman*, p. 147.

36 **"Tell them":** McCullough, *Truman*, p. 241.

36 **"In addition":** Truman, *Year of Decisions*, p. 159.

36 **"There is no":** McCullough, *Truman*, p. 244.

36 **"I went into seventy-five":** Truman, *Year of Decisions*, p. 161.

36 **"I always made":** Ibid.

37 **"I was still":** Ibid., p. 162.

37 **"Senator":** "Rear Platform and Other Informal Remarks in Illinois, Iowa, and Nebraska," May 8, 1950, in *Public Papers of the Presidents of the United States: Harry S. Truman, Containing the public Messages, Speeches, and Statements of the President, January 1 to December 31, 1950* (Washington, D.C.: U.S Government Printing Office, 1965), p. 307.

37 **"He was right":** Ferrell, *Autobiography of Truman*, p. 75.
37 **"Why don't you":** Ferrell, *Harry S. Truman*, p. 156.
38 **"I consider public":** Harry Truman remarks, *Congressional Record*, 77th Cong., 1st sess., February 10, 1941, p. 837.
38 **"We were interested":** Truman, *Year of Decisions*, p. 167.
38 **"There is no substitute":** Ibid., p. 168.
38 **"We were not":** Ibid.
38 **"In all":** Ibid., p. 186.
39 **"Now that's a matter":** "Telephone Conversation Between the Secretary of War and Senator Truman, June 17, 1943," Box 2, Atomic Bomb Collection, HSTL.
39 **"God-awful":** Ferrell, *Harry S. Truman*, p. 162.
40 **"Every effort":** Ferrell, *Autobiography of Truman*, p. 87.
40 **"Hell," he confided:** McCullough, *Truman*, p. 308.
40 **"I have been":** Ibid., p. 310.
40 **"coolest and cruelest":** Ibid.
40 **"kiss-of-death":** Ferrell, *Harry S. Truman*, p. 167.
41 **"Go all out":** Ibid., p. 168.
41 **"Are you my friend?":** Tom L. Evans, oral history by James R. Fuchs, June 13, 1963, HSTL.
41 **"Why, that's":** Ibid.
41 **"Lord," he said:** Ibid.
41 **"Bob":** Truman, *Year of Decisions*, p. 192.
41 **"To say":** Ferrell, *Autobiography of Truman*, p. 90.
41 **"Well, if that":** Ibid.
42 **"We want Wallace!":** "Texas Furnishes the Fireworks," *New York Times*, July 21, 1944, p. 12.
42 **"That really was the spark":** "Sen. Truman No. 2 Demo," *Sacramento Union*, July 22, 1944, p. 1.
42 **"The stampede":** "Second Place Race Sets Session Afire," *New York Times*, July 22, 1944, p. 8.
42 **"You don't know":** "2nd Ballot Decides," *New York Times*, July 22, 1944, p. 1.
42 **"I knew that boy":** "Truman of Missouri," *Life*, August 21, 1944, p. 75.
43 **"Who the hell":** William Leahy, interview by Jonathan Daniels, August 31, 1949, in Research Notes Used in Connection with Writing *The Man of Independence*, Part I, Notes on Interviews, Box 1, Jonathan Daniels Papers, HSTL.
43 **"Truman is a first-rate":** "Columbus Editorial Comment on Truman," editorial, *Daily Sentinel-Tribune*, July 24, 1944, p. 1.
43 **"Truman emerges":** "The Missouri Compromise," editorial, *Pittsburgh Post-Gazette*, July 22, 1944, p. 6.
43 **"However much":** "The Truman Nomination," editorial, *St. Louis Post-Dispatch*, July 22, 1944, p. 4A.
43 **"colorless":** Bill Cunningham, "Demos May Win Fall Ballot on Momentum," *Seattle Star*, July 28, 1944, p. 4.
43 **"The assumption":** "Exit Mr. Wallace," editorial, *Washington Evening Star*, July 22, 1944, A6.
43 **"Harry, I'm not":** Ferrell, *Harry S. Truman*, p. 172.
44 **"It doesn't seem":** Harry H. Vaughan, oral history with Charles T. Morrissey, January 16, 1963, HSTL.
44 **"Turn around":** Daniels, *Man of Independence*, p. 255.

Chapter 4

45 **"We all now":** "Franklin Delano Roosevelt," editorial, *Birmingham Age-Herald*, April 13, 1945, p. 1.

45 **Truman rose:** Truman, *Year of Decisions*, p. 13.

45 **"Come on":** Ernest B. Vaccaro, "Truman Gives Reporter Lift, Asks Him to Say He'd Like to Have His Door Open to Every One," *Washington Evening Star*, April 13, 1945, p. 1.

45 **"There have been":** McCullough, *Truman*, p. 352.

45 **"I'm going to miss":** Vaccaro, "Truman Gives Reporter Lift," p. 1.

38 **The staff:** Truman, *Year of Decisions*, p. 13.

46 **"It seemed still":** Daniels, *Man of Independence*, p. 27.

46 **"absolutely urgent":** Franklin Roosevelt to Harry Truman, memorandum, January 22, 1945, Box 274, President's Secretary's Files, HSTL.

46 **When he returned:** McCullough, *Truman*, p. 333; Daniels, *Man of Independence*, p. 259.

46 **"We in the State":** Charles E. Bohlen, *Witness to History, 1929–1969* (New York: W. W. Norton, 1973), p. 212.

46 **"One cannot yet":** William Leahy, diary entry for April 12, 1945, William D. Leahy Papers, LOC.

47 **"I'm not big":** Donovan, *Conflict and Crisis*, p. 15.

47 **At 10:15 a.m.:** Harry Truman, diary entry for April 13, 1945, in Ferrell, *Off the Record*, p. 17; Truman, *Year of Decisions*, pp. 14–17.

47 **"Take as long":** Edward Stettinius, diary entry for April 13, 1945, in Thomas M. Campbell and George C. Herring, eds., *The Diaries of Edward R. Stettinius, Jr., 1943–1946* (New York: New Viewpoints, 1975), p. 317.

47 **"The President," Hopkins added:** Daniels, *Man of Independence*, p. 259.

47 **"I have decided":** Edward Stettinius, diary entry for April 13, 1945, in Campbell and Herring, *Diaries of Stettinius*, p. 317.

48 **"He gave me":** Ibid., p. 318.

48 **"Do you wish":** Ibid.

48 **"I knew":** Truman, *Year of Decisions*, p. 17.

48 **"God alone":** Edward Murrow, "Buchenwald," *Evening Standard*, April 16, 1945, p. 3.

48 **Headlines that morning:** W. H. Lawrence, "Our Okinawa Guns Down 118 Planes," *New York Times*, April 13, 1945, p. 1; Philip S. Heisler, "U.S. Destroyer Sunk by Jap Suicide Bomber," *Evening Sun*, April 13, 1945, p. 4.

48 **"I saw men":** Philip S. Heisler, "Heisler Describes Jap Suicide Planes' Hits on His Warship," *Evening Sun*, April 13, 1945, p. 1.

49 **"He was confident":** William D. Leahy, *I Was There* (New York: McGraw-Hill, 1950), p. 347.

49 **"He made the impression":** Henry Stimson, diary entry for April 13, 1945, HLSP.

49 **"We shall not":** Ibid.

49 **The sixty-nine-year-old:** William Craig, *The Fall of Japan* (New York: Penguin, 1967), p. 124.

49 **"Are you sure":** Truman, *Year of Decisions*, p. 18.

50 **"It was his instinct":** Allen Drury, diary entry for April 13, 1945, in Allen Drury, *A Senate Journal, 1943–1945* (New York: McGraw-Hill, 1963), p. 412.

50 **"There is a governmental":** Frank McNaughton to Donald Bermingham, "Truman—The White House and Congress," April 14, 1945, Box 8, Frank McNaughton Papers, HSTL.

50 **"In this critical":** Ibid.

50 **"This was probably":** Ibid.

50 **"He's one of us":** Ibid.

50 **In Secretary of the Senate:** Truman, *Year of Decisions*, pp. 18–19; Harry Truman, diary entry for April 13, 1945, in Ferrell, *Off the Record*, p. 17; McCullough, *Truman*, p. 353.

50 **"Harry," one senator said:** Truman, *Year of Decisions*, p. 19.

51 **"terrible":** Frank McNaughton to Donald Bermingham, "Truman—The White House and Congress," April 14, 1945.

51 **"There will be":** Ibid.

51 **"Truman will not":** Ibid.

51 **"Truman is a good":** Ibid.

51 **"Well, isn't this":** Allen Drury, diary entry for April 13, 1945, in Drury, *Senate Journal*, p. 413.

51 **"Boys":** Truman, *Year of Decisions*, p. 19.

Chapter 5

52 **"All this very":** William Hassett Diary, entry for April 16, 1945, in Hassett, *Off the Record with F.D.R.*, p. 347.

52 **The funeral train:** Smith, *Thank You, Mr. President*, pp. 194–97; D. Harold Oliver, "Thousands Line Procession Route in Silent Homage to President," *Harrisburg Telegraph*, April 14, 1945, p. 1; "'Goin' Home,'" *Newsweek*, April 23, 1945, p. 29.

52 **"Everywhere":** William Hassett Diary, entry for April 13, 1945, in Hassett, *Off the Record with F.D.R.*, p. 340.

52 **Truman stood:** Truman, *Year of Decisions*, p. 29.

52 **A military-led procession:** "Schedule of Ceremonies," April 13, 1945, Box 1, William M. Rigdon Papers, HSTL. See also William Hassett, diary entry for April 14, 1945, in Hassett, *Off the Record with F.D.R.*, p. 341.

53 **That figure was soon dwarfed:** William S. White, "500,000 In Capital View Final March," *New York Times*, April 15, 1945, p. 1; Robert C. Albright, "500,000 Line Capital Streets to Bid Roosevelt Farewell," *Washington Post*, April 15, 1945, p. M1; Louis Lyons, "Roosevelt Goes Home," *Boston Globe*, April 15, 1945, p. D1; "Funeral Crowds Break Thru Line," *Washington Daily News*, April 14, 1945, p. 3.

53 **"I shall never":** Truman, *Year of Decisions*, p. 30.

53 **The procession:** "Many Weep Openly as Caisson Carrying Roosevelt Goes By," *Washington Evening Star*, April 14, 1945, p. 1.

53 **Body bearers placed:** Frank Kluckhorn, "Rites at Capital," *New York Times*, April 15, 1945, p. 1; Robert Klara, *FDR's Funeral Train: A Betrayed Widow, a Soviet Spy, and a Presidency in the Balance* (New York: Palgrave Macmillan, 2010), pp. 78–79.

53 **"On one side":** Tom Reedy, "The Funeral," in Donald Porter Geddes, *Franklin Delano Roosevelt: A Memorial* (New York: Pocket Books, 1945), p. 131.

53 **"He looked younger":** "Many Weep Openly."

54 **"Can you dispense":** J. B. West with Mary Lynn Kotz, *Upstairs at the White House: My Life with the First Ladies* (New York: Coward, McCann & Geoghegan, 1973), p. 56.

54 **"Please don't let":** Ibid.

54 **"She straightened":** Ibid.

54 **"Every man":** Walter Brown, "Back to Washington," undated, Box 68, WJBP.

54 **At four p.m.:** William Hassett, diary entry for April 14, 1945, in Hassett, *Off the Record with F.D.R.*, p. 342.

55 **"The only thing we have":** Kluckhorn, "Rites at Capital."

55 **A crowd:** Eben Ayers, diary entry for April 13–14, 1945, in Eben A. Ayers, *Truman in the White House: The Diary of Eben A. Ayers*, ed. Robert H. Ferrell (Columbia: University of Missouri Press, 1991), p. 9.

55 **At ten a.m. on a cool:** Christine Sadler, "Roosevelt's Body Laid to Rest in Garden of His Birthplace," *Washington Post*, April 16, 1945, p. 1; Frank L. Kluckhohn, "Grave Is Garden," *New York Times*, April 16, 1945, p. 1.

55 **"One by one":** William Hassett, diary entry for April 15, 1945, in Hassett, *Off the Record with F.D.R.*, p. 344.

55 **"We commit":** Kluckhohn, "Grave Is Garden."

56 **"Back in Washington":** Truman, *Year of Decisions*, pp. 36–37.

Chapter 6

57 **"Tragic fate":** Harry Truman, "Address of the President to the Joint Session of the Congress," April 16, 1945, Box 1, White House Official Reporter Files, HSTL.

57 **The Oval Office:** Daily Appointments of Harry Truman, April 16–20, 1945, HSTL; Truman, *Year of Decisions*, pp. 53–67.

57 **"Everyone, including Truman":** Daniels, *Man of Independence*, p. 263.

57 **Outside work:** Truman, *Year of Decisions*, pp. 27, 42–45.

57 **"I haven't been elected":** Michael D. Pearlman, *Unconditional Surrender, Demobilization, and the Atomic Bomb* (Fort Leavenworth, Kan.: U.S. Army Command and General Staff College, 1996), p. 15.

58 **Hopkins had lost:** Joseph P. Lash, *Dealers and Dreamers: A New Look at the New Deal* (New York: Doubleday, 1988), p. 364.

58 **"strange gnome-like":** Joseph Stillwell, diary entry for February 9, 1942, in Joseph W. Stilwell, *The Stilwell Papers*, ed. Theodore H. White (New York: William Sloane Associates, 1948), p. 36.

58 **"cadaverous":** Truman, *Year of Decisions*, p. 31.

58 **"How do you feel":** Ibid.

58 **"Stettinius," Truman once said:** Harry Truman, interview by Jonathan Daniels, November 12, 1949, in Research Notes Used in Connection with Writing *The Man of Independence*, Part I, Notes on Interviews, Box 1, Jonathan Daniels Papers, HSTL.

58 **"It was my feeling":** Truman, *Year of Decisions*, pp. 22–23.

59 **"an expert wire puller":** Frank McNaughton to Donald Bermingham, "Truman—The White House and Congress," April 14, 1945, Box 8, Frank McNaughton Papers, HSTL.

59 **The bald and slender:** David Robertson, *Sly and Able: A Political Biography of James F. Byrnes* (New York: W. W. Norton, 1994), p. 27.

59 **"In the back":** Walter Brown, "Back to Washington," undated, Box 68, WJBP.

59 **"able and conniving":** Harry Truman, diary entry for July 7, 1945, in Ferrell, *Off the Record*, p. 49.

59 **"All country":** Harry Truman, diary entry for July 7, 1945, in Ferrell, *Off the Record*, p. 49.

59 **"the most honest-looking":** Robertson, *Sly and Able*, p. 383.

59 **"Confusion and uncertainty":** Eben Ayers, diary entry for April 16, 1945, in Ayers, *Truman in the White House*, p. 10.

59 **"There seem":** Eben Ayers, diary entry for April 17, 1945, ibid., p. 11.

59 **"No, I need":** William Hassett, diary entry for April 16, 1945, in Hassett, *Off the Record with F.D.R.*, p. 346.

59 **"He had been":** Daniels, *Man of Independence*, p. 27.

60 **"Roosevelt's White House":** Joseph Alsop and Stewart Alsop, "Tragedy of Liberalism," *Life*, May 20, 1946, p. 72.

60 **He worked:** Harry Truman, diary entry for April 15, 1945, in Ferrell, *Off the Record*, p. 19; Truman, *Year of Decisions*, pp. 36–37.
60 **Dressed in a black:** Frank McNaughton to Donald Bermingham, "Add to the New Chief Speaks," April 16, 1945, Box 8, Frank McNaughton Papers, HSTL.
60 **"It was a neat":** Ibid.
60 **In his speech:** Truman, *Year of Decisions*, pp. 41–42; McCullough, *Truman*, p. 359.
60 **"generous and prolonged":** McNaughton to Bermingham, "Add to the New Chief Speaks."
60 **"So that there can":** Harry Truman, "Address of the President to the Joint Session of the Congress," April 16, 1945, Box 1, White House Official Reporter Files, HSTL.
60 **"Here was real sincerity":** McNaughton to Bermingham, "Add to the New Chief Speaks."
60 **"I liked what he said":** Ibid.
60 **"There's a real man":** Ibid.
61 **Roosevelt had held:** Truman, *Year of Decisions*, pp. 47–49.
61 **A record 348:** Ben W. Gilbert, "Truman Charts Policy at First Press Confab," *Washington Post*, April 18, 1945, p. 1.
61 **"All in":** "Press and Radio Conference #1 of President Harry S. Truman," April 17, 1945, Box 6, White House Official Reporter Files, HSTL.
61 **"Some of these":** Truman, *Year of Decisions*, p. 49.
61 **"One gathered":** Mark Sullivan, "Mr. Truman's Debut," *Washington Post*, April 18, 1945, p. 6.
61 **"The new president":** Eben Ayers, diary entry for April 17, 1945, in Ayers, *Truman in the White House*, p. 11.
62 **"As a veteran":** "Broadcast to the Armed Forces at Home and Abroad," April 17, 1945, Box 6, White House Official Reporter Files, HSTL.
62 **The son:** Murrey Marder, "W. Averell Harriman Dead at 94," *Washington Post*, July 27, 1986, p. A1; James Roach, "Harriman a Star on Sports Fields," *New York Times*, November 23, 1954, p 37; Judd Tully, "Harriman Art: Sold!" *Washington Post*, May 12, 1995, p. B2.
62 **"barbarian invasion":** W. Averell Harriman and Elie Abel, *Special Envoy to Churchill and Stalin, 1941–1946* (New York: Random House, 1975), p. 448.
62 **"For this reason":** Ibid., p. 447.
63 **"The Russians":** Truman, *Year of Decisions*, p. 71.
63 **"The question":** "Special Information for the President," April 13, 1945, ibid., p. 15.
63 **"Without Russia":** Truman, *Year of Decisions*, p. 72.
64 **"I intend":** Ibid.
64 **"Frankly," he began:** Ibid.
64 **"cannonball":** Winston Churchill, *The Gathering Storm* (Boston: Houghton Mifflin, 1948), p. 368.
64 **As a young man:** Raymond H. Anderson, "A Lifetime of History," *New York Times*, November 11, 1986, p. A1.
65 **"Iron Pants":** Dusko Doder, "Molotov, 'Mr. Iron Pants,' Rehabilitated by Soviets at 94," *Washington Post*, July 6, 1984, p. A21.
65 **"Molotov is a hard":** John McCloy, diary entry for May 4, 1945, JJMP.
65 **"verbal adroitness":** Churchill, *Gathering Storm*, p. 368.
65 **"I have never seen":** Ibid.
65 **"Truman then offered":** Harriman and Abel, *Special Envoy to Churchill and Stalin*, p. 451.
65 **"Molotov clung":** Ibid.
65 **At two p.m. on April 23:** Truman, *Year of Decisions*, pp. 77–79.
65 **"Overnight the atmosphere":** Ibid., p. 77.

66 **"It was," Truman declared:** Harriman and Abel, *Special Envoy to Churchill and Stalin*, p. 452.

66 **"The United States":** Truman, *Year of Decisions*, p. 80.

67 **"language that was":** Leahy, *I Was There*, p. 352.

67 **"What kind":** Albert Resis, ed., *Molotov Remembers: Inside Kremlin Politics: Conversations with Felix Chuev* (Chicago: Ivan R. Dee, 1993), p. 55.

67 **"but I wanted:** Truman, *Year of Decisions*, p. 82.

67 **"I have never":** Ibid.

Chapter 7

68 **"My chief purpose":** Henry L. Stimson, "The Decision to Use the Atomic Bomb," *Harper's Magazine* 194, no. 1161 (February 1945), p. 106.

68 **"I think":** Henry Stimson to Harry Truman, April 24, 1945, Box 28, Confidential File, Papers of Harry S. Truman, HSTL.

68 **The seventy-seven-year-old:** Godfrey Hodgson, *The Colonel: The Life and Wars of Henry Stimson, 1867–1950* (New York: Alfred A. Knopf, 1990), pp. 5–341.

69 **"The profession":** Henry L. Stimson and McGeorge Bundy, *On Active Service in Peace and War* (New York: Harper & Brothers, 1947), p. 17.

69 **"He was a man":** John McCloy to Priscilla Roberts, November 10, 1982, Box 1, Atomic Bomb Collection, HSTL.

69 **"It's the last shots":** "Democracy Can Win over Dictatorship, Stimson Declares," *Washington Evening Star*, December 11, 1941, p. B5.

69 **The day after he took:** Truman, *Year of Decisions*, p. 87.

69 **"Within four months":** Henry Stimson, "Memorandum Discussed with the President, April 25, 1945," included with Henry Stimson diary entry, April 25, 1945, HLSP.

69 **"No other nation":** Ibid.

70 **"The world in its":** Ibid.

70 **"Our leadership":** Ibid.

70 **"All recommendations":** Ibid.

70 **"I listened":** Truman, *Year of Decision*, p. 87.

70 **"Oh, I know":** Robert S. Norris, *Racing for the Bomb: The True Story of General Leslie R. Groves, the Man Behind the Birth of the Atomic Age* (New York: Skyhorse, 2014), p. 375.

70 **The mustachioed general:** Ibid., pp. 2–197.

71 **"A very alert":** F.M.S. Johnson, Efficiency Report of Leslie R. Groves, June 30, 1922, in Leslie R. Groves, Official Military Personnel File (OMPF), National Personnel Record Center, St. Louis, Mo.

71 **"His work":** John E. Harris, Efficiency Report of Leslie R. Groves, January 31, 1925, ibid.

71 **"One of the most":** F. R. Wilby, Efficiency Report of Leslie R. Groves, June 6, 1935, ibid.

71 **"General Groves":** John Lansdale, Jr., "Military Service," unpublished memoir, 1987, p. 84, Wood Library–Museum of Anesthesiology, Schaumburg, Ill.

71 **"Even if you":** Norris, *Racing for the Bomb*, p. 352.

71 **The five-story:** Alfred Goldberg, *The Pentagon: The First Fifty Years* (Washington, D.C: U.S. Government Printing Office, 1992), pp. 1–89, 183–84; Lenore Fine and Jesse A. Remington, *The Corps of Engineers: Construction in the United States* (Washington, D.C: U.S. Government Printing Office, 1989), pp. 431–39; Janet A. McDonnell, "Constructing the Pentagon," in Barry W. Fowle, ed., *Builders and Fighters: U.S. Army Engineers in WWII* (Fort Belvoir, Va.: Office of History, United States Army Corps of Engineers,

1992), pp. 107–16; Janet Eads, "New Capital Complaint: 'Pentagon Feet'—Building Is So Large Workers Thinking of Portal-to-Portal Demand," *Fort Worth Star-Telegram*, July 11, 1943, p. 10.

72 **"It is doubtful":** Goldberg, *Pentagon*, p. 1.

72 **"With regard":** Norris, *Racing for the Bomb*, p. 188.

72 **"Why," he protested:** Len Giovannitti and Fred Freed, *The Decision to Drop the Bomb* (New York: Coward-McCann, 1965), p. 50.

72 **"Now I understand":** Harry Truman, interview by Jonathan Daniels, November 12, 1949, in Research Notes Used in Connection with Writing *The Man of Independence*, Part I, Notes on Interviews, Box 1, Jonathan Daniels Papers, HSTL.

73 **"As far as is known":** Leslie Groves to Secretary of War, "Atomic Fission Bombs," April 23, 1945, National Security Archive, George Washington University, Washington, D.C.

73 **"If our scientific":** Ibid.

73 **"Atomic energy," if controlled:** Ibid.

73 **"The president did not":** Leslie Groves Memo to Files, "Report of Meeting with the President," April 25, 1945," Microfilm Roll #3, CMED.

73 **"Mr. President," Groves asked:** Norris, *Racing for the Bomb*, p. 376.

73 **"Leonard":** Leonard Reinsch, oral history by James R. Fuchs, March 13, 1967, HSTL.

PART II

75 **"We were reaching":** War Department, Washington, D.C., Immediate Release, undated (ca. August 6, 1945), Box 167, President's Secretary's Files, HSTL.

Chapter 8

77 **"All during":** "Riley Had Job on Atomic Bomb," *Platteville Journal*, September 8, 1945, p. 2.

77 **Szilard stood:** William Lanouette with Bela Silard, *Genius in the Shadows: A Biography of Leo Szilard, the Man Behind the Bomb* (New York: Charles Scribner's Sons, 1992), pp. 32, 274, and 295.

78 **"Hitler and the Nazis":** Ibid., p. 112.

78 **"The news of fission":** Michael Kort, *The Columbia Guide to Hiroshima and the Bomb* (New York: Columbia University Press, 2007), p. 15.

79 **"It howled":** Lanouette, *Genius in the Shadows*, p. 84.

79 **"Let's give it up":** Robert Jungk, *Brighter Than a Thousand Suns: A Personal History of the Atomic Scientists*, trans. James Cleugh (New York: Harcourt Brace Jovanovich 1958), pp. 83–84.

79 **The famous physicist:** Ralph E. Lapp, "The Einstein Letter That Started It All," *New York Times*, August 2, 1964, p. 169.

79 **"I haven't thought":** Lanouette, *Genius in the Shadows*, p. 199.

79 **"The one thing":** Spencer R. Weart and Gertrude Weiss Szilard, eds., *Leo Szilard: His Version of the Facts: Selected Recollections and Correspondence* (Cambridge, Mass.: MIT Press, 1978), p. 83.

79 **"We didn't know our way":** Ibid., p. 84.

79 **"We did not know how":** Ibid.

80 **"A single bomb":** Albert Einstein to Franklin Roosevelt, August 2, 1939, Box 1, Atomic Bomb Collection, HSTL.

80 **"Alex":** Lanouette, *Genius in the Shadows*, p. 209.

80 **"This," he declared:** Alexander Sachs testimony, November 27, 1945, in U.S. Congress, Senate, *Hearings Before the Special Committee on Atomic Energy: A Resolution Creating a Special Committee to Investigate Problems Relating to the Development, Use, and Control*

of Atomic Energy, Part I, 79th Cong. 1st Sess., November 27, 1945 (Washington, D.C.: U.S. Government Printing Office, 1945), p. 9.

81 **The new body:** Leo Szilard to G. B. Pegram, October 21, 1939, in Weart and Szilard, *Leo Szilard*, pp. 109–10. For accounts of this meeting, see also Henry Smyth, *Atomic Energy for Military Purposes* (York, Penn.: Maple Press, 1945), pp. 47–48; Richard G. Hewlett and Oscar E. Anderson, Jr., *The New World: 1939–1946*, vol. 1, *A History of the United States Atomic Energy Commission* (University Park: Pennsylvania State University Press, 1962), p. 20.

81 **Szilard explained:** Lapp, "Einstein Letter That Started," p. 169; Leo Szilard to Lyman J. Briggs, Memorandum, "The Possibility of a Large-Scale Experiment in the Immediate Future," October 26, 1939, in Bernard T. Feld and Gertrud Weiss Szilard, eds., *The Collected Works of Leo Szilard: Scientific Papers* (Cambridge, Mass.: MIT Press, 1972), pp. 204–6.

81 **"In Aberdeen":** Edward Teller, *Energy from Heaven and Earth* (San Francisco: W.H. Freeman, 1979), pp. 144–45.

81 **"How much money":** Richard Rhodes, *The Making of the Atomic Bomb* (New York: Simon & Schuster 1986), p. 316.

81 **"For the first":** Teller, *Energy from Heaven and Earth*, p. 145.

81 **"All right, all right":** Rhodes, *Making of the Atomic Bomb*, p. 317.

81 **"If the reaction":** Alexander Sachs, Revised Statement, November 27, 1945, U.S. Congress, Senate, *Hearings Before the Special Committee on Atomic Energy: A Resolution Creating a Special Committee to Investigate Problems Relating to the Development, Use, and Control of Atomic Energy*, Part 5, 79th Cong. 2nd Sess., February 15, 1946 (Washington, D.C.: U.S. Government Printing Office, 1946), p. 560.

81 **Work limped:** Kort, *Columbia Guide to Hiroshima and the Bomb*, p. 17.

82 **"I knew":** McGeorge Bundy, *Danger and Survival: Choices About the Bomb in the First Fifty Years* (New York: Vintage, 1990), p. 40.

82 **Across the Atlantic:** Smyth, *Atomic Energy for Military Purposes*, p. 32.

82 **"The committee considers":** MAUD Committee, "Report on the Use of Uranium for a Bomb, Outline of Present Knowledge," March 1941, in Cynthia C. Kelly, ed., *The Manhattan Project: The Birth of the Atomic Bomb in the Words of the Creators, Eyewitnesses, and Historians* (New York: Tess Press, 2010), p. 55.

83 **"I had no illusion":** Vannevar Bush, *Pieces of the Action* (New York: William Morrow, 1970), p. 59.

83 **"I would feel":** Ibid., p. 60.

83 **The president created:** Arthur Holly Compton, *Atomic Quest: A Personal Narrative* (New York: Oxford University Press, 1956), pp. 53–59.

83 **Compton's seven-page:** Hewlett and Anderson, *New World*, pp. 45–49.

83 **"Adequate care":** Rhodes, *Making of the Atomic Bomb*, pp. 29.

84 **Rather than spend:** Groves, *Now It Can Be Told*, pp. 8–15; Hewlett and Anderson, *New World*, p. 71; Steve Olson, *The Apocalypse Factory: Plutonium and the Making of the Atomic Age* (New York: W. W. Norton, 2020), pp. 28–34.

84 **The Office of Scientific Research:** Bush, *Pieces of the Action*, p. 61; Norris, *Racing for the Bomb*, p. 168.

84 **Marshall's lack:** Kenneth D. Nichols, *The Road to Trinity* (New York: William Morrow, 1987), pp. 49–50.

84 **After more than:** Groves, *Now It Can Be Told*, p. 3.

85 **Domestic construction:** Fine and Remington, *Corps of Engineers*, p. 519.

85 **"The Secretary of War":** Groves, *Now It Can Be Told*, pp. 3–4.

85 **"The basic research":** Ibid., p. 4.

85 **"In short":** Ibid., p. 20.
86 **"I doubted":** Vannevar Bush to Harvey Bundy, September 17, 1942, ibid., pp. 20–21.
86 **"I was not happy":** Groves, *Now It Can Be Told*, p. 19.
86 **On September 19, 1942:** Ibid., p. 22.
86 **Groves strove:** Ibid., pp. 27–28.
86 **"Compartmentalization":** Ibid., p. 140.
87 **One of the largest:** Ibid., pp. 33–34.
87 **"As I told you":** Ibid., p. 35.
87 **"Colonel":** Ibid., p. 36.
87 **The 59,000-acre:** Charles W. Johnson and Charles O. Jackson, *City Behind a Fence: Oak Ridge, Tennessee, 1942–1946* (Knoxville: University of Tennessee Press, 1981), pp. 6–8.
87 **Groves liked:** MDH, bk. 1, vol. 10, pp. 1.3–1.4.
87 **"The only difference":** George O. Robinson, Jr., *The Oak Ridge Story: The Saga of a People Who Share in History* (Kingsport, Tenn.: Southern Publishers, 1950), p. 30.
87 **Crews broke ground:** War Department, Public Relations Division, "Background Material: The Town of Oak Ridge," August 2, 1946, Box 168, President's Secretary's Files, HSTL.
87 **an army of 110,000:** Robinson, *Oak Ridge Story*, p. 46.
88 **"Always we were driven":** Groves, *Now It Can Be Told*, p. 96.
88 **"The construction":** MDH, bk. 5, vol. 1, p. 2.4.
88 **Proof could be found:** Robinson, *Oak Ridge* Story, p. 77.
88 **Workers used 37,562,000 feet:** Ibid., p. 79.
88 **A shortage:** Ibid., p. 77; Groves, *Now It Can Be Told*, pp. 107–9; Nichols, *Road to Trinity*, pp. 42–43.
88 **The completed plant:** Robinson, *Oak Ridge Story*, pp. 84–85.
88 **"There's equipment":** "The Atomic City," *New Yorker*, September 29, 1945, p. 48.
88 **The gas diffusion plant:** Robinson, *Oak Ridge* Story, p. 59.
89 **The larger:** MDH, bk. 2, vol. 1, p. 2.5.
89 **The completed building:** Ibid.
89 **The U-shaped:** War Department, Oak Ridge Press Release, undated, Box 167, President's Secretary's Files, HSTL; Robinson, *Oak Ridge* Story, pp. 35, 79.
89 **The top-secret town:** Robinson, *Oak Ridge* Story, pp. 48–49.
89 **"To accommodate":** Nichols, *Road to Trinity*, p. 125.
89 **Construction proved perpetual:** Ibid., p. 127.
89 **"I knew something":** James Overholt, ed., *These Are Our Voices: The Story of Oak Ridge, 1942–1970* (Oak Ridge, Tenn.: Children's Museum of Oak Ridge, 1987), p. xv.
89 **"There was no":** Helen C. Jernigan, "Happy Valley," in Overholt, *These Are Our Voices*, p. 95.
90 **"Oak Ridge croup":** Joanne S. Gailar, "Impressions of Early Oak Ridge," ibid., p. 86.
90 **"Oak Ridge might":** Ibid., p. 87.
90 **leaders battled:** Overholt, *These Are Our Voices*, p. xvi.
90 **Workers would ultimately:** War Department, Public Relations Division, "Background Material: The Town of Oak Ridge," August 2, 1946, Box 168, President's Secretary's Files, HSTL; War Department, "M.E.D. Projects Lead to Townsite Growth," undated, Box 167, President's Secretary's Files, HSTL.
90 **"Oak Ridge," as Nichols observed:** K. D. Nichols, "My Work in Oak Ridge," in Overholt, *These Are Our Voices*, p. 116.
90 **"There was a touch":** Robinson, *Oak Ridge Story*, p. 60.
90 **A fleet of 840 buses:** War Department, "Background Material: The Town of Oak Ridge," August 2, 1946.
90 **Health care:** Robinson, *Oak Ridge Story*, p. 96.

90 **Doctors delivered:** Ibid., p. 65; War Department, "Background Material: The Town of Oak Ridge," August 2, 1946.

90 **The army constructed:** Johnson and Jackson, *City Behind a Fence*, p. 126.

90 **The first academic:** Robinson, *Oak Ridge Story*, p. 63.

90 **"The school system":** Nichols, *Road to Trinity*, p. 121.

90 **The nine businesses:** Johnson and Jackson, *City Behind a* Fence, p. 35.

90 **The town had:** Robinson, *Oak Ridge Story*, p. 95; War Department, "M.E.D. Projects Lead to Townsite Growth," undated, Box 167, President's Secretary's Files, HSTL.

90 **Beyond the basics:** Johnson and Jackson, *City Behind a Fence*, p. 92.

91 **"On my first visit":** Connie J. Green, "The Oak Ridge Library," in Overholt, *These Are Our Voices*, p. 171.

91 **Residents formed:** Robinson, *Oak Ridge Story*, p. 64.

91 **Locals could thumb:** Johnson and Jackson, *City Behind a* Fence, p. 123.

91 **Others organized:** Robinson, *Oak Ridge Story*, pp. 53, 179–81.

91 **"In the beginning":** Jacinta K. Howard, " 'Music Making' on the Ridge," in Overholt, *These Are Our Voices*, p. 156.

91 **"Segregation was total":** Valeria Steele, "A New Hope," in Overholt, *These Are Our Voices*, p. 200.

91 **"There was always":** "Riley Had Job on Atomic Bomb," *Platteville Journal*, September 8, 1945, p. 2.

91 **Work went on:** "The Atomic City," *New Yorker*, September 29, 1945, p. 48.

91 **"There was," wrote the head psychiatrist":** Eric Kent Clarke, "Psychiatry on a Shoestring," in Overholt, *These Are Our Voices*, p. 185.

91 **"Eventually all":** "Riley Had Job on Atomic Bomb," *Platteville Journal*, September 8, 1945, p. 2.

92 **Army officials:** MDH, bk. 4, vol. 3, p. 2.5.

92 **"This is it":** Olson, *Apocalypse Factory*, p. 2.

92 **"All right," the general relented:** Franklin Matthias, oral history by S. L. Sanger, September 12, 1986, S. L. Sanger Papers, 1984–2015, University of Washington Special Collections, Seattle.

92 **Groves inspected:** Groves, *Now It Can Be Told*, p. 74.

92 **Similar to Oak Ridge:** MDH, bk. 4, vol. 4, p. 2.

92 **"Most of the farms":** Groves, *Now It Can Be Told*, p. 75.

92 **"While I felt":** Ibid., p. 69.

92 **The army, via purchase:** MDH, bk. 4, vol. 4, pp. 2.2, 7.1.

92 **"It was a pretty hard":** S. L. Sanger, *Working on the Bomb: An Oral History of WWII Hanford* (Portland, Ore.: Continuing Education Press, 1995), p. 23.

93 **The plan called:** MDH, bk. 4, vol. 5, pp. 2.6–2.7.

93 **"The insensible":** Hewlett and Anderson, *New World*, p. 220.

93 **The heart:** Olson, *Apocalypse Factory*, p. 91.

93 **Each cubelike:** MDH, bk. 4, vol. 5, pp. 6.13–6.14.

93 **workers pumped:** MDH, bk. 4, vol. 3, p. 3.3.

93 **The three together:** Hewlett and Anderson, *New World*, p. 216.

93 **"This Swiss cheese":** H. W. Blakeslee, "Ovens Like Piles of Cheese Turn Uranium into Plutonium, Explosive Super-Bomb," *Rochester Democrat and Chronicle*, August 21, 1945, p. 9.

93 **Workers had to construct:** MDH, bk. 4, vol. 3, p. 3.5.

93 **"The building":** Hewlett and Anderson, *New World*, p. 220.

93 **Workers staked:** MHD, bk. 4, vol. 5, p. 6.12.

93 **Officials pulled:** Earl Pomeroy, "Community of 51,000, Feverishly Active, Dies," *Oregonian*, August 9, 1945, p. 8.

94 **"We had recruiters":** Sanger, *Working on the Bomb*, p. 110.
94 **Over the course:** MDH, bk. 4, vol. 5, p. 2.6.
94 **The force hit:** Sanger, *Working on the Bomb*, p. 68.
94 **The need:** Hewlett and Anderson, *New World*, p. 216.
94 **To house:** Sanger, *Working on the Bomb*, p. 68.
94 **"It was a depressing":** Ibid., p. 93
94 **"It was so damned":** Michele Gerber, "On the Home Front," in Kelly, *Manhattan Project*, p. 190.
94 **"Well, Rob":** Sanger, *Working on the Bomb*, p. 111.
94 **Temperatures swung:** MDH, bk. 4, vol. 5, p. 4.22.
94 **"Your face":** Gerber, "On the Home Front," in Kelly, *Manhattan Project*, p. 191.
94 **"There was a beer":** "Rowdy Hanford, 'Metropolis of Race Suicide,'" *Spokesman-Review*, January 27, 1946, p. 7.
95 **Many others got:** Sanger, *Working on the Bomb*, p. 96.
95 **"We had murders":** Ibid., p. 112.
95 **"When you have":** Ibid., p. 113.
95 **The community:** MDH, bk. 4, vol. 3, pp. 2.13–2.16, 8.3–8.23.
95 **"Those of us":** John M. Findlay and Bruce Hevly, "Nuclear Technologies and Nuclear Communities: A History of Hanford and the Tri-Cities, 1943–1993," February 1995, Center for the Study of the Pacific Northwest, Department of History, University of Washington, Seattle, p. 33.
95 **"We felt":** Ibid., p. 34.
95 **Just thirty-eight years old:** Kai Bird and Martin J. Sherwin, *American Prometheus: The Triumph and Tragedy of J. Robert Oppenheimer* (London: Atlantic Books, 2008), pp. 96, 210, 258, and 632.
96 **"Adding to my cause":** Groves, *Now It Can Be Told*, p. 61.
96 **"He couldn't run":** Luis W. Alvarez, *Adventures of a Physicist* (New York: Basic Books, 1987), p. 78.
96 **"I thought":** Groves, *Now It Can Be Told*, p. 61.
96 **"As before":** Ibid., p. 64.
96 **"My two great loves":** Bird and Sherwin, *American Prometheus*, p. 81.
96 **On November 16, 1942:** Groves, *Now It Can Be Told*, pp. 65–66.
96 **"This will never":** Edwin M. McMillan, "Early Days at Los Alamos," in Lawrence Badash, Joseph O. Hirschfelder, and Herbert P. Broida, eds., *Reminiscences of Los Alamos, 1943–1945* (Dordrecht, Holland: D. Reidel, 1980), p. 15.
96 **The Los Alamos:** MDH, bk. 8, vol. 1, p. 2.7. See also Los Alamos Historical Society, *When Los Alamos Was a Ranch School* (Los Alamos, N.M.: Los Alamos Historical Society, 1974).
97 **The school's notable:** John D. Wirth and Linda Harvey Aldrich, *Los Alamos: The Ranch School Year, 1917–1943* (Los Alamos: University of New Mexico Press, 2003), p. 81.
97 **"It was late afternoon":** McMillan, "Early Days at Los Alamos," in Badash et al., *Reminiscences of Los Alamos*, p. 15.
97 **"This," Groves declared:** Ibid.
97 **The army arranged:** MDH, bk. 8, vol. 1, p. 2.7.
97 **Since the federal:** Ibid., p. 2.3.
97 **"One of the deciding":** Ibid., p. 5.10.
97 **Workers built a power plant:** Ibid., p. 2.19.
97 **The ballooning population:** Ibid., pp. 6.3–6.4.
97 **"To control":** Alvarez, *Adventures of a Physicist*, p. 129.
97 **Laborers added:** MDH, bk. 8, vol. 1, pp. 6.33–6.35, 6.37–6.43.

98 **Residents could attend:** Ibid., pp. 6.55–6.56.

98 **A school system:** Ibid., p. 2.16.

98 **"Medical service":** Groves, *Now It Can Be Told*, p. 166.

98 **Scientists could hit:** George B. Kistiakowsky, "Reminiscences of Wartime Los Alamos," in Badash et al., *Reminiscences of Los Alamos*, p. 61.

98 **Other pursuits:** MDH, bk. 8, vol. 1, pp. 6.59–6.60, 6.66.

98 **"All civilian residents":** Ibid., p. 6.66.

98 **"Almost everyone":** "In the Matter of J. Robert Oppenheimer: Transcript of Hearing Before Personnel Security Board," April 12, 1954–May 6, 1954 (Washington, D.C.: U.S. Government Printing Office, 1954), p. 13.

98 **"There were practically":** Bernice Brode, "Tales of Los Alamos," in Badash et al., *Reminiscences of Los Alamos*, p. 138.

98 **"I don't think":** Elsie McMillan, "Outside the Inner Fence," ibid., p. 43.

99 **"Los Alamos," added Alvarez:** Alvarez, *Adventures of a Physicist*, p. 129.

99 **"The fence":** Ruth Marshak, "Life at P.O. Box 1663," in Kelly, *Manhattan Project*, p. 169.

99 **"We were too many":** Laura Fermi, "The Fermis' Path to Los Alamos," in Badash et al., *Reminiscences of Los Alamos*, p. 93.

99 **"I've never drunk":** Elsie McMillan, "Outside the Inner Fence," ibid., p. 43.

99 **"Whenever things":** Ruth Marshak, "Life at P.O. Box 1663," in Kelly, *Manhattan Project*, p. 169.

99 **"We could gaze":** Bernice Brode, "Tales of Los Alamos," in Badash et al., *Reminiscences of Los Alamos*, p. 139.

99 **"I wish you":** Franklin Roosevelt to Robert Oppenheimer, June 29, 1943, in MDH, bk. 8, vol. 2, p. 3.7.

100 **"Even after":** Ibid., p. 4.1.

100 **This coincided:** Ibid., pp. 3.30, 3.36.

100 **"In the beginning":** Groves, *Now It Can Be Told*, pp. 158–59.

100 **"It was impossible":** Ibid., p. 153.

101 **The brilliant minds:** Hewlett and Anderson, *New World*, p. 235.

101 **"The force":** Groves, *Now It Can Be Told*, p. 157.

101 **The two methods:** Hewlett and Anderson, *New World*, p. 400.

101 **"Triggering devices":** MDH, bk. 8, vol. 2, p. 7.16.

101 **Scientists learned:** Ibid., p. 7.19.

101 **At a predetermined:** Ibid., pp. 14.7–14.8.

102 **The fifty-eight-year-old Arnold:** H. H. Arnold, *Global Mission* (New York: Harper & Brothers, 1949), pp. 1–29.

102 **In 1938 the general:** Thomas M. Coffey, *Hap: The Story of the U.S. Air Force and the Man Who Built It, General Henry H. "Hap" Arnold* (New York: Viking Press, 1982), p. 2.

102 **The massive four-engine:** Kenneth P. Werrell, *Blankets of Fire: U.S. Bombers Over Japan During World War II* (Washington, D.C.: Smithsonian Institution Press, 1996), p. 82.

102 **An engineering marvel:** "The Mighty B-29: Facts About the Army's Plane That Is Blasting Japan," editorial, *New York Times*, August 5, 1945, p. 67.

102 **"It was just so big":** William Cooper, oral history by Ronald E. Marcello, September 7, 1999, University of North Texas, Denton.

103 **"This brought":** Groves, *Now It Can Be Told*, p. 254.

103 **The original plan had called:** Lee Bowen, *Project Silverplate, 1943–1946*, vol.1, *A History of the Air Force Atomic Energy Program, 1943–1953*, Air Force Historical Division, July 7, 1959, pp. 99–100.

103 **Workers added:** Commemorative Booklet, 509th Composite Group, 50th Anniversary Reunion, August 5–10, 1995, pp. 36–37, in Box 1, Atomic Bomb Collection, HSTL. See

also Richard H. Campbell, *The Silverplate Bombers: A History and Registry of the Enola Gay and Other B-29s Configured to Carry Atomic Bombs* (Jefferson, N.C.: McFarland, 2005), pp. 1–2.

103 **The 509th Composite Group:** History of 509th Composite Group, Activation to August 15,1945, Microfilm Roll #B0678, pp. 1–2, AFHRA.

103 **"The Group":** Ibid., p. 2.

103 **Over the course:** Hewlett and Anderson, *New World*, pp. 723–24.

104 **That money:** Norris, *Racing for the Bomb*, p. 227; Leslie Groves, "Commencement Address, Newark College of Engineering," June 14, 1950, Box 1, Leslie R. Groves Papers, NARA.

Chapter 9

105 **"The precedents":** Groves, *Now It Can Be Told*, p. 38.

105 **On April 27, 1945:** "Notes on Initial Meeting of Target Committee," April 27, 1945, Microfilm Roll #1, CMED.

105 **"I don't like":** Groves, *Now It Can Be Told*, p. 267.

105 **"Our most pressing":** Ibid.

106 **"To enable us":** Ibid.

106 **"I have no objection":** Ibid., p. 162.

106 **Groves protested:** Leslie Groves to Robert Oppenheimer, July 29, 1943, Box 36, J. Robert Oppenheimer Papers, LOC.

106 **"You can't be replaced":** Groves, *Now It Can Be Told*, p. 31.

106 **"I want you":** Ibid.

106 **"Well," Groves said:** Ibid., p. 32.

107 **Like Groves:** War Department, Immediate Release, Brig. Gen. Thomas Farrell Bio, undated, Box 167, President's Secretary's Files, HSTL.

107 **"I emphasized":** Groves, *Now It Can Be Told.*, p. 268.

108 **"Absolutely essential":** All subsequent quotations in this chapter come from "Notes on Initial Meeting of Target Committee," April 27, 1945.

Chapter 10

110 **"I can't bear":** Tsunejirô Tamura, diary entry for March 5, 1945, in Samuel Hideo Yamashita, *Leaves from an Autumn of Emergencies: Selections of Wartime Diaries of Ordinary Japanese* (Honolulu: University of Hawai'i Press, 2005), p. 120.

110 **The forty-four-year-old:** Herbert P. Bix, *Hirohito and the Making of Modern Japan* (New York: HarperCollins, 2000), pp. 5–6, 48, 58–62, 75, 87–89; Dan Kurzman, *Day of the Bomb: Countdown to Hiroshima* (New York: McGraw-Hill, 1986), p. 81, 89.

110 **"twitchy nervousness":** Bix, *Hirohito and the Making*, p. 89.

110 **"bird in a cage":** Ibid., p. 117.

111 **He rose at seven a.m.:** Pacific War Research Society, *Japan's Longest Day* (Tokyo: Kodansha International, 1968), p. 31.

111 **shouts of banzai:** "Foe Celebrates Singapore's Fall," *New York Times*, February 19, 1942, p. 4.

111 **The press and senior:** "Can the United States Be Invaded?" editorial, *Japan Times and Advertiser*, January 9, 1942, p. 6.

111 **"Japan," as the *Asahi*:** Masuo Kato, *The Lost War: A Japanese Reporter's Inside Story* (New York: Alfred A. Knopf, 1946), p. 82.

111 **"The military used":** Saburô Ienaga, *The Pacific War: World War II and the Japanese, 1931–1945*, trans. Frank Baldwin (New York: Pantheon Books, 1978), p. 42.

112 **The 1930s proved:** Noriko Kawamura, *Emperor Hirohito and the Pacific War* (Seattle: University of Washington Press, 2015), pp. 33–34.

112 **"A withdrawal":** USSBS, *The Effects of Strategic Bombing on Japan's War Economy* (Washington, D.C.: U.S. Government Printing Office, 1946), p. 9.
112 **On May 15, 1932:** Bix, *Hirohito and the Making*, p. 252.
112 **Six years later:** Ibid., pp. 297–303.
112 **"Domestic conflicts":** Ibid., p. 429.
112 **Schools played:** Ienaga, *Pacific War*, pp. 19–32; Thomas R. H. Havens, *Valley of Darkness: The Japanese People and World War II* (New York: W. W. Norton, 1978), pp. 25–32.
112 **"War and patriotism":** Ibid., p. 23.
113 **"During recess":** Joseph Newman, *Goodbye Japan* (New York: L.B. Fischer, 1942), p. 235.
113 **As far back as 1925:** Ben-Ami Shillony, *Politics and Culture in Wartime Japan* (Oxford: Clarendon Press, 1981), pp. 11–16.
113 **The wealth of political spies:** Ibid., p. 12; Ienaga, *Pacific War*, p. 114.
113 **"Some prisoners":** Ienaga, *Pacific War*, pp. 113–14.
113 **Under the guise:** Shillony, *Politics and Culture in Wartime Japan*, pp. 91–93.
113 **"At that point":** Wilfrid Fleisher, *Volcanic Isle* (Garden City, N.Y: Doubleday, Doran, 1942), p. 317.
113 **"By the time":** Kato, *Lost War*, p. 190.
114 **The number of periodicals:** Havens, *Valley of Darkness*, pp. 64–66.
114 **"Controls on intellectual":** Ienaga, *Pacific War*, p. 97.
114 **In towns and cities:** Havens, *Valley of Darkness*, pp. 36–43.
114 **"Extravagance is the enemy":** Ibid., p. 15.
114 **The government banned:** Ibid., pp. 18–20, 30–31; Ienaga, *Pacific War*, p. 105.
114 **"Jazz was condemned":** Kato, *Lost War*, p. 190.
114 **Outside of a few industries:** USSBS, *The War Against Japanese Transportation, 1941–1945* (Washington, D.C.: U.S. Government Printing Office, 1947), p. 13.
114 **At the outbreak:** USSBS, *Oil in Japan's War* (Washington, D.C.: U.S. Government Printing Office, 1946), pp. 11.
114 **"If our reserves":** Ienaga, *Pacific War*, p. 133.
115 **"Without crude oil":** Jerome B. Cohen, *Japan's Economy in War and Reconstruction* (Minneapolis: University of Minnesota Press, 1949), p. 46.
115 **"With these materials":** Ibid., p. 33.
115 **"There would be":** Ibid.
115 **"We can fight":** Ienaga, *Pacific War*, pp. 139–40.
115 **"In war":** Ibid., p. 141.
115 **"Once you grant":** Bix, *Hirohito and the Making*, pp. 430–31.
115 **"Once an arrow":** Kawamura, *Emperor Hirohito and Pacific War*, p. 109.
116 **"As navy minister":** Ibid.
116 **"Both men":** Ibid.
116 **One of America's greatest:** USSBS, *Summary Report (Pacific War)* (Washington, D.C.: U.S. Government Printing Office, 1946), p. 2.
116 **"Japan's militarists":** Robert J. C. Butow, *Japan's Decision to Surrender* (Stanford, Calif.: Stanford University Press, 1954), p. 9.
116 **"This was a politician's":** Havens, *Valley of Darkness*, p. 101.
116 **To increase productivity:** Ibid., pp. 90–113, 150–51.
117 **"There was nowhere":** León María Guerrero, diary, introduction, July 4, 1946, courtesy of Manuel Quezon III.
117 **"A geisha":** Robert Guillain, *I Saw Tokyo Burning: An Eyewitness Narrative from Pearl Harbor to Hiroshima*, trans. William Byron (Garden City, N.Y.: Doubleday, 1981), p. 109.
117 **Authorities demanded:** Havens, *Valley of Darkness*, p. 118; Guillain, *I Saw Tokyo Burning*, pp. 118–19; Hiroyo Arakawa, "The End of a Bake Shop," in Haruko Taya Cook

and Theodore F. Cook, eds., *Japan at War: An Oral History* (New York: New Press, 1992), p. 180.

117 **"Tokyo had never":** Guillain, *I Saw Tokyo Burning*, p. 117.

117 **Vital necessities:** Havens, *Valley of Darkness*, pp. 120–23; Guillain, *I Saw Tokyo Burning*, p. 103.

117 **"The most edifying":** Havens, *Valley of Darkness*, p. 123.

118 **Bamboo replaced:** Ibid., pp. 102, 120.

118 **"Our clothes":** Aiko Takahashi, diary entry for July 22, 1943, in Yamashita, *Leaves from an Autumn of Emergencies*, p. 170.

118 **"One borrows coffins":** Kiyoshi Kiyosawa, diary entry for January 23, 1945, in Kiyoshi Kiyosawa, *A Diary of Darkness: The Wartime Diary of Kiyosawa Kiyoshi*, trans. Eugene Sovial and Tamie Kamiyama (Princeton: Princeton University Press, 1980), p. 310.

118 **Such shortages:** Cohen, *Japan's Economy*, p. 354.

118 **"Living from hand":** Ibid., p. 52.

118 **As early as 1942:** Samuel Hideo Yamashita, *Daily Life in Wartime Japan, 1940–1945* (Lawrence: University of Kansas Press, 2015), p. 160; Havens, *Valley of Darkness*, p. 130.

118 **"Everything was rationed":** Ayako Koshino, "Dressmaker," in Cook and Cook, *Japan at War*, p. 186.

118 **To survive:** Havens, *Valley of Darkness*, p. 94.

118 **"Those who could not":** USSBS, *The Effects of Strategic Bombing on Japanese Morale* (Washington, D.C.: U.S. Government Printing Office, 1947), p. 17.

118 **"It's the age":** Tsunejirô Tamura, diary entry for January 16, 1945, in Yamashita, *Leaves from an Autumn of Emergencies*, p. 113.

119 **"The trains were packed":** León María Guerrero, diary introduction.

119 **Ishii Tominosuke:** Havens, *Valley of Darkness*, p. 128.

119 **"Our stomachs":** Tsunejirô Tamura, diary entry for July 23, 1944, in Yamashita, *Leaves from an Autumn of Emergencies*, p. 86.

119 **"There's no end":** Tsunejirô Tamura, diary entry for November 11, 1944, ibid., p. 100.

119 **"We simply":** Tsunejirô Tamura, diary entry for November 20, 1944, ibid., p. 102.

119 **Even Hirohito learned:** Pacific War Research Society, *The Day Man Lost: Hiroshima, 6 August 1945* (Tokyo: Kodansha International, 1972), pp. 71–72.

119 **People swiped:** Kato, *Lost War*, p. 193.

119 **Twelve-year-old Katsumoto:** Katsumoto Saotome, interview by the author, November 21, 2019.

119 **An Osaka University:** Yamashita, *Daily Life in Wartime Japan*, p. 163.

119 **Thieves stripped:** Kiyoshi Kiyosawa, diary entry for November 9, 1944, in Kiyosawa, *Diary of Darkness*, p. 278.

119 **"There is not a house":** Kiyoshi Kiyosawa, diary entry for December 8, 1943, ibid., p. 116.

119 **"Japan," he complained:** Kiyoshi Kiyosawa, diary entry for April 19, 1944, ibid., p. 180.

119 **Workers built almost:** USSBS, *Oil in Japan's War*, pp. 6, 61–62.

119 **"Traveling through":** Kato, *Lost War*, p. 160.

119 **The government likewise:** Havens, *Valley of Darkness*, p. 102.

120 **"Suicide attack":** USSBS, *Oil in Japan's War*, p. 86.

120 **At night, people chopped:** Kato, *Lost War*, p. 193.

120 **Wealthier individuals:** Havens, *Valley of Darkness*, p. 122.

120 **"Our neighbor":** León María Guerrero, diary entry for January 26, 1945.

120 **"Don't push":** Tsunejirô Tamura, diary entry for February 5, 1945, in Yamashita, *Leaves from an Autumn of Emergencies*, p. 116.

120 **"With no firewood":** Tsunejirô Tamura, diary entry for November 11, 1944, ibid., p. 100.

120 **"I feel lucky":** Hisako Yoshizawa, diary entry for January 30, 1945, ibid., p. 197.

120 **As American bombers:** Yamashita, *Daily Life in Wartime Japan*, pp. 90–124.

120 **"Mother, as soon":** Havens, *Valley of Darkness*, pp. 165–66.

120 **"Malnutrition," one historian noted:** Yamashita, *Daily Life in Wartime Japan*, p. 121.

121 **"On sunny days":** Mitsuko Ôoka, "No Regrets," in Women's Division of Soka Gakkai, *Women Against War: Personal Accounts of Forty Japanese Women*, trans. Richard L. Gage (Tokyo: Kodansha International, 1986), p. 173.

121 **The rice crop:** Cohen, *Japan's Economy*, p. 367.

121 **America's submarine blockade:** USSBS, *War Against Japanese Transportation*, p. 6.

121 **"Human efficiency":** Kato, *Lost War*, p. 10.

121 **Worker absenteeism:** USSBS, *The Effects of Bombing on Health and Medical Services in Japan* (Washington, D.C.: U.S. Government Printing Office, 1947), pp. 90–91.

121 **The stray dogs:** Havens, *Valley of Darkness*, p. 129.

121 **The 2,007 calories:** USSBS, *Effects of Bombing on Health and Medical Services*, p. 90.

121 **Malnutrition led:** Ibid., p. 82.

121 **The infant mortality:** Guillain, *I Saw Tokyo Burning*, p. 129.

121 **New mothers:** USSBS, *Effects of Bombing on Health and Medical Services*, pp. 88–90.

121 **Older children:** Havens, *Valley of Darkness*, p. 145.

121 **"One had only":** Guillain, *I Saw Tokyo Burning*, p. 129.

121 **"Riding trains":** USSBS, *Effects of Strategic Bombing on Japanese Morale*, p. 31.

121 **Others upbraided:** Pacific War Research Society, *Day Man Lost*, p. 61.

121 **"Oftentimes, when we":** USSBS, *Effects of Strategic Bombing on Japanese Morale*, p. 214.

121 **"The leaders," a Kyoto fireman:** Ibid., p. 28.

122 **"Did you say":** Ienaga, *Pacific War*, p. 127.

122 **"Journalism," Ienaga wrote:** Ibid., p. 103.

122 **"transfer of forces":** Ibid., p. 101.

122 **"Japan may be":** Butow, *Japan's Decision to Surrender*, p. 12.

122 **"We ask for nothing":** Pacific War Research Society, *Day Man Lost*, p. 57.

122 **"Give cotton!":** Ibid., p. 73.

122 **"Turn in your silver":** Ibid.

122 **"I couldn't help":** Aiko Takahashi, diary entry for October 19, 1944, in Yamashita, *Leaves from an Autumn of Emergencies*, p. 176.

122 **"We are clearly":** Jun Takami, diary entry for May 11, 1945, in Donald Keene, *So Lovely a Country Will Never Die: Wartime Diaries of Japanese Writers* (New York: Columbia University Press, 2010), p. 82.

122 **"The whole population":** Ienaga, *Pacific War*, p. 124.

122 **"The people are":** Shillony, *Politics and Culture in Wartime,* p. 68.

123 **"Are the army":** Kawamura, *Emperor Hirohito and the Pacific War*, p. 120.

123 **"Is there any":** Ibid.

123 **"Somehow":** Ibid., p. 121.

123 **"If we ever lose":** Bix, *Hirohito and the Making*, p. 476.

123 **"Japan has lost":** Kawamura, *Emperor Hirohito and the Pacific War*, p. 129.

123 **"Under the circumstances":** Kawamura, *Emperor Hirohito and the Pacific War*, p. 128.

123 **"Hasn't Tojo":** Murlin Spencer and Russell Brines, "History to Refute U.S. Verdict on War Guilt, Tojo Declares," *Washington Evening Star*, September 10, 1945, p. 1.

123 **"Hell is on us":** Interrogation of Fleet Admiral Osami Nagano, November 20, 1946, in USSBS, *Interrogations of Japanese Officials* (Washington, D.C.: U.S. Government Printing Office, 1946), p. 2:356.

124 **"The final decisive":** General Staff of GHQ, *Reports of General MacArthur: Japanese Operations in the Southwest Pacific Area* (Washington, D.C.: U.S. Government Printing Office, 1994), vol. 2, pt. 2, p. 585.

124 **Despite interruptions:** Butow, *Japan's Decision to Surrender*, pp. 44–51.

124 **"When I think":** Bix, *Hirohito and the Making*, p. 492.

124 **"Regrettably":** Ian Nish, *The Japanese in War and Peace, 1942–48: Selected Documents from a Translator's In-Tray* (Kent: Global Oriental, 2011), p. 424.

124 **"Is that possible?":** Bix, *Hirohito and the Making*, p. 489.

124 **"There was still":** Guillain, *I Saw Tokyo Burning*, p. 187.

125 **That one raid:** USSBS, *Effects of Incendiary Bomb Attacks on Japan (A Report on Eight Cities)* (Washington, D.C.: U.S. Government Printing Office, 1947), pp. 94, 102.

125 **Rescuers fished:** For more information on the March 9–10, 1945, firebombing of Tokyo, see James M. Scott, *Black Snow: Curtis LeMay, the Firebombing of Tokyo, and the Road to the Atomic Bomb* (New York: W. W. Norton, 2022).

125 **"Tokyo," he said:** Kawamura, *Emperor Hirohito and the Pacific War*, p. 149.

125 **"Tokyo has become":** Tsunejirô Tamura, diary entry for March 16, 1945, in Yamashita, *Leaves from an Autumn of Emergencies*, p. 126.

125 **"For the first time":** Aiko Takahashi, diary entry for March 10, 1945, in Yamashita, *Leaves from an Autumn of Emergencies*, p. 179.

126 **"He was the consummate":** Kurzman, *Day of the Bomb*, p. 190.

126 **"To Suzuki":** Lester Brooks, *Behind Japan's Decision to Surrender: The Secret Struggle That Ended an Empire* (New York: McGraw-Hill, 1968), p. 26.

126 **"Don't accompany me":** Kurzman, *Day of the Bomb*, p. 191.

126 **"Japan's situation":** Butow, *Japan's Decision to Surrender*, p. 63.

126 **"Your unfamiliarity":** Ibid., p. 64.

Chapter 11

127 **"When the last":** "The President's V-E Day Radio Address," May 8, 1945, Box 190, President's Secretary's Files, HSTL.

127 **It had taken:** West, *Upstairs at the White House*, pp. 54–56.

127 **"The White House upstairs":** Truman, *Bess Truman*, p. 260.

127 **"What little":** West, *Upstairs at the White House*, p. 56.

127 **"How much":** Ibid.

128 **"When you think":** Ibid., p. 58.

128 **"This will be":** Harry Truman to Martha Ellen Truman and Mary Jane Truman, May 8, 1945, Box 19, Papers of Harry S. Truman Pertaining to Family, Business, and Personal Affairs, HSTL.

15 **Truman headed:** President Truman, Daily Diary, May 8, 1945, HSTL.

128 **"You're forty":** Transcript of Press and Radio Conference #6, May 8, 1945, Box 6, White House Official Reporter Files, HSTL.

128 **"Happy birthday":** Truman, *Year of Decisions*, 206.

128 **"All right," Truman said:** Transcript of Press and Radio Conference #6, May 8, 1945.

128 **Aides opened:** "The German Surrender, April-May 1945," Box 190, President's Secretary's Files, HSTL.

128 **"Good morning":** Transcript of Press and Radio Conference #6, May 8, 1945.

129 **"Did you ever":** Ibid.

129 **"This is":** "The President's V-E Day Radio Address," May 8, 1945, Box 190, President's Secretary's Files, HSTL.

129 **"The Japanese people":** "Statement by the President," May 8, 1945, Ibid.

130 **In war plants:** "Bells, Whistles Here Sound Victory News," *St. Louis Star-Times*, May 8, 1945, p. 1; "Capital Halts Task Only Long Enough to Hear President," *Washington Evening Star*, May 8, 1945, p. 1.

130 **Ailing Gen. John:** "Pershing Hears Truman," *New York Times*, May 9, 1945, p. 6.

130 **So did:** "Fine Birthday for Son Is Mrs. Truman's Word," *Cushing Daily Citizen*, May 8, 1945, p. 4.

130 **According to the Columbia Broadcasting System:** "Truman Sets Mark in Radio Coverage," *New York Times*, May 9, 1945, p. 6.

130 **Official word:** "Rejoicing Tempered by Grim Fight Ahead," *Press Democrat*, May 8, 1945, p. 2; Frank S. Adams, "Millions Rejoice in City Celebration," *New York Times*, May 9, 1945, p. 1.

130 **"It was not a day":** Henry Stimson, diary entry for May 8, 1945, HLSP.

130 **"The war is not":** "Rejoicing Tempered."

131 **"Nazi Germany":** E. B. Sledge, *With the Old Breed* (New York: Presidio Press, 2010), p. 223.

131 **"Oh, Jesus":** Gordon Cobbledick, "It Was V-E Day Over Here—But White Crosses Still Grow on Okinawa," *Miami Herald*, May 9, 1945, p. 1.

131 **"Some stared":** Ibid.

Chapter 12

132 **"Can Japan see":** "Will Japan See the Light?" editorial, *Honolulu Advertiser*, May 11, 1945, p. 14.

132 **The Target Committee reconvened at nine:** J. A. Darry and N. F. Ramsey to Leslie R. Groves, "Summary of Target Committee Meetings on 10 and 11 May 1945," May 12, 1945, Microfilm Roll #1, CMED. Copies of these minutes can also be found in Box 2, Atomic Bomb Collection, HSTL. Below, unless otherwise noted, all information and quotations from that meeting can be found in those minutes.

132 **"All we would produce":** Groves, *Now It Can Be Told*, p. 269.

133 **"For this weapon":** Ibid.

133 **this would require a wait:** Ibid.

133 **"Extreme care":** Ibid., p. 270.

135 **"To provide against":** Ibid., p. 271.

135 **The Target Committee reconvened two weeks:** "Minutes of Third Target Committee Meeting," May 28, 1945, Microfilm Roll #1, CMED. Copies of these minutes can also be found in Box 2, Atomic Bomb Collection, HSTL. Unless otherwise noted below, all information and quotations from that meeting can be found in those minutes.

135 **"This was too":** Groves, *Now It Can Be Told*, p. 271.

136 **"Kyoto, Hiroshima":** JCS to CINCAFPAC, CINCPAC, and Commanding General Army Air Forces, July 3, 1945, Box 22, Dale M. Hellegers Papers, HSTL.

136 **"I want to be sure":** Giovannitti and Freed, *Decision to Drop the Bomb*, pp. 40–41.

137 **Groves pushed back:** Groves, *Now It Can Be Told*, pp. 373–74. The facts Groves cited can be found in "Kyoto," June 15, 1945, Microfilm Roll #3, CMED.

137 **"The city's peacetime":** Ibid., p. 374.

137 **"If you're not busy":** Giovannitti and Freed, *Decision to Drop the Bomb*, p. 41.

137 **"He did not express":** Groves, *Now It Can Be Told*, p. 374.

137 **"I particularly wanted":** Ibid.

Chapter 13

138 **"It is clear":** Eben Ayers, diary entry for May 26, 1945, in Ayers, *Truman in the White House*, p. 29.

138 **"I gave it":** Martin J. Sherwin, *A World Destroyed: The Atomic Bomb and the Grand Alliance* (New York: Alfred A. Knopf, 1975), p. 172.

138 **"I am ready":** Joseph Stalin to Harry Truman, April 24, 1945, in U.S. Department of State, *Foreign Relations of the United States: Diplomatic Papers, 1945*, vol. 5, *Europe* (Washington, D.C.: U.S. Government Printing Office, 1967), pp. 263–64.

139 **"We were making":** Truman, *Year of Decisions*, pp. 107–8.

139 **"tide of Russian":** Winston Churchill to Harry Truman, May 11, 1945, Document No. 4, FRUS, p. 1:6.

139 **"This would be":** Ibid.

139 **"Anyone can see":** Joseph Stalin to Harry Truman, May 12, 1945, Document No. 4, ibid., pp. 1:8–9.

139 **Stalin had previously:** John R. Deane, *The Strange Alliance: The Story of Our Efforts at Wartime Cooperation with Russia* (New York: Viking Press, 1947), pp. 246–47.

140 **Truman now counted:** Tsuyoshi Hasegawa, *Racing the Enemy: Stalin, Truman, and the Surrender of Japan* (Cambridge, Mass.: Harvard University Press, 2005), p. 195.

140 **"As our forces":** Truman, *Year of Decisions*, p. 314.

140 **In expectation:** Deane, *Strange Alliance*, pp. 248–49. See also D. M. Giangreco, *Truman and the Bomb: The Untold Story* (Lincoln, Neb.: Potomac Books, 2023), pp. 36–54.

140 **The secret supply:** Richard A. Russell, *Project Hula: Secret Soviet-American Cooperation in the War Against Japan* (Washington, D.C.: Naval Historical Center, 1997), pp. 33–35, 39–40.

140 **"What they told":** Truman, *Year of Decisions*, p. 228.

141 **"The Russians complained":** Ibid.

141 **Given the deadlock:** Ibid., p. 255.

141 **"It was imperative":** Truman, *Year of Decisions*, p. 110.

141 **"Davies was not":** Ibid.,

141 **"Why don't you":** Ibid., p. 257.

141 **"I am sure":** Harry Truman to Joseph Stalin, May 19, 1945, Document No. 20, in FRUS, p. 1:21.

142 **"I made it":** Truman, *Year of Decisions*, p. 258.

142 **"He would be":** Joseph Davies to Harry Truman, "Supplemental Report in Re: Mission to London," June 12, 1945, Document No. 33, in FRUS, p. 1:69.

142 **"tired, nervous":** Ibid., p. 1:76.

142 **"England, he proclaimed":** Ibid., p. 1:69.

142 **"The Prime Minister is one of":** Ibid.

142 **"I could not escape":** Ibid., p: 1:77.

142 **"His attitude":** Ibid., p. 1:72.

142 **"Stalin is impressive":** John McCloy, diary entry for April 30, 1945, JJMP.

143 **"These German":** Harry Hopkins to Harry Truman, "Memorandum of 2nd Conversation at the Kremlin," May 27, 1945, Document No. 25, FRUS, p. 1:39.

143 **"It was better":** Harry Hopkins to Harry Truman, "Memorandum of 3rd Conversation at the Kremlin," May 28, 1945, Document No. 26, FRUS, p. 1:44.

143 **"In other words":** Ibid.

143 **"He is a realist":** Averell Harriman to Harry Truman, June 8, 1945, Document No. 30, FRUS, p. 1:61.

Chapter 14

144 **"Japan is on the verge of terrible":** DeWitt Mackenzie, "Fall of Germany Terrific Blow Against Japan," *Austin American*, May 10, 1945, p. 4.

144 **The first meeting:** R. Gordon Arneson, "Notes of an Informal Meeting of the Interim Committee, Wednesday, 9 May 1945, 9:30 a.m.–12:30 p.m.," May 17, 1945, Box 1, R. Gordon Arneson Papers, HSTL.

144 **But the committee:** Norris, *Racing for the Bomb*, p. 389.

145 **Stimson made a point:** R. Gordon Arneson, "Memorandum for the Files, May 24, 1945, Microfilm Roll #6, HBF.

145 **"The membership":** Rhodes, *Making the Atomic Bomb*, p. 630.

145 **"There was never":** Norris, *Racing for the Bomb*, p. 389.

145 **The inaugural meeting:** Minutes for all Interim Committee meetings are on file in Box 1, R. Gordon Arneson Papers, HSTL.

145 **The purpose of the committee:** Henry Stimson to Vannevar Bush, May 4, 1945, Microfilm Roll #6, HBF.

145 **"All subjects":** Giovannitti and Freed, *Decision to Drop the Bomb*, p. 61.

145 **"It was termed":** Arneson, "Notes of an Informal Meeting of the Interim Committee," May 17, 1945.

146 **"The Committee strongly":** Ibid.

146 **The group reconvened:** R. Gordon Arneson, "Notes of an Informal Meeting of the Interim Committee, Monday, 14 May 1945, 10:00 a.m.–12:30 p.m.," May 15, 1945, Box 1, R. Gordon Arneson Papers, HSTL; Leon V. Sigal, "Bureaucratic Politics & Tactical Use of Committees: The Interim Committee & the Decision to Drop the Atomic Bomb," *Polity* 10, no. 3 (Spring 1978), pp. 326–64.

146 **"The scientists," Compton said:** Karl Compton to George Harrison, May 10, 1945, Microfilm Roll #6, HBF.

146 **"The Scientific Panel":** Arneson, "Notes of an Informal Meeting of the Interim Committee," May 15, 1945.

147 **"Such a statement":** Ibid.

147 **The Scientific Panel joined:** R. Gordon Arneson, "Notes of the Interim Committee, Thursday, 31 May 1945, 10:00 a.m. to 1:15 p.m.–2:15 p.m. to 4:15 p.m.," undated, Box 1, R. Gordon Arneson Papers, HSTL.

147 **"This project":** Ibid.

147 **"As I heard":** James F. Byrnes, *All in One Lifetime* (New York: Harper & Brothers, 1958), p. 283.

147 **"The basic goal":** Arneson, "Notes of the Interim Committee," undated.

148 **"Everyone recognized":** Giovannitti and Freed, *Decision to Drop the Bomb*, p. 100.

148 **"We might say":** Arneson, "Notes of the Interim Committee," undated.

148 **"The seemingly uncooperative":** Ibid.

148 **"If information":** Ibid.

148 **"The most desirable":** Ibid.

149 **"Throughout the morning's":** Compton, *Atomic Quest*, p. 238.

149 **"If we were to warn":** James F. Byrnes, *Speaking Frankly* (London: William Heinemann, 1947), p. 261. More on Byrnes's views can be found in his personal writings in Box 1, James F. Byrnes Papers, Clemson University Special Collections and Archives, Clemson, S.C., and in James F. Byrnes, "We Were Anxious to Get the War Over," *U.S. News & World Report*, August 15, 1960, p. 65.

149 **"Nothing would have":** Stimson, "Decision to Use the Atomic Bomb," p. 101.

149 **"A nation fighting":** Norris, *Racing for the Bomb*, p. 659.

149 **"Our failure":** Ibid.

149 **"Various possibilities":** Compton, *Atomic Quest*, p. 238.

150 **"The visual effect":** Arneson, "Notes of the Interim Committee," undated.

150 **"After much discussion":** Ibid.
150 **"We would lose":** Ibid.
151 **"The program":** Ibid.
151 **"After some publicity":** Ibid.
151 **"The scientists should be":** Ibid.
151 **The committee met:** R. Gordon Arneson, "Notes of the Interim Committee, Friday, 1 June 1945, 11:00 a.m.–12:30 p.m., 1:45 p.m.–3:30 p.m.," undated, Box 1, R. Gordon Arneson Papers, HSTL.
151 **"I concluded":** Byrnes, *Speaking Frankly*, p. 261.
151 **"Under these circumstances," he said:** Byrnes, *All in One Lifetime*, p. 286.
152 **"Byrnes felt":** Giovannitti and Freed, *Decision to Drop the Bomb*, p. 106.
152 **"The present view":** Arneson, "Notes of the Interim Committee," undated.
152 **"Mr. Truman told me":** Giovannitti and Freed, *Decision to Drop the Bomb*, p. 109.
152 **"I was anxious":** Henry Stimson, diary entry for June 6, 1945, HLSP.
153 **"Namely to make":** Ibid.
153 **"The committee's function":** Stimson, "Decision to Use the Atomic Bomb," p. 101.

Chapter 15

154 **"I personally thought":** Leo Szilard, "History of the Atomic Bomb Development," May 22, 1956, Box 40, LSP.
154 **The burly general:** Norris, *Racing for the Bomb*, pp. 232–36; Lanouette, *Genius in the Shadows*, pp. 237–40.
154 **"He was a parasite":** Norris, *Racing for the Bomb*, p. 233.
155 **"It is considered":** Lanouette, *Genius in the Shadows*, p. 240.
155 **"This was the answer":** Norris, *Racing for the Bomb*, p. 234.
155 **"Few enemies":** Lanouette, *Genius in the Shadows*, p. 240.
155 **"What Is Wrong":** Leo Szilard, "What Is Wrong with Us?" September 21, 1942, Box 34, LSP. A copy of this paper can also be found in Weart and Szilard, *Leo Szilard*, p. 153.
155 **"One has to":** Ibid.
155 **"Perhaps," he concluded:** Ibid.
155 **Unlike many:** Norris, *Racing for the Bomb*, p. 234.
155 **"Nobody could":** Nuel Pharr Davis, *Lawrence and Oppenheimer* (New York: Da Capo Press, 1986), p. 163.
155 **"This weapon":** Leo Szilard to Vannevar Bush, January 14, 1944, Box 5, LSP. See also Weart and Szilard, *Leo Szilard*, p. 161.
156 **"What is the purpose":** Leo Szilard, *Reminiscences*, ed. Gertrud Weiss Szilard and Kathleen R. Windsor, in *Perspectives in American History* 2 (1968), pp. 122–23.
156 **"He had been willing":** Compton, *Atomic Quest*, p. 241.
156 **"Most of our major":** Leo Szilard, "Enclosure to Mr. Albert Einstein's Letter of March 25, 1945, to the President of the United States," in Szilard, *Reminiscences*, p. 146.
156 **"This situation":** Ibid.
156 **"I hope," Compton replied:** Szilard, *Reminiscences*, p. 124.
157 **"There I was now":** Ibid.
157 **"I see now":** Ibid., p. 125.
157 **"We were concerned":** Ibid., p. 126.
158 **"General Groves":** Ibid.
158 **"Once the bomb":** Ibid., p. 127.
158 **"How would you":** Ibid.
158 **"Russia," he said, "might be":** Ibid.
158 **"Well, you come":** Ibid., p. 128.

158 **"I certainly didn't":** Ibid.
159 **"Szilard," he wrote:** Byrnes, *All in One Lifetime*, p. 284.
159 **"His general":** Ibid.
159 **"I was rarely":** Szilard, *Reminiscences*, p. 128.
160 **"The atomic bomb is shit":** Weart and Szilard, *Leo Szilard*, p. 185.
160 **"What do you mean":** Szilard, *Reminiscences*, p. 129.

Chapter 16

161 **"We believe":** James Franck et al., "Political and Social Problems (often referred to simply as the Franck Report)," June 12, 1945, Microfilm Roll #6, HBF.
161 **Arthur Compton returned:** Hewlett and Anderson, *New World*, pp. 365–66.
161 **"By an accident":** Glenn T. Seaborg with Benjamin S. Loeb, *Stemming the Tide: Arms Control in the Johnson Years* (Lexington, Mass.: Lexington Books, 1987), p. 60.
162 **"While the authorship":** Giovannitti and Freed, *Decision to Drop the Bomb*, p. 116.
162 **"All of us":** Franck et al, "Political and Social Problems."
162 **"If no efficient":** Ibid.
162 **"It is doubtful":** Ibid.
162 **"You see what weapon":** Ibid.
163 **"The military advantages":** Ibid.
163 **"In the meantime":** Arthur Compton to Henry Stimson, "Memorandum on 'Political and Social Problems' from Members of the 'Metallurgical Laboratory' of the University of Chicago," June 12, 1945, Microfilm Roll #6, HBF.
163 **"The proposal":** Ibid.
163 **"impress the world":** Ibid.
163 **The scientists wanted:** Compton, *Atomic Quest*, p. 236.
163 **In Washington, the men:** Interim Committee Log, entries for June 12, 1945, and June 15, 1945, Box 1, R. Gordon Arneson Papers, HSTL.
163 **"This report":** Giovannitti and Freed, *Decision to Drop the Bomb*, p. 118.
164 **"We were determined":** Compton, *Atomic Quest*, pp. 239–40.
164 **"Experience with the":** Ibid., p. 240
164 **"The opinions":** J. R. Oppenheimer et al., "Recommendations on the Immediate Use of Nuclear Weapons," June 16, 1945, Microfilm Roll #6, HBF.
164 **"The committee," the minutes:** R. Gordon Arneson, "Notes of the Interim Committee, Thursday, 21 June 1945, 9:30 a.m.–1:15 p.m., 2:00 p.m.–4:15 p.m.," undated, Box 1, R. Gordon Arneson Papers, HSTL.

Chapter 17

165 **"The progress":** Marquis Koichi Kido, diary entry for June 8, 1945, in Marquis Kido, *The Diary of Marquis Kido, 1931–1945: Selected Translations into English* (Frederick, Md.: University Publications of America, 1984), p. 434.
165 **"It is his":** William Leahy to the Joint Chiefs of Staff, June 14, 1945, in Kort, *Columbia Guide to Hiroshima and the Bomb*, pp. 201–2.
166 **To take Kyushu:** John Ray Skates, *The Invasion of Japan: Alternative to the Bomb* (Columbia: University of South Carolina Press, 1994), pp. 167–70.
166 **Olympic would be:** Ibid., pp. 199–201.
166 **On that tiny:** Joseph H. Alexander, *Utmost Savagery: The Three Days of Tarawa* (Annapolis, Md.: Naval Institute Press, 1995), pp. 231–38.
167 **"You could not":** Ibid., p. 206.
167 **"casualty surge":** D. M. Giangreco, *Hell to Pay: Operation Downfall and the Invasion of Japan, 1945–1947* (Annapolis, MD: Naval Institute Press, 2009), p. 3.

167 **"It's just the damnedest":** James D. Hornfischer, *The Fleet at Flood Tide: America at Total War in the Pacific, 1944–1945* (New York: Bantam Books, 2016), p. 294.

167 **"It was war":** Holland M. Smith and Percy Finch, *Coral and Brass* (New York: Charles Scribner's Sons, 1948), p. 188.

168 **"Along the beach":** Robert Sherrod, "It Was Sickening to Watch . . . ," *Time,* March 5, 1945, p. 27.

168 **The Japanese demonstrated:** For more on the Battle of Manila, see James M. Scott, *Rampage: MacArthur, Yamashita, and the Battle of Manila* (New York: W. W. Norton, 2018).

168 **"If anything":** Bonner F. Fellers to Dorothy Fellers, February 14, 1945, Box 2, RG 44a, Bonner F. Fellers Papers, MacArthur Memorial Archives and Library, Norfolk, Va.

168 **The Japanese executed:** Donald L. Miller, *D-Days in the Pacific* (New York: Simon & Schuster, 2005), p. 297.

169 **"They would come":** Ibid.

169 **"We were surrounded":** Sledge, *With the Old Breed*, p. 253.

169 **"Every single person":** John C. McManus, *To the End of the Earth: The US Army and the Downfall of Japan, 1945* (New York: Caliber, 2023), p. 285.

169 **"Please for God's":** John D. Chappell, *Before the Bomb: How America Approached the End of the Pacific War* (Lexington: University Press of Kentucky, 1997), p. 14.

169 **"If it took":** "Results on Okinawa," editorial, *New York Times*, June 25, 1945, p. 16.

170 **Over 1,529 sorties:** Ellis A. Johnson and David A. Katcher, *Mines Against Japan* (Silver Spring, Md.: Naval Ordnance Laboratory, 1973), pp. 27–32.

170 **LeMay, in fact:** Wilbur H. Morrison, *Point of No Return: The Story of the 20th Air Force* (New York: Times Books, 1979), p. 247.

170 **"The atomic bomb was more":** Stimson, "Decision to Use the Atomic Bomb," p. 105.

170 **"I have to decide":** Harry Truman, diary entry for June 17, 1945, in Ferrell, *Off the Record*, p. 47.

170 **At three-thirty p.m.:** All subsequent quotations in this chapter come from Document No. 598, Memorandum by the Secretary of the Joint Chiefs of Staff (McFarland), "Minutes of Meeting Held at the White House on Monday, 18 June 1945 at 1530," in FRUS, pp. 1:903–10.

Chapter 18

176 **"The devastation":** Aiko Takahashi, diary entry for July 25, 1945, in Yamashita, *Leaves from an Autumn of Emergencies*, p. 186.

176 **Those six:** USSBS, *Effects of Incendiary Bomb Attacks*, p. 117.

176 **"Tokyo":** Bob Speer, "The B-29s Most of All," *Brief*, undated, p. 7, in Box 41, CLP.

176 **"I had never seen":** Aiko Takahashi, diary entry for May 27, 1945, in Yamashita, *Leaves from an Autumn of Emergencies*, p. 184.

177 **"The limitless acres":** Kato, *Lost War*, p. 6.

177 **The thirty-two:** Public Relations Office, XXI Bomber Command, Release No. 172, June 11, 1945, Microfilm Roll #A7785, AFHRA.

177 **As a result, one out of:** USSBS, *Effects of Strategic Bombing on Japanese Morale*, pp. 1, 24.

177 **"Air raids":** Ibid., p. 40.

177 **"Merely to subsist":** Kato, *Lost War*, p. 9.

177 **"Living each day":** Hisako Yoshizawa, diary entry for February 26, 1945, in Yamashita, *Leaves from an Autumn of Emergencies*, p. 199.

177 **"How long":** Hisako Yoshizawa, diary entry for June 4, 1945, ibid., p. 210.

178 **"Fire-fighting":** USSBS, *Final Report Covering Air-Raid Protection and Allied Subjects in Japan* (Washington, D.C.: U.S. Government Printing Office, 1947), p. 8.

178 **"It was officially":** Guillain, *I Saw Tokyo Burning*, p. 175.
178 **Seventy-six percent:** USSBS, *Effects of Strategic Bombing on Japanese Morale*, p. 39.
178 **"We were unprotected":** Ibid.
178 **"I did not receive":** Ibid., p. 40.
178 **"The raids almost seemed":** Ibid.
178 **"There was no":** Ibid., p. 37.
179 **"Everyone suffered":** Ibid., p. 41.
179 **Wearing Western-style:** Ibid., pp. 36, 249–50.
179 **All told, workers:** USSBS, *Final Report Covering Air-Raid Protection and Allied Subjects in Japan*, pp. 67–69, 190.
179 **"Grids were traced":** Guillain, *I Saw Tokyo Burning*, p. 173.
179 **The Philippine diplomat:** León María Guerrero, diary entry for March 26, 1945.
179 **"Tokyo was a":** Guillain, *I Saw Tokyo Burning*, p. 195.
180 **Trains were so:** Kiyoshi Kiyosawa, diary entry for March 24, 1945, in Kiyosawa, *Wartime Diary*, p. 336.
180 **Since March:** USSBS, *Effects of Air Attack on Osaka-Kobe-Kyoto* (Washington, D.C.: U.S. Government Printing Office, 1947), p. 36.
180 **Nagoya experienced:** USSBS, *Effects of Air Attack on the City of Nagoya* (Washington, D.C.: U.S. Government Printing Office, 1947), p. 12.
180 **Tokyo saw the greatest:** USSBS, *Field Report Covering Air Raid Protection and Allied Subjects in Tokyo, Japan* (Washington, D.C.: U.S. Government Printing Office, 1947), p. 158.
180 **Across Japan, more than:** USSBS, *Effects of Strategic Bombing on Japanese Morale*, p. 40.
180 **"Most people":** Havens, *Valley of Darkness*, p. 168.
180 **"The food problems":** USSBS, *Effects of Strategic Bombing on Japanese Morale*, p. 79.
180 **Those who chose:** Ibid., p. 35.
180 **An estimated 227,000:** Ibid., p. 40.
180 **"Every day":** Kafû Nagai, diary entry for May 1, 1945, in Keene, *So Lovely a Country*, p. 90.
180 **"I was like":** Katsumoto Saotome, interview by the author, November 21, 2019.
181 **"When you dig":** Hisako Yoshizawa, diary entry for July 7, 1945, in Yamashita, *Leaves from an Autumn of Emergencies*, pp. 213–14.
181 **"Thousands and thousands":** Kazuo Watanabe, diary entry for June 12, 1945, in Keene, *So Lovely a Country*, p. 76.
181 **"To each family":** Kato, *Lost War*, pp. 196–97.
181 **"Everywhere one":** Kiyoshi Kiyosawa, diary entry for April 12, 1945, in Kiyosawa, *Wartime Diary*, p. 350.
181 **"Everyone now":** Hisako Yoshizawa, diary entry for June 29, 1945, in Yamashita, *Leaves from an Autumn of Emergencies*, p. 212.
181 **"Those that I":** Kato, *Lost War*, p. 17.
181 **"To an amateur":** Ibid.
182 **"The children's lives":** in Yamashita, *Leaves from an Autumn of Emergencies*, p. 35.
182 **"They're still":** Mihôko Nakane, diary entry for June 17, 1945, ibid., 289.
182 **"It was really":** Ibid.
182 **"Everywhere there":** Kiyoshi Kiyosawa, diary entry for March 29, 1945, in Kiyosawa, *Wartime Diary*, p. 339.
182 **"If there are":** Ibid.

Chapter 19

183 **"How many people":** Musei Tokugawa, diary entry for May 20, 1945, in Pacific War Research Society, *Day Man Lost*, p. 144.
183 **"It contemplated":** Ibid., p. 158.

183 **The army planned to pitch:** Ibid.

184 **The Supreme War Council, which functioned:** For a good description of the Big Six, see USSBS, *Japan's Struggle to End the War* (Washington, D.C.: U.S. Government Printing Office, 1946), p. 4.

184 **"a jury of six":** Brooks, *Behind Japan's Decision to Surrender*, p. 34.

184 **"It has become":** USSBS, *Effects of Strategic Bombing on Japanese Morale*, p. 137.

185 **"As the war progressed":** Shigenori Tôgô, *The Cause of Japan*, trans. and ed. Fumihiko Tôgô and Ben Bruce Blakeney (New York: Simon & Schuster, 1956), p. 265.

185 **"Should I die":** Pacific War Research Society, *Day Man* Lost, p. 120.

185 **"I am resolved":** Ibid., p. 137.

185 **Historians have long:** Ibid.

185 **"From the moment":** Tôgô, *Cause of Japan*, p. 282.

186 **"Upon attending":** Ibid., p. 291.

186 **"When the enemy":** Pacific War Research Society, *Day Man* Lost, p. 158.

186 **"No external help":** Tôgô, *Cause of Japan*, p. 292.

186 **"There is only one":** Butow, *Japan's Decision to Surrender*, p. 99.

186 **"I ask all those":** Pacific War Research Society, *Day Man Lost*, p. 160.

186 **"Japan's situation":** Ibid.

186 **"His silence":** Ibid.

187 **"He was the Emperor's":** Kurzman, *Day of the Bomb*, p. 37.

187 **"This," Hirohito said:** Pacific War Research Society, *Day Man Lost*, p. 161.

187 **"By the latter":** Marquis Koichi Kido, diary entry for June 8, 1945, in Kido, *Diary of Marquis Kido*, pp. 434.

187 **"The extreme":** Ibid., p. 435.

188 **"very generous":** Ibid., p. 436.

188 **"In regard to":** Ibid.

188 **"I think the turning":** Brooks, *Behind Japan's Decision to Surrender*, p. 53.

188 **Unlike Togo:** Kurzman, *Day of the Bomb*, pp. 231–39.

188 **"Accept my son's":** Ibid., p. 233.

189 **"Our ability":** Pacific War Research Society, *Day Man Lost*, p. 172.

189 **"As a soldier":** Ibid.

189 **"And do you":** Ibid., p. 173.

189 **"The emperor himself":** Ibid.

189 **"There is no other":** Ibid.

189 **"We have heard":** Edwin P. Hoyt, *Hirohito: The Emperor and the Man* (New York: Praeger, 1984), pp. 141–42.

Chapter 20

190 **"Japan has never":** Joseph Grew congressional testimony, December 12, 1944, in U.S. Congress, *Hearings Before the Committee on Foreign Relations: Nominations—Department of State*, 78th Cong., 2nd Sess., December 12, 1944 (Washington, D.C.: U.S. Government Printing Office, 1944), p. 18.

191 **"It is of the utmost":** President Roosevelt to the Secretary of War, Memorandum, August 26, 1944, in *Foreign Relations of the United States: Diplomatic Papers, 1944*, vol. 1, *General* (Washington, D.C.: U.S. Government Printing Office, 1966), p. 569.

191 **"The elimination":** Transcript of Press Conference, January 24, 1943, in U.S. Department of State, *Foreign Relations of the United States: The Conferences at Washington, 1941–1942, and Casablanca, 1943* (Washington, D.C.: U.S. Government Printing Office, 1968), p. 727.

192 **That weariness:** Giangreco, *Hell to Pay*, p. 22.

192 **"America is not":** Max Lerner, "The Big Furlough Time," *Gazette and Daily*, July 12, 1945, p. 15.

192 **"The Japanese war":** Advertisement, *Salisbury Times*, August 9, 1945, p. 3.

192 **"You can't afford":** Advertisement, *Daily Sentinel*, June 28, 1945, p. 7.

192 **The war, which at its:** W. H. Lawrence, "A 210 Billion Debt," *New York Times*, January 12, 1943, p. 1.

192 **The conversion:** "Production Halted or to Stop on 34 Major Civilian Items," *Washington Post*, April 7, 1942, p. 22; Nona Baldwin, "Deeper Cuts Loom in Items for Home," *New York Times*, July 19, 1942, p. 27.

192 **Bobby pins:** Elizabeth MacRae Bovkin, "Take Care of Mattresses, Other Bedding," *Washington Post*, April 19, 1942, p. R6; "Shortage of Burial Caskets Is Growing," *Washington Post*, February 11, 1943, p. 4.

193 **America's ravenous:** U.S. Office of Price Administration, *Rationing in World War II* (Washington, D.C.: U.S. Government Printing Office, 1946), pp. 2–3.

193 **"Rationing," as one:** Ibid., p. 2.

193 **"About 50 million":** "Rationing Made Easy," *Washington Post*, February 17, 1943, p. B3.

193 **"Never in the memory":** Franklin Roosevelt, Radio Address to the Nation, April 28, 1942, in *The War Messages of Franklin D. Roosevelt: December 8, 1941, to April 13, 1945* (Washington, D.C: U.S. Government Printing Office, 1945), p. 42.

193 **To conserve fabric:** "'Victory Clothes' Will Be Minus Cuffs, Pleats, Some Vests," *Wall Street Journal*, January 31, 1942, p. 1.

193 **To compensate:** "Public Eager for Scrap Drive," *Washington Post*, September 13, 1942, p. 1.

193 **Many others celebrated:** "Supply of Christmas Trees to Be Reduced by Manpower Shortage and Railroad Curbs," *New York Times*, October 23, 1942, p. 15.

193 **"One to two billion":** "Thanksgiving Aids War If Turkey Fat Is Saved," *New York Times*, November 19, 1942, p. 28.

193 **Germany's defeat had led:** "Vinson Lifts Band on Racing and Eliminated the Curfew," *New York Times*, May 10, 1945, p. 1.

193 **A gray two-door:** "For Car, the First for Civilians Since February, '42, Rolls Off Line," *New York Times*, July 4, 1945, p. 15; "Reconversion Preview," *New York Times*, July 8, 1945, p. 27.

193 **A survey by the War Protection Board:** O. Max Gardner, "The Challenge of Peacetime Abundance," *New York Times*, July 8, 1945, p. 50.

194 **"Following the end":** Ibid.

194 **The sixty-five-year-old:** Steve Kemper, *Our Man in Tokyo: An Ambassador and the Countdown to Pearl Harbor* (New York: Mariner Books, 2022), pp. 1–2.

194 **His navigation:** "Ambassador Joseph Clark Grew," *Time*, November 12, 1934, cover.

194 **"unquestionably the most":** John Hersey, "Joe Grew, Ambassador to Japan," *Life*, July 15, 1940, p. 78.

194 **"I know the Japanese":** Joseph C. Grew, *Report from Tokyo: A Message to the American People* (New York: Simon & Schuster, 1942), p. 29

194 **But Grew recently:** Jospeh C. Grew, *Turbulent Era: A Diplomatic Records of Forty Years, 1904–1945*, ed. Walter Johnson (Boston: Houghton Mifflin, 1952), pp. 2:1421–38.

195 **"We must remember":** Ibid., p. 2:1429.

195 **"prince of appeasers":** Marc Gallicchio, *Unconditional: The Japanese Surrender in World War II* (New York: Oxford University Press, 2020), p. 34.

195 **"The institution":** Dale M. Hellegers, *We the People: World War II and the Origins of the Japanese Constitution*, vol. 1, *Washington* (Stanford, Calif.: Stanford University Press, 2001), p. 93.

196 **"The average American":** "U.S. Public Split on Hirohito; Many Advocate His Execution," *Washington Post*, June 29, 1945, p. 7.

196 **"Unless a definition":** J.C.S. 924/15, April 25, 1945, "Operations Against Japan Subsequent to Formosa," in Kort, *Columbia Guide to Hiroshima and the Bomb*, p. 242.
196 **"What attitude":** Hellegers, *We the People*, p. 84.
196 **"It may hold":** Ibid.
197 **"unconditional surrender" to the:** Memorandum for the Secretary of War, "Basic Objective in the Pacific War," June 9, 1945, GCMP.
197 **"We should," Marshall advised:** Ibid.
197 **An early peace:** Herbert Hoover to Harry Truman, "Memorandum on Ending the Japanese War," undated, in Joan Hoff Wilson, "Herber Hoover's Plan for Ending the Second World War," *International History Review* 1, no. 1 (January 1979), pp. 100–10.
197 **"There could be":** Herber Hoover, "Memorandum on Visit with President Truman," May 28, 1945, ibid., p. 99.
198 **"appeasement proposal":** Gallicchio, *Unconditional*, p. 56.
198 **Faced with split:** Grew, *Report from Tokyo*, p. 1437.
198 **"If the test":** Truman, *Year of Decisions*, p. 417.
198 **"This is a matter":** Henry Stimson, diary entry for June 26, 1945, to June 30, 1945, HLSP.
198 **The war secretary began work:** "Minutes of the Meeting of the Committee of the Three," June 26, 1945, Box 18, JJMP.
198 **"There is reason":** Henry Stimson to Harry Truman, "Proposed Program for Japan," July 2, 1945, copy on file with Henry Stimson, diary entry for July 2, 1945, HLSP.
198 **"The Japanese are highly":** Ibid.
199 **"Japan is not":** Ibid.
199 **"The Japanese shall not":** "Proclamation by the Heads of State, U.S.-U.K.-[U.S.S.R.]-China," undated, included with Document No. 592, FRUS, p. 1:894.
199 **"a very powerful":** Henry Stimson, diary entry for July 2, 1945, HLSP.
199 **"The president so far":** Ibid.

PART III

201 **"Our job":** Leslie Groves speech, November 19, 1945, Box 3, Thomas F. Farrell Collection, USAHEC.

Chapter 21

203 **"I'm on the way":** Harry Truman to Bess Truman, July 6, 1945, Box 14, Papers of Harry S. Truman Pertaining to Family, Business, and Personal Affairs, HSTL.
203 **At 6:01 a.m.:** William M. Rigdon, "Log of the President's Trip to the Berlin Conference, (July 6, 1945, to August 7, 1945)," July 6–7, 1945, pp. 1–2, Box 3, Rose Conway Papers HSTL.
204 **"He had to accomplish":** Daniels, *Man of Independence*, pp. 267–68.
204 **"unreconstructed rebel":** Truman, *Year of Decisions*, p. 220.
204 **"You tell Harry":** Ibid.
204 **"Oh, fiddlesticks!":** Ibid.
204 **Bess and Margaret had left:** Harry Truman, diary entry for June 1, 1945, in Ferrell, *Off the Record*, p. 40.
204 **"The Trumans were the closest":** West, *Upstairs at the White House*, p. 63.
204 **"I'm always":** Harry Truman, diary entry for June 1, 1945, in Ferrell, *Off the Record*, p. 40.
204 **"I can't help":** Harry Truman, diary entry for June 5, 1945, ibid., p. 43.
204 **"Don't think":** Harry Truman, diary entry for June 1, 1945, ibid., p. 40.
204 **Other times he entertained:** Harry Truman, diary entry for June 4, 1945, ibid., p. 42.
205 **"I sit here":** Harry Truman to Bess Truman, June 12, 1945, Box 14, Papers of Harry S. Truman Pertaining to Family, Business, and Personal Affairs, HSTL.

205 **He gifted:** "Desk Roosevelt Used Will Go to Hyde Park," *New York Times*, April 20, 1945, p. 10.

205 **With the exception of a tiny:** S. J. Woolfe, "President Truman Talks About His Job," *New York Times*, July 15, 1945, p. 48; "One Man's Office," *Newsweek*, July 9, 1945, p. 37.

205 **"I suppose I am":** Woolfe, "President Truman Talks," p. 48.

205 **The president likewise:** Truman, *Year of Decisions*, pp. 323–28.

205 **"The weakness":** Frank McNaughton to Donald Bermingham, "Add to Harry Truman (Cover) His Probable Policies," April 14, 1945, Box 8, Frank McNaughton Papers, HSTL.

205 **"blockhead":** Ferrell, *Truman in the White House*, p. 45.

206 **"Morgenthau," he colorfully :** Harry Truman, interview by Jonathan Daniels, November 12, 1949, in Research Notes Used in Connection with Writing *The Man of Independence*, Part I, Notes on Interviews, Box 1, Jonathan Daniels Papers, HSTL.

206 **To another aide:** Walter Brown, diary entry for August 4, 1945, Box 10, Walter J. Brown Papers, Clemson University Special Collections and Archives, Clemson, S.C.

206 **"If that is":** Truman, *Year of Decisions*, p. 327.

206 **"Some of my":** Harry Truman, diary entry for June 1, 1945, in Ferrell, *Off the Record*, p. 40.

206 **A Gallup poll published:** George Gallup, "Popularity of New President Greater Than FDR's at Zenith," *Washington Post*, July 1, 1945, p. B5.

206 **"His folksy":** "Truman Has Backing of Country in His First Big Three Meeting," *Newsweek*, July 16, 1945, p. 28.

206 **Unlike Roosevelt:** Bertram D. Hulen, "Truman Speeds Up Tempos of White House Activity," *New York Times*, May 13, 1945, p. E10.

206 **After work:** Eben Ayers, diary entry for May 26, 1945, in Ayers, *Truman in the White House*, p. 30.

206 **"His sincerity":** Ibid., p. 29.

206 **"The opinion":** Hulen, "Truman Speeds Up Tempos of White House Activity," p. E10.

206 **"vultures":** Transcript of Press and Radio Conference #10, June 7, 1945, Box 6, White House Official Reporter Files, HSTL.

206 **"wolves":** Transcript of Press and Radio Conference #19, August 16, 1945, ibid.

207 **"I was going":** Transcript of Press and Radio Conference #7, May 15, 1945, ibid.

207 **"If I go too fast":** Transcript of Press and Radio Conference #10, June 7, 1945.

207 **"He is making":** Eben Ayers, diary entry for June 1, 1945, in Ayers, *Truman in the White House*, p. 39.

207 **"The quality":** Cabell Phillips, "Truman Backed by Growing Public Confidence," *New York Times*, July 1, 1945, p. 41.

207 **Unlike with the previous:** "Senate Ratifies Charter of United Nations 89 to 2," *New York Times*, July 29, 1945, p. 1.

207 **While in San Francisco:** John H. Crider, "Truman Acclaimed on Arrival by Air to Close Parley," *New York Times*, June 26, 1945, p. 1; Alvin D. Hyman, "Crowds 5-Deep on Parade Route," *San Francisco Examiner*, June 26, 1945, p. 1.

207 **"You have created":** "Text of President's Address Before Final Parley Session," *New York Times*, June 27, 1945, p. 2.

207 **On his way back:** Carlos F. Hurd, "Truman Guest of Kansas City," *St. Louis Post-Dispatch*, June 28, 1945, p. 1; "Truman Can't Find White Shirts Either," *St. Louis Globe-Democrat*, June 29, 1945, p. 1.

208 **"It was necessary":** "Truman Tells Home Folks His Job Is Winning Peace," *New York Times*, June 28, 1945, p. 1.

208 **"There are two":** Ibid.

208 **"My immediate":** Truman, *Year of Decisions*, pp. 322–23.

208 **"The basic policy":** Combined Chiefs of Staff, "Estimate of the Enemy Situation (as of 6 July 1945)," July 8, 1945.
208 **"The incendiary":** Ibid.
209 **"Fanatical resistance":** Ibid.
209 **"Japan will use":** Ibid.
209 **"The Japanese believe":** Ibid.
209 **"Wish I didn't":** Harry Truman to Martha Ellen Truman and Mary Jane Truman, July 3, 1945, Box 19, Papers of Harry S. Truman Pertaining to Family, Business, and Personal Affairs, HSTL.
209 **"I wish this trip":** Harry Truman to Martha Ellen Truman and Mary Jane Truman, July 12, 1945, ibid.
209 **"How I hate":** Harry Truman, diary entry for July 7, 1945, in Ferrell, *Off the Record*, p. 49.
209 **In between packing:** Harry Truman to Bess Truman, July 3, 1945, Box 14, Papers of Harry S. Truman Pertaining to Family, Business, and Personal Affairs, HSTL.
209 **The State Department and the:** William M. Rigdon, *White House Sailor* (Garden City, N.Y.: Doubleday, 1962), p. 184.
210 **To assist on his:** Truman, *Year of Decisions*, p. 334; Rigdon, "Log of the President's Trip," List of President's Party, pp. v–vi.
210 **"The White House," Truman said:** Truman, *Year of Decisions*, p. 332.
210 **Aboard the *Augusta*:** Rigdon, "Log of the President's Trip," July 7, 1945, p. 2.
210 **The 9,100-ton:** "U.S.S. *Augusta*: Her Story," July 6, 1945, Box 137, President's Secretary's Files, HSTL.
210 **A small library:** "Books in the Library," undated, ibid.
210 **At seven a.m.:** Rigdon, "Log of the President's Trip," July 7, 1945, pp. 2–3.
211 **"He's the man":** Rigdon, *White House Sailor*, p. 188.
211 **"He took advantage":** Bohlen, *Witness to History*, p. 226.
211 **"He toured":** Rigdon, *White House Sailor*, p. 188.
211 **"Thus while the fire":** Rigdon, "Log of the President's Trip," July 10, 1945, p. 6.
211 **On Sunday he attended:** Ibid., July 8 and July 12, 1945, pp. 4, 8.
211 **Dinners proved:** Various symphonette and movie programs can be found in Box 137, President's Secretary's Files, HSTL.
212 **"He was an expert":** Robert Nixon, oral history by Jerry Ness, October 20, 1970, HSTL.
212 **"Mr. Nixon":** Ibid.
212 **"As we passed":** Rigdon, "Log of the President's Trip," July 15, 1945, p. 12.
212 **"I have always been":** David Anderson, "Truman Sees War's Havoc with Eisenhower as Guide," *New York Times*, July 16, 1945, p. 1.
212 **The president climbed:** Rigdon, "Log of the President's Trip," July 15, 1945, pp. 14–17.
213 **That first evening:** Rigdon, *White House Sailor*, p. 194.
213 **"Truman's personal":** Bohlen, *Witness to History*, p. 229.

Chapter 22

214 **"If the project":** Jimmy Byrnes to Franklin Roosevelt, March 3, 1945, Microfilm Roll #3, CMED.
214 **The test was scheduled:** Groves, *Now It Can Be Told*, p. 293.
214 **Like so much:** K.T. Bainbridge, *Trinity*, LA-6300-H, History Special Distribution, May 1976, pp. 1–3, Los Alamos Scientific Laboratory, Los Alamos, N.M.
215 **"Batter my heart":** Lansing Lamont, *Day of Trinity* (New York: Atheneum, 1965), p. 70. See also Robert Oppenheimer to Leslie Groves, October 20, 1962, Box 36, J. Robert Oppenheimer Papers, LOC.
215 **"Trinity":** Lamont, *Day of Trinity*, p. 70.

215 **To develop:** Ibid., pp. 94–96, 120–30.
215 **Ten miles:** William Laurence, *Dawn Over Zero: The Story of the Atomic Bomb* (Westport, CT: Greenwood Press, 1972), pp. 8–9, 188.
216 **To date:** Groves, *Now It Can Be Told*, p. 305.
216 **Four days earlier:** Laurence, *Dawn Over Zero*, pp. 189–90; Lamont, *Day of Trinity*, pp. 167–73.
216 **"The bomb," as one journalist:** Lamont, *Day of Trinity*, p. 175.
216 **"look for rabbits' feet":** Bainbridge, *Trinity*, p. 43.
216 **"This story":** Laurence, *Dawn Over Zero*, pp. xiii–xiv.
217 **About four p.m.:** Lamont, *Day of Trinity*, p. 190.
217 **"I knew":** Groves, *Now It Can Be Told*, p. 292.
217 **"He seemed":** Bird and Sherwin, *American Prometheus*, p. 264.
217 **"He resembled":** Lamont, *Day of Trinity*, p. 133.
217 **"Get some sleep":** Ibid., p. 196.
217 **At midnight, the duo:** Groves, *Now It Can Be Told*, p. 294.
217 **"If we postpone":** Lamont, *Day of Trinity*, p. 212.
217 **"I was devoting":** Groves, *Now It Can Be Told*, p. 294.
218 **"Groves," Farrell noted:** Lansing Lamont, interview by Thomas Farrell, tape 12 transcript, undated, Box 1, Lansing Lamont Papers, HSTL.
218 **At 3:45 a.m.:** Lamont, *Day of Trinity*, p. 213.
218 **"Prepare to fire":** Ibid, p. 218.
218 **"It is now":** Ibid., p. 220.
218 **"Our preparations":** Groves, *Now It Can Be Told*, pp. 295–96.
219 **"With the darkness":** Laurence, *Dawn Over Zero*, p. 6.
219 **"It was an eerie":** Ibid., p. 7.
219 **"Lord," Oppenheimer muttered:** Lamont, *Day of Trinity*, p. 226.
219 **"That scene inside":** Lansing Lamont, interview by Thomas Farrell, tape 12 transcript, undated, Box 1, Lansing Lamont Papers, HSTL.
219 **"Zero minus ten":** Laurence, *Dawn Over Zero*, p. 10.
219 **"Zero minus three":** Ibid.
219 **"From the east":** Ibid.
219 **"Now!":** Leslie Groves, "Memorandum for the Secretary of War," July 18, 1945, Box 1, Thomas F. Farrell Collection, USAHEC.
219 **"from about the size":** Alex Wellerstein, "The First Light of Trinity," *New Yorker*, July 16, 2015.
219 **"There rose":** Laurence, *Dawn Over Zero*, pp. 10–11.
219 **"It was golden":** Thomas Farrell, "Oppenheimer Scarcely Breathed," Atomic Heritage Foundation, Albuquerque, N.M.
220 **"The sun":** Laurence, *Dawn Over Zero*, p. 12.
220 **"My God," declared another:** Ibid., p. 191.
220 **Residents as far:** Lamont, *Day of Trinity*, pp. 240–41.
220 **"What's that!":** Lansing Lamont, "Rough Research Notes," Box 1, Lansing Lamont Papers, HSTL.
220 **Eviscerated wild:** Stafford Warren to Leslie Groves, "Report on Test II at Trinity, 16 July 1945," July 21, 1945, Microfilm Roll #1, CMED.
220 **"The thunder":** Laurence, *Dawn Over Zero*, p. 11.
220 **"I am become":** Bird and Sherwin, *American Prometheus*, p. 309.
220 **"Buddy":** Lamont, *Day of Trinity*, p. 239.
220 **"As to the present war":** Thomas Farrell, "Oppenheimer Scarcely Breathed," Atomic Heritage Foundation, Albuquerque, N.M.

220 **At base camp:** Groves, "Memorandum for the Secretary of War," July 18, 1945.
221 **"I personally":** Ibid.
221 **"We share a feeling":** Ernest Lawrence, "Thoughts by E.O. Lawrence," July 16, 1945, Box 2, Atomic Bomb Collection, HSTL.
221 **"I am sure":** Laurence, *Dawn Over Zero*, p. 11.
221 **"Now," the test:** Lansing Lamont, "Notes from Gen. Leslie Groves (1/11/65)," Box 1, Lansing Lamont Papers, HSTL.
221 **"I'm proud":** Groves, *Now It Can Be Told*, p. 298.
221 **"The war is over," Farrell interjected:** Ibid.

Chapter 23

222 **"It was a great new force":** Leslie Groves, "Memorandum for the Secretary of War," July 18, 1945.
222 **On July 16, 1945:** "Silence on Stalin," *New York Times*, July 17, 1945, p. 1.
222 **At eleven a.m., Winston Churchill:** Rigdon, "Log of the President's Trip," July 16, 1945, p. 18.
222 **"He came to call":** Truman, *Year of Decisions*, p. 340.
222 **"I nearly wept":** Martin Gilbert, *"Never Despair": Winston S. Churchill, 1945–1965* (Toronto: Stoddart, 1988), p. 61.
223 **"No," the prime minister:** Truman, *Year of Decisions*, p. 340.
223 **Truman hopped:** Michael Neiberg, *Potsdam: The End of World War II and the Remaking of Europe* (New York: Basic Books, 2015), p. 121.
223 **"Men and tanks":** Truman, *Year of Decisions*, p. 341.
223 **"This is the most":** Leahy, *I Was There*, p. 395.
223 **"I am only sorry":** Ernest B. Vaccaro and Daniel De Luce, "Big 3 Talks Now May Be Under Way," *Washington Post*, July 17, 1945, p. 1.
223 **"This one-time":** Leahy, *I Was There*, p. 395.
223 **"It is a terrible":** "Silence on Stalin: Two of The Three Big Leaders Meet in Berlin," *New York Times*, July 17, 1945, p. 1.
224 **"I never saw":** Merriman Smith, "Chief Spends Day with Churchill," *Daily News*, July 17, 1945, p. 1.
224 **Churchill followed:** "Silence on Stalin," p. 1.
224 **"It is just":** Larry Hirschback letter, July 13, 1945, in the display case at the National World War II Museum, New Orleans, La.
224 **"The course Hitler":** Winston Churchill, *The Second World War*, vol. 6, *Triumph and Tragedy* (Boston: Houghton Mifflin, 1953), p. 631.
224 **"The whole world":** John McCloy, diary entry for July 26, 1945, JJMP.
224 **"It was not hard":** Leahy, *I Was There*, p. 396.
225 **"That," the admiral:** Ibid.
225 **"After looking":** "Notes of the Trip of the Secretary of War (July 6 to July 28, 1945, inclusive)," p. 23, Microfilm Roll #128, HLSP.
225 **"There were no young":** Leahy, *I Was There*, p. 396
225 **"In that two-hour":** Truman, *Year of Decisions*, p. 341.
225 **"How the people":** John McCloy, diary entry for July 17, 1945, JJMP.
225 **"I felt," he lamented:** "Notes of the Trip of the Secretary of War," p. 24.
225 **"Operated on":** George Harrison to Henry Stimson, July 16, 1945, WAR-32887, Box 2, Atomic Bomb Collection, HSTL. See also "Notes of the Trip of the Secretary of War," p. 21.
226 **"A remotely":** Groves, *Now It Can Be Told*, p. 301.
226 **"I hope it does not":** John McCloy, diary entry for July 16, 1945, JJMP.
226 **The president sat down:** Rigdon, "Log of the President's Trip," July 16, 1945, p. 20.

226 **"There was no":** Leahy, *I Was There*, p. 396.
226 **"Both he and Byrnes":** Henry Stimson, "Notes for Diary," July 16, 1945, Microfilm Roll #128, HLSP.
226 **"As I read":** Truman, *Year of Decisions*, p. 415.
226 **"I looked up":** Harry Truman, diary entry for July 17, 1945, in Ferrell, *Off the Record*, p. 53.
227 **"Stalin looked":** Bohlen, *Witness to History*, p. 230.
227 **"You could":** Truman, *Year of Decisions*, p. 341.
227 **"I told Stalin":** Harry Truman, diary entry for July 17, 1945, in Ferrell, *Off the Record*, p. 53.
227 **"Most of the big":** Ibid.
227 **"Doctor has just":** George Harrison to Henry Stimson, July 17, 1945, WAR-33556, Box 2, Atomic Bomb Collection, HSTL.
227 **"Well," he declared:** Hodgson, *Colonel*, p. 333.
227 **"tremendously pleased":** Henry Stimson, "Notes for Diary," July 18, 1945, Microfilm Roll #128, HLSP. See also "Notes of the Trip of the Secretary of War," p. 27.
228 **"We were not":** Truman, *Year of Decisions*, p. 415.
228 **It was not until:** "Notes of the Trip of the Secretary of War," p. 36.
228 **Groves had written:** Groves, *Now It Can Be Told*, p. 303.
228 **"For the first":** Groves, "Memorandum for the Secretary of War," July 18, 1945.
228 **"We are all fully":** Ibid.
228 **"It was an immensely":** Henry Stimson, diary entry for July 21, 1945, HLSP.
228 **"I should have liked":** John McCloy, diary entry for July 21, 1945, JJMP.
228 **"The President was tremendously":** Henry Stimson, diary entry for July 21, 1945, HLSP.
229 **"Now I know":** Henry Stimson, diary entry for July 22, 1945, HLSP.
229 **"What was gunpowder?":** Giovannitti and Freed, *Decision to Drop the Bomb*, p. 249.

Chapter 24

230 **"It is impossible":** Shigenori Togo to Naotake Sato, July 25, 1945, Document No. 1233, in FRUS, p. 2:1261.
230 **On July 7:** Butow, *Japan's Decision to Surrender*, p. 123.
230 **Hirohito recommended:** Ibid.
230 **At three p.m. on July 12:** Ibid., pp. 124–25.
231 **"The war," Konoe concluded:** Ibid., p. 125.
231 **"As long as America":** Shigenori Togo to Naotake Sato, July 12, 1945, Document No. 582, in FRUS, p. 1:876.
231 **"I believe it no":** Naotake Sato to Shigenori Togo, July 12, 1945, Document No. 584, in FRUS, p. 1:877.
231 **"If indeed":** Ibid., p. 1:878.
231 **"I have expressed":** Ibid.
231 **On July 13, 1945:** Naotake Sato to Shigenori Togo, July 13, 1945, Document No. 586, in FRUS, pp. 1:879–80.
232 **"As long as the dispatch":** Naotake Sato to Shigenori Togo, July 13, 1945, Document No. 587, in FRUS, p. 1:881.
232 **At midnight, Lozovsky:** Butow, *Japan's Decision to Surrender*, p. 126.
232 **"In the final":** Naotake Sato to Shigenori Togo, July 15, 1945, Document No. 588, in FRUS, p. 1:883.
232 **"If the enemy":** Shigenori Togo to Naotake Sato, July 17, 1945, Document No. 1224, in FRUS, p. 2:1249.
232 **At three p.m. on July 18:** Charles Bohlen, "Meeting of President Truman with Generalissimo Stalin at Stalin's Villa, three p.m., July 18, 1945, on the Occasion of the President's Courtesy Call on Stalin," March 28, 1960, Document No. 1419, FRUS, p. 2:1587.

233 **But American awareness:** Richard B. Frank, *Downfall: The End of the Japanese Empire* (New York: Random House, 1999), pp. 103–4.
233 **"Things are moving":** John McCloy, diary entry for July 16, 1945, JJMP.
233 **"The gist":** James Forrestal, diary entry for July 15, 1945, in Millis, *Forrestal Diaries*, p. 75.
233 **"The President replied":** Bohlen, "Meeting of President Truman with Generalissimo Stalin," March 28, 1960, in FRUS, p. 2:1588.
233 **"It might be desirable":** Ibid.
233 **"The President," the memo noted:** Ibid.
234 **War with Russia:** Walter Brown, diary entry for July 18, 1945, Box 10, Walter J. Brown Papers, Clemson University Special Collections and Archives, Clemson, S.C.
234 **"general in form":** Naotake Sato to Shigenori Togo, July 19, 1945, Document No. 1226, in FRUS, p. 2:1251.
234 **"The Government of the USSR":** Ibid.
234 **The following day the ambassador:** Naotake Sato to Shigenori Togo, July 19, 1945, Document No. 1227, in FRUS, p. 2:1251.
234 **"Our Empire":** Naotake Sato to Shigenori Togo, July 20, 1945, Document No. 1228, in FRUS, p. 2:1253.
234 **"Do you think":** Ibid.
234 **"Our country":** Ibid., p. 2:1255.
234 **"The resulting imbalance":** Ibid., p. 2:1256.
235 **"I realize":** Ibid., p. 2:1257.
235 **On July 21:** Shigenori Togo to Naotake Sato, July 21, 1945, Document No. 1229, in FRUS, p. 2:1257.
235 **"We cannot":** Shigenori Togo to Naotake Sato, July 21, 1945, Document No. 1230, in FRUS, p. 2:1258.
235 **American code breakers:** Douglas J. MacEachin, "The Final Months of the War with Japan," December 1998, pp. 19–23.
235 **"Tokyo," as the July 17:** Magic Diplomatic Intercept No. 1210, July 17, 1945 (SRS 1732), in Kort, *Columbia Guide to Hiroshima and the Bomb*, p. 283.
235 **"Tokyo *again* says no":** Magic Diplomatic Intercept No. 1214, Jul 22, 1945 (SRS 1736), ibid., p. 284.
235 **"The response":** James Forrestal, diary entry for July 24, 1945, in Millis, *Forrestal Diaries*, p. 76.
236 **"If she should":** Stimson, "Decision to Use the Atomic Bomb," p. 101.

Chapter 25

237 **"That the war":** "Japan on the Spot," editorial, *Washington Post*, August 1, 1945, p. 6.
237 **"Atomic bombs," Szilard wrote:** "A Petition to the President of the United States," July 3, 1945, Microfilm Roll #6, HBF.
237 **"Our use":** Ibid.
238 **"In view":** Ibid.
238 **"The fact":** Leo Szilard to various research leaders, July 4, 1945, Microfilm Roll #6, HBF.
238 **Fifty-three physicists:** Szilard, *Reminiscences*, p. 130.
238 **"His colleagues":** Compton, *Atomic Quest*, p. 242.
238 **"the terms":** "A Petition to the President of the United States," July 17, 1945, Box 114, LSP.
238 **This time seventy:** Szilard, *Reminiscences*, p. 131.
238 **Szilard's advocacy:** Nichols, *Road to Trinity*, p. 186; Compton, *Atomic Quest*, p. 242.
238 **Eighteen scientists:** Untitled petition, July 13, 1945, Microfilm Roll #6, HBF.

239 **"We feel":** Petition to the President of the United States, undated, ibid.

239 **"Are not the men":** A Petition to the Administration of Clinton Laboratories, undated, ibid.

239 **"It is hard":** Evan Young to M. D. Whitaker, July 14, 1945, ibid.

239 **"I have buddies":** Compton, *Atomic Quest*, p. 243.

239 **"It was difficult":** Ibid.

239 **Military intelligence tipped:** Grover C. Thompson to John Lansdale, Jr., "Leo Szilard," July 11, 1945, Microfilm Roll #6, HBF.

240 **Daniels's questionnaire:** Farrington Daniels to Arthur Compton, "Poll on the Use of Weapons," July 13, 1945, ibid. A copy of this poll can also be found in Arthur H. Compton and Farrington Daniels, "A Poll of Scientists at Chicago, July 1945," *Bulletin of Atomic Scientists* 4, no. 2 (February 1948), p. 44.

240 **"My experience":** Compton, *Atomic Quest*, p. 244.

240 **"Washington wants at":** Ibid., p. 246.

240 **"Washington wants to":** Ibid., p. 247.

240 **"I knew all too":** Ibid.

240 **"My vote":** Ibid.

241 **"This coincides":** Arthur Compton to Kenneth Nichols, July 24, 1945, Microfilm Roll #6, HBF.

241 **"Contrary to the hopes":** Kenneth Nichols to Leslie Groves, July 24, 1945, ibid.

241 **Seven days later:** Leslie Groves to George Harrison, "Receipt of Material, August 1, 1945, ibid.

241 **"The petitions":** Leslie Groves to Harry Truman, August 16, 1963, Box 52, Post-Presidential Papers, HSTL.

241 **"As far as":** R. Gordon Arneson, "Memorandum for the Files," May 24, 1946, Microfilm Roll #6, HBF.

Chapter 26

242 **"Japan's military":** Barnet Nover, "Terms for Japan," *Washington Post*, July 1, 1945, p. 6

242 **"The Japanese soldier":** Henry Stimson to Harry Truman, "The Conduct of the War with Japan," July 16, 1945, in FRUS, p. 2:1265.

242 **"It seems to me":** Ibid., p. 2:1266.

242 **The new secretary of state:** Cordell Hull, *The Memoirs of Cordell Hull* (London: Hodder & Stoughton, 1948), pp. 2:1593–94; Joseph Grew to James Byrnes, July 16, 1945, in FRUS, p. 2:1267.

243 **"So hot":** William Philip Simms, "The $64 Question Is Whether or Not We'll Boot out Hiro," *Washington Daily News*, July 18, 1945, p. 12.

243 **"Much might be gained":** "Senator Urges Terms to Japs Be Explained," *Washington Post*, July 3, 1945, p. 1.

243 **Senator Homer Capehart:** John O'Donnell, "Capitol Stuff," *Daily News*, July 3, 1945, p. 4.

243 **"It isn't a matter":** "Senator Urges Terms to Japs."

243 **"Defeat of Japan":** "Barkley Spurns Capehart Plan," *Indianapolis News*, July 13, 1945, p. 1.

243 **"It is quite conceivable":** Walter Lippmann, "Today and Tomorrow," *Washington Post*, July 12, 1945, p. 7.

244 **"We could shorten":** "Terms for Japan," editorial, *New York Times*, July 4, 1945, p. 12.

244 **"There is no short-cut":** Ramon Lavalle, "Fight to the Finish," letter to editor, *Washington Post*, July 7, 1945, p. 4.

244 **"Operation may be possible":** George Harrison to Henry Stimson, WAR 3672, July 23, 1945, Box 2, Atomic Bomb Collection, HSTL.

244 **"Every effort":** John McCloy, "Memorandum of Conversation with General Marshall and the Secretary of War," May 29, 1945, included with John McCloy, diary entry for May 29, 1945, JJMP.

244 **Armed with the proposed:** Truman, *Year of Decisions*, pp. 416–19; Henry Stimson, diary entry for July 24, 1945, HLSP.

244 **"He said that he had":** Henry Stimson, diary entry for July 24, 1945, HLSP.

245 **"It was designed":** Stimson, "Decision to Use the Atomic Bomb," p. 104.

245 **Even an internal:** See David Lloyd to Harry Truman, January 6, 1953, Box 95, President's Secretary's Files, HSTL.

245 **In all likelihood:** Douglas J. MacEachin, *The Final Months of the War with Japan: Signals Intelligence, U.S. Invasion Planning and the A-Bomb Decision* (Central Intelligence Agency: Center for the Study of Intelligence, 1998), p. 31.

245 **By the third week:** Ibid., pp. 18–19.

245 **The Japanese reinforcement:** Giangreco, *Hell to Pay*, pp. 102, 121.

245 **Japanese leaders highlighted:** Ibid., p. 83.

246 **"This threatening development":** MacEachin, *Final Months of the War with Japan*, pp. 21–22.

246 **"We shall probably":** Giangreco, *Hell to Pay*, p. 127.

246 **"It was his opinion":** Harry Truman to James Cate, January 12, 1953, Box 95, President's Secretary's Files, HSTL.

246 **Each month:** Richard B. Frank, "Counting All the Dead," *American Heritage* 68, no. 5 (August 2023); Richard B. Frank interview by the author, October 30, 2025.

246 **"It is my suggestion":** Harry Truman, "The Story of the Atomic Bomb," undated, Box 646, Post-Presidential Papers, HSTL.

246 **"Truman made no":** McCullough, *Truman*, p. 442.

246 **"As time went on":** Groves, *Now It Can Be Told*, p. 265.

247 **"No man":** Stimson, "Decision to Use the Atomic Bomb," p. 106.

247 **"The decision":** Churchill, *Triumph and Tragedy*, p. 639.

247 **"The final decision":** Truman, *Year of Decisions*, p. 419.

247 **"We have discovered":** Harry Truman, diary entry for July 25, 1945, in Ferrell, *Off the Record*, p. 55.

247 **"Even if the Japs":** Ibid., pp. 55–56.

248 **"We faced":** Byrnes, *Speaking Frankly*, p. 262.

248 **"Even if we":** Stimson diary, entry for July 23, 1945, HLSP.

248 **"I casually mentioned":** Truman, *Year of Decisions*, p. 416.

249 **"I knew what":** Churchill, *Triumph and Tragedy*, p. 670.

249 **"How did it go?":** Ibid.

249 **Stalin's seeming lack:** McCullough, *Truman*, p. 443.

249 **At 9:20 p.m.:** Truman, *Year of Decisions*, p. 390.

249 **Shortwave radios:** "Allied Demand Broadcast in 24 Languages," *New York Times*, July 27, 1945, p. 6.

249 **"The prodigious":** Potsdam Declaration, July 26, 1945, Box 190, President's Secretary's Files, HSTL.

249 **"The full application":** Ibid.

250 **"Following are our":** Ibid.

250 **"We do not":** Ibid.

250 **"We call upon":** Ibid.

250 **"Allies Order":** "Allies Order Japan to Quit or Be Destroyed," *New York Times*, July 27, 1945, p. 1.

250 **"Last Call":** "Last Call to Japan: Surrender Now," editorial, *Philadelphia Inquirer*, July 27, 1945, p. 10.

250 **"U.S. Warns":** "U.S. Warns Nips That Nation Is Doomed," *Daily Democrat*, July 27, 1945, p. 1.

250 **"The fate of Japan":** "Potsdam Ultimatum," editorial, *Indianapolis News*, July 27, 1945, p. 10.

250 **"Quit now":** "Ultimatum from Potsdam," editorial, *Ventura County Star-Free Press*, July 27, 1945, p. 10.

250 **"Japan is finished":** "Surrender or Annihilation," editorial, *Duluth News-Tribune*, July 27, 1945, p. 12.

251 **If Japan accepted:** Truman, *Year of Decisions*, p. 421.

251 **"Maybe the Secretary's big bomb":** John McCloy, diary entry for July 27, 1945, JJMP.

251 **"All your local":** George Harrison to Henry Stimson, July 21, 1945, Microfilm Roll #4, HBF.

251 **"Aware of no":** Henry Stimson to George Harrison, July 21, 1945, ibid.

251 **"As to the matter":** Henry Stimson, diary entry for July 22, 1945, HLSP.

251 **"He told me":** Ibid.

251 **"The targets":** Joint Chiefs of Staff to Douglas MacArthur, Chester Nimitz, and Carl Spaatz, WARX 38458, Box 7, Papers of Lt. Gen. Richard Sutherland, MacArthur Memorial Archives and Library, Norfolk, Va.

251 **"Plans are to drop":** John Stone to Hap Arnold, "Groves Project," July 24, 1945, Microfilm Roll #1, CMED. A copy of this memo can also be found in Box 2, Atomic Bomb Collection, HSTL.

252 **A veteran of the European:** David R. Metz, *Master of Airpower: General Carl A. Spaatz* (Novato, Calif.: Presidio Press, 1988), pp. 302–3.

252 **"When the atomic":** Carl Spaatz, diary entry for August 11, 1945, Box 21, Carl Spaatz Papers, LOC.

252 **"If I'm going to kill":** Fletcher Knebel and Charles W. Bailey II, "Hiroshima: The Decision that Changed the World," *Look*, June 7, 1960, p. 27, copy on file in Box 5, Eben A. Ayers Papers, HSTL.

252 **Groves drafted:** Thomas Handy to George Marshall, July 24, 1945, Microfilm Roll #4, HBF.

252 **"The 509th Composite Group":** Thomas Handy to Carl Spaatz, July 25, 1945, Box 95, President's Secretary's Files, HSTL.

252 **"Hiroshima according to":** Headquarters, U.S. Army Strategic Air Forces, Guam to War Department, July 31, 1945, Microfilm Roll #1, CMED.

252 **"Targets previously assigned":** War Department to General Spaatz, Commanding General, U.S. Strategic Air Forces, Guam, July 31, 1945, ibid.

253 **"Practically all structures":** Leslie Groves to George Marshall, July 30, 1945, Box 2, Atomic Bomb Collection, HSTL.

253 **"At 10 miles":** Ibid.

253 **At six a.m.:** Pacific War Research Society, *Japan's Longest Day*, pp. 12–13.

253 **"Wait," the foreign minister:** Ibid., p. 14.

254 **"extremely impolitic":** Ibid., p. 15.

254 **"remain in a wise":** Ibid. p. 17.

254 **"wait and see":** Butow, *Japan's Decision to Surrender*, p. 146.

254 **"kill it with silence":** Pacific War Research Society, *Japan's Longest Day*, p. 16.

254 **"The government does not":** Butow, *Japan's Decision to Surrender*, p. 148.

254 **"Japs Refuse":** "Japs Refuse to Surrender," *Indianapolis News*, July 27. 1945, p. 1.

254 **"Cabinet Decides":** "Jap Cabinet Decides to Fight on Despite Destruction Ultimatum," *Los Angeles Times*, July 28, 1945, p. 1.

254 **"Demand to Be Ignored":** "Domei Says Demand to Be Ignored," *Fort Worth Star-Telegram*, July 28, 1945, p. 1.

255 **"The time schedule":** Henry Stimson to Harry Truman, WAR-41011, July 30, 1945, Box 59, George M. Elsey Papers, HSTL. The copy on file in the Truman Library has faded with time. A more legible copy can be found in Microfilm Roll #4, HBF.

255 **"Suggestions approved":** Ibid.

PART IV

257 **"Atomic energy knows neither":** Marquis Childs, "Playing with Atomic Fire," *Washington Post*, August 8, 1945, p. 7.

Chapter 27

259 **"The atomic bomb":** Leslie Groves speech, September 21, 1945, Box 3, Thomas F. Farrell Collection, USAHEC.

259 **"My job":** Paul W. Tibbets, Jr., with Clair Stebbins and Harry Franken, *The Tibbets Story* (New York: Stein & Day, 1978), p. 156.

260 **"I could see":** Ibid., p. 21.

260 **"I'm not so sure":** Ibid., p. 37.

260 **"If you want to fly":** Ibid., p. 38.

260 **"The die":** Ibid., p. 39.

261 **"A portion":** Ibid., p. 93.

261 **"A successful takeoff":** Ibid., p. 107.

261 **"If it was":** Ibid., p. 108.

261 **"Eisenhower could see":** Ibid.

261 **"All of us":** Edward Jean Smith, *Eisenhower: In War and Peace* (New York: Random House, 2012), p. 230.

262 **"If we send them":** Tibbets, *Tibbets Story*, p. 130.

262 **"Something snapped":** Ibid., p. 131.

262 **"an excellent":** James H. Doolittle with Carroll V. Glines, *I Could Never Be So Lucky Again: An Autobiography* (New York: Bantam Books, 1991), p. 310.

262 **"I've just received":** Tibbets, *Tibbets Story*, p. 131.

262 **"I didn't realize":** Ibid., p. 139.

263 **In July 1943:** Thomas Collison, *The Superfortress Is Born: The Story of the Boeing B-29* (New York: Duell, Sloan & Pearce, 1945), pp. 145–48; "14 Killed in Crash of a Bomber Igniting Seattle Packing Plant," *New York Times*, February 19, 1943, p. 21.

263 **"It was," as Curtis LeMay:** Curtis E. LeMay and Bill Yenne, *Superfortress: The B-29 and American Air Power* (New York: McGraw-Hill, 1988), p. 63.

263 **"You could hardly":** Paul Tibbets oral history by Kenneth Leish, December 1960, McDermott Library, U.S. Air Force Academy, Colorado Springs, Colo.

263 **"We got the airplane":** Ibid.

263 **"I had," he said:** Ibid.

263 **"After the excitement":** Tibbets, *Tibbets Story*, p. 151.

263 **"I'd like to ask":** Paul Tibbets, "I Dropped the Atomic Bomb on Hiroshima," undated manuscript, Microfilm Roll #38640, Paul Tibbets, Jr., Papers, AFHRA.

263 **"The penetrating nature":** Tibbets, *Tibbets Story*, p. 153.

264 **"Have you heard":** Tibbets, "I Dropped the Atomic Bomb," undated.

264 **"Now, if I told you":** Ibid.

264 **"Ours was not":** Tibbets, *Tibbets Story*, p. 155.

264 **"The organization":** Ibid.

264 **"You can't tell":** Paul Tibbets, "Training the 509th for Hiroshima," *Air Force Magazine*, August 1973, p. 51, copy on file in Microfilm Roll #38640, Paul Tibbets, Jr., Papers, AFHRA.

264 **"Paul," he concluded:** Mike Howard, "The Man Who Dropped the Bomb," *Plain Dealer Magazine*, March 25, 1984, p. 16, copy on file in Microfilm Roll #38641, Paul Tibbets, Jr., Papers, AFHRA.

265 **"We read mail":** Tibbets, *Tibbets Story*, p. 166.

265 **"You have been brought":** Ibid.

266 **"It was obviously":** Ibid., p. 170.

266 **"Calculations":** Ibid.

266 **"We would," Tibbets said:** Ibid., p. 171.

266 **"If their language":** Ibid., p. 177.

266 **Groves had initially set:** Frederick Ashworth to Leslie Groves, February 24, 1945, in Microfilm Roll #1, CMED. See also Groves, *Now It Can Be Told*, pp. 278–79.

267 **Since its capture:** Wesley Frank Craven and James Lea Cate, eds., *The Army Air Forces in World War II,* vol. 5, *The Pacific: Matterhorn to Nagasaki, June 1944 to August 1945* (Washington, D.C.: Office of Air Force History, 1983), pp. 517–20; "U.S. Tinian Airport World's Largest," *New York Times*, February 17, 1945, p. 2.

267 **Tinian's shape:** Tibbets, *Tibbets Story*, p. 181.

267 **"Tinian Island":** Ibid.

267 **In preparation:** Norman F. Ramsey, "History of Project A," September 27, 1945. A copy of that document can be found in John Coster-Mullen, *Atom Bombs: The Top-Secret Inside Story of Little Boy and Fat Man* (Privately Printed, 2004), p. 284.

267 **Along with the airmen:** Commemorative Booklet, 509th Composite Group, 50th Anniversary Reunion, August 5–10, 1995, pp. 34–35, in Box 1, Atomic Bomb Collection, HSTL.

267 **"It was an island":** Laurence, *Dawn Over Zero*, p. 200.

267 **"To the other":** Tibbets, *Tibbets Story*, p. 190.

267 **That practice:** History of the 509th Composite Group, Activation to August 15, 1945, undated, Microfilm Roll #B0678, AFHRA; Consolidated Statistical Summary of Combat Operations, Mission Nos. 1–12, August 4, 1945, Microfilm Roll #B0680, AFHRA.

268 **"These targets":** Tactical Mission Report No. Special, July 20, 1945–August 14, 1945, undated, Microfilm Roll #A7741, AFHRA.

268 **All told, thirty-eight:** Consolidated Statistical Summary of Combat Operations, Mission Nos. 1–12, August 4, 1945, Microfilm Roll #B0680, AFHRA.

268 **"These flights":** Tibbets, *Tibbets Story*, p. 192.

268 **In the latter half:** Craven and Cate, *Army Air Forces in World War II,* pp. 5:674–75.

268 **He more than tripled:** Ibid.

268 **"We are certainly":** Curtis E. LeMay to Helen LeMay, July 10, 1945, in Benjamin Paul Hegi, *From Wright Field, Ohio, to Hokkaido, Japan: General Curtis E. LeMay's Letters to His Wife Helen, 1941–1945,* ed. Alfred F. Hurley (Denton: University of North Texas Libraries, 2015), p. 370.

269 **"We hope":** "LeMay Tells Japanese People Where 'Superforts' Will Hit," *New York Times*, July 28, 1945, p. 1.

269 **Against this backdrop:** Tibbets, *Tibbets Story*, pp. 194–95; Al Christman, *Target Hiroshima: Deak Parsons and the Creation of the Atomic Bomb* (Annapolis, Md.: Naval Institute Press, 1998), p. 178.

269 **"I assured":** Ibid., p. 195.

269 **"Radar was":** Groves, *Now It Can Be Told*, p. 316.

269 **"Perched at the head":** USSBS, *The Effects of the Atomic Bombs on Hiroshima and Nagasaki* (Washington, D.C.: U.S. Government Printing Office, 1946), pp. 5–6; USSBS, *The*

Effects of the Atomic Bomb on Hiroshima, Japan (Washington, D.C.: U.S. Government Printing Office, 1947), pp. 1:8–10, 65–73.

270 **"Probably more than":** Manhattan Engineer District, "The Atomic Bombings of Hiroshima and Nagasaki," June 29, 1946, p. 7.

270 **"Hiroshima," as one intelligence:** "Hiroshima," 90.30, undated, Microfilm Roll #A7809, AFHRA.

270 **"It was a beehive":** Groves, *Now It Can Be Told*, p. 316.

270 **"worst slum":** USSBS, *Effects of the Atomic Bomb on Hiroshima*, p. 1:12.

271 **Armed with instructions:** Tibbets, *Tibbets Story*, p. 196.

271 **"No Tactical Mission":** Field Orders, Number 13, August 2, 1945, Microfilm Roll #B0679, AFHRA.

272 **"No friendly":** Ibid.

272 **"I can say":** Christman, *Target Hiroshima*, p. 182.

272 **"Her name":** Tibbets, *Tibbets Story*, p. 197.

272 **"You know":** Laurence, *Dawn Over Zero*, p. 205.

273 **"Are you sure":** Tibbets, *Tibbets Story*, p. 199.

273 **"Go ahead":** Laurence, *Dawn Over Zero*, p. 206.

273 **"There may not":** Ibid., p. 207.

273 **"With its coat":** Tibbets, *Tibbets Story*, p. 201.

273 **"From the Boys":** Ibid.

273 **"For God's sake":** Fletcher Knebel and Charles W. Bailey II, "Hiroshima: the Decision that Changes the World," *Look*, June 7, 1960, p. 28, copy on file in Box 5, Eben A. Ayers Papers, HSTL.

273 **"I wouldn't dare":** Gordon Thomas, and Max Morgan-Witts, *Ruin from the Air: The Atomic Mission to Hiroshima* (London: Hamish Hamilton, 1977), p. 289.

274 **"He was confident":** Tibbets, *Tibbets Story*, p. 201.

274 **"What the Hell":** Ibid., p. 288.

274 **"Colonel," he said:** Ibid., pp. 288–89.

274 **"It was a decision":** Ibid.

274 **"If something happened":** Ibid., p. 292.

274 **"I soon found":** Tibbets, *Tibbets Story*, p. 202.

274 **"Tonight is the night":** Laurence, *Dawn Over Zero*, p. 207.

275 **"Do your jobs":** Thomas and Morgan-Witts, *Ruin from the Air*, p. 293.

275 **"The men":** Laurence, *Dawn Over Zero*, p. 208.

275 **"All were warned":** Tibbets, *Tibbets Story*, p. 203.

275 **"May the men":** Laurence, *Dawn Over Zero*, p. 209.

275 **"I hope you don't":** Tibbets, *Tibbets Story*, p. 204.

276 **"I had known":** Ibid., p. 206.

276 **"The picture taking":** Ibid.

276 **"You guys":** Thomas and Morgan-Witts, *Ruin from the Air*, p. 298.

276 **Once in place:** AN 01-20EJA-1, "Pilot's Flight Operating Instructions for Airplanes Army Models B-29 and B-29A," May 20, 1945, pp. 20–23.

277 **"It caught immediately":** Tibbets, *Tibbets Story*, p. 207.

277 **"This is just":** Ibid., p. 209.

277 **"Dimples Eight Two":** Ibid. p. 210.

278 **"Will he ever":** Laurence, *Dawn Over Zero*, p. 210.

278 **"Come on, Paul":** Robert A. Lewis, as told to Eliot Tozer, "How We Dropped the A-Bomb," *Popular Science*, August 1957, p. 74.

278 **"No!" Tibbets declared:** Thomas and Morgan-Witts, *Ruin from the Air*, p. 302.

Chapter 28

279 **"Our people":** Richard Russell to Harry Truman, August 7, 1945, Box 735, Official File, HSTL.

276 **Dutch Van Kirk:** Dutch Van Kirk mission log, August 6, 1945, Atomic Heritage Foundation, Albuquerque, N.M. All times and elevations referenced in this chapter are drawn from this log.

279 **"It was a pleasant":** Tibbets, *Tibbets Story*, p. 211.

262 **"Colonel Tibbets":** Lewis, "How We Dropped the A-Bomb," p. 74.

280 **"Check that green":** William Parsons, "Check List for Loading Charge in Plane with Special Breech Plug," undated, in Microfilm Roll #1, CMED.

280 **"How is Parsons":** Lewis, "How We Dropped the A-Bomb," p. 74.

280 **"With the bomb armed":** Tibbets, *Tibbets Story*, p. 212.

280 **"Everything," he scribbled:** Robert Lewis, diary entry for August 6, 1945, Box 1, Atomic Bomb Collection, HSTL.

280 **With the mission safely:** Jacob Beser, *Hiroshima and Nagasaki Revisited* (Memphis, Tenn.: Global Press, 1988), p. 106.

280 **"The other planes":** Tibbets, *Tibbets Story*, p. 212.

281 **"Have you figured":** Ibid., p. 213.

281 **"The colonel better":** Robert Lewis, diary entry for August 6, 1945.

281 **"I finally gave":** Groves, *Now It Can Be Told*, p. 320.

281 **"I don't want":** Ibid.

282 **"This report":** Ibid., p. 321.

282 **"The hours":** Ibid.

282 **"I think everyone":** Robert Lewis, diary entry for August 6, 1945.

282 **"If the first priority":** Tibbets, *Tibbets Story*, p. 218.

284 **"The bomb is now":** Robert Lewis, diary entry for August 6, 1945.

284 **"Y-3, Q-3":** Tibbets, *Tibbets Story*, p. 220.

284 **"I translated":** Ibid.

284 **"It's Hiroshima":** Ibid.

284 **"Right now":** Robert Lewis, diary entry for August 6, 1945.

284 **"We had studied":** Tibbets, *Tibbets Story*, p. 221.

222 **"The early morning":** Ibid.

284 **"Do you all agree":** Ibid.

285 **"Okay, I've got":** Ibid., p. 222.

285 **"It's all yours":** Ibid., p. 223.

285 **"My eyes were fixed":** Ibid.

285 **"Goggles":** George R. Caron with Charlotte E. Meares, *Fires of a Thousand Suns: The George R. "Bob" Caron Story—Tail Gunner of the Enola Gay* (Westminster, Colo.: Web Publishing Co., 1995), p. 246.

285 **Local authorities:** USSB, *Effects of the Atomic Bomb on Hiroshima*, p. 1:84; Hiroshima Peace Culture Foundation, *Eyewitness Testimonies: Appeals from the A-Bomb Survivors* (Hiroshima, Japan: Bunkasya, 2017), p. 14.

285 **"Because Hiroshima":** Yoshiteru Kosakai, comp., *A-Bomb: A City Tells Its Story*, trans. Kiyoko Kageyama, Charlotte Susu-Mago, and Kaoru Ogura (Hiroshima: Hiroshima Peace Culture Foundation, 1972), p. 3.

285 **"When I returned":** Tadataka Sasaki, "Asking Young People to Create a Peaceful Country," in Hiroshima Association for the Success of the Atomic Bomb Exhibition, *After 60 Years, A-Bomb Survivors Speak Out: An Anthology of the Experiences of Hiro-*

shima Atomic Bomb Victims (Hiroshima, Japan: Yoshimura Printing Corporation, 2010), p. 13.

285 **"There's a B-29!":** Ibid.

286 **"The plane looked":** Futaba Kitayama, "'Oh, That's a Parachute,'" in A Citizens' Group to Convey Testimonies of Hiroshima and Nagasaki, ed., *Give Me Water: Testimonies of Hiroshima and Nagasaki* (Tokyo: Japan, 1972), p. 8.

286 **"That's beautiful!":** Ibid.

286 **"I've got the aiming":** Paul Tibbets, Jr., oral history with James Howard, Frederick Zoes, and Barry Anderson, February 7, 1945, AFHRA.

286 **"We're on target":** Tibbets, *Tibbets Story*, p. 224.

286 **"There will be":** Robert Lewis, diary entry for August 6, 1945.

286 **"It's clear":** Caron, *Fires of a Thousand Suns*, p. 247.

286 **"Bomb away":** Dutch Van Kirk mission log, August 6, 1945.

286 **"Now," Parsons said:** William Parsons to Raymond E. Leis, Jr., February 5, 1948, Box 1, William S. Parsons Papers, LOC.

286 **"Oh my God":** "Hiroshima: Jeppson's First Combat Bombing Run," *Military Trader*, February 2002, p. 19, copy on file in Box 1, Morris R. Jeppson Papers, Brigham Young University Library, Provo, Utah.

286 **"To some in the plane":** Tibbets, *Tibbets Story*, p. 225.

286 **"No one knew":** Robert Lewis, diary entry for August 6, 1945.

287 **The bomb detonated:** USSBS, *Summary Report (Pacific War)*, p. 22; Tibbets, *Tibbets Story*, p. 225.

287 **"The cockpit":** Lewis, "How We Dropped the A-Bomb," p. 210.

287 **"Everything," he said:** Laurence, *Dawn Over Zero*, p. 218.

287 **"Our B-29":** Tibbets, *Tibbets Story*, p. 226.

287 **"That's it":** Fletcher Knebel and Charles W. Bailey II, *No High Ground* (New York: Harper & Brothers, 1960), p. 204.

287 **"Fellows," Tibbets announced:** Tibbets, *Tibbets Story*, p. 227.

287 **"If Dante":** Ibid.

287 **"Holy moses":** Knebel and Bailey, *No High Ground*, p. 205.

287 **"There in front":** Robert Lewis, diary entry for August 6, 1945.

287 **"A feeling of shock":** Tibbets, *Tibbets Story*, p. 227.

287 **"My God," Lewis wrote:** Robert Lewis, diary entry for August 6, 1945.

Chapter 29

288 **"When I looked":** Yôko Ôta, *City of Corpses*, in Richard H. Minear, ed. and trans., *Hiroshima: Three Witnesses* (Princeton, NJ: Princeton University Press, 1990), p. 218.

288 **Little Boy detonated:** "Hiroshima and Nagasaki Bombing Timeline," April 26, 2016, Atomic Heritage Foundation, Albuquerque, N.M.

288 **Within one-millionth:** Committee for the Compilation of Materials on Damage Caused by the Atomic Bombs in Hiroshima and Nagasaki, *Hiroshima and Nagasaki: The Physical, Medical, and Social Effects of the Atomic Bombs*, trans. Eisei Ishikawa and David L. Swain (New York: Basic Books, 1981), pp. 22–23, 32–36.

288 **Rescuers sifting:** All artifacts mentioned can be found on display at the Hiroshima Peace Memorial Museum, Hiroshima, Japan.

288 **"We saw blue-white":** Ichiso Hori, "Caring for Injured People by Making Ointment," in Hiroshima Association for the Success of the Atomic Bomb Exhibition, *After 60 Years, A-Bomb Survivors Speak Out*, p. 56.

288 **That brilliant flash:** Averill A. Liebow, diary entries for October 19, 1945, and October 31, 1945, in Averill A. Liebow, *Encounter with Disaster: A Medical Diary of Hiroshima,*

1945 (New York: W. W. Norton, 1970), pp. 118–25, 137; USSBS, *Effects of the Atomic Bomb on Hiroshima*, pp. 2:29–31.

289 **The sudden release:** "Hiroshima and Nagasaki Bombing Timeline," April 26, 2016, Atomic Heritage Foundation, Albuquerque, N.M.

289 **Of the city's 76,327:** Committee for the Compilation of Materials on Damage Caused by the Atomic Bombs in Hiroshima and Nagasaki, *Hiroshima and Nagasaki*, pp. 342–45.

289 **The blast toppled:** USSBS, *Effects of the Atomic Bomb on Hiroshima*, pp. 1:21–26, 3:147–306.

289 **"It is no exaggeration":** Committee for the Compilation of Materials on Damage Caused by the Atomic Bombs in Hiroshima and Nagasaki, *Hiroshima and Nagasaki*, p. 61.

289 **"I felt like":** Sasaki, "Asking Young People to Create a Peaceful Country," in Hiroshima Association for the Success of the Atomic Bomb Exhibition, *After 60 Years, A-Bomb Survivors Speak Out*, p. 13.

289 **"I'm injured":** Ibid.

289 **"His back":** Ibid.

289 **"There was nothing":** Ibid., p. 14.

289 **"I couldn't even see":** Yoshito Matsushige, "I Couldn't Press the Shutter in Hell," in Hiroshima Peace Culture Foundation, *Eyewitness Testimonies: Appeals from the A-Bomb Survivors* (Hiroshima, Japan: Bunkasya, 2017), p. 72.

289 **"None of the buildings":** Setsuko Iwamoto, "That Day," ibid., p. 44.

290 **"For a moment":** Akihiro Takahashi, "The Turning Point," in Gaynor Sekimori, trans., *Hibakusha: Survivors of Hiroshima and Nagasaki* (Tokyo: Kôsei, 2010), p. 192.

290 **"I saw a train":** Hiroko Uchida, "Overcoming the Atomic Bomb Disease," in Hiroshima Association for the Success of the Atomic Bomb Exhibition, *After 60 Years, A-Bomb Survivors Speak Out*, p. 28.

290 **Flash burns:** Yoshito Matsumoto, "How I Took the Photo," in A Citizens' Group to Convey Testimonies of Hiroshima and Nagasaki, *Give Me Water*, p. 36.

290 **"Some were wearing":** Fumie Enseki, "I Chanted Sutras Before the Ashes of the A-bomb Victims," in Hiroshima Peace Culture Foundation, *Eyewitness Testimonies*, p. 31.

290 **"Everywhere I looked":** Iwamoto, "That Day," ibid., p. 46.

290 **"This wasn't":** Michiko Yamaoka, "Conveying the Spirit of Hiroshima to the Entire World," ibid., p. 142.

290 **"Water, give me":** Chisako Takeoka, "Endlessly Calling for Mother," ibid., p. 103.

290 **"Help me!":** Haruto Seo, "Flee in Flames," in Hiroshima Association for the Success of the Atomic Bomb Exhibition, *After 60 Years, A-Bomb Survivors Speak Out*, p. 42.

290 **"Wherever a puddle":** Kosaku Okabe, "Hiroshima Flash," in Kyoto Physicians' Association, *Doctors' Testimonies of "Hiroshima": A Report of the Medical Investigations into the Victims of the Atomic Bombing*, ed. and trans. Hidenori and Fusami Sugimine (Kyoto: Kyoto Physicians' Association, 1998), p. 136.

291 **"The coolness":** Akihiro Takahashi, "What Does It Mean to Live in Hiroshima?" in Hiroshima Peace Culture Foundation, *Eyewitness Testimonies*, p. 92.

291 **"Bodies were floating":** Shige Hiratsuka, "A Voice in the Flames," in Sekimori, *Hibakusha*, p. 142.

291 **"It was as if":** Ôta, *City of Corpses*, in Minear, *Hiroshima: Three Witnesses*, p. 188.

291 **"Those with burns":** Ibid., p. 189.

291 **"You can't die!":** Taeko Teramae, "Overcoming Agony and Living Courageously," in Hiroshima Peace Culture Foundation, *Eyewitness Testimonies*, p. 112.

291 **The explosion had reduced:** USSBS, *Effects of the Atomic Bomb on Hiroshima*, pp. 2:4–5.

292 **"The fires swelled":** Ôta, *City of Corpses*, in Minear, *Hiroshima*, p. 192.

292 **Downed utility poles:** USSBS, *Effects of the Atomic Bomb on Hiroshima*, pp. 2:18–19.

292 **"The public fire":** Ibid., p. 2:88.
292 **"Hiroshima," recalled:** Haruto Seo, "Flee in Flames," in Hiroshima Association for the Success of the Atomic Bomb Exhibition, *After 60 Years, A-Bomb Survivors Speak Out*, p. 42.
292 **"It was like a pillar":** Tadashi Takahashi, "Surviving the Fire Tornado," ibid., p. 25.
292 **"Help, Mummy":** Hiratsuka, "A Voice from the Flames," in Sekimori, *Hibakusha*, p. 141.
293 **"No matter":** Ibid., p. 142.
293 **"I realized":** Ibid.
293 **"Kazu," she pleaded:** Ibid.
294 **"I'm sorry, Kazu":** Ibid., p. 143.
294 **First aid teams:** USSBS, *Effects of the Atomic Bomb on Hiroshima*, p. 1:20.
294 **"No one":** Pacific War Research Society, *Day Man Lost*, p. 253.
294 **"Some carried dead":** Yoko Shineda, "Saving Our One and Only Life," in Hiroshima Association for the Success of the Atomic Bomb Exhibition, *After 65 Years, A-Bomb Survivors and War Victims Speak Out: An Anthology of the Experiences of Hiroshima Atomic Bomb Victims* (Hiroshima, Japan: Yoshimura Printing Corporation, 2015), p. 37.
294 **"I found myself":** Rikio Yamane, "Everyone in My Department Is Dead," in Hiroshima Peace Culture Foundation, *Eyewitness Testimonies*, p. 134.
294 **"I'll get a quick":** Matsushige, "I Couldn't Press the Shutter in Hell," in Hiroshima Peace Culture Foundation, *Eyewitness Testimonies*, p. 75.
295 **"The people around":** Ibid., p. 73.
295 **"Open your eyes!":** Ibid., p. 75.
295 **"I found it":** Ibid.
295 **"When I looked":** Yoshito Matsumoto, "How I Took the Photo," in A Citizens' Group to Convey Testimonies of Hiroshima and Nagasaki, *Give Me Water*, p. 36.
295 **Only three:** USSBS, *Effects of the Atomic Bombs on Hiroshima and Nagasaki*, p. 6.
295 **Of the city's 298 doctors:** Committee for the Compilation of Materials on Damage Caused by the Atomic Bombs in Hiroshima and Nagasaki, *Hiroshima and* Nagasaki, pp. 379, 516; Kyoto Physicians' Association, *Doctors' Testimonies of "Hiroshima,"* p. 99.
295 **"For all practical":** Committee for the Compilation of Materials on Damage Caused by the Atomic Bombs in Hiroshima and Nagasaki, *Hiroshima and* Nagasaki, p. 516.
295 **"Just to find":** Takahashi, "Turning Point," p. 196.
295 **"Medicine was in":** Kosakai, *A-Bomb: A City Tells its Story*, pp. 10–11.
295 **"The people who were":** Michihiko Hachiya, diary entry for August 7, 1945, in Michihiko Hachiya, *Hiroshima Diary: The Journal of a Japanese Physician, August 6—September 30, 1945*, trans. and ed. Warner Wells (Chapel Hill: University of North Carolina Press, 1955), p. 12.
296 **Within days:** Committee for the Compilation of Materials on Damage Caused by the Atomic Bombs in Hiroshima and Nagasaki, *Hiroshima and Nagasaki*, p. 519.
296 **"I was scared":** Akiyo Tagawa, "A Mother Holding Her Dead Baby," in Hiroshima Association for the Success of the Atomic Bomb Exhibition, *After 60 Years, A-Bomb Survivors Speak Out*, p. 59.
296 **"Some of the babies":** Ibid., p. 60.
296 **"The smell":** Takeshi Tanaka, "The Use of A-Bombs Must Not Be Permitted," in Hiroshima Association for the Success of the Atomic Bomb Exhibition, *After 60 Years, A-Bomb Survivors Speak Out*, p. 9.
296 **"There were few":** Army Medical College and the First Tokyo Army Hospital, "Medical Report of the Atomic Bombing in Hiroshima," November 30, 1945, National Diet Library, Tokyo, Japan.
296 **"All we had":** Setsuko Iwamoto, "That Day," in Hiroshima Peace Culture Foundation, *Eyewitness Testimonies*, p. 48.

296 **"Nurses would remove":** Tagawa, "A Mother Holding Her Dead Baby," in Hiroshima Association for the Success of the Atomic Bomb Exhibition, *After 60 Years, A-Bomb Survivors Speak Out*, p. 59.

296 **"When the nurses":** Sasaki, "Asking Young People to Create a Peaceful Country," in Hiroshima Association for the Success of the Atomic Bomb Exhibition, *After 60 Years, A-Bomb Survivors Speak Out*, p. 15.

297 **"Parents, half-crazy":** Michihiko Hachiya, diary entry for August 7, 1945, in Hachiya, *Hiroshima Diary*, p. 22.

297 **"Mother," Yoko hollered:** Shineda, "Saving Our One and Only Life," in Hiroshima Association for the Success of the Atomic Bomb Exhibition, *After 65 Years, A-Bomb Survivors and War Victims Speak Out*, p. 38.

297 **"I looked down":** Ibid., p. 39.

297 **"Let's go home":** Ibid.

297 **"When I tried":** Ibid.

297 **"We put the egg":** Ibid.

297 **Protecting the dignity:** Kosakai. *A-Bomb: A City Tells its Story*, p. 12.

297 **"We had to pull":** Teiichi Teramura, "The Unforgiveable," in Sekimori, *Hibakusha*, pp. 49–50.

298 **"We carried":** Tadaomi Furuishi, "Among the Flames," ibid., p. 165.

298 **"Each evening":** Katsuyoshi Yoshimura, "Weeds by the Roadside," ibid., p. 41.

298 **"It was a horrible":** Mitsuko Tsuchikawa, "My Child, Mother and Brother Stolen from Me by the A-bomb," in Hiroshima Association for the Success of the Atomic Bomb Exhibition, *After 65 Years, A-Bomb Survivors and War Victims Speak Out*, p. 43.

Chapter 30

299 **"Identification of the dead":** USSBS, *Effects of the Atomic Bombs on Hiroshima and Nagasaki*, p. 11.

299 **"I am certain":** Robert Lewis, diary entry for August 6, 1945.

299 **"We were still":** Tibbets, *Tibbets Story*, p. 229.

299 **"I think this is":** Ibid., p. 228.

300 **"Results clearcut":** Leslie Groves to George Marshall, August 6, 1945, in Microfilm Roll #1, CMED.

300 **"After a few":** Robert Lewis, diary entry for August 6, 1945.

300 **"You would have thought":** Tibbets, "I Dropped the Atomic Bomb," undated.

300 **"The rest of the ride":** Tibbets, *Tibbets Story*, p. 230.

300 **"The story":** Luis Alvarez to Walter Alvarez, August 6, 1945, Box 1, Lansing Lamont Papers, HSTL. A copy can also be found in Alvarez, *Alvarez: Adventures of a Physicist*, p. 8.

301 **"Attention to orders":** Commemorative Booklet, 509th Composite Group, 50th Anniversary Reunion, August 5–10, 1995, p. 18, in Box 1, Atomic Bomb Collection, HSTL.

301 **"It had been":** Tibbets, *Tibbets Story*, p. 230.

301 **"No," Groves admitted:** Groves, *Now It Can Be Told*, p. 322.

301 **"I certainly would":** Ibid.

301 **"Entire city":** Leslie Groves to George Marshall, August 6, 1945, in Microfilm Roll #1, CMED.

302 **"I was not":** Groves, *Now It Can Be Told*, p. 324.

302 **"There were suggestions":** Ibid., pp. 327–28.

303 **"Important," he began:** Transcript of Special Teletype Conference Between Leslie Groves and Curtis LeMay, August 8, 1945, in Microfilm Roll #1, CMED.

303 **"I have got here":** Eben Ayers, Press and Radio Conference, August 6, 1945, Box 188, President's Secretary's Files, HSTL.

Chapter 31

304 **"As soon as I saw":** Kay Bartlett, "Hiroshima Bomber Has No Remorse Over Act," *Tulsa Daily World*, August 3, 1975, p. 24, copy on file in Microfilm Roll #38639, Paul Tibbets, Jr., Papers, AFHRA.

304 **"In a physical":** Truman, *Year of Decisions*, p. 412.

305 **"Force is the only":** Ibid.

305 **As such, he had:** Rigdon, "Log of the President's Trip," August 2, 1945, p. 45

305 **The *Augusta*:** Ibid., p. 44.

305 **"It has been":** Harry Truman to King George VI, August 2, 1945, ibid.

305 **"Within a matter":** Smith, *Thank You, Mr. President*, p. 255.

305 **"He was happy":** Ibid.

305 **"Here was the greatest":** Ibid., p. 256.

305 **The president settled into:** Rigdon, "Log of the President's Trip," August 3–5, 1945, pp. 46–48.

306 **"No word yet":** Smith, *Thank You, Mr. President*, p. 256.

306 **"The secret":** Ibid., pp. 256–57.

306 **"O give":** Ernest Vaccaro to Eben Ayers, "Aboard U.S.S. *Augusta* with President Truman, August 5, (1945)," Box 1, William M. Rigdon Papers, HSTL.

306 **A new poll:** "Opinion Poll Shows Japs Will Fight On," *Minneapolis Sunday Tribune*, August 5, 1945, p. 5.

306 **"What is taking place":** Gladstone Williams, "Surrender or National Suicide," *Atlanta Constitution*, August 2, 1945, p. 6.

306 **"How long":** "How Long Can the Japs Hold Out?" editorial, *St. Louis Post-Dispatch*, August 4, 1945, p. 4A.

306 **"Will the Japanese":** David Lawrence, "Date of Japanese Surrender Now Big Question," *Ithaca Journal*, August 2, 1945, p. 6.

307 **"Hiroshima bombed":** Richard Edwards to William Leahy, August 6, 1945, Box 167, President's Secretary's Files, HSTL.

307 **"I could not":** Truman, *Year of Decisions*, p. 422.

307 **"Captain," he declared:** Rigdon, *White House Sailor*, pp. 206–7.

307 **"Fine! Fine!":** Ibid., 207.

307 **"Big bomb dropped":** Henry Stimson to Harry Truman, August 6, 1945, Box 167, President's Secretary's Files, HSTL.

307 **"It's time":** Rigdon, *White House Sailor*, p. 207.

307 **"Please keep":** Ibid.

307 **"Mr. President," one sailor:** Morgan Beatty to Eben Ayers, August 6, 1945, Box 1, William M. Rigdon Papers, HSTL.

307 **"There was a broad":** Smith, *Thank You, Mr. President*, p. 258.

307 **"Keep your seats":** Ernest Vaccaro to Eben Ayers, "Aboard U.S.S. *Augusta* with President Truman, Aug. 6. (1945)," Box 1, William M. Rigdon Papers, HSTL.

308 **"Now we'll finish":** Robert Nixon to Eben Ayers, "Aboard U.S.S. *Augusta* with President Truman," ibid.

308 **A follow-up:** Henry Stimson to Harry Truman, August 6, 1945, Microfilm Roll #4, HBF.

308 **"Reconnaissance planes":** Memorandum for the Press, August 6, 1945, Microfilm Roll #4, HBF.

308 **"If ever a man":** Mirriam Smith to Eben Ayers, "Aboard U.S.S. *Augusta* with President Truman, Aug. 6, (1945)," Box 1, William M. Rigdon Papers, HSTL.

308 **"Sixteen hours ago":** "Statement by the President of the United States," August 6, 1945, Box 188, President's Secretary's Files, HSTL.
309 **"Most terrible":** "Most Terrible Engine of Ruin Ever Devised May End War Soon," *Pittsburgh Press*, August 7, 1945, p. 1.
309 **"Whole Jap City":** "Whole Jap City Believed Destroyed by Explosion of Single Atomic Bomb," *Atlantic City Press*, August 7, 1945, p. 1.
309 **"Quit or Be":** "Quit or Be Atomized," *Boston Evening Globe*, August 7, 1945, p. 1.
309 **"Every effort":** "Statement by the Secretary of War," August 6, 1945, Box 188, President's Secretary's Files, HSTL.
309 **Additional releases:** These press releases can be found in Box 167, ibid.
309 **"Release at long":** Marquis Childs, "Atomic Bomb Marks Beginning—Or End," *Miami Daily News*, August 7, 1945, p. 6.
309 **"For the first time":** "Japan's Choice," editorial, *Washington Evening Star*, August 8, 1945, p. 8.
309 **"Unless the Japanese":** "Bomb to End Wars!" editorial, *St. Louis Globe-Democrat*, August 7, 1945, p. 6A.
309 **"It is a different":** "Bomb Means Short Jap War, New World, British Declare," *San Francisco Examiner*, August 7, 1945, p. 1.
309 **"Can mankind":** "Heard Round the World," editorial, *New York Times*, August 7, 1945, p. 22.

Chapter 32

310 **"That pillar of smoke":** Marquis Childs, "Playing with Atomic Fire," *Washington Post*, August 8, 1945, p. 7.
310 **"Please relay":** Pacific War Research Society, *Day Man Lost*, p. 270.
311 **"Casualties are estimated":** Ibid.
311 **"Does that figure":** Ibid., p. 271.
311 **"Why the army":** Ibid., p. 285.
311 **Lord Keeper:** Kort, *Columbia Guide to Hiroshima and the Bomb*, p. 68.
311 **"The whole city":** Butow, *Japan's Decision to Surrender*, p. 151.

Chapter 33

312 **"If there is":** "Now: Atomic Bombs or Surrender!" editorial, *Philadelphia Inquirer*, August 7, 1945, p. 10.
312 **The next atomic:** Groves, *Now It Can Be Told*, pp. 341–42.
312 **"The use of the second":** Tibbets, *Tibbets Story*, p. 236.
313 **Reporters fired:** Ibid., p. 237.
313 **"told this story":** W. H. Lawrence, "5 Plants Vanish," *New York Times*, August 8, 1945, p. 1.
313 **"We knew that he":** Wilson M'Gee, "Miamian, Trained for Doctor, Unleashed Destructive Bomb," *Miami News*, August 8, 1945, p. 12.
313 **"That bomb":** Ibid.
313 **"His father":** "Wife of Pilot 'Too Thrilled for Words' on Exploit," *Washington Evening Star*, August 8, 1945, p. A2.
313 **"I think my daddy":** Ibid.
314 **"No bomb crater":** Special Damage Assessment, Flash Report No. 9, August 8, 1945, Microfilm Roll #A7809, AFHRA.
314 **"Very few":** Ibid.
314 **"One peculiarity":** George Kenny to Douglas MacArthur, undated, Box 7, Papers of Lt. Gen. Richard Sutherland, MacArthur Memorial Archives and Library, Norfolk, Va.

314 **"Early reports":** Curtis E. LeMay, daily diary, entry for August 7, 1945, Box B7, CLP.
314 **Orders called for dropping:** Manhattan Engineer District, "The Atomic Bombings of Hiroshima and Nagasaki," June 29, 1946, p. 3.
314 **"To the Japanese People":** Translation of Leaflet, Box 1, Atomic Bomb Collection, HSTL.
315 **The main target:** Field Orders, Number 17, August 8, 1945, Microfilm Roll #B0679, AFHRA.
315 **"Niigata," as Groves explained:** Groves, *Now It Can Be Told*, p. 342.
315 **Perched on the shores:** Mission Planning Summary, Field Orders, Number 17, Microfilm Roll #B0679, AFHRA.
315 **Nagasaki, by contrast:** Ibid.; Nagasaki International Cultural Hall, comp. and ed, *Nagasaki Speaks: A Record of the Atomic Bombing*, trans. Brian Burke-Gaffney (Nagasaki: Nagasaki International Cultural Hall, 1993), pp. 3–6.
315 **Though the metro:** USSBS, *Effects of the Atomic Bomb on Nagasaki, Japan* (Washington, D.C.: U.S. Government Printing Office, 1947), p. 2:9.
315 **Population density:** USSBS, *Effects of the Atomic Bombs on Hiroshima and Nagasaki*, p. 9.
316 **Mitsubishi operated:** Ibid.
316 **"No Tactical Mission":** Field Orders, Number 17, August 8, 1945, Microfilm Roll #B0679, AFHRA.
316 **Tibbets planned:** Tibbets, *Tibbets Story*, p. 238.
316 **The twenty-five-year-old:** Charles W. Sweeney with James A. Antonucci and Marion K. Antonucci, *War's End: An Eyewitness Account of America's Last Atomic Mission* (New York: Avon Books, 1997), pp. 8–27.
316 **As such, the bomb bay:** Frederick J. Olivi with William R. Watson, Jr., *Decision at Nagasaki: The Mission That Almost Failed* (Privately Printed, 1999), p. 91.
316 **Throughout the compound:** Commemorative Booklet, 509th Composite Group, 50th Anniversary Reunion, August 5–10, 1995, p. 32, in Box 1, Atomic Bomb Collection, HSTL.
317 **"It is a thing":** William L. Laurence, "Atomic Bombing of Nagasaki Told by Flight Member," *New York Times*, September 9, 1945, p. 1.
317 **"It was painted":** Olivi, *Decision at Nagasaki*, p. 92.
317 **"Let's hope":** Robert L. Schwartz, "The Week the War Ended," *Life*, July 17, 1950, p. 102, copy on file in Microfilm Roll #38641, Paul Tibbets, Jr., Papers, AFHRA.
317 **"Then, very slowly":** Olivi, *Decision at Nagasaki*, p. 92.
317 **"We knew these cities":** Sweeney, *War's End*, p. 194.
317 **"It sat smack":** Ibid.
318 **"None of us":** Ibid., p. 195.
318 **The crews assembled:** Operations Order, Number 39, August 8, 1945, Microfilm Roll #B0678, AFHRA.
318 **"Each target":** Laurence, *Dawn Over Zero*, p. 229.
318 **A calculation:** Paul W. Tibbets, *Return of the Enola Gay* (New Hope, Penn.: Enola Gay Remembered, 1998), p. 247.
318 **"The orders":** Olivi, *Decision at Nagasaki*, p. 95.
318 **"Above all else":** Laurence, *Dawn Over Zero*, p. 229.
319 **"That was the first":** Olivi, *Decision at Nagasaki*, p. 96.
319 **"The airplane looked":** Sweeney, *War's End*, p. 202.
319 **"I want our mission":** Ibid.
319 **"Major," Kuharek announced:** Ibid., p. 203.
319 **"How long":** Ibid., p. 204.
319 **"We have 600 gallons":** Tibbets, *Return of the Enola Gay*, p. 247.

319 **"I could tell":** Ibid.
319 **"You don't need":** Ibid.
319 **"It's your call":** Sweeney, *War's End*, p. 204.
319 **"The hell with it":** Ibid., p. 205.
320 **"Before you go":** Tibbets, *Return of the Enola Gay*, p. 247.
320 **"You don't need":** Ibid., p. 248.

Chapter 34

321 **"It is the masses":** Churchill, *Triumph and Tragedy*, p. 631.
321 **The purpose of Togo's meeting:** Butow, *Japan's Decision to Surrender*, p. 152.
321 **"It was all the more":** Tôgô, *Cause of Japan*, p. 315.
321 **To confirm:** Pacific War Research Society, *Japan's Longest Day*, p. 293.
321 **"Hiroshima was subjected":** "Nagasaki Is Target for 2nd Atom Bomb," *Spokane Daily Chronicle*, August 9, 1945, p. 1.
322 **"The damage sustained":** Marquis Kido, diary entry for August 7, 1945, in Kido, *Diary of Marquis Kido*, p. 443.
322 **"Under these circumstances," Hirohito replied:** Butow, *Japan's Decision to Surrender*, p. 152.
322 **Not only could:** Brian Walsh to Jon Parshall, August 18, 2025.
322 **"Tell Suzuki":** Butow, *Japan's Decision to Surrender*, p. 153.
322 **"I have here":** Ibid.
322 **"The Soviet Government":** Ibid., p. 154.

Chapter 35

323 **"Destiny chose Nagasaki":** Laurence, "Atomic Bombing of Nagasaki Told by Flight Member," p. 1.
323 ***Bockscar* roared:** The precise takeoff time is recorded in Commander Frederick Ashworth's mission log, August 9, 1945, which is included in Norman F. Ramsey, "History of Project A," September 27, 1945. A copy of that document can be found in John Coster-Mullen, *Atom Bombs: The Top-Secret Inside Story of Little Boy and Fat Man* (Privately Printed, 2004), p. 284. The commander's log likewise is included in Frederick L. Ashworth, *An Autobiography*, unpublished, p. 482.
323 **The turbulent weather:** Sweeney, *War's End*, p. 208.
323 **"Some of these":** Olivi, *Decision at Nagasaki*, p. 98.
323 **At four a.m.:** Commander Frederick Ashworth mission log, August 9, 1945; Ashworth, *Autobiography*, p. 182.
323 **"Take it to Yakushima":** Olivi, *Decision at Nagasaki*, p. 98.
323 **"The lightning":** Ibid.
324 **"It was spectacular":** Ibid., p. 99.
324 **"God, I'm so tired":** Ibid.
324 **"Think this atomic":** Laurence, "Atomic Bombing of Nagasaki Told by Flight Member," p. 1.
324 **"From that vantage":** Ibid.
324 **"In one-tenth":** Ibid.
325 **"After a few moments":** Sweeney, *War's End*, p. 210.
325 **"We started circling":** Laurence, "Atomic Bombing of Nagasaki Told by Flight Member," p. 1.
325 **"In non-meteorological":** Sweeney, *War's End*, p. 211.
325 **"The harder":** Olivi, *Decision at Nagasaki*, p. 118.
325 **"Where the hell":** Sweeney, *War's End*, p. 211.
326 **"That's it":** Ibid.

326 **At 9:50 a.m.:** Olivi, *Decision at Nagasaki*, p. 119.
326 **Only the day before:** Craven and Cate, *Army Air Forces in World War II,* pp. 5:655.
326 **"Bomb must":** Olivi, *Decision at Nagasaki*, p. 120.
326 **"I can't see it!" bombadier:** Sweeney, *War's End*, p. 213.
326 **"No drop," Sweeney announced over:** Ibid.
326 **"I was now doing":** Ibid., p. 214.
326 **"I hoped":** Ibid.
326 **"I can't see it!" Beahan:** Ibid.
326 **"No drop," Sweeney announced :** Ibid.
327 **"As we came":** Olivi, *Decision at Nagasaki*, p. 121.
327 **"Give me the heading":** Sweeney, *War's End*, p. 215.
327 **"It's now or never!":** Olivi, *Decision at Nagasaki*, p. 120.
327 **"Reducing power":** Ibid., p. 122.
327 **"Boys getting jittery":** Ibid.
327 **"If we didn't drop":** Sweeney, *War's End*, pp. 216–17.
328 **"This is going to be pretty":** Lloyd Shearer, "Nagasaki: The Forgotten Atomic City: Kermit Beahan: The Forgotten Man," *Parade*, July 25, 1965, p. 4.
328 **"I'll guarantee":** Sweeney, *War's End*, p. 217.
328 **"We had to get":** Coster-Mullen, *Atom Bombs*, p. 74.
328 **"This is going to be a radar":** Ibid.
328 **"No change":** Olivi, *Decision at Nagasaki*, p. 124.
328 **"I've got it!":** Coster-Mullen, *Atom Bombs*, p. 75.
328 **"You own it":** Sweeney, *War's End*, p. 217.
328 **"I picked out":** Shearer, "Nagasaki: The Forgotten Atomic City," p. 4.
329 **"Bombs away":** Sweeney, *War's End*, p. 218.
329 **Ashworth recorded:** Commander Frederick Ashworth mission log, August 9, 1945.
329 **"Time seemed":** Sweeney, *War's End*, p. 218.
329 **"Even with":** Olivi, *Decision at Nagasaki*, p. 125.
329 **"The cloud":** Sweeney, *War's End*, p. 219.
329 **"I could see tongues":** J. Frederick Olivi, as told to Wilfred B. Wolfan, "Clouds of Fate Sealed the City's Doom," *Evening Republican*, August 6, 1960, p. 3.
329 **"It looked":** "Kermit Beahan, 70, Bombardier on Plane That Dropped A-Bomb," *New York Times*, March 11, 1989, p. 33.
329 **"By the time":** Beser, *Hiroshima and Nagasaki Revisited*, p. 134.
329 **"I have never seen":** Olivi, *Decision at Nagasaki*, p. 126.
329 **"Nagasaki bombed":** Sweeney, *War's End*, p. 219.
329 **"Even if we slow":** Ibid., p. 220.
329 **"We're on our way":** Olivi, *Decision at Nagasaki*, p. 132.
329 **"The flight back":** Olivi, "Clouds of Fate Sealed the City's Doom," p. 3.
330 **"Yontan tower":** Sweeney, *War's End*, p. 223.
330 **"Major," Kuharek said:** Olivi, *Decision at Nagasaki*, p. 133.
330 **"Everyone," Olivi recalled:** Ibid.
330 **"Start firing":** Ibid.
330 **"It was stick":** Ibid.
330 **"I was now barreling":** Sweeney, *War's End*, p. 225.
330 **"I was braced":** Frederick L. Ashworth, "Dropping the Atomic Bomb on Nagasaki," *Proceedings*, January 1958, p. 12–17.
331 **"It wasn't pretty":** Olivi, *Decision at Nagasaki*, p. 134.
331 **"For several moments":** Ibid.
331 **"Where's the dead":** Sweeney, *War's End*, p. 226.

331 **"Let's not mention":** Olivi, *Decision at Nagasaki*, p. 134.

331 **"How long":** Ashworth, "Dropping the Atomic Bomb on Nagasaki," p. 13.

331 **"The irony":** Sweeney, *War's End*, p. 227.

332 **"We've just dropped":** Ashworth, "Dropping the Atomic Bomb on Nagasaki," p. 13.

332 **"Well, son":** Ibid.

332 **"What do you think?":** Ibid.

332 **"Son," Doolittle said:** Ashworth, *Autobiography*, pp. 193, 199.

332 **"Ate Spam":** Olivi, *Decision at Nagasaki*, p. 135.

332 **"Not much":** Beser, *Hiroshima and Nagasaki Revisited*, pp. 136–37.

332 **"I don't think":** Olivi, *Decision at Nagasaki*, p. 136.

333 **"We were home":** Sweeney, *War's End*, p. 230.

333 **"Tinian looks good":** Olivi, *Decision at Nagasaki*, p. 137.

333 **"Come morning":** Tibbets, *Return of the Enola Gay*, p. 250.

333 **"You fucked up":** Ibid.

333 **"The awkward silence":** Ibid.

333 **"You got any more":** Robert O. Harder, *"The Three Musketeers of the Army Air Forces": From Hitler's Fortress Europa to Hiroshima and Nagasaki* (Annapolis, Md.: Naval Institute Press, 2015), p. 160.

Chapter 36

334 **"This was the day":** Raisuke Shirabe, diary entry for August 9, 1945, in Raisuke Shirabe, *A Physician's Diary of the Atomic Bombing and its Aftermath*, ed. Fidelius R. Kuo, trans. Aloysius F. Kuo (Nagasaki: Nagasaki Association for Hibakusha's Medical Care, 2002), p. 3.

334 **Many of the residents:** Nagasaki International Cultural Hall, *Nagasaki Speaks*, p. 29; USSBS, *Effects of the Atomic Bomb on Nagasaki,* p. 1:10.

334 **The morning mist:** Nagasaki International Cultural Hall, *Nagasaki Speaks*, p. 29.

334 **The pious:** Ibid., p. 65.

334 **At Nagasaki Medical College:** Takahasi Nagai, "Nagasaki Medical College on That Fateful Day," in City of Nagasaki, *Testimonies of the Atomic Bomb Survivors: A Record of the Devastation of Nagasaki*, trans. Brian Burke-Gaffney et al. (Nagasaki: City of Nagasaki, 1985), p. 1.

335 **Doctors and nurses:** USSBS, *The Effects of Bombing on Health and Medical Services in Hiroshima and Nagasaki* (Washington, D.C.: U.S. Government Printing Office, 1947), p. 2.

335 **A similar scene unfolded at:** Susan Southard, *Nagasaki: Life After Nuclear War* (New York: Viking, 2015), p. 37.

335 **"The war situation is becoming":** Yuriko Kitamura, "Recollection of Nagasaki," in Nagasaki Prefectural Girls High School 42nd Alumnae, eds., *Footprints of Nagasaki: Excerpt from "Anohi Anotoki,"* trans. Yuriko Kitamura (Nagasaki: Seibonokishi-sha, 1996), p. 62.

335 **Nagasaki had suffered:** USSBS, *The Effects of Air Attack on the City of Nagasaki* (Washington, D.C.: U.S. Government Printing Office, 1947), p. 9. See also USSBS, *Field Report Covering Air-Raid Protection and Allied Subjects in Nagasaki, Japan* (Washington, D.C.: U.S. Government Printing Office, 1947), p. 2.

335 **The most recent:** USSBS, *Effects of Bombing on Health and Medical Services in Hiroshima and Nagasaki*, pp. 2–3.

335 **Similar to other:** USSBS, *Field Report Covering Air-Raid Protection and Allied Subjects in Nagasaki*, p. 26.

335 **This was complemented:** Nagasaki International Cultural Hall, *Nagasaki Speaks*, pp. 21–22.

335 **To protect:** USSBS, *Field Report Covering Air-Raid Protection and Allied Subjects in Nagasaki, Japan*, p. 58.
336 **The war's hunger:** USSBS, *Effects of the Atomic Bomb on Nagasaki*, p. 1:11.
336 **Medical efforts:** USSBS, *Field Report Covering Air-Raid Protection and Allied Subjects in Nagasaki, Japan*, pp. 29, 32.
336 **"Enemy Drops":** Southard, *Nagasaki*, p. 31, 313.
336 **"The track":** Robert Trumbull, *Nine Who Survived Hiroshima and Nagasaki* (New York: E.P. Dutton, 1957), p. 49.
336 **"I told you":** Nagasaki International Cultural Hall, *Nagasaki Speaks*, p. 30.
336 **"We concluded":** Ibid.
337 **"I want to suggest":** Ibid., p. 31.
337 **At 10:53 a.m.:** Nagasaki International Cultural Hall, *Nagasaki Speaks*, p. 35.
337 **"Isn't that a whir":** Miyuki Fukahori, "Near Ground Zero," in Michiko Nakano, ed., *Nagasaki Under the Atomic Bomb: Experiences of Young College Girls* (Tokyo: Soeisha/Books Sanseido, 2000), p. 36.
337 **Fat Man exploded:** Nagasaki International Cultural Hall, *Nagasaki Speaks*, pp. 22–23; USSBS, *Effects of the Atomic Bomb on Nagasaki*, pp. 1:10–12.
337 **Clay roof tiles:** These are all artifacts that can be found on display at the Nagasaki Atomic Bomb Museum, Nagasaki, Japan.
337 **Doctors would later:** Masao Shiotsuki, *Doctor at Nagasaki: "My First Assignment Was Mercy Killing,"* trans. Simul International (Tokyo: Kôsei, 1987), p. 56.
337 **The explosion reduced:** Nagasaki International Cultural Hall, *Nagasaki Speaks*, p. 72.
338 **One of the hardest-hit:** Ibid.
338 **"It was like a thunderbolt":** Takashi Nagai, *The Bells of Nagasaki*, trans. William Johnston (Tokyo: Kodansha International, 1984), p. 11.
338 **"Not one leaf":** Ibid., p. 13.
339 **"The city had vanished":** Nagai, "Nagasaki Medical College on That Fateful Day," in City of Nagasaki, *Testimonies of the Atomic Bomb Survivors*, p. 2.
339 **"Everything got dark":** Takashi Nagai, *We of Nagasaki: The Story of Survivors in an Atomic Wasteland*, trans. Ichiro Shirato and Herbert B. L. Silverman (New York: Duell, Sloan & Pearce, 1958), p. 12.
339 **"Hell!" one nurse cried:** Nagai, *Bells of Nagasaki*, p. 13.
339 **The bomb had destroyed:** City of Nagasaki, *The Records of the Atomic Bombing in Nagasaki* (Nagasaki: Nagasaki Foundation for the Promotion of Peace, 1976), p. 14.
339 **The twenty neighborhoods:** Nagasaki International Cultural Hall, *Nagasaki Speaks*, p. 70.
339 **The blast ruptured:** USSBS, *Effects of the Atomic Bomb on Nagasaki*, pp. 1:16–18; USSBS, *Effects of the Atomic Bombs on Hiroshima and Nagasaki*, p. 11. For greater detail, see USSBS, *Effects of the Atomic Bomb on Nagasaki*, pp. 2:271–78.
339 **The city's medical:** USSBS, *Field Report Covering Air-Raid Protection and Allied Subjects in Nagasaki*, p. 32–34.
339 **"The explosion of the atomic":** Nagasaki International Cultural Hall, *Nagasaki Speaks*, p. 94.
340 **"Hundreds and hundreds":** Chie Setoguchi, "The Human Dam," in City of Nagasaki, *Testimonies of the Atomic Bomb Survivors*, p. 13.
340 **"I met so many":** Keshi Yamaguchi, "A Last Breath on Straw," in Nagasaki Atomic Bomb Testimonial Society, *Nagasaki: Voices of the A-Bomb Survivors* (Nagasaki: Showado Printing, 2009), p. 23.
340 **"They were stumbling":** Nagai, *We of Nagasaki*, p. 33.
340 **"For heaven's sake":** Ibid.
340 **Unlike Hiroshima:** USSBS, *Effects of Air Attack on the City of Nagasaki*, p. 11.

340 **"Visibility ahead":** Masyuki Yoshida, "Unforgettable Hell on Earth: A Fireman's Take of Horror," in Nagasaki Atomic Bomb Testimonial Society, *Nagasaki*, p. 61.

340 **In places:** Kyoko Araki, "From the Memory of Vital Water," in City of Nagasaki, *Testimonies of the Atomic Bomb Survivors*, p. 108; Keshi Yamaguchi, "A Last Breath of Straw," in Nagasaki Atomic Bomb Testimonial Society, *Nagasaki*, p. 24; Miyoko Yamaguchi, "The Mother's Life: Forty Years of Hardship," in Nagasaki Atomic Bomb Testimonial Society, *Nagasaki*, p. 75.

340 **"I saw a mother":** Kyoko Araki, "From the Memory of Vital Water," in City of Nagasaki, *Testimonies of the Atomic Bomb Survivors*, p. 109.

341 **"Burned corpses":** Nagasaki International Cultural Hall, *Nagasaki Speaks*, p. 67.

341 **Forty neighboring:** Ibid., p. 96.

341 **"I do not know how many":** Shiotsuki, *Doctor at Nagasaki*, p. 58.

341 **"Every one of them":** Ibid., p. 59.

341 **The train could approach:** Nagasaki International Cultural Hall, *Nagasaki Speaks*, pp. 99–100.

341 **"When I lifted":** Hisashi Aoki, "The Unforgettable Hell," in City of Nagasaki, *Testimonies of the Atomic Bomb Survivors*, p. 97.

341 **"Everyone was groaning":** Fumiko Wakasugi, "Starting Again from Nothing," in Mitsue Kubo, *Hibaku: Recollections of A-Bomb Survivors*, ed. Louise Hader, trans. Ryoji Inoue (Coquitlam, B.C., Canada: Nippon Printing, 1990), p. 144.

342 **"A horde":** Nagasaki International Cultural Hall, *Nagasaki Speaks*, p. 101.

342 **"When we shone":** Shiotsuki, *Doctor at Nagasaki*, p. 46.

342 **"The war is over," the twenty-five-year-old:** Ibid., p. 47.

342 **"The burns":** Ibid., p. 52.

342 **"My god," Shiotsuki thought:** Ibid.

342 **"As a result":** Ibid., p. 53.

342 **"The fires below":** Raisuke Shirabe, "August 9th: The State of Nagasaki Medical College Immediately After Atomic Bomb Explosion," in City of Nagasaki, *Testimonies of the Atomic Bomb Survivors*, p. 42.

342 **Emergency workers:** Nagasaki International Cultural Hall, *Nagasaki Speaks*, p. 95.

343 **Eighty such centers:** Ibid., p. 102.

343 **"Patients":** USSBS, *Effects of Air Attack on the City of Nagasaki*, p. 11.

343 **"On the rubble-littered":** Shitotsuki, *Doctor at Nagasaki*, pp. 60–61.

343 **"Call me":** Masayuki Yoshida, "Unforgettable Hell on Earth—A Fireman's Tale of Horror," in Nagasaki Atomic Bomb Testimonial Society, *Nagasaki*, p. 62.

343 **"Give me some":** Ibid.

343 **"Kill me!":** Ibid.

343 **"The injured":** Nagasaki International Cultural Hall, *Nagasaki Speaks*, p. 98.

343 **"Many had limbs":** Ibid.

343 **"The method":** Ibid.

343 **"Making the rounds":** Ibid.

343 **"Often we went":** Ibid.

344 **Workers used rakes:** USSBS, *Effects of the Atomic Bombs on Hiroshima and Nagasaki*, p. 11.

344 **"In the gutted":** Nagai, "Nagasaki Medical College on That Fateful Day," in City of Nagasaki, *Testimonies of the Atomic Bomb Survivors*, p. 4.

344 **"All I had":** Akira Nagasaka, "A Memorial for the Slaughtered," in Sekimori, *Hibakusha*, pp. 74–75.

344 **"With the first":** Tadao Nakazawa, "Burying My Wife," in City of Nagasaki, *Testimonies of the Atomic Bomb Survivors*, p. 174.

344 **"If only they were watermelons":** Nagai, *We of Nagasaki*, p. 124.

344 **"The heavy odor":** Ryoko Okumura, "Recollection of Summer," in Nagasaki Prefectural Girls High School 42nd Alumnae, eds., *Footprints of Nagasaki*, p. 70.

345 **"Day after day":** Emiko Kinoshita, "To My Friend with a Prayer," ibid., p. 24.

345 **"There were no coffins":** Nagai, *We of Nagasaki*, p. 65.

345 **"Please burn her":** Hisae Aoki, "Back from Death's Doorstep," in City of Nagasaki, *Testimonies of the Atomic Bomb Survivors*, p. 90.

345 **"It was an empty":** Ibid.

Chapter 37

346 **"The misery":** Matsue Atsuyuki, diary entry for August 11, 1945, in Nagasaki International Cultural Hall, *Nagasaki Speaks*, p. 80.

346 **"Valuable time":** Pacific War Research Society, *Japan's Longest Day*, p. 23.

346 **"I assured":** Marquis Kido, diary entry for August 9, 1945, in Kido, *Diary of Marquis Kido*, p. 443.

346 **"I conveyed":** Ibid., p. 444.

346 **At ten-thirty a.m., the Big Six:** Pacific War Research Society, *Japan's Longest Day*, p. 24.

347 **"I believe," he declared:** Ibid.

347 **"We can't get":** Butow, *Japan's Decision to Surrender*, p. 160.

347 **"Do we accept":** Pacific War Research Society, *Japan's Longest Day*, p. 24.

347 **"If we are lucky":** Butow, *Japan's Decision to Surrender*, p. 163.

347 **"Japan must accept":** Pacific War Research Society, *Japan's Longest Day*, p. 25.

348 **During that time:** Frank, *Downfall*, pp. 291–92.

348 **At two-thirty p.m., the cabinet:** Pacific War Research Society, *Japan's Longest Day*, p. 26.

348 **"We might win":** Ibid., p. 27.

348 **"It is far too early":** Ibid.

348 **"Japan," these leaders argued:** Ibid.

348 **"Yes, yes!":** Ibid.

349 **Six members wanted:** Kawamura, *Emperor Hirohito and the Pacific War*, p. 164.

349 **Suzuki and Togo:** Butow, *Japan's Decision to Surrender*, p. 165.

349 **At 11:50 p.m.:** Marquis Kido, diary entry for August 9, 1945, in Kido, *Diary of Marquis Kido*, p. 445.

350 **"I agree":** Pacific War Research Society, *Japan's Longest Day*, p. 33.

350 **"Japan was still":** Ibid.

350 **"We have been preserving":** Butow, *Japan's Decision to Surrender*, p. 172.

350 **"In accordance":** Ibid., p. 174.

350 **"We cannot say":** Ibid.

351 **"Your Imperial Majesty's":** Ibid., p. 175.

351 **"I have given":** Ibid.

351 **"It goes without":** Ibid., pp. 175–76.

351 **"Nevertheless," he concluded:** Ibid., p. 176.

Chapter 38

352 **"I urge Japanese":** Truman Radio Address, August 9, 1945, Box 190, President's Secretary's Files, HSTL.

352 **"During those three":** Truman, *Year of Decisions*, p. 426.

352 **"Let us carry":** Richard Russell to Harry Truman, August 7, 1945, Box 735, Official File, HSTL.

353 **"I know that Japan":** Harry Truman to Richard Russell, August 9, 1945, ibid.

353 **"Nobody is more disturbed":** Harry Truman to Samuel Cavert, August 11, 1945, Box 1573, Official File, HSTL.

353 **"It is not to be":** Leslie Groves to George Marshall, August 10, 1945, with Marshall's reply penned on the bottom, in Microfilm Roll #3, CMED.

353 **"You may wish":** Leslie Groves to Hap Arnold, August 10, 1945, in Microfilm Roll #1, CMED.

353 **"If I live to be":** Harry Truman, "Why I Dropped the Bomb," *Parade Magazine*, December 4, 1988, p. 16, copy on file in Box 1, R. Gordon Arneson Papers, HSTL.

353 **"Atomic bombs have now":** Harry Truman to the Men and Women of the Manhattan Project, August 9, 1945, Box 1573, Official File, HSTL.

354 **"Having found the bomb":** Truman Radio Address, August 9, 1945, Box 190, President's Secretary's Files, HSTL.

354 **At 7:33 a.m.:** Truman, *Year of Decisions*, p. 427.

354 **"The Japanese Government":** "Note Received from the Swiss Government," August 10, 1945, Box 190, President's Secretary's Files, HSTL.

354 **"What Japan":** Leahy, *I Was There*, p. 434.

354 **"That busted":** Henry Stimson, diary entry for August 10, 1945, HLSP.

354 **"Were we to treat":** Truman, *Year of Decisions*, p. 428.

355 **"I recommended":** Leahy, *I Was There*, p. 434.

355 **"minor matter":** Henry Stimson, diary entry for August 10, 1945, HLSP.

354 **"in order to save":** Ibid.

355 **"I do not see":** Byrnes, *Speaking Frankly*, p. 209.

355 **"We might":** Truman, *Year of Decisions*, p. 428.

355 **"I thought it was":** Henry Stimson, diary entry for August 10, 1945, HLSP.

355 **Byrnes returned:** Truman, *Year of Decisions*, p. 428.

355 **Truman summoned:** Ibid., pp. 428–29.

356 **"From the moment":** "Reply to the Swiss Government," August 11, 1945, Box 190, President's Secretary's Files, HSTL.

356 **"The ultimate":** Ibid.

356 **"He said the thought":** Henry Wallace, diary entry for August 10, 1945, in John Morton Blum, ed., *The Price of Vision: The Diary of Henry A. Wallace, 1942–1946* (Boston: Houghton Mifflin, 1973), p. 474.

356 **"Please deliver":** James Byrnes to John Winant, August 10, 1945, in U.S. Department of State, *Foreign Relations of the United States: Diplomatic Papers, 1945*, vol. 6, *The British Commonwealth: The Far East* (Washington, D.C.: U.S. Government Printing Office, 1969), p. 626.

356 **"authorize and ensure":** John Winant to James Byrnes, August 11, 1945, ibid, p. 628.

356 **"The Prime Minister and the":** Ibid., p. 629.

357 **"I congratulate":** Patrick Hurley to James Byrnes, August 11, 1945, U.S. Department of State, *Foreign Relations of the United States: Diplomatic Papers, 1945*, vol. 7, *The Far East: China* (Washington, D.C.: U.S. Government Printing Office, 1969), p. 494.

357 **"skeptical":** Averell Harriman to James Byrnes, August 11, 1945, in U.S. Department of State, *British Commonwealth*, p. 629.

357 **"He gave me":** Ibid.

357 **"noncommittal":** Ibid.

357 **"I told him":** Ibid.

357 **"In case":** Averell Harriman to James Byrnes, August 11, 1945, ibid., p. 630.

357 **"I was determined":** Truman, *Year of Decisions*, p. 432.

358 **"I stated":** Averell Harriman to James Byrnes, August 11, 1945, U.S. Department of State, *British Commonwealth*, p. 630.

358 **"Within a few":** Ibid.

358 **"I was confident":** Byrnes, *Speaking Frankly*, p. 210.

Chapter 39

359 **"It is certain":** William Leahy, diary entry for August 10, 1945, William D. Leahy Papers, LOC.

359 **At 12:45 a.m.:** Pacific War Research Society, *Japan's Longest Day*, p. 46; Butow, *Japan's Decision to Surrender*, pp. 192–93.

360 **Officials zeroed:** Pacific War Research Society, *Japan's Longest Day*, pp. 46–47.

360 **"The Allies had":** Togo, *Cause of Japan*, p. 324.

360 **"The proposed surrender":** Pacific War Research Society, *Japan's Longest Day*, p. 48.

361 **"I therefore propose":** Ibid., p. 50.

361 **"Unless we were resigned":** Togo, *Cause of Japan*, pp. 327–28.

361 **"If you persist":** Butow, *Japan's Decision to Surrender*, p. 195.

361 **"I feel," he wrote":** Marquis Kido, diary entry for August 12, 1945, in Kido, *Diary of Marquis Kido*, p. 447; Butow, *Japan's Decision to Surrender*, pp. 198–99.

361 **"If we do not":** Butow, *Japan's Decision to Surrender*, p. 196.

362 **"The premier," a relieved:** Marquis Kido, diary entry for August 12, 1945, in Kido, *Diary of Marquis Kido*, p. 448.

362 **"The course we must":** Butow, *Japan's Decision to Surrender*, p. 200.

362 **"The discussion":** Togo, *Cause of Japan*, p. 328.

362 **"Often I felt":** Ibid., p. 329.

362 **"Inasmuch as":** Pacific War Research Society, *Japan's Longest Day*, p. 73.

362 **"Will you give":** Ibid.

362 **"Impossible":** Ibid., pp. 73–74.

363 **"One look":** Ibid., p. 77.

363 **"I am having":** Ibid.

363 **The emperor gathered:** Frank, *Downfall*, p. 314.

363 **At 10:50 a.m.:** Pacific War Research Society, *Japan's Longest Day*, p. 78.

364 **"I have listened carefully":** Butow, *Japan's Decision to Surrender*, p. 207.

364 **"The whole nation":** Ibid., p. 208.

364 **"Finally," he concluded:** Ibid.

Chapter 40

365 **"In both Hiroshima":** Manhattan Engineer District, "The Atomic Bombings of Hiroshima and Nagasaki," June 29, 1946, p. 34.

365 **"Do you believe":** Frank, *Downfall*, p. 316.

365 **"Maybe," he declared:** Pacific War Research Society, *Japan's Longest Day*, p. 87.

366 **"You have power":** Ibid.

366 **"The emperor has spoken":** Ibid., p. 91.

366 **"No officer in the army":** Ibid., p. 112.

366 **The job of preparing:** Ibid., pp. 118–19.

367 **"The war situation grows more":** Ibid., p. 145.

367 **"Japan is on the verge of destruction":** Ibid.

367 **"The war situation has not developed":** Ibid., p. 158.

367 **"On the question":** Ibid., p. 155.

367 **The agreed-upon:** Ibid., pp. 159–60, 165–66.

367 **"I am most grateful":** Ibid., p. 207. See also Togo, *Cause of Japan*, p. 335.

368 **"I should have":** Butow, *Japan's Decision to Surrender*, p. 218.

368 **"I think the war minister":** Pacific War Research Society, *Japan's Longest Day*, p. 208.

368 **At the palace, a six-person:** Ibid., pp. 96–99, 106, 109–10.

368 **"How loudly":** Ibid., p. 209.
368 **"Was it all right?":** Ibid., p. 211.

Chapter 41

369 **"In this last":** Stimson, "Decision to Use the Atomic Bomb," p. 107.
369 **"Unless the Emperor":** Butow, *Japan's Decision to Surrender*, p. 211.
369 **The conspirators:** Ibid., p. 212; Pacific War Research Society, *Japan's Longest Day*, pp. 51, 75.
370 **The young officers:** Butow, *Japan's Decision to Surrender*, pp. 211–12; Pacific War Research Society, *Japan's Longest Day*, pp. 74.
366 **"No officer in the Imperial":** Pacific War Research Society, *Japan's Longest Day*, p. 112.
370 **Despite Anami's admonition:** Butow, *Japan's Decision to Surrender*, pp. 213–14.
370 **"There's no time":** Pacific War Research Society, *Japan's Longest Day*, p. 219.
370 **Hatanaka told him:** Butow, *Japan's Decision to Surrender*, p. 218.
371 **"Hold on a minute":** Pacific War Research Society, *Japan's Longest Day*, p. 219.
371 **"As commander":** Ibid., p. 221.
371 **"Time was running":** Butow, *Japan's Decision to Surrender*, p. 215.
371 **At 1:45 a.m. Ida:** Pacific War Research Society, *Japan's Longest Day*, pp. 225–27.
371 **At the palace, Imperial guards:** Ibid., pp. 230, 241, 242 and 247.
372 **Word quickly spread:** Ibid., pp. 247, 265, and 274.
372 **Across the capital:** Ibid., pp. 275–77, 284–87, and 295.
372 **"After tasting":** Ibid., p. 237.
372 **"For my supreme":** Ibid.
373 **"I believe," he wrote:** Ibid.
373 **"I am glad":** Butow, *Japan's Decision to Surrender*, p. 219.
373 **"If I don't":** Pacific War Research Society, *Japan's Longest Day*, p. 268.
373 **"Mori's been murdered":** Ibid., p. 229.
373 **"It's all over":** Ibid., p. 246.
374 **"You must do":** Ibid., p. 281.
374 **"The only thing you can":** Ibid., p. 283.
374 **"From this moment":** Ibid., p. 301.
374 **Hatanaka refused to give up:** Ibid., pp. 288–89, 302–3.
375 **"Very well," he finally:** Ibid., p. 303.
375 **"We've done":** Ibid.
375 **"When I am dead":** Ibid., p. 292.
375 **"Shall I help":** Ibid., p. 296.

Chapter 42

376 **"If the Japs":** "Sweating It Out," editorial, *Pittsburgh Post-Gazette*, August 13, 1945, p. 6.
376 **"Take precautions":** Truman, *Year of Decisions*, p. 432.
376 **Rumors of a possible:** "Rumors That Japan Has Quit War Excite Washington and Other Cities," *New York Times*, August 10, 1945, p. 2.
376 **News of a possible:** "Honolulu Goes Mad," *New York Times*, August 11, 1945, p. 4.
376 **"Londoners danced":** "White House Silent on a Time Limit," *Tampa Morning Tribune*, August 13, 1945, p. 1.
376 **"Thank God, there will":** W. H. Lawrence, "GI's in Pacific Go Wild with Joy," *New York Times*, August 11, 1945, p. 1.
377 **"I hope from the bottom":** Ibid.
377 **"With these steps":** Truman, *Year of Decisions*, p. 433.

377 **Confident of a quick:** "It Was 'I Don't Know Day' Sunday at the White House," *Tampa Tribune*, August 13, 1945, p. 7.

377 **"Reporters went":** Ibid.

377 **A similar scene unfolded outside:** "This Is Worth Waiting For," photo caption, *Washington Times Herald*, August 13, 1945, p. 20; "Crowds Here Sang, Prayed," *Washington Daily News*, August 13, 1945, p. 6.

377 **"Thank God," one soldier:** "President Waits in Vain for Reply to Surrender Note," *Washington Times Herald*, August 13, 1945, p. 1.

377 **"I don't know":** "It Was 'I Don't Know Day' Sunday at the White House," *Tampa Tribune*, August 13, 1945, p. 7.

377 **"Since I landed":** Harry Truman to Mary Jane Truman, August 12, 1945, Box 19, Papers of Harry S. Truman Pertaining to Family, Business, and Personal Affairs, HSTL.

378 **At 9:34 p.m.:** "Capital Calms Down to Await Official News on Surrender," *Washington Evening Star*, August 13, 1945, p. 2.

378 **"Here it is!":** Ibid.

378 **"President Truman":** Ibid.

378 **Celebratory gunfire:** Ibid.

378 **"On the other end":** "President Waits in Vain for Reply to Surrender Note," *Washington Times Herald*, August 13, 1945, p. 1.

378 **"Hold that flash":** "Capital Calms Down to Await Official News on Surrender," *Washington Evening Star*, August 13, 1945, p. 2.

378 **"We want Harry," people began:** "President Waits in Vain for Reply to Surrender Note," *Washington Times Herald*, August 13, 1945, p. 1.

378 **"It is safe":** "Enemy's Answer Still Is Awaited," *Washington Evening Star*, August 13, 1945, p. 1.

378 **"No word has been":** Ibid.

378 **"Might there be":** Ibid.

378 **"I do not know," he replied:** Ibid.

378 **"No word from":** "How World Waited for Tokyo Reply on Surrender," *Fitchburg Sentinel*, August 14, 1945, p. 16.

378 **"Nothing new":** Ibid.

378 **"The president has gone to bed":** Ibid.

379 **"The President directs":** George Marshall to Douglas MacArthur and Carl Spaatz, Radio No. WARX-48689, August 13, 1945, GCMP.

379 **"It is desired":** "Special Radio Teletype Conference," August 14, 1945, Box 21, Carl Spaatz Papers, LOC.

379 **The air force launched:** Craven and Cate, *Army Air Forces in World War II*, pp. 5:732–33.

379 **"calculated to remind":** "'Superforts' Stage 6-Target Wind-Up," *New York Times*, August 15, 1945, p. 8.

Chapter 43

380 **"The desire and will":** Michihiko Hachiya, diary entry for August 16, 1945, in Hachiya, *Hiroshima Diary*, p. 85.

380 **"His Imperial Majesty":** Pacific War Research Society, *Japan's Longest Day*, p. 308.

380 **The broadcast company:** Ibid., pp. 308, 320.

380 **Rumors swirled:** Yamashita, *Leaves from an Autumn of Emergencies*, p. 40.

380 **"As I walked":** Hisako Yoshizawa, diary entry for August 15, 1945, in Yamashita, *Leaves from an Autumn of Emergencies*, p. 216.

381 **"What sort":** Yamashita, *Daily Life in Wartime Japan*, p. 175.

381 **At eleven a.m., a broadcaster:** Ibid.

381 **Down in Hiroshima:** Michihiko Hachiya, diary entry for August 15, 1945, in Hachiya, *Hiroshima Diary*, p. 81.

381 **In a hotel:** León María Guerrero, diary entry for August 15, 1945.

381 **"There was complete":** Ibid.

381 **"In an instant":** Yamashita, *Daily Life in Wartime Japan*, p. 176.

381 **"To our good":** Pacific War Research Society, *Japan's Longest Day*, p. 209.

381 **"The war situation," he explained:** Ibid., 210.

382 **"The enemy":** Ibid.

382 **In rural areas:** Yamashita, *Daily Life in Wartime Japan*, p. 177; Keene, *So Lovely a Country*, pp. 101, 105.

382 **"All were expressionless":** León María Guerrero, diary entry for August 15, 1945.

382 **"As each word":** Aiko Takahashi, diary entry for August 15, 1945, in Yamashita, *Leaves from an Autumn of Emergencies*, p. 189.

382 **"The broadcast":** Michihiko Hachiya, diary entry for August 15, 1945, in Hachiya, *Hiroshima Diary*, p. 81.

382 **"I had been":** Ibid.

382 **"Only a coward":** Ibid., p. 82.

382 **"The news on the":** Havens, *Valley of Darkness*, pp. 191–92.

382 **"We all felt":** Yamashita, *Daily Life in Wartime Japan*, p. 179.

383 **"It's ended. The war":** Taiko Hirabayashi, diary entry for August 15, 1945, in Keene, *So Lovely a Country*, p. 106.

383 **"We lifted":** Atsuyuki Matsuo, diary entry for August 15, 1945, in Nagasaki International Cultural Hall, *Nagasaki Speaks*, p. 86.

383 **"Japan," the neighbor repeated:** Ibid.

383 **"I broke into tears":** Ibid.

383 **"I could see":** Nagai, *We of Nagasaki*, pp. 131–32.

Chapter 44

384 **"The bells":** John McCloy, diary entry for August 14, 1945, JJMP.

384 **"It is learned":** "White House Learns of Error After Announcing Receipt During Day of Confusion," *Washington Evening Star*, August 14, 1945, p. 1.

384 **Forty minutes later:** "How World Waited for Tokyo Reply on Surrender," *Fitchburg Sentine*l, August 14, 1945, p. 16.

384 **"The president is up":** Ibid.

384 **"Yes, sir":** "White House Learns of Error After Announcing Receipt During Day of Confusion," *Washington Evening Star*, August 14, 1945, p. 1.

385 **"It looks as if":** Edward T. Folliard, "Japs Quit Unconditionally," *Washington Post*, August 15, 1945, p. 1.

385 **"I have here":** Ibid.

385 **"Very urgent":** Ibid.

385 **"The confusion":** Ibid.

385 **Across the street:** Ibid.

385 **"The Japanese government's":** "White House Learns of Error After Announcing Receipt During Day of Confusion," *Washington Evening Star*, August 14, 1945, p. 1.

385 **Two and a half hours later:** "Byrnes First Had Word at 3 O'Clock," *New York Times*, August 15, 1945, p. 4.

385 **"A few minutes":** Byrnes, *Speaking Frankly*, p. 210.

385 **"His Majesty the Emperor":** The Japanese government's answer is included in the "Statement by the President," August 14, 1945, Box 190, President's Secretary's Files, HSTL.

386 **"It was," he said:** Byrnes, *All in One Lifetime*, p. 306.

386 **"I did not believe":** Byrnes, *Speaking Frankly*, p. 210.
386 **At 6:57 p.m.:** Thomas Reynolds, "Emperor Commanded to Ensure Disarming of All Nip Forces," *Newark Star Ledger*, August 15, 1945, p. 1; Truman, *Year of Decisions*, p. 436.
386 **"I have received":** "Statement by the President," August 14, 1945, Box 190, President's Secretary's Files, HSTL.
386 **"Allied armed forces":** Ibid.
386 **Aides handed out:** Copies of these releases can be found in the President's Secretary's Files, HSTL.
387 **"I congratulate you":** Transcript of Press and Radio Conference #18, August 14, 1945, Box 6, White House Official Reporter Files, HSTL.
387 **"That is all":** Ibid.
387 **"It was simple":** John M. Hightower, "Death Machines Stilled as New Peace Era Dawns," *Atlanta Journal*, August 15, 1945, p. 1.
387 **Car horns:** Vincent X. Flaherty, "Bedlam Reigns as Capital Celebrates," *Washington Times Herald*, August 15, 1945, p. 3; "500,000 Here Celebrate Peace with Noise and Merrymaking," *Washington Evening Star*, August 16, 1945, p. 1; Fraser Edwards, "This Is How the Peace Came to Washington," *Washington Daily News*, August 15, 1945, p. 6.
387 **"I have never seen":** "Refuse Crews Find Record Litter After Capital Celebration," *Washington Evening Star*, August 15, 1945, p. 3.
387 **"The city, as a":** Frederick R. Barkley, "President Joins Capital's Gaiety," *New York Times*, August 15, 1945, p. 3.
387 **"It was the noisiest":** "D.C. Streets Deserted on the Morning After," *Washington Times Herald*, August 15, 1945, p. 3.
387 **"We want Harry," people began to chant:** Ibid.
387 **Twenty minutes:** Truman, *Year of Decisions*, p. 437.
387 **"I'm proud of Harry":** "Call to Mother Next," *Kansas City Times*, August 15, 1945, p. 1.
387 **"The White House was the center":** Frederick R. Barkley, "President Joins Capital's Gaiety," *New York Times*, August 15, 1945, p. 3.
388 **"Ladies and gentlemen":** Ibid.
388 **"This is the day":** Ibid.
388 **"Harry, Harry":** "D.C. Streets Deserted," p. 3.
388 **"I don't deserve":** "Truman Wishes F.D.R. Could Be Here, He Tells Mrs. Roosevelt," *St. Louis Post-Dispatch*, August 15, 1945, p. 1.

Epilogue

389 **"The explosion of the atomic bomb had":** "Address to Be Delivered by Lt. Gen. Leslie R. Groves, U.S.A. (Retired) Before the Iowa Convention of the American Veterans of World War II at Waterloo, Iowa," July 31, 1948, Box 1, Leslie R. Groves Papers, NARA.
389 **A Gallup poll in August:** George Gallup, "Public Opposed to Using Gas But Approved Atomic Bombing," *Washington Post*, August 26, 1945, p. B5.
389 **"Two bombs cost":** "Quillen's Quips," *Chattanooga Times*, September 5, 1945, p. 6.
389 **The United States Strategic:** USSBS, *Effects of the Atomic Bombs on Hiroshima and Nagasaki*, pp. 3, 5.
389 **The generally agreed-upon:** These are the numbers presented in each museum.
390 **Some, like Generals:** Arnold, *Global Mission*, p. 598; Curtis E. LeMay with MacKinlay Kantor, *Mission with LeMay: My Story* (Garden City, N.Y.: Doubleday, 1965), p. 388.
390 **"I disliked seeing":** Smith, *Eisenhower*, p. 432.
390 **"I was not taught":** Leahy, *I Was There*, p. 441.
390 **"It was a question":** Undated Associated Press News Cable, Box 1, Lansing Lamont Papers, HSTL.

390 **"The whole of humanity":** Harvey Cho-ke to Harry Truman, March 14, 1958, Box 79, Post-Presidential Papers, HSTL.

390 **Thirteen years:** Tsukasa Nitoguri to Harry Truman, March 1, 1958, Box 22, ibid.

390 **"As the executive":** Harry Truman to Tsukasa Nitoguri, March 12, 1958, ibid.

390 **"I hope the Lord":** Kay Bartlett, "Hiroshima Bomber Has No Remorse Over Act," *Tulsa Daily World*, August 3, 1975, p. 24, copy on file in Microfilm Roll #38640, Paul Tibbets, Jr., Papers, AFHRA.

391 **"Does service":** David Arzt to Paul Tibbets, September 7, 1962, Microfilm Roll #38639, ibid.

391 **"Can you," another:** Mr. and Mrs. Gantner to Paul Tibbets, August 24, 1981, Microfilm Roll #38643, ibid.

391 **"With four battle":** Lloyd Whydotski to Harry Truman, July 18, 1970, Box 52, Post-Presidential Papers, HSTL.

393 **"least abhorrent":** Stimson, "Decision to Use the Atomic Bomb," p. 107.

393 **"The atomic bombs":** Bix, *Hirohito*, p. 509.

393 **"I saw misery":** Setsuko Iwamoto, "That Day," in Hiroshima Peace Culture Foundation, *Eyewitness Testimonies*, p. 49.

BIBLIOGRAPHY

ARCHIVES, LIBRARIES, AND MUSEUMS

Air Force Historical Research Agency, Montgomery, Ala.
Amherst College Archives and Special Collections, Amherst, Mass.
Brigham Young University Library, Provo, Utah
Charleston County Public Library, Charleston, S.C.
Clemson University Special Collections and Archives, Clemson, S.C.
Columbia University Oral History Archives, New York, N.Y.
Daniel Library, The Citadel, Charleston, S.C.
George C. Marshall Foundation Library, Lexington, Va.
Harry S. Truman Presidential Library and Museum, Independence, Mo.
Hiroshima Peace Memorial Museum, Hiroshima, Japan
Library of Congress, Washington, D.C.
K-25 History Center, Oak Ridge, Tenn.
MacArthur Memorial Archives and Library, Norfolk, Va.
Marlene and Nathan Addlestone Library, College of Charleston, Charleston, S.C.
McDermott Library, U.S. Air Force Academy, Colorado Springs, Colo.
Nagasaki Atomic Bomb Museum, Nagasaki, Japan
National Archives and Records Administration, College Park, Md.
National Diet Library, Tokyo, Japan
National Personnel Records Center, St. Louis, Mo.
National World War II Museum, New Orleans, La.
University of California at San Diego Special Collections and Archives, La Jolla, Calif.
U.S. Army Heritage and Education Center, Carlisle, Penn.
Willis Library, University of North Texas, Denton, Tex.
Wood Library–Museum of Anesthesiology, Schaumburg, Ill.
Yale University Library, New Haven, Conn.

SPECIFIC COLLECTIONS

Air Force Historical Research Agency, Montgomery, Alabama

Twentieth Air Force Papers
Twenty-First Bomber Command Papers
509 Composite Group Papers
Paul Tibbets, Jr., Papers

Amherst College Archives and Special Collections, Amherst, Mass.

John J. McCloy Papers

Brigham Young University Library, Provo, Utah

Morris R. Jeppson Papers

Clemson University Special Collections and Archives, Clemson, S.C.

James F. Byrnes Papers
Walter J. Brown Papers

Harry S. Truman Presidential Library, Independence, Mo.

Atomic Bomb Collection
Confidential File
Official File
President's Secretary's Files
Post-Presidential Papers
Eben A. Ayers Papers
George M. Elsey Papers
Rose A. Conway Papers
White House Chief Usher Files
White House Official Reporter Files
Charles G. Gross Papers
Dale M. Hellegers Papers
Frank McNaughton Papers
Harry H. Vaughan Papers
John Coster-Mullen Papers
Jonathan Daniels Papers
Kenneth Hechler Papers
Lansing Lamont Papers
Merle Miller Papers
R. Gordon Arneson Papers
Samuel B. Smizer Papers
William M. Rigdon Papers

Library of Congress, Washington, D.C.

Henry H. Arnold Papers
William D. Leahy Papers
Curtis E. LeMay Papers
Robert Oppenheimer Papers
William Parsons Papers
Carl Spaatz Papers

National Archives and Records Administration, College Park, Md.

Record Group 18—Records of the Army Air Forces
Record Group 77—Records of the Manhattan Project
Record Group 200—Leslie Groves Papers

National Personnel Records Center, St. Louis, Mo.

Jacob Beser Official Military Personnel File (OMPF)
Leslie R. Groves OMPF
Curtis E. LeMay OMPF
Carl Spaatz OMPF

U.S. Army Heritage and Education Center, Carlisle, Penn.

Thomas F. Farrell Papers

Yale University, New Haven, Conn.

Henry Stimson Papers

GOVERNMENT REPORTS, HISTORIES, AND MICROFILM COLLECTIONS

Assistant Chief of Air Staff–Intelligence, Headquarters Army Air Forces. *Mission Accomplished: Interrogations of Japanese Industrial, Military, and Civil Leaders of World War II.* Washington, D.C.: U.S. Government Printing Office, 1946.

Bowen, Lee, and Robert D. Little. *A History of the Air Force Atomic Energy Program, 1943–1953.* Vol. 1, *Project Silverplate, 1943–1946.* Washington, D.C.: Office of Air Force History, n.d.

Committee for the Compilation of Materials on Damage Caused by the Atomic Bombs in Hiroshima and Nagasaki. *Hiroshima and Nagasaki: The Physical, Medical, and Social Effects of the Atomic Bombs.* Trans. Eisei Ishikawa and David L. Swain. New York: Basic Books, 1981.

"Correspondence ("Top Secret") of the Manhattan Engineer District, 1942–1946." National Archives Microfilm Publications, Microfilm Publication M1109, Washington, D.C.

Craven, Wesley Frank, and James Lea Cate, eds. *The Army Air Forces in World War II.* Vol. 5, *The Pacific: Matterhorn to Nagasaki, June 1944 to August 1945.* Washinton, D.C.: Office of Air Force History, 1983.

Fine, Lenore, and Jesse A. Remington. *The Corps of Engineers: Construction in the United States.* Washington, D.C.: Office of the Chief of Military History, 1972.

Fowle, Barry W., ed. *Builders and Fighters: U.S. Army Engineers in World War II.* Fort Belvoir, Va.: Office of History, United States Army Corps of Engineers, 1992.

General Staff of GHQ, *Reports of General MacArthur: Japanese Operations in the Southwest Pacific Area*, vol. 2, pt. 2. Washington, D.C.: U.S. Government Printing Office, 1994.

Goldberg, Alfred. *The Pentagon: The First Fifty Years.* Washington, D.C.: Historical Office of the Office of the Secretary of Defense, 1992.

Greenfield, Kent Roberts, ed. *Command Decisions.* Washington, D.C.: Center of Military History, United States Army, 1987.

"Harrison-Bundy Files Relating to the Development of the Atomic Bomb, 1942–1946." National Archives Microfilm Publications, Microfilm Publication M1108, Washington, D.C.

Hewlett, Richard G., and Oscar E. Anderson, Jr. *The New World, 1939–1946.* Vol. 1 in *A History of the United States Atomic Energy Commission.* University Park: Pennsylvania State University Press, 1962.

Jones, Vincent C. *Manhattan: The Army and the Atomic Bomb.* Washington, D.C.: U.S. Government Printing Office, 1985.

MacEachin, Douglas J. *The Final Months of the War with Japan: Signals Intelligence, U.S. Invasion Planning and the A-Bomb Decision.* Central Intelligence Agency: Center for the Study of Intelligence, 1998.

Public Papers of the Presidents of the United States: Harry S. Truman, Containing the Public Messages, Speeches, and Statements of the President, January 1 to December 31, 1950. Washington, D.C.: U.S Government Printing Office, 1965.

Russell, Richard A. *Project Hula: Secret Soviet-American Cooperation in the War Against Japan*. Washington, D.C.: Naval Historical Center, 1997.

Smyth, H. D. *Atomic Energy for Military Purposes*. York, Penn.: Maple Press, 1946.

The Effect of the Atomic Bombs at Hiroshima and Nagasaki: Report of the British Mission to Japan. London: His Majesty's Stationery Office, 1946.

U.S. Congress, Senate, *Hearings Before the Special Committee on Atomic Energy: A Resolution Creating a Special Committee to Investigate Problems Relating to the Development, Use, and Control of Atomic Energy*, Part I, 79th Cong. 1st Sess., November 27, 1945. Washington, D.C.: U.S. Government Printing Office, 1945.

U.S. Department of State. *Foreign Relations of the United States: Diplomatic Papers. The Conference of Berlin, The Potsdam Conference, 1945*. Vols. 1–2. Washington, D.C.: U.S. Government Printing Office, 1960.

———. *Foreign Relations of the United States: Diplomatic Papers, 1945*. Vol. 5, *Europe*. Washington, D.C.: U.S. Government Printing Office, 1967.

———. *Foreign Relations of the United States: Diplomatic Papers, 1945*. Vol. 6, *The British Commonwealth: The Far East*. Washington, D.C.: U.S. Government Printing Office, 1969.

———. *Foreign Relations of the United States: Diplomatic Papers, 1945*. Vol. 7, *The Far East: China*. Washington, D.C.: U.S. Government Printing Office, 1969.

———. *Foreign Relations of the United States: The Conferences at Washington, 1941–1942, and Casablanca, 1943*. Washington, D.C.: U.S. Government Printing Office, 1968.

United States Strategic Bombing Survey. *A Report on Physical Damage in Japan*. Washington, D.C.: U.S. Government Printing Office, 1947.

———. *Field Report Covering Air-Raid Protection and Allied Subjects in Nagasaki, Japan*. Washington, D.C.: U.S. Government Printing Office, 1947.

———., *Field Report Covering Air Raid Protection and Allied Subjects in Tokyo, Japan*. Washington, D.C.: U.S. Government Printing Office, 1947.

———. *Final Report Covering Air-Raid Protection and Allied Subjects in Japan*. Washington, D.C.: U.S. Government Printing Office, 1947.

———. *Interrogations of Japanese Officials*, vol. 2, Washington, D.C.: U.S. Government Printing Office, 1946.

———. *Oil in Japan's War*. Washington, D.C.: U.S. Government Printing Office, 1946.

———. *Japan's Struggle to End the War*. Washington, D.C.: U.S. Government Printing Office, 1946.

———. *Summary Report (Pacific War)*. Washington, D.C.: U.S. Government Printing Office, 1946.

———. *The Effects of Air Attack on the City of Nagasaki*. Washington, D.C.: U.S. Government Printing Office, 1947.

———. *The Effects of Air Attack on the City of Nagoya*. Washington, D.C.: U.S. Government Printing Office, 1947.

———. *The Effects of Air Attack on Osaka-Kobe-Kyoto*. Washington, D.C.: U.S. Government Printing Office, 1947.

———. *The Effects of the Atomic Bombs on Hiroshima and Nagasaki*. Washington, D.C.: U.S. Government Printing Office, 1946.

———. *The Effects of Incendiary Bomb Attacks on Japan (A Report on Eight Cities)*. Washington, D.C.: U.S. Government Printing Office, 1947.

———. *The Effects of Bombing on Health and Medical Services in Hiroshima and Nagasaki*. Washington, D.C.: U.S. Government Printing Office, 1947.

———. *The Effects of Bombing on Health and Medical Services in Japan*. Washington, D.C.: U.S. Government Printing Office, 1947.

———. *The Effects of Strategic Bombing on Japanese Morale*. Washington, D.C.: U.S. Government Printing Office, 1947.

———. *The Effects of the Atomic Bomb on Nagasaki, Japan*. 2 vols. Washington, D.C.: U.S. Government Printing Office, 1947.

———. *The Effects of the Atomic Bomb on Hiroshima, Japan*. 3 vols. Washington, D.C.: U.S. Government Printing Office, 1947.

———. *The Strategic Air Operation of Very Heavy Bombardment in the War Against Japan (Twentieth Air Force)*. Washington, D.C.: U.S. Government Printing Office, 1946.

———. *The Effects of Strategic Bombing on Japan's War Economy*. Washington, D.C.: U.S. Government Printing Office, 1946.

———. *The War Against Japanese Transportation, 1941–1945*. Washington, D.C.: U.S. Government Printing Office, 1947.

BOOKS

A Citizens' Group to Convey Testimonies of Hiroshima and Nagasaki, ed. *Give Me Water: Testimonies of Hiroshima and Nagasaki*. Tokyo: Japan, 1972.

Akizuki, Tatsuichiro. *Document of A-Bombed Nagasaki*. Trans. Keiichi Nagata. Nagasaki: Nagasaki Printing, 1977.

———. *Nagasaki 1945: The First Full Length Eyewitness Account of the Atomic Bomb Attack on Nagasaki*. Trans. Keiichi Nagata. Ed. Gordon Honeycombe. London: Quartet Books, 1981.

Alexander, Joseph H. *Utmost Savagery: The Three Days of Tarawa*. Annapolis, MD: Naval Institute Press, 1995.

Allen, Thomas B., and Norman Polmar. *Code-Name Downfall: The Secret Plan to Invade Japan—and Why Truman Dropped the Bomb*. New York: Simon & Schuster, 1995.

Alperovitz, Gar. *Atomic Diplomacy: Hiroshima and Potsdam: The Use of the Atomic Bomb and the American Confrontation with Soviet Power*. New York: Simon & Schuster, 1965.

Alvarez, Luis W. *Alvarez: Adventures of a Physicist*. New York: Basic Books, 1987.

Amrine, Michael. *The Great Decision: The Secret History of the Atomic Bomb*. New York: G.P. Putnam's Sons, 1959.

Arnold, H. H. *Global Mission*. New York: Harper & Brothers, 1949.

Asbell, Bernard. *When F.D.R. Died*. New York: Holt, Rinehart & Winston, 1961.

Ayers, Eben A. *Truman in the White House: The Diary of Eben A. Ayers*. Ed. Robert H. Ferrell. Columbia: University of Missouri Press, 1991.

Badash, Lawrence, Joseph O. Hirschfelder, and Herbert P. Broida, eds. *Reminiscences of Los Alamos, 1943–1945*. Vol. 5, *Studies in the History of Modern Science*. Dordrecht, Holland: D. Reidel, 1980.

Beser, Jacob. *Hiroshima and Nagasaki Revisited*. Memphis, TN: Global Press, 1988.

Beser, Jerome, and Jack Spangler. *The Rising Sun Sets: The Complete Story of the Bombing of Nagasaki*. Bloomington, IN: Authorhouse, 2007.

Bird, Kai, and Lawrence Lifschultz, eds. *Hiroshima's Shadow*. Stony Creek, Conn.: Pamphleteer's Press, 1998.

Bird, Kai, and Martin J. Sherwin. *American Prometheus: The Triumph and Tragedy of Robert J. Oppenheimer*. London: Atlantic Books, 2005.

Bishop, Jim. *FDR's Last Year: April 1944–April 1945*. New York: William Morrow, 1974.

Bix, Herbert P. *Hirohito and the Making of Modern Japan*. New York: HarperCollins, 2000.

Blum, John Morton, ed. *The Price of Vision: The Diary of Henry A. Wallace, 1942–1946*. Boston: Houghton Mifflin, 1973.

Bohlen, Charles E. *Witness to History, 1929–1969*. New York: W. W. Norton, 1973.

Boyer, Paul. *By the Bomb's Early Light: American Thought and Culture at the Dawn of the Atomic Age*. Chapel Hill: University of North Carolina Press, 1994.

Brooks, Lester. *Behind Japan's Decision to Surrender: The Secret Struggle That Ended an Empire*. New York: McGraw-Hill, 1968.

Bundy, McGeorge. *Danger and Survival: Choices About the Bomb in the First Fifty Years*. New York: Vintage, 1990.

Bush, Vannevar. *Pieces of the Action*. New York: William Morrow, 1970.

Butow, Robert J. C. *Japan's Decision to Surrender*. Stanford, Calif.: Stanford University Press, 1954.

Byrnes, James F. *All in One Lifetime*. New York: Harper & Brothers, 1958.

———. *Speaking Frankly*. London: William Heinemann, 1947.

Campbell, Richard H. *The Silverplate Bombers: A History and Registry of the Enola Gay and Other B-29s Configured to Carry Atomic Bombs*. Jefferson, N.C.: McFarland, 2005.

Campbell, Thomas M., and George C. Herring, eds. *The Diaries of Edward R. Stettinius, Jr., 1943–1946*. New York: New Viewpoints, 1975.

Cantril, Hadley, ed. *Public Opinion, 1935–1946*. Princeton, NJ: Princeton University Press, 1951.

Caron, George R., with Charlotte E. Meares. *Fires of a Thousand Suns: The George R. "Bob" Caron Story—Tail Gunner of the Enola Gay*. Westminster, CO: Web Publishing Co., 1995.

Chappell, John D. *Before the Bomb: How America Approached the End of the Pacific War*. Lexington: University Press of Kentucky, 1997.

Chinnock, Frank W. *Nagasaki: The Forgotten Bomb*. New York: New American Library, 1969.

Christman, Al. *Target Hiroshima: Deak Parsons and the Creation of the Atomic Bomb*. Annapolis, MD: Naval Institute Press, 1998.

Churchill, Winston. *The Second World War*. Vol. 1, *The Gathering Storm*. Boston: Houghton Mifflin, 1948.

———. *The Second World War*. Vol. 6, *Triumph and Tragedy*. Boston: Houghton Mifflin, 1953.

City of Hiroshima. *The Spirit of Hiroshima*. Hiroshima: Hiroshima Peace Memorial Museum, 1999.

City of Nagasaki. *The Records of the Atomic Bombing in Nagasaki*. Nagasaki: Nagasaki Foundation for the Promotion of Peace, 1976.

———. *Testimonies of the Atomic Bomb Survivors: A Record of the Devastation of Nagasaki*. Trans. Brian Burke-Gaffney et al. Nagasaki: City of Nagasaki, 1985.

Coffey, Thomas M. *Hap: The Story of the U.S. Air Force and the Man Who Built It*. New York: Viking Press, 1982.

———. *Iron Eagle: The Turbulent Life of General Curtis LeMay*. New York: Crown, 1986.

Cohen, Jerome B. *Japan's Economy in War and Reconstruction*. Minneapolis: University of Minnesota Press, 1949.

Collie, Craig. *Nagasaki: The Massacre of the Innocent and Unknowing*. London: Portobello Books, 2011.

Collison, Thomas. *The Superfortress Is Born: The Story of the Boeing B-29*. New York: Duell, Sloan & Pearce, 1945.

Compton, Arthur Holly. *Atomic Quest: A Personal Narrative*. New York: Oxford University Press, 1956.

Conant, Jennet. *109 East Palace: Robert Oppenheimer and the Secret City of Los Alamos*. New York: Simon & Schuster, 2005.

Cook, Haruko Taya, and Theodore F. Cook. *Japan at War: An Oral History*. New York: New Press, 1992.

Coster-Mullen, John. *Atom Bombs: The Top-Secret Inside Story of Little Boy and Fat Man*. Privately Printed, 2004.

Craig, William. *The Fall of Japan*. New York: Penguin Books, 1967.

Daniels, Jonathan. *The Man of Independence*. New York: J.B. Lippincott, 1950.

Davis, Nuel Pharr. *Lawrence and Oppenheimer*. New York: Da Capo Press, 1986.

Deane, John R. *The Strange Alliance: The Story of Our Efforts at Wartime Co-Operation with Russia*. New York: Viking Press, 1947.

Detwiler, Donald D., and Charles B. Burdick, eds. *War in Asia and the Pacific, 1937–1949*. Vol. 12, *Defense of the Homeland and End of the War*. New York: Garland, 1980.

Dietz, Suzanne Simon. *My True Course: Dutch Van Kirk, Northumberland to Hiroshima*. Lawrenceville, GA: Red Gremlin Press, 2012.

Dockrill, Saki, ed. *From Pearl Harbor to Hiroshima: The Second World War in Asia and the Pacific, 1941–1945*. London: Palgrave Macmillan, 1993.

Donovan, Robert J. *Conflict and Crisis: The Presidency of Harry S. Truman, 1945–1948*. New York: W. W. Norton, 1977.

Doolittle, James H., with Carroll V. Glines. *I Could Never Be So Lucky Again: An Autobiography*. New York: Bantam Books, 1991.

Dower, John. *Cultures of War: Pearl Harbor, Hiroshima, 9-11, Iraq*. New York: W. W. Norton, 2010.

Drea, Edward J. *MacArthur's Ultra: Codebreaking and the War Against Japan, 1942–1945*. Lawrence: University Press of Kansas, 1992.

Drury, Allen. *A Senate Journal, 1943–1945*. New York: McGraw-Hill, 1963.

Eatherly, Claude. *Burning Conscience: The Case of the Hiroshima Pilot, Claude Eatherly, Told in His Letters to Gunther Anders, With a Postscript for American Readers by Anders*. New York: Monthly Review Press, 1961.

English Department of Hiroshima Jogakuin High School, ed. and trans. *Summer Cloud: A-Bomb Experience of a Girl's School in Hiroshima*. Tokyo: Sanyusha Shuppan, 1998.

Farrell, Don A. *Tinian and the Bomb: Project Alberta and Operation Centerboard*. Tinian: Micronesian Productions, 2018.

———. *Atomic Bomb Island: Tinian, the Last Stage of the Manhattan Project, and the Dropping of the Atomic Bombs on Japan in World War II*. Guilford, Conn.: Stackpole Books, 2019.

Feis, Herbert. *The Atomic Bomb and the End of World War II*. Princeton, NJ: Princeton University Press, 1966.

———. *Between War and Peace: The Potsdam Conference*. Princeton, NJ: Princeton University Press, 1960.

Feld, Bernard T., and Gertrud Weiss Szilard, eds. *The Collected Works of Leo Szilard: Scientific Papers*. Cambridge, Mass.: MIT Press, 1972.

Fermi, Laura. *Atoms in the Family: My Life with Enrico Fermi*. Chicago: University of Chicago Press, 1954.

Ferrell, Robert H. *Harry S. Truman: A Life*. Columbia: University of Missouri Press, 1994.

Ferrell, Robert H., ed. *The Autobiography of Harry S. Truman*. Columbia: University of Missouri Press, 1980.

———. *Dear Bess: The Letters from Harry to Bess Truman, 1910–1959*. New York: W. W. Norton, 1983.

———. *Off the Record: The Private Papers of Harry S. Truman*. New York: Harper & Row, 1980.

Fleisher, Wilfrid. *Volcanic Isle*. Garden City, NY: Doubleday, Doran, 1942.

Frank, Richard B. *Downfall: The End of the Japanese Empire*. New York: Random House, 1999.

Fussell, Paul. *Thank God for the Atom Bomb and Other Essays*. New York: Summit Books, 1988.

Gallicchio, Marc. *Unconditional: The Japanese Surrender in World War II*. New York: Oxford University Press, 2020.

Geddes, Donald Porter. *Franklin Delano Roosevelt: A Memorial*. New York: Pocket Books, 1945.

Giangreco, D. M. *Hell to Pay: Operation Downfall and the Invasion of Japan, 1945–1947.* Annapolis, MD: Naval Institute Press, 2009.

———. *The Soldier from Independence: A Military Biography of Harry Truman*. Minneapolis: Zenith Press, 2009.

———. *Truman and the Bomb: The Untold Story*. Lincoln, NE: Potomac Books, 2023.

Giangreco, D.M., and Kathryn Moore. *Dear Harry: Truman's Mailroom, 1945–1953: The Truman Administration Through Correspondence with "Everyday Americans."* Mechanicsburg, Penn.: Stackpole Books, 1999.

Gibney, Frank, ed. *Senso: The Japanese Remember the Pacific War: Letters to the Editor of the Asahi Shimbun*. Trans. Beth Cary. Armonk, NY: M.E. Sharpe, 1995.

Gilbert, Martin. *"Never Despair": Winston S. Churchill, 1945–1965.* Toronto: Stoddart, 1988.

Giovannitti, Len, and Fred Freed. *The Decision to Drop the Bomb*. New York: Coward-McCann, 1965.

Goldstein, Donald M., Katherine V. Dillon, and J. Michael Wenger. *Rain of Ruin: A Photographic History of Hiroshima and Nagasaki*. Washington, D.C.: Brassey's, 1995.

Groueff, Stephane. *Manhattan Project: The Untold Story of the Making of the Atomic Bomb*. Boston: Little, Brown, 1967.

Groves, Leslie R. *Now It Can Be Told: The Story of the Manhattan Project*. New York: Harper & Brothers, 1962.

Guillain, Robert. *I Saw Tokyo Burning: An Eyewitness Narrative from Pearl Harbor to Hiroshima.* Trans. William Byron. Garden City, NY: Doubleday, 1981.

Hachiya, Michihiko, *Hiroshima Diary: The Journal of a Japanese Physician, August 6–September 30, 1945.* Trans. and edited by Warner Wells. Chapel Hill: University of North Carolina Press, 1955.

Hallas, James H. *Saipan: The Battle That Doomed Japan in World War II*. Guilford, Conn.: Stackpole Books, 2019.

Ham, Paul. *Hiroshima-Nagasaki*. New York: St. Martin's Press, 2014.

Hamilton, Nigel. *The Mantle of Command: FDR at War, 1941–1942*. Boston: Houghton Mifflin Harcourt, 2014.

Harder, Robert O. *"The Three Musketeers of the Army Air Forces": From Hitler's Fortress Europa to Hiroshima and Nagasaki.* Annapolis, MD: Naval Institute Press, 2015.

Harriman, Averell W., and Elie Abel. *Special Envoy to Churchill and Stalin, 1941–1946*. New York: Random House, 1975.

Hasegawa, Tsuyoshi. *Racing the Enemy: Stalin, Truman, and the Surrender of Japan*. Cambridge, Mass.: Harvard University Press, 2005.

Hasegawa, Tsuyoshi, ed. *The End of the Pacific War: Reappraisals.* Stanford, Calif.: Stanford University Press, 2007.

Hassett, William D. *Off the Record with F.D.R., 1942–1945*. New Brunswick, NJ: Rutgers University Press, 1958.

Havens, Thomas R. H. *Valley of Darkness: The Japanese People and World War II.* New York: W. W. Norton, 1978.

Hayes, Grace Person. *The History of the Joint Chiefs of Staff in World War II.* Annapolis, MD: Naval Institute Press, 1982.

Hegi, Benjamin Paul. *From Wright Field, Ohio, to Hokkaido, Japan: General Curtis E. LeMay's Letters to His Wife Helen, 1941–1945.* Edited by Alfred F. Hurley. Denton: University of North Texas Libraries, 2015.

Hersey, John. *Hiroshima*. New York: Alfred A. Knopf, 1946.

Hiroshima Association for the Success of the Atomic Bomb Exhibition. *After 60 Years, A-Bomb Survivors Speak Out: An Anthology of the Experiences of Hiroshima Atomic Bomb Victims*. Hiroshima, Japan: Yoshimura Printing, 2010.

———. *After 65 Years, A-Bomb Survivors and War Victims Speak Out: An Anthology of the Experiences of Hiroshima Atomic Bomb Victims*. Hiroshima, Japan: Yoshimura Printing, 2015.

Hiroshima-Nagasaki: A Pictorial Record of the Atomic Destruction. Tokyo: Hiroshima-Nagasaki Publishing, 1978.

Hiroshima Peace Culture Foundation. *Eyewitness Testimonies: Appeals from the A-Bomb Survivors*. Hiroshima, Japan: Bunkasya, 2017.

Hodgson, Godfrey. *The Colonel: The Life and Wars of Henry Stimson, 1867–1950*. New York: Alfred A. Knopf, 1990.

Hornfischer, James D. *The Fleet at Flood Tide: American at Total War in the Pacific, 1944–1945*. New York: Bantam Books, 2016.

Hoyt. Edwin P. *Hirohito: The Emperor and the Man*. New York: Praeger, 1984.

Huie, William Bradford. *The Hiroshima Pilot*, New York: G.P. Putnam's Sons, 1964.

Hull, Cordell. *The Memoirs of Cordell Hull*. London: Hodder & Stoughton, 1948.

Ienaga, Saburô. *The Pacific War: World War II and the Japanese, 1931–1945*. Trans. Frank Baldwin. New York: Pantheon, 1978.

Iriye, Akira. *Power and Culture: The Japanese-American War, 1941–1945*. Cambridge, Mass.: Harvard University Press, 1981.

Janssens, Rudolf V. A. *"What Future for Japan": U.S. Wartime Planning for the Postwar Era, 1942–1945*. Atlanta, GA: Rodopi, 1995.

Johnson, Charles W., and Charles O. Jackson. *City Behind a Fence: Oak Ridge, Tennessee, 1942–1946*. Knoxville: University of Tennessee Press, 1981.

Jungk, Robert. *Brighter than a Thousand Suns: A Personal History of the Atomic Scientists*. Trans. James Cleugh. New York: Harcourt Brace Jovanovich, 1958.

Kanda, Mikio, ed. *Widows of Hiroshima: The Life Stories of Nineteen Peasant Wives*. Trans. Taeko Midorikawa. New York: St. Martin's Press, 1989.

Kase, Toshikazu. *Journey to the Missouri*. Ed. David Nelson Rowe. New Haven, Conn.: Yale University Press, 1950.

Kato, Masuo. *The Lost War: A Japanese Reporter's Inside Story*. New York: Alfred A. Knopf, 1946.

Kawamura, Noriko. *Emperor Hirohito and the Pacific War*. Seattle: University of Washington Press, 2015.

Kawasaki, Shoichiro, ed. *A Call from Hibakusha of Hiroshima and Nagasaki: Proceedings of the International Symposium on the Damage and After-Effects of the Atomic Bombing of Hiroshima and Nagasaki, July 21–August 9, 1977*. Tokyo: Japan National Preparatory Committee, 1978.

Keeling, Arlene W., and Barbra Mann Wall, eds., *Nurses and Disasters: Global, Historical Case Studies*. New York: Springer, 2015.

Keene, Donald. *So Lovely a Country Will Never Die: Wartime Diaries of Japanese Writers*. New York: Columbia University Press, 2010.

Kelleher, Brendan, and H. J. Wiesen. *Nagasaki: August 9, 1945*. Trans. Junshin Junior College English Club. Nagasaki: n.p., 1983.

Kelly, Cynthia C., ed. *The Manhattan Project: The Birth of the Atomic Bomb in the Worlds of Its Creators, Eyewitnesses, and Historians*. New York: Tess Press, 2010.

Kido, Marquis. *The Diary of Marquis Kido, 1931–1945: Selected Translations into English*. Frederick, MD: University Publications of America, 1984.

Kinnaird, Clark. *The Real FDR*. New York: Harper & Brothers, 1945.
Kiyosawa, Kiyoshi. *A Diary of Darkness: The Wartime Diary of Kiyosawa Kiyoshi*. Trans. Eugene Sovial and Tamie Kamiyama. Princeton, NJ: Princeton University Press, 1980.
Klara, Robert. *FDR's Funeral Train: A Betrayed Widow, a Soviet Spy, and a Presidency in the Balance*. New York: Palgrave Macmillan, 2010.
Knebel, Fletcher, and Charles W. Bailey II. *No High Ground*. New York: Harper & Brothers, 1960.
Kohchi, Akira. *Why I Survived the A-Bomb*. Costa Mesa, Calif.: Institute for Historical Review, 1989.
Kort, Michael. *The Columbia Guide to Hiroshima and the Bomb*. New York: Columbia University Press, 2007.
Kosakai, Yoshiteru, comp. *A-Bomb: A City Tells Its Story*. Trans. Kiyoko Kageyama, Charlotte Susu-Mago, and Kaoru Ogura. Hiroshima: Hiroshima Peace Culture Foundation, 1972.
Kozak, Warren. *LeMay: The Life and Wars of General Curtis LeMay*. Washington, D.C.: Regnery, 2009.
Kubo, Mitsue. *Hibaku: Recollections of A-Bomb Survivors*. Ed. Louise Hader. Trans. Ryoji Inoue. Coquitlam, BC, Canada: Nippon Printing, 1990.
Kurzman, Dan. *Day of the Bomb: Countdown to Hiroshima*. New York: McGraw-Hill, 1986.
Kusano, Nobuo. *Atomic Bomb Injuries*. Tokyo: Tsukiji Shokan, 1995.
Kyoto Physicians' Association. *Doctors' Testimonies of "Hiroshima": A Report of the Medical Investigations into the Victims of the Atomic Bombing*. Ed. and trans. Hidenori and Fusami Sugimine. Kyoto: Kyoto Physicians' Association, 1998.
Lamont, Lansing. *Day of Trinity*. New York: Atheneum, 1965.
Lanouette, William with Bela Silard. *Genius in the Shadows: A Biography of Leo Szilard*. New York: Charles Scribner's Sons, 1992.
Lash, Joseph P. *Dealers and Dreamers: A New Look at the New Deal*. New York: Doubleday, 1988.
Laurence, William. *Dawn Over Zero: The Story of the Atomic Bomb*. Westport, Conn.: Greenwood Press, 1972.
Leahy, William D. *I Was There*. New York: McGraw-Hill, 1950.
LeMay, Curtis E., with MacKinlay Kantor. *Mission with LeMay: My Story*. Garden City, NY: Doubleday, 1965.
LeMay, Curtis E., and Bill Yenne. *Superfortress: The B-29 and American Air Power*. New York: McGraw-Hill, 1988.
Levin, Linda Lotridge. *The Making of FDR: The Story of Stephen T. Early, America's First Modern Press Secretary*. Amherst, NY: Prometheus, 2008.
Liebow, Averill A. *Encounter with Disaster: A Medical Diary of Hiroshima, 1945*. New York: W. W. Norton, 1970.
Lifton, Robert Jay. *Death in Life: Survivors of Hiroshima*. New York: Random House, 1967.
Los Alamos Historical Society. *When Los Alamos Was a Ranch School*. Los Alamos, NM: Los Alamos Historical Society, 1974.
Maddox, Robert James. *Weapons for Victory: The Hiroshima Decision Fifty Years Later*. Columbia: University of Missouri Press, 1995.
Maddox, Robert James, ed. *Hiroshima in History: The Myths of Revisionism*. Columbia: University of Missouri Press, 2007.
Maga, Tim. *America Attacks Japan: The Invasion That Never Was*. Lexington: University Press of Kentucky, 2002.
Malloy, Sean L. *Atomic Tragedy: Henry L. Stimson and the Decision to Use the Bomb Against Japan*. Ithaca, NY: Cornell University Press, 2008.
Marx, Joseph Laurance. *Nagasaki: The Necessary Bomb?* New York: Macmillan, 1971.

Marx, Joseph L. *Seven Hours to Zero*. New York: G.P. Putnam's Sons, 1967.
Matsumoto, Yuko. *My Mother Died in Hiroshima*. San Antonio, Tex.: Press of Naylor, 1949.
McCloy, John J. *The Challenge to American Foreign Policy*. Cambridge, Mass.: Harvard University Press, 1953.
McCullough, David. *Truman*. New York: Simon & Schuster, 1992.
McIntire, Ross T., with George Creel. *White House Physician*. New York: G.P. Putnam's Sons, 1946.
McManus, John D. *To the End of the Earth: The US Army and the Downfall of Japan, 1945*. New York: Caliber, 2023.
Merrill, Dennis, ed. *Documentary History of the Truman Presidency*. Vol. 1, *The Decision to Drop the Atomic Bomb on Japan*. Bethesda, MD: University Publications of America, 1995.
Metz, David R. *Master of Airpower: General Carl A. Spaatz*. Novato, Calif.: Presidio Press, 1988.
Miller, Donald L. *D-Days in the Pacific*. New York: Simon & Schuster, 2005.
Miller, Merle, and Abe Spitzer. *We Dropped the Atomic Bomb*. New York: Thomas Y. Crowell, 1946.
Millis, Walter, with E. S. Duffield, eds., *The Forrestal Diaries*. New York: Viking Press, 1951.
Minear, Richard H., ed and trans. *Hiroshima: Three Witnesses*. Princeton, NJ: Princeton University Press, 1990.
Miscamble, Wilson D. *From Roosevelt to Truman: Potsdam, Hiroshima, and the Cold War*. Cambridge: Cambridge University Press, 2007.
Mitchell, Richard H. *Thought Control in Prewar Japan*. Ithaca, NY: Cornell University Press, 1976.
Moynahan, John F. *Atomic Diary*. Newark, NJ: Barton, 1946.
Nagai, Takashi. *The Bells of Nagasaki*. Trans. William Johnston. Tokyo: Kodansha International, 1984.
———. *We of Nagasaki: The Story of Survivors in an Atomic Wasteland*. Trans. Ichiro Shirato and Herbert B. L. Silverman. New York: Duell, Sloan & Pearce, 1958.
Nagai, Takashi, ed. *Living Beneath the Atomic Cloud: Testimonies of the Children of Nagasaki*. Compiled by Frank Zenisek. Trans. Yoshiko Hamagashira et al. Nagasaki: Nagasaki Appeal Committee, 1985.
Nagasaki Atomic Bomb Testimonial Society. *Nagasaki: Voices of the A-Bomb Survivors*. Nagasaki: Showado Printing, 2009.
Nagasaki International Cultural Hall, comp and ed. *Nagasaki Speaks: A Record of the Atomic Bombing*. Trans. Brian Burke-Gaffney. Nagasaki: Nagasaki International Cultural Hall, 1993.
Nagasaki Prefectural Girls High School 42nd Alumnae, eds. *Footprints of Nagasaki: Excerpt from "Anohi Anotoki."* Trans. Yuriko Kitamura. Nagasaki: Seibonokishi-sha, 1996.
Nakamoto, Hiroko, as told to Mildred Mastin Pace. *My Japan, 1930–1951*. New York: McGraw-Hill, 1970.
Nakano, Michiko, ed. *Nagasaki Under the Atomic Bomb: Experiences of Young College Girls*. Tokyo: Soeisha/Books Sanseido, 2000.
Neiberg, Michael. *Potsdam: The End of World War II and the Remaking of Europe*. New York: Basic Books, 2015.
Newman, Joseph. *Goodbye Japan*. New York: L.B. Fischer, 1942.
Newman, Robert. *Truman and the Hiroshima Cult*. East Lansing: Michigan State University Press, 1995.
NHK, ed. *Unforgettable Fire: Pictures Drawn by Atomic Bomb Survivors*. Tokyo: Nippon Hoso Shuppan Kyokai, 1977.
Nichols, Kenneth D. *The Road to Trinity*. New York: William Morrow, 1987.
Nihon Gensuibaku Higaisha Dantai Kyôgikai. *The Witness of Those Two Days: Hiroshima & Nagasaki, August 6 and 9, 1945*. Vols. 1–2. Tokyo: English Translation Group of "The Witness of Those Two Days," 1989.

Nish, Ian. *The Japanese in War and Peace, 1942–1948: Selected Documents from a Translator's In-Tray*. Kent: Global Oriental, 2011.

Norris, Robert S. *Racing for the Bomb: The True Story of General Leslie R. Groves, the Man Behind the Birth of the Atomic Age*. New York: Skyhorse, 2014.

O'Donnell, Patrick K. *Into the Rising Sun: In their Own Words, World War II Veterans Reveal the Heart of Combat*. New York: Free Press, 2002.

Ogura, Toyofumi. *Letters from the End of the World: A Firsthand Account of the Bombing of Hiroshima*. Trans. Kisaburo Murakami and Shigeru Fujii. Tokyo: Kodansha International, 1997.

Okuda, Sadako Teiko, with Pamela Bea Wilson Vergun. *A Dimly Burning Wick: A Memoir from the Ruins of Hiroshima*. New York: Algora, 2008.

Olivi, Frederick J., with William R. Watson, Jr. *Decision at Nagasaki: The Mission That Almost Failed*. Privately Printed, 1999.

Olson, Steve. *The Apocalypse Factory: Plutonium and the Making of the Atomic Age*. New York: W. W. Norton, 2020.

Olwell, Russell B. *At Work in the Atomic City: A Labor and Social History of Oak Ridge, Tennessee*. Knoxville: University of Tennessee Press, 2004.

Osada, Arata, comp. *Children of the A-Bomb: The Testament of the Boys and Girls of Hiroshima*. Trans. Jean Dan and Ruth Sieben-Morgen. New York: G.P. Putnam's Sons, 1959.

Overholt, James, ed. *These Are Our Voices: The Story of Oak Ridge, 1942–1970*. Oak Ridge, TN: Children's Museum of Oak Ridge, 1987.

Pacific War Research Society. *Japan's Longest Day*. Tokyo: Kodansha International, 1968.

———. *The Day Man Lost: Hiroshima, 6 August 1945*. Tokyo: Kodansha International, 1972.

Payson, Steven, ed. *Public Economies in the United States: How the Federal Government Analyzes and Influences the Economy*. Vol. 2, *Economic Analysis of Legislation, Regulation, and Taxation*. Santa Barbara, Calif.: Praeger, 2014.

Pyle, Kenneth B. *Hiroshima and the Historians: Debating America's Most Controversial Decision*. Cambridge: Cambridge University Press, 2024.

Reed, Bruce Cameron. *The History and Science of the Manhattan Project*. New York: Springer, 2014.

Reilly, Michael F., as told to William J. Slocum. *Reilly of the White House*. New York: Simon & Schuster, 1947.

Resis, Albert, ed. *Molotov Remembers: Inside Kremlin Politics: Conversations with Felix Chuev*. Chicago: Ivan R. Dee, 1993.

Rhodes, Richard. *The Making of the Atomic Bomb*. New York: Simon & Schuster, 1986.

Rigdon, William M. *White House Sailor*. Garden City, NY: Doubleday, 1962.

Robertson, David. *Sly and Able: A Political Biography of James F. Byrnes*. New York: W. W. Norton, 1994.

Robinson, George O., Jr. *The Oak Ridge Story: The Saga of a People Who Share in History*. Kingsport, TN: Southern, 1950.

Rose, Lisle A. *Dubious Victory: The United States and the End of World War II*. Kent, OH: Kent State University Press, 1973.

Rosenman, Samuel I., ed. *The Public Papers and Addresses of Franklin D. Roosevelt*. New York: Harper & Brothers, 1950.

Rotter, Andrew J. *Hiroshima: The World's Bomb*. Oxford: Oxford University Press, 2008.

Rottman, Gordan L. *Okinawa 1945: The Last Battle*. New York: Osprey, 2002.

Sanger, S. L. *Working on the Bomb: An Oral History of WWII Hanford*. Ed. Craig Wollner. Portland, OR: Continuing Education Press, 1995.

Schull, William J. *Effects of Atomic Radiation: A Half-Century of Studies from Hiroshima and Nagasaki*. New York: Wiley-Liss, 1995.

Scott, James M. *Target Tokyo: Jimmy Doolittle and the Raid That Avenged Pearl Harbor*. New York: W. W. Norton, 2015.

————. *Rampage: MacArthur, Yamashita, and the Battle of Manila*. New York: W. W. Norton, 2018.

————. *Black Snow: Curtis LeMay, the Firebombing of Tokyo, and the Road to the Atomic Bomb*. New York: W. W. Norton, 2022.

Seaborg, Glenn T., with Benjamin S. Loeb, *Stemming the Tide: Arms Control in the Johnson Years*. Lexington, Mass.: Lexington Books, 1987.

Sekimori, Gaynor, trans. *Hibakusha: Survivors of Hiroshima and Nagasaki*. Tokyo: Kôsei, 2010.

Selden, Kyoko, and Mark Selden. *The Atomic Bomb: Voices from Hiroshima and Nagasaki*. Armonk, NY: East Gate, 1989.

Serber, Robert. *The Los Alamos Primer: The First Lectures on How to Build an Atomic Bomb*. Oakland: University of California Press, 2020.

Sherwin, Martin J. *A World Destroyed: The Atomic Bomb and the Grand Alliance*. New York: Alfred A. Knopf, 1975.

Sherwood, Robert E. *Roosevelt and Hopkins: An Intimate History*. New York: Harper & Brothers, 1948.

Shirabe, Raisuke. *A Physician's Diary of the Atomic Bombing and its Aftermath*. Ed. Fidelius R. Kuo. Trans. Aloysius F. Kuo. Nagasaki: Nagasaki Association for Hibakusha's Medical Care, 2002.

Shillony, Ben-Ami. *Politics and Culture in Wartime Japan*. Oxford: Clarendon Press, 1981.

Shiotsuki, Masao. *Doctor at Nagasaki: "My First Assignment Was Mercy Killing."* Trans. Simul International. Tokyo: Kôsei, 1987.

Shoumatoff, Elizabeth. *FDR's Unfinished Portrait: A Memoir*. Pittsburgh: University of Pittsburgh Press, 1990.

Sigal, Leon V. *Fighting to a Finish: The Politics of War Termination in the United States and Japan, 1945*. Ithaca, NY: Cornell University Press, 1988.

Skates, John Ray. *The Invasion of Japan: Alternative to the Bomb*. Columbia: University of South Carolina Press, 1994.

Sledge, E.B. *With the Old Breed*. New York: Presidio Press, 2010.

Sloan, Bill. *The Ultimate Battle: Okinawa 1945—The Last Epic Struggle of World War II*. New York: Simon & Schuster, 2007.

Smith, A. Merriam. *Thank You, Mr. President: A White House Notebook*. New York: Harper & Brothers, 1946.

Smith, Edward Jean. *Eisenhower: In War and Peace*. New York: Random House, 2012.

Smith, Holland M., and Percy Finch. *Coral and Brass*. New York: Charles Scribner's Sons, 1948.

Smyth, Henry. *Atomic Energy for Military Purposes*. York, Penn.: Maple Press, 1945.

Snider, Hideko Tamura. *One Sunny Day: A Child's Memories of Hiroshima*. Chicago: Open Court, 1996.

Sodei, Rinjiro. *We Were the Enemy? American Survivors of Hiroshima*. Ed. John Junkerman. Boulder, CO: Westview Press, 1988.

Southard, Susan. *Nagasaki: Life After Nuclear War*. New York: Viking, 2015.

Steinberg, Alfred. *Mrs. R: The Life of Eleanor Roosevelt*. New York: G.P. Putnam's Sons, 1958.

————. *Sam Rayburn: A Biography*. New York: Hawthorn Books, 1975.

Stilwell, Joseph W., ed. *The Stilwell Papers*. Ed. Theodore H. White. New York: William Sloane Associates, 1948.

Stoff, Michael, Jonathan F. Fanton, and R. Hal Williams, eds. *The Manhattan Project: A Documentary Introduction to the Atomic Age*. Philadelphia: Temple University Press, 1991.

Stimson, Henry L., and McGeorge Bundy. *On Active Service in Peace and War*. New York: Harper & Brothers, 1947.

Sweeney, Charles W., with James A. Antonucci and Marion K. Antonucci. *War's End: An Eyewitness Account of America's Last Atomic Mission*. New York: Avon Books, 1997.

Szasz, Ferenc Morton. *The Day the Sun Rose Twice: The Story of the Trinity Site Nuclear Explosion, July 16, 1945*. Albuquerque: University of New Mexico Press, 1984.

Takada, Mineo. *August the Sixth, Before and After: Letters to and from Her Son*. Ed. Sylvia B. Warner. Kyoto: 高田三郎, 1979.

Teller, Edward. *Energy from Heaven and Earth*. San Francisco: W.H. Freeman & Co., 1979.

Teller, Edward, with Allen Brown. *The Legacy of Hiroshima*. Garden City, NY: Doubleday, 1962.

Thomas, Gordon, and Max Morgan-Witts. *Ruin from the Air: The Atomic Mission to Hiroshima*. London: Hamish Hamilton, 1977.

Tibbets, Paul W., Jr., with Clair Stebbins and Harry Franken. *The Tibbets Story*. New York: Stein & Day, 1978.

————. *Return of the Enola Gay*. New Hope, Penn.: Enola Gay Remembered, 1998.

Tôgô, Shigenori. *The Cause of Japan*. Trans. and ed. Fumihiko Tôgô and Ben Bruce Blakeney. New York: Simon & Schuster, 1956.

Truman, Harry S. *The Memoirs of Harry S. Truman*. Vol. 1, *Year of Decisions*. Garden City, NY: Doubleday, 1955.

Truman, Margaret. *Bess W. Truman*. New York: Macmillan, 1986.

————. *Letters from Father: The Truman Family's Personal Correspondence*. New York: Arbor House, 1981.

Truman, Margaret, ed. *Where the Buck Stops: The Personal and Private Writing of Harry S. Truman*. New York: Warner Books, 1989.

Truman, Margaret, with Margaret Cousins. *Souvenir: Margeret Truman's Own Story*. New York: McGraw-Hill, 1956.

Trumbull, Robert. *Nine Who Survived Hiroshima and Nagasaki*. New York: E.P. Dutton, 1957.

Tuchman, Barbara W. *Stilwell and the American Experience in China, 1911–1945*. New York: Macmillan, 1970

Tully, Grace. *F.D.R.: My Boss*. New York: Charles Scribner's Sons, 1949.

Wainstock, Dennis D. *The Decision to Drop the Atomic Bomb*. Westport, Conn.: Praeger, 1996.

Walker, J. Samuel. *Prompt and Utter Destruction: Truman and the Use of Atomic Bombs Against Japan*. Chapel Hill: University of North Carolina Press, 1997.

Walker, Stephen. *Shockwave: Countdown to Hiroshima*. New York: HarperCollins, 2005.

Ward, Geoffrey C., ed. *Closest Companion: The Unknown Story of the Intimate Friendship Between Franklin Roosevelt and Margaret Suckley*. Boston: Houghton Mifflin, 1995.

Weart, Spencer R., and Gertrud Weiss Szilard, eds. *Leo Szilard: His Version of the Facts: Selected Recollections and Correspondence*. Cambridge: MIT Press, 1978.

Weller, George. *First Into Nagasaki: Dispatches on Post-Atomic Japan and Its Prisoners of War*. Ed. Anthony Weller. New York: Crown, 2006.

West, J. B, with Mary Lynn Kotz. *Upstairs at the White House: My Life with the First Ladies*. New York: Coward, McGann & Geoghegan, 1973.

Wetzler, Peter. *Hirohito and War: Imperial Tradition and Military Decision Making in Prewar Japan*. Honolulu: University of Hawai'i Press, 1998.

Wheeler, Richard. *Iwo*. Edison, NJ: Castle, 2007.

Wirth, John D., and Linda Harvey Aldrich. *Los Alamos: The Ranch School Year, 1917–1943*. Los Alamos: University of New Mexico Press, 2003.

Women's Division of Soka Gakkai. *Women Against War: Personal Accounts of Forty Japanese Women*. Trans. Richard L. Gage. Tokyo: Kodansha International, 1986.

Wyden, Peter. *Day One: Before Hiroshima and After.* New York: Simon & Schuster, 1984.

Yamaguchi, Senji. *Burnt Yet Undaunted: Verbatim Account of Senji Yamaguchi*. Comp. Shinji Fujisaki. Tokyo: Japan Confederation of A- and H-Bomb Sufferers Organizations, 2002.

Yamashita, Samuel Hideo. *Daily Life in Wartime Japan, 1940–1945*. Lawrence: University of Kansas Press, 2015.

———. *Leaves from an Autumn of Emergencies: Selections of Wartime Diaries of Ordinary Japanese.* Honolulu: University of Hawai'i Press, 2005.

Youth Division of Soká Gakkai, comp., and Richard L. Gage, ed. *Cries for Peace: Experiences of Japanese Victims of World War II.* Tokyo: Japan Times, 1978.

INDEX

Page numbers in *italic* refer to illustrations.

ABOUT THE AUTHOR

A Pulitzer Prize finalist and *New York Times* best-selling author, James M. Scott is the author of *Empire of Ashes*, *Black Snow*, *Rampage*, *Target Tokyo*, *The War Below*, and *The Attack on the Liberty*, and coauthor, with Jack Carr, of *Targeted: Beirut* and the forthcoming *Targeted: Pan Am 103*. A former Nieman Fellow at Harvard, Scott is a sought-after public speaker about World War II. He has lectured on military bases, at presidential libraries, book festivals, and in universities and museums around the world, among them, the National Defense University in Washington; the National World War II Museum in New Orleans; the University of the Philippines in Quezon City; the Ronald Reagan Presidential Library in Simi Valley, California; the Clinton School of Public Service in Little Rock, Arkansas; and the U.S. Army Heritage and Education Center in Carlisle, Pennsylvania. Scott also leads battlefield tours throughout the Pacific, from Pearl Harbor and the Philippines to the Mariana Islands and Japan. He lives with his wife and two children in Charleston, South Carolina, where he is the scholar in residence at the Citadel.